Macroeconomics in Context

Macroeconomics in Context: A European Perspective lays out the principles of macroeconomics in a manner that is thorough, up to date, and relevant to students. With a clear presentation of economic theory throughout, this latest addition to the bestselling "In Context" set of textbooks is written with a specific focus on European data, institutions, and historical events, offering engaging treatment of high-interest topics, including sustainability, Brexit, the euro crisis, and rising inequality. Policy issues are presented in context (historical, institutional, social, political, and ethical), and always with reference to human well-being.

This book is divided into four parts, covering the following key issues:

- The context of economic analysis, including basic macroeconomic statistics and tools;
- The basics of macroeconomic measurements, including GDP, inflation, and unemployment, as well as alternative measures of well-being, and the particular structures of the European economies;
- Methods for analyzing monetary and fiscal policy, including an in-depth coverage of the instruments and approaches of the European central bank and some coverage of an open economy;
- The application of the tools learnt to selected macroeconomic issues, such as the euro crisis, the global financial crisis, public debt, global development, and environmental sustainability.

Far more than any other existing macroeconomic textbook, this book combines real-world relevance of the topics covered with a strong focus on European institutions and structures within an approach that explains multiple economic paradigms. This combination helps to raise students' interest in macroeconomics as well as enhance their understanding of the power and limitation of macroeconomic analysis.

Visit www.gdae.org/europeanmacro/ for online resources for both lecturers and students.

Sebastian Dullien is Professor for International Economics at HTW Berlin, University of Applied Sciences, and Senior Policy Fellow at the European Council on Foreign Relations. Prior to his appointment to the university in 2007, he worked in several positions, including economics editor for the *Financial Times Deutschland*, the German-language edition of the *Financial Times*. He has advised a number of ministries, members of the German and European Parliament, and several organizations of the United Nations.

Neva Goodwin is Co-Director of the Global Development and Environment Institute (GDAE) at Tufts University, where she is the director of the electronic *Social Science Library: Frontier Thinking in Sustainable Development and Human Well-Being*. Goodwin works toward a contextual economics theory that will have more relevance to contemporary real-world social and ecological concerns than the dominant economic paradigm does.

Jonathan M. Harris is Director of the Theory and Education Program at the Tufts University Global Development and Environment Institute, USA. His current research focuses on the implications of large-scale environmental problems, especially global climate change, for macroeconomic theory and policy.

Julie A. Nelson is Professor of Economics at the University of Massachusetts Boston and Senior Research Fellow at the Global Development and Environment Institute at Tufts University, USA. Many of her books and articles critique economic methodology from a feminist perspective. She has published in journals ranging from *Econometrica* and the *Journal of Political Economy* to *Hypatia: Journal of Feminist Philosophy* and *Ecological Economics*.

Brian Roach is Senior Research Associate at the Tufts University Global Development and Environment Institute and a lecturer at Tufts and Brandeis University, USA. He has published numerous articles on nonmarket valuation of natural resources, including drinking water quality, water-based recreation, and wildlife.

Mariano Torras teaches economics at Adelphi University in Garden City, New York, USA. A heterodox economist who specializes in ecological and development economics, Torras's recent research has been in the areas of institutional economics and economic methodology; particular attention has been on approaches to addressing climate change.

Macroeconomics in Context

A European Perspective

Sebastian Dullien, Neva Goodwin, Jonathan M. Harris, Julie A. Nelson, Brian Roach, and Mariano Torras

Routledge
Taylor & Francis Group

NEW YORK AND LONDON

First published 2018
by Routledge
711 Third Avenue, New York, NY 10017

and by Routledge
2 Park Square, Milton Park, Abingdon, Oxon, OX14 4RN

Routledge is an imprint of the Taylor & Francis Group, an informa business

Library of Congress Cataloging-in-Publication Data
Names: Dullien, Sebastian, author.
Title: Macroeconomics in context : a European perspective / Sebastian
    Dullien, [and five others].
Description: New York, NY : Routledge, 2017. | Includes index.
Identifiers: LCCN 2017009836 | ISBN 9781138185173 (hardback) |
    ISBN 9781138185180 (pbk.) | ISBN 9781315644653 (ebook)
Subjects: LCSH: Macroeconomics. | Europe—Economic conditions.
Classification: LCC HB172.5 .D85 2017 | DDC 339—dc23
LC record available at https://lccn.loc.gov/2017009836

ISBN: 978-1-138-18517-3 (hbk)
ISBN: 978-1-138-18518-0 (pbk)
ISBN: 978-1-315-64465-3 (ebk)

Typeset in Bembo
by Apex CoVantage, LLC

Brief Contents

Contents

PART IV
MACROECONOMIC ISSUES AND APPLICATIONS   493

Figures

Tables

Introduction

For students taking an introductory macroeconomics course, *Macroeconomics in Context—A European Perspective* lays out the principles of macroeconomics in a manner that is thorough, up to date, and highly readable. Whether students take this class simply to gain some understanding of how economics can be useful to them or go on to further studies in economics or business, this book will equip them with the standard tools *and* the critical understanding that they need to succeed. It introduces students both to the standard topics and tools taught in most introductory courses and to a broader and richer set of topics and tools to deepen comprehension of the economic realities of the twenty-first century.

In attempting to simplify the complexities of the real world to a comprehensible level, introductory macroeconomics textbooks too often present material that not only abstracts from reality but sometimes directly contradicts it. In this respect, it is more difficult to provide an introductory description of the macroeconomy than it is to introduce economic behavior on the microeconomic level. *Macroeconomics in Context—A European Perspective* addresses this challenge by keeping the theoretical exposition close to experience. The authors believe that students will achieve a deeper and more memorable understanding of economic theory if they can relate it to contemporary issues of interest and importance. Part of relating economic theory to contemporary issues means understanding the specific institutional context—in the case of the European edition of *Macroeconomics in Context*, the economic policy institutions found in European countries and in the European Union.

This textbook is written to encourage engaged and critical thinking about topics in economics. While demonstrating the uses of economic theory, it also provides a variety of viewpoints. Instructors who are largely satisfied with standard treatments, as well as those following the requirements of larger curricula, can be assured that the materials typically treated in Introduction to Macroeconomics courses—especially the classical and Keynesian, but also the monetarist, classical-Keynesian synthesis, new classical, and post-Keynesian approaches—are presented. At the same time, woven throughout the book are themes of great importance in everyday life as well as for an understanding of the economy. Within the broad themes of social and environmental well-being and sustainability, attention is repeatedly given to European integration, globalization, poverty and inequality, unpaid work, technology, and the environment

1

as well as the financialization of the economy, the Great Recession, and its aftermath. These elements are not add-ons but are integrated within discussions of historical, institutional, political, and social factors that affect and are affected by the economy.

A specific feature that sets the European edition of this textbook apart from most other macroeconomics textbooks is its specific focus on Europe. In contrast to many other "European editions" of textbooks originally published in the U.S., the changes go far beyond just replacing the dollar sign with a pound or a euro sign. Not only are many examples drawn from European countries, and the data presented is for European countries or the euro area as a whole, the textbook also routinely refers specifically to institutional features found in Europe that are important for macroeconomics. For example, instead of describing how the U.S. Federal Reserve conducts monetary policy by outright open-market purchases of government securities, the focus is on the European Central Bank and other EU members' central banks, which employ slightly different instruments, such as lending to banks. "Europe" in this context refers primarily to the member states of the European Union (including Britain).

For the sake of this textbook, while Brexit is explicitly discussed, Britain is still considered part of the European Union even though the country has decided to leave the EU. This choice has been made, first, because macroeconomic statistics on the EU up to 2016 still include Britain and second, because, even after leaving the European Union, Britain will share important trade linkages and similarities with other European countries. For the macroeconomic analysis, the textbook also puts a strong focus on the euro area as a whole, which, in many ways, has features of a national economy.

Macroeconomics in Context is the companion textbook to *Microeconomics in Context* (3rd ed.), published by Routledge.

CONTENT AND ORGANIZATION

Some of the innovative features of this text are apparent in even a quick scan of the table of contents, the sample course outlines on pp. 13–16, or Chapter 1. Although this textbook takes a broader and more contextual approach to economic activities, it fits these within a familiar overall organizational strategy.

- Part I, "The Context for Economic Analysis," presents the themes of the book and the major actors in the economy. Students are introduced to a range of macroeconomic questions and goals, to basic empirical and theoretical tools, and to the basic activities and institutions of a modern economy. This section concludes with an overview of supply-and-demand analysis and elasticity.
- Part II, "Macroeconomic Basics," introduces basic macroeconomic definitions and accounting methods, including gross domestic product (GDP), inflation, aggregate demand, and unemployment. These are supplemented with a discussion of how new accounting systems are being developed to measure the economic contributions of the natural environment, unpaid household labor, and other previously uncounted factors. The second half of Part II brings these abstractions down to

earth with a description of the structure of the European economies and discussion of the labor market and unemployment.

■ Part III, "Macroeconomic Theory and Policy," explores the issue of macroeconomic fluctuations. The first chapters clearly present Keynesian and classical theories of the determination of aggregate demand (*AD*) and aggregate supply (*AS*) and the effects of fiscal and monetary policies. This section develops an *AS/AD* model of output and inflation that, with inflation rather than price level on the vertical axis, is designed to be comprehensible and usefully representative of the real world. It concludes with a chapter discussing macroeconomic issues in an economy closely interlinked to that of other countries, be it European trading partners or the rest of the world.

■ Part IV, "Macroeconomic Issues and Applications," addresses the contemporary issues of financial crisis, the Great Recession, debt and deficits, the euro crisis, economic development, and the environment. While the first four chapters here are presented from a largely European or U.S. perspective, the second half of this part widens the lens to explore current global issues of poverty and inequality, economic growth, human development, and environmental challenges.

In order to focus on "contextual" discussions, we have generally placed more formal instruction in algebraic modeling techniques in optional appendices to the chapters. Also, while this book reviews the basics of supply and demand and includes "new classical" macroeconomics among the theories discussed, it devotes fewer pages to the concept of efficient markets than many books do and certainly fewer than recent books that have adopted a strongly "new classical" slant. In taking this approach, we have followed the lead of advanced researchers in the profession who convincingly argue that "micro foundations" based on the assumptions of perfect competition are of limited usefulness in explaining macroeconomic phenomena. This approach also makes the course less repetitious for students who take both Introduction to Microeconomics and Introduction to Macroeconomics courses.

WHAT MAKES THIS BOOK DIFFERENT FROM OTHER TEXTS?

This text covers the traditional topics included in most macroeconomics texts but treats them from a broader, more holistic perspective. The following chapter-by-chapter synopsis shows how this book manages both to be "similar enough" to fit into a standard curriculum and "different enough" to respond to commonly expressed needs and dissatisfactions.

Chapter 0, "Macroeconomics and Well-Being," presents graphically illustrated data on 19 variables, in each case showing where the European Union and its members stand among other countries. The related Web site www.gdae.org/europeanmacro allows users to see the same variables listed in order for all countries in the world where such data is available. The variables have been selected for intrinsic interest as well as relevance to the material in the rest of the book. This chapter is an innovation that teachers and students may choose to use in a variety of ways, including as an introduction to later topics, as a reference for use with other chapters, or as material to draw on in designing research projects.

Chapter 1, "Economic Activity in Context," presents standard macroeconomic topics such as the macroeconomic goals of living standards and stability—for the present and the future—and a basic roadmap relating macroeconomic theory to outstanding events and theories of the past century. We place these subjects in a broader context of concern for well-being. Many texts define economics as the study of choice in the face of scarcity and focus on economic growth as a (if not *the*) goal of macroeconomic policy. In this chapter, we define the well-being goals of macroeconomics as (1) improvement in living standards, (2) stability and security, and (3) financial, social, and ecological sustainability. Thus growth in GDP alone may or may not contribute to the general goal of human well-being, depending on whether it furthers these ultimate objectives.

As is the pattern in most contemporary macroeconomics textbooks, a review of microeconomic concepts comes next. Chapters 2, 3, and 4 repeat some of the material from the companion textbook, *Microeconomics in Context*, though with more emphasis on what is needed for students of the macroeconomy. Chapter 2, "Useful Tools and Concepts," introduces standard concepts of economic modeling, efficiency, scarcity, opportunity cost, the production-possibilities frontier, circular flow, and the advantages of market systems and includes a review of graphing techniques. In contrast to most standard texts, however, we place these within a broader context of concern for well-being. We discuss the institutional requirements of markets and introduce the concepts of externalities, public goods, market power, transaction costs, information and expectations, and concern for human needs and equity. The early introduction of these topics allows us to demonstrate why markets, while useful, are not on their own sufficient for organizing economic life in service of well-being.

Chapter 3, "What Economies Do," presents brief discussions of the four essential economic activities. Most textbooks discuss three essential activities—production, distribution, and consumption—but we add the activity of "resource maintenance" to draw attention to the importance of maintaining capital stocks, including stocks of natural (environmental) capital. We also incorporate a discussion of the important topic of income and wealth distribution into this early chapter. In addition to the usual economic "circular flow" diagram, introduced in Chapter 2, this chapter presents an image of economic activity as embedded in social and physical contexts and relates this approach to issues of macroeconomic concern.

Chapter 4, "Supply and Demand," contains a brief but clear exposition of traditional supply-and-demand curve analysis, including discussions of the slopes of the curves, factors that shift the curves, equilibrium and market adjustment, and a simple discussion of elasticity. Our contextual approach, however, leads to some subtle shifts in presentation. First, the model is explicitly presented as a thought experiment—as a humanly created analytical tool that may help us gain insight—rather than as a set of "laws" about "the way the world works." Second, discussions of price changes that are either too slow (i.e., "sticky") or too volatile (e.g., financial market speculation) lead students to think about how market adjustment in the real world may not be as smooth and welfare maximizing as the model is often taken to imply.

4

Chapter 5, "Macroeconomic Measurement: The Current Approach," begins Part II of the book, "Macroeconomic Basics." It presents a fairly standard introduction to national income accounting but emphasizes that the accounts have been created for specific purposes, with conventions that reflect particular assumptions or choices. It notes how the production and investment undertaken in the "household and institutions" sector have historically been deemphasized in national accounting.

Chapter 6, "Macroeconomic Measurement: Environmental and Social Dimensions," gives a more thorough introduction to alternative measures of economic performance than can be found in any other introductory economics textbook. The chapter briefly describes the Europe 2020 scoreboard, the Better Life Index, the Human Development Index, and other current approaches for assessing well-being. It includes discussions of issues in the valuation of environmental and household services and of satellite accounts for environmental and household production.

Chapter 7, "The Structure of the European Economy," is unique to this book. It describes key features of production and employment in the European economy, broken down into its primary, secondary, and tertiary sectors, and highlights differences between European countries. We include this material for several reasons. First, it makes the text more "real world" to students. Second, it provides basic economic literacy that we believe is sorely lacking among most economics students. Finally, it presents the context to illustrate several economic debates, such as the loss of manufacturing jobs, the shift out of nuclear power in some countries, and the meaning of the trend toward an ever-growing service sector, especially financial services. While this chapter is written with a European focus, its description of sectoral shifts is relevant to many economies around the world.

Chapter 8, "Employment, Unemployment, and Wages," discusses standard macroeconomic labor topics such as the definition of the unemployment rate, the different types of unemployment, and theories of the causes of unemployment. In addition, there is a special focus on labor market institutions. The chapter discusses changes in labor force participation rates, questions of labor market "flexibility," and the sources of wage differentials and inequalities.

Chapter 9, "Aggregate Demand and Economic Fluctuations," introduces the analysis of business cycles, presents the classical theory of savings–investment balance through the market for loanable funds, and develops Keynesian aggregate demand analysis in the form of the traditional "Keynesian cross" diagram. Our treatment of these topics is fairly standard, although our contextual approach places more emphasis on the possibility of persistent unemployment than do many other current textbooks—a perspective that is important in the light of the very slow recovery from the Great Recession in the U.S. and from the euro crisis in the EU.

Chapter 10, "Fiscal Policy," balances formal analysis of fiscal policy with real-world data and examples. Analysis of fiscal policy impacts is presented in fairly simple terms, with an algebraic treatment of more complex multiplier effects in appendices. While the basic analysis presented here follows the Keynesian model, the text also discusses classical and supply-side perspectives. The section on budgets and deficits should give students a basic understanding—developed further in Chapter 16—of deficits, debt, and how these affect the economy. The difference between automatic stabilizers and discretionary policy is made clear, and recent fiscal policies are discussed.

Chapter 11, "Money, Banking, and Finance," presents the basics of money and the banking system, including inflation, deflation, liquidity, and the different aggregate measures of money. Students are introduced to asset and liabilities tables, different banking institutions, and the process of money creation through the banking system. The chapter concludes with a discussion of nonbank financial institutions, financialization, and financial bubbles—topics of great relevance following the financial crisis of 2007–2008 and the euro crisis.

Chapter 12, "The European Central Bank and Monetary Policy," focuses on the role of the European Central Bank (ECB) and the implementation of monetary policy. Here we discuss the ECB's structure, functions, and monetary policy tools that it employs to influence the banking sector and the economy at large. The exposition underlines strongly the fact acknowledged in many modern academic macroeconomic models that a central bank primarily influences the short-term rate of interest, and the money supply then is created endogenously by the wider banking system. The chapter also spotlights the monetary policy in the euro area since the year 1999, with particular attention to the role of monetary policy in the 2007–2008 financial crisis and the subsequent euro crisis. Parallels with the Bank of England are also discussed in this chapter. Finally, the chapter contains an appendix that explains in detail the link between bond prices and interest rates and between nominal and real rates of interest.

Chapter 13, "Aggregate Supply, Aggregate Demand, and Inflation: Putting It All Together," addresses the tricky problem of how to teach the relationship between output and inflation to introductory students in a way that is simple yet intellectually defensible. The model presented in this chapter has many features that will be familiar to instructors. But unlike *AS/AD* models that put the price level on the vertical axis, this model has the inflation rate on the vertical axis, which makes it more relevant for discussing current events.* Unlike many new classical theory–influenced textbooks, our basic presentation is not centered on a notion of long-run full-employment equilibrium output. We emphasize, instead, how the macroeconomy adjusts dynamically in the short and medium term to often-unpredictable economic events. This also makes relating the model to current events more realistic. (Classical theory is not, however, neglected. It is also discussed in the chapter and the appendix.)

In Chapter 14, "International Linkages and Economic Policy," the foreign sector is added to the circular-flow picture, which now includes savings, investment, taxes,

---

* Regarding the theoretical underpinnings of our model, our downward-sloped *AD* curve is based on the *AD* curve developed by David Romer, "Keynesian Macroeconomics without the LM Curve," *Journal of Economic Perspectives* 14(2) (2000): 149–169 and adopted by other introductory textbook writers, including John B. Taylor, *Principles of Macroeconomics* (Boston and New York: Houghton Mifflin, 2003). Our curved *AS* is based on the notion of an expectations-augmented Phillips curve, translated into inflation and output space. The idea of a dynamically evolving economy rather than one always headed toward settling at full employment is an approach based on Keynes's own (rather than new Keynesian) thought, as explained in the appendix to Chapter 13.

government spending, exports, and imports. When talking about imports and exports, this chapter provides detailed treatment of the principles of European integration. Chapter 14 also highlights the increasingly important links between fiscal and monetary policies and in an economy open to trade and international capital flows. Finally, in introducing students to the World Bank and the International Monetary Fund, the chapter addresses the real-world political economy of international economic relations.

Chapter 15, "The Financial Crisis and the Great Recession," is another unique addition to the book. In treating a topic that, as of early 2017, continues to be an important point of reference in economic policy debates, the chapter helps add current relevance to the discussion of macroeconomic policy. Rather than develop a theoretical framework, Chapter 15 applies many of the insights introduced in earlier chapters to explain some of the likely causes and consequences of the financial crisis that led to the Great Recession. The chapter supplies an ideal context for extensive discussion of how the "real" economy relates to the financial economy and the potential problems with excessive reliance on finance. It highlights the role of the housing bubble and subprime lending, as well as financial deregulation more generally, in creating the conditions for crisis. It also contrasts the housing bubble in the U.S. with those experienced in parts of Europe, such as Britain, Ireland, or Spain. The latter part of the chapter discusses financial reform—efforts as well as new ideas—and asks some of the "big" questions that must be addressed if we are to avoid such crises in the future.

Chapter 16, "Deficits and Debt," is distinctive in a number of ways. First, it provides a current focus for the discussion of fiscal policy, allowing for greater elaboration on deficits and debt. Second, it presents the link between government debt, economic growth, and inflation or deflation. Finally, it presents and discusses European institutions to limit deficits and debts, including the Stability and Growth Pact and the Fiscal Compact.

Chapter 17, "The Euro Crisis," is another unique feature of this book. As Chapter 15 does for the financial crisis of 2008–2009, this chapter presents the economic crisis that a number of countries using the euro have experienced since 2010. It first discusses critically different explanations for the crisis. Second, it applies models developed in earlier chapters to understand the results of macroeconomic policies during the crisis. Third, it elaborates on reform proposals made to make the euro area more stable in the future.

Chapter 18, "How Economies Grow and Develop," presents basic concepts related to economic growth, such as the Rostow and Harrod-Domar models, which emphasize the importance of investment in manufactured capital. But the chapter also distinguishes between *growth* and *development* and provides examples of how investment in other types of capital—for example, human or natural capital—can be equally if not more important. It also explores in detail the question of whether most poor countries have been "catching up" with the industrialized world ("convergence") or falling behind. Country diversity is a recurrent theme; the chapter emphasizes that the "one size fits all" approach to economic development emphasizing structural reforms— such as those embodied in the Washington Consensus—has produced disappointing results and that different approaches are required in response to the circumstances in individual countries.

Chapter 19, "Growth and Sustainability in the Twenty-First Century," is an unusual chapter for a macroeconomics textbook—but a crucially important one in terms of economic education for intelligent citizenship. It examines a number of ecological challenges and includes a section on global climate change. While it covers standard theories such as the environmental Kuznets curve, it raises serious challenges to the belief that economic growth and markets can solve this century's social and environmental problems on their own. More directly, it asks whether the traditional macroeconomic goal of continued economic growth is compatible with the long-term goal of sustainability. Finally, the chapter presents ideas for alternative approaches at the local, national, and global levels that, while sustainable, do not detract from well-being.

SPECIAL FEATURES

Each chapter in this text contains many features designed to enhance student learning.

- *Key Terms* are highlighted in boldface throughout the text, with sidebar definitions for easy comprehension and review.
- *Discussion Questions* at the end of each section encourage immediate review of what has been read and relate the material to the students' own experience. The frequent appearance of these questions throughout each chapter helps students review manageable portions of material and thus boosts comprehension. The questions can be used for participatory exercises involving the entire class or for small-group discussion.
- *End-of-Chapter Review Questions* are designed to encourage students to create their own summary of concepts. They also serve as helpful guidelines to the importance of various points.
- *End-of-Chapter Exercises* encourage students to work with and apply the material, thereby gaining increased mastery of concepts, models, and investigative techniques.
- Throughout the chapters, boxes enliven the material with real-world illustrations drawn from a variety of sources regarding applications of economic concepts and recent macroeconomic developments.
- In order to make the chapters as lively and accessible as possible, some formal and technical material (suitable for inclusion in some but not all course designs) is carefully and concisely explained in chapter appendices.
- A glossary at the end of the book contains all key terms, their definitions, and the number of the chapter in which each was first used and defined.

SUPPLEMENTS

The supplements package for this book provides a set of teaching tools and resources for instructors using this text. An *Instructor's Resource Manual* and Test Bank to accompany *Macroeconomics in Context* are available. To access these electronically, send a request via e-mail to gdae@tufts.edu that contains sufficient information for us to verify your instructor status.

For each chapter, the *Instructor's Resource Manual* includes an introductory note and answers to all review questions and end-of-chapter exercises. In addition, the "Notes on Discussion Questions" section provides not only suggested answers to these questions but also ideas on how the questions might be used in the classroom. Sections titled "Web Resources" and "Extensions" provide supplementary material and links to other passages in the book or other materials that can be used to enrich lectures and discussion.

The Test Bank includes multiple-choice and true/false questions for each chapter. The correct answer for each question is indicated.

PowerPoint slides for lectures based on this textbook, slides of figures and tables from the text, tables with macroeconomic data for individual EU countries (including the UK), and a *Student Study Guide* that provides ample opportunity for students to review and practice the key concepts are available for free download at www.gdae.org/europeanmacro.

HOW TO USE THIS TEXT

The feedback that we have received from instructors who have used the first and second U.S. editions of this text has been enthusiastic and gratifying. We have found that this book works in a variety of courses with a variety of approaches, and we would like to share some of these instructors' suggestions on tailoring this book to meet your own course needs.

On pages 13–16, you will find several possible course plans based on different emphases (such as ecological, global, human development, and structural). We hope that this will help in planning the course that will best suit the needs of instructors and students.

NOTE ON DIFFERENCES FROM THE SECOND U.S. EDITION

As mentioned before, the European edition includes significant changes compared to the second U.S.–focused edition, making the book more relevant for European students. In addition to updating data in the text, tables, figures, and boxes, material specifically relevant for the European audience has been added, and material with a narrow U.S. focus has been omitted.

While Part I is the part of the book which changed least overall, there are some important adjustments here. In the data collection in Chapter 0, now a larger number of EU countries are included. Also, in most figures, the EU average is included first to allow a comparison of the students' own countries' performance with a European average and second to relate the EU to other regions in the world. In Chapters 1 to 4, the content remains largely unchanged, but some examples have been replaced.

In Chapter 5, the discussion of measurement issues follows the EU methodology of national accounts. Data is also presented for the euro area (and, in the electronic supplements, for other EU countries) instead of for the U.S. In Chapter 6, the discussion of alternative measures to GDP was expanded by a treatment of the so-called scorecard approaches used, for example, in the European "Europe 2020" policy framework. Some discussion from the U.S. edition has been shortened, especially for indicators that have not been recently updated.

Chapter 7 on the structure of the European economy has been changed significantly compared to the chapter in the original edition (which was about the structure of the U.S. economy). Not only has the data been changed, but also a slightly different focus has been put on the different sectors of the economy and different trends affecting these sectors. For example, in addition to outsourcing manufacturing jobs to developing countries and emerging markets, this chapter now discusses cross-border production chains in Europe and their implications. Chapter 8 on the labor markets now uses European definitions and European data for unemployment and labor force participation and contrasts experiences of different EU countries with each other.

Part III also contains many changes. One of the more obvious ones might be that we have altered the notation in the treatment of the Keynesian cross to make clear that the aggregate demand curve in the Keynesian cross is different from the AD curve in the AS/AD model used in later chapters (both of which were referred to as "AD" in the previous U.S. edition). To this end, we now refer to the aggregate demand/aggregate expenditure curve in the treatment of the Keynesian cross as "aggregate expenditure" or "AE," while we reserve the notation "AD" for the curve in the AS/AD model which also includes the central bank's reaction to changes in inflation.

In Chapter 10, we have changed the U.S.–centric examples and figures so that data now refers to the euro area and other European countries. Also, some more material on recent research on the size of fiscal multipliers has been added. In Chapter 11, the definitions for monetary aggregates used have been adjusted to those used in the euro area. Moreover, the discussion of the financial system has been adjusted to reflect European realities. The treatment of deflation was somewhat expanded. A new focus has also been put on the treatment of commercial banks' roles in money creation and the process through which they obtain the required reserves subsequently. This treatment is now more in line with the view in modern macroeconomic models that the central bank primarily adjusts the short-term rate of interest and both the money supply and the monetary base react (at least to a certain extent) endogenously. Chapter 12 has also been thoroughly revised and adapted to European institutions. The focus in this chapter is now on the ECB and its instruments, with a few references to practices at the Bank of England and other European central banks.

In Chapter 13, the justification for the downward-sloping AD curve has been altered to make it possible to analyze alternatively the case of a small euro-area country, a large euro-area country, and the euro area as a whole (or another economy with its own central bank): For small countries within the euro area, the negative slope of the AD curve is now explained with gains in competitiveness vis-à-vis the rest of the currency union when national inflation falls. For larger countries within the euro area and for countries with their own central bank, the negative slope is justified with the central bank's reaction function, in line with modern academic macroeconomic literature cited earlier. The applications in this chapter have been adjusted to refer to European economic events rather than to events important for the U.S. economy. Chapter 14 on international linkages through trade and finance flows now includes a treatment of the European Union as an example of regional integration. In this context, also the British decision to leave the EU ("Brexit") is discussed.

In Chapter 15, the treatment of the financial crisis in the U.S. from 2007 onward and the Great Recession has been expanded by a treatment of the housing bubbles and busts in Europe that happened during the same time. Also, the discussion of new financial regulations now also includes a discussion of changes in the EU regulatory environment for banks and other financial institutions. In Chapter 16, discussions of specific policy proposals for the U.S. have been replaced by a discussion of the effect of economic growth, inflation, and deflation on the trajectory of public debt as well as a thorough discussion of European rules for deficits and debt, especially the Stability and Growth Pact and the Fiscal Compact.

Chapter 17 is a completely new chapter on the euro crisis. The last two chapters of the book have been renumbered because of the addition of this new chapter. In Chapter 18 (formerly Chapter 17), the treatment of the Millennium Development Goals has been shortened (as the end point of 2015 for these goals has already lapsed), and new material on the recently adopted Sustainable Development Goals has been added. In Chapter 19 (formerly Chapter 18), relevant U.S.–centric examples have been replaced by European examples. The appendix on long-term demographic trends now presents data for the EU rather than the U.S.

ACKNOWLEDGMENTS

Macroeconomics in Context was written under the auspices of the Global Development and Environment Institute (GDAE), a research institute at Tufts University. The work of all contributors of written materials was paid for through grants raised by the Global Development and Environment Institute. By agreement with the authors, all royalties from sales of the book will go to support the work of the institute. We greatly appreciate the financial support that we have received from the Tides Foundation for putting together the European edition of this textbook and from the V. K. Rasmussen Foundation and others for supporting the work on the original editions.

GDAE Research Fellow Anne-Marie Codur contributed to Chapter 18 on growth and sustainability; Dr. James Devine of Loyola Marymount University, Los Angeles, contributed to the macro modeling chapters; Ben Beachy contributed to Chapter 15 on financial crisis; and Dr. Nathan Perry of Colorado Mesa University contributed to Chapter 16 on deficits and debt. Dr. Petra Dünhaupt prepared the lecturer slides.

We thank a number of instructors who were exceptionally generous in giving us detailed comments on the previous and the new editions, including Alison Butler, Willamette University; Gary Flomenhoft, University of Vermont; Robin King, Georgetown University; Dennis Leyden, University of North Carolina, Greenville; Marc Lavoie, University of Ottawa; Valerie Luzadis, SUNY-ESF, Syracuse; Torsten Niechoj, Rhine-Waal University of Applied Sciences; Eric Nilsson, California State University

San Bernardino; Chiara Piovani, University of Utah; Jan Priewe, HTW Berlin—University of Applied Sciences; Rebecca Smith, Mississippi State University; Saranna Thornton, Hampden-Sydney College; Marjolein van der Veen, Bellevue Community College; and Thomas White, Assumption College.

Essential support work on research and manuscript preparation, including data analysis for Chapter 0, was conducted by Juan Manuel Pons. We also thank the staff of Apex CoVantage, particularly Kate Fornadel, for their meticulous work in getting this book to press. At Routledge, our editor Emily Kindleysides and her assistant Laura Johnson contributed support and helpful suggestions throughout the process.

Sample Course Outlines

The timespan of an academic term imposes severe constraints on what an instructor can teach, which requires choices regarding which topics to include and how much time to devote to each. *Macroeconomics in Context* can be used as the basis for a variety of approaches, depending on how much flexibility you have and which topics and approaches are of particular interest.

To help you identify the chapter assignments that make the most sense for your class, we have put together some ideas for course outlines in what follows. Arranged in terms of broad selections and more specific emphases, they are designed to help instructors choose among chapters when there is not enough time to cover everything in this textbook.

We understand that in many departments, one primary objective of the introductory course is to teach in some detail "how (neoclassical) economists think." For instructors who choose to focus exclusively on neoclassical content, the most traditional combination of the selections described—the Base Chapters, combined with some or all of the Basic Macroeconomics Selection and the Macro-Modeling Emphasis—will provide what you need. This combination of chapters does not come close to exploiting fully the richness of *Macroeconomics in Context*, but the contextual discussions (a hallmark of this text) that are woven into the standard material will broaden the students' understanding of macroeconomic theory and provide tools for critical thinking.

Many instructors seek to combine coverage of traditional neoclassical ideas with other material. Addressing such users of *Macroeconomics in Context*, we suggest that you take advantage of the special structure of the book, which enables you to introduce traditional concepts in your introductory course while still reserving class time for other areas of interest. Ecological sustainability, for example, is an issue of increasing importance and is deeply linked to the functioning of the macroeconomy. For this focus, the Base Chapters Selection and most of the Basic Macroeconomics Selection could be combined with the "Ecological Emphasis" Selection. If your students already have a strong background in microeconomics, you can easily drop the base chapters.

Some instructors and students may have less interest in the formalities of macroeconomic modeling, in which case it might make sense to cover the Base Chapters Selection, some material from the Basic Macroeconomics Selection, and much more material from the topical emphases.

It may be worth rereading Chapter 1, Section 3, "Macroeconomics in Context," after finishing Part III, the section of the book that models economic fluctuations and policy responses. While the initial overview of controversies laid out in Chapter 1 is important to set the stage, it will probably be much better understood after the students have more exposure to macroeconomics.

Summary of Possible Course Options When Not All the Text Can Be Taught

Curriculum Focus	Likely Selections(see descriptions that follow)
Traditional macroeconomics	Base Chapters (depending on foundation in microeconomics) Basic Macroeconomics Modeling Emphasis
Strong focus on traditional macroeconomics, with other themes woven in	Base Chapters (depending on foundation in microeconomics) Basic Macroeconomics Choose from other Emphases
Strong focus on European economic policy issues	Base Chapters (depending on foundation in microeconomics) Basic Macroeconomics Choose selections from European Emphasis
Coverage of basic traditional concepts within course tailored to instructor and student interests	Base Chapters (depending on foundation in microeconomics) Choose selections from Basic Macroeconomics Choose from other Emphases

Base Chapters Selection

- Chapter 1, "Economic Activity in Context"
- Chapter 2, "Useful Tools and Concepts"
- Chapter 3, Section 1, "Introducing the Four Essential Economic Activities"
- Chapter 4, "Supply and Demand"

Basic Macroeconomics Selection

- Chapter 5, "Macroeconomic Measurement: The Current Approach"
- Chapter 8, "Employment, Unemployment, and Wages"
- Chapter 9, "Aggregate Demand and Economic Fluctuations"
- Chapter 10, "Fiscal Policy"
- Chapters 11 and 12, "Money, Banking and Finance" and "The European Central Bank and Monetary Policy"
- Chapter 13, "Aggregate Supply, Aggregate Demand, and Inflation: Putting It All Together"
- Chapter 17, "The Euro Crisis"

Ecological Emphasis

- Chapter 3, Section 2, "Resource Maintenance: Attending to the Asset Base of the Macroeconomy"

- Chapter 6, "Macroeconomic Measurement: Social and Environmental Dimensions"
- Chapter 7, Section 1, "The Three Major Productive Sectors in an Economy," and Section 2, "The Primary Sector in the European Union"
- Chapter 19, "Growth and Sustainability in the Twenty-First Century"

European Emphasis

- Chapter 7, "The Structure of the European Economy"
- Chapter 15, "The Financial Crisis and the Great Recession"
- Chapter 16, "Deficits and Debt"
- Chapter 17, "The Euro Crisis"

Global Emphasis

- Chapter 14, "International Linkages and Economic Policy"
- Chapter 18, "How Economies Grow and Develop"
- Chapter 19, "Growth and Sustainability in the Twenty-First Century"

Human Development Emphasis

- Chapter 6, "Macroeconomic Measurement: Environmental and Social Dimensions"
- Chapter 18, "How Economies Grow and Develop"

Structural Emphasis

- Chapter 7, "The Structure of the European Economy"
- Chapter 15, "The Financial Crisis and the Great Recession"
- Chapter 16, "Deficits and Debt"

Keynesian/Post-Keynesian/Institutionalist Emphasis

- Chapter 2, Section 3, "The Role of Markets"
- Chapter 4, Section 5, "Macroeconomics and the Dynamics of Real-World Markets"
- Chapter 13, Appendix A3, "Post-Keynesian Macroeconomics"
- Chapter 15, "The Financial Crisis and the Great Recession"

Macro-Modeling Emphasis

- Chapter 9, Appendix, "An Algebraic Approach to the Multiplier"
- Chapter 10, Appendix, "More Algebraic Approaches to the Multiplier"
- Chapter 13, Appendix, "More Schools of Macroeconomics"
- Chapter 14, Section 4, "Macroeconomics in an Open Economy"
- Chapter 18, Section 1, "Development and Economic Growth"

Money and Finance Emphasis

- Chapters 11 and 12, "Money, Banking, and Finance" and "The European Central Bank and Monetary Policy"

15

- Chapter 15, "The Financial Crisis and the Great Recession"
- Chapter 16, "Deficits and Debt"

Poverty/Inequality/Social Justice Emphasis

- Chapter 3, Section 3, "Distribution: Who Gets What, and How?"
- Chapter 6, Section 2, "Why GDP Is Not a Measure of Well-Being," Section 3, "Alternative Approaches to Representing Well-Being," and Section 4, "Measuring Household Production"
- Chapter 8, Section 3, "Theories of Employment, Unemployment, and Wages"
- Chapter 18, Section 3, "Understanding Poverty"

Contrasting-Schools-of-Thought Emphasis

- Have students reread Chapter 1, Section 3, "Macroeconomics in Context," after finishing Part III
- Chapter 13, Section 4, "Competing Theories," and Appendix, "More Schools of Macroeconomics"
- Chapter 19, "Growth and Sustainability in the Twenty-First Century," Section 5, "Are Stabilization and Sustainability in Conflict?"

Part I

The Context for Economic Analysis

Macroeconomics and Well-Being

What comes to your mind when you think of the word "economics"? Perhaps you think about things like inflation, unemployment, GDP (gross domestic product), supply and demand, and money. These things are definitely important in our study of economics, and we will spend much of our time in this book studying these concepts.

But the goals of economics are about much more than these. As we will see in Chapter 1, economics is *the study of how people manage their resources to meet their needs and enhance their well-being.* The term "well-being" can mean different things to different people. Traditional macroeconomic indicators like inflation, money, investment, and unemployment clearly affect our well-being. But so does our health, the quality of our environment, our leisure time, our perceptions of fairness and justice, and many other factors. In this book, we will take an inclusive approach to well-being.

If the goal of economics is to enhance our well-being, then it helps to have an idea about our current level of well-being—where we are doing well and where some improvement is desired. In this chapter, we introduce some of the most relevant data on macroeconomic indicators and well-being. Since in this book we are studying *macro*economics (as opposed to *micro*economics), we are often concerned with various measures at a national level. This chapter provides you with an overview of how a variety of countries compare across different measures of macroeconomic performance and well-being. As this book is aimed at European students, a specific focus here and in much of the rest of the book is put on the European Union, the euro area, and some of its most important member states (including Great Britain, which is still included in all official statistics on the European Union even though its government has made clear that it is going to leave the EU following a referendum on this question in June 2016). However, we recognize the importance of understanding any country within the global context. For each topic illustrated in this chapter, we present data on the European Union and some of its member states relative to other countries in order to provide some international perspective on the performance of the European economies. Different from later chapters in which we look at details of GDP (where we will mostly look at the euro area), we focus in this chapter mainly on the whole European Union with its 28 members (including the UK). The reason is that for some of the indicators, data for the EU is available, but not for the euro area. In contrast, when it comes to the details of GDP, it makes more sense to look at the euro area specifically which in many respects resembles a national economy. If you are interested in the performance of specific countries we have not included here, we provide detailed tables on the book's companion Web site: www.gdae.org/europeanmacro/.

The topics covered here preview many of the issues that are covered in more detail in later chapters. You may find some of the information in this chapter surprising. Sometimes the data-based results differ from common perceptions and media representations. But we have tried to be as objective as possible by presenting a wide range of data from reliable sources. Good data is essential for informed debates about how to enhance well-being in our communities, our country, and our planet.

NOTES ON GRAPHS

For each measure we include in this chapter, we provide a bar graph showing the data for selected countries. (Again, tables presenting the available results for all countries can be found on the book's Web site at www.gdae.org/europeanmacro/.) The countries shown here have been chosen to convey the full range of results, with a focus on the European Union and some of its member states (the EU results are presented in a different color). Major countries, such as the U.S., China, and India, are also included in each figure. Country rankings are provided, based on the available data, including the highest and lowest values for each variable. While there are more than 200 countries in the world, data is not available for all countries for each variable. Thus the number of countries ranked for each variable differs. For example, in our first chart (GDP per capita), we show that the lowest ranking for a country is 186. This tells you that reliable, accessible data on this variable is available for 186 of the countries in the world.

For each graph, the names of the countries selected appear on the left. The bar to the right of the country's name shows the value for that country, reading down from the end of the bar to the horizontal axis. Comparative data on GDP is presented in U.S. dollars, as most international data sources use the dollar rather than the euro as the main currency for cross-country comparisons. For example, we can see in the first graph that GDP per capita is roughly $16,000 in Brazil, a little under $37,000 in the EU, and almost $100,000 in Norway. If you want to find out the precise values, those are given on the book's Web site. Finally, to the right of each bar is that country's ranking for that variable. So Luxembourg has the third-highest GDP per capita, the United States the eleventh-highest, and Brazil the seventy-fourth-highest. Among the 186 countries with reliable GDP per capita data, the Central African Republic has the lowest GDP per capita.

The graphs that appear in this chapter are:

BOX 0.1 GDP PER CAPITA

What it is: Media stories of economic performance frequently refer to gross domestic product (GDP). A country's GDP per capita measures economic production per person per year, which gives us an idea of the average material living standards in the country. While GDP is perhaps the most commonly used macroeconomic metric, it does not necessarily measure well-being. We discuss how GDP is calculated in Chapter 5 and the limitations of and alternatives to GDP in Chapter 6.

The results: European Union countries cover a wide range in the ranking. Luxembourg ranks third, with a GDP per capita of around $98,000. Bulgaria ranks 69th, with a GDP per capita of $17,000. Were the EU one country, it would rank 30th, with a GDP per capita of around $37,000. In 2014, a year with still high oil prices, oil-producing Qatar had the world's highest GDP per capita at around $141,000, and the Central African Republic had the lowest, at only $590.

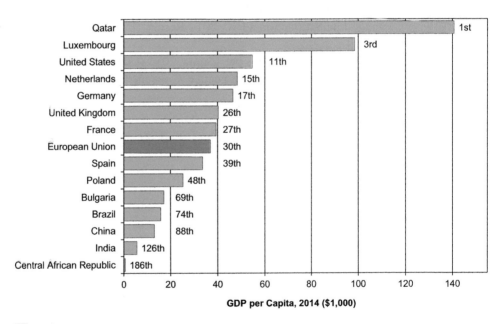

GDP per Capita, 2014 ($1,000)

Figure 0.1 *GDP per Capita, 2014 (Thousands of Dollars)*

Source: World Bank, World Development Indicators database.

Data is adjusted for purchasing power differences across countries (e.g., a dollar in India buys more than a dollar in the United States).

BOX 0.2 RECENT GROWTH RATE OF GDP PER CAPITA

What it is: In macroeconomics, we seek to explain not only why some countries have a higher GDP per capita but also what conditions lead to strong GDP growth rates. In this graph, we compare the growth in GDP per capita, after adjusting for inflation, across countries over the 10-year period 2005–2014. We discuss measuring GDP growth rates in Chapter 5 and theories of GDP growth in Chapter 18.

The results: GDP per capita over 2005–2014 grew rapidly in some countries and slowly in others and even declined in several countries. The highest growth in GDP per capita occurred in Qatar, primarily from the oil and gas industry, with high growth also in China, India, and Argentina. The fastest growth among developed countries took place in South Korea. Countries with declines in GDP per capita include Portugal, Italy, Greece, and Libya.

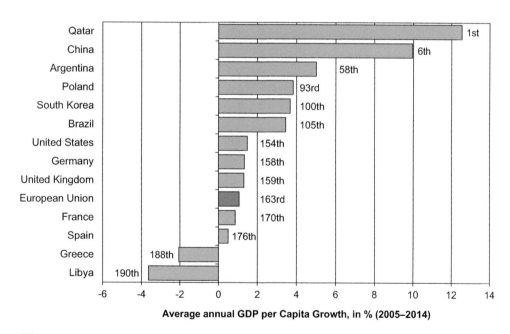

Average annual GDP per Capita Growth, in % (2005–2014)

Figure 0.2 *Growth in GDP per Capita, 2005–2014 (Percent)*

Source: International Monetary Fund, World Economic Outlook Database. April 2016 Edition.

Data is adjusted for purchasing power differences.

BOX 0.3 NET NATIONAL SAVINGS

What it is: How much a country saves and invests is widely considered an important factor in explaining differences in GDP growth rates. Here we present data on net national savings rates, which equal total national savings minus the depreciation of productive capital such as factories and machinery. A negative net national savings rate implies that a country's productive capacity may be declining. We discuss savings, investment, and growth in detail in Chapter 18.

The results: In 2014, China had the fifth-highest net national savings rate. Other countries with high savings rates include Norway, India, South Korea, and the Netherlands. Nineteen countries (among those with data) had a negative net savings rate in 2014, including the United Kingdom, Portugal, and Afghanistan.

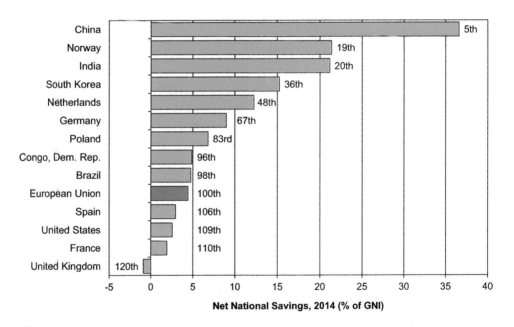

Figure 0.3 *Net National Savings Rate, 2014 (Percent of GNI)*

Source: World Bank, World Development Indicators database.

GNI is gross national income, a measure similar to gross domestic product.

BOX 0.4 GOVERNMENT DEBT

What it is: The level of government debt has been a focus of media stories in recent years. What matters is not so much the size of debt in dollars or euros but government debt relative to a country's GDP. This variable considers the amount of debt owed by the governments of different countries, including debts owed to domestic and foreign entities. What level of debt is a problem is a topic we discuss in more detail in Chapter 16.

The results: In 2014, Japan had the highest government debt in the world, measured as a percentage of GDP, followed by Greece and Jamaica. If the European Union were one single country, it would have the 24th-highest debt, but compared to other important developed countries such as the United States and Japan, this level is not overly high. Most developing countries have relatively low government debt.

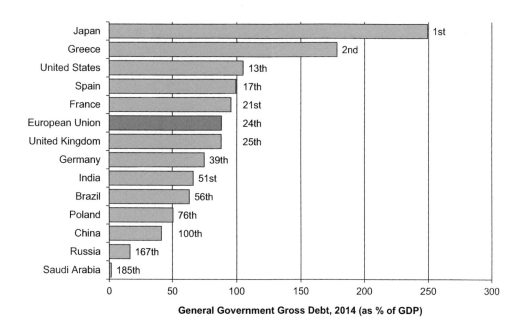

General Government Gross Debt, 2014 (as % of GDP)

Figure 0.4 *Government Debt (Percent of GDP)*

Source: International Monetary Fund, World Economic Outlook Database. April 2016 Edition.

BOX 0.5 LABOR PRODUCTIVITY

What it is: One measure of the economic efficiency of a country is labor productivity. This is calculated by dividing a country's GDP by an estimate of the total number of hours worked. Thus labor productivity tells us how many dollars of GDP are generated for each hour worked. We present more about labor productivity in Chapter 8.

The results: Data on labor productivity are available for only 36 countries. Luxembourg has the highest labor productivity in the world. On average, the European Union ranks 19th, behind countries like Canada and the United States. However, this is due mainly to low productivity in poorer EU countries such as Poland or Portugal. Less developed countries have lower labor productivity. We see that productivity in Mexico is only about 40 percent of the European Union level.

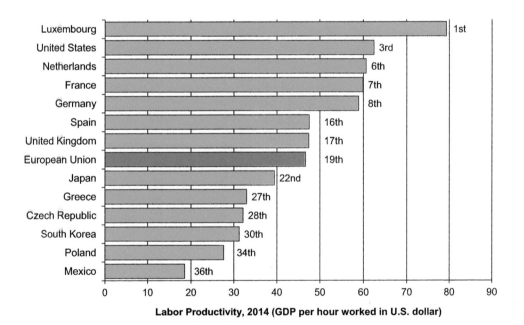

Labor Productivity, 2014 (GDP per hour worked in U.S. dollar)

Figure 0.5 *Labor Productivity, 2014 (GDP per Hour Worked)*

Source: Organisation for Economic Co-operation and Development, OECD online statistical database.

BOX 0.6 AVERAGE ANNUAL HOURS WORKED

What it is: Even if two countries have the same labor productivity, their GDP will differ if the number of hours worked is different. This graph shows the average number of hours worked each year per employee. Note that this includes only hours actually worked; vacations, holidays, and sick days are excluded. Thus the average annual hours worked in a country may be high if work expectations are more stringent and time off is limited. Work hours may also be high if workers choose to work long hours and there are very few part-time workers. We discuss work hours further in Chapter 8.

The results: Data on hours worked are available for only 36 countries. The average annual hours worked per employee is lowest in Germany. Other countries with relatively low annual work hours are the Netherlands, Norway, Denmark, and France. Work hours tend to be highest among countries with lower levels of GDP per capita. Lower hours worked correlates with the prevalence of part-time work, though the causation between these two variables could run in either direction. Other reasons include laws that mandate minimum vacation times and paid holidays. In the United States, where such laws do not exist, average work hours are higher.

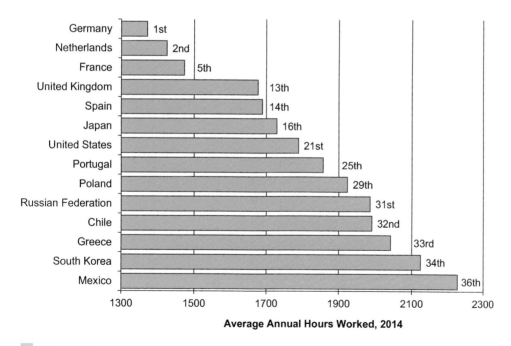

Average Annual Hours Worked, 2014

Figure 0.6 *Average Annual Hours Worked, 2014 (Lowest to Highest)*

Source: Organisation for Economic Co-operation and Development, OECD online statistical database.

BOX 0.7 UNEMPLOYMENT RATE (PERCENT OF TOTAL WORKFORCE)

What it is: The unemployment rate in a country is an important macroeconomic metric. Not only does having a job provide a source of income, but it also provides a sense of identity and contributes to overall well-being. Estimating the unemployment rate is somewhat complex. In Chapter 8, we discuss issues involved in estimating the unemployment rate including defining what it means to be in the workforce.

The results: Unemployment rates vary tremendously across countries. Qatar has the lowest official unemployment rate at 0.3 percent. While many poor countries, such as Mauritania, Lesotho, and Mozambique, have very high unemployment rates (20 percent or more), other poor countries such as Cuba and Bhutan have rather low unemployment rates, at around 3 percent. The unemployment rate in the European Union rose considerably during 2007–2009 and the euro-crisis recession, mainly because of a strong increase of unemployment in crisis countries such as Spain or Greece, with the two countries in 2014 having unemployment rates among the highest in the world.[1]

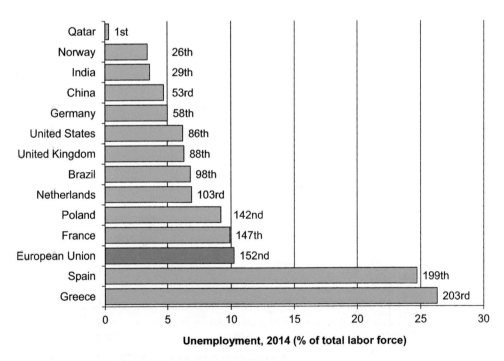

Figure 0.7 *Unemployment Rate, 2014 (Percent of Labor Force, Lowest to Highest)*

Source: World Bank, World Development Indicators database.

BOX 0.8 INFLATION

What it is: The rate of inflation summarizes how average prices change in a country in one year. For example, an inflation rate of 5 percent means that average prices increased by 5 percent that year. We discuss how to adjust data from different years for inflation in Chapter 5 and then focus on macroeconomic theories of inflation in Chapters 12 and 13.

The results: Over the period 2005–2014, Japan has had one of the lowest inflation rates in the world, with prices actually falling during some years and hardly increasing overall.[2] However, this is not necessarily a good thing, as we see later in the book. A low and stable—but not negative—inflation rate is generally considered one of the main macroeconomic policy goals. Most developed countries have generally been successful in controlling inflation in recent years. High and fluctuating inflation rates in a country are a sign of macroeconomic instability.

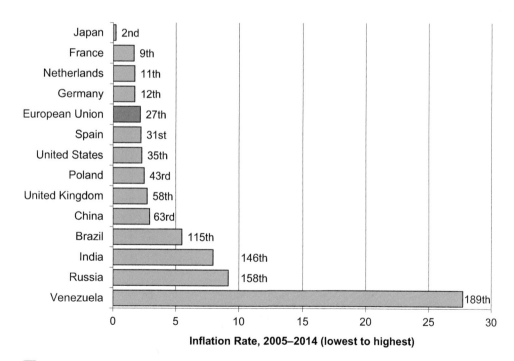

Figure 0.8 *Average Annual Inflation Rate, 2005–2014 (Lowest to Highest)*

Source: International Monetary Fund, World Economic Outlook Database. April 2016 Edition.

The average inflation rate is calculated as the average of the inflation rate for each year from 2005 to 2014.

BOX 0.9 GENERAL GOVERNMENT REVENUES (PERCENT OF GDP)

What it is: By providing and subsidizing various goods and services as well as redistributing between the rich and poor, the government can influence the well-being of the citizens, as we discuss in Chapter 10. General government revenues are funds collected by all levels of governments in the form of taxes, social security contributions, and other revenues that are available for government spending.

The results: The composition of the general government revenue varies significantly across countries. Among the countries with high government revenue (more than 50 percent) we find France, where most of its revenue comes from taxes, as well as Kuwait, which relies almost entirely on revenue from oil extraction. The European Union as a whole has a relatively high share of government revenue as percentage of GDP; however, 19 of its 28 members are below this level. The countries with the lowest government revenues (less than 15 percent of GDP) tend to be relatively poor countries in Africa, Asia, and Latin America.

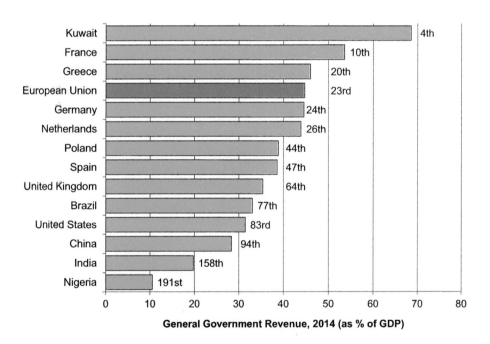

Figure 0.9 *General Government Revenue, 2014 (Percent of GDP)*

Source: International Monetary Fund, World Economic Outlook Database. April 2016 Edition.

BOX 0.10 TRADE BALANCE (PERCENT OF GDP)

What it is: In many countries, the trade balance is often a topic of media attention. When Britain decided to leave the EU, media pointed out that the country had a large trade deficit. In the case of Germany, there have been concerns that its surplus might be too large. A trade deficit means that a country imports more than it exports. Economists refer to a country's trade balance as the dollar value of its exports minus its imports, normally expressed as a percentage of GDP. Thus a negative trade balance indicates a trade deficit. A positive trade balance indicates a trade surplus. We discuss trade balances and other trade issues (such as the broader concept of the current account balance) in more detail in Chapter 14.

The results: Of the 164 countries with available data, 59 have a positive trade balance (exports exceed imports) and 105 have a negative balance. Those countries with the largest trade surpluses tend to be smaller countries (such as Macao, Luxembourg, and Singapore) or oil-producing countries (such as Qatar and Kuwait). Overall, the European Union had a trade surplus of about 2.7 percent of GDP, but with very different magnitudes between its members. Ireland had a trade surplus of almost 20 percent of GDP and the UK a deficit of 2.6 percent of GDP. The countries with the largest trade deficits tend to be poorer countries, although some poor countries do have trade surpluses.

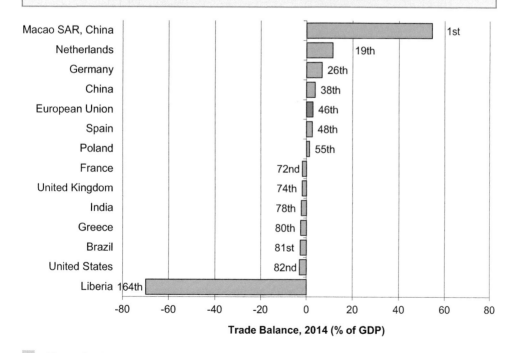

Figure 0.10 *Trade Balance (Percent of GDP)*

Sources: World Bank, World Development Indicators database; European Commission, Eurostat database; and authors' calculations.

BOX 0.11 INCOME INEQUALITY (GINI COEFFICIENT)

What it is: A Gini coefficient is a measure of economic inequality in a country. It is most commonly applied to the distribution of income (as is done in the figure), but it can also be applied to wealth distribution or other variables. It can range from 0 (everyone in the country has the same exact income) to 1 (one person receives all the income in a country). We learn more about Gini coefficients and economic inequality in Chapters 3 and 18.

The results: Scandinavian countries such as Sweden, Norway, and Finland tend to be the most equal countries in the world by income. Japan is also in this group in a number of equality measures (not all shown here but discussed in Chapter 18). On average, the European Union is in the 31st position among 146 countries with available information. Several African countries, including Botswana, Lesotho, Sierra Leone, and South Africa, are the most unequal countries in the world.

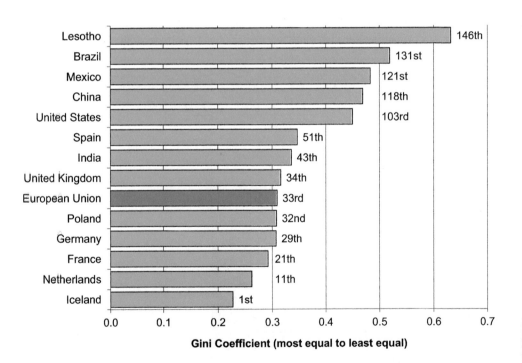

Figure 0.11 *Gini Coefficient (Most Equal to Least Equal)*

Source: Central Intelligence Agency, *CIA World Factbook.*

BOX 0.12 ABSOLUTE POVERTY

What it is: The $1.90-per-day poverty line has been defined by the United Nations as a measure of absolute poverty. One of the Sustainable Development Goals set by the United Nations is to eradicate absolute poverty worldwide. Formerly, under the Millennium Development Goals, the UN had aimed at halving the number of people in the world living in absolute poverty between 1990 and 2015. This goal has been met, mainly due to progress in China and India. We discuss poverty and economic development in Chapter 18.

The results: Note that this is the only graph in this chapter that does not include the European Union or any other developed countries (essentially no one in developed countries lives below the $1.90-a-day poverty line). A majority of people do live below that poverty line in 12 countries, including Haiti, Guinea, and Rwanda. A small portion of the population lives in absolute poverty in middle-income countries such as Albania or Uruguay.

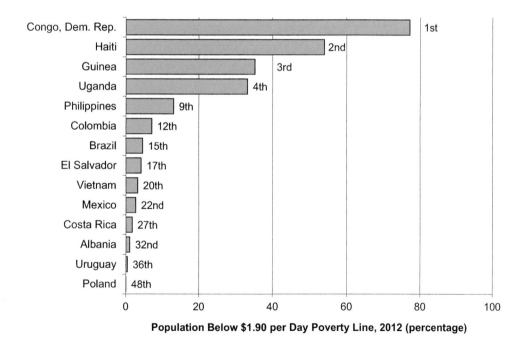

Population Below $1.90 per Day Poverty Line, 2012 (percentage)

Figure 0.12 *Percent of Population Living Below $1.90/Day Poverty Line, 2012*

Source: World Bank, World Development Indicators database.

BOX 0.13 FOREIGN AID

What it is: In 1970, the "economically advanced" countries agreed to a United Nations resolution on foreign aid to developing countries. The resolution set a target for official development assistance (ODA) of 0.7 percent of gross national income (GNI). ODA is defined as government flows to promote economic development and welfare in developing countries. The 0.7 percent target has been reaffirmed at subsequent international meetings. We discuss the role of foreign aid in promoting economic development in Chapter 18.

The results: In 2015, only seven countries met the 0.7 percent target: Sweden, the United Arab Emirates, Norway, Luxembourg, Denmark, the Netherlands, and the United Kingdom. ODA from Germany was 0.52 percent of GNI. Among the European countries, Latvia and Poland had the lowest ODA percentage, at 0.10 percent. Note that ODA does not include private charity donations or non-governmental organizations, only official aid given by governments, also including part of the support given to refugees who come to the donor countries.

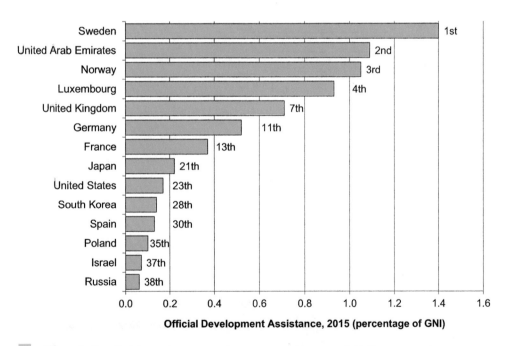

Figure 0.13 *Official Development Assistance, 2015 (Percent of GNI)*

Source: Organisation for Economic Co-operation and Development, Official Development Assistance—2015 Update.

BOX 0.14 INTERNET USERS

What it is: The percentage of people who have access to the Internet provides an indication of a country's level of technological development. As we discuss in Chapter 18, technology has long been recognized as one of the drivers of economic growth.

The results: Access to the Internet may not be as widespread as you think. While near-universal access occurs in a few countries, such as Iceland, Norway, and the Netherlands, in most developed countries, access rates are about 70–85 percent. On average, in the European Union, 78 percent of its population has Internet access. Middle-income countries generally have access rates around 30 to 50 percent. Thirty countries, most of them poor African countries, have access rates of less than 10 percent.

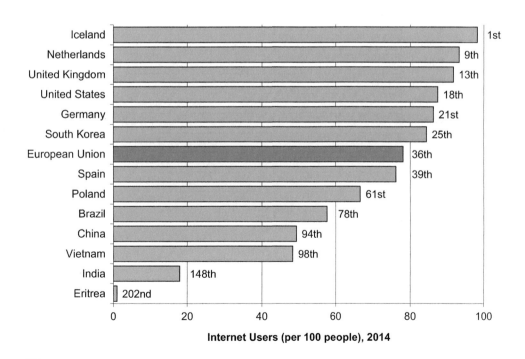

Figure 0.14 *Internet Users per 100 People, 2014*

Source: World Bank, World Development Indicators database.

BOX 0.15 EDUCATIONAL PERFORMANCE

What it is: Next we look at the educational performance of students in different countries. To compare across countries, we present data from the Programme for International Student Assessment, which administers standardized math, science, and reading tests to 15-year-olds in over 60 countries every three years. The graph below provides results from the science test. The country rankings were relatively similar for the math and reading tests, with some variations (e.g., Germany ranked 8th on the science test and 19th on the reading test).

The results: Students in Asian countries tended to achieve the highest test scores, including China, Singapore, Japan, and South Korea. Among European countries, students received high scores in Finland, Poland, and Germany. For less developed countries, scores tended to be lower.

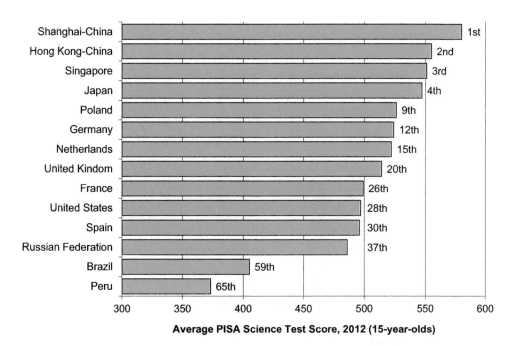

Average PISA Science Test Score, 2012 (15-year-olds)

Figure 0.15 *Average PISA Science Test Score, 2012 (15-year-olds)*

Source: Organisation for Economic Co-operation and Development, Programme for International Student Assessment, PISA 2012 Key Findings.

BOX 0.16 LIFE EXPECTANCY

What it is: Average life expectancy at birth is a common measure of health outcomes in a country. We discuss health as one component of well-being indices in Chapter 6 and as a topic of economic development in Chapter 18.

The results: Life expectancy at birth now exceeds 80 years in more than 30 countries, including Japan, France, Spain, and Greece. On average, people in the European Union have a life expectancy of around 82 years, in line with most developed countries. Life expectancy is the lowest, less than 50 years, in several African countries, including Swaziland and Lesotho.

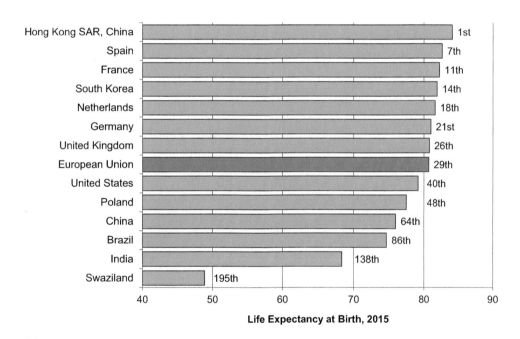

Life Expectancy at Birth, 2015

Figure 0.16 *Life Expectancy at Birth, 2015*

Source: World Bank, World Development Indicators database.

BOX 0.17 SUBJECTIVE WELL-BEING

What it is: Researchers are increasingly using surveys to measure well-being or happiness directly. The most common approach is to ask people to rate their overall satisfaction with their lives on a scale from 1 (dissatisfied) to 10 (satisfied). The responses are referred to as "subjective well-being." We discuss subjective well-being in more detail in Chapter 6.

The results: According to the most recent data, which cover 60 countries, Mexico has the highest level of average subjective well-being. Other relatively happy countries include Colombia, Qatar, Ecuador, and Uzbekistan. Among the European countries, the ones that rank higher are Sweden, the Netherlands, and Germany. Happiness levels are relatively low in countries recently having experienced conflicts such as Egypt or Iraq and in the poorest developing countries, such as Zimbabwe, as well as Eastern European countries, such as Russia, Georgia, and Estonia.

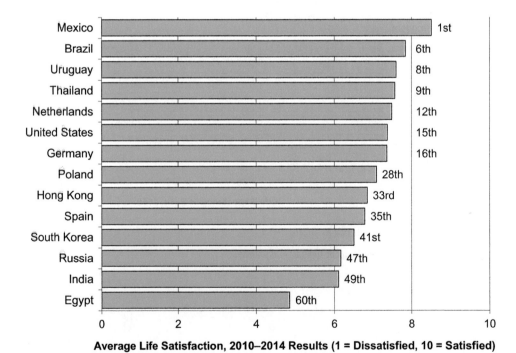

Average Life Satisfaction, 2010–2014 Results (1 = Dissatisfied, 10 = Satisfied)

Figure 0.17 *Average Life Satisfaction, 2010–2014 Results (1 = Dissatisfied, 10 = Satisfied)*

Source: World Values Survey, online database.

BOX 0.18 CARBON DIOXIDE EMISSIONS PER CAPITA

What it is: Carbon dioxide (CO_2) is the most important gas responsible for global climate change. CO_2 is emitted whenever fossil fuels are burned. Scientific analysis indicates that the accumulation of CO_2 in the atmosphere is raising global temperatures, leading to serious negative impacts on human societies and eco-systems. CO_2 per capita gives us an idea of how much the average person in a country is affecting the environment. We learn more about CO_2 and climate change in Chapter 19.

The results: The countries with the highest CO_2 emissions per capita are several oil-pro-ducing countries, including Qatar (the highest, at 44 tons per person), Kuwait, and United Arab Emirates. Were the European Union one country, it would rank 52nd, with emissions of around 7 tons per capita. Emissions per person in Greece and the Netherlands are slightly above the European Union level. While China is the world's largest emitter of CO_2 overall, on a per-capita basis, its emissions are below those in the United Kingdom, Germany, and the United States. CO_2 emissions per capita are negligible in the world's poorest countries.

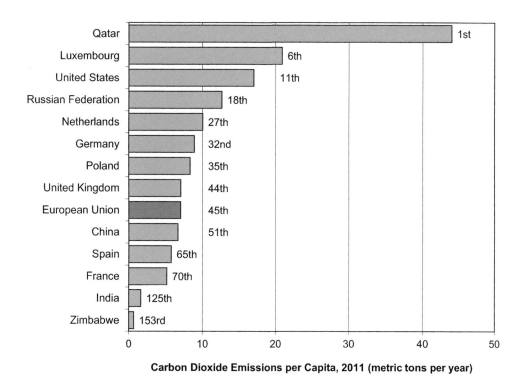

Carbon Dioxide Emissions per Capita, 2011 (metric tons per year)

Figure 0.18 *Carbon Dioxide Emissions per Capita, 2011 (Metric Tons per Year)*

Source: World Bank, World Development Indicators database.

BOX 0.19 LOCAL AIR QUALITY

What it is: While CO_2 emissions contribute to climate change, breathing air with elevated levels of CO_2 does not cause any adverse health effects. Local air pollutants, on the other hand, can cause numerous health effects, including asthma, lung cancer, and heart problems. One of the most important local air pollutants is particulate matter, which is emitted from power plants, industrial factories, motor vehicles, and other sources. Particulate matter pollution can be reduced through effective environmental regulations and technology. We discuss pollution further in Chapters 6 and 19.

The results: A country with high CO_2 emissions does not necessarily have poor local air quality. The United States is a prime example—CO_2 emissions are high, but local air quality is relatively good due to environmental laws and modern technologies. Other developed countries have as good or better local air quality. Developing countries can have good or poor local air quality, depending on their level of development, regulations, and technologies.

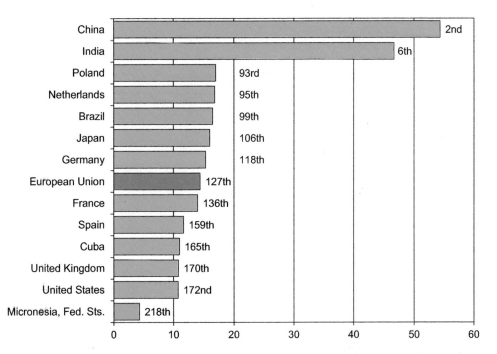

Average National Particulate Matter Concentration, 2013 (micrograms per cubic meter)

Figure 0.19 *Average National Particulate Matter Concentration, 2013 (Micrograms per Cubic Meter)*

Source: World Bank, World Development Indicators database.

Data is for particulate matter smaller than 2.5 micrometers, referred to as PM2.5. For reference, the European Union pollution standard for average PM2.5 is 25 micrograms/cubic meter ($\mu g/m^3$).

NOTES

1. Note that unemployment data in this chapter differs from that presented in Chapter 8. The reason is that in this chapter, data from the World Bank is used to make a comparison among as many countries as possible, while Chapter 8 uses the European definition of unemployment.
2. The absolute lowest rate of inflation was recorded in Zimbabwe, with prices actually falling. However, as this is a very special case (where the national currency was abandoned and prices fell after the introduction of the U.S. dollar), it is not included in the graph.

Chapter 1

Economic Activity in Context

What do you expect—and what do you want—from the economic system in which you live? Life, liberty, and the pursuit of happiness? Justice, peace, national security, a pleasant environment, and general welfare? Do you feel that you have the right to a job when you need or want one? And will you feel satisfied with access to just any job, or do you hope for one that will use your knowledge and talents, will provide you with a decent income, and will earn respect from others?

Your beliefs and expectations, taken together with those of many other people, contribute to the mood of optimism or pessimism that helps create economic booms or slumps. Other aspects of your economic behavior may contribute to the country's overall productivity. Goals are not the only determining factor for beliefs and actions, but they are an important element. This book will pay attention to goals because they are a part of what makes up the economy.

But there is another, more important reason to ask you, at the outset, about your life goals. Macroeconomics is about how economies work. This is not only interesting as an intellectual puzzle. It matters because when the economy works well, people have more opportunities to achieve their goals than when it is working badly. Depending on what your goals are, there are a variety of ways in which you could interpret what it means for an economy to be working "well" or "badly." As you read through this book, you will have plenty of opportunities to consider this idea and to think about how an understanding of basic economic principles can be used to judge or even to make economic policies. The study of economics can help us to achieve our goals as individuals and create a society in which we are satisfied to live.

1. WHAT IS MACROECONOMICS ABOUT?

economics: the study of how people manage their resources to meet their needs and enhance their well-being. The four essential economic activities are resource maintenance and the production, distribution, and consumption of goods and services.

Economics is the study of how people manage their resources to meet their needs and enhance their well-being. Individuals and societies engage in four essential economic activities: resource maintenance, production, distribution, and consumption. Resource maintenance means tending to, preserving, or improving the natural, produced, human, and social resources that form the basis for the economy and life itself. Production is using or converting some of these resources to make goods or services. Distribution refers to the sharing of products and resources among people, while consumption refers to their final use. Economists study how individuals engage in these activities, both as individuals and together through social coordination.

Often for convenience the study of economics is broken down into two parts: microeconomics and macroeconomics. This book, *Macroeconomics in Context*, is the companion to another textbook called (not surprisingly) *Microeconomics in Context*. Where **microeconomics** emphasizes the economic activities and interactions of individuals and particular organizations (such as businesses, households, community groups, nonprofit organizations, and government agencies), **macroeconomics** looks at how all of these activities join together to create an overall economic environment at the national—and often the global—level.

Economic conditions at the aggregate level create the environment in which individual economic actors make their decisions. These conditions include rates of unemployment and inflation, ecological limits and constraints, degrees of economic inequality, and social/cultural assumptions about trust and responsibility.

For example, when you seek paid work in your chosen field, your success will depend in part on both micro- and macroeconomic factors. On the microeconomic side, you will need to have prepared yourself for the work—invested in your own "human capital," an economist would say. You will need to find a particular business or other agency that can use your skills—or find direct buyers for your services if you decide to strike out on your own. You will want to find work that gives you a combination of job satisfaction, income, and benefits that you like.

But will employers in general be hiring? Some graduating classes are unlucky and flood the job market just as the national economy is "going sour"—that is, entering a **recession**. No matter how well prepared you are, finding a job can be tough during a period of high **unemployment**, when many people who seek jobs are not successful in finding them. And if you do find a job, how far will your paycheck go toward meeting your standard-of-living desires? If you start working during a period of high **inflation**, when the overall level of prices is increasing, the purchasing power of a fixed paycheck will be quickly eroded.

Macroeconomic conditions also affect personal debt. If your parents have bought a house, they will be paying back loans for a number of years. The higher the prevailing real interest rates in the economy, the more costly this borrowing will be. Your own economic well-being will also be tied to global issues such as trade flows and currency exchange rates—especially if you go to work for a business that does a lot of importing or exporting or you send money back to relatives in a home country. If you are lucky, all these factors will fall in your favor. If you are not . . . well, then you can join the chorus blaming "the economy" for your troubles.

Such macroeconomic issues are considered "short run"—economists refer to them as having to do with macroeconomic "fluctuations." Sometimes unemployment is high, and sometimes it is low, and the same goes for inflation, interest rates, trade deficits, and exchange rates.

Other macroeconomic issues have to do with the long run. Can you expect your standard of living 20 years from now, or the standard of living of your children, to be higher or lower than what you enjoy now? Are you living in a society where all people

microeconomics: the study of the economic activities and interactions of individuals, households, businesses, and other groups at the subnational level

macroeconomics: the study of how economic activities at all levels create a national (and global) economic environment

recession: a downturn in economic activity, usually defined as lasting for two consecutive calendar quarters or more

unemployment: a situation in which people seek a paying job but cannot obtain one

inflation: a rise in the general level of prices

43

macroeconomy: an economic system whose boundaries are normally understood to be the boundaries of a nation or an area, such as the euro area, when it is operating, in economic terms, like a nation.

global economy: the system of economic rules, norms, and interactions by which economic actors and actions in different parts of the world are connected to one another

economic actor (economic agent): an individual, group, or organization that is involved in economic activities

have a chance to develop themselves, or are extremes of wealth and poverty becoming more pronounced over time? What is the supply of natural resources used in production processes, and what is the quality of those resources? What other social and environmental factors affect the ability of the economy to prosper or threaten its success?

Macroeconomics seeks to explain an especially interesting phenomenon: the fact that bad things can often happen on a national or global level even though virtually no individual or microeconomic-level organization *wants* or *intends* them to happen. People generally agree that high unemployment, persistent high inflation, and destruction of the natural environment, for example, are bad things, yet they occur nonetheless.

Microeconomics and macroeconomics are terms that are applied rather loosely, covering or emphasizing different topics as times and circumstances change. Many issues have both macroeconomic and microeconomic aspects. For example, the increase of the value-added tax will affect microeconomic behavior—people may consume less or shift their patterns of consumption toward untaxed items—but it also affects government revenues, which, as we will see, are an important element of macroeconomic analysis. No one speaks of "the microeconomy" because there are too many subnational economic systems of varied sizes that are studied in the field of microeconomics. However, the term **macroeconomy** is used to refer to a national economic system or to the economy of the euro area (which resembles in many ways a national economy even if it is not quite one—see Chapter 17).

People also speak of the **global economy**, meaning the system of economic rules, norms, and interactions by which economic actors and actions in different parts of the world are connected to one another. **Economic actors (or economic agents)** include all individuals, groups, and organizations that engage in or influence economic activity. As the global economy has become an increasingly important part of the experience of more and more people, it has become more essential to include its study in introductory macroeconomics courses. You can expect to find global as well as macroeconomic issues extensively covered in this book.

Discussion Questions

1. You have evidently made a decision to dedicate some of your personal resources of time and money in college to studying economics. Why? What do you hope to learn in this course that will be helpful for you in reaching your goals?

2. Are you familiar with the following terms? While you will study them in detail in this course, see how well you can come up with a definition for them just from your previous knowledge. (It does not matter at this point if you are not familiar with them.)

unemployment	recession
inflation	economic boom
economic growth	money
development	fiscal policy
GDP	monetary policy
investment	sustainability

2. MACROECONOMIC GOALS

We have introduced the idea of an economy working "well" or "badly" and have referred to high unemployment, persistent high inflation, and destruction of the natural environment as bad things that virtually no one wants. "Bad" and "good" are value-laden terms. Do they belong in an economics textbook?

Social scientists often make a distinction between **positive questions**, which concern issues of fact, or "what is," and **normative questions**, which have to do with goals and values, or "what should be." For example, "What is the level of poverty in our country?" is a positive question, requiring descriptive facts as an answer. "How much effort should be given to poverty reduction?" is a normative question, requiring analysis of our values and goals. In our study of economics, we often find that positive and normative questions are inextricably intertwined. For example, consider the definition of poverty. To construct a definition of poverty, we need to combine facts about income distribution with a normative assessment of where to draw the poverty line. We also need to consider whether the definition of poverty should be based solely on income or whether it should include information about people's **assets** or opportunities. Life rarely offers us a neat distinction between "what is" and "what ought to be"; more often, we have to deal with a mixture of the two.

Another important thing to realize is that positive statements often carry normative implications. Consider the statement "The total share of income taxes paid by the top 25 percent of the households in Germany rose from 69.6 percent in 1992 to 76.5 percent in 2010."[1] This is a positive statement, but it seem to suggest that the top 25 percent of the income earners pay an excessive tax share and their tax burden has further increased in the recent past. But is this really true? A more complete analysis reveals that the main reason that the share of taxes paid by the top income earners in Germany and many other countries rose so much since 1990 is that they received a much larger share of income. So we need to be careful about making conclusions based on incomplete or misleading positive statements.

Much of this textbook is concerned with positive issues. Using both empirical evidence and various theories, we describe—using the best available economic research—how an economy functions at the macro level. Yet although a few people perhaps enjoy studying economic principles for their own sake, the main reason that anyone would study macroeconomics is to try to understand how we—as a society, country, and world—can reach our desired goals. Thus we cannot avoid the normative question of what goals the macroeconomy *should* achieve.

Not everyone has the same goals, either at a personal level or as part of their idea of a "good" society. However, agreement becomes easier at a more general level. Therefore, we start with the term **well-being** to describe the overall quality of life, recognizing that this broad goal has numerous normative components.

In the context of macroeconomics, we can say that three especially important components of well-being are **good living standards**, **stability and security**, and **sustainability**.

positive questions: questions about how things are

normative questions: questions about how things should be

assets: property owned by an individual or company

well-being: a term used to describe the overall quality of life

three major macroeconomic goals: the achievement of good living standards, stability and security, and sustainability.

2.1 Living Standards

One macroeconomic goal is to achieve and maintain people's living standards at a high enough level that their lives can be long, healthy, and enjoyable and offer them the opportunity to accomplish the things that they believe give their lives meaning.

The most basic living standard issues relate to the quality of people's diets and housing, their access to means of transportation and communication, and the quality of medical attention that they receive. Taking a somewhat broader view, we might also include less tangible aspects of life, such as the quality of education that people receive and the variety of entertainment that they can enjoy.

In addition, the way in which people participate in producing goods and services—as well as their consumption of them—has important implications for their health and happiness. So for working-age people, the quality of their working lives is part of their standard of living. And for people who cannot do much work because they are too young, old, ill, or handicapped, the quality of the hands-on care that they receive is a major component of their living standard.

As we will see in Chapter 6, we could add even more categories to broaden our notion of well-being, going beyond economic issues to include things like political freedom and social inclusion (see Box 1.1). Traditionally, however, macroeconomics has regarded **living standards growth** as the top concern.

living standards growth:
improvements in people's diet, housing, medical care, education, working conditions, and access to transportation, communication, entertainment, and other amenities

---

BOX 1.1 ELEMENTS OF WELL-BEING

The following are some elements that might go into a broad concept of well-being. When you think about a good life for yourself, are there elements that you would wish to add to or subtract from this list?

- Satisfaction of basic physical needs, such as adequate nutrition, health care, and a comfortable living environment.
- Security that one's basic needs will continue to be met, as well as security against aggression or unjust persecution.
- Happiness, expressed through feelings of joy, contentment, pleasure, and so forth.
- The ability to realize one's potential, including physical, intellectual, moral, social, and spiritual development.
- A sense of meaning in one's life; a reason or purpose for one's efforts.
- Fairness, including appropriate rewards for one's efforts and fair and equal treatment by social institutions.
- Freedom to make personal decisions within the limits of responsible relations with others (and the limits of their decision-making capacity, as in the case of children).
- Participation in social decision-making processes.
- Good social relations, including those with friends, family, business associates, and fellow citizens, as well as peaceful relations among countries.
- Ecological balance, meaning that natural resources are preserved and, where necessary, restored to a healthy and resilient state.

How can living standards be maintained or improved? For a long time, "raising living standards" was considered nearly synonymous with "achieving economic growth." By **economic growth**, we mean growth in the level of marketed production or output. Traditionally, this has been measured within a country by the growth of its gross domestic product (GDP)—a measure that you will hear much more about in later chapters.

economic growth:
increases in the level of marketed production in a country or region

Global economic growth has been impressive in recent decades. Figure 1.1 plots the sum of GDP for all countries from 1960 to 2015. The data from which this chart has been plotted are far from perfect—different countries have at different times used a variety of methods to calculate their GDP. The definition of GDP can also be controversial, as we explore in Chapters 5 and 6. Nevertheless, we can reasonably conclude from this picture that global production of goods and services has increased greatly over the past few decades. By this measure, the value of global production in 2015 was about 6.2 times the value in 1960.

The growth in economic production has not been equal in all countries, and material living standards are still very low in much of the world. This fact is important for people's options and their enjoyment of life. Poverty can mean that people are crowded together in unsanitary urban slums or isolated in rural huts, have barely enough to eat, receive little or no education, and never see a doctor.

Worldwide, extreme poverty is still a major concern; according to a World Bank study estimating poverty for 2012, roughly one billion people—about one-sixth of the population of the developing world—had less than $1.90 to spend per day. The production

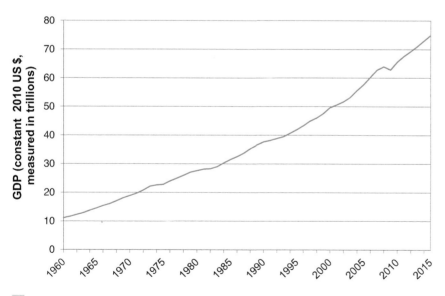

Figure 1.1 *Global Production, 1960–2015*

As measured by summing up the GDP of all countries, global production has more than sextupled in the last five and a half decades.

Source: The World Bank Group, World Development Indicators Online.

47

of more and better housing, better roads, more grain, more schooling, and more medical care—*more goods and services*—is necessary to raise living standards in such situations.

Because of this underlying concern with living standards, for many decades economists focused very strongly on measures of economic growth and the question of how it could be maintained and increased. The process of moving from a general situation of poverty and deprivation to one of increased production and plenty is what has traditionally been referred to as **economic development**. (This topic is discussed at greater length in Chapter 18.)

Generally, economic development has been thought of as a process of increasing agricultural productivity, investing in machinery and technology, and making changes in the organization of work (from home-based shops to factories, for example), so that **labor productivity** rises—meaning that people can produce more in each hour that they work.

Of course, while increased production is *necessary* in such a situation, it is not *sufficient* on its own to improve living standards for the people living in a poor country. For one thing, the increase in production may not be enough to keep pace with a growing population. Improvement in general living standards can result only if production *per person* (GDP *per capita*) on average rises.

Some of the increase in global production shown in Figure 1.1 is simply a result of more people producing goods and services. When we adjust for the growth in the world's population, we see that production per capita, measured by dividing global production by global population, has also grown over the past several decades, but not by as much. Figure 1.2 shows that global production per capita increased by about a factor of 2.6 between 1960 and 2015, according to this measure.*

economic development: the process of moving from a situation of poverty and deprivation to a situation of increased production and plenty through investments and changes in the organization of work

labor productivity: the level of output that can be produced per worker per hour

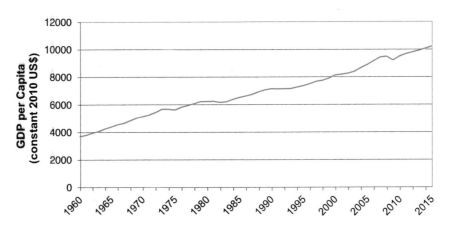

Figure 1.2 *Global Production per Capita, 1960–2015*

Global production per person has more than doubled in the last five decades.

Source: The World Bank Group, World Development Indicators Online.

---

* These figures are corrected for inflation. We examine the process by which economists correct GDP figures for inflation in Chapter 5.

If we were to disaggregate from the global figures, we would see that increases in economic production over these years vary significantly across different regions and countries. In East Asian countries, GDP per capita increased almost sevenfold. In sub-Saharan Africa, however, GDP per capita increased only about 50 percent between 1960 and 2015.

Even if GDP *per capita* is rising, other factors are still important in ensuring that economic growth benefits the world's and each country's population as a whole.

- First, it matters *what* is produced. An economy may experience "economic growth" by increasing its production of military hardware or large public monuments, for example, but these kinds of production raise living standards less than growth in production of nutritious food, widely available health care, or the quality of basic education.
- Second, it matters *how* it is produced. In some poorer countries today, many workers—including young children—work 14- to 16-hour days in unsafe, badly ventilated mines and factories; many suffer severe illnesses and early death. And in both rich and poor countries, production is often carried out in ways that deplete or degrade essential natural resources.
- Third, it matters *for whom* economic growth occurs. How are the increases in production or in incomes arising from production distributed among the population? Do some regions, or some groups of people as defined by income class, race, ethnicity, gender, or other factors, receive more of the gains from growth than others? If the benefits of economic growth go only to a tiny global or national elite, the bulk of the population may remain very poor.

Sometimes these queries about "what, how, and for whom?" are referred to as the "three basic economic questions." Even given the qualifications raised by these questions, it is generally true that in regions that are very poor, economic growth is necessary and important to increase well-being.

In richer regions, the situation may be different. In a country that is already rich, is economic growth still the key to improving living standards and increasing overall well-being? In most highly industrialized countries, populations are growing very slowly—in many countries, they are declining or on a trajectory that will soon bring about population decline.* When the population is not growing, and when the majority of families already enjoy decent housing, safe water, plenty of food, readily available heating and refrigeration, a car or two (or more), airline travel, TVs, and the like, do we really need *more* in general?

Some people would say that we do, but others believe that we should instead switch our national priorities into making sure that production is designed to increase well-being. In countries that already have a high level of production, *living standards growth* may be achievable even in the absence of *economic growth* by

---

* For more on this subject, see the Appendix to Chapter 18.

improving cultural, educational, and environmental conditions, raising the quality of work-life and the quantity of leisure, and promoting an equitable allocation of economic rewards.

We return to these questions—and to the critical issue of the relationships among economic growth, job creation, and well-being—in later chapters.

2.2 Stability and Security

While closely linked to goals for living standards, the goal of stability and security brings in a dimension that we have not yet discussed. Imagine that you are elderly, and, looking back over your life, you can say that *on average*, you enjoyed a good standard of living. This might arise from two quite different scenarios. In one scenario, you enjoy a fairly steady or gently rising living standard and are always able to plan confidently for your financial future.

In the other scenario, you are quite successful at some points in your life but also periodically have to face the real possibility of "losing it all." You do well and buy a very nice house, but then you become unemployed, and your house is foreclosed on because you are not able to make the mortgage payments. Then you start to do well again and believe you are on a solid path to a pleasant retirement, but steeply rising price levels or a jumpy stock market reduces the value of your savings and pension. Even if, after the fact and "over the long run," you can say that *on average* you have done OK in terms of your living standards, the uncertainty and anxiety of living with economic fluctuations in the second scenario would take a toll on your overall well-being relative to the more stable case.

High rates of unemployment are associated with many indicators of individual and social stress, such as suicide, domestic violence, and stress-related illnesses among those affected, and crime. Unpredictable fluctuations in employment levels and rates of inflation, interest rates, and foreign exchange rates make it difficult—and, in the worst cases, impossible—for individuals and organizations to make productive and economically sensible plans for the future. This has been a major concern for many young people who entered the work force during or after the major recession of 2008–2009 or during the euro crisis that followed.

One common pattern is for fluctuations in the level of production to occur as a cycle in which recessions (or "contractions" or "slumps") and their attendant problem of high unemployment alternate with booms (also called "expansions" or "recoveries"), which often bring with them the problem of more rapidly rising prices. This is called the **business cycle** or **trade cycle**. Even if these problems are "short run" and do not last long—people eventually find jobs or inflation slows down—fluctuations cause considerable "ill-being" while they last. So creating a stable, secure economic environment is a separate important macroeconomic goal.

In this chapter, we follow the common convention of using GDP as an indicator of prosperity. In Part II of this book, as well as later, we discuss with more precision exactly what it is that GDP does—and does not—measure. For now, we will use GDP per capita as an overall measure of economic activity. For example, consider Figure 1.3,

business (trade) cycle: recurrent fluctuations in the level of national production, with alternating periods of recession and boom

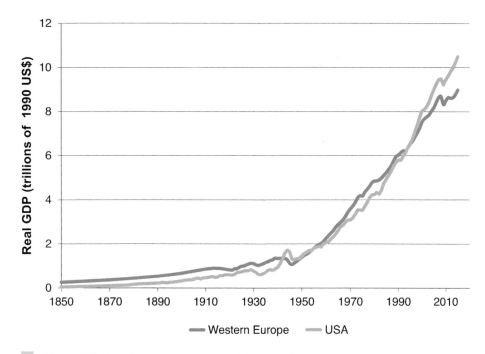

Figure 1.3 *GDP in Western Europe and the United States, 1850–2015*

GDP in Western Europe and the United States has grown over time, but it has not grown steadily. The economy has experienced alternating periods of expansion and contraction.

Source: The Maddison-Project, www.ggdc.net/maddison/maddison-project/home.htm, 2009 version. Updated with data from the IMF World Economic Outlook 2016.

which shows GDP for 12 Western European countries* and the United States since 1870. You can see that, while the general trend is upward, the curve on the graph does not indicate *steady* growth. The curve is somewhat wavy. During some periods, GDP fell as countries experienced economic contractions, and during other periods, GDP rose very steeply due to rapid economic expansion. (GDP numbers in Figure 1.3 are expressed in "real," or inflation-adjusted, and internationally comparable terms.)

One widely accepted macroeconomic goal is the achievement of sufficient economic stability to enable individuals and families to enjoy economic security and to be able to make reasonable predictions about their future. In the light of new knowledge about our dependence on the natural world, which is undergoing radical alterations due to human economic activity, the goal of security now must also include a much longer time horizon, recognizing a serious responsibility to future generations. This leads us to our third goal: sustainability.

---

* These countries are: Austria, Belgium, Denmark, Finland, France, Germany, Italy, the Netherlands, Norway, Sweden, Switzerland, and Britain.

2.3 Sustainability

We want good living standards and stability not only for ourselves right now but also for ourselves later in our lives and for our children, grandchildren, and other generations to come.

In order to understand whether we should be thinking of the goal of sustainability, we must address the questions:

- Are economic activities *financially* sustainable into the future? Or is a country incurring a high amount of debt that may create a heavy burden on its future inhabitants?
- Are economic activities *socially* sustainable into the future? Are disparities between the "haves" and the "have-nots" accelerating or diminishing? Are they based on justifiable causes or on unequal power relations? Are young people receiving the upbringing and education required to enable them to contribute to a healthy economy and society? Or is the current structure of economic activity setting the stage for future social disruption and political strife?
- Are economic activities *ecologically* sustainable into the future? Is the natural environment that supports life being treated in a way that will sustain its quality into the future? Or is it becoming depleted or degraded?

For many generations, it seemed that technological progress and economic growth were magical keys that unlocked the door to unlimited improvements in the standard of living. For example, real output per person in Western Europe in 2005 was about 10 times what it had been in 1870. "Developed" countries experienced long-run rising standards of living through industrialization, improvements in agricultural technology, and the development of service industries.

Can this process continue indefinitely? Some have argued that sustainability problems can be remedied by *more* GDP growth. For example, the issue of financial sustainability includes both concerns about the level of government debt (which accumulates whenever governments spend more than they take in) and external debt (what all people and organizations in a country owe to foreigners). Too much debt is a problem, since it means that a large proportion of a country's income in the future may need to be directed toward paying back the debt rather than other, more socially beneficial, uses. Indebtedness, however, is usually considered manageable as long as the growth of GDP is at least keeping pace with the level of debt so that debt does not increase as a percent of GDP.

Regarding social sustainability, some people believe that economic growth is also the way to relieve social ills and political strife. They reason that the bigger the pie, the bigger everyone's share can be and that rising personal incomes will naturally lead to a peaceful and productive population. Concerning ecological issues, some economists think that any current negative effects of economic growth on the environment can be remedied by additional economic growth, since higher incomes give countries the wherewithal to invest in new exploration for resources and new pollution-controlling technologies. So to the most growth-oriented economists, "sustainable growth" simply means making sure that the growth rate of GDP stays high well into the future.

In contrast to those who believe that economic growth, as traditionally defined, holds the best answers to financial, social, and environmental problems, by the end of the twentieth century, some economists had started asking whether these might instead *contribute to* these problems.

To the extent that a country's economic prosperity depends on short-sighted or unrealistic financial planning, prosperity may be unsustainable. For decades, for example, many poorer countries were encouraged to borrow heavily from richer countries in order to make progress in economic development. However, many of them did not achieve the high rate of economic growth that was supposed to result from the borrowing, and a severe "debt crisis" resulted. Some very poor countries currently spend more funds simply to pay the interest on their debt than they pay for health care for their own populations; many also pay more in principal and interest than they currently receive in grants and loans.

Some industrialized countries, including the United States, also borrow heavily to fund their activities. Many fear that such borrowing may become so excessive that dramatically higher taxes will be required in the future in order to pay interest on the debt. Those called on to pay these higher taxes—and, hence, suffer lower living standards—would be future workers like you. Setting good priorities about how we borrow—and what we borrow for—is important for long-run sustainability. This issue will be discussed in detail in Chapter 16.

Turning to social sustainability, many economists and other observers have come to question whether "development" as traditionally defined will solve the problem of global disparities in living standards. Some economists suggest that historical factors such as the legacy of colonization and political factors such as rich countries' protection of their own industries within the system of global trade mean that it is impossible to expect poorer countries to "develop" in the same way as countries that industrialized earlier. Analysts have also estimated that giving everyone in the world a U.S.-American lifestyle (which is one of the most resource-consuming lifestyles in the world), including a meat-rich diet and multiple cars per family, would require an extra two to four planets to supply resources and absorb waste! If everyone would strive toward, let's say, a Dutch or French lifestyle, the number of additional planets required to achieve this might be lower but not enough lower to change the conclusion: Not everyone can have the same consumption pattern as we have in the industrialized world today. There is, indeed, reason to question whether dwellers in rich countries will be able, in the long term, to maintain current consumption patterns.

Traditional goals of unlimited material affluence have also been called into question within richer countries, and some social scientists have suggested that consumerist and "more-is-better" values may actually contribute to personal and social discontent and the weakening of social norms of trust and reciprocity. Societies that suffer wide divisions between "haves" and "have-nots," or a general sense that everybody is just out for him- or herself, are more likely to suffer social and political breakdown—perhaps

53

to the point of violence—than societies in which. people enjoy a greater sense of social cohesion.

Regarding environmental issues, land development and certain agricultural practices have caused extinction of some species and notable decreases in genetic diversity in others. Contemporary "developed" economies are presently heavily dependent on the consumption of fossil fuels; but scientists warn that carbon dioxide emissions from the burning of fossil fuels are rapidly exacerbating global climate change.

This raises the question of whether it is sufficient to sustain the financial, economic, and ecological systems *as they are now*. Some of the ecological systems that support economic activity may already be severely degraded. In such cases, it is not enough to sustain what exists now—rather, we need to take on a goal of **restorative development**, to rebuild systems that are no longer supporting well-being in the present and the future.

Some ecologically oriented economists have suggested that instead of placing blind faith in technological progress and economic growth, society should adopt a **precautionary principle**. This principle says that we should err on the side of caution, or, as stated by one group of experts, "When an activity raises threats of harm to the environment or human health, precautionary measures should be taken even if some cause and effect relationships are not fully established scientifically."[2] Such attention to environmental sustainability need not preclude also giving attention to the goals of living standards improvement and stability, but it does clearly call into question the idea that economic growth, in itself, is always the only or the best goal.

Many economists in the twentieth century did not explicitly address the question of macroeconomic goals, content in the belief that economic growth would naturally contribute to the achievement of any other goals that we might choose. The authors of this book have found it helpful to view the economy as though it exists with a purpose; and that purpose is not simply growth in output (as has been assumed in many other macroeconomic texts) but, more broadly, human well-being in the present and the future. This requires learning how to balance ideas on how to achieve economic growth with questions about what kinds of growth actually contribute to well-being and ideas on how present and future well-being can be enhanced by restorative development.

restorative development: economic progress that restores economic, financial, social, or ecological systems that have been degraded and are no longer adequately supportive of human well-being in the present and the future

precautionary principle: the principle that we should err on the side of caution when facing a significant possibility of severe damage to human health or the natural environment

Discussion Questions

1. Which of the macroeconomic goals discussed in this section do you think should have the highest priority? Why? Are there other major goals that you think are missing from the preceding discussion?

2. No one would argue that the goal of macroeconomics is to make people *worse* off! Yet this outline of macroeconomic goals suggests that trying too hard to achieve some narrowly defined goals may lead to such a result. Why do you think that some economists would view economic growth as the major goal, while others view it as potentially in conflict with other goals such as economic, social, or environmental sustainability?

3. MACROECONOMICS IN CONTEXT

Macroeconomics, as a field of study, is not a set of principles that is set in stone. Rather, the field has developed and changed over time as new empirical and theoretical techniques have been invented and as historical events have raised new questions for which people have urgently desired answers. To give you an idea of how the various principles in this book fit into social and historical contexts, we end this chapter with a short overview of the major historical developments in macroeconomics. This is not just dusty history; you will see as you progress through this textbook that many themes keep arising in slightly new forms, while other challenges are unique to our twenty-first–century world.

3.1 The Classical Period

Centuries ago, most people in the world were involved in agriculture or in home production, such as when a family would work together to turn raw wool into cloth. Merchants were a minority, and industrial production and large-scale trade were unknown. All this changed with the coming of the Industrial Revolution, which began in England in the mid-eighteenth century. In many countries, technological progress led to new methods of production, and more productive economies both increased and diversified their output. Necessities like food and clothing used up a decreasing proportion of the average family income, while a growing fraction of the population was able to acquire more comforts and luxuries—better bedding, plumbing, housing, and transportation, to name just a few of the improvements in living standards. Academic thinkers started to try to understand and explain how these changes came about—and **classical economics** was born.

During this period, macroeconomic study focused on economic growth and distribution. The most famous classical economist was the Scottish philosopher Adam Smith (1723–1790), whose 1776 book *An Inquiry into the Nature and Causes of the Wealth of Nations* set the terms of discussion for centuries to come. Smith attributed the growing "wealth of nations" to various factors. One was changes in the organization of work, particularly the **division of labor** that assigned workers to **specialized**, narrowly defined tasks. Whereas, in family-based production, each individual had usually performed a variety of tasks, in industrial production a person would repeat one specific task over and over, presumably becoming more proficient with increased practice. Another factor was technological progress, such as the invention of new machines powered by burning coal. The third was the accumulation of funds to invest in plants and machinery ("capital accumulation"). Classical economists were also particularly concerned with theorizing about how the funds generated by selling output would come to be distributed between the people who worked in factories and the capitalists who owned the factories.

Classical economists, including Smith, David Ricardo, Thomas Malthus, John Stuart Mill, and Karl Marx, were interested in several questions that are still among the most important issues for macroeconomics: How is the total wealth generated by a society

classical economics: the school of economics, originating in the eighteenth century, that stressed issues of growth and distribution, based on an image of smoothly functioning markets

division of labor: an approach to production in which a process is broken down into smaller tasks, with each worker assigned only one or a few tasks

specialization: in production, a system of organization in which each worker performs only one type of task

55

divided between those who own the means of production and those who work for them? Is the existing division optimal? What are the forces that determine how society's wealth will be divided?

Smith is known in particular for promulgating the idea that market systems could coordinate the self-interested actions of individuals so that they would ultimately serve the social good. While Smith himself supported a number of government interventions and discussed the moral basis of social and economic behavior at length in other works, the school of classical economics has been popularly identified with the idea that individual self-interest is a positive force and that governments should let markets function without interference—that economies should be **laissez-faire**.*

laissez-faire economy: an economy with little government regulation

Say's Law: the classical belief that "supply creates its own demand"

The classical economists, with the exception of Malthus and Marx, did not much address the problem of economic fluctuations. Most of them thought that a smoothly functioning market system should be entirely self-regulating, and full employment should generally prevail. This view was summarized in **Say's Law**, named after the French classical economist Jean-Baptiste Say (1767–1832), which was said to prove that "supply creates its own demand." The example Say gave was of a tradesman, for example, a shoemaker, who sold $100 worth of shoes. Say argued that the shoemaker would naturally want to spend the $100 on other goods, thereby creating a level of demand that was exactly equal in monetary value to the supply of shoes that he had provided. If this example is extended to the whole economy, it suggests that the quantities demanded and quantities supplied of goods will exactly balance. From this, Say also deduced that the system would always generate the right number of jobs for those needing work. Classical economists discussed issues related to a country's monetary system but tended to assume that monetary issues affected only the price levels and not the level of production in a country.

3.2 The Great Depression, Keynes, and Monetarism

In practice, however, economies do not always work so smoothly. Some periods, such as the 1920s in France and the United States, the late 1990s in the U.S. as well as in many European countries, or the years just prior to the global financial and economic crisis of 2008–2009 in countries such as Britain, Ireland, and Spain, were boom years in which everyone seemed eager to invest and spend. People with extra funds would buy stocks (ownership shares in companies), invest in real estate, or deposit their funds in banks (to be lent to others) with great confidence and optimism. But it appeared that these booms frequently ended in painful recessions. Suddenly, the tide would turn, and everyone would want to sell—not buy—and stock prices would plummet. A lack of confidence in banks would lead to "bank runs" or "banking panics," such as occurred in 1930–1933 in the United States as well as many European countries, or in 2008–2009 in Iceland, Ireland, and Britain, when many people tried to withdraw their deposits all at once. With financial markets in tatters, businesses and individuals

---

* "Laissez-faire," a French term, means "leave alone" and is pronounced "lez-say fair."

would be unable or unwilling to maintain or expand their activities. Because people were cutting back on spending, produced goods would go unsold. Industries would cut back on production. People would become unemployed.

A great many people in the industrialized world suffered considerable hardship during the Great Depression that followed the 1929 U.S. stock market crash. In the United States as well as some especially hard-hit countries in Europe, GDP dropped by about 30 percent between 1929 and 1933. Industrial production fell by even more. In the U.S., the unemployment rate during the Great Depression topped 25 percent at its worst—one in four workers could not find a job. The impact in Europe varied by country, with Britain relatively lightly and Germany harder hit, but by and large, high unemployment in many countries persisted throughout the 1930s, and classical economic theory did not seem to be of much help in either explaining or correcting the situation.

The publication of the British economist John Maynard Keynes's *The General Theory of Employment, Interest, and Money* in 1936 was a watershed event. In this book, Keynes (pronounced "canes") argued that Say's Law was wrong. It *is* possible for an economy to have a level of demand for goods that is insufficient to meet the supply from production, he said. In such a case, producers, unable to sell their goods, will cut back on production, laying off workers and thus creating economic slumps. The key to getting out of such a slump, Keynes argued, is to increase **aggregate demand**—the total demand for goods and services in the national economy as a whole.

aggregate demand: the total demand for all goods and services in a national economy

Keynes suggested a number of ways to achieve this. People could be encouraged to consume more, the government could buy more goods and services, or businesses could be encouraged to spend more. Some economists thought that the best way to encourage business spending was to keep interest rates low, so that businesses could borrow easily to invest in their enterprises. But while Keynes believed that increasing investment spending would be the key to getting out of a depression, he thought that low interest rates alone would be insufficient to tempt discouraged and uncertain business leaders to start investing again. He wrote in *The General Theory* that the solution to business cycles lay in having the government take more direct control of the level of national investment. In his view, capitalist economies were inherently unstable, and only a more socially oriented direction of investment could cure this instability. This policy, however, was not generally adopted, and the Great Depression continued in many countries until the end of the 1930s.

In many countries, it was high government spending associated with national mobilization for World War II that finally brought the Great Depression to an end. Perhaps this is one reason that the followers of what came to be known as **Keynesian economics** did not follow Keynes on all points. While they retained his emphasis on deficiencies in aggregate demand, they tended to emphasize the use of **fiscal policy** to keep employment rates up. Fiscal policy is the manipulation of levels of government spending and taxation to raise or lower the level of aggregate demand.

Keynesian economics: the school of thought, named after John Maynard Keynes, that argued for the active use of fiscal policy to keep aggregate demand high and employment rates up

fiscal policy: the manipulation of levels of government spending and taxation to raise or lower the level of aggregate demand

Other economists in the years after the conclusion of World War II—most notably University of Chicago economist Milton Friedman—took a different tack. While the Keynesians argued that active government fiscal policies were the way to get *out*

57

monetarist economics: the school of economic thought that focused on the effects of monetary policy and argued that governments should aim for steadiness in the money supply rather than playing an active role

monetary policy: the use of tools controlled by the government, such as banking regulations and the issuance of currency, to try to affect the levels of money supply, interest rates, and credit

of a recession, the **monetarists** argued that bad government **monetary policies** were how economies tend to get *into* bad situations in the first place. In this view, it was primarily the U.S. government's poor use of its monetary policy tools, such as banking regulations and the issuance of currency (most often understood as "printing money"), that led to the Great Depression. They blamed government policies that encouraged overly "loose" money (i.e., easy credit, low interest rates, and high levels of money supply) for the overspending of the late 1920s. Then, they claimed, "tight" money policies (tight credit, higher-than-optimal interest rates, and low money supply) during the early 1930s turned what could have been a more minor slump into a major depression (which then spread across the world). They argued that governments should focus on keeping the money supply steady and not try to take an active role in directing the economy, even when unemployment is high. Like some classical economists, they believed that the economy would best be left to adjust on its own.

The Keynesian approach to monetary policy, in contrast, favors an active use of monetary policy together with fiscal policy to try to maintain full employment. This approach strongly influenced macroeconomic policy making in the United States and many other countries after the Second World War. The idea became popular that the government might even be able to "fine tune" the economy, counteracting any tendencies to slump with expansionary (high spending or lose money) policies, and any excessive expansion with contractionary (low spending or tight money) policies, thereby largely eliminating business cycles. A related idea was that the government could choose to "trade off" unemployment and inflation—letting the economy suffer a little more inflation to get the unemployment rate down or vice versa.

3.3 Synthesizing Classical and Keynesian Economics

In the early 1970s, this rosy picture was shattered, however, as many industrialized countries began to experience rising unemployment *combined with* increased inflation. To explain this, many macroeconomists attempted to merge elements of both classical and Keynesian economics, making a distinction between the long run and the short run as follows:

- Classical theories assert, first, that economies should naturally settle at full-employment levels of output and, second, that the primary outcome of changes in the money supply are changes in the price level or rate of inflation. In an idealized smoothly functioning market system—as we see in detail in a later chapter—any unemployment (i.e., surplus labor) should be corrected by a drop in the (equilibrium) wage. In the emerging synthesis, full employment and purely inflationary effects came to be thought of as *long-run* outcomes, which occur only after all markets have had sufficient time to adjust.

- Keynesian economists after World War II had come to accept the idea that their theories should be explainable in terms of market models, but explained unemployment as being due to the fact that markets for labor do not adjust as quickly as classical theory implies. Some Keynesian economists argued that wages are "sticky" in real-world markets and will not fall fast enough during a slump for full employment to be quickly restored. Fiscal and monetary policies were thought, in this emerging synthesis, to be effective mechanisms for coping with this *short-run* phenomenon.

Thus the dominant macroeconomic theory that emerged argued that in the short run—a period of some months or years—we are in a primarily Keynesian world in which fiscal and monetary policies can be effective. In the long run, however—after such a period of time that even "sticky" markets are able to adjust—we are in a classical world, where market adjustments ensure full employment and money only affects prices.

Economists thus explained the inflation that occurred in the first few years of the 1970s (in spite of the simultaneous presence of unemployment) as the long-run outcome of expansionary monetary policies of the previous years. It appeared that short-run active (Keynesian) government policies could have unintended negative long-term (classical) consequences.

While many economists came to agree on this general theoretical picture, debates have continued, now centered on the value of active government policies. Macro-economists at the classical end of the spectrum tend to emphasize market efficiency and a small role for government. They are suspicious about the use of monetary policy because of the possible negative effects of inflation. They also reject active fiscal policy, arguing that increases in government spending or taxation primarily lead to a larger government. Large governments, they believe, discourage private-sector activities and economic growth.

Economists on the Keynesian end of the spectrum, meanwhile, tend to emphasize the way in which unemployment can cause severe human suffering and may persist for a long time. They argue for a more active role for government. Waiting for markets to adjust on their own, they believe, may mean waiting too long. And, as Keynes himself put it, "In the long run, we are all dead."

This argument between classical and Keynesian economists is very much alive today. New developments in recent years—in particular the severe recession starting in the U.S. in 2007 and quickly spreading to the rest of the world, and its aftermath as well as the following euro crisis—have revived many of these long-running debates about the appropriate role of government fiscal and monetary policy.

3.4 Macroeconomics for the Twenty-First Century

While issues of economic growth and the business cycle preoccupied macroeconomic thinking for generations, once again, in the twenty-first century, new developments are demanding new ways of looking at the economic world.

Most recently, great suffering, including loss of homes and income, resulted in many countries from the 2008–2009 global financial and economic crisis and the following euro crisis. Deep concerns have arisen over levels of national debt in many countries, and there has been intense debate about appropriate policy responses. These issues are discussed in Parts III and IV of this book.

In a broader perspective, the persistence of substantial global poverty, as mentioned in the earlier discussion of social sustainability, has called into question the appropriateness of traditional ideas about economic development. Questions of *what, how,* and *for whom*—rather than just "how much"—are becoming ever more important in evaluating the effects of economic activity on human well-being. Increasingly unequal distributions of resources and disparities in power on local, national, and global scales are rising to the fore as critical issues for human well-being. Inequality and resource constraints have cascading effects in political instability as well as armed conflicts.

The environmental impact of fossil fuel–based economic growth has become a major focus of economic, social, and political concern, along with other environmental issues. Most previous economic theories assumed that resources and the capacity of the environment to absorb the by-products of economic growth were essentially unlimited—or at least that continued developments in technology would keep problems of depletion and pollution at bay. This has been increasingly questioned as the scale of human economic activity grows larger.

The graphs of economic growth, seen earlier in this chapter, illustrate an impressive human ability to increase production. The growth in global atmospheric carbon dioxide (CO_2, the principal gas associated with climate change) illustrated in Figure 1.4 is equally impressive but more sobering, as it shows the human ability to affect our environment significantly—sometimes in dangerous ways. CO_2 is released in fossil fuel—burning, industrial production, transportation, and heating—and the more such production takes place, the more is released. Deforestation and some agricultural practices also contribute to increases in atmospheric CO_2.

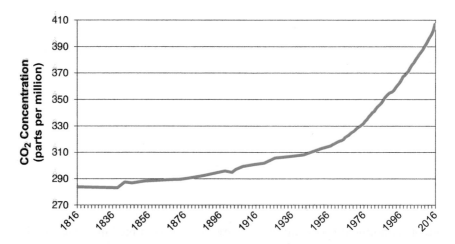

Figure 1.4 *Atmospheric Carbon Dioxide, 1816–2016*

As fossil-fuel based industrialization and deforestation have increased, so has the atmospheric concentration of the gases involved in global warming.

Source: Carbon Dioxide Information Analysis Center, http://cdiac.ornl.gov/ftp/trends/co2/siple2.013 and http://cdiac.ornl.gov/trends/co2/sio-mlo.htm.

Updated using NOAA ESRL data. ftp://ftp.cmdl.noaa.gov/ccg/co2/trends/co2_mm_mlo.txt

Unless emissions of greenhouse gases are reduced dramatically, we can expect to see a number of dangerous results from climate change, including increasingly severe disturbances to agriculture, disruptions in water supply, an expansion of the reach of tropical diseases, and threats from increasingly severe weather including hurricanes, floods, and droughts. Reconciling ecological sustainability and restoration with full employment and growth in living standards is rising in prominence as a macroeconomic issue. Related environmental issues concerning the depletion or degradation of a wide variety of critical natural resources will require new thinking about the relationship between production and living standards.

This is an exciting moment for you to be beginning the study of economics, when so much is at stake—including the kind of work, recreation, and consumption that you will be able to expect in your life—and when there is both need and opportunity for creative new ideas. If you had embarked on this course 20 years ago, you would likely have read a textbook that implied that "everything we need to know about the macroeconomy is here—just learn it." Given recent developments, it is more appropriate to invite you to contemplate and discuss how the economy works, how it doesn't, and how it should.

DISCUSSION QUESTIONS

1. Which major historical events influenced the development of macroeconomics as a field of study? In addition to the problems listed in the text, do you think there are other current problems that macroeconomics should be addressing?

2. The fact that economists do not always agree and that there are alternative "schools" of macroeconomic thought can sometimes seem confusing. It may help to think about or discuss in a group how economics compares to other subjects that you or your classmates have studied. What kinds of changes in the fields of physics or biology have occurred in the past hundred years? Are there major debates, disagreements, and unsettled issues in other fields such as psychology, sociology, or political science?

REVIEW QUESTIONS

1. What is economics?
2. How does macroeconomics differ from microeconomics?
3. What is the difference between positive and normative questions?
4. What is meant by "living standards growth"? Is this the same as "economic growth"?
5. What is economic development? What factors are important in ensuring that economic growth benefits a country's population as a whole?
6. Why are macroeconomic fluctuations a cause for concern?
7. What global developments have caused financial, social, and ecological sustainability or restoration to become increasingly prominent as macroeconomic concerns?

61

8. What is the "precautionary principle"?
9. What historical developments and concerns motivated—and what beliefs characterized—the classical economists? The school of Keynesian economics? The work of the monetarists? The synthesis of Keynesian and classical thought?
10. Name two or more global issues that will likely shape the development of macroeconomics in the twenty-first century.

EXERCISES

1. The more you pay attention to what is going on in the macroeconomy around you, the more meaningful this class will be to you. Find an article in a newspaper or newsmagazine (hard copy or online) that deals with a macroeconomic topic. Make a list of terms, concepts, people, organizations, or historical events mentioned in the article that are also mentioned in this chapter.

2. Classify each of the following as to whether it is an example of a positive question or a normative question (some may have elements of both).
   a. "What is the level of country x's national debt?"
   b. "Is the national debt too high?"
   c. "How low should the unemployment rate be?"
   d. "What policies can lower the unemployment rate?"
   e. "What kinds of production should be counted in measuring gross domestic product?"
   f. "Is it better to have low unemployment or low inflation?"

3. State whether the following statements are true or false. If false, also write a corrected statement.
   a. Macroeconomics is about the activities of government agencies.
   b. Economic growth always leads to improvements in living standards.
   c. The three aspects to consider in thinking about sustainability are financial, monetary, and ecological.
   d. Around a billion people live in absolute poverty, defined as $1.90 or less per day.
   e. Poor countries have had little problem paying back economic development loans.

4. State whether the following statements are true or false. If false, also write a corrected statement.
   a. Fiscal policy refers to government influences on credit and interest rates.
   b. Specialization and the division of labor are characteristics of industrial production.
   c. Classical economists believe that the Great Depression was caused by aggregate demand that was too low.
   d. During "bank runs" and stock market crashes, people lose confidence in the financial system and tend to cut back on their spending.
   e. Keynesian economists believe that an economy that experiences a high rate of unemployment will quickly self-correct.

5. Match each concept in Column A with a definition or example in Column B:

Column A	Column B
a. Keynesian economics	1. Lowering the income tax rate
b. Classical economics	2. Studies how economics applies at the national and global level
c. Monetary policy	3. Supply creates its own demand
d. Fiscal policy	4. Expansion in GDP as a result of new production
e. Living standards growth	5. A school that focuses on aggregate demand and encourages government action
f. Business cycle	6. Government expansion of credit availability
g. Monetarism	7. The short-run fluctuations of a national economy
h. Macroeconomics	8. The school of economic thought originally associated with the idea of laissez-faire economics
i. Say's law	9. More of the population gets access to basic health care
j. Microeconomics	10. Studies how economics applies at the level of households, businesses, and other organizations
k. Economic growth	11. A school of economic thought that argues that active government monetary policies usually make economic fluctuations worse

NOTES

1 Data from tax reports published by the German Ministry of Finance and the German Tax Payers Association.
2 This well-known formulation of the precautionary principle was spelled out in a 1998 meeting of scientists, lawyers, policy makers, and environmentalists at Wingspread, the headquarters of the Johnson Foundation in Racine, Wisconsin.

Chapter 2

Useful Tools and Concepts

Economists have developed a number of basic concepts that are useful when we want to describe how an economy works and to think about how we might make it work better, as citizens and through government action. This chapter presents some of the most important concepts in economics, including how to approach trade-offs (when we have to choose among different things that we might want); what markets really are (hint: they aren't just one thing); and the importance of such abstract things as trust and money. (You didn't think money was abstract? Wait and see!) Before we get into these concepts, however, we review economists' basic tools of investigation. The concepts and methods we discuss in this chapter reappear throughout the book and help us better understand modern macroeconomic debates.

1. OUR TOOLS FOR UNDERSTANDING

Explaining macroeconomic phenomena involves using three main modes of investigation: empirical, theoretical, and historical.

1.1 Empirical Investigation

empirical investigation: observation and recording of the specific phenomena of concern

time-series data: observations of how a numerical variable changes over time

Empirical investigation is observation and recording of specific happenings in the world. In economics, empirical investigation often involves numerical data. However, useful empirical investigation of a specific item of interest may also be represented in words or images.

When the observations take the form of showing how a variable changes over time, we call them **time-series data**. We saw important examples of time-series data in Chapter 1, in graphs that showed how GDP and atmospheric carbon dioxide (CO_2) levels have grown over time.

We will be seeing many such graphs in this book—for price levels, employment, exchange rates, and other economic variables. The accompanying Graphing Review Box (Box 2.1) will help you refresh your skills in working with data and graphs.

It is tempting to think that if two economic variables seem empirically related to each other, changes in one variable are *causing* changes in the other. Sometimes this is true. In the case of the upward trends over time that we saw for both GDP and CO_2

levels, as shown in Chapter 1, there *is* causality: Growing industrial production has led, over time, to increasing accumulations of CO_2. There are good scientific reasons to believe that the rise in accumulated CO_2 that we observed in Figure 1.4 is a direct result of years of fossil fuel–intensive economic growth, as we observed in Figures 1.1 and 1.3.

But two variables may be related empirically (or be "correlated" with each other, to use the statistical term) *without* there being a well-defined causal relationship between them. For example, countries with higher GDP tend to have higher reported levels of cancer. Does this mean that higher GDP causes cancer? No, the true relationship is between GDP and life expectancy. Higher GDP is broadly associated with longer life expectancy, and people who live longer are more likely to develop cancer at some point in their lives. The specific causes of cancer include genetics, environmental exposure, diet, and other factors. This provides an excellent example for the warning that "correlation does not necessarily imply causality." In other words, the existence of an observable relationship between two economic variables does not imply that changes in one variable *cause* the changes in the other.

BOX 2.1 GRAPHING REVIEW

Empirical analysis involves collecting and interpreting numerical data. This review covers the two most common ways that economic data is presented in this book. The first way is in a table, such as Table 2.1, which presents time-series data for the EU economy over the period 2000–2015. The table provides data each year for two variables: the annual real growth rate of GDP and the annual average unemployment rate. So we can determine from the table, for example, that in 2004, the unemployment rate was 9.3 percent and real GDP grew at a rate of 2.5 percent.

While tables can present detailed numerical data, it is not always obvious what is really happening by simply looking at a table. We could carefully study Table 2.1 to determine when unemployment is rising and when it is falling, but this is normally not the easiest way to observe trends over time. Instead, we can commonly present data in visual form, using graphs, to quickly "see" what is happening in an economy.

Figure 2.B1 presents a time-series graph of the unemployment rate. Graphs have a horizontal axis (also called the "*x*-axis") and a vertical axis (also called the "*y*-axis"). It is common practice to present time-series data with the time intervals on the *x*-axis. Presented this way, we can easily see that unemployment rose slightly from 2001 to 2004, then fell for a few years, then rose significantly to nearly 11 percent by 2013, then fell somewhat in 2014 and 2015.

You can test yourself by using the data in Table 2.1 to construct a time-series graph for the GDP growth rate. You can do this using graph paper or a spreadsheet application such as Microsoft Excel.

In addition to using graphs for time-series analysis of a single variable, we can also use graphs to explore the relationship between two different variables. This is important because it provides a way to test specific economic hypotheses. Referring to Table 2.1, we might form

Table 2.1 *Unemployment Rate and Real GDP Growth Rate, European Union (28 Member States), 2000–2015 (in Percent)*

	Unemployment rate	Real GDP growth rate
2000	8.9	3.9
2001	8.7	2.2
2002	9.0	1.3
2003	9.2	1.3
2004	9.3	2.5
2005	9.0	2.1
2006	8.2	3.3
2007	7.2	3.1
2008	7.0	0.5
2009	9.0	−4.4
2010	9.6	2.1
2011	9.7	1.8
2012	10.5	−0.5
2013	10.9	0.2
2014	10.2	1.4
2015	9.4	2.0

Source: European Commission's Ameco database, 2016

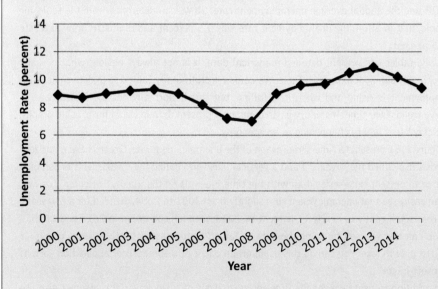

Figure 2.B1 *Unemployment Rate, European Union (28 Member States), 2000–2015*

Source: European Commission's Ameco database, 2016.

the hypothesis that unemployment rates tend to be higher when GDP growth rates are lower. We call this a **negative, or inverse, relationship**—when an increase in one variable is associated with a decrease in another variable (or vice versa, when a decrease in one variable is associated with an increase in another variable).

Figure 2.B2 plots the relationship between unemployment rates and GDP growth rates. Each "data point" on the graph tells us the values of *both* variables for a specific year. In the graph, we have kept the unemployment rate on the *y*-axis, but the *x*-axis now indicates the GDP growth rate. So the data point for 2008, for example, indicates that the GDP growth rate was 0.5 percent (by reading down to the *x*-axis), and the unemployment rate was 7 percent (by reading across to the *y*-axis). Note that there is one data point for each year. You can test yourself by figuring out which data points match which years.

A visual inspection of Figure 2.B2 can help us determine whether our hypothesis of an inverse relationship between unemployment and GDP growth rates is correct. We can see that when GDP growth rates were at their highest, 3 percent or higher, unemployment rates were lower. In general, the graph seems to support our hypothesis, but the relationship is not very strong, and there are some exceptions.

For example, in the year when unemployment was at its maximum, in 2013, GDP growth was at 0.2 percent—far from its worst performance in 2009. To determine more accurately whether our hypothesis is supported by the data, we would need to undertake statistical analysis, often called "econometrics." With this analysis, we could also test what the impact of lagged values (e.g., the past year's real GDP growth rate) are on unemployment. If you are an economics major, you will likely take a future course on econometrics.

Negative (or inverse) relationship: the relationship between two variables if an increase in one variable is associated with a decrease in the other variable (or vice versa)

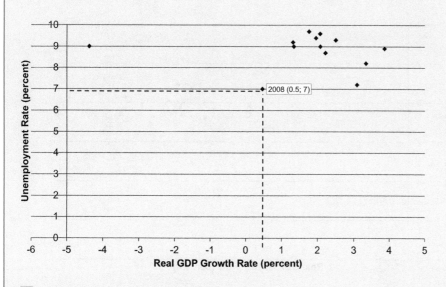

Figure 2.B2 *Relationship Between Unemployment and GDP Growth Rate, European Union (28 Member States), 2000–2015*

Source: European Commission's Ameco database, 2016.

67

Figure 2.B2 can tell us whether our two variables are related, or "correlated," but as mentioned in the text, we cannot determine whether there is a causal relationship between the two variables. While we suspect that low GDP growth causes high unemployment, we cannot prove it using a graph. The causality could potentially be in the opposite direction—that high unemployment causes low GDP growth. Even if the variables seem related in a graph, the relationship could be random, or "spurious." For example, you may have read stories about how the outcomes of sporting events are correlated with the performance of the stock market or the winners of presidential campaigns. However, it seems highly unlikely that such relationships are causal.

The opposite of an inverse relationship is a **positive, or direct, relationship**. In this case, an increase in one variable is associated with an increase in another variable—or a decrease in one variable is associated with a decrease in another.

A good example of a positive relationship is between the growth rate of GDP and the growth rate of greenhouse gas emissions, such as carbon dioxide and methane. When the economy is growing, manufacturing industries tend to produce more goods, people tend to fly and drive more, and construction activity tends to increase. All these factors tend to increase greenhouse gas emissions.

The relationship between GDP growth and the growth of greenhouse gas emission is shown in Figure 2.B3, which includes data for 1996–2013. In this case, we see a reasonably clear positive relationship—when the economy is growing rapidly, greenhouse gas emissions also tend to increase. Again, we can undertake a more sophistical statistical analysis of the positive relationship, and we cannot demonstrate causality just by looking at a graph, but the graph provides strong support in favor of a positive relationship between the two variables.

Positive (or direct) relationship: the relationship between two variables if an increase in one variable is associated with an increase in the other variable

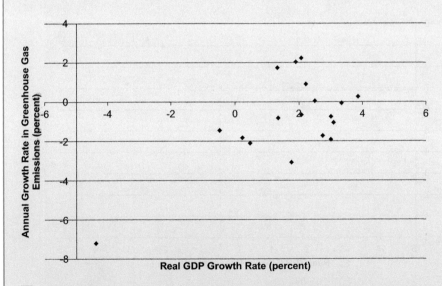

Figure 2.B3 *Relationship Between GDP Growth Rate and Greenhouse Gas Emissions Growth Rate, European Union (28 Member States), 1996–2013*

Sources: European Commission's Ameco database, 2016, and Eurostat.

Empirical investigation creates the foundation for macroeconomic analysis. Looking at the data on unemployment and GDP growth, we can see, however, that more tools are clearly needed if economists are to try to *explain* rather than simply describe macroeconomic phenomena.

1.2 Theoretical Investigation

The adjective "empirical" is usually contrasted with "theoretical," where the latter refers to statements made on the basis of abstract thought, making assumptions and logical deductions. **Theoretical investigation** is essential to macroeconomics. This book introduces a number of theories of how the macroeconomy operates.

theoretical investigation: analysis based in abstract thought

Many economic theories are based on "thought experiments." In the physical sciences, much theorizing is based on controlled experiments in the laboratory. While it is sometimes possible for economists to carry out controlled experiments at the microeconomic level (as is done in the relatively new field of "experimental economics"), this is rarely possible in macroeconomics. Thus economists tend to create theories based on assumptions about economic agents and institutions, from which, with careful reasoning, they draw out potential implications for economic behavior.

In order to make it possible to build a theory, it is sometimes useful to isolate certain aspects of economic behavior from their larger historical and environmental context in order to examine more closely the complex elements involved. A **model** is an analytical tool that highlights some aspects of reality while ignoring others. It can take the form of a simplified story, an image, a figure, a graph, or a set of equations, and it always involves simplifying assumptions. We look at some examples of economic models later in this chapter when we examine the production-possibility frontier and the basic neoclassical model. Other models appear throughout this course.

model: an analytical tool that highlights some aspects of reality while ignoring others

An important part of many models is the assumption of *ceteris paribus*, a Latin phrase that means "other things equal" or "all else constant." In order to focus on one or two variables, we assume that no other variables change. Of course, in the real world, things usually don't stay constant. Usually after a basic model is constructed, we can vary the *ceteris paribus* assumption, to see how changes in other variables will affect the model's conclusions.

ceteris paribus: a Latin phrase meaning "other things equal" or "all else constant"

Theories and models essentially simplify reality. Is this justifiable? It is if it gives us greater insight into how things actually work. A model plane, for example, cannot carry passengers or freight, but it can give aerodynamic engineers insights into how a real plane works and help them to design better features for real aircraft. In the same way, simplified models can help economists to understand the working of very complex real-world economies. Of course, economists may disagree about which models to use and as a result may come to different policy conclusions. In this text, we try to make clear what simplifying assumptions we are using to build models and to indicate when there are different economic theories that may lead to conflicting policy recommendations.

1.3 Historical Investigation

historical
investigation: study
of past events

Throughout the book, we also include a crucial third mode: **historical investigation**, which uses our knowledge of historical events to help explain macroeconomic phenomena. The Great Depression of the 1930s, major wars, the invention of computers, changing roles of women in the workforce, the financial crash of 2007–2008 and the severe recession that resulted, sometimes called the Great Recession, the euro crisis—all are examples of historical events that have had a significant macroeconomic impact.

Economists have become increasingly aware that, while gathering and analyzing data and thinking theoretically about what *could* be true are valid and important tasks, knowledge of the real-world evolution of political, economic, and social life is indispensable to understanding macroeconomics.

Discussion Questions

1. Consider the following examples of investigation. For each one, indicate which mode of investigation it most closely represents—empirical, theoretical, or historical.
   a. A biologist tries to determine the number of different species of plants found on a plot of rainforest
   b. Albert Einstein develops his theory of relativity
   c. An economist measures how GDP varies across countries
   d. A sociologist examines the impact of movements for equal pay for women on women's social and economic status
   e. An economist states that a rise in investment will lead to a fall in unemployment
2. Model building is sometimes compared to map making. If someone asks you how to get to your house, what will you put on the map you draw for them? What if the question asked has to do with the location of the highest point in town, the town's political boundaries, the public transit system, or how your dwelling links up to the local sewer system? Is it possible for a single, readable map to answer every possible question? Does the goal you have in mind for the map affect what you put on it?

2. ECONOMIC TRADE-OFFS

Three fundamental economic questions are *what*, *how*, and *for whom*. As individuals, and as members of a larger society, people make choices about *what* should be produced, *how* it should be produced, and *for whom* it should be produced. These choices involve *trade-offs* between different priorities and goals, and how these choices are made is a major focus of economic analysis.

2.1 Abundance and Scarcity

When you think of all the abundant natural resources in our world, all the human time and intelligence that exist, all the investments that have been made in organizing human societies, and the massive stock of machinery and other productive resources now accumulated, you realize that the world as a whole is wealthy indeed (even though some countries remain very poor). Although the distribution of resources is far from even across countries or among people within countries, contemporary human society as a whole still has a rich resource base on which to build. No wonder that many world religions and ethical teachings encourage an attitude of gratefulness on the part of their adherents toward the sources of life's **abundance**.

It may seem odd, then, that many economists emphasize the notion of **scarcity**—that is, the notion that there is too little to go around—when discussing society's choices concerning *what, how,* and *for whom*. What this really means is that even with all the available resources, and even with a steady eye on the goal of well-being, not everything that is socially desirable can be accomplished, at least not all at once. The current capacity of a particular hospital, for example, may allow it to increase the number of heart transplants that it performs *or* to increase the amount of care that it can provide for the severely mentally ill but not both. A given resource, such as an hour of your time, when dedicated to one beneficial activity (such as studying) will be unavailable for certain other beneficial activities (such as relaxing with your friends). Choices have to be made.

Macroeconomics is centrally concerned with how an overall economic environment emerges from the choices made by individuals and organizations and to what extent choices made by governments can make this economic environment better or worse.

2.2 Society's Production-Possibilities Frontier

Economists use the notion of a societal production-possibilities frontier to illustrate concepts of scarcity, trade-offs, and efficiency. To make matters very simple, let's assume that society is considering only two possible flows of output over the coming year, which are to be made from a given stock of currently available resources using the current state of technology. (The question of how much of the total resource stock of a society should be considered "currently available" is taken up in the next section.) The classic example is to take guns as one output and butter as the other. In more general terms, the guns-and-butter trade-off can refer to any society's more general and real-world choice between becoming a more militarized society (guns) and becoming a more civilian- or consumer-oriented society (butter).

Figure 2.1 shows a **production-possibilities frontier (PPF)** for this case. In this graph, the quantity of butter produced over a year is measured on the horizontal axis. The quantity of guns is measured on the vertical axis. The points on the PPF curve illustrate the maximum quantities of guns and butter that the society could produce. For example, point A, where the curve intersects the horizontal axis, shows that this society can produce 120 units of butter if it does not produce any guns. Moving up and to the left, point B illustrates production, over the year, of 60 units of butter and 8 units of guns. (At this level of abstraction, it is not necessary to be specific about what is meant by "units." You may imagine these as kilos of butter and numbers of guns if you like.) If the society produces no butter, how many guns can it produce? While it may seem odd to think about a society that only produces two goods, the PPF figure is nevertheless helpful for illustrating several important economic concepts.

abundance: resources are abundant to the extent that they exist in plentiful supply for meeting various goals

scarcity: resources are scarce to the extent that they are not sufficient to allow all goals to be accomplished at once

production-possibilities frontier (PPF): a curve showing the maximum amounts of two outputs that society could produce from given resources over a given time period

71

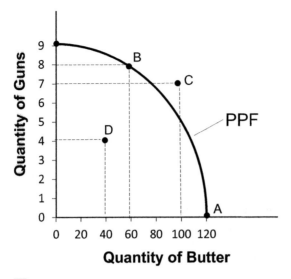

Figure 2.1 *Society's Production-Possibilities Frontier*

The PPF diagram illustrates the concept of scarcity, since combinations of goods that lie outside the frontier (such as C) are not attainable. A comparison of points that lie on the curve (such as A and B) illustrates the concept of trade-offs, since with efficient production the quantity of butter must fall if the quantity of guns produced rises. Inefficient use of resources is illustrated by points (such as D) that are inside the curve.

Scarcity

Point C in Figure 2.1 represents a production combination that is not attainable, given existing resources. To produce at that point would take more resources than this society has. The PPF is specifically defined so that only those points on or inside it represent outputs that can actually be produced.

Trade-Offs

opportunity cost:
the value of the best
alternative that is
forgone when a choice
is made

Points that lie on the PPF illustrate the important notion that scarcity creates a need for trade-offs. Along the frontier, one can get more of one output only by "trading off" some of the other. Figure 2.1 illustrates the important concept of **opportunity cost**. Opportunity cost is the value of the best alternative to the choice that one actually makes. Looking at the PPF, we see that the cost of increasing gun production is less butter. For example, suppose that the economy is at Point A, producing 120 units of butter and no guns, but then decides that it needs to produce 8 guns. Point B illustrates that after some resources have been moved from butter production into producing the 8 guns, the maximum amount of butter that can be produced is 60 units. The gain of 8 guns comes at a "cost" to the economy of a loss of 60 units of butter. Likewise, starting from a point at which the economy is producing some guns, the "cost" of producing more butter would be fewer guns.

Efficiency

An **efficient** process is one that uses the *minimum value of resources* to achieve the desired result. Put another way, efficiency is achieved when the *maximum value of output* is produced from a given set of inputs.* Points that lie *on* the PPF illustrate the maximum combinations that a society can produce. But what about points *inside* the frontier, such as point D? At point D, the economy is not producing as much as it could. It is producing 40 units of butter and 4 guns, even though it *could* produce more of one or the other or both. Some resources are apparently being wasted.

There are at least three reasons this could occur. First, the resources may be wasted because they are being left idle. For example, workers may be left unemployed, or cows could be left unmilked. Second, even if resources are fully employed, the technology and social organization being applied to the resources may be less than the best. For example, suppose the gun factory is poorly designed, so that a lot of the workers' time is wasted carting parts from one area to another. In this case, a better, more efficient organization of the workflow could increase production with no increase in resources. Third, the allocation of resources between the two production activities (i.e., guns and butter) might not be optimal. For example, if gun factories are built on the best pasture land when they could just as well be built on poorer land, the ability of the economy to graze cows and produce butter would be hampered.

When an economy is imagined to be *on* the PPF and thus producing efficiently, the only way to produce more of one good is to produce less of the other. If an economy is *inside* the PPF, by contrast, it is producing inefficiently, and improvements in the employment of resources, the application of available technology and social organization, or allocation of resources among production activities could allow it to move toward the frontier (i.e., to produce more of both goods).

The bowed-out shape of the curve comes from the fact that some resources are likely to be better suited for production of one good than the other. We can see, for example, that the society only has to give up 60 units of butter production to get the first 8 guns. Workers, for example, can be pulled out of butter production and set to work on relatively plentiful supplies of the materials most suited for guns, such as easily tapped veins of iron ore and minerals for gunpowder. Gun manufacturing plants can—if allocation decisions are made wisely—be built on land unsuitable for pasture.

However, the very last gun, gained by moving from point B up to where the PPF hits the vertical axis, comes at the cost of 60 units of butter—the same cost as the first 8 guns! To shift production entirely to guns, it is necessary to use the most productive pastureland and to redirect agricultural workers toward increasingly less accessible veins of mineral ores or to the now-crowded gun assembly lines. This shift dramatically decreases butter production while adding little to the production of guns.

efficiency: the use of resources in a way that does not waste any inputs. Inputs are used in such a way that they yield the highest possible value of output, or a given output is produced using the lowest possible value of inputs.

---

* Note that, in using the term "value of output" in this definition, economists generally mean the money value that the output can be sold for in the market. If a different definition of value were used—for example, if the reference was to the value in increasing human or ecological health or some other aspect of well-being—then some production processes might appear to be more or less efficient than they are when the measuring rod is simply market value.

Of course, we could put on the axis many other pairs of outputs besides guns and butter and still illustrate these concepts. We could look at Coca-Cola and pizza, cars and bicycles, or health care and highways.*

This classic example, however, is a good one. In the real world, such guns/butter or militarization/peacetime trade-offs can be crucially important (see Box 2.2).

What precise combination of outputs, such as guns and butter or health care and highways, should society choose to produce? The PPF does *not* answer this question. The curve shows the range of efficient possibilities but does not tell us which one of these combinations of outputs is best. To determine this, we would have to know more about a society's requirements and priorities. Is civilian satisfaction a high priority? Then the society would lean toward production of butter. Does the society fear attack by a foreign power? Perhaps then it would choose a point more toward the guns axis.

For good social decision making, this production question would have to be considered alongside questions of resource maintenance, distribution, and consumption, since all have effects on well-being. In a society with free speech and democratic discussion, there is wide room for disagreement about what the best mix of goods might be. The PPF provides a mental image for thinking about scarcity, trade-offs, and efficiency but does not, itself, tell us how to choose among the possibilities that it illustrates.

BOX 2.2 THE OPPORTUNITY COST OF MILITARY EXPENDITURES

What do military buildups and wars really cost? One way to look at this is to consider what else could have been bought with the money spent on armaments.

World military expenditures in 2015 totaled around $1.7 trillion, or 2.3 percent of world GDP. The United States is by far the biggest spender, accounting on its own for 36 percent of the global total. China, Saudi Arabia, Russia, and the United Kingdom are the next biggest military spenders. Smaller and poorer countries spend less, but some of the poorest countries—including Eritrea and Burundi—spend more on the military than they do on public services such as health care and education. Where do such countries get their weapons? The United States, Russia, China, and Germany are the leading suppliers of military goods to international markets.

Meanwhile, in large parts of the world, underdevelopment and poverty are still huge issues: Around 160 million children on the planet are showing signs of malnutrition, nearly 6 million children every year die before they reach the age of 5. Globally, 214 million people contracted malaria in 2015, and more than 400,000 died from the disease. Some of the worst consequences of deprivation and poverty could be cured with only a small share of the world's military spending. For example, experts estimate that for only $11 billion per year, one could prevent 68 million children from being malnourished. The price tag on preventing 100 million

---

* Using more advanced mathematics, we can construct equations showing the production possibilities for a society producing many different goods. This is typically done in more advanced economics classes, but the principles involved are exactly the same as in our simple two-good example.

cases of malaria through the distribution of bed-nets treated with long-lasting insecticides has been put at only $0.6 billion.

As U.S. president Dwight D. Eisenhower said in 1953, "Every gun that is made, every warship launched, every rocket fired, signifies in the final sense a theft from those who hunger and are not fed, those who are cold and are not clothed."

Sources: Stockholm International Peace Research Institute, *SIPRI Fact Sheet: Trends in World Military Expenditure, 2015,* www.sipri.org/; Copenhagen Consensus Center: Smart Development Goals, 2015, www.copenhagenconsensus.com/.

2.3 Trade-Offs Over Time

We have said that a PPF reflects possible production combinations given the stock of currently available resources and using the current state of technology. These ideas deserve more investigation. If we remember that achieving well-being involves questions of *how* and *for whom*, then the question becomes complex. For example, we generally want to conserve resources so that we can produce goods not only right now but also later in our lives. And we have an obligation to future generations to include them in our considerations of *for whom*.

Some production activities are also resource-maintenance activities, of course, and the flow of output from these adds to the stock of resources available for the future. Investments in plants and equipment can provide productive capacity not just for a few months but often for years. Production of goods and services that protect the environment or that encourage the formation of new forms of knowledge and social organization also lead to an improved resource base.

Technological progress can lead to long-run improvements in productive capacity. New technologies can create new, more efficient methods for converting resources into outputs—or even create kinds of products never before imagined. To the extent that production is of this sort, production can *add* to the production possibilities for the future. The PPF may expand over time, out and to the right, making previously unobtainable points obtainable, as shown in Figure 2.2.

technological progress: the development of new products and new, more efficient methods of production

Some productive activities contribute an ongoing flow of outputs without drawing down the stock of capital resources. Sustainable production activities, such as some agricultural and forestry processes, may not deplete the resource base and could even add to it (in which case we can term them "restorative").

But many other productive activities lead to resource depletion or degradation. The intensive use of fossil fuels is now depleting petroleum reserves, degrading air quality, and contributing to global climate change. Production processes that destroy important watersheds and wildlife habitats are also resource depleting. Mind-numbing drudgery or work in dangerous circumstances can degrade human resources by leaving people exhausted or in bad mental or physical health. These kinds of productive activities are at odds with resource maintenance.

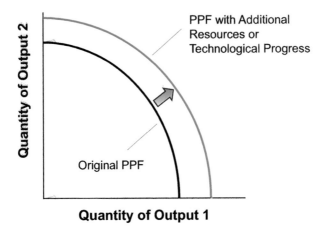

Figure 2.2 *An Expanded Production-Possibilities Frontier*

Note: When the PPF moves "out" (away from the origin), our choices are still constrained, but overall, it becomes possible to get more of both things, as compared to the "lower" PPF.

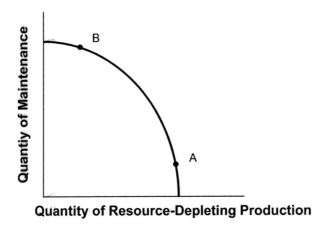

Figure 2.3 *Society's Production/Maintenance Frontier*

Note: We choose not only what to produce but how to produce it; some production methods are more resource depleting than others.

Taking a longer-term view, then, it is clear that getting the absolute maximum production, right now, out of the available resources is not an intelligent social goal. Decisions such as guns versus butter need to be accompanied by another decision about now versus later. A fuller set of questions should include: What should be currently produced, what needs to be maintained, and what investments are needed to increase future productivity?

Figure 2.3 shows a production/maintenance frontier, which illustrates the trade-off between resource-depleting kinds of production and resource-maintenance activities

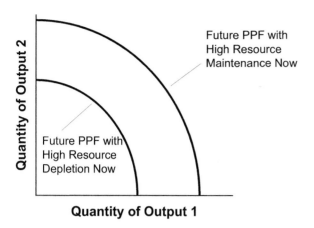

Figure 2.4 *Possible Future PPFs*

Note: Present-day decisions about how to produce will affect future possibilities concerning what can be produced.

(the latter including both conservation and investment). Point A illustrates a societal decision to engage in considerable resource-depleting production in the present year while putting little emphasis on maintenance for the future. Point B illustrates a decision to engage in a higher level of maintenance this year and in a lower level of resource-depleting production.

The consequences of choosing between points A and B are illustrated in Figure 2.4, where once again we portray a two-output (such as guns-vs.-butter) PPF. Now, however, the depiction is of some time in the future, following the current choice between A and B. As Figure 2.4 shows, a decision to maintain more for the future, by choosing point B in Figure 2.3, leads to a larger set of production possibilities in future years. A decision to engage in considerable resource depletion, by choosing point A in Figure 2.3, leads to the smaller future PPF shown in Figure 2.4.

Advances in technology, as we have noted, will always tend to push the PPF outward (as in Figure 2.2). But this will not necessarily compensate for resource depletion. In order to maintain a healthy economy for the future, we need both technological progress and resource maintenance.

Discussion Questions

1. Suppose that your study time can be allocated to studying either for this course or for another course. Your two "outputs" are your grades in each course. Draw a production possibilities curve for these two outputs. Would the curve be shaped like the PPF in Figure 2.1? Discuss.
2. Consider the following activities. Which ones do you think would expand society's PPF in the future? Which ones would shrink it? (There may be room for disagreement on some.)
   a. Increasing education spending
   b. Expanding oil **production**

    c. Building a wind-power facility

    d. Restoring wetlands

    e. Building a new interstate highway

    f. Using larger trawlers to catch more fish

3. THE ROLE OF MARKETS

As we saw in Chapter 1, one of the major areas of interest—and dispute—among economists concerns how markets function. Those who develop theories along the lines of classical economics believe that market systems function fairly smoothly and are largely self-regulating. Those who lean more toward the Keynesian side believe that market economies need some help from government policy to serve goals of human well-being. But what do economists mean by "markets"?

3.1 The Meaning of Markets

When people talk about markets, they may be referring to a number of different meanings of the word, from very concrete to very abstract. The language of economics has at least three different uses of the word "market," and the appropriate meaning must be judged from the context in which it appears. We start with the most concrete and move toward the more abstract definitions.

The most concrete and commonsense definition of a market is the idea that a **market** is a *location*—that is, a *place* where people go to buy and sell things. This is historically appropriate: Markets such as the Grand Bazaar in Istanbul or African village produce stands have flourished for ages as meeting places for people who wish to make exchange transactions. The same criterion applies today, even when the "market" has become a shopping center or mall, with many retail stores sharing one huge building, or a stock or commodity exchange, where brokers stand on a crowded floor and shout orders to buy or sell. A market, as suggested by these examples, can be defined as a physical place where there is an expectation of finding both buyers and sellers for the same product or service. In the electronic age, the market "location" may not be physical but virtual, for example the Web site eBay. Most stock exchanges have also moved to electronic trading or are expected to do so over the next years.

However, not all markets are physical places where buyers and sellers interact. We can think of markets in more general terms as *institutions* that bring buyers and sellers together. **Institutions** are ways of structuring the interactions between individuals and groups. Like markets, institutions can also be thought of in concrete or abstract terms. A hospital can be considered an institution that structures the interactions between doctors and patients. A university is an institution that structures the interactions between professors and students. But institutions can also be embodied in the customs and laws of a society. For example, marriage is an institution that places some structure on family relationships. Laws, courts, and police forces are institutions that structure the acceptable and unacceptable ways that individuals and groups interact.

market (first meaning): a physical place or Web location where there is an expectation of finding both buyers and sellers for the same product or service

institutions: ways of structuring interactions between individuals and groups, including both formally constituted establishments and patterns of organization embodied in customs, habits, and laws

Thinking of markets as institutions rather than concrete places leads to various ways of discussing *particular* markets. Many economists spend much of their time investigating one or more such specific institutional markets. They may track the trades made at various prices over time for a specific good, such as heating oil or Telefónica bonds, try to forecast what might happen in the future, or advise on the specifics of market structures. When such an economist speaks of a market, he or she most often means the institutional market for such a specific good.

In this sense, several different markets may operate under one roof, within the same organization. For example, the London International Financial Futures and Options Exchange (LIFFE) operates many markets for a variety of farm products, including milling wheat, rapeseed, and corn. Indeed, even a term such as "wheat" may be too general to define a market for some purposes, given the existence of such distinct varieties as "No. 2 dark winter wheat" and "No. 1 dark northern spring wheat." Or such an institutional market might cover a number of different physical locations, such as when an economist speaks of a market in regional terms. The "Belgian market for home heating oil," for example, may involve transactions by a number of different companies at a number of different physical or electronic locations.

In the most abstract terms, people sometimes talk of **"the market"** as a situation of idealized, unencumbered exchange. In this idealized market, buyers and sellers are imagined to come to instantaneous, costless agreements. This definition of the market may refer to all market relationships at a national or even global level. When economists speak of the merits (or limitations) of "free markets," they are often referring to the concept at this level of abstraction. What people have in mind in this case is not so much specific, institutional markets as a particular model of how markets *could* behave in an ideal case.

Economists who have a "promarket" view believe that markets should generally be left to function with very little government intervention in order to maximize economic prosperity. Other economists recognize the effectiveness of markets but believe that problems such as poverty, inequality, environmental degradation, and declining social ethics may be caused or exacerbated by unchecked and unregulated markets.

3.2 The Basic Neoclassical Model

The **basic neoclassical model**, traditionally taught in detail in most microeconomics courses at the introductory level, is a model of market exchange that—while abstracting away from many real-world factors, some of which are discussed in what follows—portrays in a simple and elegant way some important aspects of markets. Neoclassical economics arose during the late nineteenth and early twentieth centuries. It took the eighteenth-century classical idea that economies can be thought of as systems of smoothly functioning markets and expressed this idea in terms of formalized assumptions, equations, and graphs. (The prefix "neo-" in "neoclassical" means "new.")

In this model, the world is simplified to two kinds of economic actors. Households are assumed to consume and to maximize their **utility** (or satisfaction). Firms are

---

market (second meaning): an institution that brings buyers and sellers into communication with each other, structuring and coordinating their actions

"the market" (third meaning): a phrase that people often use to mean an abstract situation of pure exchange or a global system of exchange relationships

basic neoclassical (traditional microeconomic) model: a model that portrays the economy as a collection of profit-maximizing firms and utility-maximizing households interacting in perfectly competitive markets

utility: the level of usefulness or satisfaction gained from a particular activity such as consumption of a good or service

79

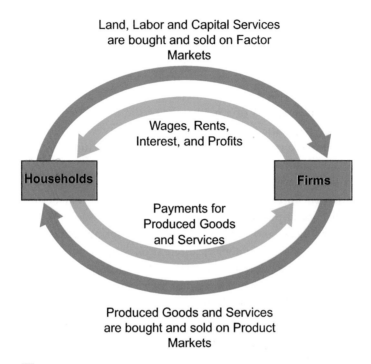

Figure 2.5 *The Circular Flow Diagram for the Basic Neoclassical Model*

Note: The neoclassical circular flow diagram represents a model in which there are only two kinds of economic actors, interacting through markets.

assumed to produce and to maximize profits. Households are considered the ultimate owners of all resources of land, labor, and capital. They rent the services of these to firms through "factor markets," receiving monetary payments in return. Firms produce goods and services, which they sell to households on "product markets" in return for monetary payments. This model can be portrayed in the circular-flow diagram in Figure 2.5. The model further assumes that there are so many firms and households involved in the market for any good or service that a situation of "perfect competition" reigns, in which prices are determined purely by forces of supply and demand.

In this idealized world, goods and services are produced, distributed, and consumed in such a way that the market value of production is as high as it can be. The model combines important *observations* about markets with *assumptions* about human values and human behavior as both producers and consumers. (In reading the following statements about the neoclassical model, see if you can recognize which parts are "positive" observations of facts and which are assumptions, which may include a "normative" slant, toward "the way things ought to be.") Full social and economic efficiency is said to arise when we can assume that:

■ The prices set by the forces of supply and demand in smoothly functioning markets carry signals throughout the economy, coordinating the actions of many individual decision makers in a highly decentralized way.

- The profit motive gives perfectly competitive firms an incentive to look for low-cost inputs and convert them into highly valuable outputs. Production decisions are thus made in such a way that resources are put to their most (market) valuable uses.
- Consumption decisions made by individuals and households maximize the "utility" or satisfaction of consumers.
- Maximizing the market value of production is assumed to be a reasonable proxy for maximizing human well-being.

We explore the working of markets in more detail in Chapter 4. Extending the model to include international trade is discussed in Chapter 14.

3.3 The Advantages of Markets

Because information and decision making in a market economy are decentralized, and producers have an incentive to respond to consumer desires, market systems can lead to a more efficient use of resources. While the workings of real-world markets are more complex, the principle of efficiency highlighted in the basic neoclassical model is of great importance.

The fact that market exchange is *voluntary*, not coerced, is often considered as an additional advantage of markets. Market systems generally offer people some choice about where they work and what they buy. Other market advocates claim that, by offering financial incentives, markets encourage people to be creative, to innovate, and to communicate with one another.

However, it is one thing to recognize that markets have advantages and another to claim that markets are *always* the best way to organize economic activity or to deny that markets may sometimes need government regulation or intervention.

Classically minded macroeconomists tend to emphasize potential efficiency gains from markets and stay fairly close to the basic neoclassical model in their theories. They tend to believe that most economic decisions should be left to "free markets."

More Keynesian-oriented macroeconomists, by contrast, tend to emphasize how real-world markets might differ from the smoothly functioning markets that exist in theory. Real-world markets require an impressive set of associated institutions to work well, they point out. And markets on their own are not well suited to addressing certain kinds of economic problems.

3.4 The Institutional Requirements of Markets

Contemporary large-scale markets do something amazing: They allow many, many separate decision makers, acting on decentralized information, to coordinate their behavior, resulting in highly complex patterns of voluntary exchange transactions. They do not, however, operate in a vacuum. Economists have identified a number of even more basic institutions that market institutions require in order to function. We classify these in four broad groups: institutions related to property and decision making; social institutions of trust; infrastructure for the smooth flow of goods and information; and money as a medium of exchange.

Institutions Related to Property and Decision Making

private property:
ownership of assets
by nongovernment
economic actors

For markets to work, people need to know what belongs to whom. **Private property** is the ownership of physical or financial assets by nongovernment economic actors. Actors must also be allowed to make their own decisions about how to allocate and exchange resources. Prices, in particular, must not be under the control of governments or powerful economic actors; generally, they should be set by the interactions of market participants themselves.

The institutions of private property and individual decision making exist both formally, in codes of law, and informally, in social norms. Social acceptance of institutions is important and not to be taken for granted. For example, some Western economists expected markets to grow quickly in the countries of the former Soviet Union as soon as communism was dismantled and opportunities for markets opened up. However, many people were accustomed to being told by the state where to work and what to do. Norms of individual initiative and entrepreneurship, it turns out, do not just arise naturally but need to be fostered and developed.

Social Institutions of Trust

A second critical institutional requirement for markets is that a degree of trust must exist between buyers and sellers. When a buyer puts down her payment, she must trust that the seller will hand over the merchandise and that it will be of the quality she expects. A seller must be able to trust that the payment offered is valid, whether it is in the form of currency, a personal check, a charge on a credit or debit card, or a promise of future payment such as an installment loan.

Cultural norms and ethical or religious codes can help to establish and maintain an atmosphere of trustworthiness. One-on-one exchanges between customers and businesses help to build trust and make future transactions smoother. Many companies have built up reputations for making quality products or providing good service. Marketers try to capitalize on the tendency of buyers to depend on reputation by using advertising to link certain expectations about quality and price to a recognizable brand name, thus creating "brand loyalty" among repeat customers.

implicit contract:
an informal agreement
about the terms of
exchange, based on
verbal discussions
and on common
norms, traditions, and
expectations

Trust may exist without social institutions of enforcement, but especially in large, complex, mobile societies in which buyers and sellers may not be individually known to one another, markets require social institutions that protect the interests of both sellers and buyers.

explicit contract: a
formal, often written
agreement that
states the terms of
exchange and may be
enforceable through a
legal system

For example, contracts are often used to define the terms of an exchange. An informal or **implicit contract** exists when the terms of an exchange are defined verbally or through commonly accepted norms and traditions. **Explicit contracts** are formal, usually written, agreements that provide a legally enforceable description of the agreed-upon terms of exchange. For formal contracts to work, there must be laws that define contracts, state the legal obligation to honor contracts, and establish penalties for those who fail to do so. There must also be a system for enforcing those laws.

In highly marketized economies, many other institutions have evolved to deal with the issue of trust. For example, credit bureaus keep track of consumer credit trustworthiness, consumer associations help to name and shame businesses that offer bad quality or overcharge customers, money-back guarantees give consumers a chance to test the quality of a good before they commit to purchasing, and escrow accounts provide a place where money can be held until goods or services are delivered. Government agencies such as the European Food Safety Authority or their national counterparts (such as the British Food Standards Agency, the French Agence nationale de sécurité sanitaire de l'alimentation, de l'environnement et du travailafety, or the Dutch Nederlandse Voedsel- en Warenautoriteit) are charged with monitoring the quality and purity of many goods that are sold.

Even in complex transactions among large groups of strangers, social norms are still essential. Detailed formal contracts are costly to write and costly to enforce. It is not practical to police every detail of every contract, and it is impossible to cover every conceivable contingency. The legal system can work smoothly only if most people willingly obey most laws and believe that it is dishonorable to cheat. In effect, relationships, social norms, and the government-created apparatus of law are institutions that must exist side by side, reinforcing one another. None of these alone can carry the whole burden of making complex contracts work and, hence, make markets possible.

Infrastructure for the Smooth Flow of Goods and Information

A third set of basic institutions for market functioning relates to making possible a smooth flow of goods and information. Most obviously, a system of **physical infrastructure** for transportation and storage is needed that provides the basic foundation for moving goods around. Such infrastructure includes roads, ports, railroads, and warehouses in which to store goods awaiting transport or sale. This sort of infrastructure can be most noticeable in its absence, as in economies ravaged by war or by natural disaster.

In addition, infrastructure needs to be in place for the flow of information. Producers and sellers need information on what and how much their customers want to buy; in a well-functioning marketized economy, this information indicates what and how much should be produced and offered for sale. At the same time, consumers need to know what is available and how much they will have to pay to get the products that are on the market. Ideally, consumers should be able to compare all potential purchases as a basis for deciding what to acquire and what to do without. It seems unlikely that this ideal condition for perfect markets will ever be reached, but Web-based exchange systems such as Amazon and eBay have brought it much closer to realization.

physical infrastructure: the equipment, buildings, physical communication lines, roads, and other tangible structures that provide the foundation for economic activity

Money as a Medium of Exchange

The final critical institution required for markets to operate smoothly is a generally accepted form of money. Coins made from gold, silver, and other metals were the most common type of money for many centuries; paper currency developed later.

Today, financial instruments such as bank account balances and electronic transfers play an even larger role. While once backed by precious metals in the central banks' vaults, the value of a euro, a British pound, or a Swedish crown is now based only on the understanding that other people will accept it in exchange. In this sense, money is also a social institution that depends on trust, as well as part of the institutional infrastructure of functioning markets. Money is discussed at greater length in Chapter 11.

3.5 The Limitations of Markets

As we have noted, the idealized model of a completely free private market (as in the basic neoclassical model) rarely exists in practice. Actual market-oriented economies always include a mixture of decentralized private decision making and more public-oriented decision making.

This is not because voters and government officials are unaware of the advantages that markets can have in helping an economy run efficiently. Rather, it is because real-world economies include a number of important, complex factors that are not taken into account in the basic neoclassical model. We discuss these issues more fully in later chapters; here we briefly define and discuss some of the major factors that are important for macroeconomics, including public goods, externalities, transaction costs, market power, questions of information and expectations, and concerns over human needs and equity.

Public Goods

public goods: goods for which (1) use by one person does not diminish usefulness to others and (2) it would be difficult to exclude anyone from benefiting

Some goods cannot or would not be provided well by private individuals or organizations acting alone. A **public good** (or service) is one whose use by one person does not diminish the ability of another person to benefit from it (referred to as "nondiminishable" or "nonrival") and whose benefit it would be difficult to keep any individuals from enjoying ("nonexcludable").

For example, if a local police force helps make a neighborhood safe, all the residents benefit. Public roads (at least those that have no tolls and that are not jammed) are also public goods, as is national defense. A system of laws and courts provides the basic legal infrastructure on which all business contracting depends. Environmental protection that makes for cleaner air benefits everyone. Some economic sectors share characteristics of public and private goods. Education and quality child care are of course private goods, as they are neither nonrival (adding more children to the same classroom lowers the quality of education) nor nonexcludable (as you can deny certain children access to specific schools or child-care facilities), but they are also to some extent public goods because everyone benefits from living with a more skilled and socially well-adjusted population.

Because it is difficult to exclude anyone from benefiting from public goods, they cannot generally be bought and sold on markets. Even if individual actors would be willing to pay for them if necessary, they have little incentive to pay because they cannot be excluded from the benefit. Economists call people who seek to enjoy a benefit without paying for it **free riders**. Because of the problem of free riders, it often makes sense to provide public goods through government agencies, supported by taxes, so that the cost of the public benefit is also borne by the public at large. The effect of taxation and government spending on the macroeconomic environment is an important theme in this book.

free riders: people who seek to enjoy the benefit of a good without paying for it

Externalities

Some market activities create **externalities**—side effects or unintended consequences. Externalities affect persons or entities such as the environment that are not among the economic actors directly involved in the economic activity. These effects can be either beneficial ("positive externalities") or harmful ("negative externalities"). Sometimes positive externalities are referred to as "external benefits" and negative externalities are referred to as "external costs." Externalities are one of the primary ways in which the true *social* value of a good or service can differ from its *market* value.

externalities: side effects or unintended consequences, either positive or negative, that affect persons or entities such as the environment that are not among the economic actors directly involved in the economic activity that caused the effect

Examples of negative externalities include a manufacturing firm that dumps pollutants in a river, degrading water quality downstream, or a bar that plays loud music that annoys its neighbors. Examples of activities that have positive externalities include child rearing by parents who, out of love for their children, raise them to become law-abiding citizens and at the same time create benefits for society at large, and people who get vaccinated against a communicable disease, which they do to protect themselves but at the same time protect those around them from the disease's spread. In both of these cases, individual actions have social benefits. Well-educated, productive citizens are an asset to the community as well as to their own families, and disease control reduces risks to everyone.

Some of the most important externalities relate to the economic activity of resource maintenance. Relying on markets alone to coordinate economic activities allows many activities to take place that damage or deplete the natural environment, because the cost of the damage often is not borne by those creating the damage and because people in future generations are not direct parties to the decision making.

If economic activities affected only the actors directly involved in decision making, we might be able to think about economic activity primarily in terms of individuals making decisions for their own benefit. But we live in a social and ecological world, in which actions, interactions, and consequences are generally both widespread and interrelated. If decisions are left purely to individual self-interest, then from a societal point of view, too many negative externalities and too few positive externalities will be created. The streets might be strewn with industrial wastes, while children might be taught to be honest in dealings only within their family but not outside it. Market values and human or social values do not always coincide.*

---

* Some people criticize the economics profession for relegating many important consequences of economic activity to the category of externalities, mistakenly assuming that this means that economists believe that anything "external" to the market is not important. In fact, economists take externalities very seriously, recognizing that their presence indicates a failure of the market to operate as it should.

85

Transaction Costs

transaction costs:
the costs of arranging
economic activities

Transaction costs are the costs of arranging economic activities. In the basic neoclassical model, transaction costs are assumed to be zero. If a firm wants to hire a worker, for example, it is assumed that the only cost involved is the wage paid. In the real world, however, the activity of reaching a hiring agreement may involve its own set of costs.

The firm may need to pay costs related to searching, such as placing an ad in print or on the Web or paying for the services of a recruiting company. The prospective worker may need to pay for preparation of a résumé and transportation to an interview. One or both sides might hire lawyers to make sure that the contract's terms reflect their interests. Because of the existence of such costs, some economic interactions that might lead to greater efficiency and that would occur in an idealized, transaction cost–free, frictionless world may not happen in the real world.

Market Power

In the basic neoclassical model, all markets are assumed to be "perfectly competitive," such that no one buyer or seller has the power to influence the prices or other market conditions that they face. In the real world, however, we see that many firms have

market power: the
ability to control or
significantly affect the
terms and conditions
of the exchanges in
which one participates

market power. For example, when there is only one firm (a monopolist) or a few firms selling a good, they may be able to use their power to increase their prices and their profits, creating inefficient allocations of resources in the process. Workers may also be able to gain a degree of market power by joining together to negotiate as a labor union. A government, too, can have market power, for example, when the defense ministry is the sole purchaser of military equipment from private firms.

Businesses may also gain power by their sheer size—many corporations now function internationally and have revenues in the tens of billions of dollars. The decisions of individual large corporations can have substantial effects on the employment levels, economic growth, living standards, and economic stability of regions and countries. Governments may need to factor in the responses of powerful business groups in making their macroeconomic decisions. National leaders may fear, for example, that raising business tax rates or the national minimum wage may cause companies to leave their country and go elsewhere. Corporations frequently also try to influence government policies directly, through lobbying, campaign contributions, and other methods. We explore the implications of corporate globalization for macroeconomic policy at more length in a later chapter.

Information and Expectations

static analysis:
analysis that does not
take into account the
passage of time

In the basic neoclassical model, in which purely decentralized decisions lead to efficient outcomes, people are assumed to have easy access to all the information that they need to make good choices. This analysis is **static**; that is, it deals with an idealized case in a timeless manner. The model does not consider the time that it might take for a person to make a decision or that it might take for a factory to gear up to produce a good. In the real, **dynamic** world, obtaining good information may be difficult, and planning for an uncertain future is a big part of anyone's economic decision making.

A manufacturing business, for example, might be considering whether to borrow funds to build an additional factory. If the company's directors were able to know exactly what the demand for its products will be in the future and what interest rates will be—along with additional information about things such as future wages, energy costs, and returns on alternative investments—the decision would be a simple matter of mathematical calculation.

But the directors will have to guess at most of these things. They will form expectations about the future, but these expectations may turn out to be incorrect. If their expectations are optimistic, they will tend to make the new investment and hire new workers. Often optimism is "contagious," and if a lot of *other* business leaders become optimistic, too, then the economy will boom. If, however, people share an attitude of pessimism, they may all tend to cut back on spending and hiring.

Because no one business wants to take the risk of jumping the gun by expanding too soon, it can be very difficult to get a decentralized market economy out of a slump. How people get their information, how they time their actions, and how they form their expectations of the future, then, are all important topics in macroeconomics that are not addressed in the basic neoclassical model. Taking these factors into account suggests why markets sometimes do not work as smoothly as that model suggests or lead to such efficient results.

dynamic analysis: analysis that takes into account the passage of time

Human Needs and Equity

Another important issue concerns distribution of income and the ability to pay for goods and services. In the basic neoclassical model, the only consumer demands for goods and services that can affect the market are those that are backed up by a consumer's ability to pay. This has several implications.

First, there is nothing in the model that ensures that resources are distributed in such a way that people can meet their basic human needs. If a few rich people have a lot of money to spend on diamonds, for example, while a great number of poor people lack the money to pay for basic health care, "free markets" will motivate producers to respond to the demand for diamonds but not to the need for basic health care.

For this reason, governments often adopt more deliberate policies of economic development, government provision, subsidies, or income redistribution to try to ensure that decent living standards become more widespread. These policies can sometimes incorporate market mechanisms and sometimes replace them.

Second, the model does not take into account nonmarketed production, such as the care given to children, the sick, and the elderly by family and friends. There is nothing in the basic neoclassical model that ensures that these sorts of production will be supplied in adequate quantities and quality.

87

Last, it is also the case that problems such as unemployment and inflation tend to affect some people more than others, so how a country deals with these problems also has distributional consequences.

market failure:
a situation in which markets yield inefficient or inappropriate outcomes

Clearly, although market systems have strong advantages in some areas, they cannot solve all economic problems. Economists sometimes use the term **market failure** to refer to a situation in which a market form of organization would lead to inefficient or harmful results. Because of the existence of public goods, externalities, transaction costs, market power, issues of information and expectations, and concerns for human needs and equity, macroeconomic systems cannot rely on "free markets" alone if they are to contribute effectively to present and future human well-being.

To some extent, *private* nonmarket institutions may help remedy "market failure." For example, a group of privately owned factories located around a lake may voluntarily decide to restrict their waste emissions, because too much deterioration in water quality hurts them all. Likewise, a widespread custom of private charitable giving may help alleviate poverty. But sometimes the problems are so large or widespread that only government, *public* actions at the national or international level seems to offer a solution. Exactly how much government action is required, and exactly what governments should do, however, are much-debated questions within contemporary macroeconomics.

DISCUSSION QUESTIONS

1. In what sense is the term "market" being used in each of the following sentences? "Go to the market and get some bananas." "The market is the best invention of humankind." "The labor market for new PhDs is bad this year." "The advance of the market leads to a decline in social morality." "The market performance of Royal Dutch Shell stock weakened last month." Can you think of other examples from your own readings or experience?
2. "Indeed it has been said that democracy is the worst form of government," said British Prime Minister Winston Churchill (1874–1965), "except all those other forms that have been tried from time to time." Some people make the same claim about more marketized forms of economic systems. What do they mean? Would you agree or disagree?

REVIEW QUESTIONS

1. What are the three main modes of economic investigation? Describe each.
2. What is a model? How does the *ceteris paribus* assumption simplify the creation of a model?
3. How do abundance and scarcity create the possibility of and the necessity of economic decision making?
4. What three requirements are met in producing along a production-possibilities frontier?
5. Draw a societal production-possibilities frontier, and use it to explain the concepts of trade-offs (opportunity cost), attainable and unattainable output combinations, and efficiency.

6. What kinds of decisions would make a PPF expand over time? What kinds of decisions would make it shrink over time?

7. What are the three different meanings of the term "markets"?

8. What are some of the assumptions of the basic neoclassical model? Why are markets said to be efficient according to this model?

9. What are the four institutional requirements of markets?

10. What is a public good? Why will private markets generally undersupply public goods?

11. What are negative and positive externalities? Give examples of each.

12. Besides public goods and externalities, describe four real-world factors that can cause market outcomes to be less than ideal.

EXERCISES

1. Consider the following data for the euro area, taken from the EU Commission's *Ameco database* 2016. Perform the graphing exercises below using either pencil and graph paper or a computer spreadsheet or presentation program.

Year	Unemployment rate(%)	Inflation(% per year)
2006	8.4	2.2
2007	7.5	2.2
2008	7.6	3.3
2009	9.6	0.3
2010	10.2	1.6
2011	10.2	2.7
2012	11.4	2.5
2013	12.0	1.3
2014	11.6	0.4
2015	10.9	0.0

a. Looking at the data listed in the chart, can you detect a trend in the unemployment rate during these years? In the inflation rate? If so, what sort of trends do you see?

b. Create a time-series graph for the unemployment rate during 2006–2015.

c. Create a scatter-plot graph with the unemployment rate on the horizontal axis and inflation on the vertical axis.

d. Using your graph in part (c), do the two variables seem to have an empirical relationship during this period, or do the points seem to be randomly scattered? If there appears to be an empirical relationship, is it inverse or direct?

2. The notion of "scarcity" reflects the idea that resources cannot be stretched to achieve all the goals that people desire. But what makes a particular resource "scarce"? If there seems to be more of it around than is needed, such as desert sand, is it scarce? If it is freely open to the use of many people at once, such as music on the radio waves, is it scarce? What about resources

such as social attitudes of trust and respect? Make a list of a few resources that clearly *are* "scarce" in economists' sense. Make another list of a few resources that are not.

3. How is the concept of efficiency related to the concept of scarcity? Consider, for example, your own use of time. When do you feel time to be more and when less scarce? Do you think about how to use your time differently during exam week compared to when you are on vacation?

4. Suppose that society could produce the following combinations of pizzas and books:

Alternative	Quantity of pizzas	Quantity of books
A	50	0
B	40	10
C	30	18
D	20	24
E	10	28
F	0	30

a. Using graph paper (or a computer program), draw the production-possibilities frontier (PPF) for pizza and books, being as exact and neat as possible. (Put books on the horizontal axis. Assume that the dots define a complete curve.)

b. Is it possible or efficient for this society to produce 25 pizzas and 25 books?

c. Is it possible or efficient for this society to produce 42 pizzas and 1 book?

d. If society is currently producing alternative B, then the opportunity cost of moving to alternative A (and getting 10 more pizzas) is _____ books.

e. Is the opportunity cost of producing pizzas higher or lower moving from alternative F to E than moving from alternative B to A? Why is this likely to be so?

f. Suppose that the technologies used in producing both pizzas and books improve. Draw one possible new production-possibilities frontier in the graph that represents the results of this change. Indicate the direction of the change that occurs with an arrow.

5. Match each concept in Column A with a definition or example in Column B:

Column A	Column B
a. A positive externality	1. An apple pie producer trusts that apple growers will supply the apples that they promise to deliver
b. Theoretical investigation	2. The annual harvest of apples in a country from 1970 to 2000
c. Time-series data	3. Producing a combination along a production-possibilities frontier
d. A public good	4. Apple growers will seek to maximize their profits
e. Opportunity cost of buying an apple	5. You do not get to have an orange
f. Scarcity	6. There is only one apple producer who is able to make very high profits

(Continued)

Column A	Column B
g. Efficient production	7. Does not take into account the passage of time
h. Technological progress	8. An orchard used to grow a full crop of apples cannot also be used to grow a full crop of pears
i. An institutional requirement of markets	9. The apple tree that you plant for your own enjoyment also pleases people passing by
j. Market power	10. Can expand a production-possibilities frontier outward over time
k. A negative externality	11. An inspection program for imported apples protects the country's orchards from a severe tree disease
l. An assumption of the basic neoclassical model	12. Einstein develops the theory of relativity
m. Static analysis	13. The production of apple pie creates water pollution that harms downstream communities

Chapter 3

What Economies Do

You cannot build a comfortable, secure house without a good understanding of construction materials, pipes, and building techniques. Likewise, we first need to examine some of the "building blocks" of any economy in order to understand how societies might be able to achieve the macroeconomic goals of good living standards, stability, and sustainability. While an in-depth analysis of specific parts of the economy is the subject of *micro*economics, not macroeconomics, some familiarity with micro-level activities is a prerequisite for a macroeconomic understanding of how all these activities add up to make a national (and global) economy.

1. INTRODUCING THE FOUR ESSENTIAL ECONOMIC ACTIVITIES

In introducing the subject matter of economics in Chapter 1, we briefly mentioned that the four essential economic activities are resource maintenance, production, distribution, and consumption. Now it is time to look at these more directly.

1.1 Resource Maintenance

resource maintenance: the management of capital stocks so that their productivity is sustained or improved

capital stock: a quantity of any resource that is valued for its potential economic contributions

natural capital: physical assets provided by nature

manufactured capital: physical assets generated by applying human productive activities to natural capital

human capital: people's capacity for work and their individual knowledge and skills

social capital: the institutions and the stock of trust, mutual understanding, shared values, and socially held knowledge that facilitate the social coordination of economic activity

Resource maintenance means tending to, preserving, or improving the stocks of resources that form the basis for the preservation and quality of life. A **capital stock** is a quantity of any resource that is valued for its potential economic contributions. Capital stocks are also often referred to as "capital assets."

We can identify five types of capital that contribute to an economy's productivity. **Natural capital** refers to physical assets provided by nature, such as soil that is suitable for agriculture or other human uses, fresh water sources, healthy ocean ecologies, a resilient and diverse stock of wild animals and plants, and stocks of minerals and fossil fuels that are still in the ground. **Manufactured capital** means physical assets that are generated by applying human productive activities to natural capital. These include such things as buildings, machinery, stocks of refined oil, transportation infrastructure, and inventories of produced goods that are waiting to be sold or to be used in further production. **Human capital** refers to individual people's capacity for productive work, particularly the knowledge and skills each can personally bring to his or her work. **Social capital** means the existing institutions and the stock of trust, mutual understanding, shared values, and socially held knowledge that facilitate the social coordination of economic activity.

Last, there is a fifth sort of resource, **financial capital**, which is a fund of purchasing power available to economic actors. While financial capital is not part of any physical production activity, it indirectly contributes to production by making it possible for people to produce goods and services in advance of getting paid for them. It also facilitates the activities of distribution and consumption. An example of financial capital would be a bank checking account filled with funds that have been either saved up by the economic agent who owns it or lent to the agent by a bank.

Notice that economists' description of "capital" is different from what you might hear in everyday use. In common usage, sometimes people take "capital" to mean *only* financial capital. We hear this in everyday references to "capital markets," "undercapitalized businesses," "venture capital," and so on. Economists take a broader view.

Capital stocks may increase or decrease as a consequence of natural forces, as in the case of a natural forest; or they may be deliberately managed by humans in order to provide needed inputs for the production of desired goods and services. When people work to increase the quantity or quality of nonfinancial resources in order to make benefits possible in the future, this is what economists mean by **investment**. Advances in technology also expand or improve the stocks of capital, including manufactured, human, and social capital, thereby increasing the productivity of economic activity.*

The activity of "resource maintenance" is about making sure that investments are sufficient to provide an economy with a good asset base for future years and future generations. You, right now, are investing in your "human capital" by studying economics.

1.2 Production

The second of the four basic economic activities is **production**. Production is the conversion of resources into usable products, which may be either goods or services. **Goods** are tangible objects, like bread or books, whereas **services** are intangibles, like TV broadcasting, teaching, or cutting hair. Popular bands that create music, recording companies that produce CDs or host downloads and streaming of music, local governments that build roads, and individuals who cook meals are all engaged in the economic activity of production. **Manufactured assets**, such as machines and buildings, are goods that are produced for investment purposes to assist in the production of other goods and services.

The economic activity of production converts some resources, which we call **inputs**, into new goods and services, which we refer to as **outputs**. This conversion is a flow that takes place over a period of time. The way in which this production occurs

financial capital: funds of purchasing power available to facilitate economic activity

investment: actions taken to increase the quantity or quality of a resource now in order to make benefits possible in the future

production: the conversion of resources to goods and services

goods: tangible objects that are produced for human use

services: intangibles that are produced by one individual or organization and offered to others

manufactured assets: goods that are produced for investment purposes to assist in the production of other goods and services

inputs: resources that go into production

outputs: the results of production

---

* This effect was noted in our discussion of production possibilities in Chapter 2.

waste products:
outputs that are
not used either for
consumption or in a
further production
process

depends on available technologies. Production processes can also lead to undesirable outputs, such as **waste products**. We consider only *useful* outputs to be economic goods and services.

Inputs include materials that become part of the produced good, supplies that are used up in the production process, and labor time. For example, were we to ask a chef how to prepare one of her specialties, say, ginger chicken, we would be given an answer in terms of ingredients (chicken, ginger, oil, etc.) and a method for combining them. The food ingredients become part of the produced good. Other inputs used in the process probably include the natural gas or electricity that provides heat and other supplies such as paper towels. The chef's labor time, as well as her skill and knowledge, is necessary for the dish to be prepared and is used in the process.

But the recipe, the chef's skills, and the stove and cooking implements that will be used neither become part of the produced good nor are "used up," although they are crucial for the production process. These can be best understood as *flows of services* arising out of *capital stocks* (see Section 2.1). The production process draws on services from social capital in the form of the social knowledge embodied in a recipe, services of the chef's human capital in the form of the chef's acquired knowledge, and services of manufactured capital in the form of the stove and implements. But unlike the materials and supplies mentioned earlier, these capital stocks are not themselves transformed or used up in production.

In the case of commercial production, the services of another form of capital—financial capital—are also vitally important. This is because the production process *takes time*. Imagine that the chef and her husband, for example, are also entrepreneurs. They need to be able to buy the ingredients, buy or rent kitchen space, and get to work well *before* they can prepare the meal and sell it. They therefore need to have financial capital available at the start of the process—either financial assets of their own or loans that they can use to pay the bills until their revenues start coming in. If, at the end of the process, they can sell the meal, cover all their expenses, and make a profit, they will end up with more financial capital than before. This is illustrated in Figure 3.1.

The reliance of commercial production on manufactured and financial capital is very important for macroeconomics, as we will see when we study issues of credit and investment. Production by noncommercial organizations such as households, nonprofit organizations, and governments is generally intended for purposes other than making a financial profit, but it also begins with resources—including financial resources, if any of the inputs are going to be bought on markets.

Figure 3.1 *The Role of Financial Capital in Commercial Production*

1.3 Distribution

Distribution is the sharing of products and resources among people. In contemporary economies, distribution activities take two main forms: exchange and transfer.

When you hand over money in return for goods and services produced by other people or when you receive a wage for the work you have provided to an employer, you are engaging in **exchange**. As we discussed in Chapter 2, markets are social institutions that facilitate exchange relations. People are generally much better off if they specialize in the production of a limited range of goods and services and meet at least some of their other needs through exchange rather than trying to produce everything they need by themselves.

Distribution also takes place through **transfer**. Transfers are payments given with nothing specific expected in return. For example, wealth is transferred from one generation to the next by inheritance. Pension payments from the government to the elderly are another example of transfers.

Distribution can take place through transfers of goods, services, or assets as well as transfers of money. The public school system, for example, distributes educational services to child and teenage students, tuition free. Parents in households transfer food and care to children. These sorts of nonmonetary transfers are called **in-kind transfers**.

1.4 Consumption

Consumption refers to the process by which goods and services are, at last, put to final use by people. In some cases, such as eating a meal or burning gasoline in a car, goods are literally "consumed" in the sense that they are used up and are no longer available for other uses. In other cases, such as enjoying art in a museum, the experience may be "consumed" without excluding others or using up material resources.

In macroeconomics, the activity of consumption is frequently contrasted with the resource-maintenance activity of *investment*. The two activities are linked by the activity of **saving**, or refraining from consumption today in order to gain benefits in the future.

For example, suppose that a subsistence farmer grows a crop of corn. To the extent that the farmer eats some of the corn, the farmer *consumes*—the corn is used up in the process of eating and is not available for future use. To the extent that the farmer sets aside some of this year's corn crop for planting next season, the farmer *saves*. This is an example in which saving is directly turned into *investment:* It puts aside a resource that will aid production in the future.

In a modern, financially sophisticated economy, the situation is more complex, but the basic idea is the same. Modern households can save by spending less money on consumption than their income would allow. Governments and nonprofit organizations can save by spending less on consumption goods than their budgets would allow. Businesses save by retaining some of their earnings instead of paying out to their shareholders (as dividends) all of what they make beyond their (noninvestment) expenses.

Savings may be used directly to purchase investment goods, for example when a business uses retained earnings to buy new software. The larger part of the flows of

distribution: the allocation of products and resources among people

exchange: trading one thing for another

transfer: the giving of something with nothing specific expected in return

in-kind transfers: transfers of goods or services

consumption: the final use of a good or service to satisfy current wants

saving: refraining from consumption in the current period

95

savings described earlier are put aside in less direct ways, by adding to the stock of financial assets available. Financial intermediaries such as banks and bond markets allow savers to lend their financial capital to other households, nonprofits, businesses, and governments that want to borrow. Some of the borrowers will use the funds to pay for the creation of new investment goods, such as buildings, factories, or a college education.

Discussion Questions

1. Think of a common activity that you enjoy. For example, perhaps you like to get together with friends and listen to music on your smartphone while popping popcorn in the microwave. List the stocks of natural, manufactured, human, and social capital that you draw on while engaging in this activity.
2. Classify each of the following according to which economic activity or activities it involves from this list: production, resource maintenance, distribution, and consumption. If any seem to include aspects of more than one activity, name the activities and explain your reasoning.
   a. Harvesting a crop of corn
   b. Attending college
   c. Building an addition onto a factory
   d. Receiving a public pension payment
   e. Cutting someone's hair

2. RESOURCE MAINTENANCE: ATTENDING TO THE ASSET BASE OF THE MACROECONOMY

The activity of resource maintenance involves sustaining and sometimes restoring the asset base of an economy. These important macroeconomic goals require care in maintaining what we have and rebuilding all kinds of capital stocks that may have become depleted or degraded. Several concepts are important for understanding the economics of resource maintenance.

2.1 Stocks Versus Flows

When noneconomists use the term "stock," they usually mean ownership shares in enterprises that are traded on the "stock market." To an economist, however, the concept of a **stock** refers to something as it is measured at a particular point in time. For example, the amount of water in a bathtub can be measured at one particular instant, and that quantity would be considered a stock. The number of computers in an office at ten o'clock on Tuesday morning is a stock, as is the number of trees in a forest at two o'clock on Saturday afternoon.

In contrast to stocks, **flows** are measured *over* a period of time. For example, the water that goes into a bathtub from a faucet is a flow; its quantity can be measured per minute or per hour. The number of computers purchased by an office over the course of this month or this year is a flow. So is the number of computers sold or junked over

stock: something whose quantity can be measured at a point in time

flow: something whose quantity can be measured over a period of time

a period of time. As trees grow or are cut down or felled by lightning, these flows add to or subtract from forest resources.

Flows are like a movie; stocks are like a still photograph. Flows can either add to stocks or decrease them. Figure 3.2 is a generalized **stock–flow diagram**, which shows how flows change the level of a stock over time by either adding to it or taking away from it.

stock–flow diagram: an illustration of how stocks can be changed, over time, by flows

For example, the balance in your checking account at the beginning of the month is a stock value. The deposits and withdrawals you make to your checking account are flows; your bank statement will tell you what the various flows were during a month. The "ending balance" listed on the statement is a stock value.

Figure 3.3 gives an alternative representation of the relation of stocks and flows, this time showing a stock at only *one* point in time. Like water flowing through the tap

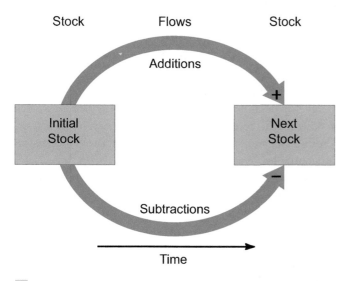

Figure 3.2 *The General Stock-Flow Diagram*

Starting from an initial quantity of a stock, flows into and out of the stock determine how great the quantity is the next time the stock is measured.

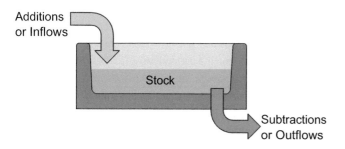

Figure 3.3 *A "Bathtub"-Style Diagram*

Like water flowing into a bathtub, flows that add to a stock will tend to raise its level over time. Like water flowing out of a bathtub, flows that subtract from a stock will tend to lower its level over time.

(additions) and the drain (subtractions) of a bathtub, flows raise or lower the level of the water in the tub (stock).

2.2 Investment and Depreciation

Investment, as mentioned earlier, is a primary form of the activity of resource maintenance. When you read the word "investment" in this textbook, the image in your mind should be of someone buying new computers for an office or planting new trees in a forest—*not* of someone playing the stock market or "investing in" corporate bonds. Those sorts of financial transactions usually merely shift the ownership of an existing financial asset from one economic actor to another; they do not add to productivity-enhancing capital stocks for the economy at large.

"*Dis*investment," or the depletion or reduction in quality of capital stocks, can also occur due to the forces of nature or human activities. When a capital stock is reduced, we say it has undergone **depreciation**. Natural capital depreciates when rivers become fouled by pollution or more trees are cut down than are naturally regenerated. Manufactured assets commonly lose their usefulness over time, as computers become obsolete, roads develop potholes, and equipment breaks. (See Box 3.1.) Human capital depreciates if skills are forgotten or not kept up to date or if age or illness renders a person less productive, and social capital can depreciate if norms of trust and peaceful interaction become less widely held.

The concept of **gross investment** is a measure of all flows into the capital stock over a period of time. **Net investment**, by contrast, adjusts this measure for the fact that some portion of the capital stock also depreciates over the same period. The capital stock at the end of the period is equal to the capital stock at the beginning of the period plus only *net* investment. If depreciation is rapid, net investment can be negative—if the replenishing flow of new investment is not sufficient to keep up with depreciation, the level of the stock will fall.

depreciation: a decrease in the quantity or quality of a stock of capital

gross investment: all flows into the capital stock over a period of time

net investment: gross investment minus an adjustment for depreciation of the capital stock

---

BOX 3.1 NO EASY FIX FOR CRUMBLING GERMAN INFRASTRUCTURE

In Germany, crumbling infrastructure is increasingly seen as an obstacle to economic growth. Since 2003, in most years, the German government has failed to spend enough on roads, canals, tracks, and public buildings to compensate for the use and wear. Roads now increasingly show potholes, and speed limits have to be imposed. About 15 percent of Germany's 70,000 local bridges are in critical condition, and many important bridges have been closed for heavy trucks. As a consequence, the number of traffic jams has risen dramatically, with an increase of almost 20 percent in 2015 alone. In the ranking of the World Economic Forum, Germany's infrastructure dropped from No. 3 in 2013 to No. 7 in 2015.

"We can see the economic damage" from shoddy roads and bridges, said Marcel Fratzscher, president of the DIW Institute for Economic Research in Berlin. "Companies say bad transport infrastructure makes Germany a less attractive place to invest." Companies' highly qualified staff often spend time in traffic jams rather than with the customer, and heavy trucks have to drive large detours, incurring additional costs. A number of economists believe that this deterioration of the public capital stock has contributed to the sharp slow-down in German productivity growth. From 1991 until the onset of the global financial and economic crisis in 2008, output per working hour in Germany rose by 1.8 percent annually. By 2015, this growth rate had come down to 0.5 percent.

Unfortunately, the problems cannot be fixed quickly. According to Fratzscher's estimate, the government is underfunding the road system by at least €10 billion annually. In order to make up for the underinvestment of the past decade and a half, much more money would be needed—according to estimates, roughly €100 billion.

While Germany has had relatively sound public finances and could easily borrow the funds necessary for these investments, politicians cringe away from such policies. One reason is legal: In 2009, German politicians changed the constitution to limit government borrowing. Moreover, during the euro crisis, they pushed other European governments to agree to write a similar limit into the euro-area rules for public budgets. A second reason is political: German politicians fear that the voters would not like to see increased government borrowing. They argue that increased public debt would be a burden for future generations yet seldom question whether a ruined infrastructure is a better thing to pass on to their offspring.

Sources: Stefan Nicola, "Crumbling German Autobahns Leave Drivers Stuck in Traffic Jams," *Bloomberg*, March 22, 2016; Sebastian Dullien, "The German Miracle Is Running Out of Road," *Financial Times*, August 29, 2013.

Resource-maintenance activities help to keep up the quantity and quality of important capital stocks. They include such activities as monitoring the water quality of a lake, repairing machinery, or keeping employees' skills up to date. Going beyond simple maintenance of the status quo, restoration means bringing back qualities that have been lost; for example, farming in such a way that the quality of the soil is actually enhanced.

Sometimes resource maintenance "activity" means *not* engaging in activity. For example, many fishing communities, sometimes under strict government regulation, have ceased fishing for species that are declining and may be in danger of extinction. Similarly, people who make voluntary decisions to minimize their gasoline consumption are helping to maintain petroleum resources as well as the health of the climate. While this may look like inactivity, including resource maintenance as an economic activity implies that minimizing some kinds of consumption can contribute to well-being.

2.3 Renewable Resources, Nonrenewable Resources, and Sustainability

In recent years, people have recognized the complexity of questions concerning the rate of depreciation of many forms of natural capital. Types of natural capital can be classified as either renewable or nonrenewable. A **renewable resource** regenerates

renewable resource: a resource that regenerates itself through short-term processes

itself through biological or other short-term processes, which may be helped by human activity. The quantity and quality of its stock depend simultaneously on the rate at which the stock maintains its productivity and grows and on the rate at which it is harvested or polluted. A healthy forest will go on indefinitely producing trees that may be harvested, yielding a flow of lumber that will be used up in production processes such as paper making.

nonrenewable resource: a resource that cannot be reproduced on a human time scale, so that its stock diminishes with use over time

Other kinds of natural capital are **nonrenewable resources**. Their supply is fixed, although new discoveries can increase the stock that is known to be available. For example, there is a finite amount of fossil-fuel reserves and a finite amount of each kind of mineral available on earth. For nonrenewable resources, there are no self-regenerating flows—at least over time spans relevant to human lives. (While oil reserves or species diversity could in principle be "renewed," the time scale for this to take place would be millions of years.) The stock can only diminish over time as a result of human use or natural deterioration.

How much of its stock of natural resources a society chooses to turn into inputs for current production processes rather than to preserve for the future is clearly a very important economic question. Even those natural inputs that are renewable—such as lumber from forests and fish from the seas—may be exhausted if so much of them is destroyed or extracted that they can no longer renew themselves. In addition, there are limits to the ability of nature to absorb polluting by-products of production processes. There are tipping points past which degraded natural capital may dramatically alter in some essential respect.

For example, in the case of climate change, rising global temperatures due to human-made emissions from the burning of fossil fuels and the use of other chemicals may bring dramatic changes during this century. Ocean levels could rise by as much as a meter or more because of melting of the West Antarctic ice cap and other factors. This would cause the flooding of many low-lying areas, including significant parts of the Netherlands, Belgium, Northern Germany, and Denmark, as well as much of much poorer countries such as Bangladesh. Some island countries, such as the Maldives, are already losing significant land mass. Resource maintenance for natural capital means tracking the size, quality, and changes in natural resources and making wise decisions about their management.

substitutability: the possibility of using one resource instead of another

Sometimes, when it is pointed out that processes of production and consumption in the industrialized countries are currently depleting many important natural capital stocks much more rapidly than they can be replenished, the issue of **substitutability** is raised. The depletion of any one resource (such as fossil fuels) is a less serious problem for future well-being if other resources (such as wind or solar energy) can be cheaply and safely substituted for it in production and consumption. The extent of substitutability that can be achieved depends both on the characteristics of the resources and on the speed of technological advances.

During the late nineteenth and the first half of the twentieth century, there was widespread confidence that technological progress would solve resource and environmental problems. In the late twentieth century, however, this faith began to fade in light of increasingly evident ecological damage. Ecologists emphasize the complexity

100

of natural systems and our relative ignorance of long-term, irreversible, or potentially catastrophic effects of economic behavior on the natural systems that support us. They suggest that, instead of placing blind faith in technological progress and economic substitutability, society should adopt a precautionary principle, as was discussed in Chapter 1.

A **sustainable socioeconomic system** creates a flow of whatever is needed (in an economic system, this is goods and services) by using its renewable capital stocks without depleting or degrading them. Although a portion of some (especially nonrenewable) capital stocks may be used up in the process of production, the overall quality and quantity of the resource base for sustaining life and well-being are preserved.

"Restorative" is a stronger word than "sustainable." We might not actually want to sustain some resources only at their present level but, instead, hope to restore the fertility of now-degraded soils and the quantity of water in important aquifers and to be able eventually to reverse the release of greenhouse gases through carbon absorption, reducing the CO_2 in the atmosphere to a less dangerous level.

A **restorative socioeconomic system** uses its resources in ways that restore desirable qualities to resources that have lost them. Although this is most obvious in the case of environmental resources, there are cases of erosion of social capital resources such as trust and trustworthiness, when corruption comes to be taken for granted in government, business, or regulatory practices. Restoration can occur through better oversight, more visible public response (for example, when white-collar criminals are given significant prison sentences) and—most difficult but most effective—aroused public consciousness of values and application of these values in social interactions.

Other examples of restorative systems are those that invest in restoring degraded portions of the built environment (bridges, communications infrastructure, etc.) or use inmate education or reentry programs to overcome the degrading impact of prison on young offenders.

sustainable socioeconomic system: a system in which the overall quality and quantity of the resource base required for sustaining life and well-being do not erode

restorative socioeconomic system: a system in which successful efforts are made to restore social, environmental, manufactured, or human capital that has deteriorated

Discussion Questions

1. Linda thinks a rich person is someone who earns a lot of money. Carlos thinks a rich person is someone who has a big house and owns lots of corporate shares and bonds. How would the distinction between stocks and flows lend clarity to their discussion?
2. Do you think that a cheap and safe substitute for the use of fossil fuels in cars will ever be found? What about a substitute for the ozone layer, an atmospheric layer that protects the earth from damaging radiation from the sun? Discuss.

3. DISTRIBUTION: WHO GETS WHAT, AND HOW?

It is important to distinguish between distribution in the form of exchange and distribution in the form of transfer—and also to understand the significance of each. In particular, macroeconomists are usually especially interested in who receives the incomes generated by production and the roles that the government plays in economic distribution. Usually, distribution is analyzed with a focus on households residing in a single country. This chapter will follow this approach, looking at the distribution within some EU countries (unfortunately, proper data on distribution among households across the whole EU is not available). The issue of distribution across countries is taken up in Chapter 18.

3.1 Labor and Capital Incomes

In exchange relations, as mentioned earlier, two actors trade with each other on mutually agreed-upon terms. One thing is delivered, and something else is expected in return, in a *quid pro quo* ("something for something") relation. In product and labor markets, exchanges typically involve a flow of goods or services from seller to buyer in return for a monetary payment. The monetary payments, in turn, create flows of labor and capital income.

For example, when customers buy shoes from a shopping mall shoe store, the incomes created include the payment of a wage to the shoe salesperson, rent to the owners of the mall, and profits to the owners of the business. **Labor income** is compensation received by workers in the form of wages, salaries, and fringe benefits. **Capital income** includes rents, profits, and interest. ("**Rent**," as economists use the term, refers not just to rent for housing but to payments for the use of any capital asset, such as machinery or an e-mail list.)

Controversy may arise over profits, rents, or interest if they are seen as excessive according to prevailing standards of fairness and equity. Most economists believe that there is a legitimate role for fair and reasonable profits and dividends, interest payments, and rents. However, persistently high profits may be a sign that a company has excessive market power, indicating that the market it is in is not competitive. Profits might not be a sign of economic health if the companies that earn them create significant negative social or environmental externalities in the process of obtaining them. Large capital incomes that arise from practices that violate the human dignity of workers are also socially harmful. When high capital incomes contribute to a concentration of wealth and power, political democracy itself may be threatened. Profits, interest, and rents are legitimate compensation, in this view, only if they are earned and used in ways that serve the common good as well as the good of the individual owner of capital.

labor income: payment to workers, including wages, salaries, and fringe benefits

capital income: rents, profits, and interest

rent: payments for the use of any capital asset

3.2 Transfers and Taxes

While incomes from production are vital to supporting economic life, distribution by means of one-way transfer also has a very significant role to play in explaining distribution in contemporary economies. Transfers are flows of money, goods, or services for which nothing specific is given in return—or at least nothing specific at the time of the transfer. Transfers can take place between individuals or between the government and individuals; macroeconomists are particularly interested in transfers involving the government.

Transfers *from* the government are often made in response to people's **dependency needs**. Our individual basic needs during some portions of our lifetimes—as infants and children or when incapacitated by age or illness—cannot be satisfied through exchange, because we have little or nothing to give at those times. During childhood, we have no choice but to rely on others—in our families, communities, and countries—to transfer to us the care, shelter, food, and education that we need to survive and flourish. We may need such transfers again later in life if we become unemployed or incapacitated by injury, ill health, or old age. Some government programs deliver specific goods and services directly as in-kind transfers, such as when public schools deliver education services, government programs provide free medical services, or international aid programs deliver food.

In the European Union, the governments of all member states run various cash transfer programs designed to help households achieve income security. Economists often distinguish between two major types.

In the case of **social insurance programs**, transfers are designed to help people if certain specific events occur. Because people cannot predict how long into old age they will live or whether unfortunate events will befall them, it is difficult for workers to know just how much to save for retirement or "a rainy day." By coming together to create a pool of social insurance, people can be ensured of basic provisioning even if their personal needs turn out to exceed their personal savings. At certain times in their lives, people contribute to these programs (through taxes or social security contributions), and at other times they receive benefits.

Social insurance programs in many European countries include public pension systems, disability benefits, or unemployment insurance. Eligibility for these programs generally depends on having been in the paid labor force for a period of time but does not depend on the income or wealth of the recipient.

Means-tested programs, by contrast, are intended to help people who simply have insufficient resources. Unlike the beneficiaries of most social insurance programs, recipients of these programs do not need to have established a substantial history of market work in order to qualify for means-tested benefits, but they must demonstrate that their other means of support (income and resources) are very low. In many European countries, examples for these programs are unemployment assistance, welfare payments, or housing subsidies.

Other funds flow *toward* the government. Income taxes are collected on wage income and on many forms of capital income. All European countries also have value-added taxes, which are basically a tax on sales of goods and services sold to consumers.* Many countries also collect taxes on real estate, calculated as a percentage of the value of the property.

A **proportional income tax** applies the same percentage tax rate to all income levels. A **regressive income tax** applies a higher tax rate to poorer households. A **progressive income tax** system is one that taxes higher-income households more

dependency needs: the need to receive care, shelter, or food from others when one is unable to provide these for oneself

social insurance programs: programs designed to transfer income to recipients if and when certain events (like retirement or disability) occur

means-tested programs: programs designed to transfer income to recipients based on need

proportional income tax: a tax in which the same share of income is collected from households, irrespective of income level

regressive income tax: a tax in which a larger share of income is collected from poorer households

progressive income tax: a tax in which a larger share of income is collected from those with higher incomes

---

* Some services and basic goods are exempt in some countries.

103

heavily, in percentage terms, than lower-income households. A progressive tax embodies the principle that those with high incomes should pay more in taxes because of their greater ability to pay without making a critical sacrifice. While a very poor household, for example, might have to give up eating some meals in order to pay even a small percentage of its income in taxes, a very rich household could pay a substantially larger percentage without much loss in well-being.

To give some examples, a 10 percent proportional tax would collect €1,000 from someone with an income of €10,000 per year and €100,000 from someone with an income of €1 million per year. If, instead, the system collected 10 percent from the poorer person and more than 10 percent from the richer, it would be progressive. If the richer person pays a *smaller* percentage, the tax is regressive. In most EU countries, the income tax is progressive, although the rates paid by the highest earners have dropped over time.

Other taxes can also be evaluated based on their proportional, progressive, or regressive impacts. Value-added taxes on basic consumer goods, for example, tend to be regressive, since poorer people spend a larger proportion of their income on such goods.

3.3 The Distribution of Income

In the previous sections, we discussed the broad *sources* of household income. But how is income distributed across households? Where do you stand in terms of outcomes of the distributional process? Is your family in the top, middle, or lower portion of the income distribution?

Eurostat publishes information on the distribution of incomes in the EU member states. Eurostat measures disposable incomes by summing up households' incomes from wages and salaries, rent, interest, profits, and cash transfer payments received from government agencies and then subtracts taxes. To get from this household income to income per person, the income is "equivalized," that is, converted into an equivalent per-capita income. To do so, Eurostat assigns weights to the people living in a household and divides the household income by these weights. The first adult in a household counts as a whole person. A second adult is only counted as 0.5 persons, as it is assumed that certain goods can be used together (kitchen utilities, furniture, bathroom, appliances), and hence two adults living together do not require twice the amount of income of a single person to attain the same standard of living. Children from the age of 14 onward count as adults; children below that age are assigned a weight of 0.3. If a single woman is now earning €30,000 per year, her equivalized income is €30,000 (as her "weight" is 1). If now a working woman earns €30,000 per year and lives together with her stay-at-home husband (who does not earn anything), the equivalized income of the two is €20,000 per person (€30,000 divided by 1.5). If, in addition, the two had two children aged 7 and 10, the equivalized income per person would only be €14,286 (€30,000 divided by 2.1).

Data for Germany, Britain, and Sweden is presented in Tables 3.1 to 3.3. To understand what these tables mean, imagine dividing up a country's population into five

Table 3.1 *Distribution of Disposable Income in Germany in 2014*

Group of population	Share of aggregate income (%)	Lower limit of each group (€)
Poorest fifth	7.5	0
Second fifth	13.5	12,819
Middle fifth	17.6	17,551
Fourth fifth	23.0	22,523
Richest fifth	38.3	29,972
Richest 5 percent	14.7	47,504

Source: Eurostat.

Table 3.2 *Distribution of Disposable Income in Sweden in 2014*

Group of population	Share of aggregate income (%)	Lower limit of each group (Swedish crowns)	Lower limit of each group (€)
Poorest fifth	8.9	0	0
Second fifth	14.8	117,076	18,115
Middle fifth	18.7	151,500	24,232
Fourth fifth	23.2	183,485	29,940
Richest fifth	34.4	225,820	37,817
Richest 5 percent	11.9	319,590	54,316

Source: Eurostat.

Table 3.3 *Distribution of Disposable Income in the UK in 2014*

Group of population	Share of aggregate income (%)	Lower limit of each group (British pounds)	Lower limit of each group (€)
Poorest fifth	7.8	0	0
Second fifth	12.8	8,144	13,088
Middle fifth	17.1	11,448	17,819
Fourth fifth	23.0	15,310	23,835
Richest fifth	39.3	20,802	32,481
Richest 5 percent	15.1	34,730	53,063

Source: Eurostat.

equal-size groups (called "quintiles"), with the poorest people all in one group, then the next poorest in the next group, and so on. The last group to be formed has the richest one-fifth (or 20 percent) of the population. The highest-income person in the poorest group in Germany would, according to Table 3.1, have a disposable (equivalized) income just short of €9,656. This group, the poorest fifth, received 7.5 percent of the income in the country. The richest fifth, those with disposable incomes of €29,972 per person or more, received 38.4 percent of total income generated in Germany.

Suppose we look at just the top 5 percent of households by income. People in this top group in Germany have an annual disposal income of more than €47,500 per (equivalized) person. In 2010, this group—which comprises one-twentieth of the total population—received almost one-sixth of the total income in Germany (14.7 percent). If we look at the top 1 percent, or the top .01 percent, we would see even more concentration of income.

If you compare the German data with that for Sweden or Britain, you find out that there is considerable variety in the degree of inequality in Europe: In Sweden, the poorest fifth of the population received around 9 percent of the total income and the top fifth "only" 34.4 percent. The top 5 percent received 11.9 percent, less than in any other EU country. The poorest person in the bottom fifth received just short of €18,115, or about 50 percent more than a German at the same relative position in his home country's income distribution.

Contrary to what many people think, the income share of the richest fifth and the lowest fifth in Britain is not very different from those in Germany. In fact, the poorest fifth in Britain actually receives a slightly larger share of total income than in Germany. Behind this interesting observation lies the fact that, according to data from Eurostat, inequality has strongly increased in Germany in the decade up to 2014 but has fallen in the UK.

In a global context, however, most countries are much more unequal than the European countries. This holds both for other industrialized countries such as the U.S. and for developing countries such as Brazil, South Africa, or Mexico.

3.4 Measuring Inequality

Lorenz curve: a line used to portray an income distribution, constructed on a graph by having percentiles of households on the horizontal axis and the cumulative percentage of income on the vertical axis

Economists frequently use a graph called a **Lorenz curve**—named after the statistician, Max Lorenz, who first developed the technique—to describe the pattern of inequality within an economy. A Lorenz curve for household income in Germany, based on the data in Table 3.1, is shown in Figure 3.4. To construct this curve, you first draw the axes, as shown in the figure. The horizontal axis represents households, lined up from left to right in order of increasing income. The vertical axis measures the cumulative percentage of total income received by households up to a given income level.

In our example, the data shown in Table 3.1 are entered into the Lorenz curve in Figure 3.4 as follows. First, point A represents the fact that the lowest 20 percent of the population received 7.5 percent of total income. Point B indicates that the lowest 40 percent of the population received 7.5 percent + 13.5 percent = 21.0 percent of total income; point C indicates that the lowest 60 percent of households received 7.5 percent + 13.5 percent + 17.6 percent = 38.6 percent of total income; point D similarly shows the income of the lowest 80 percent. The Lorenz curve must start at the origin, at the lower left corner of the graph (because 0 percent of households have 0 percent of the total income) and end at point E in the upper right corner (because 100 percent of households have 100 percent of the total income).

While Figure 3.4 shows the Lorenz curve for Germany, Figure 3.5 shows Lorenz curves for Sweden (dashed line) and the UK (solid line). Note that the curve for

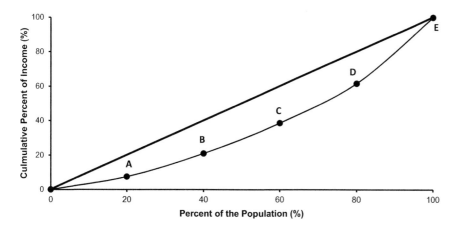

Figure 3.4 *Lorenz Curve for German Household Income, 2014*

A Lorenz curve is a way of graphically portraying an income distribution. For example, point C indicates that the poorest 60 percent of households received about 39 percent of total household income. If income were perfectly equally distributed, the Lorenz curve would be a straight line from the origin to point E.

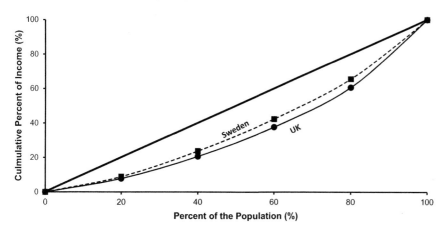

Figure 3.5 *Lorenz Curves for Disposable Income in Sweden and the UK, 2014*

The Lorenz curve for Sweden shows a more equal income distribution than that for the UK, with the curve being closer to the straight line indicating hypothetical perfect equality.

107

Sweden is somewhat closer to the diagonal than the curve for the UK. If there were a hypothetical country where income was distributed equally among all households, the Lorenz curve would be the same as the diagonal line in Figure 3.4. This diagonal line thus represents a situation of maximum equality. At the other extreme, if one household received all the income, then the Lorenz curve would hug the horizontal axis until all but the very last household was accounted for and then shoot up to point F, creating a vertical line at the right-hand side. Such a line would represent a situation of maximum inequality.

As noted, the more the curve sags, the greater is the extent of inequality in the income distribution. This observation led the economist Corrado Gini to introduce a numerical measure of inequality now known as the **Gini ratio** (or, as it is sometimes called, the "Gini coefficient"), defined as the ratio of the area between the Lorenz curve and the diagonal to the total area under the diagonal line. Referring to areas A and B in Figure 3.6, the Gini ratio is A/(A + B). Clearly, the Gini ratio can vary from 0 for perfect equality (in which everyone receives the same income) to 1 for complete inequality (in which one individual receives all the income in the society, and everyone else gets none).

According to Eurostat data, in 2014, the Gini coefficient for Germany was 0.31, for Britain 0.32, and for Sweden 0.25. Besides Sweden, in Europe, Slovenia (0.25), the Czech Republic (0.25), Slovakia (0.26), Finland (0.26), and the Netherlands (0.26) are among the most equitable countries. On the other end of the spectrum, we find countries such as Bulgaria, Romania, Portugal, and Greece (all having a Gini around 0.35). The most unequal EU country was Latvia, with a Gini of 0.36. Yet compared to countries

Gini ratio (or Gini coefficient): a measure of inequality, based on the Lorenz curve, that goes from 0 (perfect equality) to 1 (complete inequality). Greater inequality shows up as a larger area between the curved line and the diagonal.

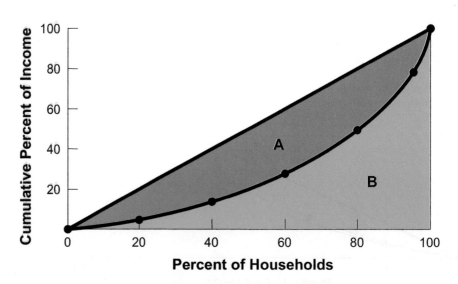

Figure 3.6 *The Gini Ratio, A/(A + B)*

The Gini ratio (or Gini coefficient) sums up the income distribution in a single number: the ratio of the area A to the sum of the areas A and B. If income were perfectly equally distributed, the Gini ratio would be equal to 0.

108

outside of Europe, even the Latvian society is still pretty equitable. According to OECD data from 2012, the Gini for the United States of America was 0.39. Some lower-income and less industrialized countries have even higher degrees of inequality, such as South Africa (0.65), Colombia (0.56), and Brazil (0.52).

Perhaps, you might object, something is wrong with the measure of income we are using. Many families prefer to produce at least some services (such as child care and cooking) for themselves. In addition, many of the things that we enjoy—such as pleasant parks, safe roads, and clean air—add to our well-being without requiring payments out of our cash income. If we were to look at the distribution of *well-being* rather than just the distribution of income, we would need to take account of these nonincome sources of important goods and services. Some of these goods may contribute to lessening inequality—for example, everyone, rich or poor, can enjoy a public park or use a public library.

Evidence suggests, however, that at least in some cases the distribution of such non-purchased goods may accentuate rather than lessen measures of inequality. Proponents of "environmental justice," for example, point out that polluting industries and toxic waste disposal sites tend to be disproportionately located near poor and minority communities. Some broader efforts to assess well-being that go beyond money incomes and GDP are described in Chapter 6.

3.5   Income Inequality Over Time

Unfortunately, for most European countries data about past trends of inequality is scarce. For many countries, household data on disposable incomes is not readily available for long periods of time. As a consequence, also estimates for the Gini are not available, questionable, or not comparable across time and across countries. However, a group of experts around the French economist Thomas Piketty have used income tax statistics to derive measures for the top income shares in different countries and their trends over time. For some countries, some data goes back to the nineteenth century. While this data does not tell us much about the incomes of the poorest part of the population (which often did not pay income taxes), the development of the share of total disposable income that went to the richest 1 percent or the richest 10 percent is still a good indication about inequality trends over time.

Even though data for the time before World War II is patchy, we can infer that in most European countries, societies were extremely unequal prior to the end of World War I. Demobilization from that war brought a first drop in the share of incomes going to the richest part of the population, and the share did not generally increase during the interwar years. For many countries, data for the years during World War II is not available, but after the war, the share of income going to the richest had fallen again. What is really interesting is what followed afterward: During the time of strong economic recovery from the devastation of the war (in many countries, we speak of an "economic miracle"), inequality fell further until the late 1970s or early 1980s. From that point on, we see a strong rebound in inequality, which has been more pronounced in some countries (for example, Britain and Germany) than others (for

109

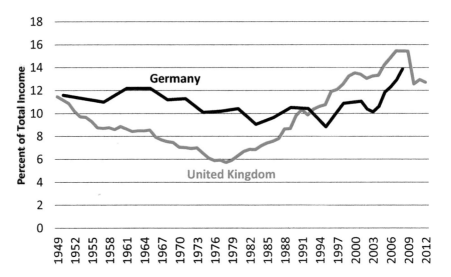

Figure 3.7 *Income Shares of the Richest 1 Percent of Households in Britain and Germany 1949–2012*

Inequality in most European countries fell after World War II until the late 1970s or early 1980s. From that point on, the share of income going to the richest 1 percent of the population has increased again.

Source: Facundo Alvaredo, Anthony B. Atkinson, Thomas Piketty, Emmanuel Saez, and Gabriel Zucman, *The World Wealth and Income Database*, www.wid.world, June 15, 2016.

example, France and Sweden). In some countries such as Britain, the very rich have seen their income share dropping since the financial and economic crisis of 2008–2009, but nevertheless, their share of national income is still much higher than it ever was between World War II and the late 1990s. Figure 3.7 illustrates the income shares of the top 1 percent for Germany and Britain.

Why has income inequality increased in many European countries over the last four decades? Economists do not completely agree on the relative importance of different factors, but there are at least seven major explanations, which probably all have contributed to the recent trends of growing inequality.

First, international trade has been increasing, and especially low-wage, formerly developing countries have started to produce and export many manufactured goods. Nowadays, China is the biggest producer of textiles and electronics, while these goods are not very much produced in Europe anymore. This competition from imports has eliminated many industrial jobs that formerly fell in the middle of the income distribution. If middle-income industrial jobs are replaced by lower-income service and retail jobs, inequality will increase.

Second, new technologies such as computers and biotechnology have become more important, increasing the income of skilled workers who understand and use the new techniques and equipment while leaving behind the less-skilled workers who remain in low-technology occupations and eliminating many low-skilled (and, increasingly, medium-skilled) jobs entirely.

Third, real interest rates have tended to be much higher from the late 1970s onward than before. As those on top of the income distribution also tend to have a larger capital stock than the poor (and especially more financial capital such as bonds or shares), a higher interest rate means that a larger share of the national income goes to the rich. If, in addition, the rich do not completely spend this income from their capital, this process is further self-enforcing.

Fourth, people today tend to marry partners who have a similar level of education, which they often did not do in the past. A doctor in the past might have married a nurse; today doctors often choose other academics as spouses. This mechanism leads to higher household incomes for the academic couples and lower income for non-academic households compared to marriages with mixed educational backgrounds.

Fifth, in many European countries, labor market deregulation and reforms to social security systems have changed the relative power of employers and employees in the workplace. Since the 1980s, many European countries have cut the benefits they pay to the unemployed or people with disabilities, and in many countries, provisions for lay-offs have been relaxed. Unions have been weakened, not only by changes to the rules of collective bargaining but also because of the shrinking number of jobs in the manufacturing sector, which used to be a stronghold of unionized labor.

Sixth, the compensation given to top executives and board members of large corporations has skyrocketed. In the U.S., where the trend is most accentuated, according to a study by the Economic Policy Institute, in 1965 chief executive officers (CEOs) of large corporations earned an average of 20 times the amount earned by the average hourly worker. In 1995, they earned 122 times as much. In 2012, they made 273 times as much.[12] In Europe, the pay between ordinary workers and CEOs has also greatly diverged. The U.S. trade union federation AFL-CIO puts the ratio between average CEO compensation and an ordinary worker's compensation at 134 for Germany, 127 for Spain, 104 for France, 89 for Sweden, 84 for the United Kingdom, and 76 for the Netherlands.

The last two issues are not simply economic. They also relate to political shifts that have increasingly eroded regulatory support for unions, as well as the aspect of culture that could be described as "what people admire." During the last quarter of the twentieth century and into the twenty-first, cultural attitudes shifted toward admiring "winners" who drew huge salaries and used their wealth in conspicuous consumption. This shift pushed into the background other traditional values of thrift, hard work, and fairness—values that even began to seem old-fashioned.

The shift in values included political changes that gave increasing power to people and institutions (most notably corporations) representing large concentrations of wealth. Both the values and the power relations of the early twenty-first century have often been compared to the situation in the 1920s. The comparison became more evident as the bursting of the financial and housing bubbles in 2008 created a close parallel to the onset of the Great Depression at the end of the 1920s. These cultural and political issues relate closely to the next topic—the distribution of wealth (as distinct from the distribution of income).

3.6 Wealth Inequality

The distribution of wealth (what people own in assets—a "stock") tends to be much more unequal than the distribution of income (what people receive over a time period—a "flow"). Most people own relatively little wealth, relying mainly on labor income or government, nonprofit, or family transfers to support their expenditures. It is possible to have *negative* wealth. This happens when the value of a person's debts (such as for a car, house, or credit cards) is greater than the value of her assets. For people in the middle class, the equity that they have in their house is often their most significant asset. By contrast, those who *do* own substantial physical and financial wealth are generally in a position to put much of it into assets that increase in value over time or yield flows of capital income—which can in turn be invested in the acquisition of still more assets.

capital gain: an increase in the value of an asset over time

The distribution of wealth is, however, less frequently and less systematically studied than the distribution of money income. In part, this is because wealth can be hard to measure. Much wealth is held in the form of unrealized **capital gains**. A household receives a capital increase in wealth if it sells an appreciated asset, such as shares in a company, land, or antiques, for more than the price at which it purchased the asset. An asset can appreciate in value for a long time before it is actually sold. No one, however, will know exactly how much such an asset has really gained or lost in value until the owner actually *does* sell it, thus "realizing"—turning into actual euros—the capital gain. Another reason it is harder to get information on wealth is that, although the government requires people to report their annual *income* from wages and many investments for tax purposes, it does not require a comprehensive report of asset holdings.

The European Central Bank collects data on wealth distribution in the euro area through surveys. The most recent such figures have been collected between 2009 and 2010, and the results indicate much more inequality than is found in the distribution of income. According to this data, the top 10 percent of households in the euro area owned almost 50 percent of all household assets, while the bottom 40 percent owned only 3.4 percent. Interestingly, two countries stick out as having an especially unequal wealth distribution: Germany and Austria. In Germany, the top 10 percent owned 55.7 percent of all household assets, in Austria 58.8 percent. The bottom 40 percent together owned just 1.7 percent of total wealth in Germany and 1.7 percent in Austria.[3] While these numbers are dramatic, recent research hints that, due to statistical problems, actual wealth inequality might be even more pronounced (see Box 3.2).

BOX 3.2 WOULD THE TOP 1 PERCENT PLEASE STAND UP?

In the public debate after the global financial and economic crisis, the top 1 percent of the population has increasingly gained attention. Protesting against expensive bank bailouts, the "Occupy Wall Street" movement claimed that "we are the 99 percent," implying that the top 1 percent were getting an unjust share of incomes and yielding undue influence on the economy.

But is the economic influence of the "top 1 percent" really as big as critics claim?

In fact, recent academic research hints that much of the data on wealth and income distribution might even *understate* the top 1 percent's influence and share of economic fruits. One issue is a sampling problem: While there is a large number of low-income earners, the number of billionaires in an economy is small. Surveying a small sample of the population (which is usually done to learn about household incomes and wealth) carries a high probability that the few billionaires are just not included in the survey.

But even if billionaires are selected to participate in the survey, they tend not to respond. Among the super-rich, often as few as 10 percent of those sampled provide complete data on their wealth and income, a much lower ratio than among the rest of the population.

In order to overcome this problem, ECB economist Philip Vermeulen has tried to enhance information from traditional household surveys with data from the Forbes list of billionaires. This adds a significant amount of information: For example, in the Netherlands' survey, there are only two households with net wealth exceeding €2 million, yet the Forbes list includes three billionaires from the country. For Italy, the richest household included in the household survey declared a net wealth of €26 million, while 14 Italian individuals are on the Forbes billionaires list, each owning at least €893 million (remember that the Forbes list looks at dollar values, so someone with less than a billion euros in wealth can be included).

Vermeulen's results underline the impression of an excessive influence of the top 1 percent. When it comes to wealth distribution, the top 1 percent own an even larger share of total wealth than previously thought. According to Vermeulen's data for a group of 10 industrialized countries, in the U.S., Germany, and Austria, the top 1 percent were the wealthiest: In the U.S., they own 37 percent of total wealth, in Austria 36 percent, and in Germany 33 percent. But even in more equal European countries, the share of wealth owned by the richest 1 percent is highly disproportionate: In Portugal, this group owns 25 percent of total wealth, in Italy 20 percent, and in France 19 percent. In the Netherlands and Finland, two countries often seen as champions of equitable distribution, the top 1 percent still owns 17 and 13 percent of total wealth.

Source: Vermeulen, Philip, *How fat is the top tail of the wealth distribution?* European Central Bank, Working Paper Series No. 1692, Frankfurt 2014.

Discussion Questions

1. In your own life so far, how big a role has exchange played in giving you what you need to live? (That is, to what extent have you received assets, goods, or services *because of something specific that you have traded in return?*) How big a role has transfer played? Do you expect this to change in the coming years?

2. What do you think is the minimum level of income that an individual or a small family would need to live reasonably well in your community? (Think about the

rent or mortgage on a one- or two-bedroom residence, etc.) What does this probably mean about where the average level of income in your community fits into the income distribution shown in Tables 3.1 to 3.3 for Germany, Sweden, and the United Kingdom?

4. THE THREE SPHERES OF ECONOMIC ACTIVITY

Economic activity takes place in three major spheres, which we designate here as the core, public-purpose, and business spheres. Economists often refer to these groups as household, government, and business spheres. In this text, however, we use the term "core" instead of "households" in order to emphasize the importance of communities, in addition to households, in the "core" activities described in what follows. (Think of the maxim "It takes a village to raise a child.") Instead of "government," we use the term "public purpose" to include both government and nongovernmental nonprofit organizations whose activities are of growing importance in modern societies. We now explore the roles of the core, public-purpose, and business spheres.

4.1 The Core Sphere

Long before the invention of money, organized markets, and systems of government, human societies organized themselves along lines of kinship and community to undertake the economic activities essential to maintaining and improving the conditions for human life. The **core sphere** is made up of household, family, and community institutions that organize resource management, production, distribution, and consumption, usually on a small scale, and largely without the use of money.

core sphere:
households, families, and communities

One distinguishing characteristic of the core sphere is how work activities are rewarded; instead of monetary rewards, work tends to be rewarded directly by what it produces. For example, work in a home garden is rewarded with tomatoes, and the reward from good child care is a happy and healthy child. People may volunteer their services to their community because they recognize that living in a healthy community is important. People play cards, soccer, or music together because they find these activities intrinsically enjoyable. Another distinguishing characteristic is that core sphere activities tend to be organized to respond to immediately perceived needs rather than, for example, to the ability to pay.

The core economy is the central location of many important economic activities that sustain human life. These include the following.

Bearing and Raising Children

Parents—even when assisted by family planning services, child-care centers, public schools, extended family, and the like—still carry the primary responsibility for fertility decisions and for caring for and nurturing children. Bearing and raising a child is the ultimate "human capital" activity—populating the society for the future. Younger children need direct feeding, dressing, bathing, holding, and responsive interaction with caring adults. Older children need less hands-on care but still need supervision and help in learning many physical, mental, and emotional skills. Much of the work of childrearing also involves the building up of "social capital"—helping children learn to function in larger communities. Community supports like playgroups and carpools can also assist in the productive activities of childrearing work.

Decisions Regarding Investment in Skills and Education

Other human-capital decisions are also often made on a household basis. How long children stay in school or whether an adult goes for further education or training is often a household decision.

Care of the Sick, Elderly, or Otherwise Needy

In countries like those of the European Union, hospitals, nursing homes, mental health clinics, and other institutions exist for people who are acutely ill or incapacitated. However, families, friends, and neighbors remain the first source of support for people with dependency needs. People who are temporarily mildly ill, recovering from surgery, or upset over life events are cared for primarily by friends and family. People with chronic mental or physical health problems may require considerable support services from their families and other people in their communities, perhaps for decades.

The Final Stage of Production of Many Goods and Services

Pasta cannot be eaten until it is cooked. A vacuum cleaner provides no services until someone plugs it in and pushes it around. Grass seed does nothing until someone plants it. Household production activities such as cooking, cleaning, and house and yard maintenance convert many goods and services (often bought on markets) into forms suitable for final use. These production processes generally involve the use of labor time, materials, and the services of household capital goods (such as stoves and lawn mowers). As we will see in Chapters 5 and 6, national accounting frameworks have been slow to recognize the importance of household production.

The Organization of Savings and Investment

Households decide how much of their cash income to allocate to saving. The next decision is how to allocate their financial savings—whether to hold them in retirement funds, real estate, money market funds, and so on. While households also save through more structured (and less voluntary) channels such as pension plans, the savings decisions of individual households are of much interest to macroeconomists. Family and friends also frequently use savings to make gifts or loans among themselves—for example, to finance food and rent in times of need or to help a friend or relative to acquire the funds for the down payment on a house or to start a business.

The Allocation of Consumption Spending

Households are the final decision makers about whether to buy denim pants or DVDs, sports cars or fuel-efficient hybrids. As we will see, the level and composition of consumption in an economy as a whole plays an important role in determining macroeconomic living standards, stability, and sustainability.

Decisions Regarding the Supply of Labor Services

Decisions to work in the labor market, to become self-employed, or to engage in household production are often made not simply by individuals but by households as part of a joint plan for family support.

The Organization of the Use of Leisure Time

In addition to putting in work time in core sphere production, people enjoy "play" time with their family, friends, and neighbors. Vacations and visits are very often planned on a family basis, and activities of recreation and relaxation are largely organized around core sphere networks of family and community. Having leisure time and the goods and services to enjoy it with friends and family is a substantial component of the standard of living.

When the core sphere is working effectively to support the quality of life, important goods and services are provided to many, many people, even if the scale of production in each specific case is quite small. Because most core sphere activities involve face-to-face interaction, the core sphere is the primary location in which the ability to form good social relations is developed.

Of course, core spheres can also work badly or inadequately. For example, responsibilities for children or elderly and ill people may be inequitably assigned between women and men. Such responsibilities may also overwhelm the personal resources of impoverished families and communities. One extreme example is the situation of parents, grandparents, or communities in sub-Saharan Africa trying to care for children orphaned by HIV/AIDS or by war. There are a huge number of these children, and the core sphere often lacks adequate resources to feed and clothe the children and their caregivers, let alone providing for education and physical safety. In richer locations, too, there are limits to what can be accomplished within small-scale, largely informal networks of personal relations. For many economic goals, more formal and larger-scale organizations are also needed.

4.2 The Public-Purpose Sphere

The **public-purpose sphere** includes governments and their agencies, as well as nonprofit organizations such as charities and professional associations and international institutions such as the World Bank and the United Nations.

public-purpose sphere: governments and other local, national, and international organizations established for a public purpose beyond individual or family self-interest and not operating with the goal of making a profit

The distinguishing characteristic of these institutions is that they exist for an explicit purpose related to "the public good"—that is, the common good of some group larger than a household or informal community. Definitions of "the public good," however, may vary widely and may even contradict one another. Although on the microeconomic scale these organizations can include nonprofit groups assembled for bowling, singing, child care, or sharing resources, those of most concern to macroeconomics are charged with purposes such as defending a country's borders, relieving poverty, providing formal health care and education, protecting the natural environment, and stabilizing global financial markets.

Organizations in the public-purpose sphere tend to be larger and more formally structured than those in the core sphere and are often more monetized. Work is often motivated by a mixture of pay and volunteerism. Jobs in nonprofit organizations often pay less than jobs of equivalent skill and responsibility in the business sphere. It is sometimes said that government employees are in "public service."

We can break down the economic functions of public-purpose organizations into two general categories: *regulation*, in which the public-purpose organization sets rules or standards for the actions of other economic entities; and *direct provision*, in which a public-purpose organization itself takes on economic activities.

Regulation

One very basic function of public-purpose organizations is to **regulate** economic activities—that is, to set the standards and "rules of the game" by which other economic actors "play." Public-purpose organizations that promote, legislate, or enforce property rights, rules about contracts or disclosure of information, laws, or norms of obligation; promulgate standards; or perform other coordinating functions create the legal and social infrastructure for economic activity.

regulation: setting standards or laws to govern behavior

Many people think of "regulation" entirely in terms of "government regulation," and it is true that the government sets many rules and standards with which other economic actors are legally obligated to comply. Government regulation of financial and securities markets, for example, plays an important role in macroeconomics. However, many nonprofit groups participate in regulating economic activity, particularly in the area of standard setting.

For example, chances are that you have taken a standardized exam like the TOEFL. This test (like others you need to take to get into certain universities, especially with international standing) is developed and administered by the Educational Testing Service, which is a large private nonprofit organization. Although we might not commonly think of such privately provided standards as "regulation," the standards implicit in these exams do, in fact, influence what is taught by institutions if they wish their students to be well prepared for taking them. Public-purpose organizations often provide the legal, social, and informational infrastructure that both support and constrain other actors in their economic activity.

117

Direct Provision

direct public provision: the supply of goods or services from government or nonprofit institutions

Direct public provision is often used to supply goods or services that cannot be supplied equitably or efficiently by private individuals or through the market. Some things are provided by the public-purpose sphere because, as a society, we believe that everyone should have access to them, regardless of the kind of family or community in which they were born and regardless of their ability to pay. Public schooling from primary school through high school is a prime example. In many European countries, there are also state-run health systems that provide medical care directly to those who need it. Many EU member states also provide highly subsidized care and education for preschool children.

Nonprofit organizations also often offer services related to education, health care, and welfare. Both governments and private charities often transfer income to people in need. Other goods and services are provided by public-purpose organizations because they are of a type that is called a "public good," as discussed in Chapter 2. Sometimes it is more efficient for a public-purpose organization to provide a good or service because of the presence of significant externalities, transaction costs, market power, or advantages to centralized information (as also discussed in Chapter 2).

Although in some instances public-purpose organizations offer goods and services for sale, much as businesses do, this is generally not their primary focus. Public-purpose organizations usually raise much of the money they need to function by soliciting (or, in the case of governments, requiring) monetary contributions in the form of taxes, donations, or membership fees.

The interplay of governments and nonprofits in providing and regulating services can be quite complex. For example, in Europe, the EU defines the framework for the exchange of securities such as stocks and bonds. It has accepted what is called the International Financial Reporting Standards as the authoritative standard for financial reporting. These principles are actually written, however, by the nonprofit International Accounting Standards Board.

The main strength of public-purpose institutions is that (like core institutions) they can provide goods and services of high intrinsic value, but (unlike core institutions) they are big enough, or sufficiently well-organized, to take on jobs that require broader social coordination. Unlike in the business sphere, the provision of goods and services itself, and not the financial results of these activities, remains the primary intended focus of public-purpose organizations.

The public-purpose sphere has its weaknesses, of course. Institutions in the public-purpose sphere are sometimes accused of being rigid, slow to adapt, and inefficient because of excessive regulation and a bloated bureaucracy. Organizations can lose sight of the intrinsic, common-good goal of providing "public service" and become more interested in increasing their own organizational budget. Because public-purpose organizations are commonly supported by taxes or donations that are often not tightly linked to the quality of their services, they may not have financial incentives to improve the quality of what they provide. Many current debates about reforms in governments and non-profits concern how incentives for efficiency can be improved without eroding these organizations' orientation toward providing goods and services of high intrinsic value.

4.3 The Business Sphere

Businesses can be defined as "entities that produce goods and services for sale at a price intended at least to approximate the costs of production."[4] The **business sphere** is made up of such firms. A business firm is expected to look for opportunities to buy and manage resources in such a way that, after the product is sold, the owners of the firm will earn profits.

Whereas the core sphere responds to its members' direct needs and the public-purpose sphere responds to its constituents, business firms are responsive to demands for goods and services, as expressed through markets by people who can afford to buy the products.

Private for-profit enterprises in many countries fall into four main legal forms: proprietorships, partnerships, corporations, and cooperatives. Proprietorships are businesses owned by single individuals or families. Partnerships are owned by a group of two or more individuals. Corporations are business firms that, through a process of becoming chartered by the government, attain a legal existence separate from the individuals or organizations who own it. Individual owners can come and go, but the corporation remains. If the corporation goes bankrupt and is forced to dissolve, the owners of a corporation cannot lose more than their investment. On the other hand, there is no legal limit to the profit they can make if the corporation is successful. This asymmetry, along with its other legal advantages, makes the corporation the preferred structure for major business activities in most countries.

Corporations that issue stock are governed by shareholders, usually according to the principle of "one share, one vote" (though there are some companies that have shares that carry multiple votes). In principle, shareholders elect a board of directors, who in turn hire professional managers to run the day-to-day operations of the corporation. (In fact, shareholders often lack the power to propose directors other than those put forward by the existing board or management. There are ongoing struggles about how or whether to increase the investors' control in this respect.) Cooperatives, in contrast to corporations, cannot issue stock and are governed by a different ownership principle. Each member of the cooperative, no matter what his or her position, has one and only one vote. In practice, cooperatives are owned by one of three groups: their workers, their suppliers, or their customers.

A strength of business organization is that, because businesses have at least one clear goal of making profit, they can sometimes operate with superior efficiency. A profit orientation drives firms to choose the most valuable outputs to produce and to produce them at the least possible cost. The profit motivation also encourages *innovation*: People are more motivated to come up with clever new ideas when they know that they may reap financial rewards. We all benefit, in terms of our material standard of living, from business efficiency and innovations that bring us improved products at lower prices.

The relative weakness of the business sphere comes from the fact that business interests may or may not coincide with overall social well-being. Firms *may* act to enhance social well-being—for example, by making decisions that consider the full needs of their customers and their workers and that take into account externalities, including those that affect the natural environment. They may be guided in these directions by the goodwill of their owners and managers, by pressure from their customers or workers, or by government regulation.

business sphere: firms that produce goods and services for profitable sale

119

Production for market exchange, however, has no *built-in* correction for market externalities. And sometimes "innovation" can take a perverse form. A prime example is the creation of new forms of mortgage "derivatives"—financial instruments based on often-unreliable home mortgages—that were widely traded by investment banks and that were instrumental in causing the financial global crisis that started in the U.S. in 2007 (discussed further in Chapter 15). In fields such as health care and education, where it can be difficult to define clear goals, businesses may increase profits by "innovatively" cutting corners on the less measurable and less-often-marketed aspects of quality of life.

4.4 A Comparative Note: Less Industrialized Economies

informal sphere:
made up of businesses operating outside government oversight and regulation. In less industrialized countries, it may constitute the majority of economic activity.

Many less industrialized economies have large **informal spheres** of small-market enterprises operating outside government oversight and regulation. Although this sphere could be classified as "business" because it involves private production for sale, it is also similar to the "core sphere" in that the activities are very small in scale and often depend on family and community connections.

In EU countries, street-level illegal drug trade and housecleaning services provided "off the books" are two examples of the "informal" sphere. In less industrialized countries, however, it is sometimes the case that *most* people are employed in small-scale agriculture, trade, and services that are not included in formal national accounts.

If we were focusing mainly on less developed countries, it would be necessary to pay a great deal more attention to the complicated reality of "informal" economic activity and perhaps to discuss it as a fourth sphere. For industrialized economies, however, we can deal with this issue by simply noting, as we have just done, that it could legitimately be classified as occurring within either the business sphere or the core sphere, leaving open the question as to which of these classifications is more appropriate.

4.5 Putting Economic Activity in Context

The four essential economic activities occur as a result of interactions within and between the three spheres. As mentioned earlier, these activities include market interactions as well as nonmarket interactions such as household production and regulation. The title of this book—*Macroeconomics in Context*—reminds us that it is important to realize that all economic activity occurs within a broader social and environmental context. This is illustrated in Figure 3.8.

The fundamental process that undergirds economic activity is an ecological one: Economic activity relies upon natural resources for material inputs into all production, transforming them into products for human use. Economic activity invariably generates pollution and waste materials. These wastes may, in turn, affect the flow of natural inputs that are available for future inputs. For example, if we overburden a river with toxic chemicals, the water may not be usable in the future for drinking water supplies.

The social context of economic activity includes politics, culture, ethics, and other human motivations, as well as institutions and history. This social context determines what constitutes acceptable economic activity. For example, we do not allow legal

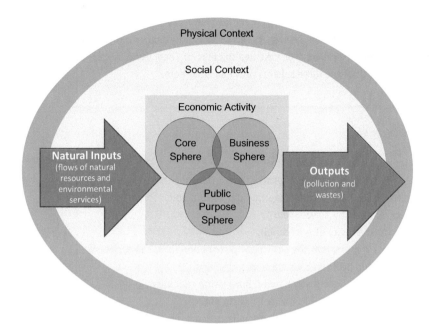

Figure 3.8 *Social and Environmental Contexts of Economic Activity*

Businesses (both foreign and domestic), households and communities (the core sphere), and public-purpose institutions (governments and nonprofit organizations) are all involved in productive activities in the economy. Economies are, in turn, embedded in a context of larger social institutions and the natural (physical) environment.

markets for human organs or illicit drugs. It also determines the relative weight that a society attaches to the different macroeconomic goals discussed in Chapter 1, such as how to assess a potential trade-off between improving material living standards and ecological sustainability.

A useful understanding of economics must take into account the interactions between the economy and its contexts, showing how the economy is dependent on these contexts and how these environmental and social spheres are in turn affected *by* the economy.

In Chapter 4, we focus specifically on the workings of the market economy, but as we proceed through the text, we will return to the issues of the relationship between the economy and its social and environmental contexts.

DISCUSSION QUESTIONS

1. Education is sometimes provided within the core sphere (at-home preschool activities and parents helping with homework), often provided by the public-purpose sphere (public and nonprofit schools), and sometimes provided by for-profit firms (including some "charter schools" or firms offering specific training programs). Can you think of some possible advantages and disadvantages of each type of provision?

2. Make a list of several things from which, over the past few days, you have eaten, drunk, been entertained by, been transported by, been sheltered by, or received other services. (For example, "dinner at Gina's," "my apartment," or "the health clinic.") Then, using the definitions in this chapter, determine which of the three spheres provided each item.

REVIEW QUESTIONS

1. What are the four essential economic activities?
2. What five types of capital contribute to productivity? Describe them.
3. How does economists' use of the term "capital" differ from common use?
4. What do economists mean by "investment"?
5. Describe the economic activity of production.
6. What are the two main forms that the activity of distribution takes? Describe.
7. Describe the relationship between consumption and saving.
8. Describe the difference between a stock and a flow, giving examples.
9. Explain the difference between gross and net investment.
10. What is the difference between renewable and nonrenewable resources?
11. What is a sustainable socioeconomic system? What is the difference between sustaining and restoring a system?
12. What are the two major forms of income received in exchange?
13. What is the main reason for transfer programs?
14. What is the difference between means-tested and social insurance programs?
15. Describe progressive, proportional, and regressive taxation.
16. What share of aggregate income does each quintile of households receive?
17. What is a Lorenz curve? What does it measure?
18. What is the Gini ratio? What does a higher value of the ratio signify?
19. Has income inequality in your country decreased or increased over recent decades? What are some of the reasons?
20. Is wealth more or less equally distributed than income? Why?
21. What are the three spheres of economic activity?
22. What are some major characteristics and functions of the core sphere?
23. What are some major characteristics and functions of the public-purpose sphere?
24. What are some major characteristics and strengths and weaknesses of the business sphere?

EXERCISES

1. Which of the following are flows? Which are stocks? If a flow, which of the five major kinds of capital does it increase or decrease? If a stock, what kind of capital is it?
   a. The fish in a lake
   b. The output of a factory during a year
   c. The income that you receive in a month
   d. The reputation of a business among its customers

e.   The assets of a bank

f.   The equipment in a factory

g.   A process of diplomatic negotiations

h.   The discussion in an economics class

2.   Which of the following are examples of exchange? Of transfer?

a.   De Beers mining company sells diamonds to wholesalers

b.   De Beers mining company takes diamonds from the mines

c.   You pay interest on credit card balances

d.   Your bank donates posters for a local community fair

3.   Statistics from the government of Thailand describe the household income distribution in that country, for 2009, as follows:

Group of households	Share of aggregate income (%)
Poorest fifth	5.5
Second fifth	8.8
Middle fifth	13.2
Fourth fifth	21.5
Richest fifth	51.0

Source: National Statistics Office Thailand, "Household Socio-Economic Survey," table 9, www.nso. go.th/eng/stat/socio/soctab6.htm.

a.   Create a carefully labeled Lorenz curve describing this distribution. (Be precise about the labels on the vertical axis.) You will need to add the shares of the poorest fifth and second fifth to get the lowest 40 percent, and so forth.

b.   Compare this distribution to the distribution in the UK, Germany, and Sweden.

4.   Match each concept in Column A with a definition or example in Column B:

Column A	Column B
a. An important function of the core sphere	1. Fish in the ocean
b. Social capital	2. Regulation
c. Progressive taxation	3. A very unequal income distribution
d. A nonrenewable natural resource	4. Taxation that collects proportionately more from the poor
e. Capital gain	5. What you are adding in the way of new computers to your office minus what has become obsolete
f. Quintile	6. A gift of food
g. An important function of the public purpose sphere	7. A house that you own increases in value over time

(Continued)

Column A	Column B
h. Net investment	8. A shared language within a community
i. Regressive taxation	9. A very equal income distribution
j. A Gini ratio close to 1	10. Raising children
k. A renewable natural resource	11. A group containing 20 percent of the total
l. Manufactured capital	12. Taxation that collects proportionately more from the rich
m. In-kind transfer	13. A factory building
n. A Gini ratio close to 0	14. Iron ore

5. Suppose that a tax system is set up as follows: Everyone gets to subtract €3,000 from their income and then pays the government 20 percent of the rest. Is this tax proportional, progressive, or regressive? Show your reasoning. (Hint: calculate what households with incomes of €10,000 per year, €50,000 per year, and €100,000 per year would pay in taxes and what percentage of their total income their taxes represent.)

6. How does inequality vary across countries? Choose two countries not mentioned in the text and write a paragraph comparing their performance on the Gini ratio and according to income share by quintile. Which country seems to have a more unequal distribution of income? For data, consult the World Development Indicators Online database (http://databank.worldbank.org/data/reports.aspx?source = world-development-indicators).

NOTES

1 Lawrence Mishel and Natalie Sabadish, "CEO Pay in 2012 Was Extraordinarily High Relative to Typical Workers and Other High Earners," *Economic Policy Institute Report*, 2013. Retrieved from www.epi.org.

2 AFL-CIO, *CEO-to-Worker Pay Ratios around the World*, 2013. Retrieved from www.aflcio.org/Corporate-Watch/Paywatch-Archive/CEO-Pay-and-You/CEO-to-Worker-Pay-Gap-in-the-United-States/Pay-Gaps-in-the-World.

3 European Central Bank, *The Eurosystem Household Finance and Consumption Survey—Statistical Tables*, July 2013.

4 U.S. Bureau of Economic Analysis, *A Guide to the NIPAs*, February 17, 2002, p. M—20. Retrieved from www.bea.doc.gov/bea/an/nipaguid.pdf.

Chapter 4

Supply and Demand

The online auction site eBay has more than 162 million active users. Every second, $2,540 (more than €2,000) worth of products—recreational vehicles, high-definition televisions, commemorative coins, T-shirts, condominiums, you name it—are traded. From its beginnings in the United States in 1995, eBay has grown into a global marketing service for individuals and small businesses. Perhaps you have bought or sold something on eBay. If you have, then you have had direct experience with a real-world market very similar, in some ways, to the sort of idealized market that forms the basis for economists' theory of supply and demand.

1. MARKETS AND MACROECONOMICS

As we discussed in Chapter 2, markets are places where individuals, businesses, and other organizations engage in buying and selling. The economic theory of supply and demand is an exceptionally useful example of a "thought experiment" that seeks to describe, in abstract terms, how people make their decisions about buying and selling.

The theory provides a simple, elegant picture of how potential sellers decide how much of a good or service to offer to sell (supply) on a market and how potential buyers decide how much to purchase (demand). The theory then goes on to show how a well-functioning market coordinates these decisions to determine price and quantity traded.

In the real world, markets sometimes work much as the theory predicts; at other times, other forces push decisions and prices away from the result predicted in the theory. When the real world corresponds closely to the theory, the result is that "the market"—not any particular individual agent or bureaucracy—determines the number of units of a good or service that are actually sold on a market, and the price at which the units sell.

1.1 Classical and Keynesian Views of Markets

The direct study of actual markets is more of a *micro*economic topic than a *macro*economic one, as we defined these terms in Chapter 1. One reason that we particularly need to introduce (or review, for those of you who have taken microeconomics) the model of supply and demand here is that understanding this model is crucial for understanding the classical approach to macroeconomics. Classical macroeconomists tend to believe that markets generally function smoothly, as portrayed in this model—at least as long as governments do not interfere.

Keynesian economists, by contrast, tend to believe that market economies need more help from government policies. They agree that the model of supply and demand has an important role to play in economics but claim that understanding the workings of the macroeconomy requires that one go beyond this model, for two reasons. First, real-world markets may deviate in important ways from the one portrayed in the abstract model. Second, explaining economic phenomena at the national level may require a different set of theoretical tools from those designed for analyzing individual markets for particular goods.

The first four sections of this chapter lay out the basic supply-and-demand model. In the last section, we return to the question of how this model sometimes may be and sometimes may not be helpful in understanding macroeconomics.

1.2 Market Competitiveness

The sort of market imagined in the classical world has two noteworthy characteristics. It is envisioned as the following:

Perfectly Competitive

perfectly competitive market: a market in which there are many buyers and sellers, all units of the good are identical, and there is free entry and exit and perfect information

In a perfectly competitive market, there are many buyers and sellers of a good, all units of the good are identical, anyone can enter or leave the market at will, and everyone has perfect information.

Self-Correcting

self-correcting market: a market that automatically adjusts to any imbalances between sellers (supply) and buyers (demand)

In a market that is self-correcting, imbalances between buyers and sellers do not persist because the market naturally adjusts without any outside influence (e.g., government).

In the real world, no market is perfectly competitive in the literal sense (although some are far more competitive than others), and although markets do tend to be self-correcting, in many cases, imbalances persist for some time. Why, then, do we make such assumptions about markets? The real world, as we know, is complex, and models are, by their nature, simplifications of this reality. Just as economists frequently invoke the *ceteris paribus* (meaning "all else equal") condition even though we know that it can never be so, the general sense in modeling is that it is acceptable to use assumptions that are not literally true as long as they can tell us something useful about reality.

eBay, for example, is a good real-world example of a market in which there are many buyers and sellers. Other kinds of markets are less perfectly competitive. If you want to buy the Microsoft Windows operating system, for example, the sole ultimate supplier is Microsoft. Microsoft's dominance means that the market for computer operating systems is far from perfectly competitive.

The market for airline tickets illustrates the idea of self-correction. When demand for flights rises sharply during the peak season, it creates a temporary shortage that is very quickly eliminated by increased prices. Labor markets often behave differently. When business demand for labor diminishes, wages tend *not* to fall accordingly—instead, some workers are laid off.

Many of the controversies in macroeconomics come down to a question of the degree to which real-world markets—and, in particular, real-world labor markets and financial markets—are similar to or differ in important ways from the perfectly competitive and self-correcting markets assumed in basic market theory.

Discussion Questions

1. Have you ever traded on eBay or a similar Internet auction site? If you have, describe to your classmates how it works.
2. Think about a case recently in which you exchanged money for a good or service. Was that market "perfectly competitive"?

2. THE THEORY OF SUPPLY

We start with an example: a simplified market for coffee, the type that people carry in a disposable cup. Let us assume, to start with, that all cups of coffee sold in the market are identical. We will also assume that the coffee sellers are all well informed and interested primarily in their potential monetary gain.

Each seller has a slightly different idea of what is an acceptable price, based on his/ her costs of production and desire to make a profit. No producer will accept less than €0.70 for a cup of coffee, but at a price of €0.70, sellers would supply 300 cups to the market. At a price of €0.80, 400 cups would be offered. In fact, it turns out that each time the price rises by 10 cents, an additional 100 cups of coffee are supplied. This precise relationship is of course unlikely in the real world, but the general principle holds true: at higher prices, sellers are motivated to offer more of the product.

2.1 The Supply Schedule and Curve

The result of this pattern is shown in Table 4.1, which we call a supply schedule. A supply schedule shows us, in the form of a table, the quantity of a good or service that would be offered by the sellers at each possible price.

From the supply schedule, we can graph a **supply curve**, as shown in Figure 4.1, which shows the same information in a different form. If we asked how much coffee would be offered for sale at a price of €1.00, for example, we could look across from €1.00 on the vertical (price) axis over to the supply curve and then drop down to the horizontal (quantity) axis to find that the answer is 600.

supply curve: a curve indicating the quantities that sellers are willing to supply at various prices

Note that the supply curve in Figure 4.1 slopes upward. This seems reasonable, consistent with an expectation that suppliers of a good or service will tend to offer more for sale the higher the price they receive. Price and quantity have a positive (or direct) relationship along the supply curve.

127

Table 4.1 *A Supply Schedule for Coffee*

Price (€/cup)	Cups of coffee supplied/week
0.70	300
0.80	400
0.90	500
1.00	600
1.10	700
1.20	800
1.30	900
1.40	1,000
1.50	1,100
1.60	1,200

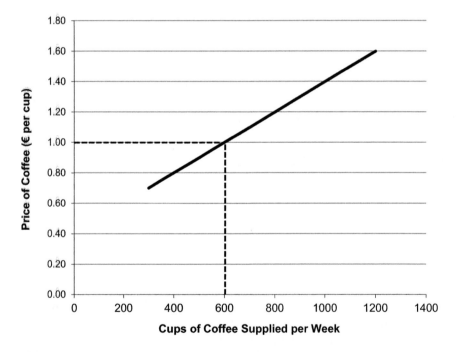

Figure 4.1 *The Supply Curve for Cups of Coffee*

The supply curve shows the same information as the supply schedule. At higher prices, more cups of coffee are offered on the market by people who are in a position to sell.

change in quantity supplied: movement along a supply curve in response to a price change

We see *movement along a supply curve* when we note, for example, that the quantity of coffee that will be offered for sale rises from 600 to 700 as the price rises from €1.00 to €1.10. This is a case of **change in quantity supplied**. It is important to refer to movement *along* a supply curve as change in the *quantity supplied* in order to avoid confusion with the topic of the next section, which deals with changes in the whole supply curve.

Check yourself by answering this question with reference to Table 4.1 or Figure 4.1: By how much does the *quantity supplied* change when the price changes from €1.10 to €1.40?

2.2 Changes in Supply

In contrast to *changes in quantity supplied*, we say there has been a **change in supply** when the whole supply curve shifts.

Why might the whole curve shift? As we noted in Chapter 2, models make frequent use of *ceteris paribus* assumptions. The supply curve shown in Figure 4.1 holds, we presume, for a given set of circumstances. But what if circumstances were different?

Suppose that more coffee sellers entered the market, with the result that 400 more cups of coffee would be offered at each price. The supply curve would shift to the right from S₁ to S₂ as illustrated in Figure 4.2. Now, at a price of €1.00, for example, 1,000 cups of coffee are offered instead of 600. We can describe the increase in supply by saying either that "supply has risen" or that "the supply curve has shifted." (It may seem confusing that a supply *in*crease shifts the supply curve *down*. Remember to start the "story" by reading across horizontally from the price axis. Then you will notice that the shift goes toward *higher* numbers on the quantity axis.)

change in supply: a shift of the supply curve in response to some determinant other than the item's price

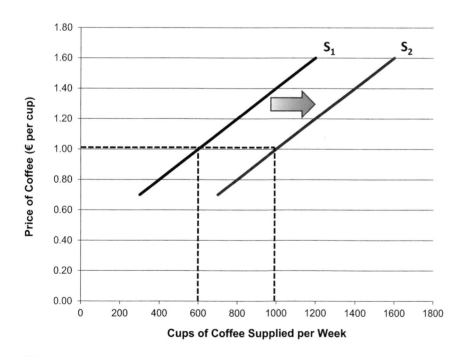

Figure 4.2 *An Increase in Supply*

The supply curve shifts outward (to the right) when sellers decide to supply a larger quantity to the market at a given price or to charge less for a given quantity.

129

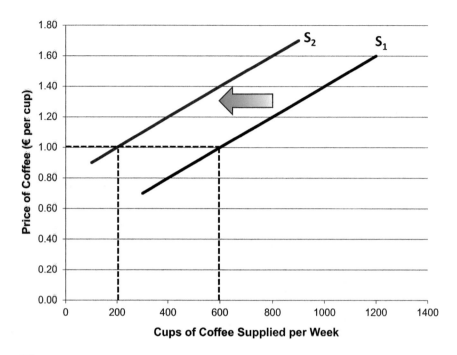

Figure 4.3 *A Decrease in Supply*

The supply curve shifts backward (to the left) when sellers decide to supply a smaller quantity to the market at a given price or to charge more for a given quantity.

We would see a similar result if a new coffee-making technology made its production less costly. With lower costs of production, suppliers become willing to accept, say, €0.40 less per cup (this is if a new coffee-making technology made its production less costly). In this case as well, 1,000 cups would be offered at €1.00, whereas before it took a price of €1.40 to elicit a supply of this size. This would also be termed an "increase in supply" and again the supply curve would shift, as illustrated in Figure 4.2.

If, instead, the number of sellers goes *down* or the cost of production for each cup of coffee *rises*, the supply curve will move to the *left* of the original one, as shown in Figure 4.3. We say that "supply has decreased" or "supply has fallen" or "the supply curve has shifted back."

Thus the number of sellers and the costs of production are among the things that can affect the location of the supply curve. Many other factors also affect the location of the supply curve. These nonprice determinants of supply generally depend on what, specifically, is being sold in a market. While we have rather arbitrarily chosen a simple coffee market for our example, the determinants of supply will vary depending on whether the item in question is an asset, a produced good, or a service and on particular characteristics of the item. For example, in the market for oil, the determinants of supply will include the success of oil exploration and discovery (a big new discovery will increase supply), while in the market for computers, technological innovations that lower chip costs will increase supply. In the market for corn, a bad harvest would reduce supply, but new, more productive varieties of corn would increase it. You can easily think of similar examples for other goods and services.

Discussion Questions

1. Explain in words why the supply curve slopes upward.
2. Verbally explain the difference between a change in *quantity supplied* and a change in *supply*. Considering the supply side of the market for lawn-mowing services, what kind of change (*increase* or *decrease* in *quantity supplied* or *supply*) would each of the following events cause?
    a. A rise in the going price for lawn-mowing services
    b. More people decide to offer to mow lawns
    c. Gasoline for lawn mowers becomes much more expensive (assume that the person doing the mowing buys the gas)

3. THE THEORY OF DEMAND

Now let us consider the market from the point of view of potential *buyers* of coffee. Potential buyers will also consider price, but of course they will prefer a lower price. Let's suppose that in this market, no potential buyers are willing to pay more than €2.30 for a cup of coffee. But a drop in the price per cup would induce more purchases of coffee. This reasonable assumption about the way potential buyers behave allows us to construct a demand schedule.

3.1 The Demand Schedule and Curve

In Table 4.2, we show the demand schedule that reflects these assumptions. A demand schedule describes, in the form of a table, the quantity of a good or service that buyers are willing to purchase at each possible price.

Table 4.2 *A Demand Schedule for Coffee*

Price (€/cup)	Cups of coffee demanded/week
0.20	1,000
0.50	900
0.80	800
1.10	700
1.40	600
1.70	500
2.00	400
2.30	300

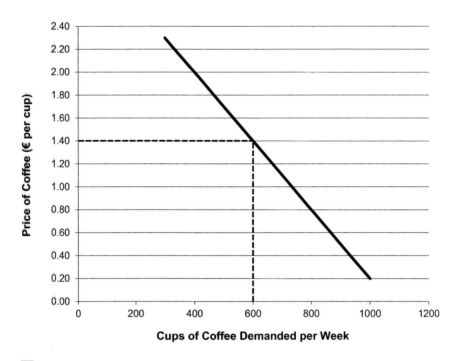

Figure 4.4 *The Demand Curve for Cups of Coffee*

The demand curve shows the same information as the demand schedule. At higher prices, fewer cups of coffee are desired by people looking to buy.

demand curve: a curve indicating the quantities that buyers are ready to purchase at various prices

From the demand schedule, we can graph a **demand curve**, as shown in Figure 4.4. Note that the demand curve in Figure 4.4 slopes downward. It seems reasonable to expect that, generally, the higher the price of a good, the fewer people will want to (or be able to) buy. Price and quantity have a negative (or inverse) relationship along the demand curve.

Suppose that the price of coffee rose from €1.40 to €2.00. According to our demand schedule, the number of cups of coffee that will be purchased falls from 600 to 400. The demand curve has not shifted, but there has been a movement *along* the demand curve. This movement is referred to as a **change in quantity demanded**.

change in quantity demanded: movement along a demand curve in response to a price change

Check yourself by answering this question with reference to Table 4.2 or Figure 4.4: By how much does the *quantity demanded* change when the price changes from €2.00 to €0.80?

change in demand: a shift of the demand curve in response to some determinant other than the item's price

3.2 Changes in Demand

As with supply, we distinguish between *a change in quantity demanded* and a **change in demand**. When there is a change in demand, the whole curve shifts.

Why might the whole curve shift? One reason might be the increasing trendiness of drinking coffee. Whereas a generation ago, one seldom saw people walking in the street holding a container of coffee, it may soon be almost as rare to see someone *not* holding one. It means that there are now many more buyers, and the change is reflected as a shift in demand. Specifically, suppose that at every price, there are now 300 more cups of coffee demanded in the market. Such a change is illustrated by the shift to the right from D_1 to D_2 in Figure 4.5. We say that "demand has risen" or "the demand curve has shifted." (Because of the curve's negative slope, in this case this also means shifting "up.")

We would see the same result if, instead of new buyers entering the market, the existing buyers each became willing to pay €0.90 more for a cup of coffee. The situation could arise, for example, if the prices of alternatives, such as tea or hot chocolate, had risen substantially. If this were to happen, the lack of reasonably priced alternatives—what economists call **substitute goods**—would likely increase the maximum price that existing coffee drinkers would be willing to pay for a cup. A classic example of substitute goods is Coke versus Pepsi. An increase in the price of a substitute good tends to increase the demand for the good in question, because people who are unwilling to pay the higher price will shift to the substitute good whose price has not risen. An increase in the price of tea or chocolate could thus lead to an "increase in demand" for coffee. The change would also be illustrated by Figure 4.5.

The coffee market may also be affected by changes in the prices of goods that are **complementary** to coffee. Complementary goods are those that are used along *with*

substitute good: a good that can be used in place of another

complementary good: a good that is used along with another good

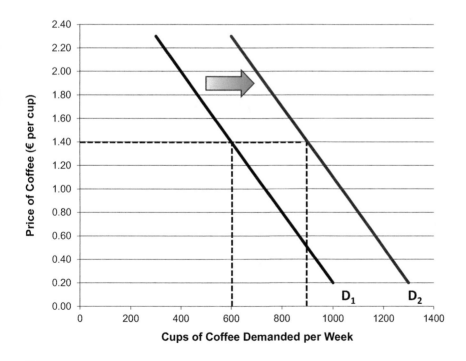

Figure 4.5 *An Increase in Demand*

The demand curve shifts outward (to the right) when more buyers want to buy at a given price or buyers are willing to pay a higher price for a given quantity.

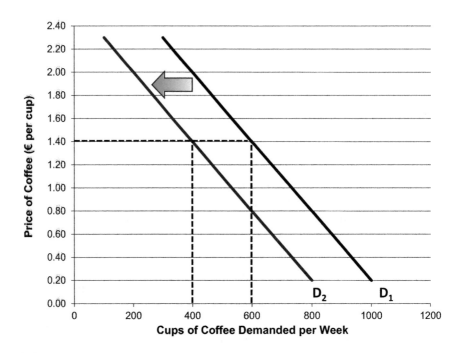

Figure 4.6 *A Decrease in Demand*

When the demand curve shifts inward (to the left), we say that demand has decreased.

the good in question. A classic example of complementary goods is hot dogs and mustard. For purposes of our example, suppose coffee is frequently consumed with sugar or pastries. An increase in the price of sugar and products that use sugar would make coffee less attractive, since the price of the "package" of coffee plus pastry is now higher. Demand for the good in question tends to decrease with an increase in the price of a complementary good. This is shown in Figure 4.6.

Thus the number of potential buyers, their ability to pay, and prices of substitutes and complements are among the things that can affect the location of the demand curve. Many other factors affect the location of demand curves, depending on the specific market in question. For example, in the market for steel, overall economic growth will increase the demand for steel, while the development of substitute materials, such as plastic composites for use in automobiles, will decrease it. Hotter weather will increase demand for ice cream but will decrease the demand for sweaters—and so forth. We can easily identify many examples of other demand shifts in everyday life.

Discussion Questions

1. Explain verbally why the demand curve slopes downward.
2. Verbally explain the difference between a change in *quantity demanded* and a change in *demand*. Considering the demand side of the market for lawn-mowing services, what kind of change (*increase* or *decrease* in *quantity demanded* or *demand*) would each of the following events cause?

a. A new office park is built, surrounded by several acres of lawn
b. There is a recession, putting many people out of work; many homeowners have less money but more time to mow their own lawns
c. The going price for lawn-mowing services rises
d. A more natural, wild yard becomes the "in" thing, as people become concerned about the effects of fertilizers and pesticides on the environment

4. THE THEORY OF MARKET ADJUSTMENT

Now that we have considered the sellers and the buyers separately, it is time to bring them together. In our hypothetical market, every cup of coffee will sell at the same price. (Remember, they are identical—why would anyone pay more or accept less than the going price?) We are now ready to ask: How many cups of coffee will be sold in the market and at what price?

4.1 Surplus, Shortage, and Equilibrium

Using the original supply and demand curves, reproduced here in Figure 4.7, we can look for the answer by considering possible prices. Suppose that we start with a high

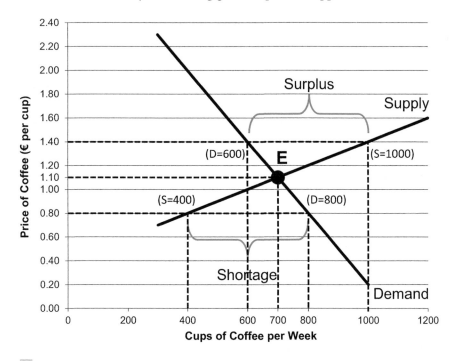

Figure 4.7 *Surplus, Shortage, and Equilibrium*

At a price of €1.40, a surplus occurs because the quantity of cups of coffee being offered for sale is larger than the quantity that people want to buy. On the other hand, at a price of €0.80, many people want to buy cups of coffee but few want to sell, so a shortage occurs. Only at market equilibrium (point E) does quantity supplied equal quantity demanded.

135

price of €1.40. At this price, 1,000 cups of coffee will be offered for sale, but consumers are collectively interested in buying only 600. Economists call a situation in which the quantity supplied is greater than the quantity demanded a **surplus**. It is illustrated in the upper part of Figure 4.7.

surplus: a situation in which the quantity that sellers wish to sell at the stated price is greater than the quantity that buyers will buy at that price

Because suppliers who are willing to sell at this price cannot find buyers, what will they do? For a number of sellers, €1.40 is more than they need to persuade them to sell. To find buyers, they will suggest a lower selling price. At €1.20, a surplus still occurs—900 cups of coffee are available at that price, but the market demands fewer than 700, so there will be further downward pressure on the price. When the price finally reaches €1.10, each and every cup made available will find a buyer. The number of cups of coffee supplied—and demanded—is equal to 700. The market price is €1.10. Economists call this a situation in which the "market clears" and an **equilibrium** is reached. "Equilibrium" describes a situation that has reached a resting point, where there are no forces acting to change it. (Economists borrowed this term from natural science.) In a market situation, equilibrium is reached when the quantity supplied is equal to the quantity demanded. The price will stop falling. Figure 4.7 illustrates the **market-clearing equilibrium** point, labeled E.

equilibrium: a situation of rest, in which there are no forces that create change

market-clearing equilibrium: a situation in which quantity supplied equals quantity demanded

What if the price had started out too low, for example at €0.80? In this case, a **shortage** would occur, in which the quantity supplied is less than the quantity demanded, as illustrated in the lower part of Figure 4.7. Because at this price 800 cups of coffee are demanded, but only 400 are supplied, the buyers who are willing to pay more than €0.80 for a cup of coffee will bid the price up. Sellers will find that they can easily get more than €0.80 for a cup of coffee, so they will raise prices. As the price rises, quantity demanded will fall, while quantity supplied will increase. At €1.10, demand is just 700 cups, exactly matched by a supply of 700.

shortage: a situation in which the quantity that buyers wish to buy at the stated price is greater than the quantity that sellers are willing to sell at that price

The **theory of market adjustment** says that market forces will tend to make price and quantity move toward the equilibrium point. Surpluses will lead to declines in price, and shortages will lead to rises in price. Surplus and shortage are both instances of **market disequilibrium**. Disequilibrium will tend to lead to changes in price and quantity. Only at equilibrium is there no tendency to change. In this example, the equilibrium price is €1.10, and the equilibrium quantity is 700.

theory of market adjustment: the theory that market forces will tend to make shortages and surpluses disappear

market disequilibrium: a situation of either shortage or surplus

4.2 Shifts in Supply and Demand

With the two curves now combined, we can investigate how market forces will cause equilibrium prices and quantities to change in response to changes in the underlying nonprice determinants of supply and demand.

In our coffee market, let us compare the original case shown in Figure 4.7 to a case in which supply has risen. How would the market result now differ, compared to the original case? In Figure 4.8, the original equilibrium is marked as E_1 with supply curve S_1. When the supply curve shifts to S_2, we see that a surplus results at the original equilibrium price of €1.10. At point E_2, with a price of €0.80, the market clears, with 800 cups of coffee being sold. As Figure 4.8 illustrates, *an increase in supply will tend to decrease equilibrium price and increase equilibrium quantity.*

136

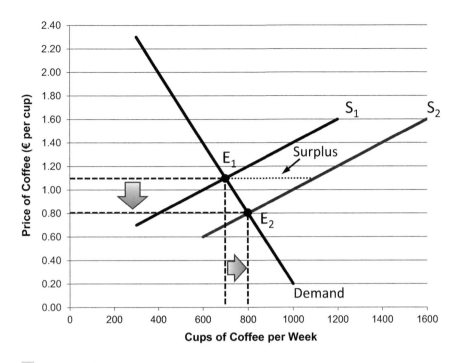

Figure 4.8 *Market Adjustment to an Increase in Supply*

With an increase in the supply of cups of coffee, there now would be a surplus at the original equilibrium price of €1.10. Market adjustment forces should cause the price to fall until a new equilibrium is established at a price of €0.80. Seven hundred cups of coffee will sell at this new equilibrium price. The equilibrium price has fallen and the equilibrium quantity has risen.

Suppose that instead of an increase in supply in this market, we have an increase in demand. In Figure 4.9, we see the effect of that demand increase: At the original equilibrium price of €1.10, a shortage results. The price will be bid up to €1.40, where 1,000 cups of coffee will be offered. As Figure 4.9 illustrates, *an increase in demand will tend to increase equilibrium price and increase equilibrium quantity.*

Notice that both supply and demand increases tend to increase the equilibrium quantity transacted. Their price effects, however, go in opposite directions. Increases in supply make the good more plentiful, driving its equilibrium price down. Increases in demand drive up the equilibrium price.

Likewise, decreases in supply and demand both tend to decrease the equilibrium quantity transacted. A decrease in supply will tend to raise the equilibrium price, as the good is harder to get. A decrease in demand will tend to decrease the equilibrium price, as fewer attempts are made to obtain the good. These effects are summarized in Table 4.3.

What if *both* curves shifted at the same time? What if, for example, there were increases in the number of sellers of coffee *and* in the number of buyers? In this case,

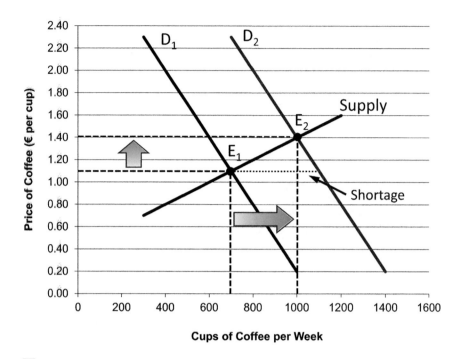

Figure 4.9 *Market Adjustment to an Increase in Demand*

With an increase in demand, there would be a shortage of cups of coffee at the original equilibrium price of €1.10. Market forces should cause the price to rise, until a new equilibrium is established at €1.40. One thousand cups of coffee will sell at this new equilibrium price. The equilibrium price has risen and the equilibrium quantity has risen.

Table 4.3 *Effects of Changes in Supply and Demand*

	Effect on equilibrium price	*Effect on equilibrium quantity*
Increase in supply	fall	rise
Decrease in supply	rise	fall
Increase in demand	rise	rise
Decrease in demand	fall	fall

price elasticity:
a measure of the sensitivity or responsiveness of quantity supplied or demanded to changes in price

the new equilibrium would be found at the intersection of two new curves rather than one new curve and one old one. Comparing the new equilibrium with the original one in the case in which both supply and demand increase, for example, the equilibrium quantity clearly rises, but the effect on the equilibrium price is ambiguous. That is, the equilibrium price may go up, go down, or stay the same depending on two factors: how far each of the curves shifts, and how steep each of the curves is (the second of these is related to the **price elasticity** of supply or demand, a concept that is discussed in what follows). In other cases, it may be the change in the price that is clear but the change in equilibrium quantity that is ambiguous—again, depending on the same two factors. You can experiment with various combinations of changes to see how they affect equilibrium. (See Box 4.1 for some examples of changes in the real-world market for coffee.)

4.3 Elasticity

When there is a change in market price, by *how much* will the equilibrium quantity change? Economists are often interested in the answer to this question. The **price elasticity of demand** measures the degree to which buyers of a good respond to a change in its price. Mathematically, it is defined as the absolute value of the percentage change in quantity demanded divided by the percentage change in price:

price elasticity of demand: a measure of the responsiveness of quantity demanded to changes in price

$$Price\ elasticity\ of\ demand = \left| \frac{(\%\ change\ in\ quantity\ demanded)}{(\%\ change\ in\ price)} \right|$$

BOX 4.1 COFFEE MARKETS IN THE REAL WORLD

After reaching a 14-year high in May 2011, wholesale coffee bean prices began to tumble. By July 2013 prices for Arabica beans, the most-consumed coffee in the world, had fallen more than 60 percent. How can our market model provide insights into changing coffee prices in the real world?

Our model suggests that falling prices can occur either due to an increase in supply or a decrease in demand or both. According to data from the United States Department of Agriculture, global coffee supplies increased over this time period. At the same time, consumption in coffee-growing countries and coffee exports both increased. So this data suggests that the main reason prices fell so much over 2011–2013 was an increase in the supply of coffee.

In the 2012–2013 growing season, Brazil, the world's largest coffee producer, had a bumper crop, with production up 14 percent over the previous year. Vietnam, the world's second-largest producer, has been scaling up its coffee production in recent years. Between 2010 and 2012, production there increased nearly 30 percent. Other major coffee-producing countries, including Colombia and Indonesia, also had production gains.

With coffee bean prices so low, you may wonder why in June 2013, Starbucks announced that it was *increasing* its prices. According to a Starbucks spokesman, the reasons for the price increase included higher costs for labor, raw materials, and rent. The cost of the actual coffee beans represents a minor portion of the total cost of producing a retail cup of coffee. Starbucks may also have raised its prices because it perceived that consumers will continue to demand its products despite slightly higher prices (i.e., that demand for coffee is inelastic).

Sources: U.S. Department of Agriculture, "Coffee: World Markets and Trade," June 2013; Kavilanz, Parija, "Next Week You'll Pay More for a Starbucks Latte," CNN Money, June 21, 2013.

The larger the quantity response is, relative to the size of the price change, the "more elastic" demand is said to be. If the response is small, demand is said to be relatively "price inelastic."

You can think of price elasticity of demand as a measure of the responsiveness of quantity demanded to changes in price.

Figure 4.10 graphs two different demand curves, along with identical supply curve shifts. In Figure 4.10(a), with the relatively flat demand curve, we see that there is a large drop in the quantity demanded associated with a small increase in price. In Figure 4.10(b), by contrast, with a relatively steep demand curve, only a small decrease in quantity demanded is associated with a substantial increase in price. The difference derives from the fact that the demand curve shown in (a) is much more price elastic than the demand curve in (b).

Goods for which there are many substitutes, which are merely wanted rather than needed or which make up a large part of the budget of the buyer, tend to have relatively price-elastic demand. Different brands of beverage, for example, will tend to be price elastic, because they can readily substitute for one another. Demand for automobiles is also price elastic—because a car is such a large expense that buyers will tend to be sensitive to price. However, goods for which there are few substitutes, that are badly needed, or that make up a small part of the buyer's budget tend to have relatively inelastic demand. We would expect demand for our earlier example of coffee to be relatively price inelastic, possibly for all three reasons!* Essential medications and gasoline are two other examples of relatively price-inelastic goods.

price elasticity of supply: a measure of the responsiveness of quantity supplied to changes in price

The **price elasticity of supply** measures the same sort of responsiveness, but this time on the part of sellers. Mathematically, it is defined as the percentage change in quantity supplied divided by the percentage change in price. When suppliers respond to a small increase in price by offering a much larger quantity of goods, we say that supply is relatively elastic. If they hardly react at all, supply is relatively inelastic. Like the price elasticity of demand, the price elasticity of supply is calculated as:

Elasticity = % change in quantity supplied / % change in price

Given that supply curves normally slope upward, price and quantity supplied change in the same direction, and thus taking the absolute value is not required.

Discussion Questions

1. Think about the market for high-quality basketballs. In each of the following cases, determine which curve shifts and in which direction. Also draw a graph and describe, in words, the changes in price and quantity. (Treat each case separately.)
   a. A rise in basketball players' income
   b. An increase in wages paid to the workers who make the balls

---

* Individual brands of coffee, by contrast, would have elastic demand, because they can substitute for one another.

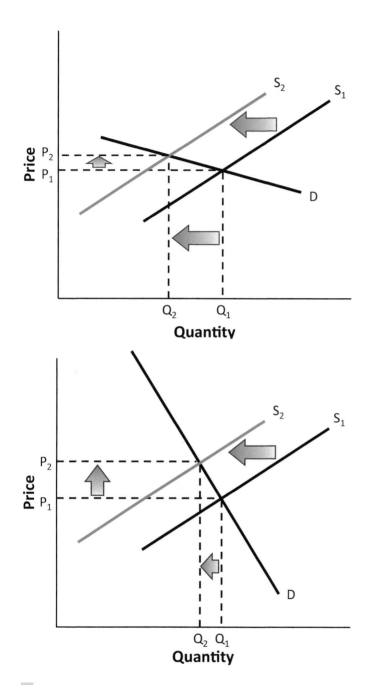

Figure 4.10a and 4.10b *Price Elasticity of Demand*

(a) Relatively Price-Elastic Demand
(b) Relatively Price-Inelastic Demand

When a small change in price leads buyers to make a large change in the quantity they demand, demand is said to be relatively elastic. If buyers' response is, instead, weak, demand is said to be relatively inelastic.

     c.   A decrease in the price of basketball hoops and other basketball gear

     d.   The country's becoming obsessed with soccer

2.   Have you ever found yourself shut out of a class that you wanted to take because it was already full? Or has this happened to a friend of yours? Analyze this situation in terms of surplus or shortage. Are classes supplied "in a market"? Do you think that it would be good if they were?

5. MACROECONOMICS AND THE DYNAMICS OF REAL-WORLD MARKETS

Although supply-and-demand analysis can be a very useful tool for understanding how markets work, few if any markets truly approach perfect competition, and seldom are they as fluid as in the simple models depicted here. Markets may be characterized by market power (as mentioned in Chapter 2 and with the example of Microsoft). Goods and services sold in markets may not be as simple as our example of cups of coffee; more commonly, there are different brands and types of product with different characteristics. Buyers and sellers may have imperfect information or be bound by long-term contracts. The role of assumptions and expectations can be significant. For example, if people were used to paying more for the services of lawyers than for the services of teachers, lawyers would be very resistant to changes in the relative prices. In general, wages, which are a special kind of price, can be affected by a variety of things aside from simple supply and demand. This special case is examined further in future chapters.

There is one additional reason to look closely at the standard market model. This is its assumption that, when the market functions in a smooth, idealized way, taking decisions out of the hands of individuals, the results are purely "objective," with no bias toward any person or group. In fact, this model does have an undeniable bias toward those with money—and a larger bias toward persons or organizations with more money. This is because "demand" in the context of supply-and-demand interactions means "willingness *and ability* to pay." So pure market results are based on the distribution of purchasing power—money—in the society.

5.1 When Price Adjustments Are Slow

An issue of particular importance to macroeconomics is the question of the speed at which real-world price adjustments take place. How long will it take our hypothetical coffee traders to reach equilibrium? Minutes? An hour? A day? The theory of supply and demand does not tell us. The graphs represent a static model. Recall from Chapter 2 that this means that the model does not take into account the passage of time.

Some markets, such as stock markets, tend to clear quickly. But other markets involve significant time delays. For example, consider the market for shirts. When you go into a clothing store, you see a rack of shirts and, on their tags, a given price. The price probably reflects a markup by the retailer over what he or she paid to a distributor to get the shirts. The distributor, in turn, probably charged a markup over the price charged by the manufacturer. Now, if the shirts were overpriced, they would not sell very well. In the terms we introduced, there would be a surplus. If the market worked as fluidly as just described, the supplier and demander would quickly be able to fine tune the price and quantity to get it just right, as we saw in our hypothetical coffee market in Figure 4.7. The price would fall, the surplus of shirts would disappear immediately, and equilibrium would be restored.

In a realistic, complicated case such as this one, however, there is actually a *chain* of markets involved—the manufacturer sells to the distributor, the distributor to the retailer, and the retailer to the final buyer. A quick adjustment of prices is unlikely. More commonly, when retailers mark down the prices on the shirts they have in stock in order to clear them out, the drop in the price will not immediately travel back up the supply chain. In the next order that the retailers place with their distributors, the retailers might just ask for a smaller quantity of shirts at the price at which the distributor is offering them—especially if the retailer were small relative to the distributor and had little power to bargain over prices. Any changes in prices or quantities at the manufacturing level would only develop over time as the manufacturers saw the level of their inventories either rise (because the shirts are not selling) or fall (because the distributors order more).

Because of the time it takes for all these things to happen, some economists believe that the most likely first response to a surplus is that manufacturers would cut *production*—perhaps laying off workers—rather than reducing their price. In such a case, the *quantity* produced adjusts to meet the quantity demanded at a given price rather than the price adjusting to clear the market. If such **quantity adjustments** happened throughout the economy, unemployment could rise.

Suppliers may also be reluctant to change the prices that they offer because of **menu costs**—literally, the costs of changing the prices listed on such things as order forms and restaurant menus. Other factors that could slow the process of price adjustment include union contracts, lengthy production processes, and information problems.

5.2 When Prices Swing Too Much: Market Instability

Other markets have adjustment processes in which prices may change rapidly. In electronic stock markets, for example, thousands of trades may take place every minute as buyers and sellers find each other and quickly negotiate a price. Such a market can probably be thought of as in equilibrium, or moving quickly toward one, nearly all the time.

Very rapid adjustments of prices, however, create their own set of problems, especially in relation to the macroeconomic goal of stability. In our hypothetical market for coffee, we assumed that people wanted coffee simply because of the taste or perhaps the energy boost, both reasonable assumptions. But there are markets in which buyers are not really interested in the *item itself* at all—only its price and the direction in which it is likely to go. **Speculation** is the buying and selling of assets with the expectation of profiting from appreciation or depreciation in their values, usually over a relatively short period of time. Speculators buy items such as stocks in companies,

quantity adjustments: a response by suppliers in which they react to unexpectedly low sales of their good primarily by reducing production levels rather than by reducing the price and to unexpectedly high sales by increasing production rather than raising the price

menu costs: the costs to a supplier of changing prices listed on order forms, brochures, menus, and the like

speculation: buying and selling assets with the expectation of profiting from appreciation or depreciation in their value

143

commodities futures (e.g., contracts to buy or sell items such as pork bellies or copper at a specific price on a future date), foreign exchange, real estate, or other investment vehicles, purely in the hopes that they will be able to sell them in the future for more than they have paid.

When many people come to believe that the price of something will rise, a **speculative bubble** can occur, in which people buy the asset because so many other people also believe that its price will continue to rise. In a mass phenomenon often referred to using terms such as "herd mentality" or "bandwagon effect," speculators' mutually reinforcing optimism causes asset values to rise far above any price that could be rationalized in terms of "economic fundamentals."

In the case of a stock price, for example, the rational economic basis for valuation should be the returns that an investor can expect from the firm of which the stock represents an ownership share, while in the case of real estate, the value should be determined by the stream of likely rents, from the present into the future. Someone who buys a home to live in should rationally select one whose costs (mortgage payments plus lost income on the money used for down payment) are similar to the rent that would be demanded for a comparable property.

During a bubble, however, people pay less attention to (or take a biased view of) such fundamental factors. Instead, demand for an asset is determined largely by purchasers' perception that they will be able to find someone to whom they can sell the asset at a higher price. Eventually, however, people begin to figure out that prices have become unrealistically high. Then demand drops, the bubble bursts, and prices fall. This happened during the "dotcom" bubble of the late 1990s in the U.S. (see Figure 4.11) and many European countries.

speculative bubble: the situation that occurs when mutually reinforcing investor optimism raises the value of an asset far above what can be justified by fundamental value

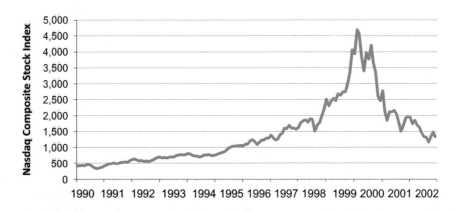

Figure 4.11 *The Stock Market Bubble of 1999–2000*

Enthusiasm about new technologies, and Internet e-commerce in particular, temporarily drove the prices of many companies' stocks very high. During the bubble, the prices of stocks as determined by supply and demand rose far above the prices that would occur if valuation had been based on the companies' actual performances.

Source: Yahoo! Finance, monthly data.

It is fairly easy, of course, to recognize a bubble after the fact. However, during the spectacular rise in stock prices that took place in the late 1990s, many otherwise rational and intelligent people convinced one another—and themselves—that the stock market boom reflected an immense jump in productivity, not a speculative bubble. This led to a major crash in stock prices during 2000–2002.

In spite of the painful lesson of this crash, soon afterward, the buildup began for another boom and bust, this time originating in the U.S. market for **subprime mort–gages**. Such mortgages are housing loans given to people whose income or credit history is not good enough to qualify them for regular mortgages.

subprime mortgage: a mortgage given to someone with poor credit

---

BOX 4.2 RECOVERY IN THE SPANISH HOUSING MARKET

The housing market is considered an important indicator of the overall economy. In the wake of the Great Recession and the following euro crisis, average house prices in Spain dropped by more than one-third between 2008 and 2014. Finally, in late 2015, the housing market began to show signs of recovery. By the beginning of 2016, prices were rising at an annual rate of more than 6 percent—as fast as they had prior to the crisis.

The rising prices are a function of both supply and demand factors. The number of homes sold nationally in 2012 was up by about 30 percent compared to the previous year. At the same time, the supply of homes was down. In the twelve months leading up to March 2016, not even 50,000 houses had been built—in a typical year prior to the crisis, almost 700,000 houses had been built.

The reasons housing prices have increased include an improvement in the overall economy, lower unemployment rates, low mortgage rates, and the tight supply. Another factor has been increased demand by foreigners: According to Mark Stucklin from Spanish Property Insight, in early 2016, demand for second homes in Spain by nonresidents has been 60 percent higher than it was, prior to the real estate boom in June 2007.

Source: Paul Day and Sarah White, "Spanish house prices rise at pre-crisis pace in first quarter," June 9, 2016; Property Wire, "Sellers reduce asking prices in Spain as the market becomes more realistic," June 3, 2016; Macrobond database.

Many banks aggressively marketed subprime housing loans to prospective home-owners from early 2004 to 2007, sometimes using fraudulent techniques and making profits by collecting fees on each loan made. Some of the world's largest banks moved aggressively into this area, bundling and repackaging the mortgages in such a way that their riskiness was not immediately apparent. This increase in credit increased demand for houses and drove up real estate prices. Eventually, however, softening of housing prices and rising adjustable interest rates caused a steep increase in the number of U.S. homeowners who were defaulting on their loans. Securities

145

based on "bundled" subprime mortgages rapidly lost market value as questions were finally raised about the actual worth of the assets on which they were based. Commercial banks lost billions of dollars, and a number of them had to close down. When credit contracted and investors panicked, the subprime crisis spread around the world, and many European countries experienced the deepest recession since World War II.

In some European countries, such as Spain, Britain, and Ireland, a domestic boom and bust in the housing market added to the downturn. Even though subprime mortgages had been rare in these countries, strong growth of bank credit also fueled demand for houses and pushed up prices in the years prior to 2008. When housing prices finally started to fall, construction companies went bankrupt, and home-owners defaulted on their loans. In Britain, Ireland, and Spain, this caused national banking crises, and in the case of Ireland, it forced the government to apply for emergency loans from the International Monetary Fund and the European partners. We will examine the global financial crisis in Chapter 15 and the following euro crisis in Chapter 16. (See Box 4.2 for a presentation of recent developments in the Spanish housing market.)

Situations of speculative bubbles and volatile (that is, rapidly changing) prices have important implications for macroeconomics, even though there is some dis-agreement among economists about the importance of market volatility. Those who take a classical point of view tend to downplay such market-related problems, believing that even if market performance sometimes seemed counter to human welfare, it would still be better than what could be achieved by any sort of regulation or intervention. Other economists, in particular those with Keynesian views or those who are particularly concerned with the economics of less industrialized countries or the fate of the less-well-off in any society, believe that some sort of regulation is needed to prevent market volatility. We discuss both the need for and nature of such regulations in later chapters.

5.3 From Microeconomics to Macroeconomics

How far does the model of supply and demand get us in explaining macroeco-nomic phenomena? That question can be broken down into two parts. First, are markets in the real world similar to the one portrayed in the model? Second, even to the extent that individual markets do behave as the model predicts, might explaining national-level economic phenomena require different theoretical tools? In other words, does it follow that what works for a market necessarily works for entire economies?

Later chapters of this book will explore these questions, starting with the ways in which we measure macroeconomic activity then examining different approaches to analyzing the behavior of the economy as a whole.

DISCUSSION QUESTIONS

1. Think of several things that you regularly buy. For which of these goods or services do prices seem to change rapidly? For which do they seem to change slowly? Can you explain why?
2. Has there been any talk of "speculative bubbles" in news reports recently? If so, what markets are being discussed? What explanations are given for why prices may be so high?

REVIEW QUESTIONS

1. Describe three characteristics of the type of market featured in classical analysis.
2. Define and sketch a supply curve.
3. Illustrate on a clearly labeled graph (a) a decrease in quantity supplied and (b) a decrease in supply.
4. Describe two factors that might cause a supply curve to shift.
5. Define and sketch a demand curve.
6. Illustrate on a clearly labeled graph (a) a decrease in quantity demanded and (b) a decrease in demand.
7. Describe two factors that might cause a demand curve to shift.
8. Describe how goods can be "substitutes." Describe how the demand curve for a good may be affected by an increase in the price of a second good that is a substitute for the first.
9. Describe how goods can be "complementary." Describe how the demand curve for a good may be affected by an increase in the price of a second good that is complementary to the first.
10. Draw a graph illustrating surplus, shortage, and equilibrium.
11. Describe, using graphs, how an increase in supply affects equilibrium quantity and price. Repeat for a decrease in supply.
12. Describe, using graphs, how an increase in demand affects equilibrium quantity and price. Repeat for a decrease in demand.
13. Describe what is meant by the price elasticity of demand and the price elasticity of supply.
14. Describe why sellers of a good might adjust the quantity of what they produce rather than the price.
15. What are some of the problems that can be created by large price swings?

EXERCISES

1. Suppose that the supply-and-demand schedules for a local electric utility are as follows: The price is in cents per kilowatt-hour (kWh), and the quantity is millions of kilowatt-hours. The utility does not operate at prices less than 13 cents per kWh.

Price	Quantity supplied	Quantity demanded
17	9	3
16	7	4
15	5	5
14	3	6
13	1	7
12	—	8
11	—	9

a. Using graph paper and a ruler or a computer spreadsheet or presentation program, carefully graph and label the supply curve for electricity.

b. On the same graph, draw and label the demand curve for electricity.

c. What is the equilibrium price of electricity? The equilibrium quantity? Label this point on your graph.

d. At a price of 17 cents per kWh, what is the quantity supplied? What is the quantity demanded? What is the relationship between quantity supplied and quantity demanded? What term do economists use to describe this situation?

e. At a price of 14 cents per kWh, what is the relationship between quantity supplied and quantity demanded? What term do economists use to describe this situation?

f. Sometimes cities experience "blackouts," in which the demand for the utility is so high relative to its capacity to produce electricity that the system shuts down, leaving everyone in the dark. Using the analysis that you have just completed, describe an *economic* factor that would make blackouts more likely to occur.

2. Continuing from the previous problem, suppose that new innovations in energy efficiency reduce people's need for electricity. The supply side of the market does not change, but at each price, buyers now demand 3 million kWh fewer than before. For example, at a price of 11 cents per kWh, buyers now demand only 6 kWh instead of 9 kWh.

a. On a new graph, draw supply and demand curves corresponding to prices of 16 cents per kWh or less, after the innovations in efficiency. Also, for reference, mark the old equilibrium point from the previous exercise, labeling it E1.

b. If the price were to remain at the old equilibrium level determined in part (c) of question 1, what sort of situation would result?

c. What is the new equilibrium price? The new equilibrium quantity? Label this point on your graph E2.

d. Has there been a change in demand? Has a change in the price (relative to the original situation) led to a change in the quantity demanded?

e. Has there been a change in supply? Has a change in the price (relative to the original situation) led to a decrease in the quantity supplied?

3. Using your understanding of the nonprice determinants of supply and of demand, analyze each of the following market cases. Draw a graph showing what happens in each situation, indicate what happens to equilibrium price and quantity, and explain why. The first case is done as an example:

Question: Market for gasoline: A hurricane hits the Gulf of Mexico, destroying many refineries that produce gasoline from crude oil.

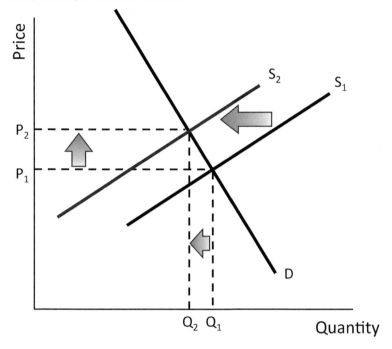

Answer:

S shifts back.

P rises.

Q falls.

The hurricane reduces the number of producers.

a. Market for bananas: New health reports indicate that eating bananas leads to important health benefits.

b. Market for shoes: A new technology for shoe making means that shoes can be made at a lower cost per pair.

c. Market for Web design services: Several thousand new graduates of design schools enter the market, ready to supply their services.

d. Market for expensive meals: A booming economy raises the income of many households.

e. Market for grapes *from California*: A freeze in Chile, usually a major world provider of fresh fruit, raises the price of Chilean grapes.

f. Market for salsa dance lessons: The only nightclub in town featuring salsa music triples its entrance fee.

g. Market for bottled water: A rumor circulates that the price of bottled water is about to triple. (Think only about the demand side.)

h. Market for Web design services: Several thousand new graduates of design schools enter the market, ready to supply their services *and*, at the same time, many firms want to create new Web sites.

149

4. Sketch a supply curve graph illustrating a student's willingness to sell his textbooks from all his classes, right now. Assume that the student will receive offers of this sort: "I'll give you [a fixed number of euros] apiece for all the books you want to sell." Carefully label the vertical and horizontal axes. Suppose that at an original offer of €30 per book, the student will be willing to sell three books, because he knows that he can replace these three for less than €30 each at a local bookstore. Mark this point on your first graph. Assume further that at €40 he would be willing to sell four books, at €50 he would supply five books, and so on. Now, on separate graphs labeled (a), (b), and (c), show this line and his offer at €30 and the precise new *point* or an approximate new *curve* that illustrates each of the following contrasts. Consider them separately, assuming no Internet resources in considering (c).
    a. He is offered €70 per book instead of €30.
    b. He discovers that the textbook materials for many of his classes are available free on the Internet.
    c. The local bookstore raises its prices substantially.

5. State whether the following statements are true or false. If false, write a corrected statement.
    a. A fall in the price of a good will cause its supply curve to shift to the left.
    b. Increased costs of supplying a good will cause the supply curve to shift to the left.
    c. A fall in the price of a substitute good will cause the demand for the good in question to fall.
    d. A decrease in supply will have a small effect on the quantity demanded if the demand curve is very elastic.

6. Consider the market for diamond rings. For each of the following, draw a graph and describe the likely effects on equilibrium price and quantity (assuming the market functions like the one described in the text). Explain your reasoning.
    a. Valentine's Day is approaching.
    b. Manufacturers discover new industrial uses for diamonds, driving up the prices that jewelers have to pay to obtain the gems.
    c. New deposits of diamonds are discovered.
    d. The price of cubic zirconium "gems" (high-quality fake diamonds) falls.
    e. People experience an increase in their wealth.

7. Suppose that a newspaper report indicates that the price of wheat has fallen. Which of the following could be possible explanations? (There may be more than one.) Illustrate *one* case on a supply-and-demand graph.
    a. A drought has hit wheat-growing areas.
    b. An increase in the price of rice
    c. Due to increasing health concerns, tobacco farmers have begun growing other crops.
    d. A new science report suggests that wheat is bad for one's health.

8. Prices of many financial assets such as stocks and foreign exchange are now readily available on the Internet. Search for a chart like Figure 4.11 for a stock index or foreign currency of your choosing and print it out. During the period covered by the graph that you found, does it seem as if this market is fairly calm or is it characterized by periods of volatility? (Caution: because price swings can be made to look relatively large or small simply by changing the scale of the graph, in answering this question, you may want to choose a fairly long time series or compare the behavior of the asset you have chosen with a similar asset.) Is there any evidence of a speculative bubble?

150

9. Match each concept in Column A with a definition or example in Column B.

Column A	Column B
a. Substitute goods	1. The stock market
b. Shifts the supply curve	2. A tiny drop in the price of a good leads to a big increase in quantity demanded
c. A "bubble"	3. Shoes and shoelaces
d. Complementary goods	4. A shoe manufacturer responds to a decline in shoe sales by cutting back on production and laying off workers
e. Speculation	5. Tea and coffee
f. Market equilibrium	6. Quantity supplied is greater than quantity demanded
g. Auction market	7. Buying an asset largely in the hope of selling it later for a higher price
h. Quantity adjustment	8. Quantity supplied is equal to quantity demanded
i. Price-elastic demand	9. A change in the number of sellers
j. Surplus	10. When investors' optimism pushes the price of an asset artificially high

Part II

Macroeconomic Basics

Chapter 5

Macroeconomic Measurement

The Current Approach

In order to make good macroeconomic policy choices, we need to have reliable information on how the economy is performing. Gross domestic product (GDP) is the metric that is most often cited to assess overall economic performance.* For example, a common definition of a recession is when an economy's GDP decreases for two consecutive quarters. Of course, other variables, such as unemployment, inflation, and interest rates, are of great interest to economists and policy makers, but they tend to rely most heavily on GDP data to guide their policy recommendations.

gross domestic product (GDP): a measure of the total market value of final goods and services newly produced within a country's borders over a period of time (usually one year)

In this chapter, we take a detailed look at GDP and related national economic data. But before we begin, a note of caution is in order. Although it is true that GDP growth improves average material living standards, which in turn contributes to well-being, it is not true that GDP growth always increases well-being. For example, if GDP grows simply because people are working longer hours, we would need to evaluate the increase in GDP against the loss in leisure time to determine whether well-being has actually increased. In Chapter 6, we look at the limitations of and alternatives to GDP as a measure of well-being in order to place our discussion of GDP "in context" with our broader discussion of well-being.

1. AN OVERVIEW OF NATIONAL ACCOUNTING

The idea of creating a system of national accounts goes back to the seventeenth century, when in both England and France, the first concepts for measuring national income were developed, and estimates were produced in order to create a more efficient tax system. These initial efforts were built upon for further estimates of national income in the following centuries; the number of countries for which estimates of national income and wealth were produced rose sharply from only 9 countries in 1900 to 33 countries by 1940.

---

* A closely related measure is gross national product (GNP). The difference between GNP and GDP concerns whether foreign earnings are included. GNP includes the earnings of a country's citizens and corporations regardless of where they are located in the world. GDP includes all earnings within a country's borders, even the earnings of foreign citizens and corporations. GDP is the more common measure used when comparing international statistics.

European System of National and Regional Accounts (ESA): a set of statistics compiled by the national European statistical agencies concerning production, income, spending, prices, and employment

The **European Statistical System (ESS)** is the partnership between the Community statistical authority, which is **Eurostat**, and the national statistical institutes and other national authorities responsible in each European Union member state for the development, production, and dissemination of European statistics.

Euro area: The countries of the European Union that use the euro as their currency

However, the modern idea of using national accounting to guide economic policies only really took hold from the 1930s onward. During the Great Depression of the 1930s, policy makers knew that national production was down, but other than a few numbers representing the volumes of railroad shipments and steel production, they had no information on *how much* it was down. Likewise, they had little way of knowing whether the policies that they were trying to implement were actually helping the economy to rebound. As a consequence, governments in both the U.S. and Europe started to commission regular estimates of national income. Interest in keeping national accounts increased further in the late 1930s and the 1940s because of the need for national economic mobilization during World War II.

After the war, countries started to create national statistical offices that were tasked with a regular compilation of national account statistics. Now every functioning country compiles national accounts using recommendations proposed by the United Nations. In the European Union, harmonization of national accounts went even further: European legislation tells the member states how they have to compute their national accounts. While the actual data compilation is still done by national offices, key data for the European Union as a whole, the euro area (all the European union countries which use the euro as their currency), and the single member states is regularly published by the European statistical authority called Eurostat. This harmonization is important, as the allocation of funds and decisions about measures against excessive public deficits (see Chapter 16) are taken based on this data. However, despite the harmonization, national statistics within Europe still differ in their reliability and coverage. For example, some countries publish more detailed accounts of the economy's capital stock than others (see the following).

The resulting dataset, which includes more than just a measurements of GDP, is referred to as the **European System of National and Regional Accounts (ESA).** It is compiled by the **European Statistical System**, a partnership between the central European statistical authority (Eurostat) and national statistical authorities.

1.1 Conventions About National Accounting Sectors

national accounting conventions: habits or agreements adopted by government agencies in order to make national accounts as standardized and comparable across different countries and time periods as possible

Before we focus on how GDP is measured, we first need to discuss some of the "conventions," or assumptions, used in the ESA. **National accounting conventions** are simply habits or agreements that are adopted by agencies in order to try to make the accounts as standardized and comparable across different countries and time periods as possible. Some of these conventions concern how data is categorized. For example, there are conventions concerning what is classified as investment versus consumption or a durable versus a nondurable good. Other conventions address how estimates are made for some components of the ESA for which readily available data is lacking. Of course, there are alternatives to the common conventions, but the emphasis is on standardization rather than always choosing the "best" approach.

One of the common national accounting conventions concerns how the entire economy is broken down into five national accounting sectors.* These sectors, as defined by the European Union rules, are:

1. *Household sector:* This includes both households and nonprofit institutions that serve households, such as nonprofit hospitals, universities, museums, trade unions, and charities. It also includes household firms. These cover sole proprietorships and many partnerships that do not have an independent legal status or full separate accounts.
2. *Nonfinancial corporations sector:* This sector covers all private and public corporate enterprises that produce goods or provide nonfinancial services to the market.
3. *Government sector:* The government sector includes all central, state, regional, and local governments and social security funds. It excludes all "business-like" government enterprises that sell goods or services in a market.
4. *Financial corporations sector:* This sector comprises all private and public entities engaged in financial intermediation such as banks, investment funds, insurance corporations, or pension funds.
5. *Rest of the world:* The entities in the first four sectors include, for the national accounts, only those located within the physical borders of the country concerned. The foreign sector (or "rest of the world") includes all entities—household, nonprofit, business, or government—located outside the borders. An individual in the United States who buys imported products from the European Union, for example, or a company located in India that sells goods or services to the European Union, figures into EU accounts as part of the foreign sector.

1.2 Conventions About Capital Stocks

Although natural, manufactured, human, and social capital are all crucial resources for economic activity, it is largely only *manufactured* capital that is currently included in the accounting of national nonfinancial assets. This might be because the national accounts were originally devised at a time when the rise of manufacturing made the accumulation of machinery and factory buildings appear to be the main road to prosperity. In the twenty-first century, the rise in importance of knowledge, along with concerns for ecological issues, suggests that additional accounts should be added—a topic we take up in Chapter 6.

The first category of manufactured capital in the national accounts is **fixed assets**. Fixed assets include equipment owned by businesses and governments, structures such as factories, office buildings, and dwellings (i.e., houses and apartment buildings). In 1995, in partial recognition of the increasingly important role of knowledge and technology in production, computer software was added as an additional type of fixed

fixed assets: equipment owned by businesses and governments, structures, dwellings, software, weapons systems, cultivated biological resources, and intellectual property products

---

* We call them "national accounting sectors" to differentiate them from the classification of the economy into sectors discussed in Chapter 7, where we refer to "production" sectors.

157

Table 5.1 *The Estimated Size of Euro Area Manufactured Capital Stock, 2013*

Type of capital	Value in trillions of euros at the end of the year
Machinery and equipment (total economy)	4.28
Other buildings and structures (total economy)	11.66
Cultivated assets and intangible fixed assets (total economy)	0.41
Dwellings (households, nonprofit institutions serving households)	14.29
Dwellings (government and corporations)	2.43
Total value of manufactured capital	**33.07**

Sources: ECB, Statistical Data Warehouse. May 18, 2016, and authors' calculations.

asset, and in 2015, knowledge created through research and development was added as a further type of fixed asset.

inventories: stocks of raw materials or manufactured goods held until they can be used or sold

A second—and much smaller—component of the manufactured capital stock is **inventories**. Inventories are stocks of raw materials, such as crude oil awaiting refining, or manufactured goods, such as the shoe inventory of a retail shoe store, that are held until they can be used or sold.

Equipment used by governments and businesses is included in "fixed assets." But what about equipment owned by households, such as cars and stoves, that is used in household production of goods and services? According to the ESA rules, all goods bought by households that are expected to last longer than one year are considered **consumer durable goods**. Consumer durables are not included in the account for assets but are sometimes reported as memorandum items.

consumer durable goods: consumer purchases that are expected to last longer than one year. These are generally items of equipment, such as vehicles and appliances, used by households to produce goods and services for their own use.

The European Central Bank's estimates of the euro value of the region's stock of manufactured assets at the end of 2013 are given in Table 5.1.

1.3 Conventions About Investment

The way that the national accounts measure investment spending may seem confusing if one does not keep in mind some basic facts. First, recall from Chapter 3 that economists generally use the term "investment" to mean additions to stocks of *nonfinancial* assets. This contrasts with the common use of the term "investment" to refer to financial investment, such as the purchase of stocks and bonds. Second, it is important to remember that investment represents a *flow*. A machine added to a factory in 2015, for example, is considered part of the national *stock* of nonresidential assets for every year from the time it is installed until the time it is junked. However, the machine was an *addition* to assets only in 2015, and hence its value would be counted as an *investment* only in that one year. Last, as was also discussed in Chapter 3, *gross* investment includes all measured flows into the capital stock over a period, while *net* investment adjusts this measure for the fact that some portion of the capital stock wears out, becomes obsolete, or is destroyed—that is, depreciates—over the period.

For example, suppose that an office complex built in 1980 is torn down this year and replaced by a new, larger office complex. Measured **gross investment** for this year would include the full value of the new office complex. **Net investment** for this year would be calculated as the value of the new office complex *minus* the value of the depreciated building that was torn down. If the new building has 10,000 square meters of space, while the old one had 6,000 square meters, for example, the economy has a net gain of only 4,000 square meters of office space. Net investment, which measures only the value of the *new* space and any improvements in quality, gives a better idea of the actual addition to productive capacity.

Gross investment in fixed assets is always zero or positive. However, if, over a period of time, the capital stock depreciates faster than it is being replaced, net investment can be negative. This can sometimes happen to manufactured capital stocks when a country is hit by major disasters such as wars or floods or during a period when new investment is very low, meaning that gross investment is less than **depreciation**.

Ideally, productive investments by all sectors would be recognized in the national accounts. But household investment in consumer durables is, by convention, not considered part of investment in the national accounts.

gross investment: all flows into the capital stock over a period of time

net investment: gross investment minus an adjustment for depreciation

depreciation: a decrease in the quantity or quality of a stock of capital

Discussion Questions

1. The ESA definitions of sectors use some conventions that are not obvious. To which sector might European statistical offices assign each of the following entities? Why?
   a. A local city government–owned golf course that charges fees similar to those at local private courses
   b. A large nonprofit hospital
   c. A German-owned manufacturing company whose offices and plants are in China
   d. A self-employed painter who is working under a limited liability incorporated structure
2. Under the ESA definitions, would spending on education be counted as investment? Would buying shares in a company be considered investment? Why?

2. DEFINING GROSS DOMESTIC PRODUCT

As we mentioned earlier, the most-referenced single number that comes out of the national accounts is GDP. A wide range of policy makers and media outlets await the announcement of newly published figures on GDP with great anticipation (see Box 5.1). The figures on the growth rate of GDP are often taken to signal the success or failure of macroeconomic policy making.

As we defined the term earlier, GDP is supposed to measure the total market value of final goods and services newly produced within a country's borders over a period of time (usually one year).

159

This definition contains several key phrases. Let us consider each of them.

Market value: For most components of GDP, we can simply refer to the market prices of goods and services to determine their contribution to GDP. However, in some cases (as we discuss later in the chapter), we do not have market prices for certain goods and services and thus need to estimate their value using another approach.

Final goods and services: A **final good** is one that is ready for use. That is, no further productive activity needs to occur before the good can be consumed (if it is a good that is used up as it is put to use) or put to work producing other goods and services (e.g., if it is a piece of equipment). The reason for limiting measurement to *final* goods and services is to avoid double counting. For example, suppose that over the course of a year, paper is produced by one company and sold to another company that uses it to make books. The books are then sold to their final buyers. Books in this case are the final goods, while the paper used in them is an **intermediate good**. By limiting the accounting to final goods, production is only counted once—the paper is only counted as part of the books.

Over a period of time: Since GDP measures a flow, it of course must be measured over a time period. Macroeconomists usually work with GDP measured on a yearly basis. Estimates of GDP are released more often than once a year—generally on a quarterly basis (the first quarter covering January through March, the second April through June, and so on).

Newly produced: Only new goods and services are counted. For example, if you buy a book published in 2010 at a used bookshop, the value of the book itself is not included in this year's GDP. Only the retail services provided by the used bookshop are "newly produced" and are part of this year's GDP.

Within a country's borders: This means that the goods and services are produced within the physical borders of the country. If a Polish citizen goes abroad to work, for example, what he or she produces while away is *not* part of Polish GDP. On the other hand, the work of a German citizen at a German-owned factory *is* part of Polish GDP if that factory is located inside the borders of Poland.

final good: a good that is ready for use, needing no further processing

intermediate good: a good that will undergo further processing

---

BOX 5.1 EUROZONE COMES OUT OF EURO-CRISIS RECESSION

Eurostat reported in August 2013 that the economy of the euro area had grown for the first time in almost two years in the second quarter of 2013, ending an 18-month recession the currency union had experienced after the deepening of the euro crisis. Real gross domestic product (GDP) for the spring quarter expanded by 0.3 percent compared to the previous quarter. The growth of euro-area GDP masked different economic fortunes across the currency area. While the German economy expanded by 0.7 percent and that of France by 0.5 percent, Spanish GDP declined by 0.1 percent and Dutch and Italian GDP by 0.2 percent.

At the time of publication, European Commission Vice President Olli Rehn interpreted the data as a sign that the European economy was on track for a gradual recovery yet warned about remaining obstacles to strong growth. "A number of member states still have unacceptably high unemployment rates; the implementation of essential, but difficult reforms across the EU is still in its early stages. So there is still a very long way to go," he said.

For the German chancellor Angela Merkel, who was facing a national election only weeks after the publication of the data, the strong GDP figures offered welcome support. First, according to the data, consumer and business spending in Germany were robust. Second, Merkel had been criticized strongly for her policies during the euro crisis, which critics saw as responsible for the deep slump the euro area went through between 2011 and 2013. The end of the longest recession in the euro area since the introduction of the common currency in 1999 was thus interpreted by her camp as a sign that her overall approach to the euro crisis was finally working. Even though this interpretation remained highly disputed in many parts of Europe, Merkel won a third term in a landslide in September 2013.

Sources: "Eurozone comes out of recession," BBC News, August 14, 2013, www.bbc.com/news/business-23692102 (accessed October 10, 2016); Angeline Benoit and Jeff Black, "Euro Area Exits Record Slump Led by Largest Economies," Bloomberg News, August 14, 2013.

3. MEASURING GROSS DOMESTIC PRODUCT

The national statistical offices as well as Eurostat publish tables showing the components of GDP, as well as many other tables dealing with assets, employment, prices, and other topics in the ESA. (Eurostat's Web site, with a large amount of statistics and further links to national statistical authorities, can be accessed at http://ec.europa.eu/eurostat/.) To understand these tabulations, however, you need to understand how aggregate *production, spending*, and *income* are related in an economic system.

Imagine a simple economy with no foreign sector, no depreciation, no inventories, and in which all the profits that companies earn end up in the bank accounts of households. In this case, three quite different measures of counting GDP would in theory all add up to the same number:

Value of Production = Value of Spending = Value of Income

Using a *production approach*, which might seem to be the most natural and direct method, we could sum up the euro value of all final goods and services produced in each national accounting sector—by the household and institutions sector, the business sector, and the government sector.

Using the *spending approach*, we could look at who *buys* the final goods and services that have been produced. Since we assumed that no goods are carried as inventory in this very simple economy, everything produced must be bought. Totaling the euro value of spending on all various kinds of goods and services by all sectors in this imaginary simple economy will indicate a second way of arriving at the figure for a country's aggregate production.

161

Last, because in this simple economy everyone who is involved in production also receives monetary payment for their contribution to it, we could, alternatively, take an *income approach*. In this approach, we total the compensation received by everyone involved in production, including workers, investors, creditors, and owners of land or equipment rented for productive use.

In this very simple economy, if, say, €10 billion worth of goods and services is produced, then the amount spent on goods and services must also be €10 billion, and the amount of payment received as income must also be €10 billion. Sometimes in dealing with national accounts, economists hence use the terms "production," "income," and "expenditure" interchangeably.

While there is a rough equivalence in theory among the product, spending, and income approaches to calculating GDP, making estimates for an actual economy requires a number of conventions and adjustments. We now consider each approach in more detail.

3.1 The Product Approach

The European statistical authorities measures the "value" of final goods and services primarily by their *market value* in their respective currency. For example, if the German business sector produces 1,000 automobiles of a certain type this year, which are then sold to final users for €20,000 each, this production contributes €20 million to GDP. As Germany uses the euro as its currency, production in Germany is measured in euros. In contrast, as the United Kingdom uses the British pound, production value there is measured in British pounds.

Rather than looking at the final sale, however, it is sometimes useful for accounting and analytical purposes to follow an alternative approach. This is to think about how much each industry contributes to the value of the final good or service. In the **value-added** approach to GDP accounting, you start with the raw materials—say, iron ore—used in producing a good or service—say, an automobile—and then see how much market value is added at each stage in the production process.

value added: the value of what a producer sells less the value of the intermediate inputs it uses, except labor. This is equal to the wages paid out by the producer plus its profits.

For example, suppose a steel manufacturer buys €500 worth of iron ore from a mining company and uses this ore to produce steel automobile frames, which it then sells to Volkswagen for €1,800 each. The difference between the price of the iron ore and the cost of any other materials needed to convert iron ore into automobile frames, including energy and equipment costs, represents value added. So if the steel manufacturer requires another €200 in additional materials and other costs to produce an automobile frame, then the difference between their total costs (€700) and the selling price (€1,800) is the value added at this stage in production (€1,100). This €1,100 is the amount that is left over after paying for inputs, and it becomes either wages to steel workers or profits to the steel manufacturing company. Similarly, we can determine the value added by Volkswagen as the difference between all its input costs (except labor) and the final selling price of the car. If the car sells for €20,000, Volkswagen's value added can be calculated by subtracting the price of the steel, rubber, glass, energy, and all other purchased inputs. Supposing that these added up to €12,000, Volkswagen's value added would be €8,000.

Eurostat maintains an extensive set of tables, called Input-Output Accounts, to keep track of the contributions to GDP by various industries in different member states of the European Union. These tables show that outputs of each industrial sector (e.g., agriculture, manufacturing, or services) can become inputs (intermediate goods) to production in other sectors.

Yet adding up all value-added contributions at each step in the production process still does not give us the final market price of the good. Many goods are taxed when they are produced or sold. All EU countries, for example, have a value-added tax (VAT) on many goods and services. Another example would be petrol, which is heavily taxed in all EU countries, and alcoholic drinks. Sometimes governments provide production subsidies, making it possible for producers to sell their goods for less than the actual cost of production. In all these cases, the market price of the good in question deviates from the value added. In order to square this, production taxes have to be added to and subsidies need to be subtracted from value added to get GDP. The fact that GDP should be the same no matter whether it is calculated using the value-added approach or adding up the final sales prices serves as a "check" on the validity of data that the national statistical authorities collect from different sources.

While finding the market value of goods may seem fairly straightforward for manufacturing industries, in practice, the idea of "market value" is often much harder to determine. In many cases, the statistical authorities use **imputation** to estimate the value of components of GDP. An imputation is a sort of educated guess, usually based on the value of similar outputs or on the value of inputs used in production.

imputation: a procedure in which values are assigned for a category of products, usually using values of related products or inputs

For example, the housing stock of a country produces a flow of services—the services of shelter. For housing units that are rented, the rent paid is the market value of the housing services. But how can we find out the value of the services generated by houses occupied by their owners? For these, the statisticians must impute a value. They use data from the rental housing market to impute what owner-occupiers might be said to be "paying in rent" to themselves.

In cases in which no similar marketed product exists, the statistical authorities often fall back on using a value-added approach, looking exclusively at the value of inputs. We know, for example, that governments purchase many intermediate goods and then produce goods and services. But rarely are government outputs—new highways, the services of parks, the services of public education, national defense, and so on—actually sold on markets. How, then, can the production of the government be valued?

In the actual GDP accounts, the value of government production is imputed by adding up the amount that governments pay their workers, the amount that they pay for intermediate goods and services, and an allowance for depreciation of fixed assets. Likewise, the production of nonprofit institutions is measured in large part by looking at their inputs. For example, data on payroll expenses form an important part of the information used in estimating the value of the services produced by nonprofit agencies.

Imputations are also used when data is difficult or impossible to obtain. Although it might be tempting to imagine the statistical authorities as all-knowing agencies that can directly observe all market transactions, gathering data is a laborious (and often expensive) process. The statistical authorities rely on a variety of censuses and surveys to obtain information, as well as on data such as government budgets and tax records. Market transactions that people take pains *not* to have observed by the government—such as illegal drug deals or work performed "off the books" to avoid taxes—hence are usually not very accurately represented in the national statistics and actually have for a long time not been represented at all (see Box 5.2). The statistical authorities update all their estimates periodically as they receive better data or improve their statistical techniques—hence you may see many slightly varying numbers quoted for, say "Spanish GDP, 2013" depending on when the data were published.

In one significant case, however, the designers of the national accounts decided not even to attempt to impute a value for production: the production of goods and services within households for their own use. The official measure of production by households does include the value of services produced by the *house itself* (i.e., the rent or imputed rent), along with production within the households to the extent that work is paid (i.e., done by hired housekeepers, babysitters, or private gardeners). But activities such as unpaid child care, cooking, or the cleaning or landscaping of a home done without pay by household members—traditionally, mostly by women—are not counted in GDP. This creates an anomaly in the accounts. For many years, textbooks noted that "if a man marries his housekeeper, GDP falls." That is, marriage would convert the woman's housekeeping work from being paid and counted to being unpaid and uncounted.

We can summarize the product approach to measuring GDP using the equation:

$$GDP = Business\ production + Household\ and\ institutions\ production$$
$$+ Government\ production + Taxes\ less\ subsidies\ on\ products$$

identity (accounting identity): an equation in which the two sides are equal by definition

This sort of equation is called an **identity** or an **accounting identity**. It holds simply because of the way in which the various terms have been defined. Once we agree on the definitions of terms, then there remains nothing controversial about an identity. (When we begin to deal with macroeconomic modeling in Chapter 9, we introduce another kind of equation, called a behavioral equation. A behavioral equation represents an economist's supposition about how an economic actor behaves—and because it may or may not hold well in practice, it can be more controversial.

Note that the rest of the world sector does not contribute to the production of GDP in this equation. Can you explain why? (Hint: Look back at the definition of GDP.)

Table 5.2 presents Eurostat's estimate in 2015 for the euro area GDP using the product approach, divided into national accounting sectors. Not surprisingly, given the conventions and accounting procedures, Eurostat attributes a very large share of productive activity to the business sector. In 2015, the business sector was estimated to have produced goods and services worth about €7 trillion, or about 77 percent of

Table 5.2 *Gross Domestic Product, Euro Area, Product Approach, 2015*

Sector and subsector	Production by sector (trillions of euros)
Households and nonprofit institutions production	0.33
Business production	7.17
Government production	1.82
Total: Gross value added	**9.33**
Taxes less subsidies on products	1.07
Total: Gross domestic product	**10.40**

Source: Eurostat, National Accounts Database. May 17, 2016.

Note: Totals may not add up exactly due to rounding.

Table 5.3 *Gross Domestic Product, Euro Area, Spending Approach, 2015*

Type of spending	Spending by category (trillions of euros)	Spending by sub-category (trillions of euros)
Household and NPISH final consumption expenditure	5.74	
Final consumption expenditure of general government	2.17	
Gross capital formation	2.03	
Gross fixed capital formation		2.05
Changes in inventories and acquisitions less disposals of valuables		−0.02
External balance of goods and services	0.46	
Exports of goods and services		4.75
Less: Imports of goods and services		4.29
Gross domestic product	**10.40**	

Source: Eurostat, National Accounts Database. May 18, 2016.

Note: Totals may not add up exactly due to rounding.

total value added of €9.33 trillion. The government sector was estimated to have contributed about 20 percent and the household sector a little more than 3 percent. Net taxes on products (taxes minus subsidies) amounted to €1.07, about 10 percent of GDP.

3.2   The Spending Approach

The spending approach adds up the value of newly produced goods and services bought by the household and institution, business, foreign, and government sectors. The estimated values for these expenditures for 2015 are listed in Table 5.3.

Purchases of goods and services by households and "nonprofit institutions serving households" ("NPISH"—these include churches and religious associations, trade unions, and political parties) are called "final consumption expenditures of households and NPISH" by Eurostat. By convention, they are all considered "final" goods and services (even though, as discussed earlier, many of these are used in household and nonprofit production processes).

Spending on fixed assets including structures, equipment, software, weapons systems, cultivated biological resources, and intellectual property products is reported under the term "gross fixed capital formation." Here, it is not differentiated between government and corporate fixed capital formation. For the household sector, only dwellings but not durable consumer goods are included in the category of fixed assets.

In a separate line, "changes in inventories and acquisition less disposals of valuables" are recorded. This includes the change in the stock of produced goods held by the business sector, as well as changes in the stock of valuables such as jewels or precious metals (not used in the production process).

Sometimes it is not easy to say what is an intermediate good and what is a final good. Recently, European statistical authorities changed the definitions to include business spending on intellectual property, as well as research and development, as investments (final goods) rather than intermediate goods. Together with other changes, this amendment raised the value of GDP by more than €300 billion—not reflecting any actual increase in production, just a change in the way production is defined (see Box 5.2).

BOX 5.2 SEX, DRUGS, AND GDP

In October 2014, euro-area GDP increased by more than €300 billion—overnight. No change took place in actual production. What happened was that Eurostat amended the rules on how business spending and illicit activities such as drug sales and prostitution should be counted in measuring GDP.

The biggest change came through a reclassification of research and development (R&D) purchases, as well as military weapon systems, from intermediate consumption (which is not counted in GDP) to investments (which is counted). In some EU countries with high R&D expenditure, such as Finland and Sweden, this change alone increased measured GDP by 4 percent.

Another change that got a lot of attention was the inclusion of illegal market activities such as prostitution or the production and sale of drugs such as cannabis, ecstasy, LSD, or heroin into the GDP calculation. According to the EU rules, as long as illegal dealings "are transactions . . .when all units involved enter the actions voluntarily," they were now counted as GDP. "Thus, purchases, sales or barters of illegal drugs or stolen property are transactions, while theft is not," the EU explains. The impact of this second change differed significantly between countries. For Italy, this new accounting rule increased GDP by 1 percent, for Britain by 0.6 percent, and for Denmark by a mere 0.2 percent.

While these changes lifted the level of GDP in both the EU and the euro area by about 3.5 percent, it was not a boost for economic growth: Eurostat revised the GDP data back from 2000 onward, so that the trend remained broadly unchanged. Reported economic growth in 2014 therefore was weak despite the revision. However, for one important indicator, this change made a difference: that is, the debt-to-GDP ratio. As GDP is now higher but the stock of debt has not changed, the national debt looks a little smaller relative to current GDP.

Sources: Silvia Merler and Pia Hüttl, "Welcome to the dark side: GDP revision and the non-observed economy," Bruegel Blog, March 2, 2015; *Financial Times*: "Sex, drugs and GDP—what's going on?" May 29, 2014.

The simple economy that we discussed when noting how, in concept, "production = spending = income" was a **closed economy**, with no foreign sector. Although sometimes countries isolate themselves from world trade (China during the 1960s being a prime example), for the most part, global economic relations have become increasingly important as advances in transportation and communication have accelerated. Because the euro area is an **open economy**, we need to take into account interactions with the foreign sector.

closed economy: an economy with no foreign sector; i.e., it neither purchases goods or services from outside its borders, nor does it sell goods or services abroad

Some of the goods and services produced inside the euro area are bought by entities in the rest of the world. If we look at single euro-area countries, sometimes the larger part of all goods and services produced inside the country is bought by entities in the rest of the world. For example, in the Netherlands in 2014, more than 80 percent of goods and services produced within the country were actually exported. The value of these exported goods must be added to the value of domestic spending in calculating GDP. In addition, some of the spending by euro-area residents is for goods and services produced abroad. Such spending is, in fact, already included in the calculation of spending by the various other sectors in Table 5.3. So the value of imported goods and services must be *subtracted* to arrive at a measure of *domestic* production.

open economy: an economy with a foreign sector

Net exports measures the overall impact of international trade on GDP. It is the difference between exports and imports:

net exports: the value of exports less the value of imports

Net exports = Exports − Imports

Net exports may be either positive (if we sell more abroad than we buy) or negative (if we buy more than we sell). In 2015, for example, we can see in Table 5.3 that the euro area exported goods and services worth €0.46 trillion (or €460 billion) more than the value of the goods and services imported. (In the table, the fact that the value of imports is subtracted rather than added is denoted by putting the number in italics.) Hence, that year, euro area net exports were positive. Note that the euro area's export and import data does not include trade within the euro area. If a French household buys a German car, this is counted as France's import and Germany's export, but at the level of the euro area, it is only counted as consumption.

Last, we come to the expenditures made by the government sector. European statistical authorities report "government final consumption expenditures," which includes spending from all levels of the government sector, including the European, national, regional, and local levels as well as social security systems, but not from publicly owned corporations selling goods and services in the market (see earlier). Public investment is not recorded here but as discussed under the category of "fixed capital formation."

Note that another item which is important in most European public budgets is missing from the GDP calculation: government transfers. Transfers are payments made by the government for which no asset, good, or service is rendered in return. Examples are welfare payments or child benefits. These are not included in the GDP calculations, as they do not correspond to newly produced goods or services.

Based on the spending by different sectors, we can summarize the spending approach with the identity:

$$GDP = \textit{Household and institution spending} + \textit{Business spending} + \textit{Net foreign}$$
$$\textit{sector spending} + \textit{Government spending}$$

Or, if we want to highlight the portions that are (by convention) considered consumption versus those considered investment, we can summarize this approach with the identity:

$$GDP = \textit{Personal consumption} + \textit{Private investment} + \textit{Government consumption}$$
$$+ \textit{Government investment} + \textit{Net exports}$$

3.3 The Income Approach

The production-related incomes (such as from wages, rents, and profits) earned by all people and organizations located inside the euro area can be summed up in a measure called **national income (NI)**.

If this were a simple economy with no foreign sector and no depreciation, the sum of the incomes from production (NI) would exactly equal GDP. But in our more complex economy, three adjustments are needed to reconcile figures on domestic income and domestic production.

First, we need to note that some domestic incomes reflect *foreign* production. For example, as mentioned, the profits of a French company may include earnings from overseas plants. Such incomes must be subtracted from NI in order to reconcile this measure with the figure for gross *domestic product*. Conversely, the income from some domestic production is received by foreign residents and so is not counted in NI. A Japanese-owned factory in France may send its profits back to its Tokyo headquarters, for example. The value of these incomes must be added to NI in order to approximate GDP.

In 2015, for the euro area, income receipts from the rest of the world exceeded income paid out to foreign residents by about €70 billion. These "net income receipts

national income (NI): a measure of all domestic incomes earned in production

Table 5.4 *Gross Domestic Product, Euro Area, Income Approach, 2015*

Types of income and adjustments	Income and adjustments (trillions of euros)
National income	8.62
Less: Net income receipts from the rest of the world	*0.07*
Plus: Depreciation *(consumption of fixed capital)*	1.84
Total: Gross domestic product	10.40

Sources: Eurostat, National Accounts Database. May 18, 2016, and authors' calculations.

Note: Totals may not add up exactly due to rounding.

from the rest of the world" are shown in Table 5.4. When net income receipts from the rest of the world are added to GDP, the result is a measure called gross national product (GNP). For many years, GNP was used as the primary measure of production in many EU countries. It measures a country's production in terms of the output produced *by its workers and companies*, no matter where in the world they were located. Based on international recommendations, most countries have by now switched their emphasis from GNP to GDP, believing that it is more important, for the purposes for which the accounts are used, to track economic activity *within the borders* of the countries concerned (even though in some cases, GDP might do a very poor job on this account—see Box 5.3).

Second, we need to account for the fact that not all of GDP creates income, since some domestic production simply goes into replacing structures, equipment, and software that have worn out or become obsolete. So we must *add* depreciation (what the statisticians call "consumption of fixed capital") to NI to get a number closer to GDP. This is a bit confusing—but it is in effect the reverse of what we did earlier, when we subtracted depreciation from gross investment to get net investment. (In calculating incomes, depreciation is typically deducted from profits.)

The third adjustment in Table 5.4 is indicated in the often-seen note, "Totals may not add up exactly due to rounding." This is referred to as the "statistical discrepancy." It reflects the fact that, no matter how diligently the statistical authorities compile the accounts, they cannot exactly reconcile the results from the income approach with the results from the product and spending approaches.

We can summarize the meaningful parts of the income approach by the identity:

GDP = National income – Net income payments from the foreign sector + Depreciation

Discussion Questions

1. The previous section explained why a country's "production" and "income" can be thought of as roughly equal in a conceptual sense. Why, in practice, does the value of domestic production actually differ from the total of domestic incomes?

2. Sometimes GDP is defined as "The total *market* value of all final goods and services newly produced in a country over time." Given the discussion, how true is this definition, really? Does GDP really count only goods and services exchanged *in markets?* Does it really account for *all* production?

BOX 5.3 WHY 26 PERCENT GDP GROWTH CAN BE A PROBLEM

In July 2016, the Irish Central Statistics Office reported that it had previously underestimated the growth of the Irish economy for 2015. According to the newly published figures, Irish GDP had increased by a whopping 26.3 percent in 2015 compared to 2014. While there was no doubt among economists that the Irish economy had been experiencing a decent recovery, the new data drew immediate criticism. The *Wall Street Journal* commented that the data should not be taken at face value. The opposition party Sinn Fein's David Cullinane said the figures showed there is "no credibility to the national account figures."

According to the Central Statistics Office (CSO), the jump was mainly caused by the reclassification of activities by foreign companies. As Ireland has a very business-friendly tax regime, some corporations had in the past years moved their legal residence to Ireland. Especially among U.S. companies, a strategy called "inversion" had been very popular. Here, a U.S. corporation buys a smaller Irish rival and then moves the legal ownership of all assets to Ireland. While the companies' core operations after such a move usually remain in the original jurisdiction, they can claim a new tax home in Ireland. As a consequence, profits of these corporations are henceforth recorded in Irish GDP. The same holds true for holding companies. Another way to reduce taxes by multinationals has been to transfer part of their intellectual property to a subsidiary in Ireland, which then charges fees for the use of this property to subsidiaries in other countries. Again, as such schemes increase profits of companies legally residing in Ireland, they increase Irish GDP.

Cases such as the revision of the Irish GDP data underline limits of using national accounts to properly represent economic activity in small open economies in a globalized world. "The reality is that the average household didn't wake up phenomenally richer this morning. Public and private debt still remain where they are," KBC Bank's chief economist Austin Hughes said. "The (new) GDP numbers are just not meaningful if the aim of the game is to truly understand what is happening in the economy," said Ulster Bank chief economist Simon Barry.

Sources: Gareth Jones, "Irish 2015 GDP growth raised to 26 percent on asset reclassification," Reuters, July 12, 2016; Eric Chemi and Nicholas Wells, "Ireland's 26 percent GDP growth just doesn't add up," CNBC Online, July 14, 2016.

---

4. GROWTH, PRICE CHANGES, AND REAL GDP

Economic growth (traditionally defined as increasing GDP) is a statistic that is closely followed by policy makers and the media. Inflation, or the growth rate of prices, is another of the macroeconomic statistics that is considered most significant. We now consider the measurement of these two factors and how they relate to each other.

4.1 Calculating GDP Growth Rates

So far, we have concentrated on calculating GDP in only one year. To calculate rates of economic growth, economists must look at how GDP changes over time. The percentage change in GDP from year to year can be calculated using the standard percentage-change formula. The standard formula, for something that takes one value in year 1 (*Value$_1$*) and another in year 2 (*Value$_2$*), is:

$$percentage\ change = \frac{Value_2 - Value_1}{Value_1} \times 100$$

So to compute the growth rate of GDP from, say, 2014 to 2015, we calculate:

$$growth\ rate\ of\ GDP = \frac{GDP_{2015} - GDP_{2014}}{GDP_{2014}} \times 100$$

For example, euro-area GDP in 2015 was estimated at €10.4 trillion, while in 2014 it was estimated at €10.1 trillion. Fitting these into the equation, we have

$$
\begin{aligned}
growth\ rate\ of\ GDP &= \frac{10.4 - 10.1}{10.1} \times 100 \\
&= .03 \times 100 \\
&= 3.0
\end{aligned}
$$

indicating that GDP grew 3.0 percent between 2014 and 2015.

4.2 Nominal Versus Real GDP

Does the number we just calculated mean that the level of aggregate production in 2015 was 3.0 percent larger than production in 2014? Not necessarily. The measure of GDP used in the previous section is **nominal or current–euro GDP**, or GDP expressed in terms of the prices of goods and services that were current at the time. The 2015 figure for GDP that we used, for example, is based on prices as they were in 2015, and the 2014 figure is based on prices that prevailed in 2014.

Not only does output change from year to year, but generally the *prices at which output is valued* change as well. If prices rose between 2014 and 2015, part of the measured GDP growth would be an increase in prices rather than in actual production. **Real GDP** is a measure that seeks to reflect the actual value of goods and services produced by removing the effect of changes in prices.

For example, suppose a very simple economy produces only two goods, apples and oranges, as shown in Table 5.5. Column (2) shows the price of each good in each

nominal (current euro) GDP: gross domestic product expressed in terms of current prices

real GDP: a measure of gross domestic product that seeks to reflect the actual value of goods and services produced by removing the effect of changes in prices

Table 5.5 *Calculation of Nominal GDP in an "Apples-and-Oranges" Economy*

(1) Description	(2) Price per kilogram (€)	(3) Quantity (kilograms)	(4) Contribution to nominal GDP [Column (2) × Column (3)] (€)
Year 1			
Apples	€1.00	100	€100
Oranges	€2.00	50	€100
			€200
Year 2			
Apples	€1.50	100	€150
Oranges	€2.00	75	€150
			€300

year, while Column (3) gives the physical production, measured in pounds. Nominal GDP is just the sum of the euro values of the goods produced in a year, evaluated at the prices in that same year:

Nominal GDP = Total production valued at current prices

As we can see in Table 5.5, in Year 1, the value of nominal GDP is €200. In Year 2, the value of nominal GDP is €300. The percentage growth of GDP from Year 1 to Year 2 can be calculated as 50 percent, applying the percentage-change formula from the previous section.

But if you look carefully, you can see that only part of the change in nominal GDP is due to an increase in production: The quantity of oranges produced rises from 50 kilograms to 75 kilograms from Year 1 to Year 2. The rest of the GDP increase is due to an increase in the price of apples, from €1.00 to €1.50. Note that the quantity of apples produced has not changed.

base year (in the constant-price method of estimating GDP): the year whose prices are chosen for evaluating production in all years. Normally real and nominal GDP are equal only in the base year.

4.3 Calculating Real GDP

Until the 1990s, most statistical authorities calculated real GDP using the "constant-price method." Because the constant-price method is relatively easy to understand and contains most of the information that you need to have as a beginning economics student, we cover it in some detail.

The constant-price method uses prices from one particular year, called the **base year**, to evaluate the value of production in all years.

Constant-price real GDP is calculated by doing the same sort of multiplying and summing exercise as shown in Table 5.5 but using the *same* prices for all years:

Constant-Price Real GDP = Total production valued at base year prices

Applying the constant-price method to our simple "apples-and-oranges" example, for instance, we might take Year 1 as the base year and express GDP in both Year 1 and Year 2 in terms of Year 1's prices. Calculations of constant-price real GDP for each year are shown in Table 5.6. While the quantities in Column (3) are the same as in Table 5.5, the prices in Column (2) are *all from Year 1*. GDP in Year 2 expressed in "constant (Year 1) euros" is the sum of quantities in Year 2 multiplied by prices in Year 1. This comes out to be €250. In the base year, real and nominal GDP are the same.

Using the percentage growth rate formula from the previous section, we can see that constant-euro *real* GDP has grown by 25 percent. Note that this is less than the 50 percent growth figure for nominal GDP. Some of the growth in nominal GDP is due to price changes not production changes.

The convention of using "constant euros," however, has a number of problems. One of the most bothersome is that it makes measured GDP growth calculations depend on which year is chosen as base. For example, what if we chose Year 2 as the base instead of Year 1? Applying Year 2 prices to both years would yield a measured growth rate of 20 percent instead of the 25 percent that we calculated using Year 1 as the base. (You can check this as an exercise.) The method also suffers from various biases, which become more important the more dissimilar relative prices and spending patterns are between the base year and a current year.

Table 5.6 *Calculation of Constant-Euro Real GDP*

(1)	(2)	(3)	(4)
Description	Price per kilogram in base year (€)	Quantity (kilograms)	Contribution to real GDP [Column (2) × Column (3)] (€)
Year 1(Base)			
Apples	€1.00	100	€100
Oranges	€2.00	50	€100
			€200
Year 2			
Apples	**€1.00**	100	€100
Oranges	**€2.00**	75	€150
			€250

*Bold type indicates base year *prices*

Since the second half of the 1990s, statistical agencies in Europe and other industrialized countries have started to calculate real GDP using the "chain-linked price" method. The concept behind the new measure is still the same—real GDP still is an attempt to measure output changes free of the influence of changing prices. Although there is still one year for which real and nominal GDP are equal, it is now called the "reference year," and real GDP is currently expressed in publications of European statistical authorities concerning the euro area in terms of "chained (2010) euros." An advantage of the chain-linked price method is that, unlike the constant-price method, it yields a unique growth rate. But the chain-linked price method requires a steep jump in computational complexity. Because these calculations are much harder than for the constant-price method, their explanation is in the Appendix to this chapter.

In Figure 5.1, you can see how measures of real and nominal GDP diverge. Because prices were generally rising over the period 1995–2015, nominal GDP grew faster than real GDP, as shown by the more steeply rising line. The difference between the rate of growth of nominal GDP and the rate of growth of real GDP is the inflation rate (discussed in the next section). Note that the reference year in Figure 5.1 is 2010; thus real and nominal GDP are the same in that year.

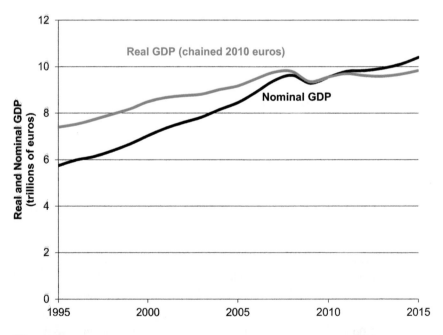

Figure 5.1 *Real Versus Nominal GDP, Euro Area, Chained 2010 Euros, 1995–2015*

Nominal GDP grows faster than real GDP when prices are rising.

Source: Eurostat.

4.4 Price Indexes and Inflation Rates

Price indexes are interesting both for how they relate to calculation of real GDP and on their own because of their relevance to the policy interest in measuring (and controlling) inflation. An **index number** measures the change in magnitude, in this case the price level, compared to another period. Generally, the value of the index number in the reference or base year is set at 100, though sometimes other values (such as 1 or 10) are used.

The price index most often reported in the news is the **consumer price index (CPI),** calculated by national statistical authorities for national price developments and by Eurostat for the euro area as a whole. The CPI measures changes in the prices of goods and services bought by households. While, traditionally, there were differences in the computational details of the CPI between EU countries, the **Harmonized Index of Consumer Prices (HICP)** uses a harmonized methodology and is used for purposes of European policy making such as the European Central Bank's setting of the interest rate (see Chapter 12).

Calculating price increases is not quite so straightforward as it might seem at first sight. For example, in Table 5.5, the price of apples increased from €1.00 per kilogram to €1.50 per kilogram. Using the standard percentage-change formula, we would say that the price of apples increased by 50 percent. However, we also see in Table 5.5 that the price of oranges did not change. So how do we calculate the overall price change in our two-good economy?

We would not simply average the two price changes to arrive at an overall price increase of 25 percent. Instead, we must realize that changes in some prices are more significant to consumers because they either purchase more of certain products (such as liters of milk) or because they spend a large portion of their incomes on something (such as rent).

Thus the CPI is calculated using a *weighted average* of the prices of the various goods and services that it tracks. The mathematics of this is worth a little explaining. A "weighted average" is an average in which the different numbers being averaged together are "weighted" to indicate their relative importance in the calculation. You are probably already familiar with this, in the calculation of your own grade point average. Each grade that you receive for a course is "weighted" by the number of credits (or hours) the course is worth. These weighted grade points are added up and then divided by the total number of credits or hours to yield your GPA. An A received for a two-credit course thus receives less emphasis in the calculation than an A received for a four-credit course.

Similarly, in measuring price levels in the economy, we want to give greater emphasis to prices for goods and services that affect consumers the most and less emphasis to the prices of relatively minor goods and services. The way to do this is to weight each price by the corresponding quantity that is sold at that price.

Once again, however, we face choices about which standards to use. Should we use as weights the quantities bought in Year 1, Year 2, or some combination? According to Eurostat standards, a *constant-weight method* should be used to calculate the CPI.

index number: a figure that measures the change in magnitude of a variable, such as a quantity or price, compared to another period

consumer price index (CPI): an index measuring changes in the prices of goods and services bought by households

175

Quantities bought during one period are chosen as the "base." These quantities are said to represent a typical "market basket" of goods bought by households. A constant-weight price index is calculated according to the following formula:

Constant Weight Price Index =

$$\frac{sum\ of\ current\ prices\ weighted\ by\ base\ quantities}{sum\ of\ base\ prices\ weighted\ by\ base\ quantities} \times 100$$

The price-index problem is analogous to the calculation of "constant-euro" GDP—only now it is a common set of *quantity weights* rather than prices from the base period that are applied to every calculation.

Consider, again, our "apples-and-oranges" economy. Table 5.7 shows how we would calculate the numerator and denominator for the constant-weight price index formula, considering Year 2 the current year and using the Year 1 "market basket" as the base. The sum of current (Year 2) prices weighted by base quantities is €250, while the sum of base prices weighted by base quantities is €200. The CPI for Year 2 is therefore calculated as (250 ÷ 200) × 100 = 125. The price index for the base year (here, Year 1) always equals 100.

The growth rate of prices—that is, the inflation rate affecting consumers—is measured by the growth rate of this price index:

$$Inflation\ rate = \frac{CPI_2 - CPI_1}{CPI_1} \times 100$$

Table 5.7 *Calculation of a Constant-Weight Price Index*

(1)	(2)	(3)	(4)
Description	Price per kilogram (€)	Quantity in base year	Sum of (prices × base quantities) [Column (2) × Column (3)] (€)
Year 1(Base)			
Apples	€1.00	100	€100
Oranges	€2.00	50	€100
			€200
Year 2			
Apples	€1.50	**100**	€150
Oranges	€2.00	**50**	€100
			€250

*Bold type indicates base year *quantities.*

So, in this case, with the price index rising from 100 to 125, the inflation rate is 25 percent.

Unfortunately, when a price index is based on constant weights, it may tend to overstate inflation for periods after the base year. When the price of a good is rising particularly quickly relative to other goods, people tend to look for cheaper substitutes. But a constant-weight index assumes that people are still buying the same quantities of the expensive goods. Various innovations have recently been made in the CPI to attempt to get around this problem. Currently, the "market basket" is updated periodically using data from ongoing household expenditure surveys (see Box 5.4 for an example from the U.S.). Some European countries have started to publish "chain-linked" price indexes and even calculate the Harmonized Index of Consumer Prices (HICP) index for their country on this basis. The mathematics of these more advanced calculations will not be presented here.

The CPI is not the only price index in use. The producer price index (PPI) measures prices that domestic producers receive for their output and so tracks many intermediate goods not included in the CPI market basket. Import and export price indexes track prices of goods traded between domestic residents and the foreign sector. Because they track different goods, these indexes—and inflation rates calculated from them—may vary.

BOX 5.4 HOW QUANTITY WEIGHTS CAN LOSE VALIDITY OVER TIME

Why do economists and statisticians make a fuss about updating the quantity weights used in calculating the consumer price index? Consider how household expenditure patterns have changed over time.

In 1901, nearly half the budget of a typical urban, working family went toward food, while 15 percent went toward shelter, and an equal proportion toward clothing. The family probably spent nothing at all on cars or gasoline—because automobiles were not yet in wide use!

By 1950, the picture had changed considerably. Now only a third of the family's spending was on food, while only 11 percent was on shelter and 12 percent on clothing. On average, families were now spending about 12 percent of their budget on expenses related to private vehicles.

In recent data on consumer expenditures, the share devoted to food has dropped even further—to 13 percent (possibly the lowest the world has ever seen). Expenditures on clothing have dropped to less than 5 percent of a household's budget, on average. Meanwhile, families are spending more on shelter (20 to 30 percent of their budget) and private vehicle expenses (16 percent of their budget) than they were in the mid-twentieth century.

Using expenditure patterns from one of these periods to "weight" the CPI in another would clearly result in biased figures. Using the 1901 expenditure pattern nowadays, for example, would mean that auto and gasoline prices would not figure into the CPI at all.

> The invention of new goods and services (e.g., MP3 players) and quality improvements in existing goods (e.g., in products for home entertainment and computing) continue to create special challenges for the economists working to measure price changes.
>
> Sources: Eva Jacobs and Stephanie Shipp, "How Family Spending Has Changed in the U.S.," *Monthly Labor Review* (March 1990), pp. 20–27; U.S. Bureau of Labor Statistics, *Consumer Expenditure Survey 2011*, data tables; and authors' calculations.

4.5 Growth and Growth Rates

We have calculated year-to-year growth rates for GDP and prices. But suppose that we want to ask how much GDP has grown over the past 5 years or 20 years? How do we calculate those numbers? The answer is rather complicated, but fortunately you can use the national account tables published by Eurostat or the national statistical authorities to answer such questions.

rule of 72: a shorthand calculation that states that dividing 72 by an annual growth rate yields approximately the number of years it will take for an amount to double

An even simpler (though less precise) way to get a grasp on the relation of annual growth rates to changes over a longer period is by using **the rule of 72**. Taking $72/x$, where x equals the annual growth rate, will give you approximately the number of years it will take for an amount to double if it grows at that constant rate (as long as the numbers you are using are not extremely high or low). For example, if real GDP grew at a constant 4 percent rate per year, it would double in about 18 years (since $72/4 = 18$).

Discussion Questions

1. The "constant-price" method of estimating real GDP uses prices for one year to calculate measures of GDP for all years. Why is it sometimes important to evaluate GDP in the current year using prices from some other year? Why can't we just always use current prices? Explain.
2. How is the "constant-price" method of estimating real GDP similar to the use of "constant weights" in the computation of the price indexes? Explain.

5. SAVINGS, INVESTMENT, AND TRADE

At a personal level, you produce goods and services, earn income, consume, save, and borrow or lend. One of the reasons you keep personal accounts might be to try to track your inflows and outflows so that you know whether you are depleting your personal assets or accumulating them. If you can save money out of your current income, you are improving your financial position for the future. However, if you spend down your savings or go into debt merely to finance a high level of consumption, you may find yourself in trouble later on. Spending down financial savings or going into debt can be a good choice for your future only if you use the funds to gain another valuable asset. Students often go into debt in order to finance their education, for example, with the idea that it will pay off later by enabling them to earn a higher income than they would have been able to otherwise.

There are analogous issues at the national level. Besides keeping track of economic growth and inflation, systems of national accounting serve another important purpose. They allow us to look at the savings-and-assets situation of a national economy as a whole (at least as far as *marketed* assets and financial flows are concerned).

5.1 The Relationship of Savings, Investment, and Trade

The category at the national level that is analogous to your personal day-to-day consumption spending is the consumption spending done by the "household and institutions" and "government" sectors. This is spending on goods and services that are presumably "used up" right now—they are not expected to help the country over the long term. The analogous category to your income is—at least roughly—GDP.

Recall that the spending approach to GDP says that

$$GDP = Personal\ consumption + Private\ investment + Net\ exports + Government$$
$$consumption\ +\ Government\ investment$$

Rearranging, we obtain

$$GDP - Personal\ consumption - Government\ consumption\ =\ Private\ investment$$
$$+\ Government\ investment\ +\ Net\ exports$$

Because saving is what is left over from income after spending on consumption (the left-hand side of the equation above), we can combine private and government investment on the right-hand side to get:

$$Saving\ =\ Investment\ +\ Net\ exports$$

Thinking about these quantities in terms of valuable goods and services, this important identity says, intuitively, that goods and services that are produced in our domestic economy in excess of what we currently use for consumption can be investment goods—additions to our stock of manufactured assets (including replacement of depreciated assets)—or can be sold to foreign countries (in excess of the value of what we import from them).

5.2 Net Domestic Product and Saving

The investment concept used in defining *gross* domestic product (GDP) is *gross* investment. To calculate what the level of production is during a year, above and beyond the production that simply replaces worn-out manufactured capital, we need another

net domestic product (NDP): a measure of national production in excess of that needed to replace worn-out manufactured capital, calculated by subtracting depreciation from GDP

concept, **net domestic product (NDP)**. NDP is GDP less depreciation (just as net investment, we saw earlier, is gross investment less depreciation):

Net domestic product = GDP − Depreciation

Similarly, we can differentiate between gross saving and net saving. To really find out the extent to which we have "put something aside for the future," we would subtract depreciation from our gross measure of saving. For example, even if our savings were positive, if they did not finance enough investment to make up for the deterioration of capital stock, we would actually start the next year in a *worse* position. Net saving is thus gross saving minus depreciation.

Net saving = (Gross) Saving − Depreciation

Net saving is a better measure than gross saving of whether we are "putting something aside for the future."

How much has the euro been "putting something aside for the future" lately? According to Eurostat data, gross savings in the euro area were €2.40 trillion in 2015, almost a quarter of euro-area GDP. But since fixed capital depreciation in 2015 was €1.84 trillion, net savings were much smaller at only €555 billion. Note that these "net savings" are usually not in the form of bank deposits or other financial assets. Most financial assets in the euro area are actually a claim against another euro-area resident and hence do not belong to net savings. If you have a bank deposit with BNP Parisbas, at the same time this bank has a liability toward you, and the saving cancels out in terms of net savings for the whole economy. Instead, "net savings" in the context of the national accounts either take the form of fixed capital or a claim against a resident outside the country or currency area under consideration.

DISCUSSION QUESTIONS

1. Suppose that the country of Atlantis is investing and exporting a great deal, while it imports little. What can you say about its level of national saving? Suppose the country of Olympus invests more than it saves. How can it do this?
2. Do you think the savings rate of the euro area is appropriate? What might be done to raise this rate by individuals, corporations, or government?

REVIEW QUESTIONS

1. For what purpose was national accounting in England and France originally begun?
2. Who compiles the European System of National and Regional Accounts?

3. What are the five accounting sectors of the economy, according to European standards? What sorts of entities are included in each sector?

4. What forms of capital assets are tracked by the European statistical authorities?

5. Explain the difference between gross and net investment.

6. Explain four key phrases that appear in the definition of GDP.

7. What are the three approaches to GDP measurement?

8. Explain why, in a simple economy, the three approaches would yield the same figure for the value of total production.

9. Explain why the following two approaches arrive at the same number for the value of a final good: (a) looking at the market price of the good and (b) counting up the value added at each stage of its production.

10. How are "market values" determined for goods and services that are not exchanged in markets or when data is not available?

11. Describe the components of GDP according to the product approach.

12. Describe the components of GDP according to the spending approach.

13. What are the major differences between GDP and national income?

14. Describe the reasoning behind the "constant-price" approach to calculating real GDP.

15. What are some problems with the "constant-price" approach to calculating real GDP?

16. Describe the reasoning behind the "constant-weight" method traditionally used in estimating the price indexes.

17. Is there only one kind of price index? Explain.

18. Explain how savings, investment, and trade are related in the national accounts.

19. Explain how a country can finance an excess of imports over exports.

EXERCISES

1. In which line (or lines) of Table 5.2 (the product approach) would the value of each of the following be counted? "Not counted in any category" is also an option.
   a. Production of fresh apples, domestically grown for profitable sale
   b. Public health inspection services
   c. Education services provided by a private, nonprofit domestic high school
   d. Child-care services provided by a child's parents and relatives
   e. Production by a French-owned company at its factory in Singapore

2. In which line (or lines) of Table 5.4 (the income approach) would the value of each of the following be counted in the macroeconomic accounts of the euro area? If it is part of "net income flows from the rest of the world," explain whether it reflects domestic (or foreign) production and whether it reflects domestic (or foreign) income. "Not counted in any category" is also an option.
   a. Wages paid by your local supermarket to its employees
   b. Profits received by a German car manufacturer from its factory in China
   c. Business spending to replace worn-out equipment
   d. Wages paid by a German car manufacturer to the employees of its factory in China
   e. Profits received by a Japanese automaker from its factory in Belgium

181

3. In which line (or lines) of Table 5.3 (the spending approach) would the value of each of the following be counted? "Not counted in any category" is also an option.
   a.   A new refrigerator bought by a family
   b.   A bottle of wine produced in France and bought by a store in New York
   c.   New computers, manufactured in Asia, bought by a Dutch accounting company
   d.   Meals produced and served in Italy to military personnel
   e.   New computers, produced in Ireland, bought by an Irish computer retail chain and not yet sold by the end of the year
   f.   A three-year-old couch bought by a used furniture store in Vienna, Austria
   g.   Cleaning services bought by a child-care facility in Berlin run by the local government (parents pay a fee at that child-care facility)
   h.   The services of volunteers in an environmental action campaign

4. Using the relations among accounting categories demonstrated in the tables and identities in the text, use the information on values in the chart that follows (measured in Neverlandian pesos) from the country of Neverland in 2015 to find values for the following categories:
   a.   Gross value added
   b.   Business production
   c.   Gross fixed capital formation
   d.   National income
   e.   Gross capital formation

Household and NPISH final consumption expenditure = 550	Business spending = 50
Household and nonprofit institutions production = 50	Exports = 225
Net income receipts from the rest of the world = 10	Imports = 125
Taxes less subsidies on products = 100	Government production = 200
Final consumption expenditure of general government = 100	Depreciation = 90
Change in inventories and acquisitions less disposals of valuables = 5	GDP = 850

5. Suppose an extremely simple economy produces only two goods, pillows and rugs. In the first year, 50 pillows are produced and sold at €5 each; 11 rugs are produced and sold at €50 each. In the second year, 56 pillows are produced and sold for €5 each; 12 rugs are produced and sold at €60 each.
   a.   What is nominal GDP in each of the two years?
   b.   What is the growth rate of nominal GDP?
   c.   What is real GDP in each year, expressed in terms of constant Year 1 euros?
   d.   What is the growth rate of real GDP (in constant Year 1 euros)?

6. Assume the same simple economy described in the previous question.
   a.   Calculate a constant-weight price index for the second year, using the first year as the base.
   b.   What is the growth rate of prices (inflation rate) from the first to the second year?

7. List the key simplifying assumptions of the traditional macro model concerning:
   a. The forms of capital included in the model
   b. The sectors of the economy
   c. Who in the economy produces and invests
8. Go to the Eurostat Web site (http://ec.europa.eu/eurostat). What are the latest figures for real GDP, current euro GDP, and the growth rate of GDP for the euro area? What time period do these represent? With which base year is real GDP expressed? In a second step, go to your country's statistical authority's Web site. How does your country compare to the euro area concerning the indicators mentioned in the first part of the question?
9. Match each concept in Column A with a definition or example in Column B:

Column A	Column B
a. A negative (subtracted) item in GDP	1. The year in which real and nominal values are equal
b. A major cause of difference between GDP and national income	2. Purchases of computer software
c. An imputed value	3. Consumption of fixed capital (depreciation)
d. An entity in the government sector	4. Unpaid household production
e. Reflects the prices of all goods and services counted in GDP	5. Implicit price deflator
f. Base year	6. National income
g. An assumption of the traditional macro model	7. Spending on imported jeans
h. Something not counted in calculating GDP	8. A measure that seeks to remove the effects of price changes
i. Real GDP	9. Uses a fixed "market basket"
j. A component of the "income approach" to GDP accounting	10. What homeowners "pay" themselves in rent
k. A constant-weight price index	11. "Governments do not produce"
l. Part of investment (gross fixed capital formation)	12. A public university

10. Go to the Eurostat Web site (http://ec.europa.eu/eurostat) and locate its information on the change of the consumer price index for the euro area ("Inflation HICP—all items")? What month is this for? By how much have prices risen over the past 12 months? For which three euro-area countries has the price increase been especially pronounced? For which three euro-area countries has it been relatively muted?
11. (If Appendix is assigned) The "chained Year 1 euro" estimate of real GDP in the apples-and-oranges example (see Appendix) is smaller than the "constant Year 1 euro" estimate of real GDP. Can you explain why? (Hint: Compare the GDP growth rates derived using the two methods.)

183

APPENDIX: CHAIN-LINKED REAL GDP

quantity index:
an index measuring changes in levels of quantities produced

The key new concept in the "chain-linked" method is an emphasis on estimating **quantity indexes** for GDP in the current year relative to the year before and relative to the reference year.

Chain-linked measures of real GDP and GDP growth are based on the use of index numbers. The ratio of two values of GDP in adjacent years, measured at a common set of prices, can be used as a quantity index to measure production in one year relative to another.

Fisher quantity index: an index that measures production in one year relative to an adjacent year by using an average of the ratios that would be found by using first one year and then the other as the source of prices at which production is valued

The calculation of chain-linked real GDP starts with the calculation of a **Fisher quantity index**, which measures production in one year relative to an adjacent year by using an *average* of the ratios that would be found by using first one year and then the other as the source of prices at which production is valued. The type of average used is a "geometric" average. Instead of adding two numbers and then dividing by two, as you would in calculating the most common type of average (the arithmetic mean), to get a geometric average, you *multiply* the two numbers together and then take the *square root*. The formula for this Fisher quantity index is:

Fisher quantity index (for year-to-year comparison)

$$= \sqrt{\left(\frac{Year\ 2\ GDP\ in\ Year\ 1\ prices}{Year\ 1\ GDP\ in\ Year\ 1\ prices}\right) \times \left(\frac{Year\ 2\ GDP\ in\ Year\ 2\ prices}{Year\ 1\ GDP\ in\ Year\ 2\ prices}\right)}$$

This index has a value of 1 in the reference year, which we take to be Year 1.

The growth rate of real GDP between the reference year and the next year can then be calculated as:

growth rate = (Fisher quantity index − 1) × 100

For example, we have already made many of the necessary calculations for the "apples-and-oranges" economy in Tables 5.5 and 5.6. Plugging these in, we get

Fisher quantity index (for Year 2 compared to Year 1)

$$= \sqrt{\left(\frac{250}{200}\right) \times \left(\frac{300}{250}\right)} = \sqrt{1.25 \times 1.20} = \sqrt{1.5} = 1.225$$

The growth rate of real GDP for the "apples-and-oranges" economy between these two years is

growth rate = (1.225 − 1) × 100 = 22.5 percent

Note that this growth rate is *between* the two growth rates (20 percent and 25 percent) we obtained by using the constant-euro method with various base years. The Fisher quantity index method gives us a unique *average* number for estimated growth.

Table 5.8 *Deriving Real GDP in Chained (Year 1) Euros*

Type of measure	Year 1	Year 2
Nominal GDP	€200	€300
Fisher quantity index (current to previous year)	—	1.225
Chain-type quantity index	100	100 × 1.225 = 122.5
Real GDP (chained Year 1 euros)	= €200	(122.5 × €200)/100 = €245

A quantity index for the current year in terms of a reference year that may be several years in the past is created by "chaining together" year-to-year Fisher quantity indexes to make a **chain-type quantity index** comparing real production relative to the reference year. The chain-type quantity index has a value of 100 in the reference year. In any subsequent year, it is set equal to the chain-type quantity index from the previous year multiplied by the Fisher quantity index calculated for the current year.

Finally, estimation of real GDP in (chained) euro terms is made by multiplying the chain-type quantity index for a year times the level of nominal GDP in the reference year and dividing by 100.

For example, suppose that we take our "apples-and-oranges" economy, making Year 1 the reference year. Year 1's chain-type quantity index is thus set equal to 100, and its nominal and real GDP are equal. These are shown in Table 5.8. The chain-type quantity index for Year 2 is the previous year's value (100) times the Fisher quantity index that we just calculated (1.225). We multiply this result, the new index number 122.5, times nominal GDP in the base year (€200) and divide by 100 to get real GDP, €245. (Whew!)

This can be continued for many years into the future—or into the past. (For example, if the Fisher quantity index calculated for Year 3 were to come out to be 1.152, then the chain-type quantity index for Year 3 would be 122.5 × 1.152.) If you want to check to see that this method actually makes some sense, calculate the percentage change in real GDP from Year 1 to Year 2 using the values in the table. You will find it does, in fact, equal 22.5 percent!

A price index can be calculated for Year 2 (using Year 1 as the reference year) as (300/245) × 100 = 122.5, showing a 22.5 percent price increase over Year 1. This kind of price index is known as a **GDP deflator** or **implicit price deflator**.

The new method has some other drawbacks as well. The sum of real components of GDP in chained-euro terms does not generally exactly add up to real GDP. Users of the data are also warned not to make comparisons of chained-euro amounts for years far away from the reference year. Many statistical authorities in Europe do not publish the final chained euro (or national currency) value but provide tables in which, for example, year-to-year growth rates in components of GDP are already calculated for the user. This is supposed to underline that the different components of GDP that have been computed by this method cannot be added together to get the overall GDP number.

chain-type quantity index: an index comparing real production in the current year to the reference year, calculated using a series of year-to-year Fisher quantity indexes

GDP deflator (implicit price deflator): a price index created by dividing nominal GDP by real GDP

Chapter 6

Macroeconomic Measurement

Environmental and Social Dimensions

1. A BROADER VIEW OF NATIONAL INCOME ACCOUNTING

As discussed in Chapter 5, GDP is a good (though not perfect) summary of the annual flow of goods and services through the market. In the 80-plus years since the introduction of national income accounting in major industrialized countries, GDP has become the official barometer of living standards and business cycles. It appears in newspapers and political debates as a measure of government performance and an indicator of economic, political, and social progress.

GDP is not just something that economists look at; rather, numbers on the size and growth rate of GDP affect critical national and international policies. It is a measure by which we judge presidents and a basis on which multilateral institutions determine how much money they will lend to developing countries. GDP numbers are widely used as a proxy for national success.

Yet GDP was never intended to play such a role. Economists dating back to Simon Kuznets, the originator of U.S. national accounting systems, have warned that GDP is a specialized tool for measuring market activity, which should not be confused with national well-being. As suggested in Box 6.1, GDP often rises with increases in things that most people would want to have less of, while it often fails to rise with positive contributions to individual and social well-being that are not bought and sold in markets.

As discussed in Chapter 3, marketed economic activity occurs within broader social and environmental contexts. These contexts can have an effect on national welfare that is no less important than marketed economic activity. The various alternatives to national accounting presented in this chapter represent our growing awareness of the importance of these social and environmental contexts of economic activity.

In Chapter 1, we mentioned that neglect of the questions of "what, how, and for whom" can mean that growth in production per capita may not lead to increased welfare. Now we can go into more detail about the problems that arise from focusing on production alone—or from focusing only on the money value of output, with too little attention to the details of what is being produced. Many economists and other analysts believe that if we are really to understand this more complete picture of the economy and what it is doing for human well-being, national governments need to start gathering new kinds of data and creating new indicators.

Before we begin to discuss specific options for adjusting, replacing, or supplement-ing GDP, we first need to ask ourselves three important questions:

1. *What should we measure?* GDP measures only economic production. Are there some things that GDP excludes that should be included as a component of well-being, such as health outcomes or environmental quality? Should some parts of GDP be excluded because they harm well-being in the short or long term?
2. *What should be used as the unit of measurement?* Although GDP is measured in euros (or other currency units), what units should be used to measure other variables of well-being, such as education, levels of violence, or air quality?
3. *Should we seek to combine disparate well-being indicators into a single "bottom-line" num-ber, or should we keep the variables disaggregated (i.e., split up into component categories)?* One tempting approach is to convert all variables to euros to allow for compara-bility. But what techniques can we use to measure variables such as environmental quality or social capital in euros, and should we even try?

BOX 6.1 THERE'S NO G-D-P IN "A BETTER ECONOMY"

The year-end numbers have been tabulated, and America is winning the race by a large mar-gin. The nation's closest competitor, China, scores only a bit more than half as high, and Euro-pean nations, Japan, and Brazil lag way behind with little chance of catching up.

 This statement is not about medal counts from the summer Olympics; it's not about citi-zens' health; and it's certainly not about student test scores in math and science. It's about GDP. The United States continues to dominate the race for the biggest economy, at least if measured at market prices.

 Gross domestic product has become the most watched and most misinterpreted of all economic indicators. It's a measure of economic activity—of money changing hands. Despite the mundane nature of this economic indicator, politicians fiercely compete with each other to see who can promise the fastest GDP growth. Government programs and investments in technology get the green light only when they are predicted to spur GDP growth. Economists, bankers, and businesspeople pop the champagne corks when they hear "good news" about quarterly GDP numbers.

 And while the United States leads in GDP, it also leads in military spending, the number of people in prison, and the percentage of people who are obese. These other first-place finishes seem at odds with America's position atop the GDP standings—that is, until you realize that spending on war, incarceration, and disease, as well as other "defensive expenditures," all count toward GDP. The arithmetic of GDP doesn't consider what the money is actually being spent on, and over time, we've been spending more and more money on remedial activities and calling this "progress."

 Counting all these negatives in GDP (not to mention omitting positive activities such as raising children, volunteering, and caring for elderly people) seems like an oversight or an accounting mix-up. But it also seems like something that could be easily fixed. Many people, including Nobel laureates in economics (and even the laureate who invented national income accounting) have issued stern warnings not to confuse GDP with national progress, and many forward-thinking economists have proposed alternative indicators of progress.

Source: Rob Dietz and Dan O'Neill, "There's No G-D-P in 'A Better Economy,'" *Stanford Social Innovation Review*, January 7, 2013.

satellite accounts: additional or parallel accounting systems that provide measures of social and environmental factors, often in physical terms, without necessarily including monetary valuation

One response to the last question has been the development of **satellite accounts**,* which are intended to supplement standard accounts by tracking data on other well-being indicators, such as health, education, and other aspects of social and environmental well-being. The latest European Union guidelines for national accounts explicitly require setting up such supplementary accounts. Consequently, European Union member states now maintain environmental accounts and publish a large amount of data under this framework (albeit with widely differing degrees of detail among the member states). Some of this data is explicitly used as input into the EU's policy making process.

Many of these satellite accounts, especially when it comes to environmental or social questions, present variables in physical units such as tons of carbon dioxide emitted or numbers of children living in poverty. Even where resources can be easily valued in euros, data in physical units may be more meaningful. Consider that we could measure the economic value of oil and gas reserves by multiplying the quantity of reserves in physical units multiplied by the market price. But suppose that the market price increases considerably at the same time that reserves are drawn down. Although the economic value of reserves could increase, that information would fail to tell us that our physical reserves have declined.

Moreover, it is often very difficult to convert variables to monetary units. How can we express changes in violence or health levels in terms of euro values? Such questions raise important methodological issues, such as whether the economic value of higher asthma rates includes only medical expenditures and lost productivity or whether other quality-of-life factors need to be considered. Some may raise ethical objections to attaching euro values to variables such as traffic deaths or biodiversity.

Nevertheless, statisticians try to keep satellite accounts compatible with standard national accounts to allow for a joint analysis of GDP and other aspects covered in the supplementary accounts. For example, the combination of environmental accounts and national accounts allows one to analyze how far certain sectors have become more energy-efficient.

---

* The United Nations differentiates between "internal" satellite accounts (those that are linked to standard accounts and typically measured in monetary units) and "external" satellite accounts (not necessarily linked and measured in either physical or monetary units). See http://unstats.un.org/unsd/nationalaccount/AEG/papers/m4SatelliteAccounts.pdf.

In addition to satellite accounts that record nonmonetary variables such as the stock of natural resources or the emission of greenhouse gases and other pollutants, European countries sometimes maintain satellite accounts to highlight certain existing components of GDP. For example, many member states maintain satellite accounts for tourism expenditure to highlight the link to broader economic activity.

Satellite accounts can be viewed as a "dashboard" approach to national accounting. The dashboard on a car provides not only a speedometer but also a gas gauge and an indicator of temperature and battery level—and we have in recent years come to recognize the value of adding an indicator of how many miles are being driven per gallon of fuel. The dashboard on an airplane contains even more indicators, and an economy is considerably more complex than an airplane.

Proponents of such dashboard approaches agree that GDP is a very useful record of national output for historical and international comparisons but believe that GDP tells us only one of the things that we want to know about the economy. Some of the things that it does not tell us are very important, and they deserve to have their own indicators. By now, there are a number of dashboard approaches used to gauge whether the messages from GDP figures are correct. One prominent example is the European Union's "Europe 2020" strategy "for jobs and smart, sustainable and inclusive growth." This strategy is based on five EU headline targets that are currently measured by nine headline indicators (such as greenhouse gas emissions, spending on research and development, employment rate, and the number of people at risk of exclusion and poverty) and regularly presented for all member states in a "scorecard."

As we delve into additional categories that we might wish to have reported in national accounts, we may find ourselves straying into areas in which measurement becomes more difficult. Thus we can add a fourth question to our list: Should we include only variables that can be measured objectively (whether in money or other units), or should we also consider subjective data? In particular, should one or more of our "dashboard" indicators present the results from surveys that ask people about their well-being? We consider this possibility in the next section.

When reading this chapter, one should keep in mind that the topics covered have very much become a "moving target." Over the past decade, a number of national and international initiatives have been started to supplement national accounts by additional official data on well-being, and many are still works in progress. In 2007, the European Commission, the European Parliament, the Club of Rome, the Organisation for Economic Co-operation and Development (OECD),* and the World Wildlife Fund hosted a high-level conference titled "Beyond GDP" in order to clarify which indicators to include in a comprehensive measurement of well-being. Building on this discussion, in 2009, the European Commission published a roadmap for the improvement of macroeconomic indicators to capture social and environmental issues in the European Union. A progress report in 2013 took stock and promised further work,

---

* The OECD is a group of the world's advanced industrialized countries, now including some developing countries, such as Mexico. The BLI was created, in part, as a response to the 2009 Stiglitz-Sen-Fitoussi Commission report discussed in the next section.

especially in making indicators available in a more timely manner. National statistical agencies in a number of EU member states also work on these issues, and the question of alternative measures of well-being has received attention up to the highest level of government in Germany, Britain, and France. Both the German parliament and the French president set up their respective high-level commissions to come up with more comprehensive ways to measure national well-being, and the British prime minister David Cameron in late 2011 announced that the nation's statistical office would start measuring subjective well-being in Britain.

As a consequence, there has been a proliferation of new indicators, more than a dozen of which have emerged in the past decade. Some concentrate on developing refined measures of national assets and production, keeping as close as possible to the framework of the European System of National and Regional Accounts (ESA). Others are working to develop wholly new indicators, hoping either to replace GDP as the major measure of economic success or to persuade the public and policy makers that GDP is useful only for some purposes and that other measures are needed to make different assessments.

Discussion Questions

1. GDP can be characterized as a (rough) measure of the amount of "throughput" taking place in an economy—as measuring the level of activity whose purpose it is to turn renewable and nonrenewable resources into new products. How does throughput relate to sustainable well-being? Is more throughput always a good thing?

2. In Chapter 3, we discussed how economies are based on natural, manufactured, social, and human capital. Only the value of manufactured capital (structures and equipment)—and, recently, software—is estimated in the current national accounts. Can you think of ways that the stocks of natural, social, and human capital might be measured? What kind of information would be needed?

2. WHY GDP IS NOT A MEASURE OF WELL-BEING

One of the most prominent attempts to reform the current set-up of GDP recording was triggered by France: Recognizing the limitations of GDP and the need to develop indicators that incorporate social and environmental factors, in 2008, French president Nicolas Sarkozy created the Commission on the Measurement of Economic Performance and Social Progress. The commission was chaired by Nobel Prize–winning economist Joseph Stiglitz. The chair of the advisory board was another Nobel-laureate economist, Amartya Sen. The coordinator of the commission was Jean-Paul Fitoussi, the former head of the French economic research institute l'Observatoire français des conjonctures économiques (OFCE). Other members of the commission included numerous prominent economists.

In September 2009, the commission produced its nearly 300-page report. It concluded that it is necessary to shift from an emphasis on measuring economic production to measuring well-being. It also distinguished between current well-being and sustainability, recognizing that whether current well-being can be sustained depends upon the levels of capital (natural, physical, human, and social) passed on to future generations.

2.1 Subjective Well-Being

As mentioned, GDP was never intended to measure welfare or well-being. Even if increases in GDP produce increases in well-being, *ceteris paribus*, many other factors may be equally or more important in determining well-being levels. In other words, well-being is clearly multidimensional. The Stiglitz-Sen-Fitoussi Commission, for example, defined eight dimensions of well-being, including material living standards, health, education, political voice, social connections, and the environment.

Objective data can be collected that provide information on many of these dimensions, such as average life expectancy, literacy rates, and air pollution levels. But such data still do not tell us exactly how these factors relate to well-being. If the goal of economics is to promote well-being, you may wonder why economists do not try to measure it directly. Until recently, most economists believed that it was not possible to obtain quantitative data on something that is inherently subjective; we cannot hook up individuals to a machine and measure their well-being in unambiguous quantitative terms. But we can take a much more intuitive approach—we can simply ask people about their well-being. Although this approach may seem unscientific, a large body of scientific research has emerged in recent decades that suggests that data on **subjective well-being (SWB)** provides meaningful information regarding social welfare levels and the factors that influence well-being.

> **subjective well-being:** a measure of welfare based on survey questions asking people about their own degree of life satisfaction

Collecting data on SWB involves surveying individuals and asking them a question such as: "All things considered, how satisfied are you with your life as a whole these days?" Respondents then answer based on a scale from 1 (dissatisfied) to 10 (satisfied). How much credence can we give to the answers to such questions?

A wide variety of efforts, such as the World Happiness Report from Columbia University's Earth Institute,[1] the Gallup World Poll, and the European Quality of Life Survey, have come up with remarkably consistent measures of "happiness" or "life satisfaction." The Stiglitz-Sen-Fitoussi Commission concludes:

> Research has shown that it is possible to collect meaningful and reliable data on subjective as well as objective well-being. Quantitative measures of [SWB] hold the promise of delivering not just a good measure of quality of life per se, but also a better understanding of its determinants, reaching beyond people's income and material conditions. Despite the persistence of many unresolved issues, these subjective measures provide important information about quality of life.[2]

The Stiglitz-Sen-Fitoussi Commission recommends using SWB data in conjunction with objective data on various well-being dimensions such as income levels and health outcomes to obtain a more comprehensive picture of welfare.

191

Most relevant for our study of macroeconomics is how SWB results correlate with standard economic measures of national welfare such as GDP. We can study the relationship in two ways:

1. Are average SWB levels higher in countries with higher GDP per capita?
2. As GDP per capita increases in a particular country over time, do SWB levels rise?

SWB data have been collected for many developed and developing countries. Figure 6.1 plots average SWB against per-capita GDP, adjusted for differences in purchasing power, for 56 countries. In general, SWB is positively correlated with higher levels of GDP, but note that the benefits of income gains decline at higher income levels, as shown by the curved trendline. However, SWB can be high in both rich and poor countries. In fact, the countries with the highest SWB levels are Mexico and Colombia, both middle-income countries.

Figure 6.1 also shows that while SWB varies among richer countries, all developed countries have relatively high SWB. There are no countries above a per-capita GDP of $20,000 per year (which translates to a slightly higher value of euros, depending on the current exchange rate) that have an average SWB below 6.0, and many poorer countries have an average SWB below 6.0. Thus it appears from this graph that for at least some developing countries, increasing GDP could lead to higher SWB levels. But income gains in richer countries are associated with much smaller increases in SWB.

The other way to analyze country-level SWB data is to consider how SWB changes as a country develops economically over time. The longest time series of SWB data

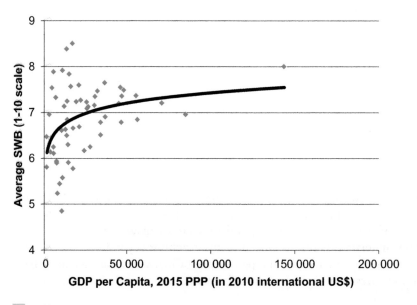

Figure 6.1 *Average Subjective Well-Being and GDP per Capita*

Sources: SWB from World Values Survey online data analysis, 2010–2014 survey wave; GDP from World Development Indicators online database.

comes from the United States, dating back to 1946. While real GDP per capita has increased by about a factor of three since 1946, average SWB levels have essentially remained constant. But an analysis of country trends in SWB over the period 1981–2007 found that average SWB rose in 45 of 52 countries, with economic growth associated with greater SWB gains for low-income countries. India is an example of a country that has experienced significant gains in SWB levels as its economy has grown in recent decades.[3]

Based on both approaches to evaluating SWB, the results imply that as people are able to meet their basic needs, such as adequate nutrition and basic health care, their happiness generally increases. Beyond that, further income gains are associated with smaller increases in SWB or no increase at all. At higher income levels, people seem more likely to judge their happiness relative to others. So even if everyone's income doubles, average happiness levels may be unchanged.

As the Stiglitz-Sen-Fitoussi Commission mentions, further work is needed to understand the relationship between SWB and other well-being measures. But the results so far suggest that SWB should be one of the indicators on our "dashboard" of well-being measures.

2.2 Critiques of GDP

Many important issues are not included adequately, if at all, in GDP. In addition, some things that are included in GDP can be misleading or represent actively harmful activities.

- A critical issue is *household production*, which is examined at more length later in this chapter. While standard accounting measures include the paid labor from such household activities as child care and gardening, these services are not counted when they are unpaid.
- Standard measures do not count the benefits of *volunteer work*, even though such work can contribute to social well-being as much as economic production does.
- A more recent criticism of GDP is that *some significant services provided for free are not counted*, even though they might increase well-being. This concerns Internet services such as Wikipedia, Gmail, or YouTube. In the case of Wikipedia, the service is not counted in GDP, as the site relies on unpaid volunteer work; in the case of Gmail or YouTube, the service is not counted as consumption since the main thing sold by Alphabet (the company running Gmail and YouTube) is advertising, and this advertising only enters into other products as intermediate input.
- *Leisure* is another important neglected factor. A rise in output might come about because people expend more time and effort at paid work. The resulting increase in measured output does not take into account the fact that overwork makes people more tired and stressed and takes away from time that they could use for enjoying other activities. But if people spend more time as leisure, increasing their well-being, this will not be reflected in GDP (except insofar as they spend money on leisure-related activities).

- Also inadequately reflected are issues around loss (or gain) of *human and social capital formation*. Social and political factors that may significantly affect well-being include the health and education levels of a country's citizens, as well as political participation, government effectiveness (or lack thereof), and issues of trust, corruption, or other aspects of the economic and social culture.

- Another significant criticism of GDP, when used as a general measure of economic progress or success, is that *interactions between the economy and the natural world are often ignored*. GDP generally does not account for environmental degradation and resource depletion, while treating natural resources that do not go through the market as having no monetary value.

defensive expenditures: money spent to counteract economic activities that have caused harm to human or environmental health

- Some outputs merely compensate for or defend against harmful events that result, directly or indirectly, from the economic activity represented in GDP. Referred to as **defensive expenditures**, these show up as positive contributions to GDP, but we do not account for the associated negative impacts. Consider, for example, an oil spill that results in massive cleanup efforts: The billions of dollars spent cleaning up after the 2011 *Deepwater Horizon* oil spill in the Gulf of Mexico turned up as positive additions to U.S. GDP, even while the environmental and human losses are mostly not reflected. When environmental issues are mostly invisible, there can be an appearance of economic growth even as the ecological basis for future economic health is being seriously undermined.

- *Products or production methods that reduce rather than increase well-being* may show up as additions to GDP. Unhealthy foods and drugs and dangerous equipment, for example, may lower, not raise, overall well-being. Even if people are willing to pay for such goods and services, either individually (perhaps influenced by advertising) or through their governments (perhaps influenced by interest-group lobbyists), such decisions might reflect poor information or bad judgment when looked at from the point of view of well-being. In terms of production methods, if people are miserable at their jobs, suffering boring, degrading, unpleasant, or harmful working conditions, their well-being is compromised. The divergence between output and well-being is especially obvious in cases in which workers' lives or health are threatened by their working conditions, even while their work results in a high volume of marketed goods and services.

- Another gap between GDP and well-being is *financial debt*. GDP counts consumption levels as rising even if the rise is financed by unsustainably large debt burdens, whether the debt is held by consumers or by governments. When debts are high enough to require painful changes in future consumption, not accounting for financial debt is similar to not accounting for unsustainable tolls exacted on the natural environment.

- Finally, increased economic activity in a given country is counted as an addition to GDP even if it *increases inequality*. Two countries with the same per-capita GDP may have a significantly different income distribution and, closely related, different levels of overall well-being. At an individual level, if someone making just €20,000 per year receives a raise of €1,000, this is counted as the same societal gain as it would be if that raise went to someone with an income of €100,000. Obviously, the additional income means much more for the individual well-being of the person with the lower salary. Although economists generally accept this concept (called the diminishing marginal utility of income), GDP counts income gains the same regardless of whether the person receiving the increase desperately needs the income or is already rich.

The foregoing examples all indicate the social dangers of pursuing policies geared only to raising GDP. A narrow national focus solely on increasing output may result in decreased leisure and less time for parenting, friendships, and community relations; it can increase levels of stress and mental illness or raise economic inequality to a socially destructive level. For all these reasons, improvements are needed in the design of measures of national success and in defining and gathering the data needed for such measures. The next two sections describe three leading alternative measures that represent one dashboard approach, one mixed approach, and one attempt to construct a composite indicator.

3. ALTERNATIVE APPROACHES TO REPRESENTING WELL-BEING

3.1 The Europe 2020 Scoreboard

After the deep recession in Europe following the global financial and economic crisis in 2008–2009, and confronted with high rates of unemployment, European policy makers decided to construct a framework for a more sustainable and inclusive growth model. In 2010, they launched a growth strategy called "Europe 2020" under which they defined targets to be reached over the coming decade in the five areas of employment, research and development, climate/energy, education, and social inclusion and poverty reduction. Building on the work of the Stiglitz-Sen-Fitoussi Commission, they came up with a scoreboard of nine headline indicators. Within the European framework of policy coordination, these indicators are now regularly monitored, and member states are asked to devise national strategies to reach previously defined targets. The scoreboard is hence not just any monitoring instrument but a set of indicators that is actually targeted by policy makers.

The Scoreboard consists of the following five dimensions and the following targets to be reached by 2020:

- **Employment:** The European Union targets to have at least 75 percent of the population aged 20–64 employed.
- **Research and Development:** At least 3 percent of GDP should be spent on research and development.
- **Climate/Energy:** Greenhouse gas emissions should be reduced by 20 percent compared to 1990. The share of renewable energy sources should be increased to 20 percent of total energy use and energy efficiency increased by 20 percent.
- **Education:** The share of early school leavers should be reduced to below 10 percent, and the proportion of individuals of age 30–34 years who have completed a tertiary or equivalent education should be increased to at least 40 percent.

195

■ **Poverty:** At least 20 million people should be lifted out of the risk of poverty or social exclusion.

GDP growth itself is not mentioned in the scorecard but is implicitly targeted, as the strategy is still about "growth," and growth is assumed to be an increase in measured GDP. Hence, the Europe 2020 scoreboard can be seen as a complementary dashboard to standard GDP measurement.

Table 6.1 presents the development of the scoreboard's indicators compared to 2008, the last year before Europe was first hit by the global economic and financial crisis and then by the euro crisis. As can be seen, over this period of time, the European Union has made some progress in the areas of research and development, environmental sustainability, and education. However, there are some dimensions of the scorecard that have actually deteriorated since 2008 and in which meeting the target by 2020 might be unrealistic. For example, the employment rate for 2014 was still below that of 2008, even though the European Union had set itself the target of increasing the employment rate to 75 percent by 2020. The performance in the dimension of poverty reduction has been even worse: While the EU had set itself the target of *decreasing* the number of people at risk of poverty or social exclusion by 20 million, this number had actually *increased* by almost 5 million.

Also, given the long economic crisis in many EU countries since 2008, the measured progress in the reduction of greenhouse gas emission was less impressive than it might seem when just looking at the reported numbers, according to which the EU had already met its target in 2014 (and remained within the target in 2015). In many countries, real GDP in 2015 had not yet reached precrisis levels. To some extent, therefore, the reduced emission of greenhouse gases is more a result of a contraction in production due to the economic crisis than a result of improvements in technology and energy-saving behavior.

3.2 The Better Life Index (BLI)

The problem of a dashboard approach is that its results are sometimes difficult to communicate. What is the conclusion about a society's well-being if the poverty rate falls by two percentage points yet the emission of greenhouse gases increases by 3 percent? In contrast to interpreting an increase or decrease of GDP by 1 percent, journalists and the general public are often at a loss what to make of changes in a complicated dashboard.

On the other hand, summing up production, poverty, inequality, environmental degradation, and other aspects of the quality of life in one single index also poses problems: In order to be added up, monetary values need to be attached to each dimension. Yet it is extremely difficult to objectively value health, inequality, or variety of species in euro terms. (We consider measurement issues at greater length in what follows, in our discussion of environmental indicators.)

The OECD has thus tried a mixed approach. With its Better Life Index (BLI), it tries to combine a large number of dimensions, many of which cannot easily be valued in monetary terms, into one single indicator without actually definitely prescribing the weight for each dimension.

196

Table 6.1 *Europe 2020 Goals and Actual Developments 2008–2014, EU 28*

Employment: 75% of the population aged 20-64 should be employed

Indicator	Unit	2008	2014	Target
Employment rate – age group 20–64	% of population aged 20-64	70.3	69.2	75

Research and Development: 3% of the EU's GDP should be invested in R&D

Indicator	Unit	2008	2014	Target
Gross domestic expenditure on R&D	% of GDP	1.85	2.03	3

Environment:
* *Greenhouse gas emissions should be reduced by 20% compared to 1990*
* *The share of renewable energy sources in final energy consumption should be increased to 20%*
* *Energy efficiency should improve by 20%*

Indicator	Unit	2008	2014	Target
Greenhouse gas emissions	Index 1990 = 100	90.3	77.3	80
Share of renewable energy in gross final energy consumption	%	11	16	20
Primary energy consumption	million tonnes of oil equivalent (TOE)	1693	1507	1483
Final energy consumption	million tonnes of oil equivalent (TOE)	1180	1061	1086

The share of early school leavers should be under 10% and at least 40% of individuals 30-34 years old should have completed a tertiary or equivalent education

Indicator	Unit	2008	2014	Target
Early leavers from education and training	% of population aged 18-24	14.7	11.2	10
Tertiary educational attainment	% of population aged 30-34	31.1	37.9	40

Poverty should be reduced by lifting at least 20 million people out of the risk of poverty or social exclusion in the EU-27

Indicator	Unit	2008	2014	Target
People at risk of poverty or social exclusion	Cumulative difference from 2008 in thousand	0	4,725	-20,000

Source: Eurostat, "Europe 2020 Headline Indicators: Scoreboard", http://ec.europa.eu/eurostat/web/europe-2020-indicators/europe-2020-strategy/headline-indicators-scoreboard, October 10, 2016.

BLI considers well-being a function of the following 11 dimensions:

1. Income, Wealth, and Inequality: The main variables used for this dimension are disposable household income and net financial wealth.* The BLI also considers the degree of inequality in income and wealth.
2. Jobs and Earnings: The main variables comprising this dimension are the unemployment rate, the long-term unemployment rate, and average earnings per employee.
3. Housing Conditions: Sufficient housing is important to provide security, privacy, and stability.
4. Health Status: The BLI includes life expectancy and a subjective evaluation of one's overall health status.
5. Work and Life Balance: The BLI measures the proportion of employees who work long (50 or more) hours per week, the time available for leisure and personal care, and the employment rate for women with school-age children.
6. Education and Skills: This is measured as the percentage of the adult (25- to 64-year-old) population that has a secondary-school degree and uses standardized testing to measure students' cognitive skills.
7. Social Connections: This dimension is measured by people's responses to a standardized question asking whether they have friends or relatives on whom they can count in times of need.
8. Civic Engagement and Governance: This dimension is based on voter turnout data and a composite index that measures citizen input into policy making.
9. Environmental Quality: The main variable used to measure environmental quality is air pollution levels, specifically levels of particulate matter. Secondary environmental variables include an estimate of the degree to which diseases are caused by environmental factors, people's subjective satisfaction with their local environment, and access to green space.
10. Personal Security: This dimension focuses on threats to one's safety. It is measured using homicide and assault rates.
11. Subjective Well-Being: This dimension measures people's overall satisfaction with their lives as well as reported negative feelings.

The BLI is designed to produce an overall well-being index. The results for each dimension are standardized across countries, resulting in a score from 0 to 10. But how do we assign a weight to the various components? One approach would be simply to weight each of the 11 dimensions equally. The BLI report makes no specific recommendations for weighting the different dimensions, but its Web site allows users to select their own weights for each of the dimensions (see www.oecdbetterlifeindex. org). The OECD is collecting user input and will use this information to gain a better understanding of the factors that are most important for measuring well-being.

---

* In addition to the main variables discussed here, most of the dimensions also consider secondary variables. For example, the dimension of income and wealth also includes data on household consumption and a subjective evaluation of material well-being.

3.3 The Human Development Index (HDI)

In contrast to the BLI, the United Nations **Human Development Index (HDI)** is calculated based on only three components of well-being: life expectancy at birth, years of formal education, and real per-capita GDP. Although they are denominated in different units—both years and money—no attempt is made to translate one into the other. Rather, relative performance is presented in a scaled index (Figure 6.2).

Like the BLI, the HDI then faces the issue of how to assign relative weights. The standard HDI approach is to give equal weight to each of the three indicators. Inclusion of standard measures of income as one-third of the indicator makes it highly, although not perfectly, correlated with GDP; of the 30 countries with the highest HDI scores in 2014, all but two were also ranked in the top 40 by national income per capita.

At the same time, the results often show that countries with similar GDP levels vary dramatically in overall human welfare, as measured by the HDI. For example, Mauritius, Belarus, and Botswana have very similar levels of GDP, but their HDI scores vary significantly. Belarus has the highest score in this group because of high education levels and relatively long life expectancy. Botswana's low life expectancy pulls down its HDI score. Vietnam, Nigeria, and Pakistan also have similar per-capita GDP values but widely varying HDI scores. Vietnam does well on the two nonmonetary measures, while Nigeria scores poorly on both of them, and Pakistan scores relatively well on longevity but not education.

Human Development Index (Scale: 0–1)		
0.90 – 1.00	—	Norway, Australia, Switzerland, Denmark, Netherlands, Germany, Ireland, United States, Canada, New Zealand, Singapore, Sweden, United Kingdom
0.85 – <0.90	—	Korea, Iceland, Israel, Luxembourg, Japan, Belgium, France, Austria, Finland, Slovenia, Spain, Italy, Czech Republic, Greece, Estonia
0.80 – <0.85	—	Poland, Argentina, Portugal, Hungary, Latvia, Croatia
0.75 – <0.80	—	Russia, Romania, Bulgaria, Turkey, Mexico, Brazil
0.70 – <0.75	—	Ukraine, Algeria, Albania, China, Thailand, Libya, Tunisia
0.65 – <0.70	—	Egypt, Indonesia
0.60 – <0.65	—	India, South Africa
0.55 – <0.60	—	Syria, Ghana, Bangladesh
0.50 – <0.55	—	Pakistan, Nigeria
0.45 – <0.50	—	Haiti, Afghanistan

Figure 6.2 *Selected Countries as Ranked in the Human Development Index*

Source: UNDP, Human Development Report, 2015 data.

The relative simplicity of the HDI has made it much easier to apply in countries with less money to spend on data collection; hence, it has been especially valuable for developing countries. It has been an annual feature of every UN *Human Development Report* since 1990. In a number of countries, the HDI is now an official government statistic; its annual publication inaugurates serious political discussion and renewed efforts, nationally and regionally, to improve lives and is followed by many development agencies interested in tracking progress. The HDI continues to be modified, with new versions that adjust for inequality and gender equity.

3.4 Other National Accounting Alternatives

Aside from the three measures just described (Europe 2020 Scoreboard, BLI, and HDI), many other proposals have been made to either supplement GDP, adjust it, or replace it. To give a sense of this landscape, we briefly describe a sample of them. Except for the first one, they are all indicators that have been developed for use in specific locales.

- The **Genuine Progress Indicator (GPI)** was one of the first comprehensive attempts to provide a single figure for well-being. It adds up personal consumption, adjusted for inequality, adds—among other things—the value of household and volunteer work as well as services from consumer durables, and subtracts costs of crime, accidents, pollution, and resource depletion. It has been computed for the United States from 1950 to 2004 and for a number of U.S. states.
- The **Happy Planet Index (HPI)** has been proposed by the New Economics Foundation in London. Like the HDI, the HPI is designed to compare the success of different countries to see how efficiently (in environmental terms) each country is able to promote the well-being of its inhabitants. The measure multiplies life expectancy by a measure of life satisfaction, then divides by ecological footprint, a measure of ecological impact.* Life expectancy is a statistic obtainable for almost all countries. Life satisfaction has been measured in a variety of ways: The HPI uses subjective well-being data from the Gallup World Poll. HPI has been calculated for 151 countries. The index tends to rise with per-capita GDP up to $5,000, after which it tends to decline, because thereafter the ecological footprint increases more rapidly than life satisfaction or life expectancy (see Box 6.2).
- Some measures have been developed for specific countries. For example, the **National Welfare Index** has been proposed for Germany. In many aspects, it is similar to the Genuine Progress Indicator, but it also includes, on the positive side, public spending on health and education, and, on the negative side, costs of alcohol, tobacco, and drug abuse, as well as the usage of nuclear energy. The indicator is presented as an index with 100 in its base year.
- Other national examples include Italy, which has a **Regional Quality of Development Index**, a composite index of 45 variables pertaining to environment, economy,

---

* A country's ecological footprint is a measure of the amount of land required to provide its inhabitants with all their natural resources and assimilate their wastes, including carbon dioxide emissions.

rights, gender equality, education, culture, working conditions, health, and political participation. France has the **Fleurbaey/Gaulier Indicator**, which is similar to GPI but tries to include even more monetary values of nonmonetary factors (job security, healthy life expectancy, environmental sustainability), using subjective valuations of these factors to create adjusted "equivalent incomes." They are aggregated and then reduced by the degree of inequality in the equivalent incomes.

- The **Gross National Happiness (GNH)** concept was proposed in Bhutan in 1972 as a guiding principle for economic development that takes a holistic approach to improving the quality of people's lives. Although the concept of GNH has been used for decades, the attempt to quantify it is recent.[4] In 2010, it was formally defined along nine different dimensions of welfare, including 33 distinct indicators. For example, the education dimension includes literacy and education rates; the psychological well-being dimension includes subjective well-being and an indicator of spirituality; and the governance dimension includes data on political participation and government performance. The index is made up of both objective and subjective data.

BOX 6.2 THE HAPPY PLANET INDEX

The Happy Planet Index asserts that the goal of society is to create long and happy lives for its members. To do this, natural resources must be used and wastes generated. The HPI is made up of three variables that reflect these concepts:

1. *Average life expectancy:* This measures whether a society's members lead long lives.
2. *Average subjective well-being:* This measures whether a society's members lead happy lives. The data is obtained from surveys that ask people how satisfied they are with their lives. Despite the simplicity of the approach, years of research have demonstrated that the results provide reasonably accurate estimates of an individual's welfare.
3. *Ecological footprint:* This measures a society's overall ecological impact. It is defined as the amount of land required to provide a society with the resources that it consumes and assimilate the waste that it generates. While it has been subject to methodological critiques, by converting all ecological impacts into a single value, it provides an overall assessment of sustainability.

Average subjective well-being, scaled between 0 and 1, is multiplied by life expectancy to obtain the "happy life years" of a society. Then the HPI is calculated as:

HPI = Happy Life Years/Ecological Footprint

The HPI has been calculated for 140 countries. The countries with the highest HPI scores are those whose citizens tend to be rather happy and long-lived but have relatively modest ecological footprints, including Costa Rica, Mexico, Colombia, and Vietnam. One interesting aspect of the HPI is that a country's HPI ranking tends to be unrelated to its GDP. The United

States ranks 108, just above Nigeria. The highest-ranking EU country is Spain, ranked 15. Denmark follows, ranked 32, the United Kingdom is at rank 34, Finland at 37, Austria at 43, France at 44, Germany at 49, and Italy at rank 60.

The interpretation and policy implications of the HPI are unclear. For example, Pakistan and Georgia have a higher HPI score than Germany or France. Does this imply that Pakistan and Georgia are more desirable to live in or more ecologically sustainable than Germany or France? Probably not. Another issue is whether a country's policies can affect happiness levels, which may be more a construction of inherent social and cultural factors than of policy choices.

But despite its limitations, the HPI has received attention as an alternative or supplement to GDP, especially in Europe. A 2007 report to the European Parliament cites several strengths of the HPI, including:

- It considers the ends of economic activity, namely, happiness and life expectancy.
- The innovative way it combines well-being and environmental factors.
- Its calculations are easy to understand.
- Data can be easily compared across countries.

So while the HPI is unlikely to become a widespread alternative to GDP, it does provide information that is not currently captured in any other national accounting metric.

Sources: K. Jeffrey et al. (2016), *The Happy Planet Index 2016: A global index of sustainable wellbeing*, London: New Economics Foundation, www.neweconomics.org; Y. Goossens et al. (2007), *Alternative Progress Indicators to Gross Domestic Product (GDP)*. London: New Economics Foundation, www.neweconomics.org.

One lesson from all these alternatives is that there is not necessarily a positive correlation between the total of final purchases in an economy (one of the things that GDP is designed to measure) and other measures of well-being in the present, or of economic possibility (even as measured by GDP) in the future. In many instances, GDP is rising while other measures stay flat or fall.

The next two sections focus on the issues surrounding two particular elements that have been seriously underrepresented in GDP. Section 4 discusses issues of accounting for household production. Section 5 takes up environmental accounting, including subsections on the methodological problems of how to assign values to things that are not sold through markets.

Discussion Questions

1. Does the Europe 2020 scorecard include anything that you think should be left out or fails to account for something that you think should be included? Think hard about what you really think human well-being is about.

2. Give examples of each of the following:
    - ■ Efforts to supplement GDP
    - ■ Efforts to adjust GDP
    - ■ Efforts to replace GDP

    Are there some alternatives discussed above that would fit into more than one of these categories? Are there some that are difficult to fit into any of them? Would you suggest any other ways of categorizing efforts that are being made to improve how we measure the success of an economy in achieving well-being for present and future people?

4. MEASURING HOUSEHOLD PRODUCTION

The preceding section described efforts around the world to improve the statistics that are used to assess a country's economic performance. Part of this movement includes interest in gathering data on household production. Many countries, including the EU member states, but also countries as diverse as the U.S., Australia, Canada, India, Japan, Mexico, and Thailand, have conducted or are conducting national time-use surveys to aid their understanding of unpaid productive activities. The United Nations Statistical Commission and Eurostat (the statistical office of the European Union) are encouraging countries to develop satellite accounts that provide the necessary information to adjust measures of GDP so that they take into account both household production and interactions between the economy and the environment while not changing the official definition of GDP.

Efforts to calculate household labor actually predate standard GDP accounts. In 1921, a group of economists at the U.S. National Bureau of Economic Research calculated that the value of household services would be about 25 to 30 percent of marketed production. Modern estimates for the early 2000s came to the conclusion that the value of household services in Germany was around €820 billion and €62.8 billion for Finland. Had these services been included in the national accounts, GDP in Germany would have been about 34 percent higher than reported under standard methodology and GDP in Finland 40 percent higher.[5] Despite numerous demonstrations of the practicality dating back almost 100 years, however, household production has never been included in official GDP accounts of major industrialized countries.

There are strong arguments to suggest that current GDP figures are less accurate for having neglected household production. Most obviously, GDP is understated—a substantial area of valuable productive activity has been overlooked (see Box 6.3). This was stressed by Simon Kuznets, the architect of national income accounting, when he presented his original set of estimates to the U.S. American Congress in 1937. With his typical candor, he noted what was missing, pointing in particular to "services of housewives and other members of the family."

Neglecting household production does not only lead to an understatement of the level of GDP but might also give a wrong impression about growth trends. One of the major economic shifts during the twentieth century was the movement of a large proportion of women from unpaid employment as full-time homemakers to paid employment outside the home. In 1870, 40 percent of all U.S. workers were women working as full-time homemakers; by 2000, the proportion had dropped to 16 percent. Trends in many European countries were similar, but timing often differed. This increase in work outside the home, as well as the increase in purchases of substitutes for home production, such as paid child care and prepared foods, was counted as an increase in GDP. The value of *lost* household production, however, was not subtracted. This failure to account for reductions in some home-produced goods and services means that GDP growth during the period was *overstated*. For example, an article in the May 2012 *Survey of Current Business* found that

> If "home production"—the value of the time spent cooking, cleaning, watching the kids, and so forth—were counted, it would raise the level of nominal GDP nearly 26 percent for 2010. Back in 1965, when fewer women were in the formal labor force and more were working in the nonmarket sector, GDP would have been raised by 39 percent. Because the inclusion of "home production" would

---

BOX 6.3 WHAT ARE STAY-AT-HOME MOMS REALLY WORTH?

What is the fair market value of all the work a typical stay-at-home mom does in a year? To answer this question, we can multiply the hours spent at different tasks by the typical wage paid to workers who perform those tasks. For the U.S., this has been tried by a number of people. For example, according to 2012 research by insure.com, the typical mom spends 14 hours per week cooking. The U.S. Bureau of Labor Statistics estimates the average wage for cooks at about $9 per hour. This implies that the annual value of a mom's cooking labor is over $6,000. Applying the same approach to other household tasks, including child care, cleaning, shopping, yard work, and driving, the annual value of a full-time stay-at-home mom is more than $60,000. Similar research by salary.com comes up with an even larger market value—about $113,000 annually!

While there are some stay-at-home dads in the United States, about 150,000, they are far outnumbered by the 5 million stay-at-home moms. But the number of stay-at-home moms has been declining in recent decades as more women have entered the workforce. While this brings additional income to households, the income is partially offset by additional expenses. In many states, the cost of full-time child care exceeds the typical annual cost of college tuition. For example, in Massachusetts, the average cost of child care is $19,000 per year.

While the additional household income and market expenditures are counted as increases to GDP, the median salary in the United States for a woman working full time is only about $37,000. So based on the values presented here, it isn't clear whether total social welfare increases or decreases when many women are compelled to enter the workforce.

Source: "What Are Stay-at-Home Moms Really Worth?" *Fiscal Times*, May 4, 2012, www.thefiscaltimes.com/Articles/2012/05/04/What-Are-Stay-at-Home-Moms-Really-Worth.aspx.

add more to the level of GDP in 1965 than in 2010, factoring in the value of these nonmarket activities was found to reduce the average annual growth rate of GDP over this period.[6]

Comparisons between countries are also made more difficult by the lack of accounting for household production in GDP. In countries of the global South, where such activities make up a much higher proportion of total production than they do in the developed countries of the global North, GDP is even more inadequate as an indicator of national production. When we focus on well-being—rather than money flows—as the goal of an economy, it becomes especially evident that there is important economic activity in households that is going unreported in national income accounts.

Why does this matter? One important reason is that the omission of most household production from the national accounts may contribute to a subtle bias in the perceptions of policy makers who base their economic decisions on them. Because household work is not measured, it may be easy to think that it is not important or not even part of the economy.

Most European pension systems, for example, make payments to people based only on their market wages and years in paid work. While in some countries, a certain time (e.g., two years) for raising children is credited for the calculation of pensions in recognition of the contribution that such unpaid work makes to social and economic life, parents who stay home for an extended period of time to look after their children regularly end up with lower pensions. Having home production counted in GDP might help make policy makers more aware of its productive contributions.[7] Interestingly, critiques of GDP for its failure to count household labor arise out of both conservative principles, which emphasize family values, and progressive ones, which seek to recognize the value of labor that has been historically and disproportionately performed by women.

4.1 Time-Use Surveys

A first step in determining a value for household production is to find out how much time people spend in unpaid productive activities. In the European Union, many national statistical authorities conduct time-use surveys, and the results for 15 of the member states are presented under the framework of Harmonised European Time Use Surveys. In these time-use surveys, adults in national samples are asked to report in detail how they used their time on one particular day.[8]

The results for the latest published survey (published in 2007) indicate that there are huge differences both between genders and between different countries on the time spent engaging in household activities, including housework, food preparation and cleanup, lawn and garden care, or household management (such as paying bills). When averaged over all responses (including those who had not spent any time on household activities), Italian women spent an average of 5 hours and 20 minutes per day on these activities, while Italian men spent only 1 hour 35 minutes on these activities. In Sweden, in contrast, women only spent an average of 3 hours 42 minutes on household activities and their male counterparts 2 hours 29 minutes. In Germany, the correspondent values were 4 hours 14 minutes for women and 2 hours 22 minutes for men.

4.2 Methods of Valuing Household Production

After time use has been measured in terms of hours spent on various activities, standard national accounting procedures require that these hours be assigned a monetary value using market or quasi-market prices. Economists have developed two main methods of assigning a monetary value to household time use: the replacement-cost method and the opportunity-cost method.

replacement-cost method (for estimating the value of household production): valuing hours at the amount it would be necessary to pay someone to do the work

In the **replacement-cost method**, hours spent on household labor are valued at what it would cost to pay someone else to do the same job. In the most popular approach—and the one used to generate the most conservative estimates—economists use the wages paid in a general category such as "domestic worker" or "housekeeper" to impute a wage. A variant of this method, which usually results in higher estimates, is to value each type of task separately: child-care time is valued according to the wage of a professional child-care worker, housecleaning by the wages of professional house-cleaners, plumbing repair by the wages of a plumber, and so forth.

opportunity-cost method (for estimating the value of household production): valuing hours at the amount that the unpaid worker could have earned at a paid job

The **opportunity-cost method** starts from a different view, based on microeconomic "marginal" thinking. Presumably, if someone reduces his or her hours at paid work in order to engage in household production, he or she is assumed to value the time spent in household production (at the margin) at least at the wage rate that he or she could have earned by doing paid work for another hour. That is, if you choose to give up €30 that you could have earned working an extra hour in order to spend an hour with your child, you must presumably think that the value of spending that hour with your child is at least €30. This leads to using the wage rate that the household producer would have earned in the market to value the time spent doing household work. In this case, estimates of the value of nonmarket production can be quite a bit higher than using the replacement-cost method, since some hours would be valued at the wage rates earned by doctors, lawyers, and other more highly paid workers.

Neither approach to imputing a wage rate is perfect. However, it would be hard to argue that perfection has been achieved in any of the other measurements and imputations involved in creating the national accounts, and many argue that imputing any value for household labor time, even using minimal replacement costs, is more accurate than imputing a value of zero.

Similar arguments have been made concerning unpaid volunteer work in communities and nonprofit organizations—the time that people spend coaching children's sports teams, visiting nursing homes, serving on church and school committees, and so on. In the German Time Use Survey from 2012–2013, on average, each person spent 21 minutes every day participating in unpaid volunteer activities. If volunteer work as well as household work were both counted in national accounts, the proportion of production attributed to the core sphere of the economy would rise considerably.

Discussion Questions

1. Do you think that national governments should incorporate a monetary estimate of the value of household production in national accounting statistics? How do you think the inclusion of household production would affect the measurement of economic activity in developed versus developing countries?

2. Think back on at least one household activity in which you have engaged in the past couple of days that in principle could be replaced by market or third-person services. How would that activity be valued by the replacement-cost method? By the opportunity-cost method? What sorts of manufactured capital goods were important, along with your labor, in the activity?

5. ACCOUNTING FOR THE ENVIRONMENT

The natural environment underpins all economic activities. To express this observation in accounting terms, consider the example of a developing country that depends heavily on natural resources. If its forests are cut down, its soil fertility depleted, and its water supplies polluted, surely the country has become poorer. But national income accounting will merely record the market value of the timber, agricultural produce, and industrial output as positive contributions to GDP.

The danger of omitting important environmental considerations from our measures of success is not limited to developing countries. The EU member states also depend in many ways on their natural resources. Soil depletion has not yet raised the cost of land-based food but is likely to do so in the future without significant changes in farming practices. The market price of fish has increased with depletion of many species. The European states share with all other countries a reliance on weather patterns that support existing lives and lifestyles; if human activities increase the level of greenhouse gas emissions that lead to serious disruptions in climate, more severe storms, and rising sea levels, more and more money will be spent in what we have described as "defensive expenditures." Serious attention is now being paid to whether these should go into our national accounting on the plus or the minus side.

Recall Figure 3.8, which indicated that the natural environment provides resources and environmental services as inflows to economic activity and that economic activity also releases waste products into the environment. How can these environmental connections be reflected in national accounting?

Environmental economists describe the economic functions of the natural world under three headings:*

1. *Resource functions:* The natural environment provides natural resources that are inputs into human production processes. They include mineral ores, crude

---

* A fourth category of environmental value stems not from use but from mere appreciation of the existence of species and environmental amenities; this is felt by some people even if they do not expect to see, for example, a blue whale or Victoria Falls. The "existence value" of a given species or resource is difficult to quantify, but it is recognized as a legitimate economic value by economists.

petroleum, fish, soil, and forests. Some of these resources, such as fish and forests, are renewable, while others, such as minerals and petroleum, are not.

2. *Environmental service functions:* The natural environment provides the basic habitat of clean air, drinkable water, and suitable climate that directly support all forms of life on the planet. Water filtration provided by wetlands and erosion control provided by tree-covered hillsides are other examples of services provided by eco-systems. People enjoy the services of the natural environment directly when they enjoy pleasant scenery or outdoor recreation.

3. *Sink functions:* The natural environment also serves as a "sink" that absorbs (up to a point) the pollution and waste generated by economic activity. Car exhaust dis-sipates into the atmosphere, for example, while used packaging goes into landfill, and fluid industrial waste ends up in rivers and oceans. Some waste breaks down relatively quickly into harmless substances. Others are toxic or accumulate over time, eventually compromising the quality of the environment.

Although for centuries these environmental functions were treated as though they were provided "free" and in unlimited amounts, more recently, the problems of deple-tion of resources, degradation of environmental services, and overuse of environmental sink functions have become increasingly apparent. The next section describes some efforts to account for them.

5.1 Environmentally Adjusted Net Domestic Product

The most basic approach to "green" accounting is to start with traditional measures and make adjustments that reflect environmental concerns. In current national income accounting, it is commonly recognized that some of each year's economic produc-tion is offset by the depreciation of manufactured, or fixed, capital such as buildings and machinery.* In other words, while economic activity provides society with the benefits of new goods and services, each year the value of previously produced assets declines, and this loss of benefits should be accounted for. Thus national accounting methods produce estimates of net domestic product (NDP), which starts with GDP and then deducts the annual depreciation value of existing fixed capital. For example, in 2015, the GDP of the euro area was €10.4 trillion. But the depreciation of fixed capital that year totaled €1.84 trillion. Thus the NDP of the euro area in 2015 was €8.56 trillion.

Extending this logic, we can see that each year, the value of natural capital may also depreciate as a result of resource extraction or environmental degradation. In some cases, the value of natural capital could increase as well if environmental quality improves; that, after all, is the point of restorative development. The net annual change in the value of natural capital in a country can simply be added or subtracted from

---

* Depreciation is simply a measure of the loss of capital value through wear and tear. For accounting purposes, it can be calculated using a "straight-line" formula according to which, for example, a new machine is esti-mated to lose 10 percent of its original value each year over a 10-year period, or by using more complex valu-ation methods.

NDP to obtain what has been called **environmentally adjusted NDP (EDP)**. Thus:

$$EDP = GDP - D_m - D_n$$

where D_m is the depreciation of manufactured capital and D_n is the depreciation of natural capital.

This measure requires estimating natural capital depreciation in monetary terms rather than physical units such as biomass volume or habitat area. The methods discussed in Chapter 5 can theoretically be used to estimate such values, but to estimate all types of natural capital depreciation in monetary terms is a daunting task that would require many assumptions. Thus the estimates of EDP that have been produced focus on only a few categories of natural capital depreciation.

One of the earliest attempts at green accounting estimated EDP for Indonesia over a 14-year period, 1971–1984.[9] This pioneering analysis deducted the value of depreciation for three categories of natural capital: oil, forests, and soil. The values of GDP and EDP over this time period are shown in Figure 6.3.[10]

environmentally adjusted net domestic product (EDP): GDP less depreciation of both manufactured and natural capital

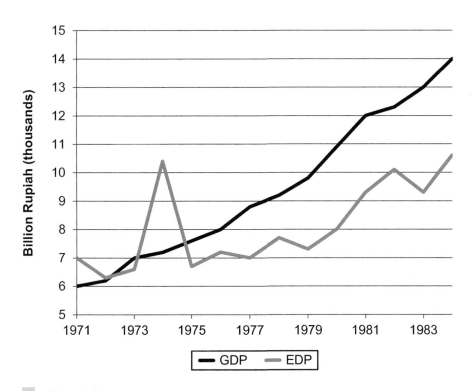

Figure 6.3 *Indonesian GDP Adjusted for Resource Depreciation*

Source: Robert Repetto, et al., *Wasting Assets: Natural Resources in the National Income Accounts.* Washington, DC: World Resources Institute, 1989.

The results suggest several important points:

- Natural capital depreciation can amount to a significant portion of GDP, in this case about 20 percent; in other words, natural capital depreciation offset about 20 percent of total economic production. Thus, GDP presents an overly positive assessment of social welfare.

- Measuring the growth of GDP to depict changes in social welfare may not produce accurate results. Over the time period covered in Figure 6.3, Indonesia's GDP grew at an annual rate of 7.1 percent. However, EDP grew at an annual rate of only 4.0 percent. So this case demonstrates that looking only at GDP to determine the trend in national welfare may lead policy makers to conclude that growth is robust. But accounting for environmental degradation shows that much of the apparent growth was at the expense of the environment.

- Monetization of natural capital must be approached carefully. Figure 6.3 indicates a noticeable spike in EDP in 1974. Does this indicate an appreciation of natural capital and an environmental improvement? Not necessarily; in fact, this spike is mainly a result of a dramatic increase in world oil prices resulting from the 1973–1974 Arab oil embargo rather than a change in the actual oil reserves in Indonesia. Similarly, in some years, the total volume of timber decreased but the market price went up, resulting in an increase in the overall value of timber resources. This increase in value masks the physical degradation of timber resources. So if we measure the value of natural capital at market prices, we may lose important information regarding the actual physical stock of those resources.*

Since this pioneering study, many countries have attempted to arrive at a valuation of their natural resources and environment (see Box 6.4). Similarly, the World Bank has developed an indicator of adjusted net savings, which seeks to measure what a society is truly saving for its future, starting with net savings (gross savings minus manufactured capital depreciation) and making adjustments for education, pollution, and the depreciation of natural capital.[11]

5.2 Valuing Environmental Factors

If assigning a monetary value to manufactured assets that are used for only a few years is difficult, think about how much more difficult it is to determine a dollar or euro measure for natural assets! Consider, for example, the value of uranium reserves still in the ground. Perhaps uranium will become more valuable a hundred years in the future because countries turn increasingly to nuclear power. Or the price of uranium may fall in the future as countries, concerned about safety and the disposal of nuclear wastes, explore other energy sources instead. The discovery of previously unknown mineral deposits, changes in policies, shifts in consumer demand, and new technologies

---

* Various suggestions have been made to overcome this barrier. For example, rather than using current market prices in a given year, one could use a five-year moving average to smooth out price spikes and dips.

are among the factors that make predicting the future over the long term very difficult and thus make it very hard to determine the value of many assets.

Other assets are difficult to value because, although we have a sense that overall ecological balance is important to human as well as other life on the planet, some forms of natural capital have no apparent *market* value. Biologists tell us, for example, that in recent decades, there has been a worldwide decline in populations of amphibians (frogs, toads, and salamanders), along with a large increase in deformities in these animals. Clearly, degradation of the natural environment is occurring. But since the market value of most frog species is zero, there are wide disagreements about how—or even whether—a monetary value can be put on these losses.*

BOX 6.4 ENVIRONMENTAL ACCOUNTING IN CHINA

In 2004, China's State Environmental Protection Agency (SEPA) announced that it would undertake a study to estimate the cost of various types of environmental damage. The initial findings released in 2006 indicated that environmental costs equaled about 3 percent of China's GDP. The report was widely criticized because it failed to include numerous categories of environmental damage such as groundwater contamination. Shortly afterward, Zhu Guangyao, the deputy chief of SEPA, released a separate report that concluded that environmental damage was closer to 10 percent of China's GDP—a value similar to what many observers were expecting.

In a 2007 report jointly produced by the World Bank and SEPA, the health and nonhealth costs of air and water pollution alone were estimated to be 5.8 percent of China's GDP.

The results indicate that much of China's recent economic growth has been partially offset by increased resource depletion and pollution. Recognizing the costs of environmental damage, the Chinese government set targets in 2006 for such variables as energy consumption per unit of GDP, releases of major air pollutants, and total forest cover. China's investment in pollution control and renewable energy is growing rapidly. However, the Chinese government's efforts to develop green GDP measures have abated somewhat in recent years, and some of the targets that were set in 2006 were not met.

Further analysis of the cost of pollution and resource depletion in China can help the government implement policies that achieve true human development.

Past policies and decisions have been made in the absence of concrete knowledge of the environmental impacts and costs. [New], quantitative information based on Chinese research under Chinese conditions [can] reduce this information gap. At the same time . . . substantially more information is needed in order to understand the health and nonhealth consequences of pollution, particularly in the water sector.

Source: World Bank and SEPA, 2007, *Cost of Pollution in China*, p. xix.

---

* Going beyond the "existence value" that some people would ascribe to amphibians, others use the analogy of how canaries are used in coal mines. Given their high sensitivity to air quality, canaries in distress indicate the danger of bad air before it rises to the level that causes humans to lose consciousness. Amphibians are highly sensitive to ground and water pollutants, including chemicals that are common in consumer products; their situation may be an important warning about dangers to human beings. But this does not resolve the question of how to value them.

As an example, suppose that a hillside is stripped of its forest covering, and the wood is sold as pulp for paper making. The lack of vegetation now means that run-off from rain increases, and "Streamside," a town at the bottom of the hill, suffers flooding and has to repair many buildings. In the national accounts as currently constructed, the logging activity contributes to GDP in this year (in the form of valuable wood products), and the activity of repairing buildings is counted as an economic activity that also adds to GDP in this year.

Or consider an alternative scenario, in which the town realizes that flooding is likely and fills sandbags to line its riverbank. It thereby avoids costly repairs. But, again, both the logging and the sandbag making are counted as adding to GDP.

What is wrong with this, of course, is that the initial environmental services of the forest in terms of water retention were not counted as part of GDP. If they had been, we would have noticed that the efforts of the town did not reflect new production so much as a *shift* in production from the "nature sector" to the human sector. Had we included the "nature sector" from the beginning, our national accounts would have shown a decrease in the production of that sector (decreased water retention) offsetting the increase in production of the human sector (that is, repairing buildings or constructing sandbag barriers).

But how should we go about evaluating the environmental services received from the trees on the hillside? Normally, economists would try to value the production of water-retention services of an existing forest by looking at some places in which this value has been translated into dollar terms. Let's imagine that near Streamside there is another town, "Sandybank," which has an identical situation with identical logging, but it has avoided damage by spending €100,000 on sandbagging. Our goal is to figure out the euro value of a year's worth of water-retention services provided by the forest near Streamside.

Suppose that the cost of repairs in Streamside, after the flooding, was €5 million. If you estimate the value of the water-retention services of the hillside forest using the **damage-cost approach**, you would say that the services are worth €5 million.

However, we could also use the experience of Sandybank as the basis for our value estimate. Using the equally plausible **maintenance-cost approach**, we could say that the value of the forest's services is €100,000. (This is similar to the "replacement-cost" approach discussed earlier in the chapter.) As often happens, the two approaches do not agree—in this case, the value of the forest's services could be estimated at either €5 million or €100,000.

Economists and environmental scientists face a similar choice in many other areas—for example, whether to measure the value of unpolluted air in terms of effects of pollution on human health (damage) or in terms of the cost of pollution-control devices (maintenance). So far, some national and international agencies have adopted one convention and some the other in their experimental environmental accounts.

If the withdrawal of environmental services makes people suffer or die, then we enter the even more controversial area of trying to assign euro values to human suffering and human lives. And many environmental effects cross national lines.

damage-cost approach: assigning a monetary value to an environmental service that is equal to the actual damage done when the service is withdrawn

maintenance-cost approach: assigning a monetary value to an environmental service that is equal to what it would cost to maintain the same standard of services using an alternative method

What is the monetary value of a global "public good" such as a stable climate? On whose account should we tally the loss of deep-sea fisheries located in international waters?

One approach to the problem of valuation is simply to use satellite accounts, as described earlier, which can be recorded in physical terms, without monetary valuation. So, for example, we might note that the forest cover in a country has declined by 10 percent without attempting to value all the ecological functions of forests. Many governments have already committed in principle to creating such accounts for their own country, and some, such as Norway, maintain extensive satellite accounts for many resource and environmental categories.

Discussion Questions

1. In Burgess County, current irrigation methods are leading to rising salt levels in agricultural fields. As a result, the number of kilograms of corn that can be harvested per hectare is declining. If you are a county agricultural economist, what two approaches might you consider using to estimate the value of the lost fertility of the soil during the current year? What sorts of economic and technological information would you need to come up with your estimates?
2. Some people have argued that the monetary valuation of environmental costs and benefits is important because "any number is better than no number"— without valuation, these factors are omitted from GDP accounts. Others say that it is impossible to express environmental factors adequately in euro terms. What are some valid points on each side of this debate? How do you think this debate should be resolved?

6. CONCLUSION: MEASURING ECONOMIC WELL-BEING

No one—and especially not their creators—would argue that alternative macroeconomic indicators have been perfected. It is quite possible to argue about whether damage cost or replacement cost should be used in evaluating environmental services, for example, or whether more direct measures of poverty should be included in the HDI. Much is still open for discussion.

No single approach has emerged as the "best" way to adjust, replace, or supplement GDP. As we have seen, any macroeconomic indicator involves numerous assumptions. One of the strengths of some of the new measures is that they allow users to see how the results change under different assumptions. For example, the BLI allows users to adjust the weights on each of the 11 well-being dimensions according to their personal preferences. Some have suggested that the best approach is to use multiple indicators, along the lines of the "dashboard" analogy mentioned earlier. One thing is clear: reliance on a single traditional GDP measure omits or distorts many crucial variables. Thus all the alternative approaches discussed in this chapter have some value in providing broader perspectives on the measurement of well-being.

DISCUSSION QUESTIONS

1. Of the various alternative indicators presented in this chapter, which one would you advocate as the best approach for measuring economic well-being? What do you think are the strengths and weaknesses of this indicator?

2. Suppose that your national government officially adopted your preferred indicator from the previous question. How do you think this would change specific policy debates in your country? What new policies do you think could be enacted?

REVIEW QUESTIONS

1. What are the two major contexts for economic activity?
2. What are satellite accounts?
3. What is subjective well-being (SWB), and how is it commonly measured?
4. Based on the scientific research, what is the relationship between the average level of SWB in a country and its GDP per capita?
5. Do average levels of SWB increase as a country develops economically?
6. What are some of the main critiques of GDP as a measure of well-being?
7. What is the Europe 2020 scoreboard, and what does it include?
8. In how far has the EU made progress reaching the Europe 2020 targets?
9. What is the Better Life Index, and how is it measured?
10. What is the Human Development Index?
11. What are some examples of household production?
12. What is the difference between the replacement-cost method and the opportunity-cost method for valuing household production?
13. What are the three main functions of natural systems?
14. What is environmentally adjusted net domestic product?
15. What are the potential problems with estimating environmental impacts in monetary terms?
16. What is the damage-cost approach to estimating the value of environmental services?
17. What is the maintenance-cost approach to estimating the value of environmental services?

EXERCISES

1. Describe in a short paragraph why measures of *output* do not always measure *well-being*. Include some specific examples beyond those given in the text.
2. Indicate whether each of the following actions or impacts would increase GDP.
   a. An individual purchases bottled water to avoid a contaminated municipal water supply.
   b. An individual obtains her drinking water from a water fountain at her workplace to avoid a contaminated municipal water supply.

    c.   A homeowner pays a lawn-care company for landscaping services.

    d.   A neighbor agrees to help a homeowner with landscaping work in exchange for assistance with plumbing work.

    e.   A paper company employs workers to plant trees.

    f.   An environmental organization provides volunteers to plant trees.

3.   Go to the European Union's "Europe 2020" Web site. Locate the scoreboard for your country. Answer the following questions:

    a.   Which dimensions have improved compared to 2008? Which have deteriorated?

    b.   For which indicators do you believe meeting the targets by 2020 is realistic?

    c.   What explains the improvements you can observe? Is it a genuine improvement or rather an unwanted side effect of other factors (such as a drop of energy consumption in a deep recession)?

4.   Go to the OECD's Web site for the Better Life Index (www.oecdbetterlifeindex.org). Note that you can adjust the weights applied to each of the 11 well-being dimensions using a sliding scale. Adjust the weights based on your personal opinions. To which factors do you assign the most weight? To which factors do you assign the least weight? Briefly summarize the rationale for your weights. Also, which countries rank the highest according to your weighted BLI?

5.   The UNDP *Human Development Report* is available at its Web site (www.undp.org). Consult this report, and choose a country that is not included in Figure 6.2. Write a paragraph describing this country's performance on the HDI as well as on three other indicators reported in the tables (such as inequality, HIV rates, or malnourishment).

6.   Suppose that you buy a bread-making machine, flour, and other foodstuffs, take them home, and bake bread with a group of young children who are in your care (unpaid). How would these activities be accounted for in current GDP accounting? How might they be accounted for in an expanded account that includes household production?

7.   Estimate how much time you spend each week doing two unpaid household production tasks (e.g., cleaning, cooking, or repairs). Then locate data on the typical wages paid to workers who perform these tasks on the Eurostat Web site (http://ec.europa.eu/eurostat/web/labour-market/earnings). Based on this data, what is the monetary value of your weekly household production for these tasks?

8.   Which of the following describe a resource function of the natural environment? An environmental service function? A sink function?

    a.   A landfill

    b.   A copper mine

    c.   Carbon dioxide (a byproduct of combustion) entering the atmosphere

    d.   Wild blueberries growing in a meadow

    e.   A suitable temperature for growing corn

    f.   A view of the Grand Canyon

9.   In 2011, the *Deepwater Horizon* oil spill in the Gulf of Mexico caused heavy damage to the fishing and tourism industries of Louisiana and other coastal states. In addition, there were long-term ecological impacts on fish and wildlife. Describe how this might be accounted for in the 2011 national accounts of the United States, if they were environmentally adjusted:

    a.   In terms of depreciation of assets

    b.   In terms of flows of produced goods and services. (Describe in detail how two approaches to assigning dollar values might be applied.)

10. Consumption of oil, gas, and coal currently fuels the EU economy but also has other effects. How might the following be accounted for in the respective national accounts, if they were environmentally adjusted?

    a. Depletion of domestic oil, natural gas, and coal reserves
    b. Release of greenhouse gases into the atmosphere
    c. Smoggy air that hides scenery and makes outdoor activity unpleasant

11. Match each concept in Column A with a definition or example in Column B.

Column A	Column B
a. Depreciation of natural capital	1. Valuing time at the wage that someone gives up
b. Satellite accounts	2. Comparison with GDP supports the diminishing marginal utility of income
c. An indicator of well-being including 11 dimensions	3. Costs of cleaning up a toxic waste site
d. An example of nonmarket production	4. The value of fish killed by toxic waste
e. Opportunity-cost method	5. Government production
f. Subjective well-being	6. The effect on copper reserves of copper mining
g. Maintenance costs	7. Better Life Index
h. Defensive expenditures	8. The service performed by a garbage dump
i. A way of measuring well-being (not production) using dollar amounts	9. Cleanup costs following an oil spill
j. Damage costs	10. Monetary or physical measures that can be related to GDP
k. Sink function	11. Europe 2020 scorecard
l. An example for the dashboard approach	12. Genuine Progress Indicator

NOTES

1 John Helliwell, Richard Layard, and Jeffrey Sachs, "World Happiness Report," www.earth. columbia.edu/sitefiles/file/Sachs%20Writing/2012/World%20Happiness%20Report.pdf.

2 Joseph E. Stiglitz, Amartya Sen, and Jean-Paul Fitoussi, *Report by the Commission on the Measurement of Economic Performance and Social Progress*, 2009, p. 16. Retrieved from www. stiglitz-sen-fitoussi.fr/en/index.htm.

3 Robert Ingelhart, Roberto Foa, Christopher Peterson, and Christian Welze, "Development, Freedom, and Rising Happiness," *Perspectives on Psychological Science* 3(4) (2008): 264–285.

4 Karma Ura, Sabina Alkire, Tshoki Zangmo, and Karma Wangd, *A Short Guide to Gross National Happiness Index* (Thimpu, Bhutan: Centre for Bhutan Studies, 2012).

5 Yvonne Rüger and Johanna Varjonen, "Value of Household Production in Finland and Germany: Analysis and Recalculation of the Household Satellite Account System in both Countries," National Consumer Research Center Working Paper 118, Helsinki, 2008.

6 Benjamin Bridgman, Andrew Dugan, Mikhael Lal, Matthew Osborne, and Shaunda Villones, "Accounting for Household Production in the National Accounts, 1965–2010," *Survey of Current Business* (May 2012): 23–36.

7 A prominent advocate of this view is Marilyn Waring, author of *If Women Counted* (San Francisco: Harper and Row, 1988).

8 See Statistics Sweden, "Harmonised European Time Use Survey," undated, retrieved from: https://www.h5.scb.se/tus/tus/default.htm.

9 Robert Repetto, William Magrath, Michael Wells, Christine Beer, Farbizio Rossini, *Wasting Assets: Natural Resources in the National Income Accounts* (Washington, DC: World Resources Institute, 1989).

10 The analysis actually refers to EDP as "NDP," which the study authors called "adjusted net domestic product." But to avoid confusion with the more common usage of the term "net domestic product"—only deducting for fixed capital depreciation—we call their environmentally adjusted values EDP.

11 See World Bank, "A More Accurate Pulse on Sustainability", June 5, 2013, retrieved from: http://www.worldbank.org/en/news/feature/2013/06/05/accurate-pulse-sustainability.

Chapter 7

The Structure of the European Economy

If the economy of the 28 member states of the European Union (as of 2016) were considered as one single country, it would compete neck and neck with the U.S. economy to be the largest economy in the world. In 2015, it produced €14.6 trillion in final goods and services—about 22 percent of the total global economic production as measured by GDP of all the world's countries. The largest share of this production came from the euro area, which recorded a GDP of €10.4 trillion—still almost 16 percent of global output. Even the largest of the European countries are dwarfed in comparison. Germany, Europe's largest economy, recorded a GDP of €3 trillion (4.5 percent of global GDP) and Britain a GDP of £1.9 trillion (about €2.6 trillion, 4 percent of global GDP).

In order to understand in more detail how a national economy functions, in this chapter, we take a closer look at the economy of the European Union, the euro area, and some of the most important European countries individually. While of course the EU is not a country, its integrated economy bears many characteristics of a national economy (for more on this, see Chapter 14). We will here consider the EU including the United Kingdom. While Britain decided to leave the EU in 2016, its economy is still very closely integrated with that of the Union, and official statistics up to the date of the actual exit include Britain as part of the EU.

In some instances, even analyzing a national economy or an economy of a supranational region such as the EU requires thinking beyond the countries' borders, because the management of a country's natural resources or financial system can affect the welfare of other countries or the entire planet. Thus while our discussion in this chapter focuses on the European economies, at times we consider these countries in a broader international framework.

Although the European economies have *grown* significantly over time, they have also *changed*. An elaboration of these changes also provides more historical context to our study of macroeconomics. A clear example is the role of agriculture. For most of European history, most people worked as small farmers. As late as 1900, in many European countries, still roughly half of the workforce was employed in agriculture. Today, the European Union as a whole is one of the world's major agricultural producers, but only around 4 percent of the workforce is directly engaged in agriculture. What is the rest of the workforce doing? You may or may not be surprised to know that around 70 percent of the workforce is engaged in producing "services" of one kind or another, with about 7 percent working in government administrations, while as of 2015, fewer than a quarter were employed in manufacturing, energy production, and construction.* This chapter provides some insight into what is going on in this complex macroeconomy.

1. THE THREE MAJOR PRODUCTIVE SECTORS IN AN ECONOMY

1.1 A Quick Review of Categories

Although macroeconomics often considers "the economy" as a whole, it is very far from being a homogeneous entity. We have already considered some ways to classify a macroeconomy into smaller units.

- In Chapter 1, we described *four essential economic activities*: production, distribution, and consumption of goods and services, and resource maintenance.
- In Chapter 3, we defined the *three economic spheres:* core, business, and public purpose.
- In Chapter 5, we saw that the European national accounts classify the economy into *five accounting sectors:* households, nonfinancial corporations, government, financial corporations, and the foreign sector.

The traditional accounting division by sector, explained in Chapter 5, was a way of defining groups according to *who* produces goods and services. In this chapter, we turn to different classification groups, which we refer to as **output sectors**, based on *what* is being produced. This is slightly confusing, but it is important to remember that these sectors are not the same ones discussed in Chapter 5.

The three productive sectors that constitute any national economy are called primary, secondary, and tertiary. The **primary sector** involves the harvesting and extraction of natural resources and rudimentary processing of these raw materials. Industries in the primary sector include agriculture, commercial fishing, and the timber industry. Mining is sometimes also considered as part of the primary sector but is sometimes counted toward the secondary sector. Generally, the products produced in the primary sector are not sold directly to households for final consumption but to manufacturers as inputs. For example, the wheat grown, harvested, sorted, and dried in the primary sector would be sold to milling and baking companies in the secondary sector, which would then process the wheat into bread.

The **secondary sector** involves converting the outputs of the primary sector into products suitable for use or consumption. The secondary sector includes manufacturing industries such as automobile production, the chemical industry, petroleum refining, the pharmaceutical industry, and electronics production. It also includes the construction of buildings and highways and utilities such as those that generate and distribute electricity.

Finally we have the **tertiary sector**, also called the service sector. This sector involves the provision of services rather than tangible goods. The tertiary sector

output sectors: divisions of a macroeconomy based on what is being produced

primary sector: the sector of the economy that involves the harvesting and extraction of natural resources and simple processing of these raw materials into products that are generally sold to manufacturers as inputs

secondary sector: the sector of the economy that involves converting the outputs of the primary sector into products suitable for use or consumption. It includes manufacturing, construction, and utilities.

tertiary sector: the sector of the economy that involves the provision of services rather than of tangible goods

---

* The shares for employment in different sectors for the euro area are very similar to those in the European Union as a whole.

includes such services as the transportation, marketing, and retailing of physical goods. It also includes direct services without the distribution of any physical goods, such as consulting, education, technology, finance, administration, and tourism.

There is no simple mapping from the three spheres that make up the economy (as described in earlier chapters) into the three output sectors just described. Firms in the *business sphere* of the economy are distributed among all three sectors. Entities from the *public-purpose* and *core spheres* can also be classified as working in one or more of the sectors. In the core sphere, for example, a household growing food in a garden is contributing to the primary sector. Production of home-cooked jam is a secondary-sector activity. The activities of care and maintenance in the home are best understood as services—thus in the tertiary sector. Much of the work of government and nonprofit organizations (in the public-purpose sphere) is accounted for in the tertiary sector, but they may also be active in each of the other two sectors.

1.2 The Relative Size of the Output Sectors in the European Economy

So what is the relative importance of each of these sectors? As you have learned in Chapter 5, to answer such questions, economists look at the value added of a sector or the incomes generated in the sector, hence *measuring production in terms of money value of output*. The italicized explanation summarizes some of what we reviewed in Chapter 6, where we noted that percentages we can get from value added of one sector do not include work that is done without pay, such as volunteer work or child care by parents. Indeed, they leave out many other issues of importance to human well-being. Nevertheless, because in many instances the most available and consistent data is to be found in the official statistics, this chapter relies on the European System of National and Regional Accounts (ESA) to classify the three output sectors in the European Union.

This means that our discussion of the relative proportions of economic production is based on the market value of goods and services. In such an analysis, a financial service that is produced in a few minutes might "count" for more than the education produced by a primary school teacher in a year—or, to use an image cited by Adam Smith, the production of a handful of diamonds could count for more than the production of a reservoir full of water.

Based on such measures, this chapter shows that in the European Union, as in most countries, the production of physical things is a relatively small, and declining, part of the measured economy. Does this mean that we are moving toward a "dematerialized" economy, more concerned with the production of services such as communication and education than manufactured goods? Is this shift toward services good news for the environment? What does it mean for our quality of life as workers, consumers, and citizens?

Market value does not tell us everything we need to know about the human value of different goods, services, and other economic activities. In some parts of the chapter, we go beyond ESA figures to discuss the parts of the existing economy that do not show up there and also to consider issues of potentially great importance for the future that are not yet well represented in current accounts.

As you will remember from Chapters 5 and 6, while most government activity is included in ESA data, with outputs valued essentially in terms of the government's cost of procuring inputs, many nonprofit as well as most core contributions to the economy are not measured in traditional national income accounting. However, we can begin to understand the relative size of the three sectors by using ESA data.

Table 7.1 presents, based on ESA data, the market value of the annual production of the three output sectors in the European Union. We see that the tertiary sector dominates the economy of the European Union, contributing 74 percent of total GDP (close to three-fourths). Note that more than a quarter of this (or 19 percent of GDP) is in the category "public administration, defense, education, human health and social work activities," which in most countries of the European Union is mainly provided by the government. If we take a look across the EU, we see that the importance of

Table 7.1 *Value Added by Output Sector in the European Union, 2015*

Industry	Value added in billion EUR	Percent of value added
Primary Sector		
Agriculture, forestry and fishing	197	1.5
Total primary sector	197	1.5
Secondary Sector		
Manufacturing	2034	15.6
Industry other than construction and manufacturing (e.g., utilities)	447	3.4
Construction	709	5.4
Total secondary sector	3191	24.4
Tertiary Sector		
Wholesale and retail trade, transport, accommodation, and food service activities	2487	19.0
Information and communication	653	5.0
Financial and insurance activities	697	5.3
Real estate activities	1455	11.1
Professional, scientific, and technical activities; administrative and support service activities	1420	10.9
Public administration, defense, education, human health, and social work activities	2505	19.1
Arts, entertainment, and recreation; other service activities; activities of household and extraterritorial organizations and bodies	477	3.6
Total tertiary sector	9694	74.0
Total economy	26164	100.0

Source: Eurostat, Gross value added and income by A*10 industry breakdowns, 2016.

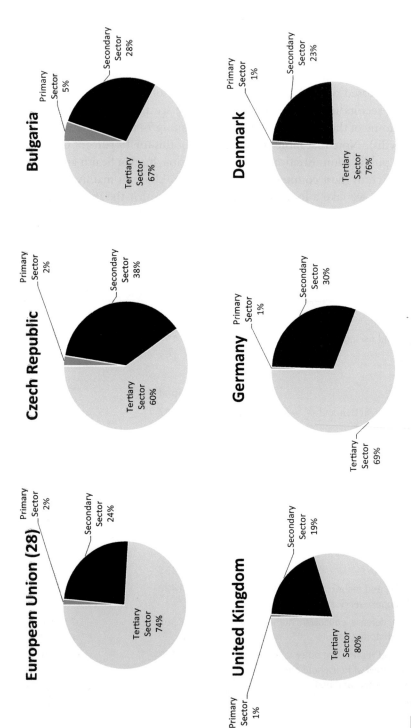

Figure 7.1 The Size of the Different Economic Sectors in Selected EU countries, in Percent of Value Added

While in all European Union countries the tertiary sector is by now the most important one, its size still differs between countries. It accounts for only slightly less than 60 percent in the Czech Republic, but is responsible for around 80 percent of value added in Great Britain.

Source: Eurostat, Gross value added and income by A*10 industry breakdowns, 2016.

the service sector differs somewhat between countries. Figure 7.1 presents the relative size of the three sectors for a handful of selected European economies. We can see that in some countries, such as the Czech Republic or Germany, manufacturing still is much more important than in the rest of the European Union, while some countries such as the UK or Denmark have especially large service sectors, and some countries such as Bulgaria still have relatively large agricultural sectors.

Does this mean that the other sectors are relatively unimportant? Not at all. The tertiary sector relies heavily on outputs from the other two sectors. Consider, for example, that a restaurant would not be able to provide food services without meat and vegetable products, furniture made from wood, and building and equipment based on rock, metal ores, or petroleum products (plastics). Some of the money that the restaurant pays for the products derived from agriculture, wood, and metal finds its way back to workers and owners in the primary sector, but the larger portion goes to secondary industries such as construction and fabrication of equipment.

Even a partner in an investment firm will need a desk in an office building, with computer and communications media, all ultimately based on outputs from the primary and secondary sectors. In the latter case, the economic value added in the tertiary sector is a giant step beyond what had been created in the other two sectors. You might wonder whether this is a sensible assessment of "value." Has the investment manager, compared to the restaurateur, contributed much more to the real wealth and well-being of the economy as is suggested by the difference in their value added? (We discuss this issue further in Section 4.2 on financialization.)

Discussion Questions

1. Think about the businesses and industries in your community. How would you classify those businesses according to each of the three sectors described above? Does your answer to this question concur with the notion that the majority of economic activity takes place in the tertiary sector?
2. Try to estimate what share of your total expenditures is spent on products from the primary, secondary, and tertiary sectors. How do you think your expenditure patterns will change in the future? For example, assuming that your income will rise after you graduate, do you think that your share of expenditures on services will increase or decrease?

2. THE PRIMARY SECTOR IN THE EUROPEAN UNION

The primary sector, as we have discussed, is concerned with the harvesting and extraction of natural resources. Countries vary widely in their natural resource endowments, and their particular resource advantages or deficits affect their economic development and future prospects. Even today, some of the countries of the European Union, such as France or Denmark, count agricultural products among their important export commodities. Others, such as the UK or Germany, have to rely on imports to feed their population. A quick look at the food, water, and energy systems illustrates the evolution of the production and use of primary-sector products in the European Union.

2.1 The Food System

Food, or the land on which it is raised, is a renewable—though, like fish, also potentially exhaustible—resource. For several millennia, European economies were agrarian economies. In 1500, in most European countries, about 75 percent of the labor force was employed in agriculture. By the mid-1700s, this figure had already dropped significantly. At that time, in England and the Netherlands, only one in two workers (50 percent) still worked in agriculture, while in most other European countries, about 60 percent of the workforce was still so employed. Now only about 4 percent of the European workforce is employed in agriculture, yet agriculture currently occupies more than 40 percent of the entire land area of the European Union and thus continues to dominate the geographic landscape of the continent. Note, however, that the share of workforce employed in agriculture varies greatly between European countries: In the UK or Luxembourg, only about 1 percent of the workforce is employed in agriculture, while for Romania, the figure still stands at 23 percent (many of whom work on small family farms that basically produce for home consumption, local sales, and extended families).

During the twentieth century, agriculture in almost all European countries underwent dramatic changes. With some differences between countries, major trends included a decline in the total farm population, a decrease in the total number of farms, an increase in average farm size, and an increase in agricultural productivity (i.e., output per acre, as well as output per worker). There are now about 11 million farms in the European Union, of which almost 40 percent are tiny, with an annual output of less than €2000. Only around 2.5 percent of the farms in the European Union have an output of more than €250,000 per year, but these large farms account together for about half of the European Union's total agricultural output. Farm receipts in the European Union on average derive a little more than half from crops and 40 percent from livestock (the rest is agricultural services).

Agricultural productivity has increased as human labor has been replaced by mechanization and as the use of modern agricultural technologies has spread. For example, since the 1960s alone, wheat yields in France have increased from around 2,200 kg per hectare to around 7,500 kg per hectare and in Portugal from less than 800 kg to more than 4,500 kg. In most European countries one farmer now provides enough food for 100 people or more.

Most of the agricultural products that people consume are not obtained directly from farmers but undergo significant processing prior to being sold to consumers. Similarly, only a tiny share of what is spent on food actually goes to farmers. While comprehensive data is not available for the EU as a whole, we can use the UK experience to gauge the importance of different parts of the agri-food sector: In the UK, out of a total consumer expenditure of about £110 billion per year on food, drink, and catering, only a little more than £10 billion end up as value added in agriculture and fishing. Significantly more goes to retailers (£30 billion) and food services—restaurants and other places serving food away from home—which account for £29 billion of value added. Food and drink processing accounts for £27 billion and wholesalers for around £12 billion. The rest goes to other sectors that sell intermediary goods to the agri-food sector, such as producers of cash registers, production lines, insurance companies, or banks.

This suggests that the impact of agriculture extends well into the secondary and tertiary sectors. Even though few people are directly employed in agriculture, in the UK, it is estimated that 15 percent of all jobs can be considered dependent on agriculture. Most of these jobs are in wholesaling, retailing, or food services.

2.2 Water

Overall, Europe has been relatively lucky when it comes to water, one of the central resources necessary for human life and a factor often underappreciated when looking at the interaction of the economic sphere with the environment. When looking at the EU as a whole, water is relatively abundant, and in general there is sufficient water available to meet demand. Unlike other regions of the world, European citizens seldom experience water shortages, and water is of a high quality. Across Europe, on average, about 500 cubic meters of fresh water per capita are taken from natural resources each year. In Northern Europe, this water is mainly used as cooling for energy production and in the manufacturing industry, while in Southern Europe, up to 80 percent of the water taken from natural resources is used for irrigation. For Europe as a whole, this so-called "abduction" of water is usually seen as sustainable, as water is a renewable resource and the amount of freshwater taken out does not exceed the rate of natural recharge (somewhat analogous to catching fish at that same rate as their populations reproduce).

However, what is true for the whole is not necessarily true for all regions and all water sources. Even in Northern Europe, rivers have frequently been overexploited, leading to damage in the rivers' ecosystems. Moreover, in recent years the number of regions which have experienced water scarcity has risen, and, increasingly, regions without a history of water scarcity have begun to be affected. While in the past, almost exclusively Southern Europe was affected by regular water shortages, today also parts of Northern Europe are hit. According to the European Environmental Agency, at least 11 percent of Europe's population and 17 percent of its territory has been affected by water scarcity, and droughts have caused damages of about €100 billion over the past three decades. Especially in Cyprus, Greece, and Spain, natural water resources are viewed as overexploited, while water levels in wells and boreholes have fallen, and in some of these countries water consumption has grown at unsustainable rates.

The problem of overexploitation carries the danger of permanently damaging the natural water supply. If below-surface aquifers in coastal areas are excessively used, the freshwater level drops and seawater flows into the aquifer. This saline intrusion diminishes the quality of the freshwater and actually might render the aquifer unusable for freshwater extraction.

Because of this danger, environmental experts have long called for more prudent management of water supplies. Fortunately there are already signs of improvement in the use of water at least in some sectors and countries. The replacement of old power plants by modern types has led to a reduction in the need of cooling water. The increase of incomes has led to the spread of modern washing machines and dishwashers, which have helped in water conservation because their water consumption is much less than that of older models (or of cleaning dishes by hand). Because of innovations and redesign, modern flush toilets (the domestic appliance with the highest water use) use only about a quarter of the water of older models. Smaller countries like Denmark and Estonia have managed to reduce household water usage significantly by increasing water prices. Technological optimists draw hope from this experience that the overexploitation of natural resources can be eventually cured by technological innovations and policy interventions.

2.3 The Energy System

Modern production and consumption systems require energy—a lot of energy. If we regarded the European Union as a single country, it would rank third in total energy consumption, behind China and the United States. In per-capita terms, the EU uses almost twice as much energy as the average person on our planet, but only about half as much as the average U.S. resident. We can also compare countries by looking at the amount of energy used per dollar or euro of GDP. A low number is generally indicative of an economy that is energy efficient in its production processes. Overall, the European Union is a bit more energy efficient than other developed countries and significantly more energy efficient than emerging market economies such as China or India.

Figure 7.2 shows the sources used to obtain energy in the European Union. We can see that the region is heavily dependent on fossil fuels; petroleum is the single most important energy source, providing nearly all the fuel for transportation. In general, carbon-based fossil fuels (petroleum, coal, and natural gas) provide more than 70 percent of all energy used in the region. As of 2013, about half of all electricity was produced by burning fossil fuels. Coal, often viewed as a fuel from an earlier industrial age, is still significant in electricity generation.

Nuclear power is primarily used to generate electricity, providing about 27 percent of the region's electricity supply. This figure is set to drop as cost considerations and the 2011 accident at the nuclear power plant in Fukushima, Japan, have caused most plans to expand nuclear power to be shelved, while Germany is phasing out nuclear energy altogether (see Box 7.1). In contrast, renewable energy's share in the energy mix has grown quickly over the past years, partly because of generous subsidies in an number of countries. While traditionally hydropower has been the most important renewable energy source, solar energy and wind power have grown strongly over the past years.

Note that European countries differ strongly in their primary sources of energy: France, for example, gets almost half of its energy (and 75 percent of its electricity)

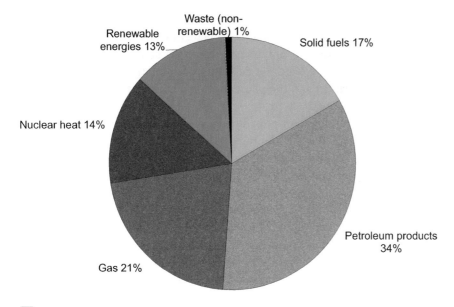

Figure 7.2 *Energy Consumption in the European Union, by Energy Source, 2014*

More than 70 percent of the energy consumed in the European Union comes from fossil fuels. The share of energy coming from renewables such as wind, solar, and geothermal energy is increasing, though, and the EU has set itself the target of producing 20 percent of its energy needs from renewable sources by 2020.

Source: Eurostat, Simplified energy balances—annual data, 2016.

from nuclear power plants and Sweden more than a third of its power from renewable sources. The Netherlands, which has natural gas resources, gets almost 40 percent of its energy needs from gas. Estonia covers almost two-thirds of its energy needs with solid fuels such as coal.

As the European Union member states have all committed to reduce their CO_2 emissions substantially over the coming decades, the trend toward renewable energies is set to continue. In principle, it is already technologically possible to produce a large share of energy needs even for industrialized economies from renewable sources. In 2010 the German Federal Environment Agency presented a blueprint on how by 2050 Germany could cover all its electricity needs from renewables. While reaching this goal would require significant investments, the agency's simulation underlined that, even for a country like Germany with a lot of manufacturing industries and suboptimal conditions for some renewables (large parts of the country tend not to get much sun during the winter), a complete shift to renewables is feasible.

Renewables have another advantage for the European Union: Their use lowers the region's dependence on imports from other parts of the world. While some countries such as the UK or the Netherlands have some oil and gas reserves, and some of the Central and Eastern European countries still have large reserves of coal, overall the EU has to import the largest share of its energy sources, including fuel for nuclear power plants. In 2013, and even taking into account the production of renewable energy, the European Union had to import fuel for about 53 percent of its energy needs. In the 1980s, the corresponding figure had only been around 40 percent. Reasons for this growing import dependence have been the depletion of domestic oil and gas reserves (in Britain and the Netherlands) and the phasing out of the use of domestic coal (for both ecological and cost reasons).

A common fallacy is that the European Union obtains most of its imported oil from the Middle East. In fact, most of the region's oil imports come from neighboring countries. The largest supplier of oil to the European Union in 2013 was Russia, which delivered about a third of the EU's oil imports. Norway has been the second most important country of origin for oil imports, with a share of 11 percent, followed by Nigeria with 9 percent. Similarly, natural gas comes mainly from Russia (41 percent), Norway (32 percent), and Algeria (14 percent).

Although energy *use* permeates every aspect of economic activity in the European Union, the *production* of energy currently employs only about 1.5 million workers, or about 0.7 percent of the employed workforce, and directly contributes a similar small share to GDP. Yet fluctuations in energy supply and prices can have significant impacts on economy-wide variables such as GDP growth, inflation, and employment. Increases in energy prices lead to downstream increases in the price of many other products and higher inflation rates. Dramatic energy price increases in recent decades, particularly in the price of oil, have precipitated recessions at both the national and international levels.

BOX 7.1 THE DILEMMAS AROUND NUCLEAR ENERGY

In many areas, European economies have been seeing a convergence in their economic policies over the past years. Not so when it comes to energy. While in all EU countries renewable energies (e.g., wind, solar, biomass) have gained market shares, the official approach to the desired energy mix differs widely, which is most evident when it comes to the use of nuclear power.

After a nuclear accident in the U.S. plant Three Mile Island in 1979 and the meltdown in the Ukrainian Chernobyl plant in 1986, in many EU countries, popular movements formed to protest against the civil use of nuclear power. As a consequence, a number of countries decided to phase out nuclear power. The Swedish parliament decided in 1980 not to build any new nuclear reactors. Italy closed down its nuclear reactors after a referendum in the second half of the 1980s. In Germany, a coalition government by the Social Democrats and the Greens negotiated a phasing out of nuclear energy with power companies in 2000.

Yet in the first decade of the 2000s, and with the increasing awareness of the threat of climate change caused by carbon dioxide emissions (which are a consequence of fossil fuel combustion), some governments had second thoughts. In 2010, the German center-right government under chancellor Angela Merkel allowed energy companies to keep their nuclear power plants running for longer than what had been initially agreed. The Italian government under prime minister Silvio Berlusconi also decided in 2008 to rethink the country's exit from nuclear power.

Then, in early 2011, a strong earthquake followed by a tsunami caused a nuclear meltdown at the Fukushima plant in Japan. Shell-shocked by these events, the German government decided almost immediately to make another U-turn in its energy policy and close all of the country's nuclear reactors by 2022. In Italy, in the summer of 2011, in a referendum, more than 90 percent of the Italians cast their votes against Berlusconi's plans for building new nuclear plants.

In contrast, in Sweden, a center-left coalition in 2016 negotiated a compromise with the opposition to allow old nuclear reactors to be replaced with new ones, tackling the dilemma that currently 40 percent of electricity in Sweden is produced by nuclear plants. The scheduled closure of these plants in the coming years would have necessitated the construction of new fossil-powered plants, which in turn would have endangered Sweden's targets for the reduction of greenhouse gases.

In France, also, nuclear power will remain important over the coming decades. In 2016, about 75 percent of its electricity was produced by nuclear power plants, and while the parliament in 2015 passed a law with goals for shifting energy production toward renewables, France continues to plan new nuclear reactors, and the government still projects nuclear power to make up as much as 50 percent of electricity production by 2025.

Sources: Guy Dinmore, "Voters reject Berlusconi reforms," *Financial Times,* June 13, 2011; Rose Jacobs, "Germany's burdensome shift to renewables," *Financial Times,* October 22, 2014; Richard Milne, "Boost to nuclear energy as Sweden agrees to build more reactors," *Financial Times,* June 10, 2016.

Discussion Questions

1. How do you obtain most of your food? Does it come from a supermarket, or do you get some from a farmers' market or grow your own? Are you surprised to learn that less than a tenth of what you spent on food goes to the primary sector, where the food is actually produced?
2. Do you think that the heavy dependence of the European Union on fossil fuels for energy is a problem? How likely is it that this might change in the future?

3. THE SECONDARY (INDUSTRIAL) SECTOR IN THE EUROPEAN UNION

When asked what makes up an economy, many people think first of manufacturing. And although the share of GDP from manufacturing has been declining in many European Union countries for several decades, the European Union remains a major manufacturer. In fact, when looked at as if it were one country, the EU in 2015 was the world's second largest manufacturer by value added, just slightly behind China and significantly ahead of the United States of America. The European Union has about 2.1 million manufacturing enterprises, which together employ about 33.5 million people.

The secondary sector includes construction and utilities as well as manufacturing. Together, these industries comprise 24 percent of GDP in the European Union (Table 7.1) and employ about 23 percent of the workforce, with about 16 percent in manufacturing and the rest in construction and utilities.

3.1 Construction and Housing

The construction industry is particularly affected by macroeconomic conditions and has a particular impact on the macroeconomy, as has been evident in the run-up to and aftermath of the global financial crisis. Construction is especially sensitive to changes in the financing conditions of households, to changes in house prices, and to changes in the government's investment spending (which often is in roads, tracks, and public buildings). In the 2000s, a number of European Union countries such as Ireland and Spain experienced a strong increase in real estate prices. As a consequence, the construction sector expanded briskly, creating jobs and income and boosting economic growth. In Ireland, the share of value added of construction in GDP rose to almost 10 percent by 2006 (see Figure 7.3). From 2004 to 2006, each year, the construction of

Figure 7.3 *Value Added in Construction as a Share of GDP, Ireland and Euro Area, 1995–2015*

The construction sector is strongly affected by macroeconomic conditions. It also has a very strong impact on the economy as a whole. A number of euro-area countries such as Ireland experienced a real estate boom in the early 2000s, which led to strong economic growth but ended in a recession when it became clear that too many houses had been constructed.

Source: Macrobond database, 2016.

around 75,000 residential units was started. When it became obvious that house prices had grown unrealistically and that developers had built too many houses, the construction industry collapsed. By 2010, value added in construction as a share of GDP had dropped to little more than 1 percent. In that year, the construction of only 4,000 new dwellings was started. The bust in the construction sector strongly contributed to the deep recession the Irish economy went through during this time. Note that value added in construction in Ireland (and other post–real-estate-bubble countries) bottomed out in 2010 and has slowly begun to recover. But the collapse from the mid-2000s peak was so severe that even by late 2015, construction in Ireland contributed only around half as much to GDP as in the euro area as a whole.

As you can see in Figure 7.3, in the euro area as a whole, construction has been much less volatile than in individual countries. The reason is that construction was very weak in Germany when countries such as Spain and Ireland experienced a boom. Since the euro periphery has started to experience a real estate bust, construction has picked up in Germany, smoothing the aggregate of the region.

3.2   Manufacturing

Even in European countries most dominated by services such as the UK, manufacturing still accounts for around 10 percent of total value added and for a similar share in total employment. For the European Union as a whole, manufacturing is responsible for almost 16 percent of value added. Table 7.2 presents a summary of the production and employment in major manufacturing industries in the region. No single manufacturing industry dominates, but the top industries include food processing, transportation equipment (mostly automobiles), metal products, and machinery and equipment. Note that the relevance of these manufacturing industries differs from country to country. In Germany, the Czech Republic, and Hungary, the automotive industry accounts for almost 20 percent of manufacturing, while Greece, Finland, and Cyprus do not have any car industry to speak of. In contrast, in Romania, but also in Italy and Portugal, the textile industry makes up 10 to 20 percent of manufacturing value added, while this industry accounts for less than 1 percent of the manufacturing sector in Sweden. We will discuss the two sectors—textiles and automobiles—in more detail, as they underline two important trends of modern manufacturing: International specialization and cross-border production sharing.

Textiles

The production of textiles is often considered one of the central drivers of industrialization: It was in the textile industry that the Industrial Revolution in Europe showed itself most during the second half of the eighteenth century and early nineteenth century. A number of innovations such as the water frame (a water-powered cotton-spinning machine), and—shortly after—of steam-powered machines such as the power loom, turned a formerly craft-based industry into a large-scale plant-centered industry. Britain had a number of advantages that allowed it to quickly dominate the world textile

231

Table 7.2 *Manufacturing Industries in the European Union, Value Added and Employment 2013*

	Gross value added in billion EUR	Employment in million
Manufacture of . . .		
food products; beverages and tobacco products	251.4	4.8
textiles, wearing apparel, leather, and related products	66.2	2.4
wood, paper, printing, and reproduction	112.4	2.5
coke and refined petroleum products	24.3	0.1
chemicals and chemical products	126.2	1.2
basic pharmaceutical products and pharmaceutical preparations	103.6	0.6
rubber, plastic products, other nonmetallic mineral products	152.5	2.9
basic metals and fabricated metal products, except machinery and equipment	238.5	4.7
computer, electronic, and optical products	101.8	1.2
electrical equipment	93.5	1.5
other machinery and equipment	209.5	3.0
motor vehicles, trailers, and semi-trailers	182.2	2.4
other transport equipment	58.2	0.7
furniture; other manufacturing	84.1	2.1
Repair and installation of machinery and equipment	79.8	1.4
Manufacturing Total	1884.0	31.5

Source: Eurostat: National Accounts employment data by industry (up to NACE A*64), 2016.

market: It had colonies in which cotton could be cheaply procured (in many cases based on slave labor), it could sell its textiles back to these colonies (aided by Britain's ability to suppress much of indigenous textile production), and it had the legal and administrative framework in place that helped it develop a capital market to enable the financing of the purchase of expensive machinery and the construction of factories. In addition, its politicians were ready to put in place protective tariffs so that domestic textile producers were shielded from competition from (initially more advanced) Indian cotton producers. Within a few decades, thousands of plants opened in Britain, and workers were lured from the countryside to factory work in cities. While working conditions during the first years of the Industrial Revolution were rather horrible (with inhumane working hours, widespread child labor, and no work safety to speak of), this transition created the foundation for further industrialization, which later led to increases in incomes and to the improvement of living conditions in the nineteenth century.

Initially, the rest of the continent lagged behind Britain in terms of industrialization. While the basic ideas and technologies of industrial textile production spread from England to France, Switzerland, and Germany, the continent did not see a proper takeoff of its textile industry before the blockade of trade between the continent and Britain during the Napoleonic wars from 1806 to 1814. With European customers being unable to buy cotton textiles from British suppliers, they turned to domestic producers, which expanded their production strongly and, in the process, built a domestic base for further industrialization on the continent.

In other parts of the world in the twentieth century, textile production has often been seen as one of the first steps toward industrialization. Textile production is usually simple enough to set up without requiring too many domestic supply industries or machine builders, yet it is complex enough for countries to start mastering industrial production processes. In Asia, countries such as Japan, South Korea, Hong Kong, and China laid the foundation of their industrialization with a successful textile sector, which was later followed by more complex industries such as electronics, steel production, ship building, or even car production.

The competition of cheap textiles from these countries led to a decline of Western textile industries. While in the nineteenth century, Britain still dominated the global cotton market, by the late 1960s, the UK's global market share had shrunk to a little more than 2 percent. Today, as in many other European countries, the textile industry in Britain has all but disappeared. In 2013, a little more than 100,000 workers (out of almost 32 million employed persons) still worked in the textile industry in Britain. In the EU as a whole in 2014, 2.4 million people worked in textile and apparel production, but this employment was very unevenly distributed. In countries such as Germany, Denmark, or Sweden, the textile industry adds less than 1.5 percent to the manufacturing sector's value added. In Bulgaria, Romania, and Italy, in contrast, it produces more than 10 percent of manufacturing value added, and in Portugal, it accounts for more than 18 percent of manufacturing value added, with similar shares of the manufacturing workers employed in the industry. However, the textile industries in these countries also have come under pressure from Asian competitors.

Asian imports can be produced at lower cost than domestic goods primarily because of lower wages. China currently dominates global textile manufacturing, but this may be changing. In recent years, textile manufacturing has been leaving China for countries with even lower wages, including Bangladesh, Cambodia, and India.

Textiles and clothing are outstanding examples of a category of manufactured items that (1) are labor intensive (i.e., their production requires a large number of labor hours in proportion to the cost of other inputs) and (2) can be produced with large numbers of unskilled laborers. These characteristics create conditions in which countries with large populations of poor people can compete on the international market.

Automobiles

In contrast to textiles, the automobile industry is a traditional manufacturing sector that has held up quite well in the European Union. In 1950, shortly after World War II, the share of Western Europe in global car production was only slightly more than 10 percent. In the 1950s and 1960s, Europe increased its market share. From the 1970s onward, other competitors, mainly from Asia, entered the market. Yet even though Europe has seen a relative decline in the production of automotives, in 2015, the European Union's share in global production of passenger cars still was more than 20 percent. If the EU were regarded as one country, it would be the second-largest car producer in the world, just behind China. The United States, which has a bigger market than the EU, is only a distant third when it comes to car production. What is more, the European automobile industry today is not only producing for the home market but is still among the world's biggest exporters. Two of the world's largest automotive groups, Volkswagen and Renault-Nissan, have their home (at least partly) in Europe.

For some of the European Union member states, motor vehicle production is still the most important manufacturing industry. In the EU as a whole, 2.4 million people work in the production of motor vehicles, and additional jobs are sustained in supplier industries (such as the producers of equipment for car manufacturers). In Germany, the Czech Republic, Hungary, and Slovakia, roughly a fifth of manufacturing value added takes place in the automotive industries.

European automobile makers long benefited from their home markets with a large, relatively prosperous population in which technological innovations could be tested. There is a long history of European customers showing a preference for domestically built cars. Volkswagen, Mercedes, and BMW have a large market share in Germany, while Fiat long dominated the market in Italy, and Citroen, Peugeot, and Renault sold well in France. Moreover, in contrast to the United States, petrol has been expensive in Europe so that European car builders concentrated more on the development of small, economical cars that were better suited for exports to third markets. In the decades since the fall of communism, and with the enlargement of the European Union toward the East, Western European automotive companies benefited from cheap labor in the new member states; basically all large European automotive groups shifted part of their production into Central European countries such as the Czech Republic, Hungary, or Slovakia. Car builders exploited cheap labor in this region in two ways: First, some large car groups bought Central and Eastern European brands, under which they produced low-cost versions of their own cars. Second, most car companies started to source certain parts and components from these formerly communist countries to lower their overall production costs (see Box 7.2). This cross-border production sharing has only been possible because of the European Union. As there are no tariffs and no customs controls between EU countries (even if, for some countries, passports are still checked when people move across borders), parts and components can be shipped across borders several times in the production process without significant costs or delays. Only because the European Union includes countries with high-skill and high-wage workers and others with low-wage workers, differences in costs could be used to increase the competitiveness of the car builders the way they did.

However, even the European car industry has been faced with a number of challenges: Since the onset of the global financial and economic crisis in 2009 and the euro crisis that followed from 2010 onward, car markets have been depressed in many European countries. With unemployment at record levels in Spain, Greece, and Italy, many households have cut back their consumption and have especially delayed car purchases. This has hurt European car producers, which could rely less on their home markets than in the past. Another challenge for European car builders is the question of how to deal with recent technological innovations, namely electric cars and self-driving cars. Electric cars are technically quite different from traditional petrol cars. For example, they usually do not have a transmission. In the past, European car builders have often been seen to be especially good and experienced in building high-quality, long-lasting transmissions. With the shift toward e-mobility, this competitive edge may be lost. When it comes to self-driving cars, U.S. companies such as Google and Tesla have long been seen as leading. It thus remains to be seen whether Europe can defend its automotive industry against competitive challenges.

3.3 Where Have All the Manufacturing Jobs Gone?

According to some measures, the size of the secondary sector in Europe has grown over the past half century. For example, the value added from manufacturing, when adjusted for inflation, is much bigger today than it was in the 1960s. For the United Kingdom (which for many is the prime example of an economy having transformed from an industry-based economy into a service-based economy), real value added in manufacturing today is about 50 percent higher than in the 1960s. In France, manufacturing value added adjusted for inflation today is about four times as large as in 1960. However, as we have seen, manufacturing's share of GDP has declined because the size of the service sector has grown so much.

Importantly, too, even though the value of manufacturing output has grown, *employment* in manufacturing has declined. While we do not have good data for the EU as a whole on this issue for an extended period of time, we know that employment in manufacturing has fallen quite substantially over the past half century in all important member states. As shown in Figure 7.4, while there were some ups and downs, in many European countries, total employment in manufacturing generally increased from 1960 until the mid-1970s. Since then, manufacturing employment has steadily declined in many countries. An exception is Germany, where from the time of its reunification in 1990, about a quarter of the jobs in the manufacturing sector were lost, but then that employment figure stabilized since the mid-2000s. From the late 1970s until 2015, Britain lost about 60 percent of its manufacturing jobs and France almost half of its manufacturing jobs.

So where have all the manufacturing jobs gone? The story is slightly different from country to country: Germany, where still one in five workers work in the manufacturing sector, is different from Britain, where only one in ten workers is employed by these industries. So, obviously more manufacturing jobs have disappeared from Britain than from Germany.

A common factor for all countries is a strong increase in productivity in the secondary sector, as industries managed to substitute manufactured capital (i.e., machinery and automation) for human labor. **Manufacturing productivity** is commonly measured as an index of the value of the goods produced per hour of labor. Manufacturing productivity in basically all industrialized countries over the past few decades has

manufacturing productivity: an index of the value of the goods produced per hour of labor in the manufacturing sector

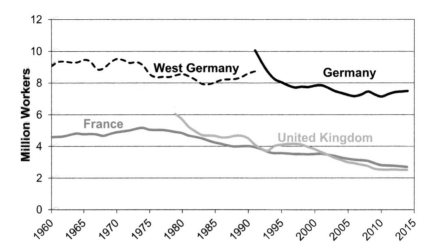

Figure 7.4 *Employment in Manufacturing in Germany, France, and the United Kingdom, 1960–2014*

The number of manufacturing jobs in most European countries has declined from the 1970s onward. While the loss of manufacturing jobs continued in France and the United Kingdom in the 2000s, German manufacturing employment has been relatively stable since the early 2000s.

Source: AMECO database, 2016.

been growing faster than overall business productivity. This increase of productivity in industrialized countries has gone hand in hand with international specialization and even stronger productivity growth in poorer countries, and especially in China. The production of light manufactures such as textiles and consumer electronics has almost completely been moved to poorer countries, especially Asia, where they could be produced very cheaply thanks to a combination of low wages and modern machineries. European companies, in contrast, now tend to produce more sophisticated manufacturing goods—high-end cars or specialized machines. The result is that consumer goods produced in Asia have become much cheaper relative to other goods and services. In 1960, the average German worker needed to save two months' worth of wages in order to buy a simple black-and-white television. Today, the average German worker needs to save only three days' wages to buy a large flat-screen color television.

The service sector, in contrast, has not seen similar increases in productivity. A barber today is not able to cut the hair of significantly more customers than 40 years ago. In addition, new services have been developed, and the health sector has become much more important for the economy as a whole. As a result, the relative importance of manufacturing jobs in European (and in fact all industrialized) economies has fallen.

Within the EU, another factor has played a role: There has been a degree of specialization between countries. Germany's economy has specialized in sophisticated manufactured goods and is now exporting many more manufactured goods to the rest of the EU than it imports. Slovakia and the Czech Republic have specialized in less sophisticated manufactured goods such as cheaper cars. In contrast, countries of Southern Europe such as Spain, Italy, and Greece have specialized in the sale of tourist services (counted as exports) to customers from Northern Europe. Britain has specialized in the sale of financial and professional services to the rest of the European Union. This specialization explains partly why manufacturing employment has held up relatively well in Germany but not in Britain or Greece. In this context, it is sometimes discussed whether Germany's huge trade surpluses constitute a "beggar-thy-neighbor policy," as one can argue that Germany's good manufacturing employment performance came at the expense of other countries (the question of trade imbalances will be covered more in detail in Chapter 14). It is also sometimes discussed whether the specialization in certain goods or services might be more beneficial than in others. For example, as discussed, some goods such as textiles come under pressure from competition of low-wage countries. A specialization in these sectors might make economic growth in the future more difficult. On the other hand, specialization in high-tech industries might help to gain more technological know-how and make economic growth easier in the future.

What does this mean for human well-being? An economist looking forward to this situation one or two hundred years ago might have said that this is exactly what progress is supposed to be about—that people can get more of what they want with less work and that they can work in the relatively comfortable environments of many service jobs instead of noisy, polluted, strenuous, and hazardous manufacturing jobs. However, in many countries, the accelerating shift of jobs from the secondary to the tertiary sector has gone hand in hand with a deterioration in the economic security and sometimes the remuneration of jobs. Unions used to be relatively strong in manufacturing industries, where workers could easily organize in large factories. In the service sector, the degree of unionization has been much lower. As a consequence, workers' bargaining power tends to be lower and job tenure is shorter. Moreover, while males with low educational attainment could earn decent wages in the manufacturing sector, this holds less and less true in today's service sector. As will be discussed further in the next section, many jobs in the service sector are not well paid (while others are well paid but are unattainable for people with low educational attainments). Many workers hence feel a deterioration of their living standards, and they often see this trend connected with the rise of the tertiary sector, even though there might be different explanations for growing inequality, as we will discuss in Chapter 8.

BOX 7.2   IS A PORSCHE STILL A GERMAN CAR?

In the mid-2000s, a dispute among economists broke out in how far Germany still had a manufacturing future. While according to international statistics, Germany had just gained world market shares and had become the world's largest exporter of goods in 2003, the labor market performance remained grim, with unemployment at record levels.

Hans-Werner Sinn, then president of the renowned Ifo economic research institute, put forward the hypothesis that despite the brilliant export performance, German manufacturing industries were not competitive. According to his reading, the German export performance was only still good because German companies had started to buy cheap parts from Central and Eastern Europe, and were only doing the final stage of assembly in Germany, using the brand "Made in Germany" to sell . In parallel, value added and employment in Germany were "hollowing out," according to Sinn. As an example, Sinn picked the Porsche Cayenne, an expensive SUV built by the German premium car maker Porsche. According to some calculations, almost 70 percent of production costs of this car were actually due to manufacturing outside of Germany.

Porsche strongly objected. The company's CEO claimed that more than half of the car's production was done in Germany. Economists criticized Sinn's view of the state of German manufacturing as too gloomy and his warnings about outsourcing of parts of the production chain as misguided.

By 2016, Sinn's claim that German manufacturing had been uncompetitive had been largely discredited. In comparison to other OECD countries and especially other Western European countries such as France, the UK, and Spain, Germany still has a comparatively large manufacturing sector, both when measured in terms of value added and in terms of employment. Moreover, in contrast to these peers, Germany's manufacturing sector's share of the economy broadly remained stable between the mid-1990s and 2016.

What Sinn picked up correctly, however, is a recent trend of economic integration in Europe: Over the past decades, cross-border production networks have formed in the EU. In manufacturing, these networks have been especially important in the integration of former communist countries of Central and Eastern Europe such as Slovakia, the Czech Republic, Hungary, and Poland. Companies especially from Germany and Austria, but also from France and Italy, have acted similarly to Porsche, outsourcing some stages of production to countries with lower wages. As a result, companies benefited from lower production costs and the countries in Central and Eastern Europe from new technologies and hence impressive productivity gains. The consensus today is that these networks have made large European manufacturing companies stronger, without negative effects on overall employment in Europe.

Sources: Ferdinand Dudenhöffer, Wie viel Deutschland steckt im Porsche?, *Ifo Schnelldienst* 24/2005, pp. 3–5; *Economist*, The problem with solid engineering, May 18, 2006.

Discussion Questions

1. During the euro crisis, in many European countries, a significant decline in housing prices could be observed. However, at the same time, the number of homes sold also declined dramatically. Shouldn't the decline in housing prices have resulted in an increase in home sales, as suggested by a basic model of supply and demand?

2. Some people cite the return from the suburbs to urban areas and the lower percentage of young people getting driver's licenses as indications that "the age of the automobile is drawing to a close." Do you think that this is true? If automobile use were to fall in half over the next 15 years, what impact would this have on the economy?

4. THE TERTIARY (SERVICE) SECTOR

Early in this chapter, we gave an intuitive explanation for why, even though people are just as dependent as they have always been on the materials extracted from nature, the primary sector has shrunk in economic importance as societies have industrialized. It was not hard to explain how manufacturing came to claim a larger part of every household budget and therefore of the total economy; however, we are still left with questions about how "services" have more recently become so significant.

Even more than the other sectors, the tertiary sector cannot be defined as a homogeneous economic category. As we saw in Table 7.1, the service sector includes a wide variety of industries, including education, retail trade, financial services, insurance, waste management, health, and entertainment. The remainder of this chapter is therefore devoted to providing some basic data on the sector, with specific attention paid to the areas of retail, financial, and insurance services and human services (including health and education).

Employment trends, wages, and other measures vary considerably across different service industries. For example, one common perception is that jobs in the service sector pay poorly. While this is true for such jobs as cashiers and receptionists, it is clearly not true for such service jobs as investment bankers and lawyers. Overall, service jobs in many EU countries pay only slightly less on average than manufacturing jobs and in some countries even marginally more. In 2014, average hourly earnings in manufacturing in the United Kingdom were £15.39, while the average pay in the service industries was £15.07 per hour. For France, the respective values were €17.81 and €17.03. The difference was bigger in the Netherlands (€19.28 vs. €17.97) and Germany (€20.91 vs. €17.06). At the same time, many jobs in finance have wages that far exceed most of those in manufacturing. For the United States, it has been shown that from the 1940s to the early 1980s, average compensation in the financial sector stayed close to the average for all domestic private industries (including manufacturing and industries in all three sectors). Starting in the early 1980s, it began to rise rapidly. By 2012, average compensation in the financial sector was 25 percent higher than the nationwide average. Similar trends have been observed in Europe. In 2015, in Britain, the average pay for financial and insurance activities reached £25.39 per hour, almost 70 percent more than the average hourly earnings for the whole economy. In Germany, the finance sector paid on average €24.93, and in France €23.62—in both cases almost 40 percent more than economy-wide average earnings.

Traditionally, most international trade has involved the exchange of physical goods, but trade in services is now expanding rapidly. While it is easy to picture a physical good moving between countries, it might be harder to imagine how *services* could be internationally traded. A service is "exported" from a country if agents in that country provide a service used by an individual or organization based abroad. For example, if someone from the U.S. stays in a hotel in Paris, this is considered an "export" of accommodation services produced in France.

A service is "imported" by a country if agents in the foreign sector provide a service used by individuals or organizations based in another country. For example, if a

German manufacturer ships its goods using freighters registered in Liberia, it is said to "import" transportation services from Liberia. Between 1980 and 2015, global trade in services increased by a factor of 12.2, while trade in goods increased by a factor of 8.1. By 2015, 22.6 percent of all international trade was in services. Improvements in information technology have made services such as customer call centers, software development, and data processing more easily transferable across national boundaries in recent years. The United Nations notes that cost savings of 20 to 40 percent are commonly reported by companies that offshore their service needs to low-wage countries.

In 2015, both the European Union with 28 member states as of 2016 (EU28) and the euro area exported slightly more in services than the regions imported, and this trade surplus has been expanding in the past several years. For both the EU as a whole as well as the euro area, the largest surpluses in services (where the region exports more than it imports) are in computer and information services as well as financial services. Within both the EU28 and the euro area, the relative strength of service exports differs. Germany, for example, has traditionally run a deficit in the trade in services, mainly because of a deficit in tourism (Germans spend more money travelling abroad than foreigners coming to Germany). Britain, in contrast, is exporting many more services than it imports. The country is especially strong in exporting professional, scientific, and technical activities, information and communication services, and financial services.

4.1 Retail Services

Few manufacturers sell their products directly to consumers. Instead, manufacturers typically sell their output to retailers, perhaps also using wholesalers as intermediaries. Retailers are categorized in the service sector because they normally do not manufacture any of the goods that they sell. Prominent retailers such as Carrefour, Metro (Media Markt, Saturn, Real, and Kaufhof), or Tesco purchase virtually all their products from suppliers in the EU and in other countries.

Retail services as a whole are not becoming a larger share of the national economy, but there have been clear changes in the structure of the retail industry. From 2000 to 2011, hypermarkets (with sales area of more than 2,500 square meters) have increased their market share, as have discounters. In almost all EU countries, concentration among retailers has increased. We can use data on concentration ratios to illustrate the ascendancy of these firms. A "five-firm concentration ratio" is calculated by dividing the domestic sales of the five largest firms in an industry by the total domestic sales in the industry. This indicator has risen for most countries. However, the structure of the retail industry still differs very much between EU member states because of different preferences, regulations, and traditions. For example, in Italy, Greece, Poland, Bulgaria, and Romania, in 2011, the largest share of edible groceries was still sold in traditional, small-scale retail stores, while in the Netherlands, Denmark, and Estonia, this share was only around 10 percent. As a consequence, concentration also differed greatly between countries. In 2011, the five largest retailer groups only made up 24 percent of sales in

Italy, while the share of the five largest retailer groups in Denmark (not the same ones as in Italy) reached 83 percent.

In some countries, large retailers have come to dominate their industries by offering consumers a large number of choices and low prices. In the parlance of microeconomics, the retail industry in these countries is clearly oligopolistic, meaning that it is dominated by a small number of companies. The economic scale of the largest retailers has become so large that the behavior of individual firms has implications at the macroeconomic level. In 2012, Walmart was the world's largest retailer (and largest company) by revenue, with sales of $482 billion (more than Poland's GDP), and the world's largest nongovernment employer, with 2.3 million employees.

Some researchers believe that a major reason that productivity increased so much in the United States in the late 1990s (when productivity there increased much faster than in Europe) is a result of Walmart's pressure on suppliers to increase their efficiency. As another example of Walmart's pervasive reach, the decline of the American textiles industry can be attributed in part to Walmart's foreign sourcing of low-priced apparel. Consider that an estimated 10 percent of Chinese imports to the United States are for Walmart. Economy-wide impacts like these blur traditional distinctions between microeconomics and macroeconomics and demand new lines of research and analysis.

European retailers tend to be smaller, not least because of cultural and regulatory differences between countries, which has made rolling out a single business model across the whole continent more difficult. In 2014, Carrefour, Europe's largest European retailer, had global sales of "only" about €100 billion and about 380,000 employees. Some experts claim that the lower productivity growth observed in European retail is a result of continuously segmented markets. Others defend the model of small-scale grocery stores predominant in some EU countries as an important element of culture and tradition worth preserving even if it comes with economic costs in the form of higher grocery costs and lower productivity.

4.2 Finance and Financialization

Financial and insurance activities are often analyzed together. With a number of banking crises since the late 2000s, this sector has had a crucial impact on the European economy and will hence be presented in some detail. The most common job categories in financial and insurance activities are bank tellers, loan officers, and insurance agents. Combined, in the EU28, these sectors accounted for 5.3 percent of value added in 2015 and collectively employed more than 6 million people (about 3 percent of the workforce). In some countries the importance has been larger: In Britain, financial and insurance activities made up 7.2 percent of value added and in Luxembourg 28.4 percent. 4 percent of Britain's workforce and 10 percent of Luxembourg's workforce were employed in finance.

Moreover, for many countries, the importance of the financial sector has grown over the past decades until the onset of the financial crisis in 2008–2009. While we do not have good data for the EU as a whole or even the euro area going back over a longer period, for some individual countries, we see an increase in the importance of the financial sector over several decades: In Britain, value added in financial and insurance activities in 1970 was a mere 5 percent of GDP. It then rose to almost 11 percent in 2009 but has fallen since. In Ireland, the share rose from 8.5 percent in 1995 to more than 11 percent in 2009 and has fallen slightly to around 10 percent in 2013. Taking an even longer perspective, in the United States, from 1947 to the present, the percentage of value added from finance and insurance has more than tripled, from 2.4 percent to 7.7 percent.

Of special interest among such services today—because they are closely associated with the market dysfunctions implicated in the Great Recession—are the **financial institutions** that manage **financial assets**. A large share of these assets are not directly held by households or nonfinancial corporations but by financial institutions, which include banks, credit unions, pension and retirement funds, mutual funds, securities brokers, and insurance companies. Financial institutions are divided into two types, according to the services that they provide (though many institutions now provide both types of services). Monetary financial institutions, such as banks and credit institutions, accept deposits from the general public and then use the deposits to make loans. Other financial institutions, such as insurance companies, pension funds, brokerage firms, and mutual fund companies, sell financial products such as insurance or money management. They then invest their revenues in a variety of financial assets. Pension funds, in particular, hold extensive financial assets that they manage for the present and future benefit of retirees and workers; thus in many countries, they are the largest investors, employing the services of a variety of financial institutions.

Financial assets include stocks (shares in ownership of companies); bonds (certificates indicating that the holder has lent money to a government entity or a business, which will repay the loan over time, with interest); foreign currencies (held when the investor expects either that his own currency will depreciate or that a foreign currency will rise in relative value); and money market accounts (specially designed savings accounts at banks, which pay higher interest than normal savings accounts but often place restrictions on withdrawals or set a minimum deposit level).

According to standard economic theory, the principal function of banks and other financial institutions is to *intermediate* the movement of funds throughout the economy; specifically, they move funds between savers and investors. When we deposit money in banks, they redirect these funds back into the economy in the form of loans that pay higher rates of interest to cover the banks' costs of operation and give them a profit. When these loans are used to open new businesses or expand existing ones, resulting in increases in production and employment, intermediating institutions such as banks are helping the real economy to function. The "**real economy**" refers to the part of the economy that is concerned with actually producing goods and services, as opposed to the financial side of the economy (sometimes called "the paper economy"), whose activities focus on buying and selling on the financial markets.

Given that the primary role of the financial sector is to facilitate activities in the real economy, and given huge technology improvements this sector has made through the invention of ATMs, information technology, and online banking over the past decades,

financial institution: any institution that collects money and holds it as financial assets

financial assets: a variety of holdings in which wealth can be invested with an expectation of future return

real economy: the part of the economy that is concerned with actually producing goods and services

there is no inherent reason to expect the financial sector to grow significantly over time relative to the size of the overall economy. Yet as we have seen, the relative size of the financial sector has increased considerably. How did this happen? The explanation is complex and multidimensional and is considered further in Chapter 11 and, especially, Chapter 15. At this point, consider an image that may help you to visualize the situation.

Imagine that the financial sector is a hot air balloon; the basket tethered beneath it is the real economy (or at least that part of the real economy that is related to, and uses the services of, the financial sector). The relationship is essential for the financial sector: without such a relationship, it would just float up into the sky, without any substance. It also has value for the real economy: It gives the economy a "lift" by allocating savings to useful investments. However, since the early 1980s, a process of **financialization** has allowed the balloon to inflate more and more. Less and less of its connection to what is going on in the real economy has to do with the traditional circulation of financial capital: from production, through savings, then back to production of real-world goods and services. Instead, the connection is increasingly about the expansion of financial claims within the balloon, including "bubbles" of temporary inflation in the prices that people are willing to pay for financial assets, as well as the creation of large amounts of debt.

financialization: a process in which the financial sector of the economy is increasingly able to generate and circulate profits that are not closely related to the real economy

This can generate huge incomes for a small group of people. Part of this income is spent in the real economy, paying for luxury cars, villas, and the services of personal trainers and celebrity chefs, but much of it feeds back into the expansion inside the balloon. As the production of goods and services in the rest of the economy does not increase as quickly as the financial sector, an increasing share of goods and nonfinancial services can be bought by those who work in the financial sector or earn profits from that sector.

The simplest way of understanding the financialization that has affected many advanced economies in recent decades is as a combination of two things: (1) huge increases in debt throughout the economy along with (2) inflation in the price of assets, unconnected with any inflation in the price of real goods and services. This is what occurred in many countries until 2007, when both asset prices and debt levels throughout the economy ballooned relative to incomes. In some countries in which the financial sector was deregulated earlier, this trend had started already in the 1980s. In other countries, debt levels only started to increase in the 1990s. Until the onset of the global financial crisis, however, debt levels rose in most industrialized countries. Even after the crisis of 2008–2009, debt levels have come down only moderately and not so in all countries.

Figure 7.5 illustrates this development for the case of private household debt: In almost all EU countries, household debt as a multiple of net disposable income rose strongly over the past two decades. In the UK, household debt in 2014 stood at 156 percent of disposable income, up from 111 percent in 1997. In Portugal, household debt reached 141 percent of disposable income, almost three times as much as in 1995, when it stood at 55 percent. Germany is an outlier here, with a slight fall of household debt from 97 percent of disposable income in 1995 to 94 percent in 2014.

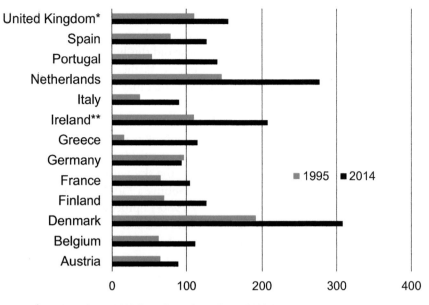

* gray bar refers to 1997 data; ** gray bar refers to 2001 data

Figure 7.5 *Household Debt as a Share of Net Disposable Income in Selected European Countries, 1995 and 2014*

In almost all EU countries, debt levels of private households increased strongly between 1995 and 2014. Most of this debt is mortgage debt, but debt from consumer loans and student loans have been increasing, too.

Source: OECD, Household debt (indicator). doi: 10.1787/f03b6469-en, 2016.

When looking at the composition of household debt, the largest share in all countries is mortgage debt, followed by consumer credit and, increasingly, student loans.

A similar upward trend can be observed when it comes to the debt levels of non-financial corporations. At the end of 2014, for the EU as a whole, financial liabilities of nonfinancial corporations stood at 287 percent of GDP. As a long time series is not available for the European Union as a whole, the trend must be approximated by looking at the individual member states: In the UK, total financial liabilities of nonfinancial corporations had risen from 215 percent in 1995 to 286 percent in 2014; in Spain, the increase was from 163 percent of GDP to 326 percent of GDP, and in France from 207 to 391 percent of GDP.

Debt levels have moderated since the financial crisis of 2008. Many households have substituted debt reduction for new spending. As discussed in Chapter 15, in some cases, declining household income and growing inequality between households played an important role in the credit boom, as consumers compensated for limited incomes by relying on credit cards and other loans to extend their ability to continue spending.

The financial economy, as we will see in Chapter 15, found ways to use household debt, especially mortgages, as collateral to expand its own activity, while regulatory easing and the rise of new kinds of financial institutions made it possible for money to be lent out with very little collateral. ("Collateral" is a valuable asset used as a basis for a loan.) A wide variety of financial firms entered the game of taking in funds and then turning them around to invest in high-yield assets.

Financial firms may sell stock (shares in the company) to raise capital, but in recent years, borrowing became a more popular way to increase the funds held by a financial firm. The higher the ratio of borrowed funds to funds contributed by stockholders, the greater a firm's financial **leverage**. Leverage essentially means using borrowed money to increase the investment power of one's own money, and it leads to higher "return on equity" (ROE), because the return can be calculated with factoring in only the (generally low) interest rates on borrowed funds that are involved. With a large cushion of borrowed funds, a financial institution could, for example, hold €1 million as collateral while lending out €25 million. These loans could go to other institutions, which, in turn, held back a few percent and lent out the rest. Such loans are described as "highly leveraged" (€1 million can leverage €25 million or more). This possibility made it appealing for banks and other financial institutions to keep borrowing more money in order to have a greater stake in other investments. However, it also created significant risks: If a firm is leveraged 25-fold, then a loss of just over 4 percent will be sufficient to bankrupt it.

leverage: the use of borrowed money to increase the investment power of one's own money

Financialization really takes hold when the loans themselves are increasingly viewed as desirable investments. This leads to a situation in which much of the financial sector is leveraging itself to invest in financial assets that are themselves different types of loans, and increasingly these loans are bundled into other complex financial instruments. To repeat a saying that is popular in the sector, "Finance mostly finances finance."* The relative size of the financial economy increases as companies substitute this type of financial investing for "real" investment (i.e., purchasing of fixed assets like machines or computers).

As noted, the two sources of hot air for the financialization balloon are debt and asset price inflation. In real markets, the price of a good or a service comes from an intersection of several considerations, including the cost of supplying it and how willing and able people are to pay for it. In financial markets, the cost of supply is often nothing more than the time and inventiveness of the manager who invents or promotes a financial asset that most people do not understand (and are most often not intended to understand). These assets can, at least for a while, be extremely profitable; hence the very large salaries received by the people who work on Wall Street or equivalent centers in London and other financial capitals.

For the United States, there are a number of facts about profits and compensation in the financial sector that have been widely reported and that underline the degree of financialization:

■ Profits in the financial sector in the United States represented 14 percent of total corporate profits in 1981; 30 years later, this figure was about 30 percent.

---

* This phrase originated with Jan Toporowski, a professor at the University of London.

- From 1948 to 1982, average compensation in the financial sector ranged between 99 percent and 108 percent of the average for all domestic private industries. This figure began to rise starting in 1983, reaching 181 percent in 2007.
- In the economy as a whole, over a 25-year period, the market value of financial assets, taken together, grew from about 4 times GDP to a little more than 10 times GDP.
- In 1970, the value of financial assets in the United States barely exceeded the value of fixed assets. The value of financial assets was 68.7 percent greater than tangible fixed assets in 1983 and rose to more than triple that level by 2009.[1]

For European countries, often long-term statistics about the size of the financial sector are not available or not comparable across countries. Moreover, the trend of financialization has been especially pronounced in the U.S. Yet to a certain extent, similar developments can be observed in some European countries. In most EU countries, the financial sector's share of total (economy-wide) profits exceed its contributions to both value added and employment. For example, in the United Kingdom, operating profits of the financial sector have regularly been more than 10 percent (and even more than 17 percent in 2009) of total operating profits in the economy even though value added in the sector has mostly been only slightly above 7 percent. Overall, in the euro area, banking assets have by now reached more than 500 percent of annual GDP. This is a huge increase compared to the size of the banking sectors that could be observed in single countries in the 1980s. In 1981, in Belgium, banking assets were a mere 112 percent of GDP, in France 60 percent of GDP, in Italy 116 percent of GDP, in Spain 101 percent of GDP, in the Netherlands 98 percent of GDP, and in Germany 103 percent of GDP.

If the cost of production in the financial sector is different from the supply side in the real economy, the demand side of the financial economy is even more different. Financial markets do not operate like markets for real goods and services, in which an increase in the price of a good tends to depress demand. In financial markets, instead, an increase in the price of an asset can spur people to borrow more, which in turn causes prices to rise further. To understand this whole system, it is important to understand that *the value of an asset is what you think someone else is willing to pay for it*. Whether the asset is a tulip bulb (as in the bizarre incident of tulip mania in the seventeenth century) or a piece of real estate or some complex bundle of derivatives, as long as the balloon is inflating, the prospective buyer of an asset may pay a price that bears no relation to anything on the ground, as long as he or she believes that the price will keep going up, and the next buyer will be willing to pay still more. When the speculative fever breaks, prices can decline even more rapidly—the financial "bubble" bursts, with bad consequences for the real economy.

The process of financialization has affected stock markets throughout the world. Average holding times for stocks have fallen as large financial institutions engage in rapid trading of stocks in search of short-term gains. Investors on the New York Stock Exchange (NYSE) held stocks for an average period of about five years in 1975, two years in 1991, but only five months in 2008.[2,3] This is in contrast to an approach that focuses on the ability of a business to generate revenues and generally involves holding stocks for longer periods. Short-term investing makes markets more vulnerable to "bubbles," when investors looking for a quick profit drive stock prices to excessive heights, leading to a subsequent crash.

The modern stock market, however, plays a relatively small role in financing investment in the real world. The majority of transactions in the stock market consist of investors transacting with other investors, while a relatively small proportion of stock purchases actually finance new investments in productive activities. Genuinely new activities, such as start-up businesses, tend to be financed through "angel" investors who have personal knowledge of the business; in the case of many small business start-ups, the initial funding very often comes from family and friends. Once a new business has begun to have a track record, the next stage of financing is likely to come from venture capitalists (also outside of the public stock markets), who spend their working lives scrutinizing new businesses and investing in a number of them, with the understanding that many will fail but with the hope that a few will make it big. Finally, when a business is considered mature enough to go public, the venture capitalists and the CEO will agree on the best time to make an initial public offering (IPO). This is the main opportunity for funds invested through the stock market to make a real difference in business activity.

In contrast, established corporations do not depend on the stock market as much as is generally thought when they decide to invest in new or expanded activities. Most of the major corporations of today have accumulated large pools of retained earnings, which they can invest in new activities. In fact, in the euro area as a whole, since the global financial and economic crisis of 2008–2009, the corporate sector had more profits than it spent on capital investment. The result is that liquidity from corporations is invested in financial assets and further fuels bubbles and volatility.

4.3 Human Services: Health

We now return to the real-world portion of the tertiary sector within the macroeconomy with a consideration of human services. Human services include education, health care, social work, and child care. These services can be provided by private businesses, nonprofit organizations, or governments—or may be delivered outside of the market through the work that is done in the core sphere. In most European countries, a large share of the marketed portion of these services is either directly provided by the government or heavily subsidized. This is a stark contrast to the United States of America, where many of these services are privately procured and financed.

In all developed countries, health-care expenditures have grown strongly over the past decades. Part of this is due to medical progress. When the chancellor of the German Reich, Otto von Bismarck, introduced the first public universal health insurance (which paid for medical treatment and hospitalization) in 1883, the portfolio of available therapies was rather small. There was no possibility for elaborate surgeries, and not many drugs were yet available (antibiotics were only invented half a century later). As a consequence, potential costs remained rather limited. Today, complicated surgeries like hip replacements or kidney transplants are often routine work. Many infectious diseases can be cured with well-tailored but expensive antibiotics or other drugs. Chronic diseases such as HIV infections, diabetes, or even kidney failure can be managed over years. Demographics have changed. People today live much longer than 130 years ago, and they tend to have fewer children. As a consequence, the share of elderly people among the population has strongly increased. As old people tend to have more ailments, this leads to higher demand (and higher total costs) for medical services.

All of this is reflected in an increase in health-care spending, both in absolute terms and as a share of GDP. Even in 1970, in most European countries, spending for health care (both public and private) was seldom more than 5 percent of GDP. By 2013, in the more developed EU countries such as the Netherlands, Sweden, Germany, France, or Denmark, spending on health care was around 11 percent of their GDP, and in slightly poorer countries such as Spain, Italy, or Portugal about 9 percent of GDP. (Britain in a way is an outlier, belonging to the high-income group but only spending 8.5 percent of GDP on health.) As inflation-adjusted GDP has at least doubled in many EU countries since 1970, this translates into a fourfold increase of real health spending.

Part of this spending on health care ends up as value added in the manufacturing or construction sectors: Medical equipment and drugs must be produced, and hospitals must be built. However, a larger share of these costs ends up as value added in the tertiary sector in the form of wages for doctors, nurses, therapists, and administrators. In the EU as a whole, in 2013, value added in the health-care sector amounted to more than 5 percent of GDP. About 6 percent of the workforce was employed in health care. If we add together employment in health care and other social work (as is often done by statisticians), the share in overall employment rises to 11 percent—or in other words: In the EU, one in nine workers is employed in health care and social work.

Beyond the similarities of increasing health-care costs, however, there are a number of important differences in the organization of the health-care system across European countries, including in the quality of health-care systems, which differs strongly between countries. While the government plays a large role in all EU countries, the details differ. In the United Kingdom, for example, the largest part of the health-care system is directly run by the government under the National Health Service (NHS). In Germany, every resident has to have insurance (usually from a public insurance company), but most of the health services are provided by private doctors and hospitals, who are then reimbursed by the patient's health insurance. Other countries such as Spain have parallel systems of government-run provision and private clinics.

As growing health-care costs are seen as a pressing issue for government budgets in many European countries, there are frequent efforts at reform in health-care systems. During the euro crisis, some health-care systems have seen severe cut-backs, sometimes damaging their effectiveness. According to analyses by the World Health Organization, some of the European health systems are among the best of the world.

On the other hand, some of the health-care systems in poorer EU member states such as Romania, Bulgaria, or Latvia (which also tend to spend a lower share of GDP on health care) rank very low in international comparisons.

When compared to the United States of America, which spends much more on health than European countries (16.4 percent of GDP in 2013), the European systems are usually seen as being more efficient. According to health indicators, health outcomes in Western Europe are better than in the U.S. Life expectancy at birth has generally been a couple of years higher in Western Europe than in the U.S., and infant mortality in the U.S. has been significantly higher than in Western European countries (in 2013, 6.5 out of 100,000 infants died in the United States, while the corresponding figures were only 2.7 for Sweden, 3.3 for Germany, 3.5 for France, and 3.8 for the United Kingdom). The main difference between Europe and the United States when it comes to health care is that the systems in the EU member states usually are much more universal, covering everyone, and that the government plays a larger role in trying to limit costs, for example, by negotiating drug prices with pharmaceutical companies.

4.4 Human Services: Education

As with health care, the financing of education systems varies a lot between European countries, even though the public sector finances the largest share of education. In many countries such as Sweden, Finland, Estonia, Latvia, Belgium, Austria, Italy, Poland, and France, less than 10 percent of the spending on primary and secondary education is paid for by the private sector. The country with the largest share of private expenditure for primary and secondary education in the EU is Britain, which has a long tradition of privately financed schools, but even there, more than 80 percent of expenditure on primary and secondary education comes from public budgets.

Differences are much larger when it comes to tertiary (university) education. Here, countries differ strongly in their approach of requiring students to pay tuition fees, even at public universities. In the United Kingdom, the fees that students face now routinely reach several thousand pounds per year. In contrast, in Germany, Denmark, Finland, and Sweden, there are no tuition fees, and in France and Belgium, tuition fees are nominal and far below €1000 per year. These different approaches are reflected in the share of tertiary education paid for by public budgets. In Sweden, Germany, and Belgium, almost 90 percent of all tertiary education expenses are covered from public funds; in the UK, just about half.

Also, the level of funding (both public and private) for education differs a lot between European countries. At the bottom end are countries such as Latvia or Hungary, where only a little more than 4 percent of GDP is spent on education. On the top are countries such as the UK, where expenses for education amount to 6.3 percent of GDP, or Belgium, where 5.9 percent of GDP is spent on education.

Huge variations can also be found in educational attainment. According to a standardized test developed by the OECD to measure the performance of 15-year-olds in mathematics, reading, and science (the so-called PISA test), a number of European

249

countries such as the Netherlands, Estonia, Finland, and Poland score among the best in the world, while others rank below the average of industrialized countries. Interestingly, the performance seems not to be directly related to spending on primary and secondary education. Estonia, for example, only spends 3.2 percent of its GDP on primary and secondary education, but its students score among the top. The United Kingdom spends 4.5 percent of its (higher) GDP on primary and secondary education, yet British students score only mediocrely in the PISA test. Here it is important to keep in mind that—as we discussed in Chapter 5—for government-provided services, the value added in national accounts is calculated by looking at the costs only but not on whether the money is well spent. If one teacher's salary were to increase strongly, value added in education would increase, even if the students did not learn a single bit more!

A final huge difference in the education system can be found in the enrollment of small children in early childhood education. In some (especially Northern) European countries, almost universal enrollment in early childhood education can be found, while some other countries have a much lower coverage ratio. For example, in Denmark, according to the OECD, more than 90 percent of 2-year-olds are already in early childhood education, while not even a third of Austrian or British children of the same age are enrolled in such institutions. Also, financing of child-care institutions varies greatly: Again, in the Nordic countries, many of these child-care facilities are heavily subsidized and government provided, while in Britain, parents have to foot most of the bill.

Overall, more than 23 million people in the European Union are employed in education, representing almost 8 percent of all employees. They are tasked with the education of more than 28 million students enrolled in primary schools, more than 40 million in secondary schools, and almost 20 million students in the higher education system. By 2014, among the 25- to 54-year-old population in the EU, about 30 percent had a university degree. And while in the past more men than women went to university, this has completely changed. Of the younger generation (age 30 to 34), in 2014, more than 42 percent of women had a university degree but less than 34 percent of men did.

5. CONCLUDING THOUGHTS

This chapter has provided a bird's-eye view of the European economy. We have looked at primary-sector activities that provide the raw materials on which everything else depends, noting that the importance of these activities is belied by the small percentage of GDP devoted to them. We have looked at secondary-sector activities that process physical materials, turning them into goods for sale. And we have looked at the tertiary sector, which accounts for almost three-fourths of the economic activity in the European Union.

The "marketed" section of the economy (including goods and services produced by the government), on which we have concentrated here, is not the whole picture. Seemingly inherent in our economic system is a drive to find ever more ways to replace what we do for ourselves with marketed services or products. The replacement of much home cooking with fast food, take-out, and rapid meal delivery is a prime example. Still, the services that people provide as friends, neighbors, family members, and citizens continue to be a large part of the economy, though unmeasured by flows of money and therefore missing from GDP. Recall from Chapter 6 that even the most conservative estimates of the total value of household production are 25 to 30 percent of standard GDP. In a more fully accounted economy, covering the core as well as the business and public-purpose spheres, the tertiary sector would still loom very large—much of the (nonmonetized) economic activity in the core sphere is services—but its expansion would be largely in the areas of "private social services" and "entertainment."

As we continue our analysis of the macroeconomy, we will focus primarily on the portion of the economy that is measured by standard GDP. We will be concerned primarily with aggregate figures, concentrating for example on total consumption, total investment, and total government spending. The material covered in this chapter, as well as in the preceding two, may help us to bear in mind the realities that lie behind the abstractions that are necessary to develop macroeconomic theory. Before delving into that theory, we need to review one other important area of the real economy—employment and unemployment—the topic of the next chapter.

DISCUSSION QUESTIONS

1. Economic theory suggests that goods and services provided in competitive markets by private enterprises will result in lower prices. But we have learned that health-care costs in the United States are actually much higher than in Europe, although Americans do not have better health outcomes than people in countries that provide public health care. How would you explain this result?
2. What can be the benefits of a growing financial sector? Why is a growing financial sector not always beneficial for the economy as a whole?

REVIEW QUESTIONS

1. List and define the three major output sectors of the European economies, as discussed in this chapter.
2. Approximately what percentage of the EU GDP is produced in each of the three sectors? How has this allocation changed over time?
3. How do "technological optimists" view the debate about natural resource constraints?
4. What are some of the potential future natural resource constraints on economic activity?
5. Summarize how agriculture in the European Union has changed over the past century.
6. Does the declining share of the primary sector imply that it is becoming less important?
7. What is the largest source of energy in the European Union?
8. Why does the number of new housing starts in most countries show a cyclical pattern?
9. Contrast the recent history of the European textile and automobile industries.
10. Are some politicians correct when they say that European manufacturing jobs have been shifted to Asia?
11. Is the service sector synonymous with low-paying jobs?

12. What is meant by "financialization"? What data suggest that advanced economies have become more financialized in recent years?
13. Summarize the state of health care in the European Union.
14. What trend was emphasized in the chapter concerning retail services?

EXERCISES

1. Match each statement in Column A with a percentage in Column B.

Column A	Column B
a. Share of the employed persons in the EU who work in education	1. around 11 percent
b. The tertiary sector's share of GDP	2. 74 percent
c. The percentage of EU energy needs covered from petroleum products	3. 1.5 percent
d. The share of value added of Irish construction in GDP just before the real estate bubble burst	4. 24.4 percent
e. The share of energy needs the European Union covers with imports	5. almost 10 percent
f. The secondary sector's share of GDP in the EU	6. 53 percent
g. The percentage of GDP spent on health care in most high-income European countries	7. 34.4 percent
h. The primary sector's share of GDP in the EU	8. almost 8 percent

2. Search the Internet or other news sources for a recent article discussing the loss of European jobs to other countries. Based on what you have learned in this chapter, present an analysis of the article. Can you find any statements in the article that you think may be inaccurate?
3. Eurostat's databases are the sources of much of the data presented in this chapter. Go online and locate the relevant databases. Find the percentage of GDP attributed to the primary, secondary, tertiary, and government sectors for your home country. How does the country compare to the EU? How has the size of the sectors changed over recent years?
4. Match each statement in Column A with an answer in Column B.

Column A	Column B
a. The largest of the three economic sectors by value added	1. Cyclical
b. The smallest of the three economic sectors by value added	2. Fiat
c. An example of a business in the primary sector	3. Primary
d. An example of a business in the secondary sector	4. Carrefour
e. An example of a business in the tertiary sector	5. Declining
f. The current trend regarding the size of the secondary sector	6. Tertiary
g. The current trend regarding the size of the tertiary sector	7. A local farmer's market
h. The typical trend regarding the number of housing starts	8. Increasing

NOTES

1 Data from Bureau of Economic Analysis, "Corporate Profits by Industry"; *Statistical Abstract of the United States*; Economic Policy Institute, Briefing Paper #331, 2011.
2 Data from Eurostat Labour Force Survey, 2016.
3 World Federation of Exchanges, *Average Holding Period for Stocks*. Retrieved from http:// world-exchanges.org/; http://topforeignstocks.com/wp-content/uploads/2012/11/Stock-Holding-Periods-1991-2010.png.

Chapter 8

Employment, Unemployment, and Wages

As discussed in Chapter 1, a primary goal of the macroeconomy is to support a good standard of living.* This normally involves making it possible for people to gain the income needed to purchase goods and services. Nonmarket factors such as household production, publicly produced goods and services, leisure time, and a healthy environment play an important role in determining living standards, but for most people in developed economies, income from work is the main factor needed to support individuals and families. Also, many studies show that being integrated in the social net of employment is important for many people to feel needed and content. In this chapter, we focus on paid employment and on levels of employment and unemployment in the economy as a whole.

The second macroeconomic goal that we cited was stability and security. Unemployment can be a major threat to people's stability and security. This chapter focuses specifically on understanding the phenomenon of unemployment. Later chapters consider the macroeconomic conditions that affect unemployment levels.

The third macroeconomic goal is to sustain and restore the various forms of capital that are essential for future as well as present well-being. This chapter discusses the ways in which the availability of natural and manufactured capital, in particular, is relevant for future employment and income.

What does all of this mean for your future? Do you, for example, feel that your future work experience will be similar to that of your parents? During some periods in history, expectations of work remained stable for decades. But expectations have changed—according to an international 2014 survey, many respondents in industrialized countries believe that today's children will be worse off than their parents. For example, 20 percent of the British respondents indicated that today's youth will have a better life than their parents, while 54 percent said that their lives will be worse. In Spain, only 16 percent believed in a better future, while 62 percent predicted a decreasing standard of living![1]

There are many reasons for this sense of turbulence and change, including the globalization of markets, the increasing scale and concentration of many businesses,

---

* The terms "standard of living" and "well-being" are often used interchangeably, but there is a distinction. "Standard of living" refers to the tangible aspects of one's life, while "well-being" refers to the overall state of one's life, including social and psychological aspects as well as tangible aspects.

changing relations between states and corporations, the information revolution and other rapid changes in technology, and the impact of, first, the Great Recession (the recession of 2007–2009, so named because of its severity and lasting impact), and then the euro crisis that started in 2010. This chapter and subsequent chapters will explore what macroeconomics can tell us about how these and other forces are affecting the nature of employment, the levels and impacts of unemployment, and the longer-term future of work and incomes.

1. EMPLOYMENT AND UNEMPLOYMENT

We have seen in previous chapters how official data is used to draw a macro portrait of a country's economy—and how this data may emphasize some aspects (especially the economic activities that involve markets) and ignore or downplay others. We start this chapter with a similar look at the official data on work issues. This data does not cover everything that we might want to know, but it is important to know how to read the official data and what they can tell us.

1.1 Measuring Employment and Unemployment

Labor market statistics are among the most confusing in Europe. Not only does the European statistical office, Eurostat, publish monthly data on unemployment rates and the number of unemployed, but so do national statistical offices. To make things worse, in many cases, the data does not match. If you follow, for example, general news in the UK or Germany about the unemployment situation, you will be confronted with a different number than you find at the Eurostat Web site.

The explanation for this cacophony is that national and European statistics have often been designed for different purposes and often use different definitions for who to count as "unemployed" and who not. For example, many countries report the number of claimants to national unemployment benefits, as this number is important for national budgets. Very often, however, for receiving unemployment benefits, you have to meet additional criteria than just being out of work. In many European countries, you need to have paid contributions into the unemployment insurance for a certain period of time before you can claim benefits. Hence, if national news presents the number of claimants, this might be lower than what Eurostat presents as the number of unemployed. In other cases, the national definition of unemployment is just different from the international definition. For example, in Germany, someone who works 5 hours per week but is looking for a full-time job would be counted as unemployed, while European statisticians count the same person as "employed."

For the past years, Eurostat has tried to push for more harmonization across countries. It has implemented the definitions recommended by the International Labour Organization (ILO), a body that tries to improve working conditions around the world, and many European countries by now report prominently unemployment figures according to that standard. Hence, if you want to see a clear picture of the labor market in a given European country and compare whether unemployment is better or worse than in another country, you are best advised to look at the Eurostat data first.

Eurostat gets its data from a combination of surveys and additional data from national authorities. Every quarter, together with national statistical authorities, it conducts a survey among European households. In 2014, this survey covered about 1.6 million individuals. The results are published in the quarterly labor force survey data on the Eurostat Web site. Using national data, for example, on the number of recipients of national unemployment benefits, Eurostat extrapolates this quarterly data to get monthly data on the unemployment rate that is published every month.

Survey methods differ between countries, but similar questions are asked. In the UK, for example, most of the initial interviews are conducted face to face, with follow-up interviews usually done by telephone. Questions are asked about work status, but also about specific demographic variables such as marital status or ethnicity. Based on a number of work-related questions, the person interviewed is classified as employed, unemployed, or not in the labor force.

It is worth noting that official labor force, employment, and unemployment statistics only include persons 15 years or older who live in a private household. Hence, children are excluded, as are people who are in compulsory military service or live in prison or in a mental institution. Trends in employment statistics over time, then, need to be analyzed in the light of considerations such as changes in age demographics, military policy, and rates of disability and incarceration. Thus in principle, the abolition of compulsory military service can lead to changes in unemployment and employment numbers.

employed person (Eurostat definition): a person who did any work for pay or profit during the week before he or she is surveyed or who worked in a family business

Those who are included in the labor force statistics are categorized using a number of questions on their work status. First, it is asked whether the person surveyed worked for pay or profit during the reference week. Anyone who answers "yes" will be classified as **employed**. If someone did *any* paid work last week—even if he worked for only an hour or two at a casual job—the interviewer will code him as "employed." If the person answers "no," more questions will be posed. For example, if you have a paid job but just did not happen to put in any hours last week because you were sick, on vacation, or on certain kinds of leave, you will be coded as working and "employed." Also, if you did *unpaid* work in a family-run business, such as a retail store or farm, you will be classified as "employed."

BOX 8.1 UNEMPLOYMENT FIGURES HIDE TRUE DEGREE OF JOBLESSNESS IN EUROPE

According to official figures, by 2016, the situation in European labor markets had significantly improved from the depth of the euro crisis. By the summer of 2016, unemployment had fallen by 2 percentage points from its peak reached three years earlier.

However, not all of this decrease was due to unemployed people having found new jobs. In a number of countries, while unemployment fell, the number of workers who had given up looking for a job had actually increased, indicating that not all of the improvement in unemployment figures actually represented an improvement in economic conditions.

In Italy, for example, the share of people in the working-age population who were stating that they were "available for work but not seeking" rose from 13.1 percent in 2013 to 14.4 percent in 2015. Some of these people were living off financial support by family members, but others were relying on off-the-book jobs. According to Giuseppa Ragusa from the LUISS Guido Carli University, this creates different problems: This group does not pay income taxes and does not pay contributions to the pension system, increasing the burden for those who have formal jobs.

Not all countries with high unemployment also have a high number of discouraged workers. In Spain, for example, the share of discouraged workers never exceeded 5.1 percent and has fallen with the reduction in unemployment. One reason might be that unemployment benefits are much more generous in Spain than in Italy, one of the European countries with the least generous unemployment benefits. In order to be eligible for unemployment benefits in Spain, an unemployed person has to be actively looking for work.

Source: Carol Matlack, "Discouraged Workers Dog Europe's Recovery," *BloombergBusinessweek*, March 17, 2016.

Note that the "family business" situation is the only case in which unpaid work currently counts as being employed in the official statistics. If you are occupied with caring for your children or other family members or doing community volunteer work, you will *not* be considered "employed." Terms such as "labor," "work," and "employment" in official statistics generally refer only to *paid* work.

If the answers to the household survey do *not* result in someone being classified as "employed," the person concerned will be further classified depending on answers on job search and availability (see Figure 8.1). If a person has been seeking employment and is available right away or a person has secured a job in the future but would have been available to start right away, they are counted as **unemployed**. Activities such as reading job ads, contacting employers, and sending out résumés count as a job search. The question about whether you could start a job concerns whether, in fact, you are *available* for work. If, for example, you are a college student searching during spring break for a summer job, but you are not available to start the job until June, you would answer "no" to the availability question—and not be counted as unemployed.

unemployed person (Eurostat definition): a person who is not employed but who is actively seeking a job and is immediately available for work

If you are either employed or unemployed, Eurostat classifies you as part of the **labor force**. But what if you are neither "employed" nor "unemployed"—if you do not have a job but are not actively seeking one? Then you are classified as **inactive**. People in this category are often taking care of a home and family, in school, disabled, or retired. Note that people can be classified as "inactive" even if they are far from being inactive, such as stay-at-home mothers or fathers.

labor force (Eurostat definition): all those who are either employed or unemployed

Notice, in Figure 8.1, that the vast majority of EU28 residents who are not "employed" are "inactive" (136 million) or are not part of the surveyed population (about 125 million). The latter group is made up mainly of children under 15 and those aged 75 years or older. In comparison, about 22.8 million people in 2015 were formally counted as "unemployed."

inactive person (Eurostat definition): someone who is neither "employed" nor "unemployed"

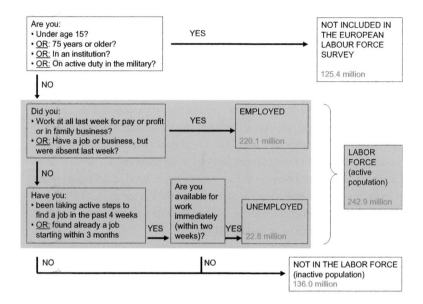

Figure 8.1 *Who Is in the Labor Force? (2015 Data)*

The labor force survey asks people a series of questions to determine if they are employed, unemployed, or not in the labor force.

Source: Eurostat, "Statistics Explained: Labour market and Labour force survey (LFS) statistics," Brussels, October 2016.

1.2 The Unemployment Rate

unemployment rate: the percentage of the labor force made up of people who do not have paid jobs but are immediately available and actively looking for paid jobs

Having made estimates, based on the survey responses, of the total number of employed and unemployed people in the country, Eurostat calculates the official **unemployment rate**. This follows the formula:

$$unemployment\ rate = \frac{number\ of\ unemployed\ people}{number\ of\ people\ in\ the\ labor\ force} \times 100$$

For example, for 2015, looking at Figure 8.1, you can see that Eurostat estimated that in the EU28, 220.1 million people were employed and 22.8 million people were unemployed. The unemployment rate was thus calculated as 9.4 percent:

$$unemployment\ rate = \frac{22.8\ million}{242.9\ million} \times 100 = 9.4$$

The unemployment rate represents the fraction of the officially defined labor force that is made up of people who are not currently working at paid jobs but are currently looking for and available for paid work.

The unemployment rate reported in the media is often "seasonally adjusted." Over the course of a year, some swings in unemployment are fairly predictable. For example, agriculture and construction tend to employ fewer people in the cold winter months, and tourism employs a lot of seasonal workers in the summer. Eurostat releases "seasonally adjusted" figures that attempt to reflect only shifts in unemployment that are due to factors *other than* such seasonal patterns.

Eurostat also estimates unemployment rates for various demographic groups, occupations, industries, geographical areas, and single member states. Historically, unemployment rates have generally been substantially higher for immigrants than for the local population, for teenagers than for older people, and for less educated people than for the more educated. Unemployment rates often have differed somewhat by gender, though not with any consistent pattern. They also have differed strongly between countries, again without consistent patterns. In the early 2000s, Germany had especially high rates of unemployment, while the Netherlands was doing much better. By 2015, this pattern had reversed. Some representative unemployment rates are given in Table 8.1.

Table 8.1 *Unemployment Rates for Different Groups, EU28, 2015*

Group	Unemployment rate
All Workers	9.4
Country of Residence (selected)	
Germany	4.6
Czech Republic	5.1
United Kingdom	5.3
Netherlands	5.9
Sweden	9.4
France	10.4
Italy	11.9
Spain	22.1
Greece	24.9
Age	
Less than 25 years	20.3
25 to 74 years	8.3
Education	
Up to lower secondary education (usually up to about 10 years of school)	16.3
Upper secondary and postsecondary, nontertiary education (e.g., 12 years of school, vocational school)	7.5
Tertiary education (usually bachelor's degree or higher or equivalent)	5.2
Gender	
Adult male	9.3
Adult female	9.5

Source: Eurostat, "Statistics Explained: Unemployment Statistics," October 2016.

Discouraged Workers and Underemployment

The fact that some "inactive" people might want jobs but have given up looking for them has long troubled employment analysts. To the extent that people give up looking, the official unemployment rate *underestimates* people's need and desire for paid jobs.

In recent years, statistical authorities have added questions to the survey to try to determine how many people in the "inactive" population may want employment, even if they are not currently searching for work. The Eurostat survey hence includes a question for the economically inactive population on why a person has not been seeking employment. In 2015, for the EU28, 5.1 percent of the inactive population (which would amount to about 9 million people) stated that they had not looked for work, as they believed no work was available for them. This group is called **discouraged workers**. They may have become discouraged because their skills do not match available openings, because they have experienced discrimination, or because they have been turned away time after time. Recently, the number of discouraged workers has hugely increased in Europe. In 2007, the year before the onset of the global economic and financial crisis, only 4 percent of the inactive population was classified as discouraged workers. Moreover, the share of discouraged workers differs widely across the EU countries. For example, in Bulgaria and Italy, more than 12 percent of the inactive population stated in 2015 that they had stopped looking because they thought no work was available for them. In Germany, in contrast, the figure was only 1.6 percent and in Austria only 0.8 percent.

Another part of the inactive population that might want to work but currently is not working is made up of those who are seeking work but who are not available immediately. Many people in this group look after children or relatives and would have to make arrangements before they could begin a job. In the EU28, this group has been estimated to number 2.2 million in 2015.

Another part of underemployment includes those who currently are on a part-time job but would like to work more hours. In the EU28, roughly 38 million people were working part time in 2015. Many of these do so because they chose a part-time job, maybe because they have to look after children or relatives. Others might only be able to work part time for health reasons. Some might have decided that they would like to have more spare time and do not need the wage from full-time employment. However, according to the surveys from Eurostat, a significant number of part-time workers actually would like to work longer hours but are not able to do so because their employers do not allow them to do so and no other jobs are available. The number of such **underemployed part-time workers** has been estimated at roughly 10 million in 2015 in the EU28. In this group, women are overrepresented: According to Eurostat, about two-thirds of underemployed part-time workers are women.

A final form of underemployment is if someone is employed but works in a position that does not match her skills. Suppose that you paint your aunt's living room for cash while you are waiting to hear back on job applications for management or computer positions. Eurostat counts you as already employed, but you are not fully using your skills. While underemployment due to underutilization of skills is certainly of

discouraged workers: people who want employment but have given up looking for a job

underemployed part-time workers: part-time workers who would like to work additional hours and are available to do so

considerable concern for both efficiency and quality-of-life reasons, Eurostat surveys do not currently attempt to measure this sort of underemployment.

What indicator, then, should we look at to see whether the national employment situation is "bad" or "good"? Probably, the unemployment rate is still the single best available indicator for the labor market situation. However, we should also make use of the other indicators on underemployment made available by Eurostat.

Discussion Questions

1. How would Eurostat classify you, personally, on the basis of your activities last week? Can you think of an example in which someone you think of as *working* would not be considered by Eurostat to be officially "employed"? Is it true that people who are *not working* are generally counted as "unemployed"?
2. Do you know anyone who is a "discouraged worker"? How about someone who is an "underemployed part-time worker"?

1.3 Labor Force Participation

An important labor force statistic is the **activity rate** (sometimes also called "labor force participation rate"), which indicates the fraction of potential paid workers who either are in paid jobs or are seeking and available for paid work. We can calculate the activity rate by dividing the number of people officially in the labor force by the number of people of working age who are not institutionalized or in the military:

activity rate or labor force participation rate: the percentage of potential workers either with a job or actively seeking a job or the labor force as a percentage of the civilian noninstitutional population

$$activity\ rate = \frac{number\ of\ people\ in\ the\ labor\ force}{number\ of\ people\ of\ working\ age,\ not\ institutionalized\ or\ in\ the\ military} \times 100$$

Activity rates are usually reported for different definitions of working age (e.g., 15 to 64 years old or 15 to 74 years old). In 2015 the activity rate in the EU28 for those aged between 15 and 64 was about 72.5 percent. Note, however, that the activity rate differs widely across EU countries. There are some countries in which activity rates are rather low. In Italy, for example, the activity rate in 2015 was only about 64 percent. In Romania and Bulgaria, the rates reached 66 and 69 percent, respectively. In contrast, in Sweden, the activity rate reached almost 82 percent, in the Netherlands 80 percent, and in Germany 78 percent.

If we look into the details, we find that the differences are mainly due to female labor market participation. In the first half of the twentieth century, it was common in basically all industrialized countries for men to be the "breadwinners" of families while most women stayed home to care for children and engage in other household production. Thus men were much more likely to be part of the labor force, according to the definition presented in Figure 8.1. Women's participation in the labor market also explains the most important trends in activity rates during the past half century: In all industrialized countries for which we have data available, labor force participation increased very strongly between the 1970s and today and in all countries, this increase is mostly due to women entering the labor force.

261

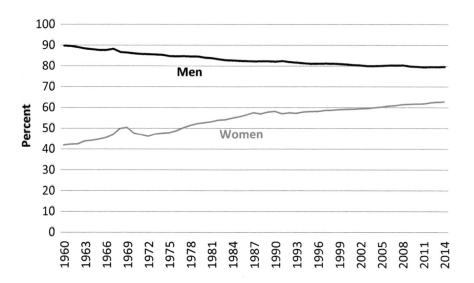

Figure 8.2 *Male and Female Labor Force Participation Rates, Industrialized Countries (OECD), Aged 15 to 64, 1960–2014*

In the industrialized world, the labor force participation rate for men has declined slightly over the last several decades, while significantly more women have entered the labor force.

Source: OECD, Dataset: LFS by sex and age—indicators, July 2016.

The women's rights movement during the 1960s and 1970s contributed to this expansion in women's labor-market activities. Other factors include the expansion of publicly provided child care, the expansion of the service sector (discussed in Chapter 7), and reductions in the average number of children per family. As one example, in the Netherlands, the overall activity rate in 1971 was a mere 58 percent—more than 20 percentage points less than today. Since then, the activity rate among women in the Netherlands increased from a mere 30 percent to 74 percent today.

In Sweden, the activity rate among women was recently calculated at 79 percent, while it was only 55 percent in Italy and 57 percent in Romania (see Figure 8.3). In other words: In Italy, only about one in two women between the ages of 15 and 64 actually had a paid job or was looking for one.

In contrast, the activity rate among men has decreased somewhat. In Germany, in 1970, almost 90 percent of men aged 15 to 64 were part of the labor force. Today, only 83 percent are. Part of this trend can be explained by the expansion of higher education: As more people attend college today than 40 or 50 years ago, fewer young people are counted as economically active. Another—albeit less significant—reason might be a cultural change: Today, it is much more accepted than in the 1970s if men stay home for some period of time to look after their children. A number of European countries now encourage this trend by subsidizing men staying home when children are young.

Differences in national policies toward families and publicly provided or subsidized child care also at least partly explain the differences in female labor market

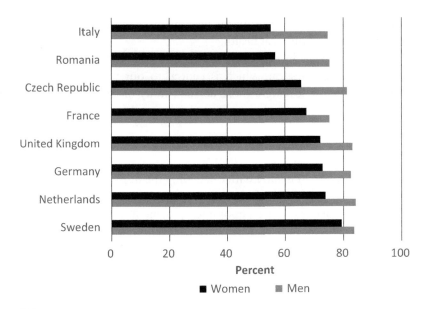

Figure 8.3 *Labor Force Participation of Men and Women in Selected EU Countries, in Percent, 2014*

Most of the difference in overall labor force participation in EU countries stems from differences in female labor force participation, which is much higher in countries such as Sweden, the Netherlands, or Germany than in Italy or Romania.

Source: OECD, Dataset: LFS by sex and age — indicators, July 2016.

participation between different EU countries: Sweden is traditionally known for its policies of publicly providing child care and helping families to combine work and family. In Italy, in contrast, child care is often not widely available, and in many regions, traditional views on family structures still hold.

Discussion Questions

1. What was the labor force experience of your grandparents (or others whom you know in that generation)? Of your parents (or others in their generation)? What do you expect your own labor force participation to be like? Do the patterns in your family reflect the national pattern of changes discussed in the text?

2. What evidence have you seen—in your own family or in the media—of increasing "flexibility" in labor markets? Do you think that these changes have been beneficial, harmful, or both?

2. A CLOSER LOOK AT UNEMPLOYMENT

The unemployment rate is one of the most important indicators that economists use to judge the state of a country's economy. As we see below, a degree of unemployment is expected and even considered healthy in an economy. But being unemployed for a long time, against one's wishes, has a significant negative impact on people's well-being, including their mental and physical health.[2]

A recession has a major impact on increasing unemployment. Why do recessions occur? We briefly address this question, which is central to our understanding of employment and unemployment, leaving a more detailed study of the phenomenon to Part III of this book.

2.1 Types of Unemployment

Although statisticians are concerned mainly with calculating the number of the unemployed, economists are more concerned with the causes of unemployment. Economists often apply a three-way categorization of types of unemployment, which—while not closely related to Eurostat categories—can be helpful in thinking about some of the major causes of unemployment.

Frictional Unemployment

frictional unemployment: unemployment that arises as people are in transition between jobs

Frictional (or search) unemployment merely reflects people's transitions between jobs. The fact that some people are unemployed does not necessarily mean that there are no jobs available. In early 2015, for example, while there were 614,000 people unemployed in the Netherlands, there were also about 130,000 job vacancies—that is, jobs looking for people! (Data on job vacancies for the EU as a whole is unfortunately not available, as data for some important member states such as France is missing.) Even in a well-functioning economy, it may take many weeks for people and suitable jobs to find each other. An unemployment rate of 0 percent could only happen if everyone who wants a job always takes one immediately, or at least within Eurostat's quarterly survey periods. Not only is this unlikely, but it is also in some ways undesirable. Everyone benefits if people take the time to find good job matches—work that puts their skills and talents to good use. Because information about job openings takes time to find, and employers may want to spend time interviewing and testing applicants, making a good job match is not an instantaneous process.

For the most part, economists do not worry too much about frictional unemployment because some frictional unemployment—about 2 to 3 percent—is inevitable, and much of it tends to be short term. Things such as innovative Web technologies for matching job offers to job seekers may reduce frictional unemployment by reducing search time.

Many job seekers rely on public unemployment insurance programs to ease their income needs while they spend time searching for work. In most EU28 countries, public unemployment benefit schemes are in place under which those who lose a job will get a partial compensation for their wage income lost. However, these schemes differ greatly among countries. In some countries such as Luxembourg or Slovenia, replacement payments can reach 80 percent of former wages, while in the UK, for an average earner, they are less than 20 percent. In some countries such as Lithuania,

Romania, or Poland, benefits are only paid for up to 26 weeks; in other countries, payments might run for two years or more.

Structural Unemployment

Structural unemployment arises when a widespread mismatch occurs between, on the one hand, the kinds of jobs being offered by employers and, on the other, the skills, experience, education, or geographic location of potential employees. One important cause of structural unemployment is sectoral shifts, such as those described in Chapter 7, in which employment has been falling (relative to total population size) in the primary and secondary sectors, with the largest number of new jobs opening up in the tertiary (service) sector. Modern European economies may have a lot of new openings for computer programmers and nurses' aides in the capital cities, for example. But these will not do you much good if you live in rural area and your skills are in welding or wood carving.

Major transitions in the kinds of work that are available—whether caused by new technologies or by sectoral shifts—are inevitably painful. Many manufacturing jobs have traditionally enjoyed institutional arrangements—including unionization and job characteristics negotiated with the help of unions—that increased the compensation and the quality of those jobs. People who had developed valuable skills in one job may find that their labor commands a lower price in other types of work. Many displaced workers, particularly older ones, may never find the kind of pay and satisfaction that they had at their earlier occupations. Older displaced workers are more likely than younger ones to stay unemployed for long periods or to exit the labor force. This observation holds especially true for those workers in formerly communist countries in Central and Eastern Europe who lost their jobs during the transition from a planned economy to a market economy in the early 1990s: Many older workers actually never managed to secure a permanent new job.

Governments at all levels have tried various policies to prevent or alleviate structural unemployment. The governments of some countries, notably Germany and France, as well as Japan in the 1980s and 1990s, have enacted industrial policies that directly encourage the development and retention of certain key industries through loans, subsidies, and tax credits. Many of these policies (such as the German subsidy for hard coal) are now being phased out, and EU rules prevent national governments from introducing new subsidies for existing industries. Nowadays, public policies in the EU mainly focus on retraining displaced workers and increasing their mobility. A number of measures are financed out of the EU budget, such as the Youth Guarantee, under which the EU financed a scheme to guarantee all unemployed people under 25 to get a concrete offer for a traineeship, apprenticeship, (temporary) job, or continued education from 2013 onward. There has been some question, however, as to whether these measures have actually been successful in getting displaced workers into good new jobs. Business policies at the firm level are also relevant: Firms can help prevent structural unemployment if they make retaining or retraining their loyal employees a priority, even while responding to changes in technology and trade.

structural unemployment: unemployment that arises because people's skills, experience, education, or location do not match what employers need

265

Cyclical Unemployment

cyclical unemployment: unemployment caused by a drop in aggregate demand

Cyclical unemployment is unemployment due to macroeconomic fluctuations—specifically, unemployment that occurs due to a recession. During recessions, unemployment rises as demand for the products of business falls off. During recoveries, this kind of unemployment should decrease.

recession: traditionally defined as occurring when GDP falls for two consecutive calendar quarters

Traditionally, a **recession** has been defined as a situation in which GDP falls for at least two consecutive calendar quarters. For the euro area, the nonprofit Centre for Economic Policy Reform (CEPR) dates the beginning and end of recessions. The CEPR determinations are strongly based on GDP data, though they also consider other indicators, such as the individual components of output and labor market data.

Whereas frictional unemployment and a degree of structural unemployment are almost always present in an economy, cyclical unemployment is variable and is the kind of unemployment that can effect anyone, regardless of her or his education. Hence it is a significant source of insecurity for broad parts of the population. This is why a great deal of macroeconomic theorizing has to do with the causes of cyclical unemployment and the appropriate policy responses. In severe recessions, such as the one experienced in many countries during the global financial and economic crisis of 2008–2009, or during the euro crisis, cyclical unemployment becomes unacceptably high and may remain high even after the economy is no longer formally in recession. This is what has been called a "jobless recovery": Even after GDP starts to recover, job growth is very slow.

As we see later in this chapter and in the following chapters, economists have different theories about what to do in response to high unemployment. As discussed in Chapter 1, these debates trace back to the Great Depression of the 1930s and the differences between classical economics and the theories of John Maynard Keynes. We pursue these issues in much greater detail starting in Chapter 9. First, however, we will delve into patterns of unemployment and the workings of the labor market.

2.2 Patterns of Unemployment

Figure 8.4 shows the monthly unemployment rate in the euro area and the EU28 from the mid-1990s onward (note that data for the EU28 is only available from 2000 onward). Unemployment was at a low of 7.2 percent in the euro area and 6.8 percent in the EU28 in 2008 and at a high of 12.1 percent in the euro area and 11 percent in the EU28 in 2013. Notice in the figure that the EU28 (as well as the euro area, which is part of the EU) experienced two recessions between the mid-1990s and 2016, both occurring in short succession after 2007.

During the global financial and economic crisis the unemployment rate rose dramatically from around 7 percent in 2008 to around 10 percent in the winter of 2009–2010. When the economy started to recover in early 2010, unemployment fell slightly. However, shortly after, Europe was hit by the euro crisis (discussed more in detail in Chapter 18), and unemployment rose further, reaching the record of 12.1 percent for the euro area and 11 percent for the EU28 in April 2013. Although the unemployment rate has fallen after that peak, even in 2016, unemployment remained

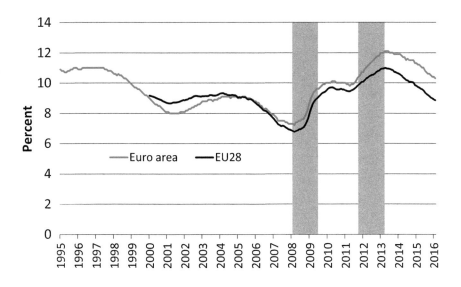

Figure 8.4 *The Monthly Unemployment Rate in the EU28 and the Euro Area, 1995–2016 (Euro Area Recessionary Periods Shaded).*

Unemployment rises during recessions (shown in grey) and decreases during economic recoveries.

Source: Eurostat.

elevated, especially in the euro area, with more than 10 percent of the labor force out of work in the summer of 2016.

The situation looks even more dramatic for single countries within Europe. As one can see in Figure 8.5, the unemployment rate in Spain in the summer of 2016 was still more than twice the precrisis level of 2007, at around 20 percent. Unemployment in Greece was even higher, with almost 25 percent of the labor force still out of work.

Even though cyclical unemployment can in principle affect anyone in the economy, some groups tend to be more strongly affected. In general, it is the young or the less well educated who are hit the hardest. Figure 8.6 illustrates this for the case of Spain. As you can see, while unemployment jumped both for those under 25 and for those 25 and older, the increase among the young was much more pronounced. At the peak of the crisis, more than 55 percent of Spaniards between 15 and 24 who were part of the labor force had no employment. In contrast, for those aged 25 and up, the unemployment rate never rose above 24 percent. Some young Spaniards who missed out on initial entry into the labor market may continue to be disadvantaged by the lack of important skills and experience.

Clearly, cyclical unemployment can cause considerable economic hardship. Thus, avoiding or minimizing cyclical unemployment is an important goal of economic policy. This goal cannot be achieved without a good understanding of why macroeconomic fluctuations occur and what kinds of policies might be used to dampen them. These concepts will be discussed in Part III of this book.

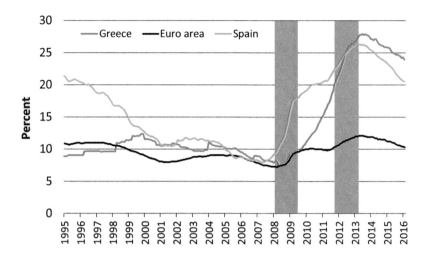

Figure 8.5 *Unemployment Rate in Crisis Countries, Spain and Greece, Compared to Euro Area Average, 1995–2016*

Unemployment is unequally distributed in the euro area. Especially in countries strongly affected by the euro crisis, unemployment has increased after 2008.

Source: Eurostat.

Figure 8.6 *Unemployment Rates Among Those Under 25 and Those Aged 25 to 74 in Spain, 1995–2016*

In general, the young and less well educated are more severely hit by cyclical unemployment. In Spain, the unemployment rate among those under 25 years old jumped by more than 30 percentage points after 2007.

Source: Eurostat.

Discussion Questions

1. Reflecting on your experience or that of someone you know, how long might it normally take for someone to find a job in your area? Comparing your answers in a group, do you find different opinions? What might be some of the factors that make frictional unemployment last a longer or shorter period of time?

2. Do you know of places in your city or region (or country) that have been hit particularly hard by unemployment and underemployment recently or in past decades? Do you know why this hardship occurred? Would you characterize this unemployment as frictional, structural, or cyclical?

BOX 8.2 THE DANGERS OF LONG-TERM UNEMPLOYMENT

In many European countries the long period of slow growth and recession, which started with the global financial and economic crisis from 2007 onward and extended into the euro crisis, has led to new records in long-term unemployment. In Greece, the country hardest hit by the crisis, by 2014, a staggering 73.5 percent of the unemployed had been without a job for more than a year. In parts of Greece, this share actually reached almost 80 percent.

In the euro area as a whole, about half of the roughly 16 million unemployed in 2016 were counted as long-term unemployed. The long-term unemployment rate is especially high among the old, the young, and the unskilled.

Economists do not fully agree why the share of long-term unemployment in Europe has been so high. Neo-classical economists tend to focus on so-called rigidities in the labor market. According to them, one reason for the long duration of unemployment is that the jobless do not easily move to other countries or even other regions. Sometimes, they blame generous unemployment benefits for this immobility, as they think incentives for moving to find other jobs are impaired by these payments. Another argument is that European labor market legislation usually favor those with long job tenure. As a consequence, only a few workers change jobs in any given month, which makes it difficult for the long-term unemployed to reenter the labor market.

Keynesian economists, in contrast, state that it is the sheer duration of the crisis in Europe that has led to the high rates of long-term unemployment. When companies are just not hiring because of falling sales and a dismal economic environment, people who have lost their jobs have little chance of re-entering employment.

What economists generally agree on, however, is the negative effect of high long-term unemployment. According to Mark Carney, the governor of the Bank of England, "when people are unemployed for too long, they lose their skills, so called hysteresis." Fewer skills means that long-term unemployed have an even worse chance of finding a new job, and if they do, they will remain less productive than other workers. This mechanism actually can lead to lower long-term growth of an economy.

Beyond these economic factors, long-term unemployment has important negative social effects. The long-term unemployed usually report a significantly lower level of subjective well-being, and this effect tends to linger even if a long-term unemployed finally finds a new job. Moreover, long-term unemployment is one of the most important risk factors for people falling into poverty.

Sources: *Economist*, "Why long-term unemployment in the euro area is so high," August 2, 2015; Szu Ping Chan, "Why there's little hope for Greece's unemployed," *The Telegraph*, July 9, 2015.

3. THEORIES OF EMPLOYMENT, UNEMPLOYMENT, AND WAGES

Employment and wages are fundamental components of macroeconomic analysis. As of 2015, income from wages and salaries accounted for around 63 percent of national income in both the euro area and the EU28. (The other sources of income mostly derive from various kinds and degrees of ownership of productive assets—such as buildings, land, or other resources or stocks, which are ownership "shares" in companies.) Labor income is what makes it possible for most households to purchase many of the things that they need and want. We now take a look at the different explanations for how wages are set and how overall employment and unemployment levels are determined.

3.1 The Classical Theory

You will recall from Chapter 1 that "classical" approaches to economics favor the workings of free markets, without government intervention. The classical approach to understanding wages and employment assumes that markets behave as described by the idealized supply-and-demand model presented in Chapter 4, characterized by perfect competition.

This model, as applied to the labor market, is shown as Figure 8.7a. "Quantity," on the horizontal axis, can be understood to mean either quantity of labor *services* or the amount of labor hours supplied and demanded. We can think of this quantity as being measured, for example, by the number of full-time equivalent days worked over a given time period. The "price" of labor is the wage, in this case, per day (we assume that this is a "real" wage, i.e., adjusted for inflation.) Workers supply labor, while employers demand it. This very simple model assumes that every unit of labor services is the same, and every worker in this market will receive exactly the same wage. The equilibrium wage in this example is W_E and the equilibrium quantity of labor supplied is at L_E.

Because the market pictured in Figure 8.7a is free to adjust, there is no involuntary unemployment. Everyone who wants a job at the going wage gets one. There may be many people who would offer their services on this market *if* the wage were higher—as the portion of the supply curve to the right of L_E demonstrates. But, given the currently offered wage rate, these people have made a rational choice not to participate in this labor market.

Within this model, the only way that involuntary unemployment can exist is if something gets in the way of market forces. The presence of a legal minimum wage is commonly pointed to as one such factor. As illustrated in Figure 8.7b, if employers are required to pay a minimum wage of W★ ("W-star"), which is above the equilibrium wage, this model predicts that they will hire fewer workers. At an artificially high wage W★, employers want to hire only L_D workers. But at that wage, more people (L_S) want jobs. There is a situation of surplus, as we discussed in Chapter 4. In this case, the market is prevented from adjusting to equilibrium by legal restrictions on employers. Now there are people who want a job at the going wage but cannot find one—that is, they are unemployed.

In the real world, where issues of motivation, labor relations, and power are also important, the classical idea that minimum wages cause substantial unemployment can be called into question. In a well-known study, economists David Card and Alan

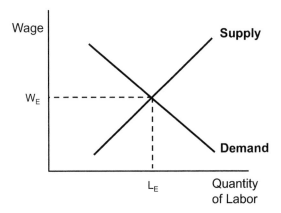

Figure 8.7a *The Classical Labor Market Model*

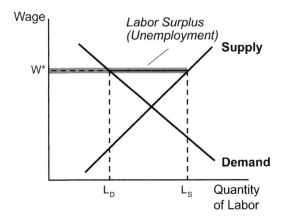

Figure 8.7b *Unemployment in the Classical Labor Market Model*

271

Krueger found that a moderate increase in the minimum wage in New Jersey did not cause low-wage employment to decline and may have even increased it.[3] The study came under fire from economists who believed (given the analysis shown in Figure 8.7a) that such a result simply could not be true. But the classical world assumes perfect competition, whereas real-world employers may have enough power in the labor market to be able to pay workers less than they are worth. Labor markets seem to be more complicated than a simple supply-and-demand model suggests. Several other studies have since confirmed Card's and Krueger's findings for other regions and other countries, including a number of EU countries.

In any case, the minimum wage affects only a portion of the workforce—people who are relatively unskilled, including many teenagers—but unemployment tends to affect people at all wage levels. Classical economists suggest other "market interference" reasons for unemployment, as well. The economy might provide fewer than the optimal number of jobs, they believe, because:

- Regulations on businesses reduce their growth, restricting growth in the demand for labor.
- Labor union activities and labor-related regulations (such as safety regulations, mandated benefits, or restrictions on layoffs and dismissals) increase the cost of labor to businesses, causing them to turn toward labor-saving technologies and thus reducing job growth.
- Public "safety net" policies, such as disability insurance and unemployment insurance, reduce employment by making unemployment less devastating.

Labor-market recommendations that are derived from a classical point of view tend to focus on getting rid of regulations and social programs, which are seen as obstructing proper market behavior. Like other classical proposals, such labor-market proposals assume that the economy works best under the principle of laissez-faire ("leave it alone"). But alternative explanations of the workings of labor markets suggest a different perspective. In considering some of these alternative explanations, we will step away from the assumptions of a single, homogeneous market in which all jobs and all workers are alike and the labor market is characterized by perfect competition. Labor markets are also influenced by many other factors, including history, psychology, power, resources, productivity, and technology.

3.2 Alternative Perspectives on Labor Markets

In Chapter 1, we identified the Keynesian (pronounced "Canesian") perspective as a major alternative to the classical view. Keynes, among many other economists, pointed out aspects of real-world human psychology, history, and institutions that make it unlikely (as well as often undesirable) that wages will fall quickly in response to a labor surplus. Wages may eventually adjust as suggested in the classical model, but too slowly to keep the labor market in equilibrium. And even if wages do fall, this will not necessarily result in full employment, for reasons we will discuss.

272

The incidence of unemployment, as well as the different rates of pay going to different groups, has much to do with people's memory of recent history. When one category of work is paid more highly than another, people who were receiving those higher wages are often able to hold out for a long time against other forces (including supply and demand) that would tend to reverse the relationship. Employers may be slow to reduce wages because they fear that workers will strongly resist such a move—perhaps with strikes or other labor actions. The observed failure of wages to adjust as quickly or completely as predicted has inspired a number of theoretical explanations. Some of these fall into the category of **"sticky wage" theories**. In addition to psychological resistance to wage cuts, a minimum wage might also make wages "sticky," or wages may also become set at particular levels by long-term contracts, such as many large employers negotiate with labor unions.

"sticky wage" theories: theories about why wages stay at above-equilibrium levels despite the existence of a labor surplus

A fairly recent attempt to explain wages that differ from the equilibrium point is efficiency wage theory, which points out that managers must attract, train, and motivate workers if their enterprise is to be productive; it is thus costly for the employer to lose the employees they have found and trained. Moreover, when workers are better paid, they may be healthier and better nourished and therefore more able to do quality work. (This is especially true when talking about wage rates at the low end of the scale.) Efficiency wage theory is a good fit with many observations. Workers may be more highly motivated and may have a lower propensity to quit if they know they are getting "a really good deal" from their employer than they would be if they are getting barely enough to motivate them to take the job or just the same as they could get anywhere else. Workers with a lower likelihood of quitting are more valuable to an employer because the employer saves on the costs of training new workers. Workers may also work more efficiently if they believe that they could lose their "really good deal" if they are caught shirking. Employers may therefore find it to their advantage to pay employees more than would be strictly necessary to get them to work. This theory can be illustrated by looking back at Figure 8.7a, where W★ could be read as the **efficiency wage**.

Legally or contractually set wages, fear of worker unrest, and efficiency wages are all possible explanations for "sticky wages." What sort of policies result from such theories? More government activity to relieve unemployment-related hardship may be proposed, such as the policies we discuss in Part III of this book, or programs of unemployment benefits or job creation.

efficiency wage theory: the theory that an employer can get a higher quality of workers and motivate them to put forth more effort by paying them somewhat more than they could get elsewhere

Some economists also argue that a moderate level of economy-wide price inflation tends to relieve some "sticky wage" unemployment. How could this be so? Suppose that you are working for €12 per hour now, and your employer wants to cut your wage to €10 per hour. You would probably resist if asked to accept this wage cut—especially if you see that other people are not suffering such wage cuts. But suppose, instead, that your wage stays at €12 per hour, and, over time, inflation reduces the purchasing power of your wage to €10 per hour (in terms of prices of the base year). Your nominal wage has stayed the same, but your real wage (and thus your real cost to your employer) has fallen. Because this has happened more subtly—and is felt more economy-wide—than a cut in your personal nominal wage, you may not feel as compelled to resist.

According to some theories, such a drop in the wage (in real terms) should cause employment to increase.

While some Keynesian theorists emphasize sticky wages, Keynes's critique of classical views actually went much further. In more general terms, the Keynesian perspective challenges the entire classical assertion that unemployment results mainly from wage levels that are too high. Rather than blaming unemployment on "the wage being too high," Keynes and his followers focus on the issue of insufficient demand for labor—which they perceive as the direct result of *insufficient demand for goods and services.* (It is often said that "the demand for labor is a derived demand"—meaning that it is derived from the demand for the output produced by labor.)

Thus, to Keynes and his followers, fixing the problem of unemployment in a recession or depression is not just a matter of making labor markets work more smoothly. Rather, total demand—what economists refer to as **aggregate demand**—for goods and services in the economy has to increase in order to stimulate hiring. In this analysis, falling wages would not improve labor market conditions but would make things worse, because workers would have less money to buy goods and services, leading to lower levels of business sales and further layoffs. Unlike the classical economists, Keynes believed that government policies could be effective in response to an economic downturn. We consider these theories and policies in Part III of this book.

aggregate demand: the total demand for all goods and services in a national economy

3.3 Longer-Term Issues: Productivity, Resources, and Technology

An important macroeconomic issue is the share of total income received by labor. Data that track the share of national income received as wages indicate that this share has declined in recent years. For the average of industrialized countries, labor's share of total income tended, between 1960 and 1980, to fluctuate around a long-run value of approximately 70 percent. By 2015, it had decreased to 63 percent in the EU28 and to 61 percent in the United States.

One explanation for this could be that workers have become less productive—but statistics on average output per hour worked indicate that wages have in fact not been keeping up with growing labor productivity. The formal definition of **labor productivity** is the market value of the output of a given amount of labor, normally one hour or one full-time employee. Labor productivity growth in the countries that later became the European Union averaged 4.5 percent annually between 1960 and 1973 but has slowed since to 1.6 percent until 2006 and 0.4 percent between 2007 and 2015.

labor productivity: the market value of the output that results from a given amount of labor

As labor becomes more productive, one would expect that wages would rise accordingly. As shown in Figure 8.8, which presents the growth of labor productivity and real wages since 1960, this was approximately true from 1960 up to until about 1980. Over this period, wages and productivity both increased by a real factor of about two. But since then, a gap between productivity growth and real wage growth became evident. This **wage–productivity gap** has increased over time.

As suggested in Chapter 3, the decline in the bargaining power of unions in many countries of the European Union is one obvious explanation for the widening wage–productivity gap. Workers have not had the power to insist that their wages keep up

wage–productivity gap: the gap between the growth of labor productivity and the growth of wages

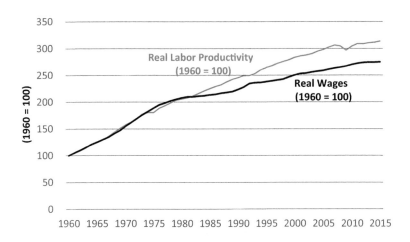

Figure 8.8 *Real Wages and Labor Productivity, European Union Countries, 1960–2015*

Wages increased along with labor productivity from 1960 up to about 1980. Since then, wage growth has not kept pace with productivity gains.

Source: AMECO database, July 17, 2016.

with the increasing value of their output. At the same time, when we consider the share of income going to labor, we also must realize that the productivity of labor depends in part on other aspects of production.

There are a number of important determinants of labor productivity, including health and education (as aspects of human capital), work organization, and levels of cooperation in the workplace (which are aspects of social capital). This section focuses on two other determinants of labor productivity: technology, which can expand the stocks of manufactured, human, and social capital, and natural resources.

Technology and Wages

Obviously, a main reason for the upward trend in labor productivity shown in Figure 8.8 is an improvement in technology. But can technology also be part of the reason that median wages have not kept pace with productivity gains?

Ever since the beginning of the Industrial Revolution, technology has been recognized by workers as a double-edged sword. On the one hand, it has created circumstances wherein each worker has more natural and manufactured capital to work with, raising workers' productivity and hence their earnings. On the other hand, technology can effectively replace workers, leading to **technological unemployment**; ever fewer workers are needed to produce a given quantity of output.

Fears of technological unemployment have been raised repeatedly during the last two and a half centuries. While these fears have been valid in specific areas—for example, computers have made many secretarial jobs obsolete—the total quantity of jobs has not declined as a proportion of the population. Indeed, in the twentieth century, the number of jobs in the European Union increased significantly as women

technological unemployment: unemployment caused by reduced demand for workers because technology has increased the productivity of those who have jobs, effectively reducing the demand for workers

275

successfully entered the labor force and increased the activity rate, as mentioned earlier. Technological unemployment, to those who experience it, is as painful as any other type of unemployment; however, it does not become a society-wide issue if the total number of jobs keeps pace with the size of the population, and workers can adapt to the new circumstances with the help of education or retraining.

skill-biased technical change: the theory that relative wage gains will be the greatest for those workers who possess the education and skills to use modern technologies

Technology can also affect wages and the distribution of wages across different types of workers. One theory, referred to as **skill-biased technical change**, proposes that workers who possess the education and skills needed to use modern technologies will see relative increases in employment and wages. For example, workers who are able to use computers and other digital technologies may gain an advantage over workers who lack such skills. If these skilled workers are a minority of the work force, they could obtain wage gains while most workers' wages stagnate. Note that *average* wages may increase while the *median* wage stays relatively constant if all the gains accrue to those at the top.* Skill-biased technical change has been hypothesized to be one of the reasons for an overall increase in inequality in many industrialized countries. Evidence suggests that skill-biased technical change may be part of the explanation for rising wage inequality but not the most important factor, particularly in recent years.

BOX 8.3 WHAT IS THE FUTURE OF WORK?

Discussions about the future of work tempt us to try to imagine what a better world would be like and to ask ourselves whether the economy of the future is trending in such a direction. Questions along these lines were posed to Andres McAfee, an MIT business school researcher who coauthored the book *Race Against the Machine*. Asked for an optimistic view of the future, McAfee described a "digital Athens" in which a highly automated and productive economy would greatly reduce the need for human labor—"So the optimistic version is that we finally have more hours in our week freed up from toil and drudgery." When asked if he saw a digital Athens on the horizon, he responded that, instead, "the people at the top of the skill, wage, and income distribution are working more hours," while added leisure is going to those who don't want it—the unemployed.

McAfee was also asked, "What is your advice to the individual, or to the parent educating a child?" His response: "To the parent, make sure your kid's education is geared toward things at which machines appear not to be very good. Computers are still lousy at programming computers. Computers are still bad at figuring out what questions need to be asked. I would encourage every kid these days to buckle down and do a double major, one in the liberal arts and one in the college of sciences."

Source: "When Machines Do Your Job," interview with Andres McAfee, *Technology Review* (September/October 2012): 71.

---

* The median wage is the wage received by workers at the exact middle of the wage distribution. Thus the median wage can remain constant or decline while wages in the top half of the distribution increase.

Natural Resources and Wages

The availability and prices of natural resources can also affect wages. Labor and natural resources represent two inputs in production processes, along with other types of capital, so productivity depends on a combination of inputs.

First, consider the possibility that natural resources are becoming scarcer and/or more expensive to extract, as discussed in Chapter 1. If natural resources, as one input into production processes, become more expensive, producers will seek to substitute other inputs that have become relatively less expensive. Thus the demand for labor would be expected to increase, and wages should rise. But we also have to consider the macroeconomic impact of a rise in natural resource prices. In recent years, higher prices for oil and other natural resources have had a negative impact on economic activity, contributing to higher unemployment.

As mentioned, technology also represents an input into production processes. If natural resources become more expensive, that creates an incentive for research into ways to use these resources more efficiently or to seek substitutes. Technological improvements or resource substitution could offset the negative impacts of natural resource scarcity on wages and the overall economy.

Productivity gains could also be the basis for reducing work hours. Figure 8.8 shows that labor productivity has roughly doubled between 1970 and 2015. One interpretation of this result is that the European Union can now produce twice the quantity of goods and services with the same amount of labor used in 1970. But an alternative possibility is that we can now produce the same quantity of goods and services produced in 1970, but with *half the amount of labor.*

Consider this statement in light of the notion of labor flexibility. Suppose that workers had the choice between taking productivity gains as either wage increases or labor time decreases. Theoretically, European workers could be living at the same material living standards of 1970, but working only six months of every year! Of course, some workers may always choose more pay over shorter hours, but allowing for more choice in how and when we work accords with standard economic theory, stated as follows:

> According to economic theory, we should let each worker choose how many hours to work. If workers choose shorter hours, it is because they get greater satisfaction from more free time than they would get from more income. According to the basic principle of market economics, interfering with individuals' choices between more free time and more income reduces total well being, just as interfering with individuals' choices between two products would reduce total well being by forcing some people to buy the product that gives them less.[4]

Assuming that many workers are willing to work shorter hours for an equivalent reduction in pay, as mentioned in Section 2.2, this would reduce their overall consumption and thus rates of natural resource degradation and extraction.

While some European countries have experimented with cutting the overall hours worked per week to reduce unemployment by redistributing the total volume of work among more employees (such as France with the introduction of the 35-hour workweek in the 2000s; see Box 8.4), currently, in many European countries, part-time jobs are much less attractive than full-time jobs because hourly wages are often low and fewer benefits are provided. Some countries have enacted policies to promote higher-quality part-time jobs. One example is the Netherlands, where discrimination against part-time workers is illegal, and employers must offer the option of shorter work hours unless they can prove that it would impose an economic hardship on their business.

Some analysts have proposed that giving people more flexibility to set their work hours is an important way to achieve a more sustainable society. We will discuss the issue of policies needed for sustainability in more detail in Chapter 18.

BOX 8.4 THE FRENCH 35-HOUR WORKWEEK

There are two reasons why one might want to think about the reduction of the standard work-week: First, reducing the weekly working time frees time for other activities. Second, in times of high unemployment, a reduction of the average working time might help to distribute the volume of work more equitably, hence lowering unemployment.

In France, the idea of shortening the working week in order to lower unemployment started to be seriously discussed in the 1970s. In 1982, the government under the socialist president François Mitterand shortened the length of the workweek by one hour to 39 hours and introduced a fifth week of annual vacation, both without reduction in workers' pay. While the planned progression to shorter working times was interrupted by a crisis of business confidence and capital flight in the mid-1980s, the debate lived on. In 1993, a center-right government passed a law providing financial incentives for the reduction of working times.

Then in 1998, a coalition led by the socialist prime minister Lionel Jospin passed a law reducing the workweek to 35 hours for companies with more than 20 employees, from February 2000 onward, and for smaller firms from 2002 onward. Later legislation provided detailed provisions on how to move to the 35-hour workweek. According to these rules, it was intended that employees would in the end earn roughly the same in a 35-hour workweek as they had previously in a 39-hour workweek. In order to make the transition not too burden-some for firms, rebates for social security contributions were introduced and premiums for overtime were reduced.

The exact effect of the transition to the 35-hours workweek is still disputed more than a decade after it took place, with estimates ranging between a few hundred and 700,000 jobs actually created because of the shorting of the weekly working times.

Employers and conservative economists were never happy with the reduction in working time. They claimed that, while the transition might have initially created some jobs, the shortening of the working week without a proportional reduction of wages had eroded French competitiveness relative to other countries with stagnating or falling wage costs, such as Germany. As the conservative British prime minister David Cameron put it in 2014, ridiculing the French: "They think 'Well, let's have a 35-hour working week for everybody and then we share out the jobs that are available,' what we find happens then is that your businesses become more expensive to run than anybody else's, you lose out to the competition and you have less jobs in the economy."

On the other hand, research shows that the reduction in the working week has led to a more equitable distribution of domestic (unpaid) work by men and women living in families with children. Moreover, especially women tend to spend more time with their children, indicating that the reduction in the workweek might have simplified combining family and careers in France. Even Mr. Cameron's *Quality of Life* advisory group was hence positive toward a shorter working week.

Up to today, the 35-hour workweek continues to be controversial in France. After the socialists lost the elections in 2002, the newly elected center-right government weakened the financial incentive for companies still working with a 39-hour workweek to make the transition toward the 35-hour one. Under the conservative president Sarkozy in 2007, a "work more to earn more" scheme exempted overtime premiums from income taxes and social security taxes in order to give an incentive for workers and employers to increase working time again. Under the following socialist government, however, Sarkozy's tax breaks on overtime were scrapped again.

Sources: Philippe Askenazy, "Working time regulation in France from 1996 to 2012," *Cambridge Journal of Economics*, 2013, Vol. 37 (2), pp. 323–347; Ariane Pailhé, Anne Solaz, Arthur Souletie, "The Effects of the French 35-Hour Workweek Regulation on Intra Household Time-Allocation," paper presented at the Population Association of America 2013 Annual Meeting, New Orleans; Camille Logeay, Sven Schreiber, "Testing the effectiveness of the French work-sharing reform: a forecasting approach," *Applied Economics*, 2006, Vol. 38 (17), pp. 2053–2068.

DISCUSSION QUESTIONS

1. Which arguments seem most convincing to you, those of classical labor market theorists, "sticky wage" theorists, or Keynesian economists concerned with aggregate demand? What are some strengths and weaknesses of each argument?
2. Can you think of other impacts, positive and negative, of allowing workers more flexibility in setting their work hours? Would you support any specific policies to promote more choice of work hours?

REVIEW QUESTIONS

1. What population is included in the official household survey that measures employment and unemployment?
2. What questions are asked to determine whether someone is "employed"?

3. What makes a person count as "unemployed"?

4. How is the unemployment rate calculated?

5. What are underemployed part-time workers? Discouraged workers?

6. What does employment flexibility mean from the perspective of workers? From the perspective of employers?

7. What is the labor force participation rate, and how is it calculated? How has it changed in recent decades for men and women in the European Union?

8. How can high levels of unemployment be explained in the Keynesian model?

9. List and describe the three types of unemployment.

10. What policies may be used to combat frictional and structural unemployment?

11. What is the relationship between the average duration of unemployment and the unemployment rate?

12. Describe the classical theory of unemployment.

13. What are some of the reasons that an economy might offer less than the optimal number of jobs, according to classical theory?

14. Describe how "sticky wages" could lead to unemployment.

15. What are some reasons that wages might be "sticky"?

16. What are "efficiency wages," and why might payment of them lead to unemployment?

17. What has been the relationship between labor productivity and average wages in the European Union since 1960?

18. How can changes in technology affect prevailing wage rates?

19. What is skill-biased technical change?

20. How can the price and availability of natural resources affect prevailing wage rates?

EXERCISES

1. The small country of Nederland counts its unemployed using the same methods as the European Union. Of the population of 350 people, 70 are under age 15, 190 are employed in paid work, and 70 are adults who are not doing paid work or looking for work because they are doing full-time family care, are disabled, or are in school. 10 are above the age of 75 and retired. The rest are unemployed. (No one is institutionalized, and the country has no military.) Calculate the following:
   a. The number of unemployed
   b. The size of the labor force
   c. The unemployment rate
   d. The labor force participation rate (overall, for both sexes)

2. The population of Tatoonia is very small. Luis works full time for pay. Robin works one shift a week as counter help at a fast-food restaurant. Sheila is 78 years old and retired. Shawna does not work for pay but is thinking about getting a job and has been looking through employment postings to see what is available. Bob has given up looking for work after months of not finding anything. Ana, the only child in the country, is 12 years old.

   a.   How would a household survey, following EU methods, classify each person?

   b.   What is the activity rate in Tatoonia?

   c.   What is the unemployment rate in Tatoonia?

3.   Suppose an economy is suffering unemployment due to wages that are "too high," as theorized by classical economists.

   a.   Draw and label a graph illustrating this case, in which the going wage is €20, the equilibrium wage is €15, 50 million people want to work, but only 30 million are employed.

   b.   Describe some of the assumptions about labor markets that underlie this graph.

4.   A computer software company advertises for employees, saying "We offer the best-paid jobs in the industry!" But why would any company want to pay more than it absolutely *has to* in order to attract workers? Can this phenomenon help to explain the existence of unemployment? Explain in a paragraph.

5.   Locate the most recent update of unemployment and employment statistics for the European Union at the Eurostat Web site. In a paragraph, describe how the labor force, overall unemployment rate, and unemployment rates by country of residence, gender, and education differ from the numbers (for 2015) given in the text.

6.   Match each concept in Column A with a definition or example in Column B.

Column A	Column B
a. "Not in the labor force"	1. The theory that unemployment is caused by insufficient aggregate demand
b. Classical labor market theory	2. Occurs during a recession
c. Underemployed part-time workers	3. Unemployment due to factors other than seasonal reasons
d. Frictional unemployment	4. Occurs when the skills, experience, and education of workers do not match job openings
e. Employed	5. Wages and employment levels are determined by supply and demand, with no involuntary unemployment
f. Seasonally adjusted unemployment	6. Immediately available for and currently looking for paid work
g. Unemployed	7. Military personnel
h. "Sticky wages"	8. A policy response to structural unemployment
i. Structural unemployment	9. Worked 15 hours or more in a family business
j. Keynesian theory	10. Occurs as people move between jobs
k. Cyclical unemployment	11. Part-time workers who would like to work additional hours and are available to do so
l. Not included in the household survey covering employment	12. Unemployment may occur because wages are slow to fall
m. Technological unemployment	13. Occurs when technology reduces the overall need for workers
n. Paid parental leave	14. A retired person

NOTES

1 Ipsos MORI Global Trends Survey, *People in Western Countries Pessimistic about Future for Young People*, April 14, 2014. Retrieved from www.ipsos-mori.com/researchpublications/researcharchive/3369/People-in-western-countries-pessimistic-about-future-for-young-people.aspx.

2 Rainer Winkelmann, "Unemployment, Social Capital, and Subjective Well-Being," IZA Discussion Paper No. 2346, Bonn, Germany, September 2006.

3 David Card and Alan B. Krueger, "Minimum Wages and Employment: A Case Study of the Fast-Food Industry in New Jersey and Pennsylvania," *American Economic Review* 84(4) (1994): 774–775.

4 Charles Siegel, *The End of Economic Growth* (Berkeley, CA: Preservation Institute, 2006), p. 29.

Part III

Macroeconomic Theory and Policy

Chapter 9

Aggregate Demand and Economic Fluctuations

What makes an economy experience GDP expansion or contraction, high or low employment, and good or bad business conditions? These questions have been very much in the forefront of discussion in the European Union and many other countries since the financial crisis of 2007–2008, the ensuing recession, widely known as the Great Recession, and the euro crisis that followed. In a sophisticated contemporary economy such as that in the euro area, a decline in demand for goods and services by consumers and businesses generally leads to recessionary conditions and higher unemployment. In Chapter 15, we discuss the events of the financial crisis and its aftermath and in Chapter 17, the euro crisis in more detail. But before getting into these specifics, we need to develop a general theory of how the demand for goods and services varies over time and how this affects economic conditions.

1. THE BUSINESS CYCLE

Part III of this textbook focuses in particular on the goal of economic stabilization—that is, keeping unemployment and inflation at acceptable levels over the business cycle. For the moment, we set aside consideration of our two other goals—the goal of improvement in true living standards and the goal of maintaining the ecological, social, and financial sustainability of a national economy—to focus on stabilization. As we see, one crucial key to understanding macroeconomics is how the amount that individuals and businesses want to spend overall (or "aggregate demand," as we called it in Chapter 1) influences and is influenced by other macroeconomic variables. One of the key debates in macroeconomic policy is between Keynesians, who believe that aggregate demand needs active guidance if the economy is to be stable, and more classically oriented economists, who believe that aggregate demand can take care of itself.

In Chapter 1, we introduced the notion of the "business cycle," while in Chapter 8, we considered in detail how employment and unemployment vary over the cycle. Now we look in more detail at business cycles, or recurrent fluctuations in the level of national production, with alternating periods of recession and boom.

1.1 What Happens During the Business Cycle

Figure 9.1 shows the pattern of real GDP growth over the period 1995–2015 for the euro area as a whole.* In most years, as you can see, GDP grew. But during two periods—2008 to 2009 and from 2011 to 2013—GDP shrank. The level of real GDP actually went *down* from one calendar quarter to the next. As noted in Chapter 7, economists talk about a "recession" when economic activity declines for two consecutive quarters, relying on GDP statistics to make this judgment.

In other periods, you can see that GDP grew quite steadily. From the mid-1990s until the onset of the global financial and economic crisis of 2008, GDP in the euro area mostly expanded briskly, with a period of slower growth around the year 2000. But then, in 2008, the global financial and economic crisis hit, and the economy plunged into a severe recession, lasting from the second quarter of 2008 to the second quarter of 2009. In the middle of 2009, a recovery started, but it was interrupted by the euro crisis, which cast the euro area into a new recession in 2011 that lasted until 2013. It took until the end of 2015 to regain the precrisis level of GDP for the euro area as a whole, and in a number of member states, GDP remained below that level for quite a while afterward. Also, unemployment shot up during the crisis and has remained elevated for years in a number of euro-area countries. The goal of macroeconomic stabilization policy is to smooth out such variations.

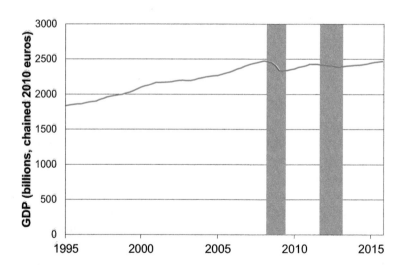

Figure 9.1 *Euro Area GDP and Recessions*

After 2008, the euro area experienced two recessions within five years. During these periods, real GDP fell.

Source: Eurostat quarterly data 1995–2015, and CEPR.

---

* For the euro area, quarterly GDP data is only available from 1995 onward. On the companion Web site to this book, you can find charts with data on GDP, unemployment, and inflation for various euro-area countries.

As we discuss the ins and outs of stabilization policy, you need to keep in mind three "stylized facts." Economists call these "stylized facts" because, while they form a very important base for the way we think about the economy, they are not always literally true. Just as we use simplifying assumptions in microeconomics to draw supply-and-demand curves, we start from a simplified version of reality in constructing our macroeconomic theory.

Stylized Fact #1: During an economic downturn or contraction, unemployment rises, while in a recovery or expansion, unemployment falls. This is fairly easy to understand, since when production in an economy is falling, it would seem natural to assume that producers need fewer workers—because they are producing fewer goods. Similarly, in an expansion, unemployment falls.* This relationship is sometimes expressed by an equation called **Okun's law**. In the early 1960s, economist Arthur M. Okun estimated that for the U.S., a 1-percentage point drop in the unemployment rate was associated with an approximately 3-percentage point boost to real GDP. While for the euro area, the exact numerical relationship between GDP growth and unemployment is different, the underlying logic holds: When growth accelerates, unemployment falls. As the equation for Okun's "law" seems not to be stable, it should best be regarded as a rule of thumb than a law.

Okun's "law": an empirical inverse relationship between the unemployment rate and real GDP growth

We can see some strong evidence of this inverse relationship between output growth and employment by comparing Figure 9.1 with Figure 9.2, which shows the

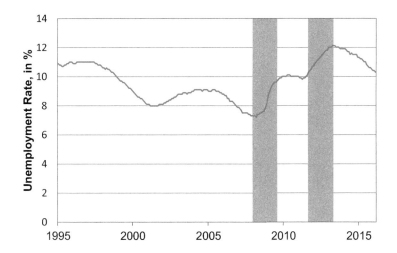

Figure 9.2 *Euro Area Unemployment Rate and Recessions*

During the 2008–2009 and 2011–2013 recessions, unemployment shot up sharply and continued to increase after the recession formally ended, reaching a peak of 10 percent in 2010.

Source: Eurostat monthly data 1995–2015, and CEPR.

---

* In a "jobless recovery," real GDP growth is slow (below average), so it does not create jobs fast enough to counteract the normal increase in the labor force due to population growth and decrease in labor demand due to increased output per worker.

unemployment rate from 1995 to 2015, including the two recessions that occurred after 2008. As output turns downward in Figure 9.1, unemployment shoots dramatically upward in Figure 9.2. The inverse relation, however, is not perfect. Sometimes, as in the recession of 2008–2009, unemployment continues to increase even after GDP started to rise again. In other instances, such as in the early 2000s, unemployment increases even without a recession, when GDP growth turned weak but GDP did not contract. But, by and large, rising GDP is generally associated with increased employment.

Stylized Fact #2: An economic recovery or expansion, if it is very strong, tends to lead to an increase in the inflation rate. During a downturn or contraction, pressure on inflation eases off (and inflation may fall or even become negative). The reasoning behind this result is that, as an economy "heats up," producers increasingly compete with one another over a limited supply of raw materials, labor, and so on. Prices and wages tend to be bid up, and inflation results or intensifies. In a slump, this upward pressure on prices slackens or even reverses, so inflation may be lower or even, in some cases, negative (deflation). Figure 9.3 shows the inflation rate over the period 1995–2015, including the same two recessions highlighted in Figures 9.1 and 9.2.

As you can see, the "stylized fact" that inflation tends to fall during a recession seems to be borne out by the actual data for this period. The two recessions shown in Figure 9.3 were accompanied by distinct downturns in the inflation rate. But fluctuations in the inflation rate also occurred during other periods, with both increases and downturns occurring during economic upswings. Business cycle–led variations in the degree of competition for workers and resources are only *one* cause—and, in recent

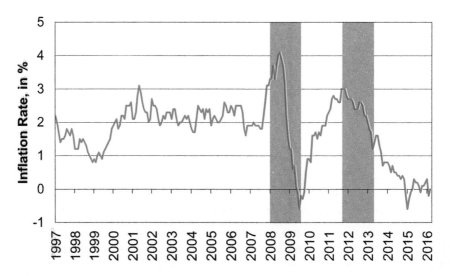

Figure 9.3 *Euro Area Inflation Rate and Recessions*

During the 2008–2009 and 2011–2013 recessions, inflation fell sharply. Inflation generally reflects the business cycle, along with other factors.

Source: Eurostat monthly data 1995–2015; CEPR.

decades, not always the most important cause—of variations in inflation. We look at this issue more closely in Chapters 12 and 13. But for the discussion of business cycles in this and the following two chapters, we assume that booms lead to at least a threat of rising inflation.

Stylized Fact #3: Over the business cycle, business investment moves in parallel with GDP, but it varies much more strongly than GDP or household consumption. The reasoning behind this result is, first, that investment can be more easily postponed than other types of spending and, second, that investment plays a central role in the business cycle (as we discuss later in this chapter). For example, people have to continue eating or paying their rent even in an economic downturn. But businesses can decide to continue producing with an old machine and forego investment altogether for a while. Figure 9.4 shows the change in gross capital formation compared to one year earlier in the euro area and compares it to the change in GDP over the same period for the years 1995–2015, including the same two recessions highlighted in Figures 9.1, 9.2, and 9.3.

What can be easily seen is that investment growth accelerates at the same time as overall GDP growth. In periods of strong GDP growth such as 1998–2000 or 2005–2007, investment grew even faster than GDP. In 1998–2000, it was mainly investment in the booming Internet and telecommunication industries at that time which explains the upswing; in 2005–2007, investment in housing in some euro-area countries helps explain the boom. In the two recessions of 2008–2009 and 2011–2013, investment contracted much more strongly than GDP.

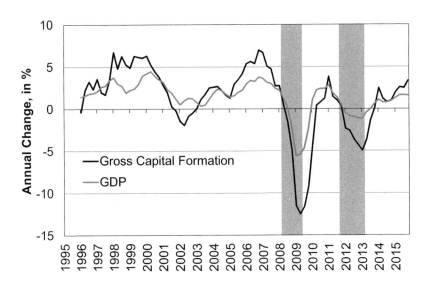

Figure 9.4 *Investment Growth, GDP Growth, and Recessions in the Euro Area*

Since 1995, investment has moved in tandem with GDP, albeit changes have been stronger. During the 2008–2009 and 2011–2013 recessions, investment fell much more strongly than GDP.

Source: Eurostat quarterly data 1995–2015; CEPR.

1.2 A Stylized Business Cycle

When analyzing business cycles, it is often convenient to separate the issue of economic fluctuations from the issue of economic growth. In Figure 9.1, the most striking pattern is the overall growth trend in GDP. For the analysis in Part III of this book, it will be more helpful to mentally remove the upward trend and to think of business cycles in terms of the stylized picture shown in Figure 9.5. (We return to the subjects of growth and development in Part IV.)

During a contraction, GDP falls until the economy hits the trough, or lowest point. During an expansion, GDP rises from a trough until it reaches a peak. In Figure 9.5, the idea that there is a range of output levels that represent "full employment" is represented by the gray area labeled with the value Y^*. Given the different kinds of unemployment discussed in Chapter 8, there is some controversy about exactly what "full employment" means over the business cycle, so we have used a range rather than a specific level of GDP here to indicate **"full-employment output"** for modeling purposes. (Sometimes you may also see this referred to as "potential output.")

At full-employment output, the economy is, presumably, not suffering from an unemployment problem. But neither is the unemployment rate actually zero (as measured by Eurostat), due to the existence of at least some short-term, transitory, or "frictional," unemployment.

What economists generally do agree on is that there have been—historically, at least—episodes when economies have "overheated" and output has gone above this range—giving rise (by Stylized Fact #2) to inflationary pressures. Thus Figure 9.5 shows employment at the peak levels at the top of, or possibly slightly exceeding, the "full employment" band. And there have also been times when economies have fallen into troughs, with (due to Stylized Fact #1) unacceptable levels of unemployment.

"full-employment output" (Y^*): for modeling purposes, a level of output that is assumed to correspond to a case of no excessive or burdensome unemployment but the likely existence of at least some transitory unemployment

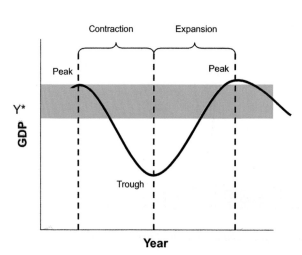

Figure 9.5 *A Stylized Business Cycle*

In this hypothetical economy, GDP contracts from peaks to troughs and expands from troughs to peaks. A range of output indicating "full employment" is indicated by Y*.

In terms of the business cycle model shown in Figure 9.5, the goal of stabilization policy is to keep an economy in the gray area, avoiding the threats of inflation and unemployment.

1.3 The Downturn Side of the Story

It will take this entire chapter and the next four to build up a workable theory of the business cycle! Because this is a large and complex topic, we need to take things one step at a time. We start by looking at the case of economic downturns.

The biggest downturn for most countries was, of course, the Great Depression. Production in all major economies dropped dramatically from 1929 to 1930 and unemployment soared, reaching more than 40 percent in some countries by some measures. Not only were times bad—they stayed bad. In many countries, unemployment stayed in the double digits all through the 1930s. And as social safety nets as we have them today in most European countries were unknown in the 1930s, many unemployed experienced poverty, misery, and hunger. Table 9.1 presents some data on unemployment rates in different countries during the Great Depression.

Another severe economic downturn hit industrialized countries in 2008. Starting from a fall in housing prices and a drop in economic activity in the U.S., the downturn quickly spread to all OECD countries. While not as serious as the Great Depression, this "Great Recession" resembled it in that, unlike most recessions of the past, it persisted for more than a few quarters, and GDP contracted sharply. In the euro area, a second recession followed very quickly after the Great Recession, now triggered by the euro crisis. The severe recession of 2008–2009 was caused in large part by the financial crisis in the U.S. in 2007, which quickly spread to other countries around the world. The euro crisis can be seen as a later consequence of the financial crisis, as problems in the banking sector led to large bailout packages in some euro countries, which in turn led to a dangerous increase in the public debt-to-GDP ratio and triggered investors' doubt about debt sustainability. These two recessions hence illustrate

Table 9.1 *Unemployment in Industry During the Great Depression*

	1929	1932	1935
France	1.0	15.4	14.5
Germany	13.3	43.8	16.2
Netherlands	2.9	25.3	31.7
Norway	15.4	30.8	25.3
Sweden	10.2	22.4	15.0
UK	10.4	22.1	15.5
U.S.	5.3	36.3	30.2

Source: Barry Eichengreen and Tim Hutton, "Interwar Unemployment in International Perspective," Institute for Research on Labor and Employment, University of California Berkeley Working Paper, 1988.

the vulnerability of the global economy to excess "financialization," a topic that we discussed in Chapter 7 and to which we return in Chapter 15.

Notice that in our stylized business cycle in Figure 9.5, there is no scale on the "year" axis. The timing of the cycle is not regular or predictable, so economists in the early years of the Great Depression differed on how to interpret it. Most economists in the 1930s, trained in the classical school, reassured public leaders that this sort of cycle was merely to be expected. They believed that the economy was in the "trough" stage but that it would soon start to expand again. In the long run, they assured officials, the economy would recover by itself, as it had recovered from other downturns in the past.

In response, British economist John Maynard Keynes quipped that "in the long run, we are all dead." He meant that simply waiting for the economy to recover would lead to an unacceptably long period of severe economic damage—which indeed is what happened during the Great Depression. In 1936, Keynes presented a theory on how economies can fall into recessions and stay there for a long time—and some ideas about how public policy might help economies get out of the trough more quickly. We start our detailed study of business cycle theory with models that illustrate classical and Keynesian theories concerning recession and depressions.

Discussion Questions

1. What impressions do you have of the Great Recession that began in 2008? How about the euro crisis? What were its impacts on people you know or have heard about? How do you think it compares to the Great Depression of the 1930s?
2. Do you know in what phase of the business cycle we are at present? Is the euro-area economy currently in a recession or an expansion? What does this mean for employment, inflation, and GDP growth?

2. MACROECONOMIC MODELING AND AGGREGATE DEMAND

For economists, explanations often take the form of theoretical mathematical models. A theoretical model (as we saw in Chapter 2) is a "thought experiment" to help us see the world, which necessarily highlights some aspects of a situation. At the same time, due to simplifying assumptions, it neglects others. A mathematical model expresses the theory in terms of equations, graphs, or schedules. Models contain variables. These are abstract (simplified) representations of important macroeconomic measures—usually related to ones that we can observe empirically, such as GDP or the unemployment rate. Macroeconomists make simplifying assumptions about variables, for example, assuming that all the various interest rates that might coexist in the economy can be summarized as if they were a single one, referred to as "the interest rate." Mathematical models relate these variables together using algebraic formulas, graphs, or tables in such a way as to make clear how these variables affect one another, according to the theorist's understanding.

2.1 Simplifying Assumptions

In Chapter 5, we saw that the economy could be described in terms of four sectors: household, business, government, and foreign. Household expenditures on consumption, business expenditures on investment, government spending, and exchange with the foreign sector expressed as net exports were summed up to obtain total GDP.

This approach simplifies the economy—for example, by assuming that only businesses and the government carry out investment in equipment—and the models of aggregate demand we now develop simplify even further:*

- For the models in Part III of this book, we assume that the full-employment output level *does not grow.* In designing models, it is often useful to separate different issues into different models. Chapter 18 of this text examines economic growth and ignores business cycles. In Part III, we take an opposite but complementary approach, concentrating on cycles and abstracting from growth.
- For the initial analysis in this chapter, we assume that the only actors in the economy are *households* and *businesses.* We also assume that all income in the economy goes to households in return for the labor or capital services that they provide. (In the real world, businesses often hold onto some of their profits as "retained earnings" rather than paying them all out to households, but we ignore that here.) We reintroduce the government in Chapter 10 and discuss the foreign sector in Chapter 14.
- For the remainder of the present chapter, we concentrate on the difference between the classical and Keynesian theories about the behavior of economies that face a threat of *recession* and rising unemployment due to (potentially) insufficient aggregate demand. Booms and inflationary pressures are discussed in later chapters. While modern macroeconomic models are often not purely "Keynesian" or "Classical" anymore (current schools of thought include "New Keynesian," "Post-Keynesian," "Neoclassical," and "New Classical," discussed further in Chapter 13 and its Appendix), the polarization helps us understand the underlying arguments.

These simplifications allow us to make some important points while still keeping the stories, with their accompanying math and graphs, reasonably simple.

2.2 Output, Income, and Aggregate Demand

Recall from Chapter 5 that whether GDP is measured by the product approach, the spending approach, or the income approach, the number will be the same (in theory). For the macroeconomic models that we now develop, we will assume that a single variable, which we will denote as "Y," represents GDP expressed as "output,"

---

* As noted in Chapter 5, household investment in consumer durables are not specifically accounted for in national income calculations.

"product," or "income" interchangeably. The top arrow in Figure 9.5 illustrates that, in our simplified macroeconomy, production by firms generates labor and capital incomes to households.

But things get more interesting when we examine the flows from income into spending and from spending (aggregate demand) to supporting a given level of output in the economy. A macroeconomy is in an *equilibrium* situation when output, income, and spending are all in balance—when they are linked in an unbroken chain, each supported by the other at the equilibrium level, as illustrated in Figure 9.6.

aggregate expenditure (*AE*): (in a simple model without government or foreign trade): what households and firms *intend* to spend on consumption and investment: $AE = C + I_I$

The Keynesian model is based on the idea that aggregate demand or **aggregate expenditure**, which we denote as *AE*, may (at least temporarily) fall out of balance with the other flows. Aggregate expenditure in the economy depends on the spending behavior of the economic actors in the economy. Households make consumption spending decisions, and together the household sector generates an aggregate level of consumption, *C*. We assume that households always consume at the level that they plan to, given their incomes—that what they end up spending is always exactly equal to what they *intended* to spend.

But for firms, the situation can be more complicated, as we will see as this chapter progresses. Purchases of final goods by business firms are considered investment, as discussed in Chapter 5. We will denote total investment for a given year as *I*. But, as we will see, total actual investment is not always the same as what business firms *plan* to invest. We call the amount they *plan* to invest over the course of a year *intended investment*, I_I.

Because the only actors we are looking at right now are households and businesses, we begin our modeling of aggregate expenditure with the equation:

Aggregate Expenditure = Consumption + Intended Investment
$$AE = C + I_I$$

AE is the level of spending that results if people are able to follow their plans.

Remembering that if "output," "income," and "spending" are all just different ways of looking at GDP, it must also be true in this simple economy that GDP is equal to consumption plus total (actual) investment:

$$Y = C + I$$

behavioral equation: in contrast to an accounting identity, a behavioral equation reflects a theory about the behavior of one or more economic agents or sectors. The variables in the equation may or may not be observable.

$Y = C + I$ is an *accounting identity*. At the end of any year, when *actual* flows of output, income, and spending are tallied up in the national accounts, the spending by households and businesses *must* (in an economy with no government or foreign sector) be equal to GDP. This equation is true in the same way that, in business accounting, net worth is defined as equal to assets minus liabilities.

The equation $AE = C + I_I$, in contrast, represents something different. It is what is called a **behavioral equation**, used by economists for modeling purposes—we do not have a national agency that looks into business leaders' minds and measures their *intentions*! We work with *both* of these equations later in this chapter. The accounting identity involves the *actual* level of investment, while the behavioral equation involves the level of *planned, desired, or intended* investment. While in this simple world households always *actually* spend what they have *intended* to spend (so we do not need a separate symbol for "intended consumption"), Y and AE will only be the same if actual investment (I) is equal to intended investment (I_p). As we will see, this will not always be the case.

The link from income (Y) to spending (AE) is the potential weak link in the chain illustrated in Figure 9.5. This is because the people who get the income do not just automatically go out and spend it all. This creates the problem of *leakages*.

2.3 The Problem of Leakages

The household sector, we have assumed, receives all the income in the economy. Households spend some of this income on consumption goods and save the rest, according to the equation:

$$S = Y - C$$

where S is the aggregate level of saving. Saving is considered a "leakage" from the output-income-spending cycle, because it represents income that is *not* spent on currently produced goods and services. This is illustrated in Figure 9.7, which shows that some funds are *diverted* from the income-spending part of the cycle into savings.

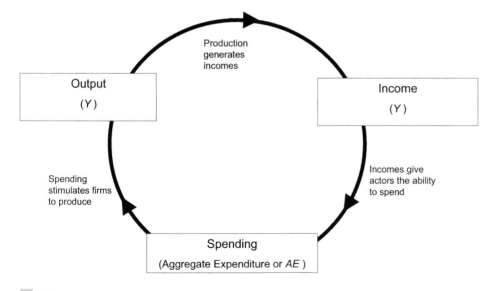

Figure 9.6 *The Output-Income-Spending Flow of an Economy in Equilibrium*

A macroeconomy is said to be in equilibrium when the incomes that arise from production give rise to a level of spending that, in turn, stimulates producers to produce the original level of output.

The other side of the coin, however, is that businesses need funds if they are going to be able to buy investment goods. (Remember, we have assumed that they do not hold onto any of the income they receive but pass it all along to households as wages, profits, interest, or rents.) In our simple model, we assume that firms must borrow from the savings put away by households in order to be able to finance investment projects.

You can think of households depositing their savings in banks, with firms taking out loans from the banks to buy structures or equipment. In this way, firms can reinject funds to the spending stream in the form of investment. This "injection" of spending through investment is also illustrated in Figure 9.7.

If the amount that households want to save is equal to the amount that firms want to invest, then these two flows will balance each other out:

> *In equilibrium:*
> *leakages = injections*
> $S = I_I$

If the flows are in balance, then Figure 9.7 is just a more complicated version of the equilibrium situation portrayed in Figure 9.6. The income–spending flow is more complex, but all income still ends up feeding into AE, thus supporting the initial level of output (you can mentally fill in the missing part of the circle). This is the kind of equilibrium you might encounter while pumping air into an inner tube that has a leak: The inner tube stays the same size because you put in more air just as quickly as it is leaking out.

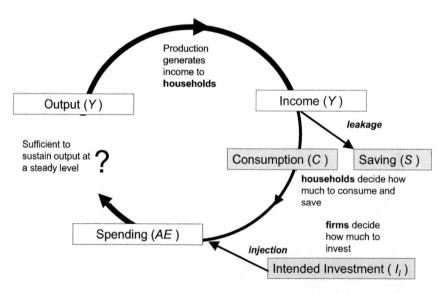

Figure 9.7 *The Output-Income-Spending Flow With Leakages and Injections*

When households save rather than spend part of their incomes, funds are diverted from the income-spending flow. When firms spend on investment goods, this creates a flow into the spending stream.

This can be seen mathematically as well. If we add C to each side of the equilibrium condition, we get $C + S = C + I_I$. But from the equation that defines saving (S), we know that the left side equals Y, while from the definition of aggregate expenditure, we know that the right side equals AE. Therefore, when leakages equal injections:

In equilibrium:
$Y = AE$

This equation says that spending is exactly sufficient to buy the output produced—the economy is in a macroeconomic equilibrium. But households and firms are two different sectors—what happens if their plans *do not* match?

Suppose that businesses suddenly lose confidence about the future and cut back on their plans for expansion (that is, they reduce I_I). Or suppose that intended investment is unchanged, but households suddenly decide to consume less and save more, so that the flow into savings is larger than what firms want to use for investment. In either case, leakages will exceed injections. If the savings leakage in Figure 9.7 is larger than the investment injection, the result is that AE will be smaller than income and output:

In the case of insufficient aggregate expenditure:
leakages > injections
$S > I_I$
$Y > AE$

The question mark in Figure 9.7 indicates that planned spending may or may not be sufficient to support the existing level of output. If the economy is not in macroeconomic equilibrium, something will have to adjust.

Here we reach the dividing point between classical and Keynesian economists. These two theories tell very different stories about how this adjustment comes about. We start with the classical story.

2.4 The Classical Solution to Leakages

In the classical model, we are essentially in a perfectly balanced world, where output is always at its full-employment level. We saw in Chapter 8, looking at business cycles from an employment perspective, that classical economists believed that falling wages in flexible labor markets would bring the economy back to full employment.

For the moment, we put this labor-market story into the background and ask our business cycle question in another way: How does an economy (which we assume to be running at a full-employment level of production) keep leakages into saving *exactly equal to* injections coming from investment spending? Or, to express this another way, how can the economy respond to a sudden shift in saving or intended investment that might cause insufficient (or excessive) aggregate expenditure? The classical argument is again, not surprisingly, that flexible markets will keep the economy at a full-employment level of spending and output.

In this case, the relevant market is what economists call the market for *loanable funds*. In our very simple model, households save out of income from current production. Because they can earn interest on any savings they deposit in a bank rather than stuff under a mattress, they will prefer the bank. In this market, households are the *suppliers* of loanable funds and firms are the *demanders* of loanable funds. The classical theory about the market for loanable funds is illustrated in Figure 9.8. The vertical axis is the interest rate paid from firms to households, which acts as the "price" of loanable funds.

Classical economists assume that households make their decisions about how much to save by looking at the going rate of interest in this market. The higher the interest rate, the more worthwhile it is to save, because their savings earn more. The lower the interest rate, the less appealing it is to save. So the supply of loanable funds (saving) curve in Figure 9.8 slopes upward.

To firms, however, the payment of interest is a cost. So when interest rates are low, this model assumes, firms will want to borrow more for investment projects because borrowing is inexpensive. High interest rates, in contrast, will discourage firms from borrowing. The demand curve in Figure 9.8 thus slopes downward. Where the curves cross determines the equilibrium "price" of funds—here, the interest rate of 5 percent—and the equilibrium quantity of funds borrowed and lent.

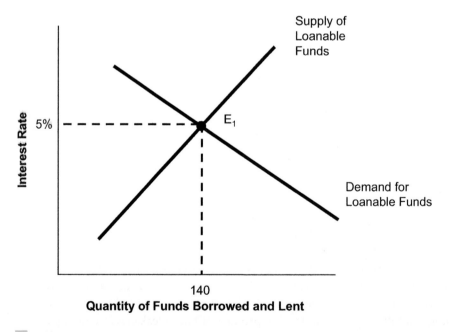

Figure 9.8 *The Classical Model of the Market for Loanable Funds*

In the classical version of the macroeconomic model, household saving creates the supply of loanable funds and firms' borrowing for investment creates the demand for loanable funds. At the equilibrium interest rate, the amount households save and the amount businesses invest are equated.

In Figure 9.8, the amount saved by households and lent out is 140—which is also the amount borrowed and invested by firms.* (All numbers in our simple models are made up and set to be easy numbers to handle. You could think of the unit for our numbers for Y, AE, C, I, and S as billions of real euros in a fictional economy.)

In Figure 9.9 we illustrate what happens in the classical model if, after starting from a position at point E_0 (which we assume corresponds to a full-employment balance of S and I), firms suddenly change their plans, deciding to spend less on investment. The demand-for-loanable-funds curve shifts leftward. If the interest rate remained at 5 percent, we would see a big drop in investment. But because the interest rate falls to 3 percent, part of the drop in investment will be reversed as firms take advantage of the cheaper loans. And because the interest rate is now lower, some households will choose to save less and consume more (indicated by the movement downward along the supply curve).

In the end, saving and (both intended and actual) investment will still be equal, though at a lower level—in Figure 9.9, the level drops to 60. Aggregate expenditure will still be equal to the full-employment level—though now it is made up of somewhat less investment and somewhat more consumption than before the shift in investment plans. In short, the fall in intended investment was balanced by an increase in consumer spending (a decrease in saving).

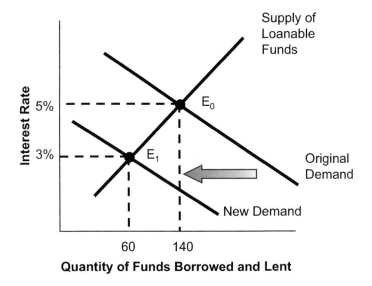

Figure 9.9 *Adjustment to a Reduction in Intended Investment in the Classical Model*

In the classical model, smooth adjustments in the market for loanable funds keep saving equal to investment, even if firms or households change their behavior.

---

* In the real world, households and institutions, firms, governments, and the foreign sector all borrow and lend for various reasons, and much of the supply and demand for loanable funds reflects transactions in existing assets that have little to do with current flows of production and income. This model abstracts from these complications to focus on flows of savings and investment.

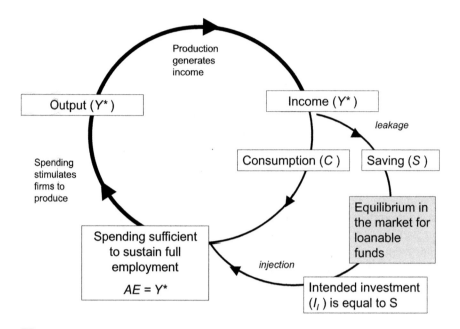

Figure 9.10 *Macroeconomic Equilibrium at Full Employment in the Classical Model*

Leakages always equal injections in the classical model because of smooth adjustments in the market for loanable funds. The economy is always in equilibrium at a full-employment level of output (Y*).

In the classical model, both households' saving activity and firms' investment spending are assumed to be quite sensitive to changes in the interest rate, which serves as the "price of loanable funds." An adjustment in the interest rate, according to this theory, will quickly correct any threat of imbalances between the leakage of savings and the injection of investment. The interest rate is assumed to adjust smoothly in a free-market economy.

With saving and intended investment always in balance, there is no reason to think that the economy would ever diverge from full employment. The economy is thus self-sustaining at full employment due to the smooth working of the market for loanable funds (see Figure 9.10). We assume (for now) that the level of output that corresponds to full employment is clearly known. As we did in Figure 9.4, we use the symbol Y^* to denote this full-employment level (or range) of output and income.

In the real world, things do not always work out so smoothly (see Box 9.1). This became evident in the Great Depression, when the economy clearly did fall into a situation of severe and prolonged unemployment. People came to be dissatisfied with the classical theory. Could there be something wrong with this story? Could another theory do a better job of explaining the depression—and, even better, point toward how the economy might get out of it? This issue has particular relevance today, because we have recently been through a similar experience—stubbornly high unemployment that does not automatically readjust to full employment.

BOX 9.1 SMALL BUSINESS LOANS DURING THE EURO CRISIS

According to the theory of loanable funds, banks act as intermediaries between the savings of households and the borrowing of businesses. If demand for funds falls, because for example companies decide to cut back on investments in a recession, this theory predicts that interest rates will fall. As a consequence, on the one hand, households will save less; on the other hand, companies will increase investments again.

However, this is not what was observed in many countries during the euro crisis. While the interest rates in the money market (the market in which banks lend to each other) fell close to 0 in 2014, investments did not increase. One reason was that banks did not necessarily pass on these lower borrowing costs to their customers. "One reason is macro[-economic] uncertainty, but that isn't as bad as it was," says Dario Perkins, economist at Lombard Street Research in London. In addition, banks were lacking the capital base they needed to make more loans, as regulation requires them to hold a certain amount of equity capital before they can make more loans.

According to Federica Lucisano, chief executive of Lucisano Media Group, which acquires and distributes films and TV programs, "the main problem is that [...] local banks still grant financing at high rates."

As a consequence, many companies have looked into ways to circumvent banks. As Pietro Colucci, CEO of Kinexia, a small renewable energy company based in Milan, explains: "Our choice was to explore other financing instruments such as private bond placement." While this kind of financing provides some relief, it cannot substitute for all bank lending. Many small companies usually are unable to place bonds, as their credit needs are too small relative to the costs of bond placement. This creates, in effect, two separate markets for loanable funds, with small companies generally placed at a disadvantage, facing more difficulties and higher costs in obtaining credit.

Sources: Sarah Gordon and Peter Wise, "Eurozone companies urge capitals to reform econo-mies," *Financial Times*, September 23, 2014.

Discussion Questions

1. Who are the actors in this simple macroeconomic model? What is the role of each in determining the flow of currently produced goods and services? What is the role of each in the classical market for loanable funds?
2. Explain verbally why, in the classical model, the demand for loanable funds curve slopes downward. Explain verbally why the supply of loanable funds curve slopes upward.

3. THE KEYNESIAN MODEL

Keynes's major contribution was to develop a theory to explain why aggregate expenditure (or aggregate demand) could stay persistently low. He called it *the General Theory*, because he believed that the case of full employment (Y^*) represents only a special case, one that may not often be achieved. In this section, we present the basics of his theory using (for the moment) the very simple closed-economy, no-government, no-growth model introduced earlier.

3.1 Consumption

Many things may affect the level of aggregate consumption in an economy, but one thing that very clearly affects it is the level of current aggregate income. Households are able to spend more on consumption goods and services when the economy is generating a lot of income than they can when it is not (see Box 9.2). So Keynes used in his model a very simple *consumption function* that expresses aggregate consumption as the sum of two components: an "autonomous" part and a part that depends on the level of aggregate income. In algebraic form, the Keynesian consumption function is expressed as:

$$C = \bar{C} + mpc\ Y$$

where $\bar{C}$ is "autonomous" consumption and *mpc* is called the "marginal propensity to consume" (explained in what follows). We first discuss the economic significance of these two parts of the function and then put the function to work.

Autonomous consumption is the part of consumption that is not related to income. It can be thought of as a minimum level of income that people feel required to spend for basic needs. It can also be seen as reflecting the amount of consumption spending that people will undertake no matter what their current incomes are, reflecting their long-term plans, their commitments and habits, and their place in the community.

But, of course, much of consumption does reflect current income and its changes. The term **"marginal propensity to consume"** (*mpc*) reflects the number of *additional* euros of consumption spending that occur for every *additional* euro of aggregate income. Using the notation Δ (the Greek letter delta) to mean "change in," *mpc* can be expressed as:

marginal propensity to consume: the number of additional euros of consumption for every additional euro of income (typically a fraction between 0 and 1)

$$mpc = \Delta C/\Delta Y = \textit{(the change of C resulting from a change in Y)} \div \textit{(the change in Y)}$$

In the following example, we use an *mpc* of 8/10 or 0.8. This means that for every additional €10 in aggregate income, households will spend an additional €8 on consumption. Logically, the *mpc* should be no greater than 1. An *mpc* greater than 1 would mean that people increase their consumption by *more* than the addition to their income. An *mpc* of about 0.8 has been the standard, historically, in Keynesian modeling exercises—though such a value may not correspond well to actual data on consumption in every time period.

Recall that any income not spent by the household sector is saved. Based on the consumption function, a savings function can be derived using the equation for savings and substituting in the equation for consumption:

$$S = Y - C = Y - (\bar{C} + mpc\ Y) = -\bar{C} + (1 - mpc)\ Y$$

The term ($1-mpc$) is called the "**marginal propensity to save**":

$$mps = 1 - mpc = \Delta S/\Delta Y$$

marginal propensity to save: the number of additional euros saved for each additional euro of income (typically a fraction between 0 and 1)

BOX 9.2 CONSUMER SPENDING RISES WITH INCREASED INCOME DESPITE POLITICAL UNCERTAINTY

By September 2016, Spain had been without a working government for almost a year. As the acting prime minister, Mariano Rajoy, had not been able to form a coalition with a majority in parliament after the election in late 2015, no law had been passed since October 2015. Moreover, political uncertainty was lingering: As political parties were not really making progress in agreeing on a new majority coalition, the country was drifting toward the possibility of a third election in just over a year.

Nevertheless, the Spanish economy was weathering the absence of a working government relatively well. When the national statistics office published revised GDP data for the second quarter of 2016 in August, growth turned out to be a robust 0.8 percent relative to the previous quarter for the fourth quarter in a row, putting annual GDP growth for 2016 as a whole at more than 3 percent, well above the European average and all other large European economies.

Drivers of the recovery were strong increases in private consumption and business investment. With unemployment falling strongly and a tax cut enacted in 2015, households' disposable incomes had increased strongly, and people were spending this money. Compared to one year earlier, consumption was up 3.6 percent in the second quarter of 2016.

Sources: *Reuters*, "Spanish economy powers ahead as politicians dither," August 25, 2016; Tobias Buck, "Spanish economy prospers despite continued political stalemate," *Financial Times*, September 5, 2016.

For example, if households spend 80 percent of additional income, or €8 out of an additional €10 in income, then they must save 20 percent (= 100 percent – 80 percent), or €2 out of €10. So if the *mpc* is 0.8, the *mps* must be 0.2.

If we assign number values to the parameters $\bar{C}$ and *mpc*, we can express the relation between income and consumption stated in the consumption function by a schedule, as in Table 9.2. Various income levels are shown in Column (1). For now, we set autonomous consumption at 20 (as shown in Column [2]). With an *mpc* set equal to 0.8, Column (3) shows how to calculate the second component of the consumption function. Adding together the autonomous and income-related components yields total consumption, shown in Column (4). We also show in Column (5), for later reference, the implied level of saving. For example, the shaded row indicates that when income is 400, $C = 20 + 0.8\,(400) = 20 + 320 = 340$. Saving is calculated as $400 - 340 = 60$. Consumption and saving both rise steadily as income rises.

Table 9.2 *The Consumption Schedule (and Saving)*

(1)	(2)	(3)	(4)	(5)
Income (Y)	Autonomous consumption $\bar{C}$	The part of consumption that depends on income, with mpc = 0.8	Consumption C = 20 + 0.8 Y	Saving S = Y − C
		= 0.8 × column (1)	= column (2) + column (3)	= column (1) − column (4)
0	20	0	20	−20
100	20	80	100	0
200	20	160	180	20
300	20	240	260	40
400	20	320	340	60
500	20	400	420	80
600	20	480	500	100
700	20	560	580	120
800	20	640	660	140

We can also see the relationships among consumption, income, and saving in this model in the graph in Figure 9.11. (For a review of graphing techniques, see Box 9.3.) The horizontal axis measures income (Y), while the vertical axis measures consumption (C). The consumption function crosses the vertical axis at the level of autonomous consumption ($\bar{C}$) of 20. The line has a slope equal to the *mpc* of 0.8. Figure 9.11 also includes a 45° line, which tells us what consumption would be if people consumed all their income instead of saving part of it. So the vertical distance between the 45° "consumption = income" line and the consumption function tells us how much people save. We can see, for example, that at an income of 100, households, in this model, consume all their income. At levels of income lower than 100, consumption is higher than income, and they "dissave."* At an income of 400, how much do people save? Check for yourself that the information given in Table 9.2 and Figure 9.11 for income levels of 0, 100, and 400 are in agreement.

---

* When the household sector "dissaves," it depletes assets (or increases debts) in order to pay for consumption. In this case, consumption exceeds income, and savings are *negative*. This happens only very rarely. According to OECD data, in the 2000s, there were a few years of negative household savings in the UK, Ireland, Denmark, Estonia, and Greece and one year of negative household saving rates in Spain. These years mostly coincided with times of large increases in the value of residential real estate when households felt richer. In all other industrialized countries, household saving rates remained positive.

304

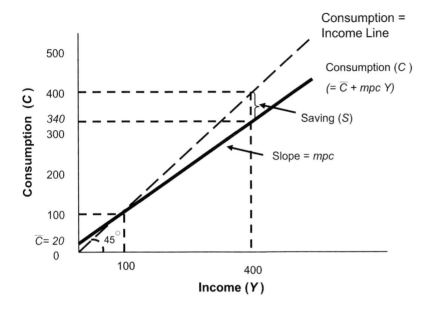

Figure 9.11 *The Keynesian Consumption Function*

In the Keynesian model, consumption rises with income according to the equation
$C = \bar{C} + mpc\ Y$.

A number of factors can cause the consumption schedule for a macroeconomy to change. Among the significant ones are:

- *Wealth.* When many people in a country feel wealthier—perhaps because the stock market or housing prices are high—the household sector as a whole may tend to spend more, even if households' actual annual incomes do not change.
- *Consumer confidence.* When people feel less confident about the future—perhaps due to political turmoil or the fear of a coming recession—they may tend to hunker down and spend less on consumption goods.
- *Attitudes toward spending and saving.* If many people decided to consume less for reasons of health, cultural shifts, or the environment, consumption would also be depressed.
- *Consumption-related government policies.* High levels of saving can be a source of capital for economic growth. Sometimes, a country's leaders will urge people to lower their consumption levels and raise their saving levels in order to allow for more investment without inflation or capital imports. (An exercise at the end of this chapter asks you to look at some implications of such a policy.) At other times, leaders urge people to consume in order to boost the economy. Tax systems may be designed to encourage saving or to encourage certain types of consumption.
- *The distribution of income.* Poorer people tend to spend more of their income than richer people, because just covering necessities can take most or all of their income (or more, forcing them into debt). So a redistribution of income from richer people to poorer people tends to raise consumption and depress saving.

Some of these factors may be best thought of as changing $\bar{C}$ in the Keynesian consumption function, causing the consumption schedule to shift up or down, while others may change the *mpc*, causing the schedule to become steeper or flatter.

BOX 9.3 GRAPHING WITH A SLOPE-INTERCEPT EQUATION

Linear equations are of the form $Y = a + b X$. On a graph, the variable Y is measured on the vertical axis and the variable X is measured on the horizontal axis. X and Y are called "variables" and a and b are called "parameters." The parameter a is called "the intercept" and shows where the line representing the linear relationship between X and Y crosses the vertical axis. The parameter b is "the slope" and determines the steepness of the line. It reflects "rise over run": that is, starting from any point on the line and moving to any other point off to the right on the same line, the slope is the ratio of the number of units the line moves *upward* (*rises*) to the number of units the line moves *sideways* (*runs*).

The consumption function, $C = \bar{C} + mpc\, Y$, is of this same form, only with different variable and parameter names. The consumption function relates the variable C to the variable Y. It has an intercept of $\bar{C}$ and a slope of *mpc*.

Note that the classical model assumes that people make their decisions about how much income to consume and how much to save based largely on the interest rate, but the Keynesian model does not mention the interest rate because the effects of interest rates on saving are, in fact, ambiguous. If you saw that a very high interest rate is prevailing in the loanable funds market, you might want to take advantage of it and increase your rate of saving, at least for a while. In this case, you would be acting as classical economists assume: A higher interest rate causes you to save more and consume less.

But what if you are saving primarily to finance your college education or your retirement, so you have a certain target level of accumulated wealth in mind? A higher interest rate also means that you can reach this target *faster* (and so revert to higher consumption sooner) or that you can reach the target in the same amount of time while saving *less*. Common sense suggests that the amount that people save depends mainly on their ability to save, based on their income as well as their needs and plans, rather than primarily on the current interest rate.

In fact, a more significant impact of changes in interest rates on household behavior comes from their effect on what households may *pay* in interest rather than on what households earn. While the simple classical model assumes that households are only on the saving and lending side of the market, in reality, households frequently borrow to spend on capital goods for household production. When interest rates are high, households may postpone buying houses, cars, major appliances, and other consumer durables.

In any case, the simple Keynesian function that we are working with leaves out the interest rate entirely. The most important thing to remember about the

Keynesian consumption function is that some income generally "leaks" into saving (and so does not create aggregate expenditure) and that, unlike in the classical model, the interest rate is *not* considered an important factor in determining the size of this leakage.

3.2 Investment

In the real world, firms may take into account a number of things when thinking about how much to invest. The cost of borrowing (the interest rate) is certainly one factor, as are other things, such as the prices of investment goods, their own accumulated assets and debt, and the willingness of people and banks to lend to them. (Not everyone can qualify for a loan.) Keynes thought that, in general, interest rates were somewhat important in explaining the level of investment. But he argued that, in the case of a severe slowdown of economic activity such as the Great Depression, a low interest rate would not be enough to motivate business firms to invest in building up new capacity.

The most important factor in explaining aggregate investment spending, Keynes thought, is the general level of optimism or pessimism that investors feel about the future, or what he called "animal spirits." If firms' managers believe that they will be able to sell more of the goods or services that they produce in the future, and at a good price, they will want to invest in equipment and structures to maintain and expand their capacity. If they do not see such a rosy future ahead, then why would even a very low interest rate persuade them to invest? The borrowed funds will have to be repaid; the major question for the borrower is "are my prospects for success good enough to allow me to repay this loan?" The interest rate will marginally change the amount to be repaid but is not the major determinant of the answer to this question.

Because Keynes saw investment as future directed rather than related to any current, observable economic variables, the "function" for intended investment in the simple Keynesian model just says that investors intend to invest whatever investors intend to invest. All of intended investment is considered "autonomous" in this model. We can denote this as:

$$I_1 = \overline{I}_I$$

where $\overline{I}_I$ is "autonomous intended investment." Don't worry too much about whether to put a bar over the symbol—we have introduced it here just to show you that it is similar in concept to the $\overline{C}$ in the consumption function. Just as $\overline{C}$ can go up or down depending on consumer confidence, $\overline{I}_I$ can go up or down depending on investor confidence.

Figure 9.12 graphs investment against income for the case where $\overline{I}_I = 60$. Because investment does not depend on income, the graph is horizontal. The lack of attention to interest rates is a limitation of the simple Keynesian model. In later chapters, we depart from this simplification and consider the effects of interest rates on investment.

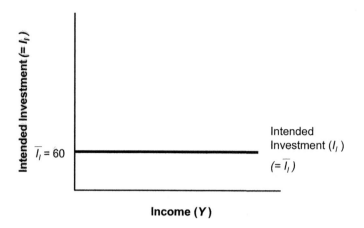

Figure 9.12 *The Keynesian Investment Function*

In the simplest Keynesian model, intended investment is a constant, no matter what the level of national income, being determined instead by long-term profit expectations.

Table 9.3 *Deriving Aggregate Expenditure From the Consumption Function and Investment*

(1)	(2)	(3)	(4)
Income (Y)	*Consumption (C)*	*Intended investment (I_I)*	*Aggregate expenditure $AE = C + I_I$ = column (2) + column (3)*
0	20	60	80
300	260	60	320
400	340	60	400
500	420	60	480
600	500	60	560
700	580	60	640
800	660	60	720

3.3 The Aggregate Expenditure Schedule

Earlier we defined *AE* as the sum of consumption and intended investment. We can now add intended investment to the consumption schedule and curve to get a schedule and graph for aggregate expenditure. In Table 9.3, Columns (1) and (2) just repeat Table 9.2. In Column (3), we have set intended investment at 60, for any level of income, in line with the notion that it is all "autonomous." Column (4) calculates the level of aggregate intended spending in the economy. We can see that when, for

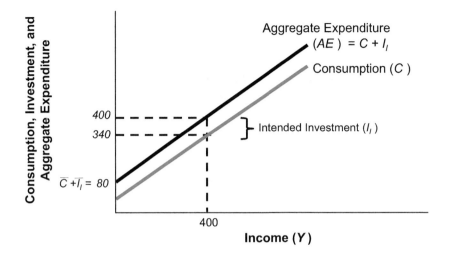

Figure 9.13 *Aggregate Expenditure*

The AE curve is derived by adding the autonomous intended investment to consumption at each income level. So at each level of Y, AE is the vertical sum of C and I_I.

example, $Y = 400$, households and businesses together plan to spend 400 on consumption and investment.

Figure 9.13 shows the relationship between income and aggregate demand. The AE line lies exactly 60 units vertically above the C line, at every level of income. Its intercept is the sum of autonomous consumption and intended investment. Its slope is the same as that of the consumption function. We can see that when, for example, $Y = 400$, then $C = 340$ and $AE = 400$.

The AE curve shifts up or down as autonomous consumption or autonomous investment changes. Suppose that intended investment is 140 instead of 60. Table 9.4 calculates AE for selected levels of income like those that we used before but at this higher level of I_I. Because neither $\overline{C}$ nor the *mpc* has changed, Column (2) is the same as in earlier tables.

This aggregate demand schedule is graphed in Figure 9.14. The intercept is now 160, which is equal to $\overline{C}$ of 20 plus $\overline{I}_I$ of 140, while the slope is still equal to the *mpc*. Notice that now, at an income level of 400, aggregate demand is 480 instead of 400. With investment increased by 80, aggregate demand at any income level increases by 80 as well.

Figure 9.14 could also be used to illustrate an increase in $\overline{C}$ from 20 to 100 (an increase of 80) while intended investment remains at 60. Any combination of $\overline{C}$ and $\overline{I}_I$ that sums to 160 would yield this graph. In economic terms, any increase in autonomous consumer and investor desired spending increases aggregate expenditure.

309

Table 9.4 *Aggregate Expenditure With Higher Intended Investment*

(1)	(2)	(3)	(4)
Income (Y)	Consumption (C)	Intended investment (I_l)	Aggregate expenditure (AE)
0	20	140	160
300	260	140	400
400	340	140	480
500	420	140	560
600	500	140	640
700	580	140	720
800	660	140	800

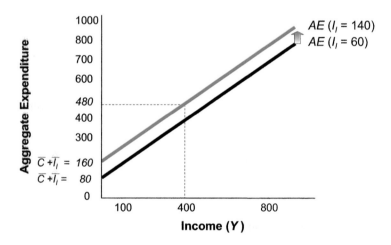

Figure 9.14 *Aggregate Expenditure With Higher Intended Investment*

If intended investment increases (or autonomous consumption increases), the aggregate expenditure curve shifts upward.

3.4 The Possibility of Unintended Investment

The key to the Keynesian model is understanding why and how *unintended* investment can occur and how firms respond when they see it happening. Unintended investment occurs when aggregate expenditure is insufficient, because firms will not be able to sell all the goods that they produce.

Recall (from Chapter 5) that a country's manufactured capital stock includes structures, equipment, *and inventories*. Many firms normally plan to keep as inventory a level

Table 9.5 *The Possibility of Excess Inventory Accumulation or Depletion*

(1)	(2)	(3)	(4)	(5)	(6)
Income (Y)	Aggregate expenditure (AE)	Excess inventory accumulation (+) or depletion (−) = column (1) − column (2)	Intended investment (I_I)	Investment (I) = column (3) + column (4)	Check that the macroeconomic identity still holds: Y = C + I
300	320	−20	60	40	300
400	400	0	60	60	400
500	480	20	60	80	500
600	560	40	60	100	600
700	640	60	60	120	700
800	720	80	60	140	800

of supplies that they expect to use soon and products that they have not yet shipped. *Unintended* inventory investment occurs when these inventories build up unexpectedly. A manufacturing firm, for example, experiences *excess inventory accumulation* when it cannot sell its goods as quickly as expected and the goods pile up in warehouses. Conversely, a firm that sells its goods faster than expected experiences *excess inventory depletion*, as the goods "fly off the shelves" and the warehouse empties out.

Actual investment (I, as measured in the national accounts) is the sum of what businesses plan to invest, plus what they inadvertently end up investing if *AE* and *Y* do not match up exactly:

I = intended investment (I_I) + excess inventory accumulation or depletion

In Table 9.5, Columns (1) and (2) repeat information from Table 9.3 for intended investment of 60 and selected levels of income. Column (3) calculates levels of *unintended* investment. If, for example, income and output are 600, but aggregate expenditure is only 560, excess inventory accumulation of 40 will occur. Or, if income and output are 300, but firms and households want to buy 320, inventories will be depleted by 20 to meet the demand. Only at an income level of 400 is there a balance between income and spending.

Columns (4) to (6) are included in Table 9.5 to show that both the equation $AE = C + I_I$ and the identity $Y = C + I$ hold at all times in this model. Column (5) of Table 9.5 calculates actual investment (I) as the sum of intended and unintended investment. Notice that the figures in Column (6) match those in Column (1)—when we include *unintended*, excess inventory accumulation or depletion, the basic macroeconomic identity $Y = C + I$ is still true.

Figure 9.15—often called the "Keynesian cross" diagram—illustrates this case for two income levels. The *AE* curve, as we know, represents the sum of consumption and

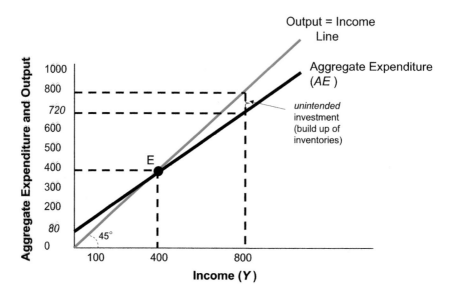

Figure 9.15 *Unintended Investment in the Keynesian Model*

If income and output in an economy are above the level of aggregate expenditure, excessive inventories accumulate. This is illustrated for the income level of 800.

investment at any income level. The dashed line is a 45° line that (as in our earlier diagram about consumption, income, and saving) illustrates equality between the values on the two axes. With income on the horizontal axis and output on the vertical axis, all points on this 45° line represent situations in which output equals income. At an income level of 800, the *AE* curve indicates that aggregate expenditure is 720. But the "output = income" line indicates that output is 800 and so exceeds spending. There is unintended inventory buildup of 80, as indicated by the vertical distance between the *AE* curve and the 45° line, at this income level. (Check to see that this is consistent with Table 9.5.)

At an income level of 400, where the *AE* line crosses the 45° line, there is full macroeconomic equilibrium, because output, income, and spending are all at the same level. Unintended investment is 0.

At levels of income and output above 400 in Table 9.5 and Figure 9.15, business firms' managers are unhappy because more and more of their goods are gathering dust. For levels of income and output below 400, their inventories are being depleted below intended levels. These are *not* equilibrium levels of income, and the economy will not stay at any of those income levels—things will change.

3.5 Movement to Equilibrium in the Keynesian Model

If firms are unhappy about unsold goods, they will do something to correct the situation. If inventories are building up more than intended, they will cut back on production. Their cutbacks in production will continue until they are no longer seeing inventories build up excessively—that is, until the level of what is actually produced matches what they can sell. Reductions in Y will continue until $Y = AE$. This is a little more complicated than it may at first seem, though, since any reduction in output leads to reduced income, which leads to reduced consumption, so that AE is a moving target. We look at this complication in Section 3.7, but for now we continue with the main story.

In Figure 9.15, suppose that the economy were (for reasons explored later) initially at an income and output level of 800. From Figure 9.15 and Table 9.5, we can see that this is not an equilibrium—producers are seeing excess inventory accumulation of 80 because AE is only 720. Producers will cut back on production. The equilibrium point E is obtained when aggregate output has fallen to 400 and AE has also fallen to 400.

So, what has happened here? If you look back at Table 9.2, you can see that at the initial income level of 800, there was a "leakage" into saving of 140. But firms, we have assumed, only want to spend 60 on investment. Leakages exceeded injections by 80, aggregate expenditure was insufficient, and inventories of 80 built up. Firms cut back on production. They continued to cut back until inventories were back where they wanted them.

Yet when the economy arrives at an equilibrium, the balance between saving and investing has been restored! Why is this so? Intended investment has not changed—it has been at 60 all along. But now that income has dropped, households have less income to use for consumption and saving, and so saving has dropped from its initial level of 140 to only 60. (See Table 9.2 to check that this is the level of saving at an income level of 400.) It is changes in aggregate income, and the resulting changes in consumption and saving, that have caused leakages and injections to become equal again.

We can also see in the schedules and graphs what would happen if AE were for some reason to be *above* the current level of output. If output were to start out at 300, for example, desired spending of 320 (see Table 9.5) would cause produced goods to "fly off the shelves" and deplete inventories. According to this model, this situation would motivate firms to increase production. As production rises, income, consumption, and saving would also all rise. Again, equilibrium would be reached when Y and AE both equal 400 and S and I both equal 60.

3.6 The Problem of Persistent Unemployment

Now that the pieces of the model have been explained, the model can be put together to illustrate what Keynes taught about the Great Depression. Assume that 800 represents the full-employment level of output for this economy, as illustrated by the vertical "full-employment range" Y^* in Figure 9.16. If intended investment is 140 (the higher AE line in Figure 9.16), the economy is at an initial full-employment equilibrium at E_0. (Refer to Table 9.4 and Figure 9.14 to confirm that at this level of income, $Y = AE$.)

But at the start of the Great Depression, the 1929 stock market crash and other events caused business and investor confidence to plummet. (Consumer confidence

313

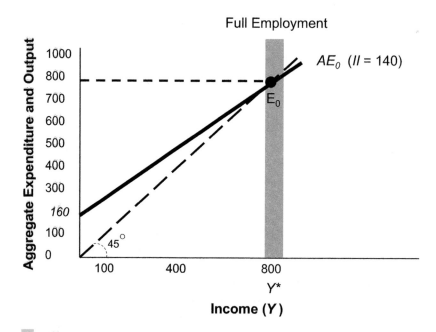

Figure 9.16 *Full Employment Equilibrium With High Intended Investment*

Supposing that Y = 800 represents full employment, an intended investment level of 140 generates spending sufficient to maintain this as an equilibrium.

and financial wealth also plummeted, but we are simplifying the story by concentrating on firms.) Producers became very uncertain about whether they would be able to sell what they produced, so they cut back radically on their investment spending. A similar mechanism can be argued to have worked at the onset of the Great Recession in 2008–2009: The banking crisis in the U.S. and its global repercussions caused such a high degree of uncertainty that businesses all over the world cut back their investment plans radically.

Such a cutback in investment plans is modeled in Figure 9.17 as a drop in aggregate demand caused by a drop in intended investment from 140 to 60. (Note that 60 is the number used in Table 9.3, so that AE_1 in Figure 9.16 is identical to the AE curve in Figure 9.13.) With the drop in AE, income of 800 is no longer an equilibrium. Consistent with the adjustments toward equilibrium that we just discussed, output, income, and spending contract until a new equilibrium (E_1) is reached at a level of 400.

An income and output level of 400, however, is far below the level of production required to provide full employment for workers. Massive unemployment results. And in the Keynesian model, there is no automatic mechanism (as there was in the classical model) that rescues the economy from this situation. The economy experiences a contraction, settling at a new, persistent, self-reinforcing, low-income, and high-unemployment equilibrium, as shown in Figure 9.18.

To say that a macroeconomy is "in equilibrium" just means that output, income, and spending are in balance. The basic idea about an equilibrium is that there tend

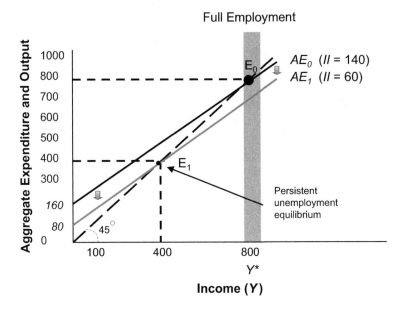

Figure 9.17 *A Keynesian Unemployment Equilibrium*

A fall in investor confidence causes the equilibrium level of output to fall. The initial excess of leakages over injections caused by low investment spending is corrected by a contraction in output, income, and saving. At E1, leakages and injections are again equal.

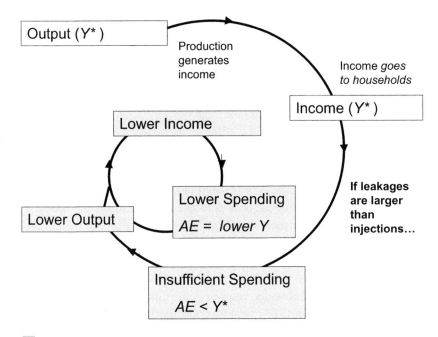

Figure 9.18 *Movement to an Unemployment Equilibrium*

An excess of leakages over injections causes aggregate expenditure to be insufficient for a full-employment level of output. Output and income fall until equilibrium is restored.

to be forces (such as, in this model, firms' desire to avoid unintended inventories) that are likely to push an economy toward equilibrium and tend to keep it there after it is achieved. But achievement of an equilibrium is not the same thing as full employment—the equilibrium level at which output, income, and spending balance may or may not be at full employment.

In Keynes's view, there was nothing that would "naturally" or "automatically" happen to pull an economy out of such a low-employment situation. A full-employment equilibrium such as E_0 in Figure 9.16 is possible, but it is merely one of a large number of possible equilibria (seen in the model as different points along the 45° line). Equally possible is a persistent unemployment equilibrium such as E_1 in Figure 9.17. Because Keynes, unlike classical economists, did not equate equilibrium with full employment, he believed that there is often a need for action to stimulate aggregate demand. Such policies are the topics of Chapters 10 and 12.

3.7 The Multiplier

In the preceding example, intended investment dropped from 140 to 60 because of a fall in investor confidence—a decline of 80 units. But output dropped from 800 to *400*—a decline of *400* units. Why is the decline in output so much bigger than the decline in investment spending that caused it?

The intuition behind this result is that, while the drop in investment spending leads to a drop in aggregate expenditure, which leads directly to a contraction in output, there are also feedback effects through consumption. Because consumption depends on income, and income depends on *AE*, which depends on consumption, additional effects "echo" back and forth. For example, reducing production in a factory does not merely involve laying off assembly-line workers. The laid-off factory workers now have less income to spend at stores. This means that the stores will also need to lay off some of their employees, who then also have less income. And so on. This process is illustrated in more detail in Table 9.6.

In the first row of Table 9.6, for example, the drop in intended investment (step 1) leads to an immediate drop in *AE* of 80 (step 2). Firms see inventories piling up and cut back production by 80. But this decreases the income going to households, because firms are now paying less in wages, interest, dividends, and rents. Consumers react (in step 3) to a change in income according to the relationship $\Delta C = mpc\ \Delta Y$. With 80 less in income, they reduce their spending by 64. How do they manage to keep their budget in line when they have only reduced their spending by 64 but their income went down by 80? See if you can think of the answer before you check the footnote.*

The second and later rows show how decreases in consumption decrease aggregate expenditure, output, and income and thus depress consumption even further. Note

---

* They economize by reducing both consumption and saving. They reduce their saving by 16 (which corresponds to the remaining 20 percent of the income change).

Table 9.6 *The Multiplier at Work*

Change in intended investment	Change in aggregate expenditure and in output and income	Change in consumption $\Delta C = mpc\ \Delta Y = .8 \times$ Column (2)
1. Investors lose confidence. $\Delta I_I = -80$	2. Reduced investment spending leads directly to $\Delta AE = -80$. Producers respond to reduced demand for their goods by cutting back on production. $\Delta Y = -80$	3. Less production means less income. With income reduced by 80, households cut consumption by $mpc\ \Delta Y$ $= .8 \times -80\ \Delta C = -64$
	4. Lowered consumption spending means lowered AE $\Delta AE = -64$ Producers respond. $\Delta Y = -64$	5. Households cut consumption by $mpc\ \Delta Y$ $= .8 \times -64$ $\Delta C = -51.2$
	6. $\Delta Y = -51.2$	7. $mpc\ \Delta Y = .8 \times -51.2$ $\Delta C = -40.96$
	8. $\Delta Y = -40.96$	9. $\Delta C = -32.77$
	10. $\Delta Y = -32.77$ etc. Sum of changes in Y $= -80 + -64 + -51.2 + -40.96 +$ $-32.77 + \ldots = -400$	11. $\Delta C = -26.21$ etc.

that in each round, the decrease in Y gets a little smaller. Fortunately, a convenient result from mathematics means that we do not need to calculate the sum of all these changes in Y by continuing to extend the table, row after row (in theory, forever—although the numbers get very tiny after a while).* A result from the mathematics of infinite series implies that, in the end, the total change in Y is related in the following way to the original change in I_I:

$$\Delta Y = \frac{1}{1 - mpc} \Delta \bar{I}_I$$

which means, in this case,

$$\Delta Y = \frac{1}{1 - 0.8}(-80) = \frac{1}{0.2}(-80) = 5(-80) = -400$$

---

* Column 2 of the table can be summarized as:

$\Delta = \Delta I_I + mpc\ \Delta \bar{I}_I + mpc\ (mpc\ \Delta \bar{I}_I) + mpc\ (mpc\ (mpc\ \Delta \bar{I}_I)) + \ldots$
$= (1 + mpc + mpc^2 + mpc^3 + \ldots.)\ \Delta \bar{I}_I$

But the infinite series $(1 + x + x^2 + x^3 + x^4 + \ldots + x^\infty)$ where $x < 1$ can be simplified to $1/(1-x)$.

The expression $1/(1 - mpc)$ is called "the income/spending multiplier"—or, for short, the multiplier—and is abbreviated *mult:*

$$mult = \frac{1}{1 - mpc}$$

In this case, with $mpc = 0.8$, the multiplier is 5. The initial decrease in intended investment causes, in the end, a decrease in income that is five times its size. We can express this mathematically as $\Delta Y = mult\ \Delta \bar{I}$.

The value of the multiplier would be the same if it had been a decrease in consumer confidence, acting through a change in $\bar{C}$ that started this cascade in incomes, instead of a decrease in investor confidence. Mathematically, this means $\Delta Y = mult\ \Delta \bar{C}$ as well. In Chapter 10, we add consideration of factors that change aggregate demand other than investor and consumer confidence.

Discussion Questions

1. If you received a raise of €100 per month, how would you increase your spending per month? How much would you change your saving? What is your *mpc*? What is your *mps*?
2. Describe verbally how, in the Keynesian model, an economy can end up in an equilibrium of persistent unemployment.

4. CONCLUDING THOUGHTS

In classical economic theory, an economy should never go into a slump—or at least it should not stay in one very long. Any deficiency in aggregate expenditure would be quickly counteracted by smooth adjustments in the market for loanable funds. Keynes, by contrast, theorized that deficiencies in aggregate expenditure, due to drops in investor (or consumer) confidence, could explain the deep, long-term slumps that many countries experienced during the Great Depression (as well as some of the other economic depressions that various economies have experienced throughout history). Modern Keynesians argue that this theory also explains the Great Recession that began in 2008.

Any excess of "leakages" over "injections" into the aggregate expenditure stream would, Keynes theorized, lead to progressive rounds of declines in consumption and income until savings are so low that a new, lower-output-level equilibrium is established. He believed that some kind of government action was required to get the economy out of its slump and to achieve a higher equilibrium level. In Chapter 10, we explore how the U.S. economy did, in fact, get out of the Great Depression, as well as some of the policies that were instituted in response to the Great Recession in the EU as well as the U.S.

It is also worth taking a moment to consider the implications of this model as it relates to contemporary controversies over consumerism and the environment. In the

Keynesian model, it does, indeed, appear that keeping consumption and spending at high levels is necessary to keep the economy humming. The idea that cutting back on consumption spending would be "bad for the economy" is based on the Keynesian notion that reductions in aggregate spending lead to recessions or depressions and that these could potentially be deep and persistent. Would our cutting back on the kinds of consumption that are environmentally damaging lead to recession and job losses? Or could we perhaps substitute other kinds of economic activity and job creation? We revisit this assumption in later chapters to see whether it really is the case that what is good for the environment (and for future generations) has to be "bad for the economy."

DISCUSSION QUESTIONS

1. Which theory—classical or Keynesian—seems more realistic in describing today's economy? Explain why.
2. Have you ever read articles or editorials that claim that high consumption is essential for a healthy economy? Does the Keynesian model seem to confirm or challenge this idea? What are some arguments for the opposite point of view?

REVIEW QUESTIONS

1. During a business-cycle recession, which of the following typically rises: the level of output, the unemployment rate, the level of investment, or the inflation rate?
2. During the 1930s, how did economists' opinions about the Great Depression differ?
3. In the model laid out in this chapter, who receives income? Who spends? Who saves?
4. What is the definition of aggregate expenditure? How does it differ from measured GDP?
5. What conditions comprise equilibrium in a macroeconomy?
6. Saving is described as a "leakage" from the circular flow. How is it a leakage?
7. How can an increase in saving (if not balanced by an increase in intended investment) cause a shrinkage of the output-income-spending flow?
8. Describe the classical market for loanable funds. Who are the actors, and what do they each do?
9. Describe how the problem of leakages is solved in the classical model.
10. How did Keynes model consumption behavior? Draw and label a graph.
11. List five factors, aside from the level of income, that can affect the level of consumption in a macroeconomy.
12. Why isn't the interest rate included in the Keynesian consumption function?
13. What did Keynes think was the most important factor in determining investment behavior?
14. What determines aggregate expenditure in the Keynesian model? Draw and label a graph.
15. Do firms always end up investing the amount that they intend? Why or why not?

16. Draw a "Keynesian cross" diagram, carefully labeling the curves and the equilibrium point.

17. Describe how adjustment to equilibrium occurs in the Keynesian model.

18. Does a macroeconomy's being "in equilibrium" always mean it is in a good state? Why or why not?

19. What is "the income/spending multiplier"? Explain why a drop in autonomous intended investment or in autonomous consumption leads to a much larger drop in equilibrium income.

EXERCISES

1. Carefully draw and label a supply-and-demand diagram for the classical loanable funds market. Assuming that the market starts and ends in equilibrium, indicate what happens if there is a sudden drop in households' desire to consume.
   a. Which curve shifts and in what direction?
   b. What happens to the equilibrium amount of loanable funds borrowed and lent? (You do not need to put numbers on the graph—just indicate the direction of the change.)
   c. What happens to the equilibrium interest rate?
   d. What happens to the equilibrium amount of investment?

2. Suppose that you see a toy store increasing its inventories in early December, right before the Christmas/Chanukah/Kwanzaa season. Is this a case of excess inventory accumulation? Why or why not?

3. Suppose that the relation between consumption and income is $C = 90 + 0.75 Y$.
   a. For each additional euro that households receive, how much do they save? How much do they spend?
   b. What is the level of consumption when income is equal to 0? 360? 500? 600? (You may want to make a table similar to Table 9.2 in the text.)
   c. What is the level of saving when income is equal to 0? 360? 500? 600?
   d. As income rises from 500 to 600, by how much does consumption rise? What formula would you use to derive the *mpc* from your answer to this question if you did not know the *mpc* already?
   e. Graph this consumption function, along with a 45° "consumption = income" line. Label the slope and intercept, and show how the level of savings when income is equal to 600 can be found on this graph.

4. Draw a Keynesian cross graph and assume that the macroeconomy starts and ends in equilibrium. Label the initial aggregate expenditure line AE_0. Then show what happens in the diagram when a rise in consumer wealth raises $\bar{C}$ (autonomous consumption) in your diagram. (This event might happen if the stock market or the housing market enjoys large price increases. You do not need to put numbers on the graph—just indicate the direction of the change.)
   a. How does the AE line shift? Label the new line AE_1.
   b. What is the *initial* effect of this change on inventories? How will firms change production in response to this change in inventories?
   c. What happens to the equilibrium level of production, income, and spending? Does each rise, fall, or stay the same?

5. What happens in the Keynesian model if households decide to be "thriftier"—that is, spend less and save more? Do the following multistep exercise to find out.

   a. Suppose that the economy starts out in a situation we already developed in the text: $\bar{C} = 20 + .8Y$ and $I_1 = 60$ (see Table 9.3). Carefully graph the resulting AE curve, labeling the levels of aggregate expenditure that result when income is equal to 0, 300, 400, and 500. Label the curve AE_0, add the 45° line, and label the equilibrium point E_0.

   b. What is the equilibrium level of income in this initial case? What is the equilibrium level of saving?

   c. Now suppose that people decide they want to save more of their income and spend less of it. In fact, their new level of autonomous consumption is 0, so the new consumption function is just $C = .8Y$. Calculate the levels of consumption and aggregate demand that would result from incomes of 0, 300, 400, and 500. (You might want to set up a table similar to Table 9.3, but using this new equation for consumption. Intended investment is still 60.)

   d. If income stayed at the equilibrium level determined in step (b) of this question, would people now be saving more? How much more? Show your work.

   e. Add the AE curve that arises from your calculations in step (c) on the graph that you drew earlier. Label this curve AE_1 and the new equilibrium point E_1.

   f. What is the new equilibrium level of income? What is the new equilibrium level of saving? Compare your answers to your answers in step (b).

   g. Explain why this phenomenon arising from the Keynesian model is called "the paradox of thrift." Can you explain why this "paradox" arises?

6. Suppose that the behavior of households and firms in an economy is determined by the following equations:

   $$C = 90 + 0.75Y$$
   $$\bar{I}_i = 35$$

   a. Show in a table what the levels of C and AE would be at income levels of 0, 500, and 600.

   b. If, for some reason, income equaled 600, would there be unintended inventory investment? If so, would inventories be excessive or depleted, and by how much?

   c. If, for some reason, income equaled 500, would there be unintended inventory investment? If so, would inventories be excessive or depleted, and by how much?

   d. What is the equilibrium level of income and output?

   e. What is the income/spending multiplier equal to in this model?

   f. If intended investment were to rise by 25, by how much would equilibrium income increase? Use the income/spending multiplier.

7. (Appendix) Suppose that the behavior of households and firms in an economy is determined by the following equations:

   $$C = 50 + 0.9Y$$
   $$\bar{I}_i = 50$$

Answer the following questions, using algebraic manipulations *only.*

   a. What is the equation for the AE curve?

   b. What is the level of equilibrium income?

   c. If intended investment increases by 10 units to 60 units, by how much will equilibrium income rise?

8. Match each concept in Column A with a definition or example in Column B.

Column A	Column B
a. mult $\bar{I}_I$	1. Peak
b. An injection	2. An inverse relationship between unemployment and rapid GDP growth
c. An assumption evident in the equation $AE = C + I_I$	3. Households save more when income rises
d. Okun's "law"	4. $I - I_I$
e. Classical assumption about saving	5. The proportion of an additional dollar that households spend on consumption
f. Unintended investment	6. $\bar{C} + \bar{I}_I$
g. The turning point from a business cycle expansion to contraction	7. The amount that equilibrium GDP rises when autonomous investment rises
h. *mpc*	8. Households save more when the interest rate rises
i. The intercept of the *AE* curve	9. No government sector
j. A Keynesian assumption about saving	10. Intended investment

APPENDIX: AN ALGEBRAIC APPROACH TO THE MULTIPLIER

The formula for the multiplier in the simplest Keynesian model can also be derived using tools of basic algebra, starting with rearranging the equation for *AE*:

$$AE = C + \bar{I}_I$$

We can substitute in the Keynesian equation for consumption, $C = \bar{C} + mpc\ Y$, and use the fact that in this model all investment is autonomous, to get

$$AE = (\bar{C} + mpc\ Y) + \bar{I}_I$$
$$= (\bar{C} + \bar{I}_I) + mpc\ Y$$

The last rearrangement shows that the *AE* curve has an intercept equal to the sum of the autonomous terms and a slope equal to the *mpc*. Changes in either of the variables in parentheses, by changing the intercept, shift the curve upward or downward in a parallel manner.

By substituting this into the equation for the equilibrium condition, $Y = AE$, we can derive an expression for equilibrium income in terms of all the other variables in the model:

$$Y = (\bar{C} + \bar{I}_I) + mpc\ Y$$

$$Y - mpc\, Y = \bar{C} + \bar{I}_I$$

$$(1 - mpc)\, Y = \bar{C} + I_I$$

$$Y = \frac{1}{(1 - mpc)}(\bar{C} + \bar{I}_I)$$

If autonomous consumption or intended investment increases, these each increase equilibrium income by $mult = 1/(1 - mpc)$ times the change in autonomous consumption or investment.

To see this explicitly, consider the changes that would come about in Y if there is a change in $\bar{I}_I$ from $\bar{I}_{I_0}$ to a new level, $\bar{I}_{I_1}$, while autonomous consumption (and the mpc) stays the same. We can solve for the change in Y by subtracting the old equation from the new one:

$$Y_1 = \frac{1}{1 - mpc}(\bar{C} + \bar{I}_{I_1})$$

$$-\left[Y_0 = \frac{1}{1 - mpc}(\bar{C} + \bar{I}_{I_0}) \right]$$

$$Y_1 - Y_0 = \frac{1}{1 - mpc}(\bar{C} - \bar{C} + \bar{I}_{I_1} - \bar{I}_{I_0})$$

But $\bar{C}$ (and the mpc) is unchanged, so the first subtraction in parentheses comes out to be 0. We are left with:

$$Y_1 - Y_0 = \frac{1}{1 - mpc}(\bar{I}_{I_1} - \bar{I}_{I_0})$$

or

$$\Delta Y = mult \Delta\, \bar{I}_I$$

where $mult = 1/(1 - mpc)$. Similar analysis of $\Delta\bar{C}$ (holding intended investment constant) would show that the multiplier for that change is also $mult$.

Chapter 10

Fiscal Policy

Economic theory has real-world implications, as we can see by looking at some recent economic history. After the default of the U.S. investment bank Lehman Brothers in September 2008, the world economy went into a shock. Banks stopped lending, companies stopped investing, and world trade collapsed. In the first months immediately after the default, exports in major economies plummeted, much as they had in the Great Depression of the 1930s. In a rare coordinated policy move, governments of the most important industrialized countries and of many emerging markets passed enormous economic stimulus packages. They cut taxes, increased spending on infrastructure, increased transfers for the unemployed, and created incentives for people to consume more. For example, in Germany, an "Abwrackprämie" (scrapping bonus) of €2,500 was paid to consumers who got rid of their old car and bought a new one. Similar schemes were enacted in Britain and France.

The commonsense idea behind policies such as these is that more spending, either by government or by individuals and families who receive tax cuts, will create demand for goods and thereby expand employment and output. In terms of the macroeconomic theory sketched out in Chapter 9, these policies are intended to increase aggregate demand, generating positive multiplier effects. And in fact, in most European countries, after the stimulus packages were enacted, the economy embarked on an initially rather brisk recovery, surprising many economic observers at that time.

Unfortunately, this was not the end of the story. In early 2010, investors panicked about the high level of public debt and deficits in Greece and the euro crisis (which will be covered more in detail in Chapter 17) set in. In a coordinated attempt to improve investor confidence, the EU countries started to reduce their borrowing by cutting government expenditure and increasing taxes. As a result, many economies in the euro area slid back into recession, and unemployment increased further. It was not until 2013 that the euro area managed to get out of recession. And from 2013 to 2016, growth remained rather lackluster.

During the whole period, there was a fierce debate on the exact mechanics of these economic developments and the government policy responses. Conservative economists had argued from the beginning that the stimulus policies would only increase the deficit and national debt and would not be effective in helping the economy to recover. Proponents of the stimulus responded that it was essential to prevent an already very weak economy from slipping into Great Depression–like conditions. A similar debate emerged when it came to the "austerity" packages of spending cuts and tax increases in Europe. Conservative economists argued that the negative effect on output would be limited but that the policies would improve investors' confidence, which in turn would produce positive effects for economic growth. Critics of austerity policies, in contrast, argued that large reductions in public expenditure combined with tax increases would push the countries concerned deeper into recession. As you can see, in terms of economic theory, this argument reflects the difference between classical and Keynesian views of how economies operate.

We return to the specifics of these debates—and an evaluation of the results of economic stimulus and of austerity policies—in future chapters. Our goal in this chapter is to develop a basic theory of government spending and taxes and their effects on the economy, using the principles of aggregate demand and the multiplier developed in Chapter 9.

1. THE ROLE OF GOVERNMENT SPENDING AND TAXES

Economists often disagree about which tax and spending policies are best in different economic situations. These debates are over **fiscal policy**—what government spends, how it gets the money that it spends, and the effects of these activities on GDP levels. To understand these issues, we need to extend the simple macroeconomic model of Chapter 9 to include the role of government.

fiscal policy: government spending and tax policy

If the role of the government is added, the equation for aggregate expenditure used in previous chapters becomes:

$$AE = C + I_I + G$$

Government spending on goods and services, including spending by federal, state, and local governments (G), is added to aggregate expenditure (AE). Taxes do not appear directly in this equation, but, as we will see, they have an impact through their effect on consumption spending.

government spending (G): the component of GDP that represents spending on goods and services by federal, state and local governments

We examine the effects of these changes to our model one at a time, starting with the impact of a change in government spending.

1.1 A Change in Government Spending

Government spending has a direct impact on the level of GDP. Government purchases of goods and services increase aggregate expenditure, boosting equilibrium output. In Chapter 9, we showed how a decline in intended investment (I_I) lowered the AE line, leading to equilibrium at a lower level of income. This suggests that government spending might be used as an antidote to low investment spending.

Suppose that we start with the macroeconomic equilibrium presented in Table 9.5 and Figure 9.17 in Chapter 9. Remember that this was an unemployment equilibrium. If we start at an unemployment equilibrium, additional aggregate expenditure will be needed to return to full employment. Our first model assumed no government role;

hence initial government spending equals 0. Thus a simple policy would be to increase government spending on goods and services from 0 to 80. As you can see in Table 10.1 and Figure 10.1, the addition of 80 units of government spending causes the equilibrium to shift up by 400, to the full-employment Y^* of 800. Why does this happen?

Table 10.1 *An Increase in Government Spending*

(1) Income (Y)	(2) Consumption (C)	(3) Intended investment (I_I)	(4) Original aggregate expenditure $(AE_0 = C + I_I)$	(5) Government spending (G)	(6) New aggregate expenditure $(AE_1 = C + I_I + G)$
300	260	60	320	80	400
400	340	60	400	80	480
500	420	60	480	80	560
600	500	60	560	80	640
700	580	60	640	80	720
800	660	60	720	80	800

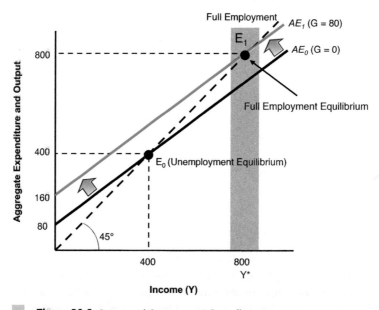

Figure 10.1 *Increased Government Spending*

An increase in government spending has a similar effect to an increase in private fixed investment. It shifts the AE line upward as government spending rises. This increases the equilibrium levels of income and output. The increase in Y is larger than that of G because of the multiplier effect, which occurs due to the induced consumption that occurs as the economy expands along the AE line.

Let's look at a simple example—a new building construction program. Government money is spent on goods such as concrete and steel as well as paying workers. This directly creates new aggregate expenditure. In addition, there are multiplier effects—construction workers will use their incomes to buy all kinds of consumer goods and services. The multiplier effects add to the original economic stimulus resulting from the government spending.

The effect is exactly the same as the multiplier for intended investment that we discussed in Chapter 9. The initial change in government spending (ΔG) becomes income to individuals (ΔY), which leads to a round of consumer spending (ΔC) equal to ($mpc*\Delta Y$), which in turn becomes income to other individuals, leading to another round of consumer spending, and so forth. The whole process can be summarized using the same formula as in Chapter 9 but now applied to government spending rather than intended investment:

$$\Delta Y = \frac{1}{1 - mpc} \Delta G$$

or:

$$\Delta Y = mult \, \Delta G$$

Using the same *mpc* and multiplier as before (we had chosen the example where *mpc* = 0.8, resulting in *mult* = 5) allows us to predict the impact of government spending on economic equilibrium. The multiplier applies to government spending in exactly the same way that it does to changes in intended investment. Therefore, an increase in government spending of 80 leads to an equilibrium shift of 80 × 5 = 400. Looking at it the other way, if we start with the goal of an increase of 400 in Y, we can divide 400 by 5 to find the needed quantity of ΔG: 400/5 = 80.

Note that at the original *AE* level, there is an equilibrium at 400, where $AE_0 = Y$, and there is significant unemployment. After the addition of 80 in government spending (G), the new equilibrium is at the full-employment level of 800, where $AE_1 = Y$. (You can check other levels in the table to make sure that it is the only level at which $AE_1 = Y$.) Figure 10.1 shows the same thing graphically. The aggregate expenditure schedule moves up by 80 at each level of income, so that the horizontal intercept of the *AE* line moves up from 80 to 160. The slope of the *AE* line remains the same, since there has been no change in the *mpc*. The change in equilibrium income is equal to the change in government spending times the multiplier.

Using the multiplier, we can easily calculate the effect of further changes in government spending. For example, suppose that government spending were reduced from 80 to 60. This negative change of 20 in G would lead to a change of (5 ×−20 = −100) in equilibrium Y. Income would fall from 800 to 700.

So we can see that an increase in government spending will raise the level of economic equilibrium, while a decrease in government spending will lower it. The multiplier effect, which is the same size in both directions, gives the policy extra "bang for the buck"—in this case, a change in government spending leads to five times as great a change in national income.

While we have used a multiplier of 5 to illustrate our hypothetical example, in real life, the multiplier is rarely this large (as we will see later in the chapter and also in the algebraic presentation in Appendix A2), but there will usually be some multiplier effects from a change in government spending. The exact size of this multiplier is subject to much debate among economists but is generally estimated to be below 2.0.

1.2 Taxes and Transfer Payments

To complete the picture of fiscal policy, we need to include the role of taxes and transfer payments. If voters and government officials do not want to raise government spending on goods and services, they have another option. To raise GDP, the government could cut taxes or increase **transfer payments**. Transfer payments are government grants, subsidies, or gifts to individuals or firms. Examples of transfer payments include unemployment insurance, public pension payments, and subsidies to, for example, energy or agricultural corporations.

transfer payments: payments by government to individuals or firms, including pension payments, unemployment compensation, and subsidies

Tax reductions are often chosen as a policy tool for macroeconomic stabilization. As noted, tax reductions played a large role in most stimulus packages passed in 2008 or 2009. (Tax reductions, of course, tend to be politically popular in addition to providing economic stimulus.) Increases in transfer payments would have the same general positive effect on aggregate demand. The opposite policies—increasing taxes or decreasing transfer payments—would have a negative effect on economic equilibrium, similar to a reduction in government spending.

Changes in taxes and transfer payments, however, do not have exactly the same effect as changes in government spending on goods and services. The mechanism by which tax and transfer changes affect output differs from the process discussed earlier for government spending. While government purchases *directly* affect aggregate demand and GDP, the effect of taxes and transfer payments is *indirect*, based on their effect on consumption or investment. There are many kinds of taxes and transfers, including corporate taxes, tariffs, and inheritance taxes, but we focus here on the effects of changes in personal income taxes and transfers to individuals.

For example, let's say consumers receive a tax cut of 50. If they spent it all, that would add 50 to aggregate expenditure. But according to the "marginal propensity to consume" (*mpc*) principle, consumers are likely to use a portion of the tax cut to increase saving or reduce debt. With the *mpc* of 0.8 that we used for our basic model in Chapter 9, the portion saved will be $0.2 \times 50 = 10$, leaving 40 for increased consumption. Thus the effect on aggregate expenditure would be only 40, not 50 (since saving is not part of aggregate expenditure).

The same logic would hold if consumers received extra transfer income of 50. They would spend only 40 and save 10. The reverse would be true for a tax increase or a cut in transfer payments. With a tax increase or benefit cut of 50, individuals and families would have less to spend and would reduce their consumption by 40.

Economists define **disposable income** (Y_d) as the income available to consumers after paying taxes and receiving transfers:

$$Y_d = Y - T + TR$$

where T is the total of taxes paid in the economy and TR is the total of transfer payments from governments to individuals.

Changes in taxes or transfer payments directly affect disposable income but only indirectly affect consumption and aggregate expenditure. Hence their impact on economic equilibrium is less than that of government spending, which affects aggregate expenditure directly.

For this reason, the multiplier effects of changes in taxes and transfer payments are smaller than the multiplier impacts of government spending. If taxes are "lump sum"—that is, set at a fixed level that does not change with income—then we can write $T = \bar{T}$. The **tax multiplier** for a lump-sum tax works in two stages. In the first stage, consumption is reduced by $mpc \, (\Delta \bar{T})$, which can be expressed as:

$$\Delta C = -(mpc) \, \Delta \bar{T}$$

In the second stage, this reduction in consumption has the regular multiplier effect on equilibrium income. The combined effect can be expressed as:

$$\Delta Y = (mult) \, \Delta C = -(mult) \, (mpc) \, \Delta \bar{T}$$

The tax multiplier is equal to $\Delta Y / \Delta \bar{T} = -(mult)(mpc)$. Mathematically, $(mult)(mpc)$ always works out to exactly 1.0 less than the regular multiplier. (You can use the multiplier formula from Chapter 9 to work out why this is true.) Using the figures from our previous example, where $mpc = 0.8$ and $mult = 5$, the tax multiplier would be $-(0.8) \times 5 = -4$. (For a more detailed algebraic account of the tax multiplier for a lump-sum tax, see Appendix A1.)

Just as a tax increase has a contractionary effect, a tax cut will have an expansionary effect. Historically, tax cuts played an important role in U.S. economic policy in the 1960s, 1980s, and 2000s, as well as in the response to the recession of 2007–2009. In Europe, almost all countries enacted tax cuts in the crisis of 2008–2009. In all cases, the effect on GDP was expansionary, although there is debate about the exact mechanism through which this occurred—not all economists accept the simple tax multiplier process that we have discussed.

Transfer payments, which as we noted are a kind of "negative tax," affect the level of output through a similar logic. An increase in transfer payments, like a tax cut, will give people more money that they can spend. But the expansionary effect occurs only when they actually do spend—so, according to the *mpc* logic, the impact of an increase in transfer payments is reduced by whatever portion of the extra income people decide to save. The multiplier impact of a change in transfer payments is therefore the same as that of a change in taxes, except in the opposite direction. A cut

disposable income: income remaining for consumption or saving after subtracting taxes and adding transfer payments

tax multiplier: the impact of a change in a lump-sum tax on economic equilibrium, expressed mathematically as $\Delta Y / \Delta \bar{T} = -(mult) \, (mpc)$

in transfer payments, like an increase in taxes, will be contractionary, tending to lower economic equilibrium.

In the real economy, income taxes are generally proportional or progressive—that is, they increase with income levels (as discussed in Chapter 3).* In our model, the effect of a proportional tax would be to *flatten* the aggregate expenditure curve, since it has a larger effect at higher income levels. (See Appendix A2 for a more detailed treatment of the impact of a proportional tax—we omit analysis of progressive taxes, which is a bit more complex.) This in turn will affect the multiplier, reducing it somewhat.

How can we explain the effect of a proportional tax on the multiplier? Taxes that rise with income will tend to lower the proportion consumed out of each euro increase in income. For example, with a 15 percent tax, each extra euro of income will be reduced to 85 cents of disposable income. Applying our original *mpc* of 0.80 to the remaining 85 cents, we get $0.8 \times 0.85 = 0.68$, indicating that 68 cents will be devoted to consumption (and 17 cents to saving). The result is similar to having a lower *mpc*, which also means a lower multiplier. This will dampen the effect of income changes on aggregate expenditure and economic equilibrium.

You might wonder what would be the effect of an increase in government spending that is exactly balanced by an increase in taxes. Since we have shown that the multiplier effect of taxes goes in the opposite direction from that of government spending, it might appear that the effects would cancel each other out. But this is not the case. Because the tax multiplier is smaller than the government spending multiplier, there is a net positive effect on aggregate expenditure and equilibrium. The difference between the two multipliers equals 1, so the net multiplier effect will also equal 1. In the example we have used, the government policy multiplier is 5, and the tax multiplier is 4, so the **balanced budget multiplier** $= +5 - 4 = 1$. Thus the impact on economic equilibrium is exactly equal to the original change in government spending (and taxes). So we can say that $\Delta Y = \Delta G$.**

For example, an increase of €50 billion in government spending, balanced by an equal increase of €50 billion in taxes, would be expected to lead to a net increase in equilibrium output of €50 billion. One way of thinking about this is to consider that the original government spending boosts GDP, but the negative multiplier effects generated by the tax increase cancel out the positive multiplier effects of the government spending. This results in a weaker net effect than government spending of €50 billion alone, which would lead to $\Delta Y = (mult)\Delta G = 5\Delta G$, or €250 billion in this example.

balanced budget multiplier: the impact on equilibrium output of simultaneous increases of equal size in government spending and taxes

1.3 The Circular Flow With Government Spending and Taxes

We can modify the simple circular flow model introduced in Chapter 9 (Figures 9.6 and 9.7) to add government spending and taxes. A circular flow including government spending and taxes is shown in Figure 10.2. As noted, transfer payments are considered

---

* Not counting "loopholes" that sometimes allow the very wealthy to characterize some of their income in ways that allow them to pay *lower* effective tax rates than do other groups.

**Technically, simultaneous changes in government spending and taxes of equal size do not imply that the overall budget is balanced. What is required for this is that *total* spending and *total* taxes be equal.

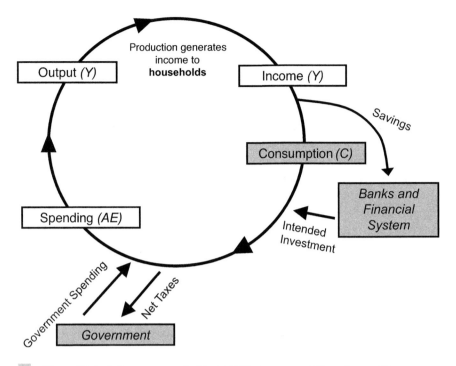

Figure 10.2 *A Macroeconomic Model With Government Spending and Taxes*

The model shows two sets of leakages and injections into the circular flow: savings (leakage) and intended investment (injection), and net taxes (leakage) and government spending (injection). These may or may not balance out at a full-employment level of output.

negative taxes, so we do not include a separate arrow for transfers. Instead, we show **net taxes**—taxes minus transfer payments—as a leakage from the circular flow and government spending as a reinjection to the circular flow.

net taxes: taxes minus transfer payments

This model thus has two leakages—savings and net taxes—and two injections—intended investment and government spending. As discussed in the previous chapter, savings and investment flow through the financial system and may or may not balance. Similarly, taxes and government spending may or may not balance, depending on whether the government has a deficit, a surplus, or a balanced budget.

This model represents a useful, simplified way of thinking about the complex macroeconomic system. If the overall leakages and injections balance, the system should be at a full-employment equilibrium. From a Keynesian perspective, the objective of government policy is to achieve such a balance by varying government spending and net taxes to offset any imbalances in savings and investment. Classical economists are more skeptical about the ability of government to achieve this and more concerned that government action will unbalance rather than balance the circular flow. We discuss some of these policy implications in much more detail in later chapters.

In Chapter 14, we introduce one more modification of the circular flow diagram to take into account the foreign sector, showing the effect of imports and exports. But first, we examine some of the implications of government policies aimed at balancing out the circular flow.

1.4 Expansionary and Contractionary Fiscal Policy

The three fiscal policy tools discussed earlier—changes in government spending, changes in tax levels, and changes in transfer payments—affect income and employment levels as well as inflation rates (discussed further in what follows and in Chapter 13). They also, of course, affect the government's budgetary position. The budget could be balanced, in surplus, or in deficit, depending on the combination of spending and tax policy that is employed.

Increasing government spending is an example of what economists refer to as **expansionary fiscal policy**. Other expansionary fiscal policies are increasing transfer payments or lowering taxes. Whether through a direct impact on aggregate demand or through giving consumers more money to spend, these policies should increase aggregate demand and equilibrium output.

If that were the whole story, macroeconomic policy would be simple—just use sufficient government spending or tax cuts to maintain the economy at full employment. But there are complications. One problem is that in order to spend more, the government has to raise taxes, borrow, or "print money." (Issues of how government finances its expenditures are discussed later in this chapter and in subsequent ones.) Raising taxes tends to counteract the expansionary effects of increased spending. Borrowing money creates deficits and raises long-term government debt that, as we will see, may or may not be a problem (these issues are discussed in depth in Chapter 16).

Another problem is that too much government spending may lead to inflation. The goal of expansionary fiscal policy is to expand the economic activity to its full-employment level. But what if fiscal policy overshoots this level? It is easy to see how this might occur. For politicians, government spending on popular programs is easy, but raising taxes to pay for them is hard. This can lead to budget deficits (discussed in Section 2), but it can also cause excessive aggregate expenditure in the economy. Excessive expenditure could also, in theory, arise from high consumer or business spending, but usually government spending, alone or in combination with high consumer and business expenditures, is partly to blame when the economy "overheats." The result is likely to be inflation.

According to our basic analysis, the cure for inflation should be fairly straightforward. If the problem is too much aggregate expenditure, the solution is to reduce aggregate expenditure. We could do this by reversing the process discussed in the previous section and lowering government spending on goods and services. A similar effect can be obtained by reducing transfer payments or by increasing taxes. With lower transfer payments or higher taxes, businesses and consumers will have less spending power. Lower spending by government, businesses, and consumers will result in a lower equilibrium output level, and there will no longer be excess demand pressures to create inflation.

expansionary fiscal policy: the use of government spending, transfer payments, or tax cuts to stimulate a higher level of economic activity

Thus we have identified another important economic policy tool—**contractionary fiscal policy**. This is a weapon that can be used against inflation, though it would generally be unwise to use it at times of high unemployment. (The problem of what to do if unemployment and inflation occur at the same time—something that is not shown in our simple model—is discussed in Chapter 13.) Of course, too large a spending reduction could overshoot in a downward direction, leading to excessive unemployment and, possibly, a recession.

Although the effects of contractionary fiscal policy can be painful, it would be wrong to assume that expansionary fiscal policy is always beneficial and contractionary policy always harmful. Contractionary policy can be useful when previous policies have "overshot" the goal or when the economy is suffering from excessive inflation. We discuss this issue of policy choice extensively in this and the following chapters.

contractionary fiscal policy: reductions in government spending or transfer payments or increases in taxes, leading to a lower level of economic activity

Discussion Questions

1. What recent changes in government spending or tax policy have been in the news? How would you expect these to affect GDP and employment levels?
2. In general, tax increases are politically unpopular. Would you ever be likely to favor a tax increase? Under what circumstances, if any, might a tax increase be beneficial to the economy?

2. PUBLIC BUDGETS IN EUROPE

In this textbook, we have often taken the perspective of the euro area as a whole as our point of reference instead of looking at single national economies. This usually makes sense, as in a number of dimensions, the euro area resembles a traditional national economy such as that of the U.S. For example, it has a common central bank which sets monetary policy for the whole euro area (see Chapter 12). It has also a common external exchange rate (see Chapter 14). Yet when it comes to describing the public budget, the relevant point of reference is still the single European nation state. The euro area does not have a public budget of its own. The EU budget (large parts of which are spent in the euro area) is very small compared to national budgets in Europe and hence has little influence on macroeconomic variables. It amounts to about 1 percent of euro-area GDP, compared to public spending of on average more than 40 percent of GDP. Hence, the following section will focus on public finances in selected EU member states.

The EU member states' budgets include spending on goods and services, transfer payments, and taxes. (In our analysis, we look at the total of national public spending, including lower levels of government such as regions or municipalities.) Thus we can divide total government expenditures, or **government outlays**, into two categories. Total government outlays include not only government spending on goods and services (G) but also government transfer payments:

government outlays: total government expenditures, including spending on goods and services and transfer payments

Government Outlays = G + TR

333

Recalling the earlier discussion, only government spending directly affects aggregate demand. Transfer payments do so only indirectly through their effect on consumption. As we see in what follows, however, both types of outlay affect the public budget, since both represent funds that the government must pay out.

On the revenue side, government income comes from taxes (T). When revenues are not sufficient to cover outlays, the government borrows to cover the difference. The actual financing of a deficit is accomplished through the sale of **government bonds** by national governments. Government bonds are interest-bearing securities that can be bought by firms, individuals, or foreign governments. In effect, a government bond is a promise to pay back, with interest, the amount borrowed at a specific time in the future.

Sources of government revenue and outlays for selected EU countries are shown in Figures 10.3 to 10.5. As you see, the size of governments as well as the main source of

government bond:
an interest-bearing security constituting a promise to pay at a specified future time

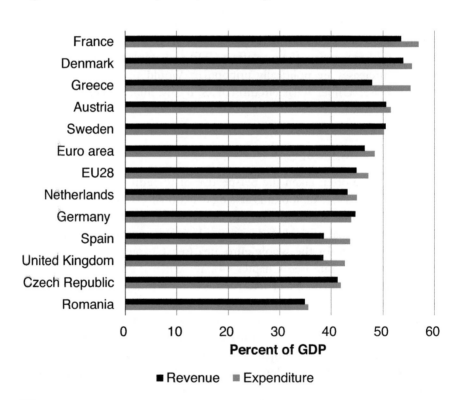

■ Revenue   ■ Expenditure

Figure 10.3 *General Government Expenditure and Revenue, Selected EU Countries, in Percent of GDP, 2015*

The size of the government sector varies strongly between European countries, with government expenditure amounting to more than 55 percent of GDP in France and Denmark and only around 35 percent of GDP in Romania. With very few exceptions, EU member states in 2015 had expenditures significantly higher than their revenues. In order to bridge this gap, they borrowed by issuing government bonds.

Source: Eurostat, Government revenue, expenditure and main aggregates (table gov_10a_main), 2016.

334

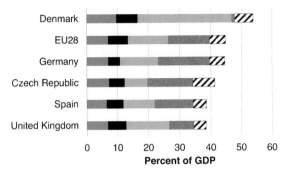

■ VAT
■ Taxes on products other than VAT
■ Taxes on income, wealth, etc.
■ Social security contributions
☑ Other revenues

Figure 10.4 *Sources of Government Revenues for Selected EU Countries, in Percent of GDP, 2015*

EU countries also have chosen quite different approaches for financing their budgets. Denmark relies heavily on taxes on income and wealth, while Germany and the Czech Republic collect a large share of public revenues from social security contributions.

Source: Eurostat, Government revenue, expenditure and main aggregates (table gov_10a_main), 2016.

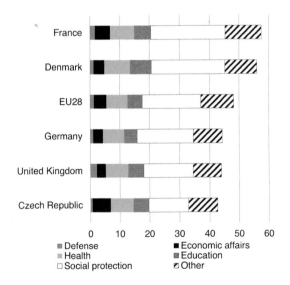

■ Defense   ■ Economic affairs
■ Health   ■ Education
□ Social protection ☑ Other

Figure 10.5 *General Government Expenditure and Revenue, Selected EU Countries, in Percent of GDP, 2014*

Not only does the size of the government sector vary among EU countries, but so do priorities. Britain, for example, spends much more on defense than Denmark, even though its overall government spending is smaller.

Source: Eurostat, General government expenditure by function (tablegov_10a_exp), 2016.

revenue differ between countries. Figure 10.3 shows government revenue and expenditure as a share of GDP for 2015. In some countries such as France or Denmark, the government collects more than half of GDP in taxes and other revenues and spends even more. In other countries such as Romania, government revenue is only a little more than 35 percent of GDP.

Note that these figures cover the general government sector. In the national statistics in some countries, social security systems are presented as separate entities, and they often have dedicated revenue, for example through social security contributions. In order to make the government sectors of different countries comparable, however, they have been included in the government sector here. In contrast, in line with Eurostat conventions, government-owned corporations that engage in market activities (such as state-owned banks) are not counted as part of the government sector.

Despite the variations in the size of governments across EU countries, it is important to note that all over the Union, government spending is a major part of the economy. This is mainly due to the European consensus of having a welfare state covering the most important lifetime risks of the population such as illness, age, and unemployment. If we expand our comparison beyond Europe, we find that with the exception of Estonia and the Slovak republic, even EU countries with a relatively low share of government expenditure to GDP have a larger government sector than, for example, Korea or the United States.

Figure 10.4 presents the revenue for selected EU countries from different taxes for 2015. Some countries such as Denmark or the UK collect only a small share of their revenue from social security contributions, while other countries such as Germany or the Czech Republic collect much more through such contributions. In contrast, value-added taxes (VAT) play a much larger role in Denmark than in most other EU countries. Similarly, taxes on products other than VAT (e.g., alcohol or gasoline) play a larger role in Denmark than in other countries. Taxes on income and wealth are much less important in Germany and Spain than in other countries.

If you look at the composition of government expenditure for 2014 (presented in Figure 10.5), you also see significant variations in how governments spend their funds. While all countries spend a significant share of their outlays on social protection and health, the amount they spend on these activities still differs. Denmark and France, for example, spend much more on social protection than the Czech Republic or the United Kingdom. As a share of GDP, Denmark spends almost 70 percent more on education than Germany.

Part of the government expenditure is interest paid on public debt accumulated in the past. If interest rates are low, the burden of these outlays on public budgets remains limited. If interest rates are higher (as they were in most countries in the 1990s), however, they can become a heavy burden on government budgets and even lead to crises (one crisis in which an increase in interest rates on public debt played a role, the euro crisis, is covered in Chapter 17).

Clearly, government borrowing and interest payments on the debt have economic impacts. What is the nature of these impacts? To answer this question, we need to look more carefully at the nature of government deficits.

2.1 Deficits and Surpluses

First, we need to define what we mean by the **government budget surplus or deficit**. This can be calculated by subtracting total government outlays from total government tax revenues. A positive result indicates a surplus; a negative one, a deficit.

$$Budget\ Surplus\ (+)\ or\ Deficit\ (-) = T - Government\ Outlays$$
$$= T - (G + TR)$$

Showing the government's budget deficit as a percentage of nominal GDP is a simple way to correct for the effects of both inflation and the ability of the economy to handle the deficit. The larger the economy—as measured by GDP—the easier it is to manage a given deficit, since both the fiscal and budgetary impacts of the deficit will be relatively smaller compared to the size of the economy. A bigger economy means that people will have higher incomes, and a larger flow of savings is likely to be available to purchase more government bonds, making it easier for the government to borrow.

Rules differ between EU states in terms of how much the various levels of government (or social security systems) can borrow. In order to make the data comparable, we therefore usually look at the deficit or the surplus of all levels of government combined, including health, unemployment, and pension systems. Although regional or provincial governments may have some ability to borrow, usually central governments have the largest flexibility to conduct budget operations. As they have more freedom to change tax rates and can borrow more easily in the financial markets, they are usually in a position to conduct **deficit spending**. However, in contrast to countries outside the euro area such as the United States or Japan, euro-area countries' conduct of fiscal policy (and especially their ability to run large deficits) is constrained by a set of European Union rules, including the so-called Stability and Growth Pact and the Fiscal Compact. We return to this point in later chapters.

Economists sometimes use the term "**countercyclical**" to describe a government policy of increasing spending and cutting taxes in lean times and doing the reverse when the economy strengthens. When governments are unable or unwilling to borrow, they tend to follow a more **procyclical policy**, in which both recessions and booms are reinforced rather than counterbalanced. This is not the intended result but simply a result of the fact that tax revenues usually fall when times are bad, leading to cuts in expenditure, and that tax revenues increase in good times, inducing politicians to spend more. Such procyclical policies occurred when austerity measures were implemented in European countries during the euro crisis. Even though the countries concerned were already experiencing weak economic growth or were in an outright recession, governments saw themselves forced to cut expenditure, thus deepening the downturn.

Over the years, the size of deficits in euro-area countries has varied considerably, and for some countries the fiscal position has moved from deficit to surplus and back (Figure 10.6). For example, Spain and Ireland were recording surpluses in the years prior to the onset of the global financial and economic crisis in 2008. Germany has long

budget surplus: an excess of total government revenues over total government outlays

budget deficit: an excess of total government outlays over total government revenues

deficit spending: government spending in excess of revenues collected

countercyclical policy: fiscal policy in which taxes are lowered and expenditure is raised when the economy is weak, and the opposite occurs when the economy is strong

procyclical policy: fiscal policy in which taxes are lowered and expenditure is raised when the economy is strong, and the opposite is done when the economy is weak

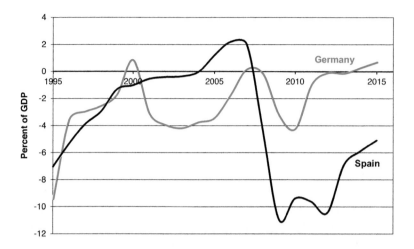

Figure 10.6a *Surplus (+) or Deficit (-) of Germany and Spain as a Percent of GDP*

Spain recorded a fiscal surplus prior to the euro crisis. However, falling tax revenue, costs of stimulus packages and bank bailouts, as well as rising costs of unemployment insurance, pushed the balance into deficit. Germany managed to pay back some debt in 2000 when the government auctioned off mobile phone licenses expensively to phone companies but then recorded significant deficits for much of the 2000s before it managed to retire some debt in 2015.

Source: AMECO Database, 2016.

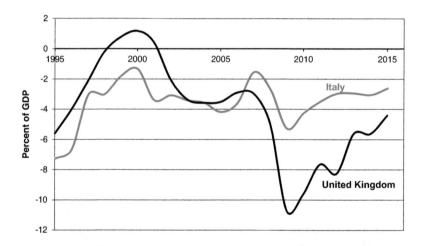

Figure 10.6b *Surplus (+) or Deficit (-) of Britain and Italy as a Percent of GDP*

Since the mid-1990s, Italy has never recorded a budget surplus. However, Italy's deficit remained under control during the crisis starting in 2008, reflecting pro-cyclical cuts in expenditure. In Britain, in contrast, the government passed a large stimulus package and allowed the deficit to reach more than 10 percent of GDP before switching to austerity policies to reduce the deficit.

Source: AMECO Database, 2016.

recorded significant deficits but recorded a small surplus in 2015. Some other countries such as Greece have recorded significant deficits for a very long time. Especially with the onset of the euro crisis (which has been interpreted as a debt crisis by many economists), this has led to an extensive debate about the impact of deficits on the economy. We focus on these issues in greater depth in Chapter 16 and Chapter 17. As we see, there is much continuing controversy among economists and the general public about the significance of budgetary policy and deficits and many different ideas about the best way to handle issues of government spending, taxes, and transfer payments.

2.2 Automatic Stabilizers

Deficits and surpluses are not just a result of active fiscal policy. A significant portion of the variations in government spending and tax revenues occurs "automatically" due to mechanisms built into the economic system to help stabilize it.

BOX 10.1 WHY EUROPE HAS STRONGER AUTOMATIC STABILIZERS THAN THE U.S.

When one compares the economic structures of industrialized countries before the Great Depression of the 1920s and 1930s with the structure prior to the global financial crisis of 2008–2009, one large difference is the size of the government sector and especially the existence of social safety nets such as public unemployment insurance or welfare payments.

These changes have positive consequences beyond reducing the misery among the unemployed during the recession. As tax receipts usually fall in a recession with falling incomes, and the government pays increased unemployment benefits to those losing their jobs, disposable incomes nowadays fall much less with an initial drop in economic output than was the case during the Great Depression.

Recent estimates suggest that in Europe, these "automatic stabilizers" work much better than in the United States. Using the tax rules and eligibility criteria for unemployment benefits in place in 2008, it can be shown that 47 percent of the impact of a job loss on disposable incomes is buffered by the tax and transfer system in the European Union but only 34 percent in the United States. Perhaps not very surprisingly, within Europe, this figure also varies strongly. In Estonia, less than 25 percent of losses in disposable incomes are compensated for by these automatic stabilizers, while the figure reaches more than 80 percent in Denmark. In general, Southern and Eastern European countries have much less effective automatic stabilizers than Western and Northern European economies.

Other factors such as tax structure also affect stabilization, but most of the difference between the size of automatic stabilizers in the United States and Europe can be explained by significantly more generous unemployment benefits in the EU. Also within the EU, countries with more generous unemployment insurances tend to have stronger automatic stabilizers.

Source: Mathias Dolls, Clemens Fuest, Andreas Peichl, Automatic stabilisers and the economic crisis in Europe and the U.S., VoxEU, September 17, 2010.

---

automatic stabilizers: tax and spending institutions that tend to increase government revenues and lower government spending during economic expansions but lower revenues and raise government spending during economic recessions

Even if no specific budgetary action is taken, the government's budget will vary over the business cycle. Suppose that the economy is entering a recession. As aggregate expenditure falls, the government deficit generally rises. Tax revenues decline as people have less income on which to pay taxes due to the slowing economy. In addition, as more people receive unemployment insurance, transfer payments related to programs such as food stamps increase. This cushions the fall in personal disposable income—and thus the fall in consumer spending.

If the government does not actively move to balance its budget, these automatic changes in spending and taxes tend to moderate the recession. In effect, the recession creates an automatic response of expansionary fiscal impacts—increased spending and lower tax revenues. It will also, of course, tend to increase the government deficit (or reduce any surplus).

Similarly, if aggregate expenditure is rising during an economic expansion, tax revenues rise. Fewer people receive unemployment or other transfer payments. This means that personal disposable income does not rise as quickly as national income. This, in turn, puts a damper on increases in consumer spending—and limits the inflationary overheating that can arise from increased aggregate expenditure.

cyclical deficit (surplus): the portion of the deficit (or surplus) that is caused by fluctuations in the business cycle

Automatic stabilizers are, therefore, inseparable from cyclical budget imbalances. Economists often say that the portion of the deficit (surplus) that is the result of automatic stabilizers is the **cyclical deficit (or surplus)**. It is, in effect, the part of the budget balance that is sensitive to fluctuations in the macroeconomy.

This phenomenon helps explain why, for example, the Spanish and Irish governments were able to enjoy budgetary surpluses in the mid-2000s. It also helps to explain why the German government in 2015 was able to run a small surplus. It is true that the policies of the respective governments, such as prudent spending, contributed to the surplus. But at least as important is the increase in tax revenues because of growing business profits, personal incomes, and falling costs because of low unemployment. In some instances (like that of Spain in the 2000s), with hindsight, economists now reckon that the government actually overspent, even in times of surplus. Here, the argument is that the government has very large amounts of tax revenue because of the business cycle (i.e., real estate–related taxes during the housing boom) that they thought were permanent revenue and spent lavishly.

In addition to the automatic stabilizers, the government budget has another aspect that levels the fluctuations of output. This is the steadiness of government spending. Unlike business investment, consumer spending, or net exports, many areas of government spending do not change drastically from year to year. This adds an element of stability to the economy's aggregate expenditure.

2.3 Discretionary Fiscal Policy

discretionary fiscal policy: changes in government spending and taxation resulting from deliberate policy decisions

Sometimes, the automatic stabilization effect of government spending and taxes cannot smooth economic ups and downs as much as is needed. Relatively severe problems of recession or inflation often give rise to proposals to use an active or **discretionary fiscal policy** to remedy the situation. This issue is controversial among economists.

Some economists, as we will see, believe that the government should *never* use an activist fiscal policy, believing that it is likely to do more harm than good. Other economists argue that activist fiscal policy is essential, especially to respond to severe economic problems such as deep recession.

Regardless of economists' advice, the fact is that governments are making fiscal policy all the time, whether in a planned or unplanned manner. Every year, the government revises its budget, including levels of spending and taxation. These spending and tax levels have effects on the economy, and it is important to try to understand them.

As Figure 10.7 shows, government receipts and outlays tend to fluctuate over time. For example, in 2009, when the European economy went into recession, outlays as a percentage of GDP increased. This was due on the one hand to the stimulus packages passed, but also to the fact that GDP contracted, increasing the *ratio* of public expenditure to GDP. These responses to recession included both an automatic stabilization effect (including increased unemployment compensation, as noted) and a discretionary policy component.

Historically, the first major experience with expansionary fiscal policy in many countries occurred during World War II. In the U.S., before the war, President Franklin D. Roosevelt's New Deal had initiated some government spending programs intended to put the unemployed to work during the Great Depression. But these programs were dwarfed by the magnitude of war spending in the 1940s. As a result, U.S. unemployment, which had been as high as 25 percent in 1933 and 19 percent in

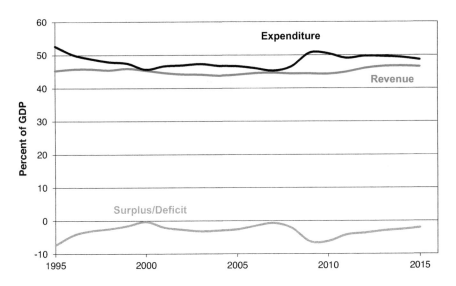

Figure 10.7 *Euro Area Government Expenditure, Revenues, and Surplus/Deficit, as a Percent of GDP, 1995–2015*

Overall, governments in the euro area have operated at a moderate deficit for most of the last few decades, with particularly high deficits during the global financial and economic crisis.

Source: AMECO Database, 2016.

1938, fell to about 2 percent in 1943.* Similarly, in Europe, the mass unemployment of the Great Depression was replaced with expanded military and civilian employment as war spending escalated on both sides.

After the conclusion of World War II, government spending in the industrialized world never returned to prewar levels, and the beneficial effects of the expanded government role—steady economic growth with relatively low unemployment levels—seemed to justify this. In the 1960s, economists became even more optimistic about the benefits of fiscal policy. At that time, it was suggested that it would be possible for the government to "fine-tune" the economic system using fiscal policy to ratchet aggregate demand up or down in response to changes in the business climate.

"Fine-tuning" was largely discredited in the 1970s and 1980s, as the economy of many EU countries, as well as the U.S., struggled with inflationary problems that were partly a result of sharp increases in oil prices but were also seen as having been worsened in some countries by excessive government spending (we look at this in more detail in Chapter 13). In addition, many economists argued that problems of **time lags** made fiscal policy unwieldy and often counterproductive.

time lags: the time that elapses between the formulation of an economic policy and its actual effects on the economy

To understand the problems with fine-tuning and time lags, we can use a commonsense example. Imagine that when you wake up, it is too cold in your apartment, so you turn up the temperature on the thermostat. It might take so much time for the apartment to warm up that you do not get the benefits before you leave for work. You might become impatient, raising the temperature again. As a result, the apartment gets too hot during the day, so when you get home, you have to turn the thermostat down again. Thus delayed responses make your management of the apartment's temperature less effective. The best strategy is to set the thermostat at a single temperature (or, with a programmable thermostat, a specific daily pattern) and then to resist fiddling with it.

Similarly, time lags can make active fiscal policy less effective as a way to stabilize the economy. There are two types of lags: *inside* and *outside* lags. Inside lags refer to delays that occur within the government, while outside lags refer to the delayed effects of government policies. There are four major types of inside lags:

1. *A data lag:* It may take some time for the government to collect information about economic problems such as unemployment.
2. *A recognition lag:* Government decision makers may not see an event as a problem right away.
3. *A legislative lag:* Discretionary fiscal policy must be instituted in the form of legal changes in the government's budget. The government's economists may want to increase spending or decrease tax rates, but they have to convince both the president and Congress to act to solve the problem.
4. *A transmission lag:* These legal changes take time to show up in actual tax forms and government budgets. One solution is that changes can be made retroactive to

---

* Employment figures for that era covered a labor force in which a much lower proportion of women were seeking jobs than is the case today. During World War II, an unusually large number of women were employed, filling jobs left vacant by men who were serving in the armed forces.

speed up their implementation—for instance, a tax cut legislated now may apply to income received during the previous year. However, this is not always done.

In addition, even if all these lags have been overcome, it takes time for the new policies actually to affect the economy (the "outside lag"). Suppose, for example, that the government responds to a rise in unemployment with increased government spending or a tax cut. By the time these policies are in place and create an economic stimulus, the economy may have recovered on its own. In that case, the additional aggregate expenditure will not be needed and is likely to create inflationary pressures.

Despite these problems with discretionary fiscal policy, governments have continued to use it, with mixed results. Government fiscal stimulus, with or without a formal economic justification, was widely applied in a number of European countries as well as the U.S. and Japan during the 1960s and 1970s. Most widely remembered cases include the German stimulus packages of the mid-1960s, the fiscal expansion in the 1970s in Italy, and the massive stimulus spending in France in the early 1980s under president François Mitterrand. While the experiences of the 1960s have been generally interpreted as positive, the expansionary policies of the 1970s and 1980s are now seen as more problematic, with impacts including pushing up inflation and the public debt level. This perception might explain why Europeans were reluctant to use fiscal stimulus from the mid-1980s onward until the Great Recession of 2008–2009.

In the U.S., in contrast, expansionary policy was used from 1980–1987 and in the early 2000s as well as in the Great Recession. One reason for the U.S. government's willingness to use fiscal stimulus might have been the specific details of American stimulus packages: By and large, all major stimulus packages included a significant amount of tax cuts, a policy especially popular in the U.S. Such tax cuts as part of stimulus packages were implemented under Presidents Kennedy, Reagan, and George W. Bush, as well as by the Obama administration as part of a stimulus policy in response to recession.

Using fiscal policy to stabilize the economy made a global revival during the Great Recession of 2008–2009: During this time, all major economies passed large stimulus packages, and these packages nowadays are credited by many with having prevented a further deterioration of the world economy.

It is sometimes difficult to evaluate the extent to which fiscal policy is expansionary or not. In economically good times, governments are often faced with an increase in revenue (as the population's income increases), and one common reflex of politicians is to use this money for increased spending or tax cuts. In this case, an increase in spending does not appear to cause any increase in the deficit, because it is covered by the increased revenues. Nonetheless, the underlying fiscal position of the government has deteriorated, and a new downturn in economic activity will now lead to a larger deficit. In order to see how the fiscal position has really changed, economists have come up with the concept of a **structural deficit (or surplus)**. We can (loosely) think of the structural deficit as the deficit that would occur if the economy were at full employment, with current spending and tax legislation in place. Only changes in the structural budget balance truly reflect the direction of fiscal policy—that is,

structural deficit (surplus): the portion of the deficit (or surplus) that results from tax and spending policy dictated by the government at its discretion whether it is stimulative or contractionary—since other changes are related to the automatic stabilizers.

BOX 10.2 GLOBAL STIMULUS IN THE GREAT RECESSION

While a number of countries such as the United States and Ireland had already seen their economies weaken during 2007, by the end of 2008, it had become clear that this was not a standard downturn. After the failure of the U.S. investment bank Lehman Brothers in September, trade and investment globally collapsed, and all major economies entered a deep recession.

Shocked by the magnitude and speed of economic contraction, governments all over the world started to pass stimulus packages consisting of tax cuts and increases in government expenditure. Among the G20 countries alone (the 20 most important economies), stimulus packages amounted to $2 trillion, almost 1.5 percent of global GDP. Never before had governments around the world passed a similar stimulus in such a synchronized way.

Most of these packages were actually passed in a timely way and were enacted less than six months after Lehman Brothers' bankruptcy. While for the OECD as a whole, the stimulus was roughly balanced between measures affecting government expenditure (hence increasing government spending and transfers) and government revenue (hence cutting taxes), the picture differed strongly between countries. In the UK, for example, the stimulus package focused almost inclusively on cutting taxes. In Japan, in contrast, about 75 percent of the stimulus package came in the form of increased government outlays.

Many developing countries and emerging economies channeled a large part of their stimulus into infrastructure investment. In developed countries, a significant share of the funds also went into transfers to unemployed individuals or into labor market measures. For example, in the United States, the maximum duration an individual could receive unemployment benefits was increased from 26 to 99 weeks. In Germany, subsidies were paid to companies that kept their staff on the payroll but reduced their weekly working hours.

Overall, many observers credited the global stimulus response with preventing a much worse depression and with the partial recovery of the world economy. However, as the stimulus packages together with bank rescues necessary during the crisis also pushed up public debt levels, politicians in many countries felt forced to turn to a policy of cutting deficits by increasing taxes and lowering public expenditure, resulting in contractionary fiscal policies that were seen by many as a reason for continuing slow economic growth after 2010.

Sources: International Labour Organization, A Review of Fiscal Stimulus, *EC-IILS Joint Discussion Paper Series No. 5*, Geneva, 2011; OECD, The Effectiveness and Scope of Fiscal Stimulus, *OECD Economic Outlook*, Interim Report March 2009, Paris, pp. 105–150.

---

supply-side economics: an economic theory that emphasizes policies to stimulate production, such as lower taxes. The theory predicts that such incentives stimulate greater economic effort, saving, and investment, thereby increasing overall economic output and tax revenues.

Changes in tax policy—tax cuts, for example—also are classified as discretionary (in contrast to changes in tax revenues resulting from business–cycle fluctuations). Proponents of tax cuts sometimes appeal to **supply-side economics** (most prominently introduced during the government of Margaret Thatcher in the UK from

1979 onward and in the U.S. under the Reagan administration in the 1980s) to support their policies. The supply-side argument for tax cuts is essentially that lower tax rates encourage more work, saving, and investment, thereby creating a more dynamic economy. According to the most enthusiastic advocates of supply-side economics, output will grow so rapidly in response to a cut in tax rates that total tax revenues will actually increase, not decrease. This is different from the logic of increased aggregate demand that we have discussed, which implies that tax cuts will create an economic stimulus but are likely to raise the government deficit.

The economic record seems to show that tax cuts do indeed create an economic stimulus—but debate continues among economists as to whether this effect is demand led (as implied by our fiscal policy model) or based on supply-side effects. And in general, tax cuts have usually led to lower revenues and higher deficits.

Discussion Questions

1. Do you think that your country's government is mostly responsible for persistent budget deficits? Are budget deficits necessarily bad?
2. Why doesn't the government run surpluses every year instead of deficits? Wouldn't doing so be better for the economy?

3. POLICY ISSUES

3.1 Crowding Out and Crowding In

A common concern of fiscal policy critics is that government spending gets in the way of consumption and private investment. We have already seen that while government expenditures boost aggregate demand, the tax revenues required to finance such expenditures have the opposite effect. But the expenditure effect is stronger, euro for euro, than the tax effect, which is why the effects do not exactly cancel each other out and why the balanced-budget multiplier equals 1 instead of 0.

That would be the end of the story if raising taxes were the only means of financing government expenditures. Yet we know that the government frequently runs deficits and, when it does so, it must borrow money. It borrows from the capital markets. If one follows the theory of a market of loanable funds intermediating savings between households on the one hand and governments and firms on the other hand (as discussed in Chapter 9), government borrowing in theory leaves less money available for private investment. The reduced availability of loanable funds can have the effect of raising interest rates, which, by making borrowing more expensive, makes investment less likely, *ceteris paribus*. Economists therefore say that borrowing to help cover budget deficits may have the effect of "**crowding out**" private investment. Economists who favor the classical approach often claim that replacing dynamic private investment with "clumsy" government spending is wasteful and inefficient.

Figure 10.8 uses the classical model of the loanable funds market, introduced in Chapter 9 (Figure 9.8) to illustrate how government demand for loanable funds could

crowding out: a reduction in the availability of private capital resulting from government borrowing to finance budget deficits

345

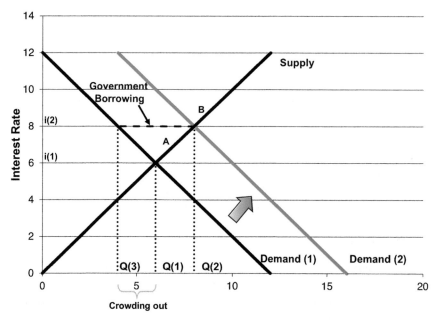

Figure 10.8 *Crowding Out in the Loanable Funds Market*

According to classical theory, government borrowing crowds out private investment, as the government is competing for the same funds in the market for loanable funds as the firms do for their investment.

crowd out private borrowing. The supply curve (*S*) represents savings or, more concretely, the supply of loanable funds. For a given supply, the interest rate will be pushed up from i_1 to i_2 when the government borrows money to pay for a budget deficit, represented by a shift in the demand curve from D_1 to D_2. The result is that private investment is now more expensive and saving becomes more attractive.

The difference between Q_2 and Q_3 represents the amount of funds borrowed by the government. Because this additional demand raises the interest rate, private investment becomes less attractive, and some is "crowded out." Q_3 now represents the quantity of loanable funds available for private investment. The amount of "crowding out" is shown on the graph as the difference between Q_1 and Q_3. The implication of this analysis is that government deficit spending is counterproductive to the aim of promoting private investment.

John Maynard Keynes acknowledged the potential for crowding out. He did not, however, believe that deficit spending would crowd out private spending to a significant degree if, as during the Great Depression, there was considerable slack in the economy. In other words, if owners of capital are reluctant to invest anyway, there is no reason for government borrowing to drive up interest rates. Remember that in the Keynesian view, recessionary conditions are characterized by an excess of savings over investment. If there is a large excess of savings, there is no reason to worry that government borrowing will absorb too much of the available loanable funds.

346

Keynes also minimized the importance of crowding out for other reasons. First, recall from Chapter 9 that, according to Keynes, investment decisions are not dependent only on the rate of interest. He believed that investment decisions also are a function of expectations of future profit, what he called "animal spirits." In good economic times, investors purchase more capital goods because their growing profits reinforce an optimistic outlook about the future. And they are likely to do so despite the historical tendency for interest rates to *rise* in good economic times. The opposite might well be true in recessions. Despite low interest rates, business spending will be lower due to growing pessimism. For the reasons noted, government borrowing to finance deficits may not raise interest rates during a recession, and even if it does, this might not have any significant effect on investment, since investors will not want to invest anyway—at least until the economy starts to recover.

Modern Keynesian economists also point out that the theory of loanable funds is outdated in advanced financial systems. As will be discussed in Chapter 11, the banking sector can create the money demanded by the other sectors. If one follows this argument, there is no fixed amount of loanable funds; instead, the amount of loanable funds will depend on firms' willingness to invest and the banking sector's creation of funds to finance this investment. As long as government spending does not lead to an overheating of the economy by pushing aggregate expenditure beyond the economy's capacity limits, there will be no crowding out.

Finally, there is significant scope for complementarity between public and private investment. According to this argument, certain government expenditures on, say, transportation, energy, or communications networks enhance the potential profits of private investment by providing critical infrastructure. Rather than being a substitute for private investment, government spending supports the productivity of private investment and is therefore likely to encourage more of it. When such government spending generates more investment, it is called **crowding in**.

crowding in: the process in which government spending leads to more favorable expectations for the economy, thereby inducing investment

During the Great Depression, Keynes argued that the economy could be stuck in a potentially permanent low-level equilibrium (i.e., the unemployment equilibrium we saw in Chapter 9) and that the government needed to run deficits to finance the spending necessary to stimulate aggregate demand and thus attract renewed investment spending on capital goods. This argument has been reflected recently by the demands of some to end austerity policies in Europe and instead increase infrastructure spending even if this requires additional borrowing in order to get the sluggish euro-area economy moving again.

3.2 Different Multiplier Effects

Another issue of considerable policy controversy is which items in the budget deserve priority. A principal goal of government spending—especially discretionary spending—is to stimulate the economy. The multiplier ensures that every additional euro of government spending increases aggregate demand by more than one euro. But we have also seen that much of the effect can be offset by taxes. In addition, it is unrealistic to assume that the multiplier effect is the same regardless of the type of government expenditure.

As seen earlier, the larger the *mpc*, the greater the multiplier. Until now, we have assumed that the *mpc* is uniform—that is, that it represents the marginal propensity to consume of all individuals and groups in society. But there may be significant variations in the *mpc* depending on which income groups are involved.

The typical wealthy individual is capable of saving a significant percentage of his income, a much greater percentage than that of most poor people. Of course, what is saved is not consumed; the average poor person spends a higher percentage of each additional euro received than would a rich person. In other words, a poor person's *mpc* tends to be higher. Because a higher *mpc* translates to a larger multiplier, Keynes argued that in general the multiplier is largest when government spending is directed toward those who have the highest *mpc*. Spending that benefits the poor or unemployed is thus likely to have larger multiplier effects.

Summarizing all these arguments, we can conclude that multipliers

- Are not stable over time but might be larger in a recession, when crowding out is less of a problem
- Are larger if the spending benefits poor households
- Are larger if the government spends money on investment for infrastructure, as in this case, crowding in of private investment might happen

In fact, this is exactly what modern research on fiscal multipliers shows. Table 10.2 presents results from a meta-study on the size of fiscal multipliers (which summarizes a large number of independent studies on the issue). As we see, for most measures, the size of the multiplier varies strongly over the business cycle. Fiscal policy seems not to be very effective in influencing output when the economy is already booming.

Table 10.2 *Different Multiplier Effects*

Fiscal measure	Multiplier		
	In an upswing	*Over the business cycle*	*In a downturn*
Unspecified public spending	0.6	0.7	1.5
Public consumption	0.5	0.5	1.8
Public investment	0.3	1.5	1.9
Military spending	−0.2	0.2	2.1
Changes in taxation	0.3	0.4	0.4
Transfers to households	0.4	0.4	2.6

Source: Sebastian Gechert and Ansgar Rannenberg, Are Fiscal Multipliers Regime-Dependent? A Meta Regression Analysis, IMK Working Paper 139, Düsseldorf, 2014.

In contrast, some measures are quite effective when the economy is in a recession. While, overall, the multipliers listed here are smaller than those seen in earlier examples because of offsetting effects and leakages (discussed in Appendix A2), the effects of increased transfers to households, public investment, and public consumption are all significantly large. Note, in contrast, the relatively small multipliers for changes in tax cuts. As anticipated by Keynes, tax cuts in this case get less "bang for the buck" due to the generally smaller *mpc* exhibited by the beneficiaries of such policies.

3.3 Applying Fiscal Policy

We have now identified a number of different fiscal policy approaches that can be used by the government to respond to various economic conditions. We have also noted some of the differences in opinion among economists as to the effectiveness and appropriate use of fiscal policy. In future chapters, we examine the application of fiscal policies to specific problems, including the financial crisis and recession that began in 2007 in the U.S. and led to a global recession in 2008–2009.

Before doing this, we need to add another very important aspect of the economy to our analysis: money, credit, and monetary policy. Monetary policy is a very important factor affecting, among other things, interest rates and inflation. We need to understand how money is created, how the creation of money is influenced by the central bank, and how this relates to other macroeconomic factors. This is the topic of Chapters 11 and 12.

After we have added an analysis of money and monetary policy, we will return to a consideration of the issues of unemployment and inflation and appropriate policies to respond to them in Chapter 13. We will then introduce the international economy in Chapter 14. In Chapter 15, we discuss the economic crisis of 2007–2008 and its aftermath. In Chapter 16, we focus on issues of debt and deficits.

REVIEW QUESTIONS

1. What is the impact of a change in government spending on aggregate expenditure and economic equilibrium?
2. What is the impact of a lump-sum change in taxes on aggregate expenditure and economic equilibrium? How does it differ from a change in government spending?
3. Give some examples of expansionary and contractionary fiscal policy.
4. How is the budget surplus or deficit defined? How has the budget position of the euro area (and your country) varied in recent years?
5. What is meant by an automatic stabilizer? Give some examples of economic institutions that function as automatic stabilizers.
6. What are some of the advantages and disadvantages of discretionary fiscal policy? Give some examples of the use of discretionary fiscal policy.
7. What is a cyclical deficit? What is a structural deficit? How are they different?
8. What is crowding out? How specifically does crowding out happen? Explain. What is crowding in?

EXERCISES

1. Using the data in Table 10.1, determine the economic equilibrium for a government spending level of 60.

2. Using Table 10.1 and the formulas and numbers given in the text for the multiplier and tax multiplier, calculate the effect on equilibrium GDP of a government spending level of 100 combined with a tax level of 100. What does this imply about the impact of a balanced government budget on GDP, compared to government spending alone?

3. Go to the European Commission's Directorate for Economic and Financial Affairs' Web site (http://ec.europa.eu/economy_finance/eu/forecasts/index_en.htm). Locate the most recent economic forecast. Consult the most recent summary table on "Structural budget balance." Are euro-area governments as a whole predicted to run an expansionary or a contractionary fiscal policy this year? Given the change in the unemployment rate, should this be called a procyclical or countercyclical fiscal policy? Which countries in the EU (now including non–euro-area countries such as the UK and Sweden) are running an expansionary fiscal policy? Which run a contractionary fiscal policy?

4. Which of the following are examples of automatic stabilizers, and which are examples of discretionary policy? Could some be both? Explain.
   a. Tax revenues rise during an economic expansion
   b. Personal tax rates are reduced
   c. Government spending on highways is increased
   d. Farm support payments increase
   e. Unemployment payments rise during a recession

5. Match each concept in Column A with a definition or example in Column B.

Column A	Column B
a. Tax multiplier	1. Reduction in income tax rates
b. Disposable income	2. Unemployment compensation
c. Expansionary fiscal policy	3. $Y - T + TR$
d. Contractionary fiscal policy	4. $G + TR$
e. Government outlays	5. Reduction in government spending
f. Automatic stabilizer	6. Intended investment
g. Injection into the circular flow	7. $-(mult)\,(mpc)$

APPENDIX: MORE ALGEBRAIC APPROACHES TO THE MULTIPLIER

A1. AN ALGEBRAIC APPROACH TO THE MULTIPLIER, WITH A LUMP-SUM TAX

A lump-sum tax is a tax that is simply levied on an economy as a flat amount. This amount does not change with the level of income. Suppose that a lump–sum tax is levied in an economy with a government (but no foreign sector). Because consumption in this economy is $C = \bar{C} + mpc\, Y_d$ while disposable income is $Y_d = Y - \bar{T} + TR$, we can write the consumption function as:

$$C = \bar{C} + mpc\, (Y - \bar{T} + TR)$$

Thus aggregate expenditure in this economy can be expressed as:

$$
\begin{aligned}
AE &= C + I_I + G \\
&= \bar{C} + mpc\, (Y - \bar{T} + TR) + I_I + G \\
&= (\bar{C} - mpc\, \bar{T} + mpc\, TR + I_I + G) + mpc\, Y
\end{aligned}
$$

The last rearrangement shows that the AE curve has an intercept equal to the term in parentheses and a slope equal to the marginal propensity to consume. Changes in any of the variables in parentheses, by changing the intercept, shift the curve upward or downward in a parallel manner.

By substituting this into the equation for the equilibrium condition, $Y = AE$, we can derive an expression for equilibrium income in terms of all the other variables in the model:

$$Y = (\bar{C} - mpc\, \bar{T} + mpc\, TR + I_I + G) + mpc\, Y$$

$$Y - mpc\, Y = \bar{C} - mpc\, \bar{T} + mpc\, TR + I_I + G$$

$$(1 - mpc)\, Y = \bar{C} - mpc\, \bar{T} + mpc TR + I_I + G$$

$$Y = \frac{1}{1 - mpc}(\bar{C} - mpc\, \bar{T} + mpc\, TR + I_I + G)$$

If autonomous consumption, intended investment, or government spending change, these each increase equilibrium income by $mult = 1/(1 - mpc)$ times the amount of the original change. If the level of lump-sum taxes or transfers changes, these change Y by either negative or positive $(mult)(mpc)$ times the amount of the original change.

To see this explicitly, consider the changes that would come about in Y if there were a change in the level of the lump-sum tax from T_0 to a new level, T_1, if everything else stays the same. We can solve for the change in Y by subtracting the old equation from the new one:

$$Y_1 = \frac{1}{1 - mpc}(\bar{C} + I_I + G - mpc\, \bar{T}_1 + mpc\, TR)$$

$$\left[Y_0 = \frac{1}{1 - mpc}(\bar{C} + I_I + G - mpc\, \bar{T}_0 + mpc\, TR) \right]$$

$$Y_1 - Y_0 = \frac{1}{1 - mpc}(\bar{C} - \bar{C} + I_I - I_I + G - G - mpc\, \bar{T}_1 + mpc\, \bar{T}_0 + mpc\, TR - mpc\, TR)$$

But $\bar{C}, I_I, G, TR$ (and the *mpc*) are all unchanged, so most of the subtractions in parentheses come out to be 0. We are left with (taking the negative sign out in front):

$$Y_1 - Y_0 = -\frac{1}{1 - mpc} mpc \, (\bar{T}_1 - \bar{T}_0)$$

or

$$\Delta Y = -(mult)(mpc)\Delta \bar{T}$$

As explained in the text, the multiplier for a change in taxes is smaller than the multiplier for a change in government spending, because taxation affects aggregate demand only to the extent that people *spend* their tax cut or pay their increased taxes by reducing *consumption*. Because people may also *save* part of their tax cut or pay part of their increased taxes out of their *savings*, not all the changes in taxes will carry over to changes in aggregate demand. The tax multiplier has a negative sign, since a *decrease* in taxes *increases* consumption, aggregate demand, and income, while a tax increase decreases them.

A2. AN ALGEBRAIC APPROACH TO THE MULTIPLIER, WITH A PROPORTIONAL TAX

With a proportional tax, total tax revenues are not set at a fixed level of revenues, as was the case with a lump-sum tax, but rather are a fixed *proportion* of total income. That is, $T = tY$ where t is the tax rate. The equation for AE becomes

$$\begin{aligned} AE &= \bar{C} + mpc \,(Y - tY + TR) \, I_I + G \\ &= (\bar{C} + mpc \, TR + I_I + G) + mpc \,(Y - tY) \\ &= (\bar{C} + mpc \, TR + I_I + G) + mpc \,(1 - t) \, Y \end{aligned}$$

With the addition of proportional taxes, the AE curve now has a new slope: $mpc(1 - t)$. Because t is a fraction greater than 0 but less than 1, this slope is generally flatter than the slope we have worked with before. A *cut* in the tax rate rotates the curve *up*ward, as shown in Figure 10.9.

Substituting in the equilibrium condition, $Y = AE$, and solving yields:

$$\begin{aligned} Y &= (\bar{C} + mpc \, TR + I_I + G) + mpc \,(1 - t) \, Y \\ Y - mpc \,(1 - t) \, Y &= \bar{C} + mpc \, TR + I_I + G \\ (1 - mpc \,(1 - t)) \, Y &= \bar{C} + mpc \, TR + I_I + G \end{aligned}$$

$$Y = \left[\frac{1}{1 - mpc(1 - t)}\right](\bar{C} + mpc \, TR + I_I + G)$$

The term in brackets is a new multiplier, for the case of a proportional tax. It is smaller than the basic (no proportional taxation) multiplier, reflecting the fact that now any

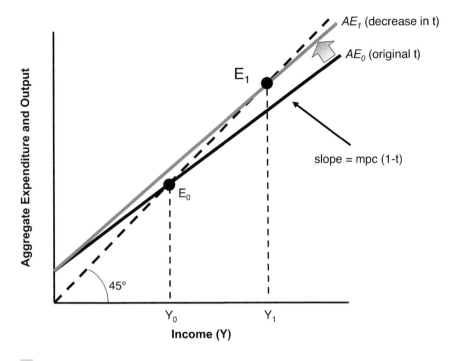

Figure 10.9 *A Reduction in the Proportional Tax Rate*

In the case of a proportional tax, a tax cut reduces the tax rate t, which increases the slope of the AE curve and raises equilibrium income from Y_0 to Y_1.

change in spending has smaller feedback effects through consumption. (Some of the change in income "leaks" into taxes.) For example, if *mpc* = 0.8 and *t* = 0.2, then the new multiplier is $1/(1-0.64)$, or approximately 2.8, compared to the simple model multiplier $1/(1-0.8)$, which is 5. Changes in autonomous consumption or investment (or government spending or transfers) now have less of an effect on equilibrium income—the "automatic stabilizer" effect mentioned in the text.

Is there a multiplier for the tax rate, *t*? That is, could we derive from the model a formula for how much equilibrium income should change with a change in the rate (rather than level) of taxes? For example, if the tax rate were to decrease from 0.2 to 0.15, could we calculate the size of the change from Y_0 to Y_1 illustrated in Figure 10.9? Yes, but deriving a general formula for a multiplier relating the change in *Y* to the change in the tax rate requires the use of calculus, which we will not pursue here. (If you are familiar with calculus, you can use the last formula to calculate the change in *Y* resulting from a change in *t*.)

Chapter 11

Money, Banking, and Finance

Everyone would like to have more money, right? Well, maybe not. In 2004, it was very easy to be a millionaire in Turkey—many times over. A million Turkish lira were worth about €0.50. A 20 million-lira bill was worth about €10. People routinely just put their thumb over the last six digits when looking at a value expressed in liras. *Guinness World Records* named the Turkish lira the world's least valuable currency. But you could have lots of it!

1. WHY MONEY?

So far, this book has said very little about money, finance, or interest rates. This is in line with early views on money, according to which money is a mere facilitator in the process of employing scarce resources—including labor—in the production of goods and services that contribute to economic well-being. But in modern economies, money is more than a mere facilitator. As one could observe quite clearly during the Great Recession, if there are problems in the banking system, deep and long-lasting recessions might be the consequence. If companies would like to invest but do not get the loans necessary to do so, they often cannot realize their plans. The same applies to households who want to build or buy a home: Without finance, such plans cannot be realized. Hence, money, finance, and interest rates are clearly important macroeconomic issues.

What is the relation of money and finance to economic behavior? Before we get into the details of how money and credit work in a sophisticated contemporary economy, let's picture a few simpler—and dramatically different—scenarios, drawn from real-world situations and events, that inform how economists have come to think about money and the macroeconomy.

1.1 Money and Aggregate Demand

Let's start with a case of an economy in which inflation is low to moderate. Suppose further that this economy has a banking system that is sophisticated and in reasonably good shape. You are a businessperson who has a great idea about how to expand your business. Or, in your role as a household member, you are interested in buying a home for your family. But you do not have the cash. You go to a bank and ask for a loan. The bank will evaluate your creditworthiness, see whether expanding its balance sheet is sensible within its business strategy and regulatory requirements, and then either deny you a loan or offer you a loan on particular terms. If you receive a loan offer and accept the terms, you will take out the loan and go out and spend. If you are denied the loan, or if you think the terms are too unfavorable, you will forgo expanding your business or buying the house.

To the extent the central bank of a country (or, in the case of the euro area, a group of countries) can affect the volume and terms of loans made by banks, it can thus affect the level of spending in the economy. We have seen in Chapters 9 and 10 how the level of spending (or aggregate expenditure) in an economy is related to levels of employment and output. **Monetary policy** that affects the behavior of banks, then, may also be a significant factor in achieving the goals of macroeconomic stabilization and low unemployment.

But not all economies enjoy low inflation rates and stable banking systems. Our next two cases illustrate these topics.

monetary policy: the use of tools controlled by the central bank, such as interest rates on funds commercial banks borrow from the central bank, or the purchase of government bonds by the central bank to affect the levels of interest rates, credit, and money supply

1.2 "Running the Printing Press"

Consider a country with a very simple government and banking system. The country's government is housed in a single building and pays its employees and its bills in cash. In the basement of the building is a printing press that prints paper money. The government finds it very difficult to collect enough taxes to pay its operating expenses, so it just runs the printing press every time an employee needs to be paid or a bill comes due.

How would this affect the economy? If the national economy is very large and growing, relative to the size of government expenditures, the fresh bills may just be absorbed into circulation without much impact. But if the economy was stagnant and expenditures were large, there would soon be a classic situation of inflation caused by "too much money chasing too few goods." As more and more money is put into circulation, prices will rise at an increasingly rapid rate.

If this goes on for long, a situation of hyperinflation (often defined as any annual inflation rate higher than 100 percent) can result. Germany after World War I, Hungary after World War II, Bolivia in the mid-1980s, Argentina during various periods, Ukraine in the early 1990s, and Zimbabwe in 2008–2009 all experienced famous hyperinflations.

In Germany in the 1920s, for example, the economy was in tatters after the war, and the government found it impossible to collect taxes in sufficient amounts to support its operations, let alone pay the reparations demanded by the victors. So it resorted to running the printing presses. Inflation reached a high of 41 percent—per *day!* In 1920, a German postage stamp cost 4 marks; in 1923, the same stamp cost *50 billion* marks.

> ## BOX 11.1 EXPERIENCES OF HYPERINFLATION
>
> During the period of German hyperinflation in the 1920s, a story was told of someone taking stacks of deutsche marks, the German currency, to town in a wheelbarrow in order to make a modest purchase, and—after leaving it for a moment—returning to find the wheelbarrow stolen and the bills stacked on the ground. Other stories told of people in a bar ordering their beers two at a time, because the time it took for the price of beer to rise was less than it would take for the beer to get warm.
>
> After the fall of the Soviet Union, in the 1990s, Russia suffered from severe inflation. Many people who had saved money in cash found that it had become nearly valueless. A Russian colleague told one of the authors of this text how his mother had thought, at the beginning of the 1990s, that she had enough money saved to take care of her in old age. She watched the value of her stash of bills go down and down until finally, in desperation, rather than watch it disappear, she took it to the store and bought a bag of sugar.

barter: exchange of goods, services, or assets directly for other goods, services, or assets, without the use of money

In such a situation, it obviously becomes very difficult to keep a sophisticated economy going. People tend to resort to **barter**—exchanging goods, services, or assets directly for other goods, services, or assets—to try to avoid having to deal with a rapidly inflating currency. It becomes impossible to think about making a deposit at a bank or to work out reasonable terms for a loan, and so normal patterns of saving and lending are disrupted. If they can, people may try to acquire—or at least keep their accounts in—a "hard," noninflating currency issued by a foreign country. Hyperinflation is obviously not a good situation; production tends to be lowered and unemployment raised by the chaos that hyperinflation causes in an economy.

Hyperinflation usually ends when the nearly valueless currency is abandoned, and people exchange very large denominations of the old currency for small denominations of a new currency. If the new currency is accompanied by a credible government promise to stop "running the printing press," the episode of hyperinflation draws to a close. This is what happened after the hyperinflation of the early 2000s in Turkey; the old lira was abandoned in favor of a new currency that removed six zeros. By 2016, the new Turkish lira had a fairly stable value of about €0.33.

Even if inflation does not reach hyperinflation levels, high inflation can be disruptive to an economy. Over time, high inflation can wipe out the value of people's savings, and it hurts people who are on fixed incomes (such as nonindexed pensions). It redistributes wealth from creditors to debtors, since people now repay debts in money that is worth less than the money that they originally borrowed. It creates "menu costs"—literally, the cost of time and effort made to update printed menus and other sorts of price lists. Rising or variable inflation rates create a great deal of uncertainty, which can make it very difficult for households and businesses to make sensible plans regarding savings, retirement, investment, and so on. For these reasons, stabilization of a country's price level is among the important goals of macroeconomic policy.

1.3 Deflation and Financial Crises

Now consider an economy in the opposite situation, in which people are not willing to spend, maybe because they want to hold on to their money or because banks do not want to lend. In this case, prices must be bid *down*. A situation of generally falling prices is called **deflation**. Why would deflation be a problem? While deflation makes people's savings *more* valuable and *helps* people who are on fixed incomes, it is still disruptive. In this case, wealth is redistributed from debtors to creditors. You borrow "cheap" money but later have to pay back with money that is "expensive." Deflation also creates menu costs, and it creates uncertainty. When people come to expect deflation, it may also cause them to cut back on spending. Why buy a big item such as a car or computer now if you believe you will be able to buy the same item for less next year?

deflation: when the aggregate price level falls

Deflation is often touched off by a financial crisis in which many people lose access to the opportunity to obtain loans and perhaps access to their own deposits at banks as well. If you cannot withdraw money from your account at a bank, and you cannot get a loan, then you cannot pay for things. If many people are in this situation, the economy grinds to a halt—or at least slows down considerably. Because less money is spent, prices fall. Once prices start to fall, business failures follow: With debts fixed in nominal currency terms (e.g., in dollars or euros), falling prices means an increasing debt burden. Business failures in turn lead to bad loans and more banking failures.

The Great Depression was accompanied in the United States by just such a collapse in the banking system. The "bank runs" or "banking panics" of 1930–1933, in which people rushed to try to withdraw their deposits all at once, caused many banks to fail. Because deposit insurance did not yet exist, people's accounts at those banks were wiped out. The price level dropped 25 percent in just a few years. Falling prices bankrupted businesses and farmers and thus made conditions even worse.

But deflation is not merely "ancient history." Japan also experienced deflation touched off by a financial crisis in late 1989 after a speculative bubble in real estate and stocks came to a sudden end. Japanese banks had, it turned out, racked up huge amounts of bad loans—loans on which they would never be able to collect. Some banks were ordered to shut down, while others teetered. People became justifiably leery of spending with the future so uncertain. Because banks had to write down their capital because of losses on their loan portfolios, they were unable to lend as much, and because spending was shrinking, the Japanese economy slid into recession. Over the next decade and a half, prices steadily fell at a rate of about 1 percent per year (see Box 11.2).

In early 2016, a certain fear of deflation was also present among central bankers in the euro area. Because of the global financial and economic crisis of 2008–2009 and the following euro crisis, unemployment had remained stubbornly high for an extended period of time in a number of euro-area countries. In some countries, wages and prices had fallen, and surveys were showing that people increasingly expected permanently lower inflation. Central bankers feared that low rates of inflation actually might turn into outright deflation at some point. To avert this danger, the ECB enacted a number of highly unconventional monetary policy measures, such as quantitative easing and negative interest rates (see also Chapter 12).

Deflation can be very damaging when looked at from the perspective of the real potential productivity of an economy. Businesses might have great ideas for expansion, and people may want to work and spend, but they are held back by the falling price level: With the prospect of debt becoming harder to service over time, companies will not borrow and banks will not lend. Hence, investment will be postponed or cancelled and people not employed. For this reason, as well as the problems discussed already with rapid inflation, stability of the monetary system is an important policy goal for governments and is closely related to both the goal of price stability and the goal of raising living standards.

BOX 11.2 DEFLATION IN JAPAN

Following a banking crisis in 1989, the Japanese economy slid into a situation of recession and deflation, which it was not able to shake for more than two decades. A very slow growth rate has been accompanied by generally falling prices, which have made it very difficult to keep the economy on track.

"As deflation became entrenched, consumers adjusted accordingly. Instead of splurging on a bottle of Chanel fragrance, they started to buy perfume by the ounce from peddlers online. Companies adjusted, and designer denims gave way to no-frill jeans that went for $10 instead of $100 ... Consumers grew accustomed to expecting that the longer they waited, the cheaper goods would become. And they held back on spending. That led to even less demand and more years of deflation."

In 2013, the new Japanese government of Prime Minister Shinzo Abe (pronounced ah-bey) tried to revive Japan's deflated economy with economic stimulus and monetary expansion. But "for companies to feel confident enough to start raising prices, Japan's consumers have to start spending again, and data confirming that trend is mixed."

In July 2013, "prices rose in Japan last month at their fastest pace for almost five years, offering some hope for ending years of debilitating deflation that has stymied growth. The consumer price index was up 0.7 percent from a year earlier, the biggest rise since a 1.0 percent increase in November 2008. Hideo Kumano, chief economist at Dai-ichi Life Research Institute, commented: "today's CPI data shows signs of exit from deflation, but we still need to see improvement in the job market and redistribution of wealth . . . to declare deflation is over."

"The definition of exit from deflation can be political, but the key is 'sustainable' rises in prices, which is difficult to achieve without improvement in the job market and salaries," Kumano said."

Sources: Hiroko Tabuchi, "Getting Japan to Spend," New York Times, June 29, 2013; Miwa Suzuki, "Japan Price Rise Offers Hope for Deflation End," Yahoo News, August 30, 2013.

Discussion Questions

1. Which of the three conditions just described—low inflation, high inflation, or deflation—best characterizes the euro-area economy right now? Do you know of any country currently in one of the other conditions?

2. Unemployment and inflation are usually considered the "bads" that can come with business cycles. Compare the costs to society of unemployment to the costs to society of inflation.

3. What are the main problems about deflation? Isn't it great if the purchasing power of savings increases?

2. WHAT IS MONEY?

You have no doubt that the bills and coins you have in your wallet are "money." Economists would agree with you on that. But in other ways, the manner in which economists use the term is very different from the way it is used in popular speech. Money, to an economist, is something that plays three specific roles in an economy, and the cash in your pocket is only one form of money.

2.1 The Roles of Money

Money is a special kind of financial asset (a form of financial capital) that has three important functions.

First, it is a *medium of exchange*. When you sell something, you accept money in return. When you buy something, you hand over money to obtain the good or service that you want. Without a functional medium of exchange, an economy would have to operate as a barter system, as mentioned in the earlier example of German hyperinflation. You would have to trade tangible objects or services directly in order to get other goods or services in exchange. This could be quite inconvenient—there would have to be what is called a "double coincidence of wants." For example, if you want pizza and can offer Web design services, you would need to hunt around for pizza makers in need of Web design. Such merchants may or may not exist, but even if they did, you would certainly have to spend some considerable time finding them. With money, on the other hand, you can sell your services to anyone who wants them and use the money you receive to buy pizza from anyone who supplies it.

Second, money is also a *store of value*. That means that, even if you hold onto it for a while, it will still be good for transactions when you are ready to use it. This is obviously a necessary property, since the pizza makers are unlikely to accept your money in exchange unless they know that, a month from now, their landlord will also accept the same money when they pay their rent. In serving as a store of value, money serves as a way of holding wealth—like any other form of financial or real capital that is held because it is worth something. The thing that makes money distinct from other assets is its **liquidity**, that is, the ease with which it can be used in exchange. Money is highly liquid—you can take it to the store and use it immediately. If you own a car, shares in a business, or a valuable piece of jewelry, these are also ways of storing your

liquidity: the ease of use of an asset as a medium of exchange

wealth, but they are not liquid. You must convert the value stored in them to money before you can buy something else.

The third role of money is that it is a *unit of account*. Things are often assigned money values even if they are not actually being bought and sold. When a firm estimates the value of unsold inventories in its warehouses in order to calculate its profits or losses, for example, or a town assesses the euro value of a house even though there are no plans for it to be sold, they are using money as a unit of account.

Some ways in which we commonly use the term "money" differ from how economists use it. For example, we might say that someone "makes a lot of money" because he has a high annual *income*. Income, however, is a *flow* variable, measured (as described in Chapter 3) over a period of time. Money is a *stock* variable—a particular kind of asset. A person who makes a lot of income over a year may acquire a large stock of money—or he may not. If the income is quickly spent on goods and services, the person may have high *income* (over the year) but accumulate little *money* (measured at a point in time).

We may also say that someone "has a lot of money" if she has accumulated a lot of *wealth*. But this is also not technically correct. A wealthy person may hold a lot of her assets in the form of corporate shares, real estate, or Renaissance paintings rather than as spendable, liquid money. Middle-class families are sometimes described as "house rich but cash poor" exactly for this reason. If they attempt to hold a high proportion of their assets as home equity, they may end up with very little in the way of funds that they can actually spend—that is, *money*. Liquidity issues aside, holding money (a particular financial asset) is not the same as holding a tangible asset with useful physical properties. Money is thus not the same thing as wealth or income. This is an important distinction, on which we will elaborate in later chapters.

2.2 Types of Money

commodity money: a good used as money that is also valuable in itself

intrinsic value: value related to the tangible or physical properties of the object

Throughout much of history, **commodity money** was the most common type of money. Commodity money is, or is made up of, something that contains **intrinsic value** and is also used in exchange. Coins made of gold or silver are probably the most familiar example. Decorative beads, shells, fishhooks, and cattle have served the purpose in some cultures. In prisons and prisoner-of-war camps and in the black market in many countries in Europe after World War II, cigarettes sometimes developed into a medium of exchange. "Prices" for chocolate or other goods and services were quoted in terms of numbers of cigarettes required in exchange. (Cigarettes thus had exchange value in this system even to nonsmokers, for whom they had no intrinsic value.)

To be used as money, a commodity must be *generally acceptable, standardized, durable, portable, scarce*, and, preferably, easily *divisible*. Standardization is important so that disputes do not arise about the quality and value of the money. Coins stamped by the government are a popular kind of money because the stamp is a sign that they are of equal weight and purity of mineral content. Gold and silver have historically been popular because coins made from them are durable. The scarcity of gold and silver was also an important factor. Coins made of, say, wood, in an area with many forests would rapidly lose value, as everyone could just make their own. Divisibility is also important. Heavy gold ingots might be useful for buying expensive real estate but are not very useful for buying pasta for dinner. Smaller coins and coins made of less valuable minerals were historically minted to provide a medium of exchange for smaller purchases.

Gold and silver coins, while fairly portable, can still be inconvenient to carry around in large quantities. Individual banks, state governments, and national governments have at various times issued paper monies that represent claims on actual commodities, usually gold or silver. For many years, starting in the late 1830s, most European countries had their national currencies by law backed by gold. The exchange rate between different currencies was computed from their respective value relative to gold, and international transactions were finally settled in gold reserves.

This system of gold-backed currencies broke down with the start of World War I, as many of the war parties resorted to the printing press to finance war expenditure. It was briefly reinstated between 1925 and 1931 before being finally abandoned in Europe for good in the Great Depression. After World War II, most of European gold had ended up in the U.S. in exchange for war-related supplies, and the European countries decided not to reintroduce a backing of their currencies by precious metal.

So what is the basis of value of the coins and euro banknotes we use today? The basis of value is—precisely and no more than—the expectation that the euro bill will be acceptable in exchange. The currency and coins we use now are what are called **fiat money**. "Fiat" in Latin means "let it be done," and a legal authority does something "by fiat" when it just declares something to be so. *A euro bill is money because the government declares it to be money.* In other words, its intrinsic value is no more than the value of the piece of paper of which it is made; but fiat money possesses **exchange value**, which is the value of the goods or services that such money can pay for in the market.

fiat money: a medium of exchange that is used as money because a government says it has value and that is accepted by the people using it

Fiat money is what some people call a "social construction"—something that works in society because of how people think and act toward it, not because of something it intrinsically "is." Fiat money works well as long as people are generally in agreement that it has value. Later, we examine some cases in which people have stopped agreeing—when people have lost confidence in the value of their money.

exchange value: value that corresponds to the value of goods or services for which the item can be exchanged

As economies have become more and more sophisticated, even carrying around paper money is inconvenient for many purposes. Nowadays, you are likely to make many of your transactions by other means, such as making electronic funds transfers from your bank. Funds in your bank, in turn, can be created by your commercial bank by the stroke of a pen when granting you a loan. This type of money, which is purely based on a promise to pay by someone other than the central bank, is called **credit money**. Understanding what types of transactions are said to involve "money" requires understanding how various assets differ in their liquidity as well as the distinction between money and credit.

credit money: money that is backed by a promise to pay by someone other than the central bank

2.3 Measures of Money

Because different assets have different degrees of liquidity, it is difficult to draw distinct lines between which assets are "money," which are "near-money," and which are "not money." As a result, economists have devised various ways of defining and measuring the volume of money that is circulating in a given economy.

Coins and bills are obviously "money." In the euro area today, coins are procured by national governments and produced in a number of mints around the euro area. Not all countries have their own mint, but each country has distinct designs on the backs of the euro coins. Banknotes are printed in more than a dozen different printing companies, and the national central banks share the responsibility for producing the bills. When economists measure a country's "money supply," only currency that is *in circulation* is included—that is, not currency sitting in a vault at the mint or at a bank. In January 2016, euro currency in circulation totaled €1.045 trillion (an average of about €3200 per person living in the euro area, including babies and pensioners).

But checking accounts are also extremely liquid. People can pay for almost everything using debit cards and electronic transfers of funds from their checking accounts (and in some euro countries, still paper checks). In fact, a number of euro countries have restrictions in place that transactions above a certain value *must* be made by bank transfer, and, in 2016, it was decided that €500 bills should be phased out. (One reason for this was that such large bills are often used by persons wishing to use money for illegal transactions.) Many people can also now move funds from their savings accounts (or, in some countries, money market accounts) to their checking accounts and back without limits and without prior notice. The most commonly used measure of the amount of money in an economy at a given point in time, called M1, includes not only currency in circulation but also the value of deposits which are redeemable at any time ("overnight deposits").[1] In January 2016, checkable deposits totaled €5.623 trillion (more than five times the currency in circulation), so M1 totaled €6.668 trillion.

M1: a measure of the money supply that includes currency and overnight deposits

But what about time deposits that mature soon? In many cases, against a fee, these can be converted into cash at short notice as well. A measure called **M2** includes everything in M1, plus deposits with an agreed maturity of up to two years and deposits redeemable at notice of up to three months. M2, which totaled €10.273 trillion as of January 2016, is almost twice the size of M1. When economists talk about "the money supply," they usually mean either M1 or M2.

M2: a measure of the money supply that includes all of M1 plus deposits with an agreed maturity of up to two years and deposits redeemable at a notice of up to three months

While not quite as liquid as M1, M2 types of money are liquid enough to be labeled "near-money." If we include some—quantitatively less important items—such as money market funds or debt securities with a maturity of up to two years, we arrive at M3. Prior to the introduction of the euro, Germany's central bank, the German Bundesbank, gave special attention to the development of M3 for its interest rate decision. As a consequence, many European economists still follow more the development of M3 than that of M2.

Specialists even use other broader categories of money. The principal reason for the different classifications is to allow for different points on the liquidity continuum

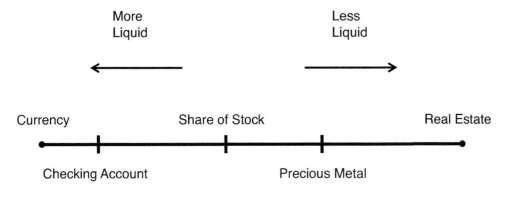

Figure 11.1 *The Liquidity Continuum*

Items more to the left are more liquid or, in other words, more easily used to purchase something of value. The farther to the right on this continuum, the less liquid the item is. Currency is as liquid as it gets, and real estate is usually about the most difficult asset to convert to money (seldom taking less than a few months).

that distinguish money from other kinds of assets (see Figure 11.1). While it is clear that currency is money and that real estate is not, the line separating money from nonmoney assets is not clearly defined.

What about using a credit card to make a purchase? From the user's point of view, using a credit card often seems to be like using a debit card or cash from one's pocket. In economists' terms, however, one does *not* use "money" when paying with a credit card. When paying on credit, you are, technically speaking, taking out a temporary loan from the credit card company. Only one day a month, when you send a check or electronic transfer to your credit card company from your checking account, do you make a "money" transaction.

Discussion Questions

1. Suppose that you asked someone who has not taken an economics class why a euro bill has value. What do you think he or she would say? Would he or she be correct?
2. What do you commonly use to make payments? Cash? Credit cards? Online payments? In which of these cases are you using "money"?

3. THE BANKING SYSTEM

It is easy to understand how the mints and printing houses scattered around the euro area create currency and how they could create more or less of it. But how does currency make its way into people's wallets? How are bank deposits such as checking accounts created? How can the volume of currency and deposits be influenced over time, as a matter of macroeconomic policy? To understand the answer to these questions, we need to know more about how a contemporary banking system works.

As will be explained in the following section, deposits are created by commercial banks, and currency is put into circulation by the interaction of commercial banks with the central bank. For the euro area, the role of the central bank is fulfilled by the so-called Eurosystem, which consists of the national central banks of the euro member states (such as the Bundesbank and the Banque de France) and the European Central Bank (ECB). As the decisions are taken by the ECB, for simplicity, we will refer to the ECB as the relevant central bank in this chapter. Most countries have combined systems of commercial banks and a central bank, which work at least roughly like the system described in this chapter. The workings of this combined system are discussed in greater detail in Chapter 12. Here we start by looking at commercial banks.

3.1 Commercial Banks

In the discussion of the market for loanable funds in Chapter 9, we assumed that some agents lend and others borrow, but we paid no attention to how borrowers and lenders would find each other. An individual might go to a relative or friend for a loan. But when the borrower is operating in a more impersonal way—perhaps because the borrower is a business, not an individual, or does not have personal contacts with individuals who can make the needed loan—an intermediary is needed to put together would-be lenders with would-be borrowers.

financial intermediary: an institution such as a bank, savings and loan association, or life insurance company that accepts funds from savers and makes loans to borrowers

A commercial bank is a type of institution called a **financial intermediary**. Individuals and organizations deposit funds with financial intermediaries, for safekeeping, to provide the convenience of making bank transfers, paying with a debit card, writing checks, or to earn interest. The financial intermediaries use the funds deposited with them to make loans to individuals and organizations that seek to borrow funds. Commercial banks as a special type of financial intermediaries can also create money by extending loans without prior deposits, as described in what follows.

Commercial banks are for-profit businesses, meaning that they seek to make earnings on their activities. They do so by charging interest (and perhaps other fees) on the loans they make. One of their functions is to screen the parties seeking loans in order to determine their creditworthiness. Lending is a risky business—not all loans made will be paid back in full. Demanding physical assets as collateral can alleviate some of the risk.

For example, mortgages and home-equity loans are collateralized by the value of a house; if the owner defaults on the loan, the bank may take possession of the house. Consumer loans are made on the basis of available income and job security of the applicant. Other loans are made on the basis of an evaluation of, say, the strength of a business plan and a business's record in paying back past loans. Banks may charge different interest rates depending on the riskiness of a loan or deny a loan request outright.

To understand what happens in a banking system, we start with a private bank's simplified balance sheet, shown in Table 11.1. A balance sheet is a standard double-entry

Table 11.1 *A Simplified Balance Sheet of a Commercial Bank*

Assets		Liabilities	
Reserves	€10 million	Deposits	€100 million
Government bonds	€20 million		
Loans	€70 million		

accounting representation of a commercial bank's assets and liabilities. It must "balance" in that assets and liabilities must add up the same amount. The right-hand side of a balance sheet, as shown in Table 11.1, lists an organization's liabilities. An **economic liability** is anything that one economic actor owes to another. The funds that you deposit in a bank are listed among the bank's liabilities, because it has an obligation to repay these funds to you.

Except in the case of banking panics, depositors are not likely all to show up at the same time, demanding their funds in cash. Although the bank must keep some funds on hand to meet depositors' withdrawal needs, normally it can use most of the deposits that it holds to obtain earnings.

Assets of an organization are listed on the left-hand side of a balance sheet, as shown in Table 11.1. **Bank reserves**, shown as an asset, include vault cash that the bank keeps on hand to meet likely short-term calls, such as depositors' withdrawals. Reserves also include deposits that the commercial bank has made in an account at the European Central Bank (discussed in Chapter 12). The bank owns these ECB deposits in the same way that bank customers "own" the deposits on their liability side. Banks are required to maintain a certain share of their customers' deposits with the ECB.

One relatively safe way for the bank to earn some interest is to lend money to national governments (i.e., to the French treasury or the German government). Recall from Chapter 10 that governments borrow from the public when they need to finance a government deficit or refinance part of the debt. They do so by issuing government bonds, which give the buyer the right to specific payments in the future. Depending on the duration of the loan, these securities may be called "bills" or "bonds." Government securities in the euro area also have their specific national names (German bonds might be referred to as "bunds," French bonds as "OATs" for "Obligations assimilables du Trésor"). We will use the term "government bonds" to represent any type of government security.

Very active markets exist for trading government bonds, especially from larger EU member states such as Germany, Italy, France, or the UK, and a particular bond may change hands many times before it is paid off. Banks tend to keep some of their assets—in the euro area, about one-tenth, on average—in government bonds, because, under normal circumstances, bonds earn interest but are also relatively liquid. If it looks as if depositors will want more cash back than a bank has in its vault, the private bank can quickly sell some of its government bonds on the open bond market.

The major asset of a commercial bank—and the major way that it makes its earnings—is its portfolio of loans other than government bonds: funds that are owed

economic liability: anything that one economic actor owes to another

bank reserves: funds not lent out or invested by a private bank but kept as vault cash or on deposit at the central bank

to the bank by businesses, households, nonprofits, or sub-national levels of government. Unlike government bonds, which can be liquidated quickly if necessary, some of these may be business loans, home mortgages, or consumer loans that will not be repaid for years.

Such assets are generally far less liquid than vault cash or bonds. This can potentially be problematic in difficult times. The health of a commercial banking system depends on having depositors who are confident about the safety of the funds that they have entrusted to the banking system and are not trying to withdraw their funds more rapidly than such loans are repaid. If confidence in the banks diminished and many customers wanted to withdraw their money, some banks might find themselves with insufficient liquidity (i.e., too many of their assets in long-term loans) to service all requests, further undermining confidence in the system.

3.2 Bank Types

So far, we have mainly talked about "commercial banks." In fact, this is a term under which a number of different bank types can be found that have different business models and different functions. The banks with which most people are familiar are known as retail banks, which perform the functions that we have already described: keeping money in secure deposits, providing payment, and extending loans (Table 11.2). Savings banks are also similar to retail banks but usually have a narrow regional focus and specialize in the provision of home loans to their customers and loans to small and medium-sized businesses. Another type of bank seen in many European countries are collective banks, which are similar to retail banks but are collectively owned by their customers. In many European countries, there are also public banks, which usually are tasked with the support of certain sectors (e.g., agriculture) or regions of the economy.

Table 11.2 Bank Types

	Chief functions
Retail	Safekeeping of money, checking accounts, loans
Savings banks	Similar to retail bank but specializing in loans, particularly mortgages and loans to small and medium-sized businesses
Cooperative banks	Same as a retail bank but cooperatively owned by customers
Private	Caters almost exclusively to high-net-worth individuals; functions extend beyond traditional banking into variety of financial services
Investment	No traditional banking functions; involved in underwriting and issuing securities, assistance with company mergers and acquisitions, market making, and general advice to corporations
Universal	Covering both investment and retail banking services
Central	Overseeing the monetary stability of the national economy by setting interest rates and providing liquidity to commercial banks

Private banks are exclusive, catering to high-net-worth individuals and companies. Their functions range widely from traditional banking to many forms of investment, some of which is moderate to high risk. Investment banks mostly deal with companies instead of individuals and do not offer any traditional banking services. For example, they help companies place stocks or bonds in the markets or sell options to hedge against changes in the exchange rate.

While in some countries, investment banks have long been separated from normal commercial banking, in many European countries, "universal banking" has been the norm—a single bank providing commercial banking services as well as investment banking services. In Europe, BNP Paribas, Crédit Agricole, and Société Générale of France; HSBC of the United Kingdom; Deutsche Bank of Germany; and ING Bank of the Netherlands are examples of such universal banks.

Central banks are entirely different institutions. They exist to ensure monetary stability in the economy. Many central banks are also tasked with regulating and supervising the banking system. For example, the central bank for the euro area, the European Central Bank (ECB), was given this task in 2014. Chapter 12 deals specifically with the ECB.

Banks and their activities have been and still are heavily regulated. Banks face rules about how much equity capital they must have relative to their assets, in which asset types they may invest how much, and even how qualified their management has to be. For a long time after World War II, in many countries, even binding ceilings for interest rates on deposits and loans were the norm. In the U.S., until its repeal in 1999, the Banking Act of 1933 (called the Glass-Steagall Act) required that traditional banking functions be strictly separated from the financial and investment activities of private banks and investment banks.

After a few decades of deregulation of bank activities from the mid-1990s onward, the recent past has seen a new tightening of rules. Excessively risky activities by banks had played a central role in the genesis of the global financial and economic crisis of 2008–2009 as well as in the euro crisis that followed. Consequently, policy makers have started to introduce stricter regulations again. Among others, banks are now required to have much more of their own capital at stake when they lend out money or engage in other risky activities. Moreover, in the European Union, in 2016, discussions were continuing as to how far excessively large and complex banks can be broken up by regulators.

3.3 How Banks Create Money

As we saw earlier, in the euro area, physical money is procured by national central banks and printed and coined in a variety of places across Europe. Yet this knowledge does not solve the issue of how this money gets from the central bank into your pockets. We have also discussed that the largest part of money today is not in the form of coins and banknotes but in the form of deposits. But we have not answered the question yet of how this deposit money comes into use.

To answer these questions, we need to take a closer look at the operation of commercial banks, and especially the credit creation process. If you have ever taken out a loan from a bank, you know that the money you borrow is not generally delivered to you as a bundle of cash. Rather, the bank credits your bank account with the amount of the loan, or it creates a new transaction account in your name. Consequently, when banks make loans, they increase the money supply, because transaction accounts make up part of M1 and the broader money supply. This answers the second part of our question: Deposit money is created when banks make loans.

If you now make payments through a bank transfer or by paying with your debit card (e.g., for a refrigerator), a certain amount from your account is transferred to the retailer's account. The overall money supply (which includes overall cash in circulation plus overall deposits) remains unchanged.

But how does cash now enter the picture? In order that customers can withdraw cash, commercial banks turn to the central bank and borrow cash. In this process, central banks require commercial banks to provide some collateral and usually charge an interest rate (we will turn to the details in Chapter 12). The commercial bank fills its ATMs with the cash and allows customers to withdraw from their account. Note that this process does not change M1 or the broader money supply: When withdrawing cash, your deposit at the bank shrinks by the same amount you withdraw, and the money supply remains unchanged.

Yet getting cash from the central bank is not the only interaction of your bank with the central bank. In many jurisdictions, including the euro area, commercial banks are required to hold a certain share of their deposits as reserves (the so-called **reserve requirements**).[2] Reserves are commercial banks' funds in a special account at the central bank. For the money-creation process, it is important to understand that these reserves do not need to be available at the time when a deposit or a loan is made but have to be put in the account within a certain time. In the euro area, for example, the amount of required reserves is computed based on the customers' deposits in a commercial bank at the end of one month. In the reserve maintenance period starting roughly six weeks later, the bank then has to present reserves meeting these requirements.

So practically, at the end of the month, a bank sums up how much money customers have in their accounts and computes how many reserves it must get hold of. Based on this figure, it either borrows reserves from other banks or, against collateral and with an interest rate, from the central bank. Understanding this process is important, as it shows that (contrary to what is sometimes thought) the reserves are not a constraint to banks' lending activities, as the loan is made by banks before they are required to have the reserves to do so.

You might now ask why central banks require commercial banks to hold reserves. This is a good question, given that, prior to the 1930s, many banking systems operated without reserve requirements and given that the Bank of England as well as the central banks of Canada and New Zealand have abandoned minimum reserve requirements altogether. Central bank experts usually state that minimum reserve requirements increase the commercial banks' borrowing needs from the central bank and hence facilitate the conduct of monetary policy (covered in the next chapter).

reserve requirements: the fraction of bank deposits that banks *must* keep as reserve

In addition to required reserves, banks sometimes hold excess reserves. These are reserves they are not required to hold but that they keep voluntarily. While banks usually try to minimize excess reserves, since they are costly and do not earn as much interest as other assets, in periods of financial crisis, banks prefer to hold onto excess reserves.

In Chapter 12, we explore in greater detail how the European Central Bank influences the banking system's process of money creation.

Discussion Questions

1. How do banks lend money that they do not physically possess to their customers? To what extent are they creating money in the process?
2. Does it bother you that banks hold only a small fraction of the value of their deposits on reserve? Why or why not?

4. MONEY AND FINANCE

In the past, the average person with a little extra money had few options for what to do with it other than putting it in the bank. Today, however, people have numerous financial investment alternatives available. Many people, including those classified as "small investors," find themselves with funds that they do not need at the moment and would like to use to accumulate a nest egg. But how can they choose among the many different options, including mutual funds, individual stocks, bonds, or other assets? This book does *not* attempt to offer specific advice on this question. However, a better understanding of the economy as a whole and of finance in particular will help you to make informed economic decisions. In this section, we begin to look at the relationship between investment decisions that are good for the investor and those that make the economy as a whole more productive—and how these may sometimes diverge.

4.1 Functions of Finance

The primary and most long-standing function of our financial system is the provision of money to support investment in real capital. Such "real" investment is the same as the "intended investment" that we saw in Chapter 9, which is an important reinjection into the circular flow that comes from the financial system. The banking system is involved in this key function, but here we are interested in the broader financial system, of which banks form only a part.

In recent years, finance for other purposes has grown in importance. **Portfolio investment**, once available only to rich individuals, is much more widespread today. This refers mostly to investing funds in securities such as stocks or bonds. To an economist, portfolio investment is merely another form of saving, a means of postponing consumption while hoping to earn a greater return than in a traditional bank. It is not "true" investment in the sense of the national accounts covered in Chapter 5, because when one buys a stock or a bond, ownership of an existing

portfolio investment: the purchase of financial assets such as stocks and bonds

369

security is simply transferred from one person to another—there is no addition to the economy's stock of capital.

A century ago, only the wealthy partook of this form of financial planning. Indeed, only a minority of the population earned enough to save significantly. As this changed, most people saved money in traditional banks instead of securities. Only more recently, over the past three or four decades, have stocks and bonds been "democratized" in the sense that a sizable percentage of the population, at least in some countries, now owns such assets. The change is largely due to the introduction of collective (also called "pooled" or "commingled") investment vehicles, such as mutual funds, and their association with capital-backed pension plans.

Finance now provides not only a variety of ways to invest but also more choices for long-term saving. It also supports speculation, that is, buying securities in the hopes of short-term gain. Individuals who speculate are not truly saving—they hope to exploit changes in prices to achieve short-term profit. The financial system offers them a vast and growing array of possible securities, each with its own market. The opportunities for speculation are therefore substantial. Speculators, unlike "true" investors, entrepreneurs, or businesspeople, do not directly contribute to economic well-being. As we will see, however, at a large enough scale, speculative activity has the potential to influence the economy through its impact on income, wealth, and spending.

As long as speculators are risking their own funds, the economic impact of their activity is limited. Most potential problems emerge when they borrow funds for the purpose. Speculators may borrow money in order to exploit what they see as market opportunities based on short-term price movements. This can create problems when speculators use excessive **leverage**—investments based on borrowed funds. As we see in greater detail in Chapter 15, borrowing excessively to finance risky speculative ventures carries the potential to destabilize the entire financial system and, with it, the economy. Another possible problem, not unrelated, occurs when lenders extend large lines of credit to borrowers who would not ordinarily satisfy minimum loan criteria. Both of these were recurrent problems during the most recent financial crisis.

Finally, public finance relates to how governments finance their activities. We say relatively little about this in the present chapter. Chapter 10 has already covered government finance with particular attention to taxes and spending, and Chapter 16 elaborates on the subject of government deficits and debt.

leverage: the use of debt to increase the potential rate of return of one's investment (at greater risk)

4.2 Nonbank Financial Institutions

nonbank financial institution: a financial institution that performs a number of services similar to those offered by banks but that is not a licensed bank and is not subject to banking regulations

There was a time when banks were responsible for most, if not all, economic matters relating to money. Today, many other types of financial intermediaries exist; indeed, over the past few decades, banks have been declining in importance relative to these **nonbank financial institutions**. In many of the EU countries, most savings today go through such institutions, which invest in stocks, bonds, and other assets. Note, however, that there are large differences among EU countries: In the Netherlands, roughly half of the households own private pension claims with a median value of €53,000. In Slovakia, in contrast, only 15 percent of the households own this type of wealth, and the median value among these households is a mere €3,000. Consequently, in some European countries, nonbank financial institutions play a major role in investment financing, while in other countries, banks are still the dominant way of financing real investment.

For instance, many people have their money in what are known as **collective investment vehicles** (CIVs), which basically offer people alternatives to saving money in a bank. Many types of CIVs fall into the category of **pooled funds**, which accept investments from many different investors and reduce the cost of making decisions about investing by managing them all together.

The best-known example of a CIV is a mutual fund, in the UK sometimes referred to as unit trust. Many individuals place their savings in such funds, which offer customers a variety of "baskets" or "pools" of investments. They purchase "shares" of a given fund instead of individual stock shares or bonds. Some funds are invested in high-growth stocks with moderate to high risk, for example, while others are mostly in government bonds. The number of possibilities is large, as thousands of pooled funds exist, invested not only in different classes of stocks and bonds but in commodities and other assets (as well as combinations of two or more of these forms of asset).

Pooled funds have lower fees than funds managed by a broker, because they do not have a paid manager looking after an individual investor's money (yet they have paid managers looking over the pool of funds who are paid for this service). At the same time, many believe that they offer better returns than bank savings accounts. The returns, however, may vary greatly, depending in large part on the riskiness of the investments that compose the fund.

Index funds (or index trackers) are pooled funds that do not have a manager making decisions about in which specific shares or bonds to invest but that try to replicate a given market index such as the EUROSTOXX 50 index for Europe's 50 most important stocks or national stock market indexes such as the German DAX 30, the British FTSE, or the Dutch AEX. These funds are usually managed by some kind of software, and the administrative fees are much smaller than for actively managed funds.

Hedge funds are a special category of CIV that often engages in highly speculative investments, promising greater earnings potential than most other funds, along with higher risk. Because they carry greater risk, hedge funds are only permitted to do business with particular (high-net-worth) individuals and institutions. Hedge funds are not necessarily commingled; though it is unusual, a hedge fund can be created by a single very large investor.

Pension funds are another type of CIV that accumulates savings from workers, sometimes including a matching contribution from employers, usually over a long period, to be disbursed as benefits in retirement. Access to the funds before retirement is highly restricted, with significant penalties for early withdrawals. To encourage workers to participate (thereby voluntarily deferring a percentage of their pay that they could otherwise use for current consumption), such funds are granted generous tax breaks in many European countries, both through reducing taxable income by the amount of the employee's contribution and by deferring taxes on earnings. Given the

collective investment vehicle or pooled fund: an investment vehicle that pools investments from many different sources, making investment decisions for them all as a group

index fund: a type of pooled fund that tries to replicate a common stock or bond market index. As this fund does not require active management by a manager, fees are usually lower than in other types of pooled funds

hedge fund: a type of pooled fund that often engages in highly speculative investments and to which access is generally restricted to wealthy clients

pension fund: a fund with the exclusive purpose of paying retirement benefits

different rules in different EU countries and given the differences in the generosity of national public pension systems, coverage varies widely across Europe.

Some of the largest investors in the world are pension funds that pool the retirement and health savings accounts of workers in the U.S. public sector. For example, the California Public Employees Retirement System (CalPERS) had about $279.5 billion in investments as of January 2014. This is the equivalent of 1.5 times the annual Irish GDP. CalPERS' income comes from returns on its investments and from the health-care and pension plans of more than a million workers and their employers, which include government agencies at the state or local level as well as public schools. CalPERS provides health-care benefits to about 1.6 million beneficiaries and their families and retirement benefits to about 553,000 individuals. With their large investments, these U.S. pension funds often can influence corporate behavior (even far beyond U.S. borders) and have been pivotal in removing CEOs who have performed poorly. They have also taken seriously environmental issues such as climate change and are gradually adjusting their assets to remove investments that will be disadvantaged as markets adjust to both the dangers of business as usual and the opportunities for businesses that help in mitigating or adjusting to a changed climate.

insurance company: a company that pays to cover all or part of the cost of specific risks against which individuals and companies chose to insure themselves

Another example of a nonbank financial institution is an **insurance company**. You might not think of insurance companies as similar to banks, but over time they have come to resemble them in some ways. The principal difference is that instead of making a deposit with an insurance company, you pay it a premium (monthly, quarterly, or annually) that is meant to protect you against a particular risk (or, in the case of certain capital life insurance policies, pay out a certain amount at a certain date in the future). The company, however, must have sufficient funds available to pay to beneficiaries that have the bad fortune (fire, flood, theft, accident, ill health, etc.) against which they had been insured. It must therefore earn a return sufficient to cover the cost of these payouts. In this way, an insurance company resembles a bank: It holds a pool of money that it lends to governments and companies and sometimes even invests in stocks or other riskier investments. The difference is usually that insurance companies can much better predict by statistical models when payouts will become due (especially for life insurance), and most European insurances have hence taken a longer-term perspective on their investments. However, in the U.S., some insurance companies have engaged in very risky business. The huge insurance company American International Group (AIG), for example, put billions into risky investments and had to seek a government bailout during the financial crisis of 2008–2009 (discussed further in Chapter 15). A special type of

reinsurer: a company that sells insurance to insurance companies to share the risk in case of large damages caused, for example, through natural disasters

insurance company is a **reinsurer**. These companies sell insurance to insurance companies for catastrophic events such as floods, earthquakes, or hurricanes that might devastate whole regions and that are too costly to be borne by typical insurance companies alone. Some of these reinsurers are remarkably farsighted. SwissRe, for example, has used both its statistical expertise and its painful experiences with disasters related to climate change to be a strong spokesman for policies to avert further catastrophic weather.

Brokerage services also fall into the category of nonbank financial institutions. **Securities brokers**, for example, keep an inventory of different financial assets—mostly stocks and bonds—that result from playing the role of middleman in transactions between buyers and sellers. They earn a commission, a percentage of the transaction, for the service of linking the buyer and the seller. Their service provides another option for customers who might otherwise put all their savings in a bank account. From the customer's point of view, funds invested with a broker are very liquid—in other words, a broker can easily convert a stock or bond into cash for a client. But since the broker is earning his own fees based on what products the client buys, questions have recently been raised about whom the broker is most likely to be serving: the buyer or the seller. The sellers are apt to be large organizations with close, sometimes financially rewarding relationships to the broker. In some instances, brokers have encouraged the purchase of stocks or other assets that they knew were unlikely to offer the advertised return because they themselves stood to gain from the transaction.

securities broker: an agent responsible for finding a buyer for sellers of different securities, thereby offering enhanced liquidity to the seller

In many European countries, there are also **building societies**. The idea of these financial institutions is that members first save over a number of years and then, after a certain period of time, are entitled to borrow from the funds of other savers at preferential interest rates to buy or build a dwelling. While in some countries such as Germany and Austria, building societies still operate along these lines, in other countries such as the UK, this part of the financial system was deregulated in the 1990s, and the building societies have started to offer regular banking services. A number of former building societies, having turned toward more risky business models, were central to the development of the financial crisis of 2007–2008 in Britain. The prime example here is Northern Rock, which experienced a bank run in 2007 and was later nationalized by the British government.

building society: a financial institution which collects savings from its customers and offers them at preferential rates to other customers so that they can buy or build a residence

In addition to these rather old types of nonbank financial institutions, a number of specialized financial institutions have developed over the past years that blur the line between banks and nonbanks. Some of them have taken on functions that are usually reserved for banks, but because of carefully crafting their business, they do not fall under banking regulation. The institutions are often referred to as **shadow banks**. One example of these entities is money market funds. These funds collect savers' money and lend the money collected to other banks or large corporations, usually for the short term. Shares in these funds are tradable, so by selling shares, savings are in principle available at any time. As long as debtors repay, there usually is not much movement in the price of the shares. Debtors have to repay the agreed principal plus interest. Hence, both from the side of the saver and from the side of the borrower, this service looks like a banking service. These types of shadow banks have grown, as they were a way to get around the rather strict bank regulation. At the same time, the financial crises in industrialized countries between 2007 and 2009 have demonstrated that these shadow banks can endanger the stability of the financial system and hence the economy at large.

shadow bank: credit intermediation that involves entities and activities outside the regular banking system

These different examples of institutions engaged in nonbanking finance represent an industry that has been growing in size and importance relative to banking. Their activities do not directly affect the money supply unless it is very broadly defined, because loans from these entities, unlike transactions using bank accounts, are not liquid (and are therefore usually classified as "nonmoney assets"). Nevertheless, as we will see in chapters to follow, they play a critical role in the national economy, as well as in the conduct of monetary policy (discussed in Chapter 12).

All nonbank financial institutions offer customers alternatives, often much more attractive than traditional bank savings. And they exemplify the manner in which the role of money has, over time, shifted from being a mere facilitator of real economic activity to playing an active and essential part in the real economy, with profound economic implications and consequences. We explore the phenomenon in much greater detail in the coming chapters.

4.3 Financialization and Financial Bubbles

By almost any measure, modern economies are much more dependent than ever on finance. Total financial assets in the euro-area banking sector roughly doubled from 2003 to 2013 to a total of €57 trillion (almost six times euro-area annual GDP). For the UK and the U.S., the figures are even more mind-boggling: Financial assets have surpassed the equivalent of 10 times the respective national GDP for both countries. The value of financial transactions is even larger. For the U.S., this value was *73 times* GDP already in 2009, primarily as a result of rapid growth in high-frequency trading, which permits speculators to buy and then quickly sell large quantities of assets. That the economy depends so much on finance does not necessarily pose a problem in itself. However, it may contribute to widening economic inequalities, and other difficulties occur when financial investment behavior ceases to be prudent. When economies grow on the basis of mass investment in assets with questionable foundations yet rise in price, the growth is unstable and destined to be of short duration. Such irrational speculative price rises are called bubbles.

Possibly the most famous historical example of a speculative bubble is the Dutch tulip frenzy (called a tulipomania) in the early 1600s. Different tulip types had different values, and since no one knew which type would bloom from a given tulip bulb, mass speculation ensued. Initially only the wealthy Dutch were buying them, but eventually the rest of the population caught the fever. Because everyone was buying tulips, their price rose rapidly, until the peak in March 1637, when some select bulbs sold for several times the yearly income of a skilled craftsman. Shortly thereafter, however, confidence in their value vanished. Almost overnight, the tulip market crashed, and many speculators were ruined.

Almost three centuries later, the U.S. stock market also experienced a speculative bubble. Many at the time believed that the rapid increase in stock prices during the 1920s was entirely justified, attributing it to a "new reality" evidenced in the establishment of the Federal Reserve in 1913 along with government policies to extend free trade, fight inflation, and relax antitrust laws. But what was really driving the bubble was the same factor underlying the Dutch tulip craze—the "herd instinct" that causes people to follow what everyone else is doing and to believe what everyone else believes. In the 1920s it seemed as if everyone was buying stocks. This drove up share prices, in turn making stocks much more attractive. The period was also characterized by heavy borrowing, especially by the U.S. middle class. Toward the end of the 1920s, a substantial share of consumer debt was taken on in order to buy stock shares (instead of consumer goods). In October 1929, the stock market crashed, and the Great Depression followed, which spread from the U.S. to the rest of the world quickly.

In recent years, and especially since the start of deregulation of international capital flows and many other aspects of finance from the 1970s onward, many other bubbles have developed. Spectacular cases are those in in East Asia in 1997, the 1999–2000 "dot-com" stock market bubbles, and the housing bubbles in the United States, Britain, Ireland, Spain, and other European countries in the late 2000s. At the root of all of them is a widespread belief in the value of an asset or assets that is reinforced by speculative borrowing. Bubbles are characterized by a rapid increase in prices that are not generally accompanied by an equally rapid improvement in economic conditions. In other words, a defining feature of such bubbles is that there is seldom any economic basis for them. The buying begets more buying, and the appreciation in the asset values is fleeting.

Despite having so much experience with bubbles, why do we fail to learn from past mistakes? Speculative bubbles form for two reasons: one psychological and one economic. The psychological explanation has to do with the faith or "blind optimism" that people exhibit, even when confronted with evidence to the contrary. As discussed in Chapter 4, and contrary to traditional economic theory, people are not always rational. One of the mistakes commonly made is extrapolating values over time. In other words, if home prices in Dublin have risen 30 percent in the past year, some might rush to buy property in Dublin, believing that the trend will continue. Another common mistake, as we have noted, is the tendency to follow the herd. Even someone who doubts that prices could continue to increase might find it difficult to resist buying an asset when everyone he knows has already done so (and has already made money!). The same phenomenon is at play among money managers. Those who take a conservative or contrarian position during a bubble risk performing worse than nearly everyone else, as long as the bubble continues to expand—which may be a period of several years or even more than a decade. This accounts for the tendency of fund managers to "follow the herd" in the investment advice given to clients.

Many bubbles are fueled by easy credit. If banks are willing to extent credit, investors and speculators might be lured into borrowing for their purchases of stocks or real estate, in the hope of reaping returns that are higher than they could obtain from bank savings. As we have seen, such behavior multiplied throughout the macroeconomy drives up asset prices on the strength of greater demand for them, leading to the inflation of a financial bubble. Excessive credit expansion was a major factor in the housing bubble of the 2000s (discussed in detail in Chapter 15).

4.4 Finance and the Macroeconomy

How exactly are all these possibilities of bank-based and non–bank-based finance linked to the macroeconomy? Remember our output-income-spending flow with leakages and injections from Chapter 9. At that point, we explained how intended investment is an injection and how the demand for capital goods creates the income necessary to produce savings to finance these investments. Finance is an essential element of this circuit. Of course, some firms can save funds out of their retained profits and can use these funds directly to buy capital goods. But for new firms or for firms with investment plans larger than their retained profits, finance is crucial to actually realize their investment plans. This does not necessarily mean that macroeconomically, savings have to be collected prior to the investment undertaking. As we have discussed, banks can create deposit money by extending loans with "the stroke of a pen," and this money can be used to make purchases of capital goods by their clients. However, if banks and nonbanks are not willing (or not able) to provide funds to firms and households, potential investment plans cannot turn into intended investment and cannot become an injection to the output-income-spending flow.

Hence, there is a clear relationship between the amount of credit and finance extended by the financial sector (both banks and nonbanks) and the level of aggregate expenditure in the economy (see Figure 11.2). Everything else being equal, the larger the volume of finance extended for real capital investment activities, the higher the amount of injections and the higher aggregate expenditure.

Yet "everything else being equal" here is an important qualification: As we have discussed, with the growth of the financial sector in many modern economies, a significant share of finance is not used anymore to finance real capital expenditure. Instead, banks give loans to hedge funds, and hedge funds might hold shares of commercial banks. Households might own shares of money market funds that have given a loan to the bank, which has lent the money further to the hedge fund. This cascade of finance

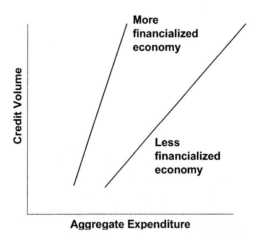

Figure 11.2 *Credit and Aggregate Expenditure*

A larger amount of credit disbursed tends to lead to more aggregate expenditure: Money is usually borrowed by households and firms to finance spending on consumer goods, residential properties, or new equipment. However, the more financialized an economy, the more of the credit goes into nonproductive activities without an impact on aggregate expenditure. For a financialized economy, therefore, the Credit-AE-curve is further to the left.

of course does not by itself create more injection into the economy and hence does not increase GDP. Hence, if an economy experiences "financialization" as discussed earlier, the same volume of credit and finance outstanding will result in less aggregate expenditure than in a case of a less financialized economy (see again Figure 11.2).

4.5 The International Sector

What we have neglected so far is the international aspect of finance, that is the cross-border trading of financial assets. While within a single country (and within the euro area), most financial assets are denominated in domestic currency, trading in financial assets from outside the currency area comes with an extra complication: Foreign assets might be denominated in another currency. In this case, the value of a—let's say—Japanese stock in the eye of the French investor does not only depend on the stock price in Japanese yen but also on the euro–yen exchange rate. While some investors might hence invest in foreign assets because they believe in the good performance of—for example—a Japanese car company, others invest abroad to speculate on changes in the exchange rate.

Just as domestic finance can funnel funds from savers to investors and hence extend credit to borrowers, trading financial assets across borders means that one country borrows and another country acquires claims.

Indeed, the financial system itself has become globalized. Although international trade has increased in the past four decades, the rapid expansion in cross-border financial flows is even more impressive. As we will see in Chapter 14, financial flows and trade are closely related. To put it as simply as possible, countries with a trade deficit must borrow from countries with trade surpluses. And some countries that persistently run a deficit get to the point at which they must borrow from other countries not only to continue purchasing imports but also to service (i.e., pay interest on) their debt.

When you hear economists or reporters speak about "global imbalances" or "imbalances in the euro area," they are referring to a world that is increasingly polarized; deficit countries come to depend on borrowing from surplus countries in order to support their appetite for imports, and surplus countries rely on the deficit countries to continue purchasing their exports in order to boost their domestic economies and employment. For years prior to the euro crisis, countries such as Spain, Portugal, Greece, or Estonia have run huge trade deficits, while Germany and the Netherlands have run huge trade surpluses. In the international debate, there is little doubt, for example, that other countries' demand over the years for South Korean exports has lifted that country into the group of the world's prosperous countries; other Asian countries—most notably China—have been trying to emulate that success. In Europe, at the same time, it is very much disputed which role the huge German trade surplus has played in the country's recovery from a period of weak growth in the early 2000s. While German economists tend to claim that the large surplus was merely a result of the high quality of German manufactured goods and the high demand for them, economists from other euro-area countries often claim that these surpluses indeed were central to bringing down unemployment in Germany. They underline that basic arithmetic prohibits *every* country from exporting its way to growth (since everyone's exports must be someone else's imports), and the debt that finances the purchases made by the deficit countries only mounts as global imbalances become greater.

These imbalances play an important part in the growing "financialization" of the global economy. The implications for growth, employment, inflation, inequality, and sustainability are potentially huge. We look into this in much greater detail in the chapters that follow.

DISCUSSION QUESTIONS

1. What is the difference between the real, monetary, and financial economies? In what way are they related to each other? Should growth in one imply growth in the others?
2. Do you think that it is a good idea to allow commercial banks to invest in stocks? In real estate? In junk bonds? Explain.

REVIEW QUESTIONS

1. Describe three scenarios that could describe economies in very different situations, with regard to their banking systems and price (in)stability.
2. Describe the three roles played by money.
3. Describe at least three different types of money.
4. Describe at least two measures of money.
5. Draw up and explain the components of a balance sheet for a private bank.
6. What characteristics are needed to make commodity money effective?
7. What is meant by leverage? What are its advantages and its dangers?
8. What are "pooled funds"? Describe two different kinds of pooled funds. What is the primary advantage of the pooling process?
9. What is a financial bubble? Give some examples, and explain some of the causes of financial bubbles.
10. What does it mean to say that foreign currency can be a store of value but not a medium of exchange?

EXERCISES

1. Search for the "World Economic Outlook Database" on the Internet and locate the most recent version. Use this database to select inflation data (units of percentage change) for the euro area, Japan, the United States, and your home country for the period 2000 to 2015. Construct a table of annual inflation rates for these countries. Now construct a graph using annual inflation rates on the vertical axis and the year on the horizontal axis. Plot the annual inflation rates

from your table in three separate lines on the same graph. How would you compare the experiences of these three countries based on your graph?

2. Use the statistics section on the ECB's Web site (www.ecb.int categories), to locate monetary data for M1 money and M2 money (monthly data of each stock, seasonally adjusted). How do the two series relate in size? How do the changes in the two series compare to one another? Does your understanding of the definitions of M1 and M2 help you make sense of what you observe?

   Note: If you want to use a tablet or mobile phone, you can also use the ECB's app "ECBstatsApp" for this task!

3. Determine whether each of the following belongs on the asset side or the liability side of the balance sheet identified in parentheses.
   a. €20,000 loan for a new automobile (balance sheet for an individual)
   b. 10-year government bonds (balance sheet for a bank)
   c. €1,000 checking account (balance sheet for a bank)
   d. €500 in euro notes—also known as cash! (balance sheet for an individual)
   e. €10,000 student loan (balance sheet for a bank)

4. Assume a required reserve of 0.01 (1 percent) to complete the following:

Assets			Liabilities
Reserves	€100,000	Loans from the ECB	€200,000
Loans	€1,000,000	Deposits	€1,800,000
Bonds	€900,000		
Total	€2,000,000	Total	€2,000,000

   a. Calculate the required reserves for this bank.
   b. Calculate the initial excess reserves for this bank. What can the bank do with these excess reserves?

5. Assume a required reserve of 0.20 (20 percent) to complete the following:

Assets			Liabilities
Reserves	€3,000,000	Deposits	€11,500,000
Loans	€6,000,000		
Bonds	€2,500,000		
Total	€11,500,000	Total	€11,500,000

   a. Calculate the required reserves for this bank.
   b. Calculate the excess reserves for this bank.

6. State whether the following statements are true or false. If false, also write a corrected statement.
   a. Inflation erodes the value of savings.
   b. Inflation creates "menu costs."

    c.   Inflation reduces uncertainty.

    d.   Inflation hurts people on fixed incomes.

    e.   Inflation redistributes wealth from debtors to creditors.

    f.   While inflation carries huge costs, deflation is generally harmless.

7.   Match each concept in Column A with a definition or example in Column B.

Column A	Column B
a. Excess reserves	1. The ease of use of an asset as a medium of exchange
b. Barter	2. A measure of the money supply that includes currency and overnight deposits
c. Deflation	3. An institution such as a bank, savings and loan association, or life insurance company that accepts funds from savers and makes loans to borrowers
d. Required reserves	4. A good used as money that is also valuable in itself
e. Liquidity	5. When the aggregate price level falls
f. Commodity money	6. A medium of exchange that is accepted as money because the government says it has value
g. Fiat money	7. A measure of the money supply that includes all of M1 plus deposits with an agreed maturity of up to two years and deposits redeemable at a notice of up to three months
h. M1 money	8. Exchange of goods, services, or assets directly for other goods, services, or assets, without the use of money
i. M2 money	9. The portion of bank reserves that banks must keep on reserve
j. Financial intermediary	10. The portion of bank reserves that banks are not legally required to keep

NOTES

1   Note that the exact definitions for monetary aggregates differ between jurisdictions. For example, in the U.S., travellers' checks are counted toward M1.

2   Note, however, that this is not true for the UK: In Britain, commercial banks are not required to hold any reserves with the central bank, but they may do so.

Chapter 12

The European Central Bank and Monetary Policy

Since the onset of the global financial and economic crisis in 2008, central banks have taken center stage. During the crisis, all over the world, central banks provided huge amounts of liquidity to commercial banks to instill confidence. As it became clear that the crisis would have significant effects on the real economy, they also slashed interest rates, and many central banks later took extraordinary measures to keep interest rates low in an effort to stimulate their economies.

Moreover, in Europe, the European Central Bank (ECB) has also played an important role in defusing the euro crisis. When in the summer of 2012 investors doubted the sustainability of the common European currency, the euro, and financial capital was fleeing many European countries, Mario Draghi stepped up and told the audience at an investors' conference in London that "the ECB is ready to do whatever it takes to preserve the euro. And believe me, it will be enough." Later that year, Mario Draghi presented plans for how the ECB could buy government bonds of embattled euro-area governments. The market panic subsided. Nowadays, his actions in 2012 are widely credited with overcoming the euro crisis.

In this chapter, we examine the structure and policy making of the central banks in Europe and especially the European Central Bank. We will first start with the dealings of the central bank with the macroeconomy in the normal course of the business cycle. In a second step, we will look at some of the unorthodox measures introduced by central banks and the ECB during the especially weak economic conditions after the global financial and economic crisis of 2008–2009 and during the euro crisis. The specific reasoning behind Mario Draghi's promise and how he contributed to defusing the sovereign debt crisis in the euro area, in contrast, will not be covered in this chapter, but in Chapter 17.

1. THE EUROPEAN CENTRAL BANK

Not long ago, in the 1990s, each EU country had its own central bank, and each central bank was issuing a national currency. Germans were paying with German marks, the French with French francs, and the Dutch with their guilders. The interest rates for German commercial banks borrowing from the Bundesbank were decided in Frankfurt and those for French banks borrowing from the Banque de France in Paris.

If a Dutch company wanted to buy supplies from a German partner, it had to change its guilders into German marks first.

However, European governments felt that fluctuations in the exchange rate between countries were an important obstacle for creating a truly single market for Europe. After decades of discussion, in the Maastricht Treaty of 1992, it was thus agreed that the member states of the European Union would introduce a common currency to replace their national currencies. Further, criteria on inflation as well as government debt and deficits were defined that countries had to fulfill if they wanted to join the new common currency. As some member states at that time (such as Denmark and the UK) were wary of such an integration step, these countries were given the possibility to opt out and keep their national currencies.

The ECB took over the management of the first batch of 11 national currencies on January 1, 1999. This first wave of members included Germany, France, Italy, Spain, Ireland, the Netherlands, Austria, Belgium, Portugal, Finland, and Luxembourg. From this moment onward, decisions on interest rates and other conditions for commercial banks' dealings with the national central banks were decided centrally in the ECB headquarters in Frankfurt. Also at this point, the exchange rates between the national currencies entering the euro were irrevocably fixed.

At the beginning of 2002, national coins and notes in circulation were then replaced by euro notes and euro coins, which are now the sole legal tender in the euro area. Other EU member states joined the euro in the years following, and in 2016, 19 EU countries were part of the euro area.

Even though the decisions about interest rates and other important parameters of monetary policy are now taken by the ECB, national central banks in the countries using the euro still exist, such as the Bundesbank, the Banque de France, or the De Nederlandsche Bank. These national central banks within the euro area implement the decisions of the ECB in their respective territories. They are in charge of dealing with national commercial banks, delivering cash, and providing the decision-making level in the ECB with information about the economic and financial situation in the member states. The heads of the national central banks are also allowed to vote in interest rate decisions of the ECB (even though on a rotating basis). The whole setup of the euro members' national central banks and the ECB on top is officially called "Eurosystem." For simplicity (and in line with the common use of the terms), we will use the term ECB both for the ECB itself as well as for the Eurosystem.

In setting its monetary policy, the ECB has been given a primary mandate by the European treaties to "maintain price stability." The treaties go on, stating that "[w]ithout prejudice to the objective of price stability, the [ECB] shall support the general economic policies in the Union." This is usually interpreted as obliging the ECB to focus primarily on price stability, and if this goal is not put into jeopardy, to support other goals such as stimulating employment and economic growth. The term "price stability" is further qualified by the ECB and is interpreted currently as annual consumer price inflation "of below but close to 2 percent." Note that the ECB's mandate is very different from that of other central banks. The United States Federal Reserve, for example, has a broader mandate: It is supposed to aim at "maximum employment, stable prices, and moderate long-term interest rates." However, it is sometimes criticized for prioritizing price stabilization above the other goals.

In setting its policies, the ECB is completely free from influence of national governments or European institutions. In fact, its independence is guaranteed by the European treaties, which can only be changed by unanimous vote of all 28 EU members. It is also prohibited from giving loans to governments or to finance governments' budget deficits. Some people reckon that the ECB is thus the most independent central bank in the world.

As the European Union in 2016 had 28 members but the euro area only 19, there are 9 EU countries that were not members of the euro area and still had their own currencies. Some of these, such as the UK and Denmark, will most likely never become members. In these countries, the national central banks are not bound by the ECB's decisions, but they can set their own interest rates and employ other tools of monetary policy freely. Even before Britain's decision to leave the EU, the Bank of England, the UK's central bank, for example, cut its interest rate more aggressively during the financial crisis of 2008–2009 than the ECB and embarked much earlier on so-called "quantitative easing" (which will be described in detail later in this chapter).

While the Bank of England or the Swedish Riksbank differ in institutional detail from the ECB, the process of influencing the economy is broadly similar to that of the ECB. This chapter will thus talk about the ECB, but you can use your insights for analyzing the British or Swedish economy as well.

Discussion Questions

1. What is the ECB, the Eurosystem, and a national central bank in the euro area? Why was the ECB created?
2. The Bank of England has also been given independence from government interference by an Act of the British Parliament. How far do you think this type of independence compares to that of the ECB?

2. MONETARY POLICY

2.1 How the ECB Influences the Money Market Interest Rate

As we have seen, the main goal of the ECB is to "maintain price stability." Yet the central bank has no direct influence over consumer prices. Prices are set by corporations and households in markets (and by governments for regulated prices), and the ECB has no control over any of these actors. Instead, the ECB is usually trying to influence the corporations' and households' price-setting behavior indirectly. Its main instrument to do so is its main refinancing rate, the interest rate at which commercial banks can borrow funds from the ECB.

If the ECB feels that inflation is picking up because the economy might be in danger of overheating, it increases the interest rates. When commercial banks have to pay more for the funds they can get at the ECB, they will tighten their credit supply and increase the interest rates they charge to their customers. As a consequence, there will be less credit creation compared to a situation of unchanged interest rates. As we have seen in Chapter 11, the banks' credit creation is also reflected in an increase in the monetary aggregates, so an increase in the interest rate should also slow the growth of the money supply.

In contrast, if the ECB feels that inflation is too low because the economy is not growing strongly enough and corporations cannot increase prices, it cuts interest rates. When commercial banks can get funds more cheaply, it is hoped that they will provide more and cheaper loans to their customers, who in turn will spend more on structures, dwellings, machines, or new consumer goods. While this mechanism often works well, there is no definite way the ECB can actually force banks to lend out more or corporations and households to borrow. Especially after the onset of the economic and financial crisis of 2008–2009, banks did not extend loans even though the ECB was offering them cheap funds (see below). We will look first at the normal operating procedures of the ECB that were in place until the crisis (and still are the mainstay of its operating today) and only later turn to the changes and additions made over the past years.

The decisions about monetary policy tools, including the interest rates, are taken by the ECB's Governing Council. This Council consists of six members of the ECB's Executive Board and the (currently 19) heads of the national central banks. The members of the Executive Board have permanent voting rights, but the voting rights of the heads of the national central banks rotate, so that at any given moment, 15 of them have the right to vote. Usually, the Governing Council meets every two weeks on Thursday. Every six weeks, it decides on changes in its monetary policy, and the decision is then explained at a press conference shortly after the meeting.

As mentioned, the most important instrument of the ECB's monetary policy is the main refinancing rate. This is the interest rate at which the ECB auctions off liquidity to commercial banks in its weekly main refinancing operations. Under these operations, commercial banks provide the ECB with some collateral (bonds with low probability of default), and the ECB lends to the banks a certain share of the collateral's value for usually one week (even though there are some longer-term refinancing operations as well). The commercial banks can then either hold these funds as reserves in their account at the ECB, use it to make payments to other banks (if customers transfer money), or change them into cash to distribute to their customers. They can also lend the funds to other commercial banks.

A simplified balance sheet for the ECB is shown in Table 12.1. Because currency is issued by the ECB, it is the central bank's main liability. You will recall from

Table 12.1 *A Simplified Balance Sheet of the European Central Bank*

Assets		Liabilities	
Loans to banks	€1800 billion	Currency in circulation	€1000 billion
		Bank reserves	€800 billion

Chapter 11 that a liability refers to anything that someone owes to anyone else. Currency is technically a liability to the ECB because it is legally redeemable for equivalent value: You can get new currency for old. Moreover, commercial banks can exchange it against reserves in their account at the ECB. These reserves held by commercial banks are the ECB's other major liability. Commercial banks need the reserves in their account at the ECB either to fulfill their minimum reserve requirements (see Chapter 11) or to make payments to other banks. Currency in circulation and bank reserves together are sometimes called the monetary base, because they are the liabilities of the central bank on which the creation of other monetary aggregates such as M1, M2, or M3 is based.

monetary base: the sum of total currency plus bank reserves

Let us now take a look at the process of money creation and central bank lending to commercial banks. Assume that ABC Bank makes a €10 million loan to Castello Construction. In a first step, it credits the amount to the current account of Castello Construction as a deposit and books the loan as an asset (Table 12.2). In this first step, the monetary aggregate M1 has increased by €10 million. At this point, the ECB's balance sheet has not changed yet, so the monetary base has not changed.

As we have discussed in Chapter 11, a few weeks after having made the loan, ABC bank will need to prove to the ECB that it has adequate reserves to fulfill the minimum reserve requirements. In order to do so, it will in the meanwhile try to borrow some reserves from other commercial banks who might have excess reserves they want to get rid of. If this is not successful, it will bid for reserves in the weekly main refinancing operations with the ECB. Usually, the ECB calculates the amount of reserves it lends through these options so that they are adequate for the banking system to come up with the required reserves to back their outstanding loans.

In any case, if ABC bank neither manages to borrow reserves from another bank nor manages to secure adequate reserves at the ECB's main refinancing operations, it can still go to the ECB and borrow from the marginal lending facility (more on this below). Under this facility, banks can borrow against a slightly higher interest rate than they would pay under the main refinancing operation, but they can be sure that they can get the funds needed (provided they can present some acceptable collateral).

Table 12.3 shows the impact of the balance sheets of ABC bank and the ECB if ABC bank borrows either through the main refinancing operation or through the marginal lending facilities the funds necessary to fulfill the reserve requirements of 1 percent. Note that this operation has not changed the monetary aggregate M1 (as bank reserves are not part of M1), but has increased the monetary base by €100,000.

Table 12.2 *ABC Bank Makes a Loan to Castello Construction*

Change in ABC Bank's Balance Sheet

Assets		Liabilities	
Loans to Castello Construction	+ €10 million	Deposits	+ €10 million

Table 12.3 *ABC Bank Borrows the Required Reserves From the ECB*

(a) Change in the ECB's Balance Sheet

Assets		Liabilities	
Loans to commercial banks	+ €100,000	Bank reserves	+ €100,000

(b) Change in ABC Bank's Balance Sheet

Assets		Liabilities	
Reserves	+ €100,000	Loans from the ECB	+ €100,000

Note that one aspect in the process of creation of monetary base is very similar to that of deposit money: In both cases, money is created by "the stroke of a pen" (or, probably more adequately today, by "the stroke of a key"). In the case of creation of M1 by the banking sector, the commercial bank creates "money" by crediting new deposits to its borrower. In the case of the creation of bank reserves, the ECB creates these reserves by crediting funds to the commercial bank's account at the central bank.

What is impressive in this process is that the amount of money that can be used for payment purposes (M1) has increased by much more than the amount of reserves the ECB has created—in our example, 10 times more! This is broadly in line with what we observed in Chapter 11: The largest part of the money supply is deposit money created by banks. This deposit money is created by the commercial banking system and has no backing in physical currency in circulation.

But how much money can be created on a single euro provided by the ECB? A simple answer might be to use the reserve requirements as a guideline. According to this notion, if commercial banks have to hold 1 percent of their deposits in reserves, then €1 of reserves can support €100 in deposits.

However, this misses that some of the money created by the banking system is actually exchanged into cash and carried around. This money cannot be used to fulfill the banks' minimum reserve requirements. This very simple analysis also neglects that sometimes banks keep excess reserves, either because they fail to lend them to other banks or because they decide to keep them in case they have liquidity needs. Hence, empirically, the ratio between M1 and the monetary base is much smaller. In January 2016, M1 amounted to €6.668 trillion and the monetary base to €1.826 trillion (currency in circulation was €1.045 trillion and banks' reserves around €800 billion). Hence, for every euro of base money, there was about €3.60 in M1. This ratio is also called the **money multiplier**, which is defined as:

money multiplier: as the ratio of the money supply to the monetary base, it tells how much bigger the money supply is relative to the monetary base

$$money \; multiplier = \frac{money \; supply}{monetary \; base}$$

Note that in the past, the causality of money creation was often thought to run exactly opposite to the mechanism presented in this chapter. In the times before modern central banks, when money was commodity money made from gold, the monetary base (in this case, the amount of gold coins in circulation) had to increase before more loans could be made. Of course, commercial banks could also create credit money by extending loans to households and firms. Just as today, they could credit some borrower a certain amount to her account. Yet at least if banks were required to actually hold a certain amount of physical gold relative to their deposits, they had to come up with gold prior to making the loan. If the supply of gold in the economy did not increase, banks could not increase their lending. Money supply could increase only if new gold was found. From this time stems the (now usually discarded) notion that the money multiplier should be interpreted as the amount of M1 that is created after the monetary base is exogenously expanded by one euro.

2.2 Other Monetary Policy Tools

As we have seen, the main instrument of the ECB is the main refinancing rate, the price at which commercial banks can get funds from their central bank. As the banks can lend the funds onward to other banks, and banks can usually decide whether to borrow from the ECB or from other commercial banks, the interest rate in the interbank money market in the euro area is usually very close to this main refinancing rate. However, sometimes, commercial banks might misestimate the amount of reserves they can get from other banks or the demand of other banks for reserves. In these circumstances, the interest rate in the interbank money market might fluctuate away from the main refinancing rate.

In order to make sure these fluctuations are not too large, the tool kit of the ECB comprises two standing facilities that are open to the commercial banks permanently: the marginal lending facility and the deposit facility. Under the marginal lending facility, banks can always borrow reserves, yet at a slightly higher rate than under the main refinancing operations (provided, of course, that they can offer the ECB some good-quality collateral). The deposit facility allows them to park excessive reserves at the ECB, and they will usually get an interest rate on these deposits. As the marginal lending facility is an alternative for commercial banks to get reserves instead of borrowing in the interbank money market, the rate charged in this facility is usually the upper border of interest rates charged in the money market. As putting reserves into their account in the deposit facility is an alternative to lending to other commercial banks, the interest rate of the deposit facility is usually the bottom for interest rates in the money market. Figure 12.1 underlines this principle: As you can see, the money market rate has most of the time been very close to the main refinancing rate but always remained in the corridor between the deposit rate and the interest rate charged at the marginal lending facility.

In the years since the start of the euro crisis, the ECB has added new instruments to its tool box. Among others, it has loaned large amounts of reserves to commercial

387

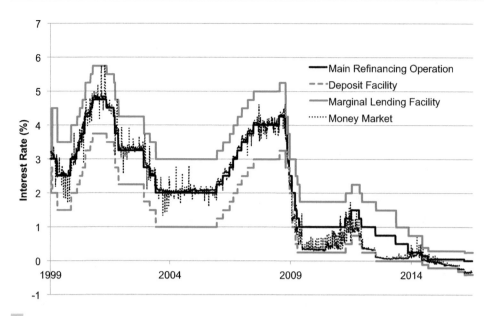

Figure 12.1 *Money Market Rate and ECB Interest Rates*

The money market interest rate generally remains close to the ECB's main refinancing rate and does not leave the corridor between the rates of the deposit facility and the marginal lending facility.

marginal lending facility: a facility under which commercial banks can always borrow reserves at short notice from the ECB

deposit facility: a facility in which commercial banks can deposit excess reserves and on which interest is paid

banks in operations with very long maturities (several years instead of the usual one week). It has also started to buy directly government bonds and corporate bonds from commercial banks. Finally, it has started to move its deposit interest rate into negative territories. These unconventional measures will be covered in Section 4.1, as they can be seen as crisis-related measures with which the ECB has reacted to the commercial banks' reluctance to increase loans to nonfinancial corporations and households.

In this section, we have discussed the technical question of *how* the ECB or another economy's central bank can change the interest rate in the overnight money market and how it provides reserves to the commercial banks in its territory. Now we can move on to the more interesting questions of *why* it may—or may not—want to do so.

Discussion Questions

1. Describe in words how the money supply increases in the euro area and which role the ECB plays in the process.
2. The setup of the ECB's instruments with the main refinancing operation, the deposit facility, and the marginal lending facility is often also called a "corridor system." Can you explain in your own words why interest rates in the money market usually do not move out of the corridor created by these rates?

3. THE THEORY OF INTEREST RATES, MONEY, AND AGGREGATE EXPENDITURE

So far, we have discussed how the ECB influences the short-term interest rate for which banks can borrow reserves. But how is the economy affected when there is a change in the interest rates at which banks can borrow?

3.1 The ECB's Interest Rates and Other Interest Rates in the Economy

As we have seen, the ECB can influence the interest rate in the money market. However, if you have ever taken out a consumer loan or considered getting a mortgage, you might have noticed that the interest rate your bank has offered you is much higher than the ECB's main refinancing rate. There are several factors which explain this gap: First, most loans from the banking sector to households or firms are not short-term loans but longer-term loans. Remember that the banks usually borrow from the ECB for one week, but consumer or corporate loans usually run at least over several months, if not years, and mortgages sometimes for up to 30 years. Second, the commercial bank needs to make some provisions in case a borrower does not pay back the loan. Third, the commercial bank needs to make a profit in order to cover costs for credit administration, staff, and services.

Nevertheless, even if consumer rates are generally higher than the short-term rate in the interbank market, they tend to rise or fall with changes in the short-term interest rate. As a general rule, an expansionary monetary policy lowers interest rates throughout the economy. Conversely, contractionary monetary policy tends to raise interest rates throughout the economy.* As lower interest rates make loans cheaper, usually an expansionary monetary policy leads to faster credit growth throughout the economy. Conversely, as higher interest rates make loans more expensive, contractionary monetary policy usually leads to slower credit growth or even credit contraction throughout the economy. Thus central bank monetary policy affects businesses and individuals throughout the economy.

3.2 Interest Rates and Investment

Economists are particularly interested in interest rates because of their effect on investment. To the extent that individuals or businesses make investments using borrowed funds, higher interest rates make investing more expensive and hence less attractive. Even if investment is financed directly out of savings, it might be affected by a change in the interest rate. If interest rates are high, it might be more attractive to put deposits into an interest-bearing account rather than to buy a new piece of machinery or build a house. Residential investment, in particular, has historically been especially sensitive

---

* Things get more complicated when we consider the duration of loans and the difference between short- and long-term interest rates. We address this issue in the Appendix.

to variations in interest rates. In many euro countries, investment in homes is financed by mortgages with interest rates which are fixed over a long period of time, up to 15 years. A small change in the interest rate can add up, over time, to a very big difference in the total cost of buying a house.

The case for interest rate effects on intended business investment in structures, equipment, and inventories (sometimes referred to as "nonresidential investment") is a bit more mixed. We saw in Chapter 9 that Keynes did not think that changes in the interest rate would be sufficient to get the economy out of the Great Depression. Investor pessimism during that period was very deep. Trying to encourage businesses to invest when they see no prospect of selling more of their goods has been referred to as attempting to "push on a string."

accelerator principle: the idea that high GDP growth leads to increasing investment, and low or negative GDP growth leads to declining investment

The idea that business fixed investment primarily responds to changes in sales much more than to changes in interest rates has been called the **accelerator principle**. If businesses see their sales rising, they may need to expand their capacity—that is, invest in new equipment and structures—in order to keep up with demand for their product. Since the best macroeconomic indicator of expanded sales is a rising GDP, this principle says that the best predictor of investment growth is GDP growth. Conversely, a small decline—or even just slowing down—of demand may lead to a disproportionate drying up of intended investment, as firms come to fear being caught with excess capacity. To the extent the accelerator principle is in force, changes in the interest rate may have only a relatively minor effect on levels of investment.

Given a particular level of optimism or pessimism, however, firms can be expected to pay at least some attention to interest rates in deciding how much to invest. Higher interest rates tend to limit the amount of investment by firms that may need to borrow money to invest. Using the string analogy, it is easier to pull on a string than to push it—tighter monetary policy is likely to restrain overall investment. Combining this logical assumption with the empirically observed sensitivity of residential investment to interest rates, our simple model of macroeconomic stabilization says that, *all else being equal*, lower interest rates will lead to higher intended investment spending (and vice versa for higher interest rates). Intended investment is inversely related to the interest rate, r, as shown in Figure 12.2.

Changes in investor confidence, related to actual spending (via the accelerator principle) or to expected levels of spending, can be portrayed as shifting this intended investment curve. An increase in investor confidence, for example, shifts the curve to the right (from I_I to I_I') as shown in Figure 12.3. At any given interest rate, firms now want to invest more (I^{**} rather than I^*). A decrease in investor confidence shifts the curve to the left.

3.3. Monetary Policy and Aggregate Expenditure

Our basic model of aggregate expenditure (or aggregate demand), developed in Chapters 9 and 10, can now be expanded to include the effect of monetary policy. In an economy with low or moderate inflation and a stable banking system, expansionary monetary policy lowers interest rates, which tends to raise intended

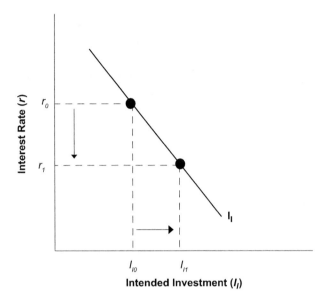

Figure 12.2 *The Intended Investment Schedule*

All else equal, if the interest rate falls (from r_0 to r_1), intended investment should rise (from I_{I0} to II_{I1}).

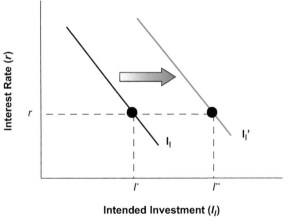

Figure 12.3 *An Increase in Investor Confidence*

If firms become more confident about future sales and want to increase their capacity, the intended investment schedule shifts to the right.

investment (Figure 12.2). Because intended investment spending, I_I is part of aggregate expenditure $AE = C + I_I + G + NX$, this increase in investment should shift the AE schedule upward and raise the equilibrium levels of aggregate expenditure, income, and output, as shown in Figure 12.4. The chain of causation can be summarized as:

Hence, we get a negative relationship between the ECB's main refinancing rate and aggregate expenditure, as depicted in Figure 12.5: Higher interest rates lead to lower levels of aggregate expenditure, while lower interest rates lead to higher levels of aggregate expenditure.

If the economy is headed toward a recession, then monetary policy that is relatively loose, lowering the interest rate in order to help maintain output, can have a desirable stabilizing effect. Sometimes such an **expansionary monetary policy** is called an **accommodating monetary policy**, especially (though not exclusively) when the ECB is reacting to a specific economic event that might otherwise tend to send the economy into recession.

Contractionary monetary policy, in contrast, would be prescribed if the economy seems to be heading toward inflation. In that case, the ECB seeks to slow growth and "cool down" the economy by increasing interest rates. In the aggregate demand

expansionary monetary policy: the use of monetary policy tools to increase the money supply, lower interest rates, and stimulate a higher level of economic activity

accommodating monetary policy: loose or expansionary monetary policy intended to counteract recessionary tendencies in the economy

contractionary monetary policy: the use of monetary policy tools to limit the credit and money supply, raise interest rates, and encourage a leveling off or reduction in economic activity

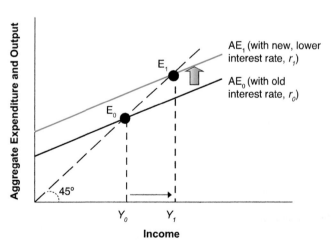

Figure 12.4 *Expansionary Monetary Policy and the AE Curve*

In this model, expansionary monetary policy lowers interest rates, raises investment spending, and raises aggregate expenditure, income, and output.

392

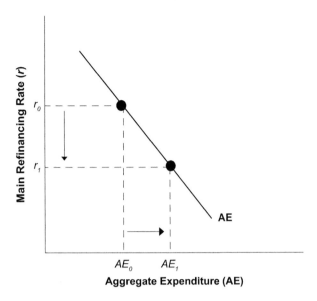

Figure 12.5 *The ECB's Main Refinancing Rate and the AE Curve*

Everything else being equal, lower interest rates lead to higher investment spending and higher aggregate expenditure. The AE curve is downward sloping.

model, this will lower intended investment, shift the *AE* schedule downward, and lower the equilibrium levels of aggregate demand, income, and output.*

You might now ask: Why does the ECB care about aggregate expenditure and aggregate demand? Didn't we learn that the primary mandate of the ECB is to maintain price stability? The answer is that there is a close link between aggregate expenditure and inflation. Everything else being equal, higher aggregate expenditure also tends to lead to higher inflation. With higher demand for goods and services, from a certain point onward, bottlenecks in the economy develop, and firms start increasing prices. If the central bank manages to "cool down" the economy, inflationary pressure usually disappears. Similarly, when firms have a lot of spare capacity, they might attempt to cut prices to lure demand from competitors, and inflation will fall. This link between inflation and aggregate demand will be discussed in detail in Chapter 14, but for the moment, you should keep in mind that the ECB tries to steer inflation indirectly by influencing aggregate expenditure.

The ECB's reaction function to inflation is depicted in Figure 12.6: We have the main refinancing rate on the horizontal axis and the inflation rate on the vertical axis. The reaction function of the ECB is now upward sloping: If the ECB sees inflationary pressure rising, it will increase the interest rate. If it sees inflationary pressure abating, it will cut interest rates.

---

* In Chapter 14, we look at how monetary policy can also change *AE* by affecting international capital flows, the relative values of national currencies, and net exports.

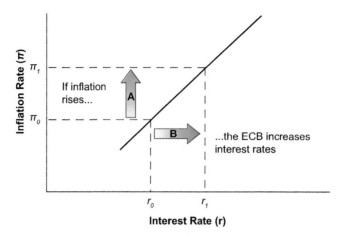

Figure 12.6 *The ECB's Reaction Function*

As the ECB's primary objective is to keep inflation low and stable; it will react to increases in inflationary pressure with hikes in its main refinancing rate.

Discussion Questions

1. What sorts of interest rates are relevant to your own economic activities? Do you think that ECB policies affect their levels?
2. Is it always true that a cut in interest rates leads to an increase in investment and aggregate demand? Why or why not?

4. MONETARY POLICIES IN PRACTICE

4.1 The ECB and Investment, 1999–2015

The effect of the ECB's policy on investment can be illustrated with several recent historical examples. In early 2001, the ECB's main refinancing rate stood at 4.75 percent. But there were signs that the economy might be heading into recession: The "dot-com" stock market bubble had burst, and the U.S. economy, an important export partner, was heading into a recession. In April 2001, the ECB cut the main refinancing rate by a quarter percentage point, citing diminishing inflation risks and a moderation of GDP growth. In late August, it cut interest rates again after having received more news of a slowing economy and easing inflationary pressure. Only a couple weeks later, on September 11, 2001, terrorists hijacked four airliners in the United States and steered two of them into the World Trade Center in New York. These terrorist attacks were a major negative shock to business and consumer confidence in all industrialized countries, and the ECB reacted with further rate cuts. Throughout the period 2001–2003, the ECB steadily pushed interest rates down, as shown in Figure 12.7. The main refinancing rate reached a low of 2 percent in early 2003.

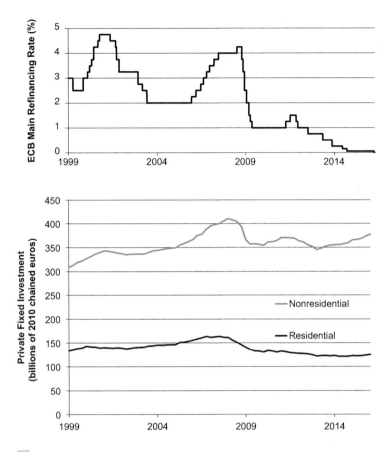

Figure 12.7 *Monetary Policy and Investment, 1999–2015*

In 2001–2003, from 2008 on, and after 2011, interest rate cuts helped spur residential and nonresidential investment, although the responses were slow.

Source: Eurostat and ECB, 2016.

What was the consequence for investment and aggregate demand? The bottom half of Figure 12.7 shows the data for residential and nonresidential private fixed (i.e., noninventory) investment. Investment might seem to move in the direction *opposite* of that predicted by the theory of investment presented earlier (Figure 12.2). As interest rates steadily fell through 2001 and most of 2002, both residential and nonresidential investment *fell slightly.*

But recall that the theory said that "all else being equal," a lower interest rate should lead to higher intended investment—and all else was *not* equal during this period. Businesses had too much capacity and inventory and were pessimistic about sales. Moreover, the global security situation, with the terror attacks of 2001 being followed by the wars in Afghanistan and Iraq, caused uncertainty among the business community and kept them from investing. In terms of the model, Figure 12.8 shows this pessimism shifting the intended investment schedule to the left, from I_{I0} to I_{I1}'. The

395

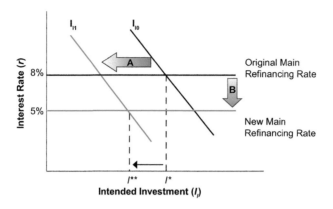

Figure 12.8 *Expansionary Monetary Policy in an Environment of Pessimism*

If investors become pessimistic (shift A), the level of intended investment can still fall, even though ECB actions lower the interest rate (shift B). The net effect is that intended investment falls from I* to I**.

lower interest rates due to ECB action may have kept investors from cutting back even more, but the lower rates were not enough to prevent the downturn in nonresidential (and overall) investment, shown on the graph as a shift from I★ to I★★. A similar argument might be true for residential investment: With unemployment increasing and the private households' economic future appearing more uncertain, people cut back on their plans to buy a home. Without the rate cuts of the ECB, even more households might have decided not to construct a new house.

Both residential and nonresidential investment started to pick up in 2004. By the end of 2005, the ECB believed that the recovery was well under way and would continue. Moreover, it felt that again, inflationary pressures were building in the economy. For the next three years, the ECB steadily increased its main refinancing rate in an attempt to keep the economy from "overheating."

In late 2008, the ECB shifted again to an expansionary monetary stance, as can be seen in Figure 12.7. Already during 2008, construction had cooled significantly, driven especially by a slowdown in euro-countries that had previously experienced a housing boom, such as Spain or Ireland. However, the ECB during this time still thought that inflationary pressures were the main problem and even hiked interest rates in mid-2008. Then in the fall of that year, the global economic environment deteriorated sharply. While problems in the U.S. housing market had emerged from late 2006 onward, the whole extent only became clear in 2008. As we discuss in Chapter 15, during the 2004–2007 period, banks had aggressively moved into the marketing of "subprime" mortgages (loans given to people whose incomes or credit histories ordinarily would not be good enough to qualify them for mortgages). When borrowers found it impossible to pay back these loans, the value of mortgages held by banks and other investors fell drastically, creating a financial crisis and pushing the economy toward recession. On September 15, the mortgage crisis led to the default of the investment bank Lehman Brothers. This default sent shock waves through the global

396

financial system, and credit supply dried up, even for relatively safe activities such as exports of goods and machinery (see Chapter 14). The economy in most industrialized countries experienced the deepest recession since World War II. The ECB reacted by cutting its main refinancing rate from 4.25 percent to 1.0 percent in only seven months. None of the euro-area countries had seen similarly low interest rates in the decades before the euro introduction in 1999.

Feeling uncomfortable with such historically low interest rates, when investment started to pick up again in 2011, the ECB quickly started to hike interest rates again. However, this shift in monetary policy proved to be premature. During 2011 and into 2012, investors' fear of possible defaults of some euro-area governments and a breakup of the euro area, as well as harsh austerity packages passed to alleviate financial investors' fears, led to a contraction of aggregate demand in the euro area, and indications grew that the euro area was heading for a second recession in very short succession, a so-called double-dip recession (the euro crisis will be covered in detail in Chapter 17). The ECB reacted again with interest rate cuts, taking the main refinancing rate from 1.5 percent in mid-2011 to almost 0 percent in 2016.

Unfortunately, rate cuts at this time did not prove enough to stabilize the economy, and the ECB started to embark on a number of unconventional measures. In 2012, the ECB president Mario Draghi promised publicly to do "whatever it takes" to preserve the euro and announced that the ECB would buy government bonds of countries in dire financial straits. In 2014, the ECB additionally started to move the deposit rate into negative territory. Thus, when commercial banks were holding excess reserves in their ECB account, they were charged a fee instead of being paid interest. The idea was to induce banks to lend to firms and households instead of holding reserves in their account at the ECB.

In 2015, with the recovery remaining weak and signs that the private sector's inflation expectations were falling increasingly short of the ECB's target of "below but close to 2 percent," the ECB resorted to an unusual approach known as **quantitative easing (QE)**. Instead of following its regular main refinancing operations, under QE, the ECB buys government bonds and other financial assets (mostly bonds). The main objective here is not just to keep short-term interest rates low but to also lower longer-term interest rates. The first of these is supposed to get banks to lend more to firms and the second to get households and other investors to invest in more risky assets and to provide corporations with finance through nonbanks. Among the large central banks in the world, the ECB was the last to resort to QE. Both the Bank of England and the U.S. Fed had tried these policies successfully after the financial crisis of 2008–2009 and had managed to return to a normal operation of monetary policy by 2016.

quantitative easing (QE): the purchase of financial assets including long-term bonds by the ECB, creating more monetary reserves and lowering long-term interest rates

Together with negative interest rates on its deposit facility, by 2016, the ECB had managed to push the yields for German government bonds below 0 percent for maturities up to seven years. In short, investors were actually *paying* more for a government bond now than they would be repaid in a few years' time.

Even in 2016, in the euro area, normalization of monetary policy was still seen to be quite a time off. While the economy had recovered and investment was slowly picking up again, unemployment remained high, and inflation hovered around 0 percent. Given the risks of deflation discussed in Chapter 11, the ECB was contemplating even more expansionary measures. At the same time, a public debate erupted about the risks and legitimacy of the ECB's latest actions. Some politicians, especially from Germany, criticized the low interest rates as a way to "expropriate savers." Other critics warned that such a massive program of monetary expansion could have undesired effects, such as fueling further financial bubbles or causing inflation to suddenly rise. To evaluate these concerns, we need to look a little further into monetary theory.

BOX 12.1 ECB PRESIDENT DEFENDS STIMULUS

In a speech at a think-tank event in Berlin on October 25, 2016, the president of the European Central Bank, Mario Draghi, vehemently defended the ECB's policy of buying large amounts of government bonds under its quantitative easing program as well as actions that had pushed short-term interest rates into negative territory. According to him, these policies had been successful, as they had removed the threat of a vicious spiral of falling prices and ever weaker aggregate demand.

Ever since the ECB announced its quantitative easing program in 2015, it had been confronted with criticism. While some economists criticized that the planned expansion of the central banks' balance sheet by €1.7 trillion would eventually cause high inflation, others complained that the resulting low interest rates on government bonds would take the pressure off governments to conduct structural reforms. Others had voiced concerns that the low interest rates would endanger the stability of the banking sector, as banks' profits might be hurt, and banks might be induced to engage in overly risky activities. Finally, some had worried that the expansion of money supply would push up asset prices while depressing interest rates for small savers, hence increasing inequality.

Mario Draghi rebutted all these fears in Berlin: "We have every reason to believe that, with the impetus provided by our recent measures, monetary policy is working as expected: by boosting consumption and investment and creating jobs, which is always socially progressive," he said.

On earlier occasions, Draghi had appealed to European governments to support his battle against the weakness of aggregate demand in the euro area instead of criticizing the ECB. "Countries that have fiscal space should use it," Mr. Draghi said. "Germany has fiscal space." Germany at that time was running budget surpluses, and the German government had repeatedly resisted demand for more public spending to boost the euro-area economy.

Sources: Claire Jones, Draghi hits back at critics of QE and negative rates, *Financial Times*, October 25, 2016; Tom Fairless, ECB Stands Pat on Stimulus as Draghi Defends Policy, *Wall Street Journal*, September 8, 2016

4.2 The Liquidity Trap and Credit Rationing

As noted, the ECB rate hit historical lows in 2009 and was further reduced to almost 0 by 2013. Banks were provided with plenty of liquidity through unconventional instruments. Measured by the nominal interest rate, this was the most expansionary monetary policy in Europe's postwar history. Insofar as inflation and inflation expectations were falling and recovery was very slow, there was a strong case for continued loosening.

However, the medicine seemed to be very slow to be working. Loans from euro-area banks to the private sector continued to contract until early 2015. Why was there such a weak reaction to such a strong monetary stimulus? Two reasons might explain the weak reaction. First, while nominal interest rates have been low, real interest rates have not been that low. Real interest rates denote the difference between nominal rates and inflation. In fact, it is the real interest rate that matters for the investment decision of firms. To understand this, let's have a look at an example. Let us assume firm E produces bolts and can initially sell them for €1 per piece. For its investment, it borrows €100 at a nominal interest rate of 5 percent, so that it has to repay €105 a year from now. In a situation in which prices remain unchanged (inflation at 0 percent), it has to sell 105 bolts to repay the loan. In this case, the real interest rate is 5 percent. Now assume that prices increase by 5 percent and the firm can sell the bolts next year for €1.05. In this scenario, it now has to sell only 100 bolts in order to repay its loan. The real interest rate is now 0 percent. It is easy to understand that the interest rate is much less burdensome in the second scenario.

In the euro area, while nominal interest rates have been historically low in the years after 2012, real interest rates have not, as inflation fell quickly and had been around 0 percent in 2015 and 2016. While in past recessions, prior to the introduction of the euro, real interest rates sometimes were strongly negative, they were not so in 2016. As it is very difficult to move interest rates far below 0 percent (economists even used to talk about a "zero lower bound" for interest rates), one argument might be that at the current economic situation, interest rates would need to be even lower, but the ECB is constraint by the zero bound.

The second argument is the possibility of a liquidity trap. Remember our earlier analogy of pushing on a string. As the ECB continues to add to the monetary base and cut interest rates, there is a possibility that it will just create more "slack in the string"—despite having plenty of reserves, they will not find their way into credit creation and hence useful investment and job creation. In the 1930s, Keynes introduced the term **liquidity trap** for a situation in which it is impossible for a central bank to drive interest rates down any lower. In the past few years, the euro area appears to have hit this monetary policy wall.

liquidity trap: a situation in which interest rates are so low that the central bank finds it impossible to reduce them further

In a situation of a liquidity trap, even though the ECB cuts interest rates and tries to flood the banking system with reserves, banks still do not expand loans to firms and households. Recall that, for expansionary monetary policy to work in the predicted way, banks have to respond by making new loans. But what if banks do not find many of their customers creditworthy or their usual customers are not very interested in taking out new loans? Another impediment might be that the capital position of banks is weak due to past losses, and hence they might be reluctant to expand their balance sheet (in Chapter 11, we have discussed that banks are required by regulators to hold a certain amount of capital relative to their loans portfolio). Instead of using extra funds to make more loans, banks may tend to engage in **credit rationing** in order to ensure their own profitability. This means that they will lend to the customers whom they deem most creditworthy, using restrictive standards to decide who merits getting a loan. If this happens, some firms and individuals will get the funds that they need,

credit rationing: when banks deny loans to some potential borrowers in the interest of maintaining their own profitability while others—and particularly smaller firms and lower-income individuals—may be frozen out. In this case, monetary policy may have significant distributional effects: in the simplest terms, making the rich richer and the poor poorer.

The possibility of a liquidity trap, or of reluctance among bankers and investors to lend and borrow, means that the ECB faces limitations in its ability to stimulate a sluggish economy (see Box 12.1). We can also show how these problems translate into our graph showing the relationship between the interest rate and aggregate expenditure. Figure 12.9 shows the curve originally presented in Figure 12.5 for the case of problems with the monetary transmission mechanism (through a liquidity trap and/ or unwillingness of bankers and investors to lend and borrow): From a certain level of interest rates downward, further cuts in the interest rate do not have short-term effects on credit, and hence aggregate expenditure, and the *AE*–interest rate curve here becomes vertical.

This does not necessarily mean that the ECB's efforts are fruitless. Over a longer period, low interest rates may help businesses to pay back debt and banks to accumulate profits. At some point, the *AE*–interest rate curve might become slowly more normal again. As of 2016, evidence indicated that the ECB's policies had at least led banks in the euro area to make new loans to households (even if not yet to firms), and the overall amount of loans outstanding was increasing. But at the same time, the low interest rates raised concerns that some of the money might go to the wrong places, creating bubbles in asset prices. Moreover, there was concern that the increase

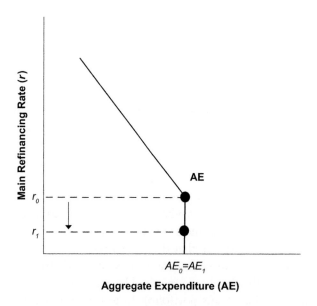

Figure 12.9 *The ECB's Main Refinancing Rate and the AE Curve When There Are Problems in the Banking Sector*

If there are problems in the banking system, from a certain point onward cuts in the interest no longer translate in an increase of aggregate demand.

in excess reserves might in the future lead to a sudden outbreak of inflation. Finally, some experts worried that the negative interest rates might depress banks' profitability and further keep them from lending.

Discussion Questions

1. What is quantitative easing? How is it different from the ECB's main refinancing operations? What other "unconventional" tools has the ECB employed since the outbreak of the euro crisis? Has the ECB had favorable results with its policies since the 2008–2009 financial crisis?
2. Explain the liquidity trap. Do you think that the theory accurately describes the events after the Great Recession and in the euro crisis?

5. THE THEORY OF MONEY, PRICES, AND INFLATION

Section 4 laid out a description of the ECB's roles and activities as it is mainly understood by many eminent macroeconomists today. This description is not universally accepted, as other arguments can be made that are based on a different understanding of the relationship between interest rates, money, and the macroeconomy. This section will present some of these additional ideas and tools for monetary analysis.

5.1 The Quantity Equation

One way of thinking about the relationship between the real economy, money, and prices is based on what economists call the **quantity equation**:

$$M \times V = P \times Y$$

In this equation, Y is, as usual, real output or GDP. P indicates the price level as measured by a price index, for example the GDP deflator discussed in Chapter 5. The multiplication of these two variables means that the right-hand side of the equation represents nominal output (if necessary, review Chapter 5 for an explanation of the difference between nominal and real output).

On the left-hand side, M measures the level of money balances, such as the M1 measure discussed earlier. V, the only really new variable here, represents the velocity of money. The **velocity of money** is the number of times that a euro changes hands in a year in order to support the level of output and exchange represented by nominal GDP. In other words, since the money in circulation is insufficient to "purchase" everything entailed by GDP, velocity represents how often, on average, each dollar changes hands in order for there to be sufficient funds to purchase all the goods and services produced in the economy. (Remember that we are talking about both cash and bank deposits—so "changing hands" could be literal, as when you pay for a pizza with cash, or virtual, as when a bank clears a check on one account, making the funds available to another account holder.)

quantity equation:
$M \times V = P \times Y$
where M is the money supply, V is the velocity of money, P is the price level, and Y is real output

velocity of money:
the number of times that a euro would have to change hands during a year to support nominal GDP, calculated as $V = (P \times Y)/M$

401

Since nominal GDP and M1 are observable, velocity can be calculated as the ratio of the two,

$$V = \frac{P \times Y}{M}$$

For the quantity equation to become the basis for a *theory* rather than merely represent definitions of variables, an assumption needs to be made about velocity. Supporters of different economic theories all have subscribed to the irrefutable arithmetic of the quantity equation. Where they have differed is over assumptions regarding the behavior of one or more of the variables.

Two theories we discuss in what follows—classical and monetarist—assume that velocity is constant—changing very little, if at all, with changing conditions in the economy. If this is true, then the level of the money supply and the level of nominal GDP should be tightly related. We denote this assumption that velocity is constant by putting a bar over V. The **quantity theory of money**, then, is characterized by the relation

quantity theory of money: the theory that money supply is directly related to nominal GDP, according to the equation $M \times \bar{V} = P \times Y$

$$M \times \bar{V} = P \times Y$$

where $\bar{V}$ is read "V-bar." More Keynesian-oriented theories, however, while they may make use of the quantity equation, do not assume that velocity is constant. Their analyses are not based on the quantity theory.

5.2 Competing Theories

Classical monetary theory is based on the quantity theory of money, plus the assumption that output is always constant at its full-employment level.* That is,

$$M \times V = P \times Y^*$$

where Y^*, as usual, denotes full-employment output. In this case—in contrast to the aggregate demand model described in Section 4—changes in the money supply can have *no* effect on the level of output. The inability of changes in the money supply to affect real output is called **monetary neutrality**. The only variable on the left-hand side that is not constant is the money supply, while the only variable on the right-hand side that is not constant is the price level. Thus, all that a change in the money supply can do is change prices. Rather than an increase in the money supply increasing output, in this model, an increase in the money supply has no effect other than to cause inflation.

monetary neutrality: the idea that changes in the money supply may affect only prices while leaving output unchanged

---

* We simplify here, but to be precise, the classical view is that the economy will always *tend* toward full-employment equilibrium in the long run. Please review Chapter 9 for a comparison between the classical and Keynesian views on this point.

Classical economists, then, tend to see no need for discretionary monetary policy. On the contrary, they consider it counterproductive. In the case of an economy that is not growing, classical theory would prescribe a stable money supply level to avoid unnecessary changes in prices. In a growing economy, classical theory says that the money supply should grow at the same rate as real GDP in order to keep prices stable. If we assume that the rate of real GDP growth is fairly constant, then the money supply should just grow at a fixed rate, say 3 percent per year. A central bank that enforces this is said to be following a **money supply rule**.

Another famous theory based on the quantity equation is **monetarism**, propounded by Milton Friedman and Anna Jacobson Schwartz in their book *A Monetary History of the United States, 1867–1960*, published in 1963. While Keynes had argued that insufficient investment and aggregate demand caused the Great Depression, Friedman and Schwartz argued that it was caused by a severe contraction in the money supply.

Friedman had earlier propounded the quantity theory of money and has become known for his saying that "inflation is always and everywhere a monetary phenomenon." But unlike the pure classical theorists, he thought that *bad* monetary policy could have, at least temporarily, *bad* effects on the real economy. During the early years of the Great Depression, he and Schwartz pointed out, both the money supply and the level of nominal GDP fell sharply. This empirical observation can be seen as consistent with the quantity theory of money:

$$M \times \bar{V} = P \times Y$$

$$\downarrow \quad \underset{change}{no} \quad \downarrow \quad \downarrow$$

money supply rule: committing to letting the money supply grow at a fixed rate per year

monetarism: a theory associated with Milton Friedman, which claims that macroeconomic objectives are best met by having the money supply grow at a steady rate

They argued that the contraction in the money supply caused the reductions in both the price level and real GDP—an assertion that remains controversial. Because of his belief in the potential for bad monetary policy to cause harm, Friedman was one of the most vocal proponents of the idea that central banks should simply follow a fixed rule of having the money supply grow at a steady rate. In this regard, he and most classical theorists would have been in agreement.

The quantity equation can also be used to shed light on the problem of very high inflation, described early in Chapter 11. Suppose that the level of output in an economy is stagnant or growing only very slowly. At the same time, suppose that the central bank is causing the money supply to grow very quickly, that is, by printing money to help the government finance the budget deficit. If people come to expect high inflation, money may become a "hot potato"—people want to hold it for as short a time as possible because it loses value so quickly. They will try to turn money into noninflating assets—real estate, hard currency, jewelry, or barterable goods—as quickly as they can. This means that the velocity of money also increases. A situation of hyperinflation in a stagnant economy can be illustrated as:

$$M \times \bar{V} = P \times \bar{Y}$$

$$\uparrow \quad \uparrow \quad \uparrow \quad \underset{change}{no}$$

where the bar over Y indicates that output is stuck at a level below full employment. With output stagnant and both money supply and velocity increasing, inflation must result.

While we imagined a printing press in the government's basement in our earlier story about hyperinflation in Chapter 11, a sophisticated economy can also essentially "run the printing presses" if the agency that issues government debt and the central bank work together. For example, suppose that the euro-area governments issue new debt, and the ECB immediately buys the same amount of new debt and injects new money into the economy. The effect is the same as if the ECB had just printed new currency, except that the increase in bank reserves is in the form of "a stroke of the pen" instead of freshly printed paper. This is called **monetizing the deficit**. In the euro area, however, the ECB is prohibited from buying new government debt. Even when it decided from its own considerations to buy government debt (i.e., under the quantitative easing program), it only bought already outstanding ("old," not "new") government debt.

monetizing the deficit: when a central bank buys government debt as it is issued (equivalent to "running the printing presses")

Note also that in the theory presented in the first sections of this chapter, the quantity equation holds. Economists adhering to the view presented (that the ECB sets the interest rate as a reaction to inflationary pressure and, through this behavior, influences AE) would acknowledge the validity of the quantity equation. However, they would also state that the link between interest rates and the development of monetary aggregates such as M1 or M2 is not stable and that the monetary aggregates at best provide some additional information about how AE will develop. Therefore, they do not put much emphasis on analyzing the monetary aggregates M1 or M2 in simplified macroeconomic models.

Discussion Questions

1. What is the difference between the quantity *theory* of money and the quantity *equation*?
2. Has inflation been reported to be a problem in any recent news reports? Check recent inflation data at http://ec.europa.eu/eurostat/de. How do you think this is related to recent ECB monetary policy?

6. COMPLICATIONS AND POLICY CONTROVERSIES

As we have seen, even the goal to "maintain price stability" is not trivial to achieve, as the central bank cannot influence inflation directly. Instead, it can use its tools to influence economic activity, and inflation is only affected indirectly. Yet in the real world, central banks actually might have to take more issues into account beyond price stability. For example, it is generally accepted that central banks should also look after the stability of the financial sector, at least to make sure that the monetary transmission mechanism does not become damaged. Moreover, lately, there has been a debate whether the ECB might have gone too far with its policies. This section questions how the mandate of the ECB should best be fulfilled, whether this mandate is still appropriate, and what alternatives could be imagined.

6.1 The ECB's Dilemma

This chapter has described that, in order to reach price stability, the ECB should increase interest rates in a boom to keep the economy from overheating and cut interest rates in a bust. In order to keep inflation stable, it should thus just try to keep employment at the "full-employment level." This may seem very straightforward, but policy making can have many complications. For one thing, there is the controversial question of what exactly the "full-employment" level of employment is at any given time. Suppose, for example, that the ECB starts to get nervous about inflation too early in an economic upswing. Perhaps the unemployment rate could have fallen to, say, 6 percent, with little increase in inflation, if the recovery had been allowed to continue, but the ECB switches into inflation-fighting mode at an unemployment rate of, say, 8 percent. By halting the recovery too early, the ECB may end up being blamed for causing unnecessary suffering. But if conditions in the economy are such that letting unemployment fall to 6 percent would cause a large rise in inflation, then if the ECB lets the recovery continue, it will instead end up being blamed for inflation.

There is also considerable controversy over what rates of inflation can be considered acceptable. Some economists find only inflation rates from 0 percent to 2 percent acceptable; others do not see an urgent need for monetary control unless inflation is 5 percent or higher. Some economists are outright afraid of deflation; some others believe that a certain fall in the price level does not hurt much and does not justify unorthodox policy measures such as quantitative easing or negative interest rates.

Another practical problem is that monetary authorities have to pay attention to issues of timing. In Chapter 10, we discussed the "inside lags" of decision making and implementation as well as the "outside lag" of an enacted policy having an effect on aggregate demand. In the case of fiscal policy, the "inside lags" tend to be rather long, while governments and parliaments try to agree on a budget, but the "outside lag" is relatively short. For monetary policy, the case tends to be reversed. The ECB's Governing Council meets every two weeks. While it takes interest rate decisions usually every six weeks, it could also do so more frequently. A monetary policy decision only requires discussion and a majority among the Governing Council's 21 voting members, unlike the much more extensive discussions required to get a tax or spending change through parliaments. Hence decisions about monetary policy can generally be made more quickly than decisions about fiscal policy. But monetary policy only has an effect on aggregate demand, as people change their plans—often their very long-term plans—about investment and spending. So the "outside lag" is generally thought to be longer. There is a danger that the effects of a policy intended to counteract a recession may not be felt until the next boom, or the effects of policies intended to counteract a boom might not be felt until the next recession, exacerbating the business cycle instead of flattening it out.

6.2 The ECB and Its Mandate

Moreover, just keeping consumer price inflation stable might not be enough. After the global financial crisis of 2008–2009, a number of economists started to question whether central banks around the world had actually paid enough attention to asset price bubbles, such as those in real estate. Some economists were arguing that just looking at consumer price inflation had led central banks such as the U.S. Fed and the ECB not to increase interest rates early enough in the 2000s and that the central banks had thus contributed to the built-up of real estate bubbles, which finally led to the crisis. However, this position is still disputed. While most economists agree that asset price bubbles pose a major threat to the economy, it is not clear what central banks should do against them.

The main problem is that among the central banks' traditional instruments, none is really able to pop bubbles without causing collateral damage. Take, for example, the main refinancing rate. Of course, central banks could have increased interest rates much earlier to counter asset price bubbles. However, this would have dampened investments throughout the economy, including firms' investment in new machinery. As the economy as a whole was not overheating during that time, this might have led to excessive unemployment and actually a fall of inflation short of the inflation target of the central bank.

Since 2009, many central banks around the world have been given additional tasks and tools to ensure financial system stability. For example, under the European Banking Union, which was initiated in 2012 and came into effect in 2014, the ECB now holds responsibility for the supervision of all commercial banks in the euro area (even if it has left the day-to-day business of supervising smaller banks with national authorities). However, its mandate is still the original one to "maintain price stability." In normal times, it probably could argue that maintaining financial system stability is a precondition to conduct monetary policy and hence to maintain price stability. However, should there ever be a conflict between maintaining price stability (as measured by consumer prices) and preventing asset price bubbles, the ECB would have a hard time explaining why it might neglect the price stability target for stability of asset prices.

Another contentious issue has been whether the ECB has actually gone too far with its use of unconventional monetary policy instruments. In the recent crisis, some people have warned that the ECB's policies might in the end lead to hyperinflation. According to their argument, the increase in excess reserves in the banking system might at some point in the future suddenly lead to large amounts of credit creation and suddenly increase monetary aggregates such as M1 or M2. This increase would then lead to a jump in prices, which could turn into hyperinflation. However, no signs of this have materialized in the euro area yet. Other countries such as the U.S. or the UK, where central banks for a while also increased excess reserves by quantitative easing, have by now even managed to exit this policy and have increased interest rates again without any problems of hyperinflation or even strongly increasing inflation.

The decision of the ECB to move the deposit rate into negative territory and contribute with its purchases of government bonds to negative yields for bonds of several euro-area governments has also been much criticized. Especially in Germany, bankers and politicians have publicly demanded a change in the ultra-lax policy stance. According to their view, the negative interest rates redistribute between savers (mainly in the "Northern" countries of the euro area such as Germany) and borrowers (to be found in the "Southern" countries of the euro area such as Spain, Greece, or Italy). Also, according to these critics, the ultra-low interest rates endanger the business model of traditional savings banks that take in deposits (for which they do not charge a fee) and lend out this money. If they now do not find enough borrowers but have to pay a fee at the ECB if they park the funds, this would lead to losses. The reply of Mario Draghi but also many Anglo-Saxon economists was to underline that the negative return on government bonds is not necessarily a result of the ECB's monetary policy but rather of an imbalance of investments and savings (see Box 12.1).

Related to this critique was the question whether the ECB might take too much pressure off governments to reform. Some—again, especially German economists and senior staff in the German ministries—have argued that ECB policy has led to very low government bond yields even for countries with high debt levels. According to these critics, these low interest rates lower the incentives of governments to implement structural reforms and cut budget deficits decisively. In contrast, defenders of the ECB underline that the ECB does not have the mandate to impose structural reforms or permanent budget cuts on member states and question whether slightly higher interest rates would really lead to more reforms.

Linked to this debate, but usually coming from a different political direction, is the question about the mandate of the ECB. Among the large central banks, the formal mandate of the ECB is especially narrow. The U.S. Fed, for example, has been given the mandate to "promote maximum employment, price stability, and moderate long-term interest rates," while the Bank of Japan is tasked with looking after both price stability and financial system stability. In many developing countries and emerging markets, the respective central banks have also been tasked to look after certain dimensions of economic development as well as price stability.

Especially the Fed is often referred to as an example by those who wish a broader mandate for the ECB. These people argue that the ECB has often reacted with a too-restrictive monetary policy. For example, the ECB increased interest rates in the summer of 2008, when the U.S. as well as a number of euro-area economies were already in recession, because it felt that inflationary pressure was still too high. Also, the ECB was the first major central bank to increase interest rates after the global financial crisis, already in 2011, again because it felt that inflationary pressure warranted a more restrictive monetary policy. In both cases, the ECB had to retract soon and cut interest rates again. According to proponents of a broader mandate, in these cases, being tasked with both employment and price stability goals would have allowed the ECB to forego interest rate increases.

Defenders of the ECB's current mandate point out that, in practice, the difference of the ECB's and the Fed's mandates are smaller than the wordings suggest. They argue that since price stability can only be reached by keeping aggregate demand close to full employment, the employment target is already implicit in the ECB's target. Moreover, if inflation as well as long-term inflation expectations are kept low, long-term interest rates will remain moderate. A final point also plays in favor of those defending the status quo: The mandate of the ECB can only be changed by

407

a change in the EU treaties, something for which the unanimous consent of all 28 member states is needed.

BOX 12.2 INTERNATIONAL MONETARY FUND PROPOSES HIGHER INFLATION TARGET

Shortly after the global financial and economic crisis, economists at the International Monetary Fund challenged the existing orthodoxy that central banks should try to keep inflation around 2 percent, a target that had been adopted by most central banks in the industrial world. In a paper coauthored by the IMF's chief economist, Olivier Blanchard, the experts state that the crisis had "exposed flaws in the pre-crisis policy framework" and that the "architecture of postcrisis macroeconomic policy" should be rethought.

One of the proposals put forward was to increase the inflation target from 2 to 4 percent. The argument: It is difficult for central banks to lower interest rates below 0 percent. If the economy is now hit by a crisis and the central banks need to lower interest rates strongly, it has more room to do so if nominal interest rates are higher to start with. In an environment of inflation around 2 percent, nominal interest rates can usually be expected to be lower than if inflation were normally around 4 percent. Hence, an inflation target of 4 percent would give a central bank more room for maneuver in times of need.

Blanchard's proposal was controversial. Some economists argued that higher inflation would come with economic costs, as price lists would have to be updated more often, and the risk of economically incorrect prices would increase, which in turn would lead to distortions in the economy. According to Blanchard, these fears are excessive. "Nobody knows the cost of inflation—between 2 percent and 4 percent—so I think people could get used to 4 percent and the distortions could be small," said Mr. Blanchard.

Yet central banks did not take up the proposal. Ben Bernanke, then chairman of the U.S. Federal Reserve, reacted at a conference in Tokyo, stating that it would be a "very risky transition" if the Fed did anything to reduce its commitment to keeping inflation around 2 percent. The Bank of Japan governor Masaaki Shirakawa added, "Looking back at the serious economic downturn after the failure of Lehman Brothers, very few think that reducing interest rates by a few percentage points, enabled by having a higher target rate of inflation, would have materially changed the recovery path of the economy."

Sources: Robin Harding, Fed and BoJ reject higher inflation target, *Financial Times*, May 26, 2010; Chris Giles, IMF floats plan to raise inflation targets, *Financial Times*, February 12, 2010.

DISCUSSION QUESTIONS

1. What are some arguments in favor of having the ECB having a broader mandate? What are some arguments against it?
2. How does the issue of time lags affect fiscal and monetary policy?

REVIEW QUESTIONS

1. Draw up and explain the components of the balance sheet of the ECB.
2. Show what happens to the ECB's balance sheet and the balance sheet of a commercial bank when the commercial bank borrows from the ECB.
3. Describe how decisions by a bank to extend loans finally lead to an increase in reserves in the banking sector and why the increase in reserves is usually lower than the increase in initial loans.
4. Describe two tools the ECB uses to keep money market interest rates close to its main refinancing rate.
5. Describe how a change in the ECB's main refinancing rate might lead to changes in the money supply M1.
6. How is investment related to the interest rate? What other factors affect investment? Use a graphical analysis to show these relationships.
7. Show the effects of an expansionary monetary policy in a Keynesian cross diagram.
8. Describe how ECB policy operated during the 2000–2015 period.
9. What is the quantity equation? What is the quantity theory of money?
10. What is monetarism?
11. Discuss how monetary expansion can lead to high inflation, using the quantity equation.
12. Explain how problems in the banking sector, such as insufficient capital, can affect the transmission mechanism between interest rate cuts and aggregate demand.

EXERCISES

1. Suppose that the QRS bank has extended loans by €2,000,000 to its customers and credited the money to the customers' overnight accounts.
    a. Show how this affects the balance sheet of QRS Bank.
    b. Assume that QRS Bank did have €10,000,000 in required reserves but did not have any excess reserves before making the new loans. If minimum reserve requirements are 1 percent, how many additional reserves does QRS bank need to get now in order to fulfill the minimum reserve requirements?
    c. Assume that QRS Bank borrows these required additional reserves from the ECB. How does its balance sheet change through these loans? How does the ECB's balance sheet change?
    d. Assume that one of QRS's customers makes a transfer of €1,000,000 to an account in TUV bank. How does this change the balance sheets of QRS bank and TUV bank? Assuming that prior to the transfer, neither QRS bank nor TUV bank had excess reserves, to what extent do these two banks now fulfill their minimum reserve requirements? Is there a way that they can fulfill their minimum reserve requirements without borrowing more reserves from the ECB?
2. Suppose that the ECB increases its main refinancing rate by 0.25 percentage points.
    a. Assuming that the level of business confidence remains unchanged, show on a graph how this interest rate increase will change the level of intended investment.

409

b.   What would you expect to happen to money supply M1? Explain.

c.   What is the effect on aggregate expenditure and output? Show on a carefully labeled graph.

d.   What is the effect on equilibrium consumption and saving? (You may need to refer to Chapter 9 to answer this.)

3.   Suppose that investor confidence falls, and the ECB is aware of this fact. Using the model presented in this chapter, show (a) through (c) below graphically:

a.   How a fall in investor confidence affects the schedule for intended investment.

b.   What the ECB could do, influencing the money market, to try to counteract this fall in investor confidence.

c.   The effect on *AE* and output if the ECB is able to *perfectly* counteract the fall in business confidence.

d.   Is the ECB likely to be as accurate as assumed in part (c)? Why or why not?

4.   Suppose that the level of nominal GDP in Estilvania is €30 billion and the level of the money supply is €10 billion.

a.   What is the velocity of money in Estilvania?

b.   Suppose that the money supply increases to €15 billion and nominal GDP rises to €45 billion. What has happened to velocity?

c.   Suppose that the money supply increases to €15 billion and nominal GDP rises to €40 billion. What has happened to velocity?

d.   Suppose that the money supply decreases to €8 billion and both the price level and real GDP fall, leading to a decrease in nominal GDP to €26 billion. What has happened to velocity?

5.   Match each concept in Column A with the best definition or example in Column B.

Column A	Column B
a. Expansionary monetary policy	1. The idea that changes in the money supply affect only prices, not output
b. Fiat money	2. Residential investment
c. Accelerator principle	3. Standardization
d. Monetary neutrality	4. A euro coin made of minerals worth €.10
e. Velocity	5. The ease with which an asset can be used in trade
f. Liquidity	6. The ECB increases its main refinancing rate
g. Commodity money	7. A silver coin
h. A good property for money to have	8. The ECB's mandate
i. To maintain price stability	9. Bank deposits at the ECB
j. Bank reserves	10. Currency in circulation and overnight deposits
k. M1	11. The number of times that a unit of money changes hands in a year
l. Very sensitive to interest rates	12. Relates investment to GDP growth
m. Contractionary monetary policy	13. The ECB lowers its main refinancing rate

6.   The president of the ECB regularly gives testimony before the European Parliament's Economic and Monetary Affairs Committee about the state of monetary policy. Find the most recent such testimony at www.ecb.europa.eu/. What does the president of the ECB identify as the most significant issues facing the economy? How is the ECB proposing to deal with them?

7.   (Appendix A1) Suppose that you have a bond with a face value of €200 and coupon amount of €10 that matures one year from now.

   a.   If the going interest rate is 3 percent, how much can you sell it for today?

   b.   If the going interest rate is 8 percent, how much can you sell it for today?

   c.   What does this illustrate about bond prices and interest rates?

8.   (Appendix A2) Suppose that the nominal prime interest rate for a one-year loan is currently 6 percent.

   a.   If inflation is 1 percent per year, what is the current real interest rate?

   b.   Suppose that many people believe that the inflation rate is going to rise in the future—probably up to 2 percent to 3 percent or more within a few years. You want to borrow a sum of money for ten years and are faced with deciding between

      1.   A series of short-term, one-year loans. The interest rate on this year's loan would be 6 percent, while future nominal interest rates are unknown.

      2.   A 10-year fixed-rate loan on which you would pay a constant 6.25 percent per year. If you agree with most people and expect inflation to rise, which borrowing strategy do you expect might give you the better deal? Why? Explain your reasoning.

APPENDIX

A1. BOND PRICES AND INTEREST RATES

The ECB usually influences short-term interest rates in the money market through changes in the interest rates at which commercial banks can borrow from the central bank. Yet for investments of firms and households into fixed capital, usually longer-term interest rates are more important. These interest rates are usually indirectly also affected by the ECB's decision to change short-term interest rates. To understand this link, it is important to take a look at the market for government bonds.

A **bond** represents debt, but, as a particular kind of financial instrument, bonds have some characteristics worth mentioning. When the government (or a business) borrows by selling a bond, it makes promises. It promises to pay the bondholder a fixed amount of money each year for a period of time and then, at the end of this time, to repay the principal of the loan. The fixed amount paid per year is called the *coupon amount*. The date that the principal will be repaid is called the *maturity date*. The amount of principal that will be repaid is called the *face value* of the bond.

So far, it seems simple enough—a €100 bond at 5 percent, for example, specifies that its issuer will pay you €5 a year for 10 years and then pay you €100 at the end of 10 years. What makes bond markets more complicated, though, is that bonds are often sold and resold, changing hands many times before they mature. During the period to maturity, many factors affecting the value of the bond may change, and so the *bond price*—the price at which bondholders are willing to buy and sell existing bonds—may change.

bond: a financial instrument that pays a fixed amount each year (the coupon amount) as well as repaying the amount of principal (the face value) on a particular date (the maturity date).

For example, suppose that you bought the bond just described at its face value of €100. The *bond yield to maturity*, or annual rate of return if you hold a bond until it matures, would obviously be 5 percent (€5 annually is 5 percent of the €100 bond price). Suppose that after a couple of years, you want to sell your bond (perhaps you need the cash), but meanwhile, the rate of return on alternative (and equally safe) investments has risen to 10 percent. People will not be interested in buying your bond at a price of €100, because they would get only a 5 percent return on it, whereas they could get a 10 percent return by investing their €100 elsewhere. To sell your bond, you will need to drop the price that you demand until your bond looks as attractive as other investments—that is, until the €5 per year represents a 10 percent yield to maturity.

Conversely, if the return on alternative investments has fallen, say to 2 percent, the €5 per year on your bond looks pretty good, and you will be able to sell it for *more than* €100. Bond prices and bond yields are thus inversely related.*

Euro-area governments issue a variety of different kinds of bonds (to complicate things, even bonds with similar characteristics have different names, depending whether the French, Italian, or German government has issued them). Some of these bonds (often called bills) have a zero coupon amount and mature in one year or less. Because the holder receives no coupons, they are sold at a discount from their face value. Other bonds pay a coupon amount every six months and have maturities that range from 2 to 30 years. France has even issued a bond with a maturity of 50 years. In the real economy, then, there are many different "government bond" prices—and interest rates. It is only for the sake of simplicity of modeling that we assume only one type of bond and one interest rate.

Although many people and organizations buy and sell government bonds on what is called the "secondary market" (the "primary market" being the governments' initial offering of the bonds), the ECB's policies have a significant impact (and even had this impact prior to the implementation of outright bond purchases under the quantitative easing policy) on bond prices. As commercial banks can use the government bonds as collateral to borrow from the ECB, a lower interest rate gives them an incentive to borrow from the central bank and to buy government bonds. Hence, with a lower main refinancing rate of the ECB, banks tend to buy more government bonds. Their price increases, and the yield for bonds falls. If the ECB increases its main refinancing rate, this deal becomes less attractive, and commercial banks might try to sell some bonds to repay their loans from the ECB.

A simplified (secondary) bond market is shown in Figure 12.10(a). The price of bonds (and the corresponding nominal interest rate) is on the vertical axis and the

---

* If the bond has one year left to maturity, for example, its value one year from now is €105. We can use the formula [Value next year] / (1 + interest rate) = [Value now] to find out what you could get by selling the bond today. If the interest rate on alternative investments is 10 percent, then €105/(1 + .10) ≈ €95.45. The lower the bond price, the higher the bond yield, and vice versa. Conversely, if the return on alternative investments has fallen, say to 2 percent, the €5 per year on your bond looks pretty good, and you will be able to sell it for *more than* €100. If the interest rate is 2 percent, then €105/(1 + .02) ≈ €102.94.

quantity on the horizontal. The supply curve, in this case, is determined by the willingness of investors (including commercial banks) to sell bonds—that is, to exchange their government debt for cash, which means, in effect, to *stop* lending to the government. The demand curve is determined by investors' (again including banks') willingness to buy bonds—that is, to lend to the government. The effect of an ECB interest rate cut is illustrated in Figure 12.10(b). The cut in the main refinancing rate shifts

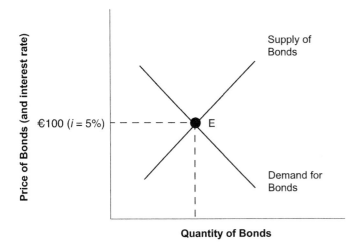

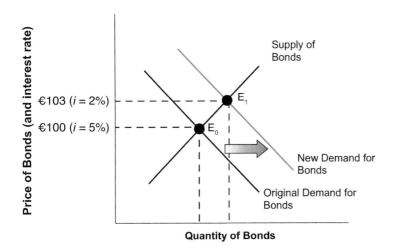

Figure 12.10 *The Market for Government Bonds*

When the ECB cuts its main refinancing rate, the demand curve for government bonds shifts out. This raises the price of bonds, lowering their interest rate.

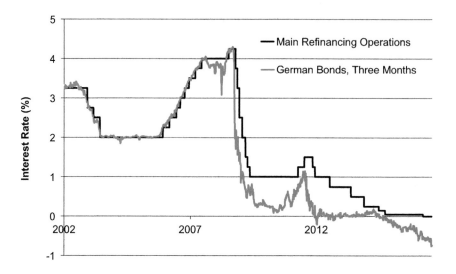

Figure 12.11 *The ECB Main Refinancing Rate and Three-Month Interest Rate on German Government Bonds, 2000–2016*

The money market and the market for short-term government bonds are closely related.

Source: Macrobond, daily data.

the demand curve for government bonds to the right. As a result, the price of bonds rises. Because bond prices and interest rates are inversely related, the rise in the price of bonds means that the going interest rate on them falls.*

Although this explanation focuses on the market for government bonds, it is actually parallel to the earlier discussion of the ECB, the money market interest rate, and the rates for loans to firms and households. The interest rate for three-month German government bonds and the main refinancing rate are graphed together in Figure 12.11, and they track each other closely. The bottom line of this story is the same as that given by the link between short-term interest rates and those charged for bank loans in this chapter: An ECB rate cut drives down interest rates.

A2. SHORT- VERSUS LONG-RUN AND REAL VERSUS NOMINAL INTEREST RATES

In the model of interest rates and aggregate demand discussed in Section 3 of the text, we assumed that the ECB, through setting its main refinancing rate, could change the interest rate that influences investment spending. In Figure 12.8, we used the symbol r

---

* The exact relationship depends on the time to maturity of the bond. The longer this time, the greater the impact of an interest rate change on the bond price.

to denote a generalized interest rate. In real life, however, many different interest rates have to be taken into account.

Here we present some basic facts about short-run versus long-run and real versus nominal interest rates. We also note the difference between the ECB's focus on the short-term, nominal interest rate and the interest rate that investors often consider the most relevant: that is, the long-term, real interest rate.

In Section 4.1, we discussed the ECB main refinancing rate as the principal interest rate the ECB influences. This is a short-term, nominal interest rate. It is short term because while this rate is quoted in annualized terms (that is, what borrowers would pay if they kept the loan for a year), the loans are actually made on one day and paid back one week later (the standing facilities even have a maturity of only one day). The main refinancing rate—like any interest rate that you normally see quoted—is a *nominal* interest rate, not adjusted for inflation. The interest rates determined in markets for loanable funds are always nominal rates.

But if you are considering undertaking a substantial business investment project or buying a house, the interest rate that you should be taking into account, if you are a rational decision maker, is the *real* interest rate over the life of the business loan or mortgage. The **real interest rate** is:

$$r = i - \pi$$

real interest rate: nominal interest rate minus inflation, $r = i - \pi$

where r is the real interest rate, i is the nominal interest rate, and π is the rate of inflation.

For example, suppose that you borrow €100 for one year at a nominal rate of 6 percent. You will pay back €106 at the end of the year. If the inflation rate is 0, then the purchasing power of the amount that you pay back at the end of the year is actually €6 more than the amount you borrowed. However, if inflation is 4 percent during the year, the €106 that you pay back is in "cheaper" euros (euros that can buy less) than the euros that you borrowed. The real interest rate on your borrowing will be only 2 percent. The higher the inflation rate, the better the deal is for a borrower at any given nominal rate (and the worse it is for the lender).

If inflation is fairly low and steady—as we assumed in the aggregate demand model—then this difference between real and nominal interest rates is not of crucial importance. If inflation is steady at, say, 2 percent, then both lenders and borrowers mentally subtract 2 percent to calculate the real rate that corresponds to any nominal rate. If the ECB lowers the main refinancing rate from 8 percent to 5 percent, for example, then it correspondingly lowers the real rate from 6 percent to 3 percent.

In recent decades, inflation has been fairly low, usually close to 2 percent. But inflation is not always so predictable. When inflation is high or variable, it is very important to realize that investors' decisions are in reality influenced by the **expected real interest rate**, r_e:

$$r_e = i - \pi_e$$

expected real interest rate: the nominal interest rate minus expected inflation, $r_e = i - \pi_e$

where i is the nominal rate the borrower agrees to pay and π_e is the *expected* inflation rate.

415

The actual real interest rate (r) can be known only with hindsight. That is, only *after* information on inflation has come for last month or last year can you calculate what the real interest rate *was* in that period. But you never know with certainty what the real interest rate is right now or what it will be next year. The more changeable inflation is, the harder it is to form reliable expectations about real interest rates.

Since investors are usually interested in long-run, real interest rates, while the ECB controls primarily short-run, nominal interest rates, the impacts of various ECB policies on the economy may not be as straightforward as our basic models imply.

Chapter 13

Aggregate Supply, Aggregate Demand, and Inflation

Putting It All Together

If you read the financial pages in any newspaper (or sometimes the front pages if economic issues are pressing), you will see discussion about government budgets and deficits, interest rate changes, and how these affect unemployment and inflation. You may also see news about changes in the availability of certain crucial resources—particularly energy resources—and about how the impact of such changes in resource supplies spread throughout the country's economy. How does economic theory help to make sense of it all?

In Chapter 9, we started to build a model of business cycles, focusing at first on the downturn side of the cycle and the problem of unemployment. In Chapters 10, 11, and 12, we explained economic theories concerning fiscal and monetary policy. So far, our models have focused on the "demand side," illustrated by shifts of the aggregate expenditure (*AE*) curve. In this chapter, we complete the demand-side story so that it includes explicit attention to the potential problem of inflation. Then we move on to the issue of the actual productive capacity of the economy, or "supply-side" issues. Finally, we will arrive at a model that we can use to "put it all together."

1. AGGREGATE EXPENDITURE AND INFLATION

The *AE* curve in the Keynesian model used in the previous three chapters was graphed with income on the horizontal axis and output on the vertical axis. We mentioned that if output is above its full-employment level, there may be a threat of rising inflation, but nothing in the figures incorporated this idea. The graphs that we used all measured income, output, and aggregate expenditure (or aggregate demand) without considering changes in price levels. It is time now to remedy that omission.

1.1 The Aggregate Demand (*AD*) Curve

We can develop a different approach to aggregate demand by viewing it in a graphical format that compares output to inflation. In order to distinguish this approach from the approach in former chapters, we will introduce an *AD* curve which shows the effect of inflation on the macroeconomic equilibrium level. To show this graphically,

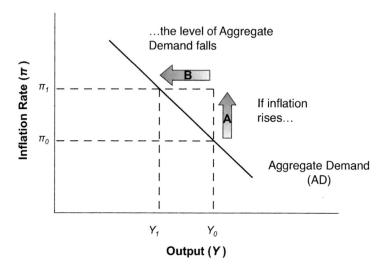

Figure 13.1 *The Aggregate Demand Curve*

This analysis shows the impact of different inflation levels on aggregate demand.

we put inflation on the vertical axis, and output (Y) on the horizontal axis.* This is shown in Figure 13.1. The *AD* curve shown here differs from the Keynesian *AE* curve (used in former chapters), since it takes into account changes in inflation and the reaction of the central bank to different levels of inflation, but the points on this new curve all correspond to points where the Keynesian *AE* curve crosses the 45° line.

This view of aggregate demand assumes that higher inflation rates will tend to reduce total demand. The channel through which this happens differs for the type of economy in question. Here, we need to distinguish between economies that have their own central bank that can set interest rates at its discretion and that have a floating exchange rate with other countries, and countries that are part of the euro area and hence cannot set their own interest rates (as the interest rate for the whole euro area is instead set by the ECB). Examples of the first group are countries such as the U.S. and Japan or, in Europe, the UK, Sweden, or Switzerland. Examples of the second group are all countries in the euro area, such as Germany, France, Austria, the Netherlands, Slovakia, Ireland, or Portugal.

For countries with their own central bank and a floating exchange rate, the downward–sloping *AD* curve can be explained by the central bank's reaction to different levels of inflation. As we have discussed in the previous chapter, all major central banks put at least some weight on controlling inflation. If inflation increases, central bankers will increase interest rates, which in turn will dampen aggregate demand. If

---

* Some versions of the *AD* curve in other textbooks use "price level" rather than inflation on the vertical axis. The authors of this text believe that using inflation better represents the reality of an economic system in which prices are rarely constant and in which central banks aim at a target rate of inflation, not a specific price level.

inflation falls, central bankers will cut interest rates, which tends to increase aggregate demand. This process is shown graphically in Figure 13.1. Monetary policy here mainly works through its influence on intended investment but also on consumption and on (net) exports. (We will cover more in detail in Chapter 14 how a cut in interest rate can lead to more exports.)

The mechanism is slightly different for a small country within the euro area, such as Ireland or Slovakia. As the ECB looks at the overall inflation for the euro area, any changes in price trends in these countries are most likely not going to have much of an impact on the ECB's interest rate decision (Ireland's share in the euro area's GDP is less than 2 percent, Slovakia's share less than 1 percent). So if inflation falls in these countries but not in the rest of the euro area, the ECB will most likely keep its main refinancing rate unchanged. But there is another channel through which falling inflation in these countries impacts aggregate demand: If inflation in Ireland falls short of that in the rest of the euro area, Irish goods and services get cheaper relative to those produced in other euro-area countries. This is called a **real depreciation** and will be covered more in detail in Chapter 14. As a consequence, Irish exports to the rest of the euro area increase and Irish imports contract. Total demand for goods and services produced in Ireland increases.

But what about countries in the euro area that are big enough to influence the ECB's decision? Germany (almost 30 percent of euro-area GDP) or France (more than 20 percent of euro-area GDP) come to mind as such cases. Here, both arguments apply: First, if inflation in one of these economies falls, even if it does not fall in the rest of the euro area, the impact on overall inflation is large enough that the ECB is likely to cut rates. Second, goods and services in these economies become more competitive relative to those in other euro-area countries and (net) exports to the rest of the euro area increase.

Thus, the model can be used to either analyze the impact of changes in inflation for one economy inside the euro area or to analyze the euro-area economy as a whole. In both cases, the *AD* curve looks similar, as shown in Figure 13.1, even if the mechanics behind the downward slope are different.

Note that there might be a threshold beyond which a further fall in inflation does not increase aggregate demand anymore. As we have discussed in Chapter 11, there might be a point below which a further cut in the central banks' interest rate does not have much immediate impact anymore, either because banks are reluctant to lend or because there are not enough borrowers banks deem creditworthy. Another possibility is that the central bank runs into the problem of having lowered the interest rate to zero and not being able to push it further into negative territory. In these cases, the *AD* curve would become vertical from a certain level of inflation downward.

real depreciation: domestic products gaining price competitiveness because of lower inflation than in partner countries or because of a depreciation of the nominal (money value) exchange rate

1.2 Shifts of the *AD* Curve: Spending and Taxation

The downward slope of the *AD* curve shown in Figure 13.1 is based on the indirect impacts of inflation on aggregate demand, as discussed earlier. What determines the position of the curve? As discussed in our original Keynesian *AE* analysis, the position

419

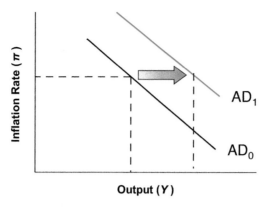

Figure 13.2 *The Effect of Expansionary Fiscal Policy or Increased Confidence on the* AD *Curve*

If government spending increases, taxes decrease, consumers or investors become more confident, or net exports increase, demand for goods in the economy rises.

of the *AE curve* depends on specific levels of government spending, taxation, autonomous consumption, autonomous investment, and autonomous net exports. As the *AD* curve is derived from the *AE* curve, these factors also influence the position of the *AD* curve. Changes in these variables will therefore cause the *AD* curve to shift.

For example, if the government were to undertake expansionary fiscal policy, this would shift the *AD* curve to the right, as illustrated in Figure 13.2. At any level of inflation, there would now be aggregate demand sufficient to support a higher level of output.

An increase in autonomous consumption or investment would have a similar effect, as would an autonomous increase in net exports. Recall that autonomous consumption is the part of household spending that does not depend on income, and autonomous investment is the part of business spending that does not depend on the interest rate. These are often used to represent consumer and business "confidence." Thus an increase in consumer or investor confidence could also cause the rightward shift in Figure 13.2. Conversely, of course, contractionary fiscal policy, reductions in consumer or investment confidence, or reduction in autonomous net exports would shift the *AD* curve to the left.

1.3   Shifts of the *AD* Curve: Monetary Policy

As we have noted, the ECB (and any other central bank) usually responds to higher inflation by increasing interest rates, and this is reflected in the slope of the *AD* curve. This kind of policy response, which aims to keep inflation near a target level, is a rather passive sort of monetary policy. A more active form of central bank intervention occurs when the central bank leaders decide to change policy more fundamentally—either by changing their inflation target or by shifting their focus to fighting unemployment.

For example, before the advent of the euro, countries who wanted to join had to bring inflation down below a certain threshold (one of the "convergence criteria"). Countries such as Italy or Spain, which used to have higher inflation rates than Germany or the Netherlands, had to shift their monetary policy to a much tighter stance. Compared to their previous policy, the same level of inflation would result in higher real interest rates set by their central banks. This would have the effect of dampening investment and hence shifting the *AD* curve to the left.

Alternatively, in a severe recession, the ECB might decide that the economy requires additional stimulus. If the ECB instituted significant expansionary monetary policies, driving interest rates down further than its normal reaction function would warrant, this would, in theory, have the effect of boosting investment and shifting the *AD* curve to the right.

To summarize:

■ The *AD* curve indicates levels of equilibrium GDP at different possible rates of inflation, including the normal policy reaction of the central bank.
■ The *AD* curve can be shifted by changes in levels of autonomous consumer spending, autonomous investment, fiscal policy, net exports, or by major changes in monetary policy.

Discussion Questions

1. "The negative slope of the *AD* curve means that higher levels of output will lead to lower levels of inflation." Is this statement correct or not? Discuss.
2. Does the ECB always want the inflation rate to be as low as possible? Why or why not?

2. CAPACITY AND THE AGGREGATE SUPPLY CURVE

As we have noted in earlier chapters, increases in aggregate expenditure can push output up toward the full-employment level. In our current analysis, an increase in aggregate expenditure is shown by a rightward shift in the *AD* curve. But what happens when output reaches—or maybe even exceeds—the full-employment level? In a graph such as Figure 13.2, for example, there is nothing in the model that seems to prevent expansionary policies from just shifting the *AD* curve, and output, up and up and up.

Obviously, this cannot be true in the real world. At any given time, there are only certain quantities of labor, capital, energy, and other material resources available for use. The euro-area labor force, for example, comprises just over 168 million people. The euro area simply cannot, then, produce an output level that would require the work of 200 million people. This is a *hard capacity constraint:* What happens as an economy approaches maximum capacity can be modeled using the aggregate supply (*AS*) curve. The *AS* curve shows combinations of output and inflation that can, in fact, occur within an economy, given the reality of capacity constraints.

2.1 The Aggregate Supply (AS) Curve

Figure 13.3 shows how aggregate supply is related to the rate of inflation. Starting from the right, at high output levels, we can identify five important, distinct regions of the diagram.

maximum capacity output: the level of output an economy would produce if every resource in the economy were fully utilized

First (starting on the right in Figure 13.3), the vertical **maximum capacity output** line indicates the hard limit on a macroeconomy's output. Even if every last resource in the economy were put into use, with everybody working flat out to produce the most they could, the economy could not produce to the right of the maximum capacity line.

Just below the maximum capacity level of output, the *AS* curve has a very steep, positive slope. This indicates that, as an economy closely approaches its maximum capacity, it is likely to experience a substantial increase in inflation. If many employers are all trying to hire many workers and buy a lot of machinery, energy, and materials all at once, workers' wages and resource prices will tend to be bid upward. But then, to cover their labor and other costs, producers will need to raise the prices that they charge for their own goods. Then, in turn, if workers find that the purchasing power of their wages is being eroded by rising inflation, they will demand higher wages, which leads to higher prices, and so on. The result is a phenomenon called a **wage-price spiral**, in which higher wages and higher prices lead to a steep rise in self-reinforcing inflation.

wage-price spiral: when pressure on wages creates upward pressure on prices and, as a result, further upward pressure on wages

In the real world, such steep increases in inflation are usually the result of dramatic pressures on producers, such as often occur during a national mobilization for war.

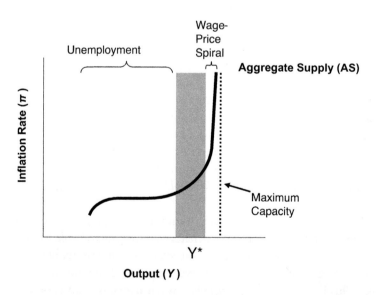

Figure 13.3 *The Aggregate Supply Curve*

As the economy approaches its maximum capacity, inflation levels tend to rise as excessive demand for workers, goods and services, and production inputs pushes up wages and prices.

During World War II, for example, many governments pushed their economies very close to their maximum capacity—placing big orders for munitions and other supplies for the front, mobilizing the necessary resources by encouraging women to enter the paid labor force, encouraging the recycling of materials on an unprecedented scale, encouraging the planting of backyard gardens to increase food production, and in general pushing people's productive efforts far beyond their usual peacetime levels. As a result, unemployment plummeted. Governments, knowing that such pressures could lead to sharply rising inflation (as shown in the wage-price spiral region of Figure 13.3), usually kept inflation from getting out of hand by instituting **wage and price controls**—direct regulations telling firms what they could and could not do in the way of price or wage increases.

The shaded area to the left of the wage-price spiral region in Figure 13.3 indicates, as it did in the national income equilibrium graphs in Chapters 9 and 10, a range of full-employment levels of output. While it is controversial to say exactly where that level may be, it can be thought of as an output level high enough that unemployment is not considered a national problem. And because it must be low enough to allow for at least a small measurable level of transitory unemployment, the *full-employment* level of output is slightly lower than the *maximum capacity* level of output.

As the economy approaches its maximum capacity, inflation levels tend to rise as excessive demand for workers, goods and services, and production inputs pushes up wages and prices.

Within the full-employment range, Figure 13.3 shows a gently rising *AS* relationship. This is because, even well before an economy approaches the absolute maximum capacity given *all* its resources, producers may tend to run into "bottlenecks" in the supply of *some* resources. Agricultural workers may be plentiful, for example, but professional and technical workers may be in short supply. Or fuel oil may be plentiful, but there may be a shortage of natural gas. Shortages in the markets for particular kinds of labor and other inputs may lead to an acceleration of inflation in some sectors of the economy. Because the measured inflation rate represents an average for the economy as a whole, some aggregate increase in inflation may be observed.

This sort of increase in inflation that comes with high (but not extremely high) production is what economists expect to happen when the economy nears a business cycle "peak." Note, however, that the *AS* curve has been drawn flatter toward the left of the *Y** range, indicating that combinations of full employment and stable inflation may also be possible.

When the economy is in recession or recovering slowly from a recession, output is below its full-employment level. The flat *AS* line shown in Figure 13.3 for this region indicates that, under these conditions, there is assumed to be no tendency for inflation to rise. Because a considerable amount of labor and other resources are unemployed, there is no pressure for higher wages or prices. It is also likely that because wages and prices tend to be slow in adjusting downward, inflation will not fall either—at least not right away.

When the economy is hit not by a regular recession but by a really deep recession, such as the one experienced in most industrialized countries in the 2008–2009

wage and price controls: government regulations setting limits on wages and prices or on the rates at which they are permitted to increase

423

global financial and economic crisis or those experienced by countries severely struck by the euro crisis such as Greece, Ireland, or Portugal, output is so far below the full-employment level that inflation starts to drop and may even become negative (deflation). In this situation, demand is so weak that a large number of companies go bust. As the more expensive firms tend to be pushed out of the market first, this lowers measured inflation. Also, in such a situation, workers and their unions might agree to wage cuts, which lowers firms' costs and allows them to further reduce their prices. Here, the *AS* curve in Figure 13.3 slopes downward again as a further fall in aggregate demand accelerates the process of disinflation or even deflation.

2.2 Shifts of the *AS* Curve: Inflationary Expectations

When people have experienced inflation, they come to expect it. They then tend to build the level of inflation that they expect into the various contracts into which they enter. If a business expects 5 percent inflation over the coming year, for example, it will add 5 percent to the selling price that it quotes for a product to be delivered a year into the future, just to stay even. If workers also expect 5 percent inflation, they will try to get a 5 percent cost-of-living allowance just to stay even. A depositor who expects 5 percent inflation and wants a 4 percent real rate of return will be satisfied only with a 9 percent nominal rate of return.

In this way, an expected rate of inflation can start to become institutionally "built in" to an economy. As a first approximation, it is reasonable to assume that people expect something like the level of inflation that they have recently experienced (an assumption that economists call "adaptive expectations"). Thus inflation can be, to some degree, self-fulfilling.

Because different contracts come up for renegotiation at different times of the year, the process of building in particular inflationary expectations will take place only over time. Because of the time that it takes for prices and wages to adjust, we need to make a distinction between short-run and medium-run aggregate supply responses.

The *AS* curve in Figure 13.3 was drawn for a particular level of expected inflation in the *short run*. Before people have caught on to the fact that the inflation rate might be changing, their expectations of inflation will continue to reflect their recent experience. The rate of inflation at which the *AS* curve becomes horizontal is the expected inflation rate. In this model, an economy in recession, or on the horizontal part of the *AS* curve, will tend in the short run to roll along at pretty much the same inflation rate as it has experienced in the past. Only tight labor and resource markets caused by a boom will tend to increase inflation, which will come as a surprise to people and will not immediately translate into a change in expectations. For the purposes of this model, you might think of the short run as a period of some weeks or months.

Over an unspecified longer period of time—the *medium run*—however, a rise in inflation due to tight markets tends to increase people's expectation of inflation.* If

---

* As distinguished from the *long run,* discussed in the Appendix.

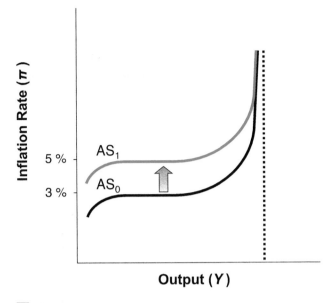

Figure 13.4 *The Effect of an Increase in Inflationary Expectations on the Aggregate Supply Curve*

If people come to expect higher inflation, these expectations get built in to wage and price contracts, leading to a generally higher level of inflation throughout the economy.

they expected 3 percent inflation but over a period of time they experience 5 percent inflation, the next time that they renegotiate contracts, they may build in a 5 percent rate. Figure 13.4 shows how the *AS* curve shifts upward as people's expectation of inflation rises. Note that the maximum capacity of the economy has not changed—nothing has happened that would affect the physical capacity of the economy to produce. All that has happened is that now, at any output level, people's expectation of inflation is higher.

Similarly, if people experience very loose markets for their labor or products or lower inflation due to lack of aggregate demand and recessionary conditions, over the medium run, the expected inflation rate may start to come down (see Box 13.1). Employers may find that they can still get workers if they offer lower wages. Unions might agree to lower wage increases, as their members might be afraid of unemployment, and low wage increases in a situation of low inflation still guarantee stable purchasing power. Producers may raise their prices less this year than last year or cut prices because they are having trouble selling in a slow market. When people start to observe wage and price inflation tapering off in some sectors of the economy, they may change their expectations about inflation. As people react to the sluggish aggregate demand that occurs during a recession, they will tend, over time, to lessen their expectations about wage and price increases. The graph for this would be similar to Figure 13.4 but would show the *AS* curve shifting downward instead of upward.

425

2.3 Shifts of the *AS* Curve: Supply Shocks

supply shock:
a change in the
productive capacity
of an economy

The *AS* curve also shifts when the capacity of the economy changes. A **supply shock** is something that changes the ability of an economy to produce goods and services. Supply shocks can be beneficial, as when there is a bumper crop in agriculture or a new invention allows more goods or services to be made using a smaller quantity of resources. Increases in labor productivity also allow an economy to produce more goods and services.

In such cases, the real capacity of the economy expands, as shown in Figure 13.5. The line indicating maximum capacity shifts to the right, showing that the economy can produce more than before. We model the beneficial supply shock as moving the *AS* curve both to the right and downward. It moves to the right because capacity has increased. It moves downward because beneficial supply shocks are often accompanied by decreases in prices. As computer technology has improved, for example, the price of any given amount of computing power has dropped rapidly. To the extent that computers play a significant role in the economy, this tends to undermine inflation.

Supply shocks can also be adverse. Natural occurrences, such as hurricanes or droughts, and human-caused situations, such as wars, that destroy capital goods and lives are examples of adverse supply shocks. They reduce the economy's capacity to produce and, by concentrating demand on the limited supplies of resources that remain, tend to lead to higher inflation. Adverse supply shocks would be illustrated in a graph such as Figure 13.5, but with the direction of all the movements reversed.

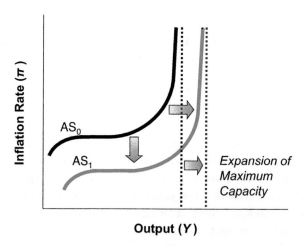

Figure 13.5 *A Beneficial Supply Shock: Expansion of Output Capacity*

An expansion of output capacity could be a result of new technology or improved labor productivity.

426

Discussion Questions

1. Describe in words how the *AS* curve differs from the *AD* curve. What does each represent? What explains their slopes?
2. In some euro-area countries, certain wage contracts are automatically linked to inflation, meaning that workers get automatic pay raises if consumer prices increase. Why does this practice have important macroeconomic consequences?

3. PUTTING THE *AS/AD* MODEL TO WORK

Economists invented the *AS/AD* model to illustrate three points about the macroeconomy:

1. Fiscal and monetary policies affect output and inflation:
   - *Expansionary fiscal and monetary policies* tend to push the economy toward higher output. If the economy is approaching its maximum capacity, they will also cause inflation to rise.
   - *Contractionary fiscal and monetary policies* tend to push the economy toward lower output. Inflation is unlikely to fall quickly, but a persistent recession will tend to lower inflation over the long term.
2. *Supply shocks* may also have significant effects:
   - Adverse supply shocks lower output and raise inflation.
   - Beneficial supply shocks raise output and lower inflation.
3. *Investor and consumer confidence and expectations* also have important effects on output and inflation.

Bearing these principles in mind, we will see how this model helps to explain some major macroeconomic events.

3.1 An Economy in Recession

In Figure 13.6, we bring together the *AS* and *AD* curves for the first time. The (short-run) equilibrium of the economy is shown as point E_0, at the intersection of the two curves. Depending on how we place the curves in the figure, we could illustrate an economy that is in a recession, at full employment, or in a wage-price spiral. (We temporarily omit the maximum capacity line, but we reintroduce it when we discuss inflation.)

In this specific case, the fact that E_0 is to the left of the full-employment range of output indicates that the economy is in a recession. Private spending, as determined in part by investor and consumer confidence, along with government and foreign-sector spending, are not enough to keep the economy at full employment. The fact that the curves intersect on the flat part of the *AS* curve indicates that inflation (in the short run) is stable. So in this situation, unemployment is the major problem. What can be done?

Figure 13.6 models the real-world situation in many industrialized countries in the global financial and economic crisis of 2008–2009. Unemployment rose quickly

427

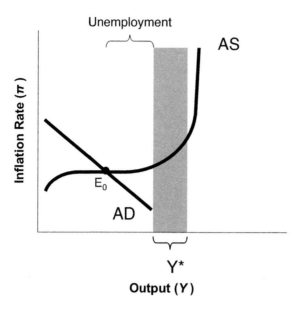

Figure 13.6 *Aggregate Demand and Supply Equilibrium in Recession*

The position of the AD curve indicates a low level of aggregate demand, leading to an economy with unemployment at equilibrium E_0. At this point on the AS curve, inflationary pressures are low.

in many countries, but inflation was very low. In this situation, the governments of the major OECD countries passed stimulus packages with tax cuts and spending increases, which mostly came into effect in early 2009. For Germany, the stimulus package was estimated to have a total volume of €75 billion (3 percent of GDP), for Spain of around €40 billion (3.5 percent of GDP), for the Netherlands around €10 billion (1.5 percent of GDP), and for the United Kingdom of around £20 billion (1.4 percent of GDP). In absolute terms, the U.S. passed the largest package among industrialized countries, worth $800 billion (or 5.6 percent of GDP). The goal of these stimulus programs was to promote employment both through its direct impact and multiplier effects, expanding private spending and employment. This effect is shown in Figure 13.7 as a rightward shift of the *AD* curve.

As noted in Chapter 10 (Box 10.2), the stimulus packages helped European economies to recover from recession and saved or created millions of jobs. While economists are not in agreement about how large the multiplier effects of the program were, many argue that without the program, European economies would have continued to plunge deeper into recession. In most countries, however, the effects were not large enough to bring the economy back to full employment. This is reflected in Figure 13.7 as an *AD* shift that moves output toward but not into the full-employment zone.

How about the effect of this expansionary program on inflation? As the *AS/AD* model would lead us to expect, inflation did not rise because the economy did not

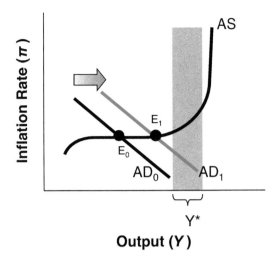

Figure 13.7 *Expansionary Fiscal Policy in Response to a Recession*

An expansion of government spending, as well as a program of tax cuts, shifts the AD *curve to the right. This reduces unemployment, but since the economy is in the flat portion of the* AS *curve at equilibrium* E_1, *it has little effect on inflation.*

move beyond the flat portion of the *AS* curve. Some economists and political commentators warned that such a high level of government spending and deficits would certainly cause serious inflation—but as of late 2016, almost a decade after the initiation of the stimulus program, inflation remained low in all industrialized countries (see Box 13.1).

In the euro area, however, another problem emerged shortly after the stimulus packages had stabilized the economies: the euro crisis struck. Adding to the fiscal burden from the stimulus packages, governments had found themselves forced to rescue their ailing banks with public money. With the revelation that Greece had understated its public debt and deficit for many years, investors became aware of the risk of sovereign default. The interest rate they demanded for holding government debt skyrocketed and confidence collapsed.

In a panicked attempt to counter these sentiments, national governments started to cut back public deficits quickly. All across the euro area, austerity packages with cuts to public expenditure and tax increases were enacted.* The *AD* curve shifted back to the left, for some countries even beyond the point E_0 (the situation in the recession of 2008–2009).

The reaction in the United States was different. The Federal Reserve was not happy with the slow growth of the U.S. economy and stepped in early with the further monetary stimulus known as "quantitative easing" (as discussed in Chapter 12). The hope

---

* The euro crisis will be covered in detail in Chapter 17.

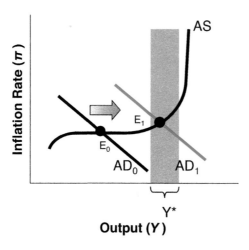

Figure 13.8 *A Greater Expansion of Aggregate Demand*

If aggregate demand increases by a larger amount, it can bring the economy back into the full-employment zone. At equilibrium point E_1, the AS/AD model indicates the possibility of a slightly higher inflation level.

was that a combination of this monetary expansion plus recovering confidence on the part of consumers and businesses could lead to a more complete recovery.

While the recovery proved slower than in previous decades, as of 2016, the U.S. economy had moved into a recovery. Economists debated the stability of the recovery, but unemployment had fallen back to below 5 percent by the summer of 2016, and the Fed had ended its quantitative easing program and had even cautiously started to increase interest rates again. This development is shown in Figure 13.8. Here we see that a larger *AD* shift brings the economy back into the full-employment zone. At this point, the model predicts that there could be at least a slight increase in inflation. Compared with the more dismal performance of the euro-area economy, the overall effort of U.S. policy makers can thus be judged a success.

As we see later in this chapter, not all economists agree with this analysis. Some classical economists argue that inflation has merely been delayed but will eventually cause major problems and perhaps force a return to recession. We will look into the theoretical issues involved later (without providing any definite judgment on the debate).

BOX 13.1 WHAT HAPPENED TO INFLATION?

Despite the ECB's target of maintaining an inflation rate of "below but close to 2 percent," by 2016, the rate of change in consumer prices in the euro area had dropped to only slightly more than 0 percent. Over some months in the spring of 2016, average prices for the typical consumption basket were actually even lower than 12 months earlier.

Reasons for the lack of price pressure were plentiful: First, companies in the euro area had for a long time been operating far below their full capacity. Competition was fierce, and excess capacity led to price cuts in certain sectors. Second, because of persistently high unemployment in many euro-area countries, wage increases had been subdued. As a consequence, firms could cut costs and could use the savings to lower their prices. Finally, energy prices had collapsed. Between the summer of 2014 and early 2016, oil prices had fallen by almost two-thirds, and as a number of contracts for other sources of energy are linked to the oil price, this increasingly was reflected in the general price development.

But the reason that caused most concern among the ECB's central bankers was a fourth factor: people's expectations of future inflation were gradually changing. Both surveys and prices for inflation-linked bonds were indicating that financial market participants were expecting the period of low inflation to continue over several years. One of the reasons for changing expectations was the long period during which the ECB has consistently missed its inflation target: By the summer of 2016, inflation had been significantly below 2 percent for three years.

The fear among policy makers is that lower inflation expectations will make it much more difficult to bring inflation up to its target in the future. Inflation expectations enter into unions' wage demands and into firms' price setting. If people get accustomed to the absence of inflation, the expectation of zero price increases might hence become a self-fulfilling prophecy. While low or zero inflation might seem like a good thing to consumers, policy makers are concerned with the risks of a deflationary situation that would make it difficult for the economy to recover from recessionary conditions.

Sources: *Reuters*, People may be losing faith in ECB's ability to fix inflation -ECB research, August 26, 2016; Samya Beidas-Strom, Davide Furceri and Bertrand Gruss, Combating Persistent Disinflation: A Challenge for Many Central Banks, *IMF News Article*, September 27, 2016.

Although inflation has recently been low in both Europe and the United States, we do know that there have been other times in economic history when inflation has been a major problem. What does the *AS/AD* model indicate about policy in such periods? We explore this topic next.

3.2 Stagflation

In the 1950s and 1960s, neither unemployment nor inflation was a major problem in most Western European countries. Even though some countries such as Germany experienced a recession in the mid–1960s, overall economic growth was robust and unemployment low (in no major European country were unemployment rates significantly above 5 percent, and they were as low as 1 or 2 percent in Germany, France, and the UK). Inflation was on average higher than today and fluctuating more strongly, but broadly perceived to be under control. Single years with high inflation in some countries were followed by years with much lower inflation, without large increases in unemployment.

At that time, policy makers by and large believed that they could manage the economy and keep unemployment at desired low levels by allowing for a little more or a little less inflation. The trade-off between unemployment and inflation became known as the Phillips curve, after the economist who had first identified an empirical relationship between unemployment and inflation. Working on data from 1861 to 1957, Alban William Phillips had found that for the UK, periods of high inflation coincided with periods of low unemployment and vice versa. If one looks at data for the U.S. in the 1960s, this relationship also seems to be evident during this time period (see Figure 13.9). Even though Phillips did not make such a claim, the Phillips curve relationship seemed to suggest that policy makers could continue to "trade off" inflation and unemployment—that they could, by use of appropriate fiscal and monetary policies, choose to settle the economy at any point along the curve. Policy makers could push up inflation to keep unemployment low or perhaps sacrifice some employment to push down inflation—or so it was thought at the time.

This conceived wisdom was shattered in the 1970s. In this decade, in many industrialized countries, inflation shot up without any fall in unemployment, and in some countries inflation and unemployment even went up strongly at the same time. Behind this development was the so-called "oil-price shock." In 1973–1974, the member

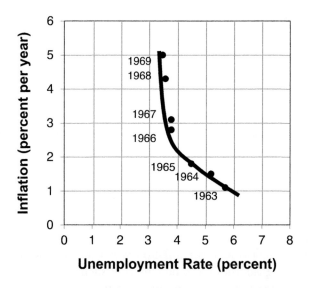

Figure 13.9 *The Phillips Curve for the U.S. in the 1960s*

In the 1960s economist A.W. Phillips identified an inverse relationship between inflation and unemployment. While this basic relationship still holds true, events of the 1970s and later showed that inflation can be much more variable than the simple Phillips principle implies.

countries of the Organization of Petroleum Exporting Countries (OPEC) cut production, greatly increased the price at which they sold their oil, and even temporarily stopped shipping oil to certain countries. The price of oil, a key input into many production processes, suddenly quadrupled. The result was a strong increase in inflation and unemployment in many European countries. The developments of the early 1970s came as a shock to Phillips curve–minded economists and policy makers. From 1969 to 1970, unemployment and inflation both rose, and both stayed fairly high through the 1970–1973 period. This combination of economic stagnation (recession) and high inflation came to be known as **stagflation**.

How can we explain this effect? The impact of the oil-price shock is shown in Figure 13.10. The economy starts off in a recession at point E_0, which is substantially to the left of the initial maximum capacity line. The cut in foreign oil production meant that oil-importing countries now suffered from a reduced capacity to produce goods, which is shown in Figure 13.10 by the maximum capacity line and AS curves shifting to the left. Even if labor resources were fully employed, an economy with reduced access to other inputs would not be able to produce as much. At the same time, the rise in oil prices had an immediate and direct effect on inflation, shifting the AS curve up as well, as also shown in Figure 13.10. Both inflation and unemployment got worse.

Different European countries dealt with the problem in different ways. As we can see in Figures 13.11a and 13.11b, the pattern of unemployment and inflation was very different between Italy (and other Southern European countries) and Germany. Both countries were hit by the oil-price shock of the 1970s, yet in Italy, inflation rose strongly (reaching annual rates of almost 20 percent) with unemployment being

stagflation: a combination of rising inflation and economic stagnation

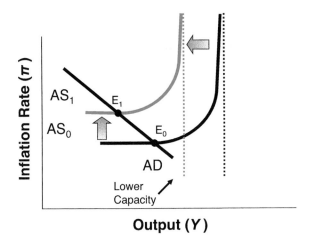

Figure 13.10 *The Effect of the Oil-Price Shock of the 1970s*

A drastic increase in the price of a key resource reduces the economy's total capacity and shifts the AS curve up and to the left. Both inflation and unemployment get worse at equilibrium point E_1.

433

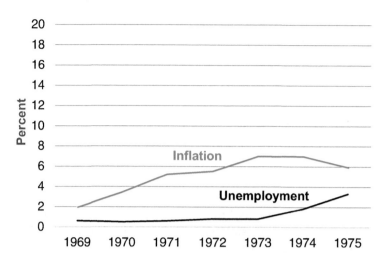

Figure 13.11a *Inflation and Unemployment in Germany, 1969–1975*

The oil-price shock of the 1970s pushed inflation in Germany only up a few percentage points, and price pressure quickly subsided again. However, unemployment more than doubled.

Source: AMECO database, 2016.

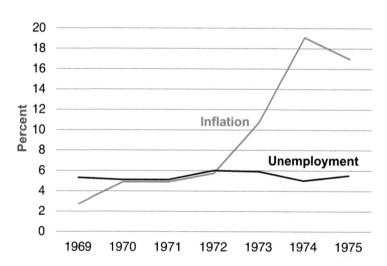

Figure 13.11b *Inflation and Unemployment in Italy, 1969–1975*

In Italy, inflation surged during the oil-price shock of the 1970s. However, unemployment remained almost unaffected.

Source: AMECO database, 2016.

almost unaffected, while in Germany, unemployment rose, but inflation quickly came down again. How can we explain these different outcomes using our *AS/AD* model?

Germany demonstrates the standard case of a monetary policy reaction discussed earlier: Inflation shot up due to the increased oil prices (the shift in the *AS* curve), but

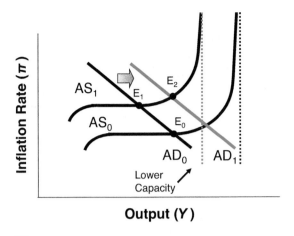

Figure 13.12 *The Italian Reaction to the Oil-Price Shock of the 1970s*

Initially, the oil-price shock has led to increased unemployment and higher inflation (a movement from E_0 to E_1). Yet, the Italian government reacted with expansionary fiscal and monetary stimulus, which pushed inflation further up (to E_2).

the German central bank, the Bundesbank, as a reaction, directly increased the interest rates (moving us on the *AD* curve from E_0 to E_1). The result is an increase in both inflation and unemployment.

In Italy, the reaction of the government and the central bank was different (as shown in Figure 13.12): As policy makers did not want to accept a large increase in unemployment, they increased public spending. The central bank did not counteract this increase in aggregate demand by increasing interest rates but even helped by using expansionary monetary policy to finance part of the increased government expenditure. So in addition to the shift of the *AS* curve up and to the right (because of the oil-price shock), the *AD* curve shifted right (because of expansionary fiscal and monetary policy), bringing the economy to point E_2. The result in Italy was thus even higher inflation, but—at least for the moment—no increase in unemployment.

3.3 A Hard Line Against Inflation

This was still not the end of the inflationary story of the 1970s. Countries such as Italy that had accommodated the inflationary shock in the mid-1970s had seen inflationary expectations permanently shifted upward. The horizontal part of their *AS* curve was now significantly higher than prior to the oil-price shock. The result was a permanently higher rate of inflation. Having recently experienced a wage-price spiral, people had built expectations of higher inflation into their wage and price contracts. As Karl Otto Pöhl, former president of the Bundesbank, the German central bank, once commented, inflation is like toothpaste—once you squeeze it out of the tube, you cannot get it back in. On an annual basis, between 1973 and the end of the decade, Italy did not experience any single year with inflation below 10 percent. In Germany and Switzerland, in contrast, inflation had come down to low single digits by 1978 again.

Then oil prices jumped again in 1979 and 1980. In U.S. dollar terms, in 1979, the price of oil was *ten* times higher than it had been in 1973. Measured in Italian lira and other Southern European countries, the price increase was even larger (as these currencies had lost value relative to the U.S. dollar). The high rates of inflation experienced in many countries in the late 1970s were already very damaging to the economies concerned. As we noted in Chapter 11, high rates of inflation can wipe out the value of people's savings and make it very difficult for households and businesses to plan, save, and invest.

High rates of inflation were not only a European phenomenon. In the U.S., inflation had also risen to uncomfortable levels (peaking in March 1980 at almost 15 percent). Even though the economy was already in a recession and the unemployment rate was above 7 percent, the Federal Reserve, under the chairmanship of Paul Volcker, took deliberate and drastic action to bring the long-term inflation rate down by implementing very contractionary monetary policies. Most European central banks followed this move and also increased interest rates in the early 1980s; some others such as the Banque de France followed a similar policy later in that decade. The effects of these "tight money" policies can be seen in Figure 13.13.

As discussed earlier, contractionary monetary policy shifts the *AD* curve to the left. The *AS/AD* model predicts that the immediate effect of this policy will be to send the economy even deeper into a recession, with output falling even farther below its

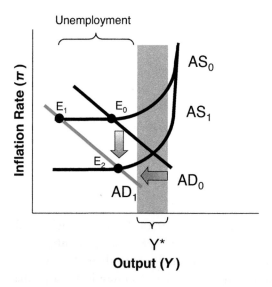

Figure 13.13 *The Effects of the Fed's "Tight Money" Policies in the 1980s*

A very restrictive monetary policy drives the AD curve sharply to the left, pushing unemployment to very high levels. But a resulting decrease in inflationary expectations shown in aggregate supply curve AS₁ lowers inflation and allows the economy to recover to equilibrium point E₂.

full-employment level, as shown by equilibrium point E_1. But there is a further effect on inflationary expectations.

These contractionary policies were usually accompanied by stories in the media about how central bankers were really committed to bringing down inflation, no matter the cost. Because people found this commitment credible (especially after they had observed that central banks were willing to accept a deep recession to bring down inflation), their expectations of inflation also came down. The effect of this decrease in inflationary expectations is shown as a downward shift in the AS curve to AS_1, showing a reduction in inflation. Such recessions with falling inflation are, in fact, what happened in many European countries and also in the U.S. during the 1980s.

Disinflation worked fastest in the U.S. By 1983, the U.S. inflation rate had fallen to 4 percent, but at a significant human and economic cost. Unemployment during 1982 and 1983 rose to nearly 10 percent. The disinflation process was slower in most parts of Europe. While inflation in Germany also dropped below 5 percent in 1983, in Italy, Ireland, Sweden, France, and Spain, inflation fell below this threshold only in the second half of the 1980s. With a few exceptions, and with slight differences in the timing, this fall in inflation coincided with a strong increase in unemployment. In Italy, between 1975 and 1987, unemployment rose from 5.5 to 9.6 percent. In France, unemployment over this period increased from 3.3 to 8.9 percent, in the UK from 3.2 to 11.2 percent.

Different countries experienced very different developments of unemployment in the years that followed. In some countries such as the U.S., the economy recovered and employment increased, as shown by equilibrium point E_2. By the late 1980s, unemployment in the U.S. had come down to almost 5 percent, a lower level than experienced ever since the first oil-price shock of 1973. In contrast, the experience in some European countries was much more dismal: Unemployment remained elevated in many European countries, including France, Italy, Ireland, and Spain, well into the 1990s.

Why this was the case remains disputed among economists. Some claim that inflexible European labor markets were to blame. According to this argument, firms in many countries are reluctant to hire new workers due to the legal difficulties of getting rid of them again if business declines. It therefore takes a long time of high economic growth before firms actually start hiring and unemployment falls again. In the meanwhile, unemployed workers lose their skills and become less productive. According to this narrative, during the long period of low growth and high unemployment in the 1980s and 1990s, part of the cyclical unemployment has turned into structural unemployment, resulting in lower potential output.

Other economists claim that central bankers did not lower interest rates enough once inflationary pressure had subsided. According to this view, excessively tight monetary policies in the late 1980s and early 1990s limited the speed of Europe's recovery. This behavior of central bankers might be explained by the experience of the 1980s, which had shown that after inflationary expectations become established, they can be reduced only by policies that cause major economic pain. This may have led policy makers to be very wary of encouraging any new inflationary wage-price spiral.

437

3.4 An Overheated Economy

So far, we have looked at the possibility that adverse supply shocks such as the oil-price shocks can lead to a surge in inflation. However, it is also possible for inflation to be caused by an overheated economy and an excess of aggregate demand. While such situations have been rather rare in Europe over the past 40 years, there is one prominent example: The German reunification boom in the early 1990s.

From World War II until 1990, Germany was divided into two parts: The Western part (occupied by the U.S., Britain, and France after World War II) had a capitalist economy, and GDP per capita had increased quite impressively in the postwar years. The smaller Eastern part (occupied by the Soviet Union) had a communist planned economy, and the improvement in living standards there had been much less than in the West. Due to a lack of investment, the capital stock in the East was deteriorating, and basic commodities were often in short supply.

Both parts of Germany were divided by a heavily fortified border, including the famous Berlin Wall. With the crumbling of the Soviet Union in the late 1980s, the East German government also came under pressure. Reacting to inadequate supplies of consumer goods and the absence of democratic elections, East Germans took to the streets. On November 9, 1989, the East German government gave in to the pressure and opened the borders to West Germany. Elections were called slightly later, and the newly elected democratic East German government quickly negotiated a reunification with the West. On July 1, 1990, an "economic and currency union" was formed between the two German states, and on October 3, 1990, East Germany joined the West German Federal Republic of Germany.

The reunification had enormous economic consequences. First, East Germans were allowed to convert their savings into (West) German marks. As they had not been able to buy many consumer goods before (due to lack of supply), they immediately went on a spending spree. In addition, West German firms experienced a jump in confidence. The German chancellor at that time, Helmut Kohl, promised "blooming landscapes in the East," and companies rushed to expand their capacities to produce for the new market in the East. Finally, confronted with the sorry state of East German infrastructure, the German government passed a huge public investment program. For political reasons, the Kohl government did not want to increase taxes, so all this additional expenditure was paid for by new borrowing.

What happened? Let us have a look at West Germany only. In our model, the additional demand of consumer goods by Eastern Germans and the demand for new infrastructure and new capital goods shift the AD curve strongly to the right. In this case, the impact was so large that the curve was shifted beyond the full employment area. We can see the effect in Figure 13.14: The AD curve shifts right and the economy moves from E_0 to E_1. The model hence would predict an increase in inflationary pressure. This is indeed what happened. Unemployment fell sharply, from almost 8 percent to a little more than 5 percent. At the same time, inflation accelerated from less than 3 percent in 1989 (when the Berlin Wall came down) to more than 6 percent in early 1992.

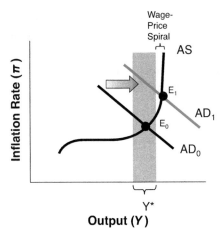

Figure 13.14 *Excessively High Aggregate Demand Causes Inflation*

Expansionary policy causes the economy to "heat up." In the short run, people respond by increasing output, but tight markets for labor and other resources cause inflation to rise as well at equilibrium point E_1.

What happened next? Shortly afterward, the German economy was hit by a number of negative shocks. The Bundesbank increased interest rates sharply (some economists claim much more sharply than warranted by their normal reaction function), and both consumer and investor confidence plummeted. In the fall of 1992, many European countries experienced a currency crisis (the European Monetary System crisis or "EMS crisis") and went into a recession. As many of these countries were important trading partners for Germany, German exporters struggled, further reducing demand for German goods. In the *AS/AD* model, these factors all contribute to a strong leftward shift of the *AD* curve. As a result, inflation fell and unemployment shot up.

3.5 Austerity Policies and Structural Reforms

Let us now fast-forward through the rest of the 1990s and the first decade of this century (parts of it will be covered in later chapters on the Great Recession of 2008–2009). In the euro crisis, two sets of policies were enacted, which we can also analyze with our *AS/AD* model: austerity packages and structural reforms. We will cover the euro crisis more in detail, so we will limit our exposition here to the bare basics: From 2010 onward, investors got concerned about the debt sustainability in a number of euro-area countries. As a consequence, they required higher interest rates when they lent to governments, firms, and households in the countries concerned. The EU told the countries concerned to react by cutting public spending, increasing taxes, and implementing structural reforms, making markets more flexible. What would our *AS/AD* model predict as a result of these policies?

Let us start with the loss in investor confidence: A loss of investor confidence means that some firms and some individuals will now have a hard time getting loans.

This is represented in Figure 13.15a by a shift of the AD curve to the left from AD_0 to AD_1. The economy hence moves from E_0 to E_1. Output falls and unemployment increases. Then governments, following EU rules, cut public expenditure and increase taxes. Again, this moves the AD curve further to the left, now from AD_1 to AD_2. The economy moves from the equilibrium in E_1 to the equilibrium in E_2. Output further falls and unemployment further decreases.

Structural reforms are in principle supposed to make markets more flexible and hence increase potential output. While it is very much disputed whether the reforms enacted during the euro crisis really are those that could increase potential output, let us assume for a moment that they fulfill this purpose. In this case, they would lead to a shift of the AS curve downward and to the right (see Figure 13.15b). The economy

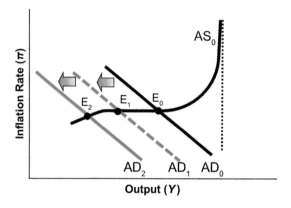

Figure 13.15a *A Loss of Investor Confidence in the* AS/AD *Model*

When investors lose confidence in one country and cut credit lines to the country's firms, the AD *curve shifts left. GDP contracts and unemployment increases.*

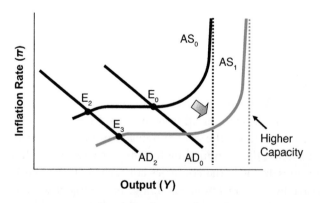

Figure 13.15b *Structural Reforms in the* AS/AD *Model*

If the government reacts to the fall in output with reforms that increase potential output, in a second step, the AS *curve shifts right. GDP increases again, but prices fall. It is not clear, however, whether a return to the initial GDP level is possible.*

440

would now move along the *AD* curve from the equilibrium in E_2 to the equilibrium in E_3. Inflation would fall, output would increase, and unemployment would fall.

What has been the empirical evidence on the impact of these policies? In fact, the performance under austerity programs differed a lot between euro-area countries. While Greece has done very poorly, Ireland has done much better. As of early 2016, GDP in Greece still was about 25 percent lower than in 2008. In Ireland, GDP in early 2016 actually was more than 20 percent *higher* than in 2008 (even though the reliability of the data was questioned—see Box 5.3). In Ireland, as of early 2016, unemployment had fallen to 8.5 percent. While this is still significantly higher than prior to the crisis, it is far below the 2012 peak of more than 15 percent. In Greece, as of early 2016, unemployment still stood above 24 percent. While this was slightly lower than at the peak of the crisis, it was still more than three times the level of 2007. Inflation fell in both countries but actually much more strongly in Greece. Figure 13.16 and Figure 13.17 show the development of inflation and unemployment in Greece and Ireland from 2011 to 2016.

How can one explain these different performances? For one thing, austerity packages were different in size. Greece cut public expenditure much more than Ireland. Yet this is not the whole story. We have noticed already that for small countries in the euro area, the downward-sloping *AD* curve can be explained by making exports more competitive relative to the partners' products. In Ireland, the share of exports and imports to GDP is much higher than in Greece. Hence, aggregate demand can be expected to react much more strongly to a fall in inflation in Ireland than in Greece. In Figure 13.18a and Figure 13.18b, this is represented by different slopes of the *AD*

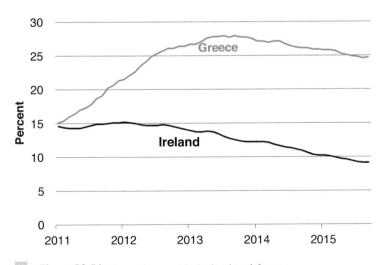

Figure 13.16 *Unemployment in Ireland and Greece*

During the euro crisis, unemployment in both Ireland and Greece was significantly above precrisis levels. However, as of 2016, unemployment in Ireland has come down significantly, while it has remained stubbornly high in Greece.

Source: Eurostat, 2016.

441

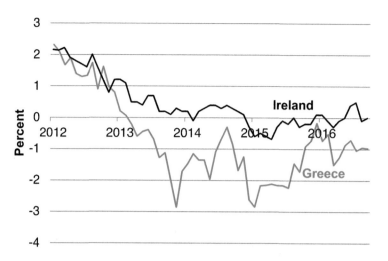

Figure 13.17 *Inflation in Ireland and Greece*

Inflation fell in both Ireland and Greece after austerity packages and structural reform measures were enacted. However, inflation fell further in Greece than in Ireland.

Source: Eurostat, 2016.

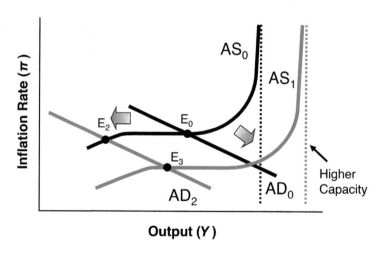

Figure 13.18a *Macroeconomic Results of Austerity and Structural Reforms in Ireland*

As Ireland is a very open economy, falling inflation caused by structural reforms boosted exports and aggregate demand. As a consequence, structural reforms were able to counteract part of the negative impacts of austerity.

curve. In Greece, the AD curve is steeper, as the economy is structurally in a position in which it is not able to benefit much from falling inflation. The equilibrium E_2 in Figure 13.18a, reached after the combination of austerity policies and structural reforms, is one of lower inflation but not much less unemployment than with austerity

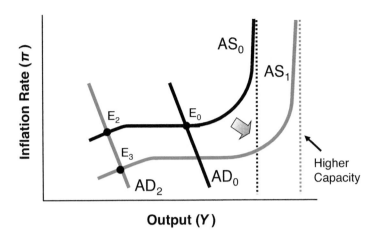

Figure 13.18b *Macroeconomic Results of Austerity and Structural Reforms in Greece*

As aggregate demand in Greece does not react much to changes in inflation, structural reforms have not been able to increase employment significantly. The combination of austerity and structural reforms has led to lower inflation but also high unemployment.

alone. In Ireland, the *AD* curve is much flatter, as exporters benefit more strongly from increased price competiveness. Here, as shown in Figure 13.18b, the equilibrium reached after austerity and structural reforms is one of much less unemployment than after austerity only.

Discussion Questions

1. Under what circumstances can aggregate demand be increased without leading to problems with inflation? Under what circumstances is an increase in aggregate demand likely to cause inflation?
2. Stagflation—a combination of unemployment and inflation—seems to be the worst of both worlds. What policies were used to respond to the stagflation of the late 1970s and early 1980s? What factors led to improving economic conditions in the later 1980s and the 1990s? Why do you think that "austerity" policies in recent times seem to have been less effective in promoting economic recovery?

4. COMPETING THEORIES

The *AS/AD* model has given us insight into some of the major macroeconomic fluctuations of the past several decades. But there remains much room for controversy. Was it necessary to enact expansionary fiscal policy in order to get the European economies out of the 2008–2009 recession? Was it a good idea for the ECB to lower interest rates to zero (and below for deposits) in 2015–2016 to try to promote recovery? Economists differ greatly in their views on these issues, and their theoretical backgrounds tend to inform their answers to these and other more contemporary questions.

Here we review the ways in which classical and Keynesian economics address these questions. Additional theories—some of which take positions between these two poles—are reviewed in the Appendix to this chapter.

4.1 Classical Macroeconomics

As discussed in previous chapters, economists with ties to the classical school tend to believe in the self-adjusting properties of a free-market system. In the classical view, labor markets clear at an equilibrium wage (Chapter 8). Classical markets for loanable funds cause savings and investment to be equal at an equilibrium interest rate (Chapter 9). In theory, then, a smoothly functioning economy should never be at anything other than full employment.

In terms of the *AS/AD* model, the classical theory implies an *AS* curve that is quite different from the one that we have been working with, as shown in Figure 13.19. In such an economy, output would always be at its full-employment level (now shown as a distinct value rather than a range). The *AD* level would determine the inflation rate but nothing else.

The rationale for this vertical *AS* curve is as follows. At the full-employment level, people are making their optimizing choices about how much to work, consume, and so on. If for some reason the economy were to produce at less than the full-employment level, the unemployed workers would bid down wages and full employment would be restored. If the economy were to produce at more than its full-employment level, wages would be bid up, and employment would drop back to its full-employment level. Such processes are assumed to work so quickly and smoothly that the economy will return to full employment fairly quickly.

What, according to the classical model, is the effect of aggregate demand-management policies? As we can see in Figure 13.19, expansionary fiscal or monetary policy

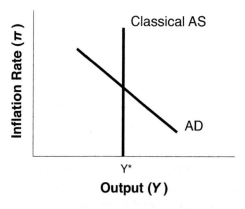

Figure 13.19 *The Classical View of AS/AD*

The vertical AS curve represents the classical view that the economy will tend to return to full employment automatically.

can have no effect on the output level. Classical economists believe that increased government spending just "crowds out" private spending (as discussed in Chapter 10), in particular spending on investment. Because the economy is already at its full-employment level of Y^*, more spending by government just means less spending by consumers and businesses.

Similarly, in the classical view, monetary expansions are believed to lead only to increased inflation. As we saw in our discussion of classical monetary theory in Chapter 12, the classical prescription is that the central bank should just choose a certain growth rate of the money supply or level of the interest rate to support and stick to it, without concerning itself about unemployment and output. Classical theory tends to support politically conservative policies that emphasize small government and strict rules on monetary policy. Classical economists would tend to say that the fiscal expansionary policies put into place in 2009 were unnecessary for the purposes of macroeconomic stabilization but that the actions of major central banks to bring down inflation in the early 1980s were a good idea.

4.2 Keynesian Macroeconomics

The original Keynesian belief was that market economies are inherently unstable. The Keynesian notion of the influence of "animal spirits" on investment refers to the tendency of private decision makers to become overly optimistic and create booms in investing and production. And the higher the boom, the deeper the crash. Firms that have overextended and overproduced during an upswing need time to regroup, sell off inventory, and so on before they will be ready to go on the upswing again. Households that have overextended and overspent during a boom also need to regroup and perhaps pay down debt before they will be willing to restart an optimistic spending bandwagon.

This view of perpetual business cycles is a fundamentally different worldview from those that presume an automatic "settling down" of the economy at a full-employment equilibrium. Keynes did *not* believe that macroeconomic phenomena could be explained by assuming rational, optimizing behavior by individuals and then extrapolating from models of individual markets to the macroeconomy. Modern Keynesians argue that this inherent tendency toward market instability requires active government intervention and that the alternative—simply waiting for the market to correct itself—risks major economic damage and long-term depression.

It is important to note that Keynesians do not only favor expansionary fiscal and monetary policies. They believe that they are needed in case of recession, but under different circumstances, such as the inflationary periods that we have discussed, contractionary policy may be called for. Keynesians thus find the kind of analysis that we have presented in this chapter very useful for determining what type of policy is needed in different circumstances. The traditional model of Keynesian business cycles must be modified to deal with new events such as supply shocks (discussed earlier) and sustainability issues (discussed in Chapter 18). These require models that are flexible

445

enough to address new issues as they arise. Such models are best built on the understanding that economies are subject to a variety of forces, many of which can swamp the market equilibrium logic that would be expected to lead to a classical situation of full-employment equilibrium.

In the modern era, the debate between economists who favor classical approaches and those who argue for Keynesian analysis has continued. The global financial and economic crisis of 2008–2009 and its aftermath (including the euro crisis) have provided new fodder for these arguments about economic analysis and policy (see Box 13.2).

BOX 13.2 CLASSICAL AND KEYNESIAN VIEWS OF RECESSION AND RECOVERY

The most recent economic crises have provided a new arena for the long-running debate between classical and Keynesian views in economics. In the United States the Great Recession of 2007–2009 and the slow recovery afterward, and in Europe the euro crisis and its aftermath, have provided ample new evidence on the impact of macroeconomic policies.

Two major responses to the initial crisis—the fiscal stimulus programs of 2009–2010 in many countries and policies of ultralow interest rates and "quantitative easing" by major central banks—are right out of the Keynesian playbook of expansionary fiscal and monetary policy. At the same time, policies of "austerity" (drastic spending cutbacks) implemented in many European countries after the onset of the euro crisis reflect the classical perspective that excessive government spending is a problem, not a solution, and that budget deficits need to be eliminated. Thus the discussion has focused on the relative success or failure of these policies.

Keynesians argued that the stimulative fiscal and monetary policies implemented in the United States prevented a much worse recession, saving or creating millions of jobs (Blinder and Zandi, 2010) and putting the country on a (slow) road to recovery. They believed that the results, in terms of employment creation, were limited mainly because the stimulus was not large enough and that the stimulus was essentially reversed after the 2010 Republican congressional victories. Although Keynesians generally supported the Fed's expansionary policies, they suggested that they are subject to the "liquidity trap" identified by Keynes—the tendency of banks and individuals to hold on to money in bad times, limiting the effectiveness of expansionary monetary policy (Krugman, 2011, 2013). Meanwhile, they pointed to the deepening recession in Europe as proof that the "classical medicine" of budget austerity was counterproductive.

Classical economists, by contrast, saw the government efforts at economic stimulation as a failure, one that would saddle the country with an increased burden of debt. According to Allan Meltzer (2011),

> U.S. fiscal and monetary policies are mainly directed at getting a near-term result. The estimated cost of new jobs in President Obama's jobs bill is at least $200,000 per job . . . once the subsidies end, the jobs disappear—but the bonds that financed them

remain and must be serviced. Perhaps that's why estimates of the additional spending generated by Keynesian stimulus—the "multiplier effect"—have failed to live up to expectations.

As of 2016, the U.S. economy was performing much better than most European economies, which were still well below their production levels of 2007, with unemployment rates in some countries still remaining at Great Depression levels of more than 25 percent. Predictions by classical economists of the beneficial effects of budget austerity in Europe and of accelerating inflation in the United States had not come true (Morris, 2013). U.S. budget deficits were falling (in June 2013, the federal government even briefly ran a surplus)—something that Keynesians attributed to the success of their policies, while classical economists pointed to budget cuts imposed as part of the "debt ceiling" deal of 2011 under which the deficit had been brought down.

Does this situation amount to a vindication of Keynesian policies or merely a temporary and partial success that will look different in a long-term perspective? Will the United States end up crippled by debt, or will economic recovery make debt management much easier? Will European economies rebound based on conservative budget policies, or will these countries eventually turn to more expansionary approaches? The economic argument will continue, and new policies and new data will be grist for the mill of continued economic debate.

Sources: Alan S. Blinder and Mark Zandi, "How the Great Recession Was Brought to an End," 2010, www.economy.com/mark-zandi/documents/End-of-Great-Recession. pdf; Paul Krugman, "Keynes Was Right," *New York Times*, December 29, 2011, and "Deficit Hawks Down," *New York Times*, January 25, 2013; Allan H. Meltzer, "Four Reasons Keynesians Keep Getting It Wrong," *Wall Street Journal*, October 28, 2011; Harvey Morris, "Europe Urged to Make a U-Turn on Austerity," *International Herald Tribune*, April 10, 2013.

DISCUSSION QUESTIONS

1. What is the effect of expansionary fiscal and monetary policies in the classical model?
2. Which do you think gives a better description of economic realities: classical or Keynesian macroeconomic theory? Explain.

REVIEW QUESTIONS

1. What does the *AD* curve represent, and why does it slope downward (differentiate between countries with a central bank of their own and euro-area countries without a national central bank deciding on monetary policy)? In what respect is the *AD* curve different from the *AE* curve?
2. What shifts the *AD* curve?

447

3. What does the *AS* curve represent, and why does it have the shape that it has?
4. What shifts the *AS* curve?
5. Describe, using the *AS/AD* model, a combination of events that might cause an economy to suffer from "stagflation."
6. Describe, using the *AS/AD* model, the impact of an adverse supply shock.
7. Describe, using the *AS/AD* model, how ECB policy might bring down inflation over time.
8. Describe, using the *AS/AD* model, the effects of austerity and structural reforms.
9. What does the *AS* curve look like in the classical model, and why?
10. What underlying dynamic did Keynes believe is behind the business cycle? Illustrate with an *AS/AD* graph.

EXERCISES

1. For each of the following, indicate which curve in the *AS/AD* model shifts (initially), and in which direction(s):
    a. A beneficial supply shock
    b. An increase in government spending
    c. A monetary contraction designed to lower the long-run inflation rate
    d. An increase in taxes
    e. An adverse supply shock
    f. A fall in people's expectations of inflation
    g. A decrease in consumer confidence
2. Suppose the inflation rate in an economy is observed to be falling. Sketching an *AS/AD* model for each case, determine which of the following phenomena could be the cause. (There may be more than one.)
    a. The government gives households a substantial tax cut.
    b. Agricultural harvests are particularly good this year.
    c. Businesses are confident about the future and are buying more equipment.
    d. The ECB is trying to move the economy toward a lower long-run inflation rate.
3. Suppose that an economy is currently experiencing full employment, and inflation is only slightly higher than had been expected.
    a. Draw and carefully label an *AS/AD* diagram that illustrates this case. Label the point representing the state of this economy $E_{(a)}$.
    b. Suppose that investors' confidence is actually only in the middle of an upswing. As investor confidence continues to rise, what happens to inflation and output? Add a new curve to your graph to illustrate this, as well as explaining in words. Label the point illustrating the new situation of the economy $E_{(b)}$.
    c. What sort of tax policy might a government enact to try to counteract an excessive upswing in investor confidence? Assuming this policy is effective, illustrate on your graph the effect of this policy, labeling the result $E_{(c)}$.
4. Suppose that an economy is in a deep recession.
    a. Draw and carefully label an *AS/AD* diagram that illustrates this case. Label the point representing the state of this economy E_0.

b. If no policy action is taken, what will happen to the economy over time? Show on your graph, labeling some new possible equilibrium points E_1, E_2, and E_3. (Think about which curve shifts over time, and why, when the economy stagnates. Assume that no changes occur in investor or consumer confidence or in the economy's maximum capacity output level.)

c. Suppose that the changes you outlined in (b) occurred very rapidly and dramatically. Is government policy necessary to get the economy out of the recession?

d. Write a few sentences relating the above analysis to the dispute between classical and Keynesian macroeconomists.

5. Check recent inflation rates at www.ecb.europa.eu/. What do you think explains the recent pattern of inflation? How does this relate to *AS/AD* analysis, and to the debate among different schools of thought, as discussed in Box 13.2?

6. Empirical data on the macroeconomy for the euro area as well as other EU countries can be found on the European Commission's Web site. Go to http://ec.europa.eu/economy_finance/eu/forecasts/index_en.htm and locate the statistical appendix. Jot down data on the *unemployment rate* and the *deflator of gross domestic product* for recent periods. Plot a few points on a graph to show how the economy has performed recently.

7. Match each concept in Column A with a definition or example in Column B.

Column A	Column B
a. Aggregate supply	1. A rightward shift in the AD curve
b. Real depreciation	2. A suggested relationship between inflation and unemployment
c. Increase in autonomous consumption	3. People's feelings about prices, based on experience or observation
d. Maximum capacity output	4. The economy's total production in relation to inflation
e. Beneficial supply shock	5. A sudden shortage of a key resource
f. Reduction in autonomous investment	6. A self-reinforcing tendency of wages and prices to rise
g. Aggregate demand	7. Domestic products gaining price competitiveness because of low inflation or a depreciation of the nominal exchange rate
h. Inflationary expectations	8. Government regulations to prevent wages and prices rising
i. Phillips curve	9. The economy's total production if all resources are fully utilized
j. Wage-price spiral	10. A burst of technological progress
k. Wage and price controls	11. Total spending on goods and services in an economy
l. Vertical AS curve	12. A leftward shift in the AD curve
m. Adverse supply shock	13. Represents the classical model of an economy at full employment

APPENDIX: MORE SCHOOLS OF MACROECONOMICS

A1. NEW CLASSICAL ECONOMICS

In the simple classical model presented in this chapter, the economy is nearly always at or close to full employment. Faced with the empirical evidence of widely fluctuating output and unemployment rates, some modern-day economists—often called "new classical" economists—have come up with a number of theories that seek to explain how classical theory can be consistent with the observed fluctuations.

At one extreme, some economists have sought to redefine full employment to mean pretty much whatever level of employment currently exists. Assuming that people make optimizing choices and markets work smoothly, one might observe employment levels rise and fall if, for example, technological capacities or people's preferences for work versus leisure shift over time. Some new classical economists, who have worked on what is called **real business cycle theory**, have suggested that "intertemporal substitution of leisure" (i.e., essentially, people voluntarily taking more time off during recessions) could be at the root of the lower employment levels observed during some historical periods.

Economists of the **rational expectations** school (which originated during the 1970s and 1980s) proposed a theory as to why monetary policy only affects the inflation rate and not output. The basic idea is that people have perfect foresight (i.e., they are perfectly rational), so their decisions already factor in the effects of predictable central bank policy, rendering it ineffective. This model can be explained by using the AS/AD model with a classical-type vertical AS (as shown in Figure 13.17). This vertical AS is interpreted to be the real supply curve for the economy, while in the short term the ordinary, curved AS reflects people's inflationary expectations.

Figure 13.20 shows the effects of an expansionary monetary policy in this classical world. Starting at E_0, the central bank acts to shift the AD curve to the right by increasing their inflation target, from AD_0 to AD_1. Economists of the rational expectations school predict that actors in the private economy will anticipate this expansionary move by the central bank and interpret it to mean that higher inflation is likely. As a result, they immediately raise their inflationary expectations. This rise in expected inflation, shown by the upward shift of the standard AS curve from AS_0 to AS_1, cancels out the expansionary effects of the policy. Output will not change, and the economy stays on the classical AS curve—but at a higher level of inflation. Possibly a very unexpected move by the central bank might have a temporary effect on output, but as soon as people understand what policies the central bank is carrying out, the policies will become ineffective due to changes in expectations.

Other new classical economists accept that unemployment is real and very painful to those it affects. However, they see aggregate demand policies as useless for addressing it. Rather, they claim that unemployment is caused by imperfections in labor markets (the "classical unemployment" described in Chapter 8). To reduce unemployment, new classical economists prescribe getting rid of government regulations (such as rigorous safety standards or minimum wages) that limit how firms can

real business cycle theory: the theory that changes in employment levels are caused by change in technological capacities or people's preferences concerning work

rational expectations theory: the theory that people's expectations about central bank policy cause predictable monetary policies to be ineffective in changing output levels

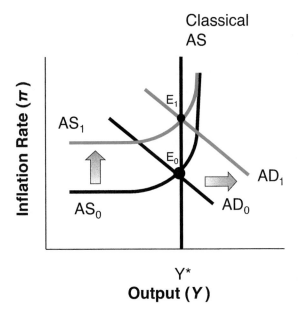

Figure 13.20 *A New Classical View of Economic Fluctuations*

"New classical" economists suggest that an expansionary move by the ECB, shifting the AD curve to the right, will be accompanied by an increase in inflationary expectations, shifting the AS curve up. The net effect, at E_1, is an increase in inflation with no change in equilibrium output.

do business, restricting union activity, or cutting back on government social welfare policies that make it attractive (according to the new classical economists) to stay out of work. Market pressures, they believe, will be enough on their own to support full employment—if given free rein.

A2. THE NEOCLASSICAL SYNTHESIS AND NEW KEYNESIAN MACROECONOMICS

Somewhere in the middle ground is what has been called the "classical-Keynesian synthesis" or **neoclassical synthesis**. (It is a bit confusing that the terms "neoclassical" and "new classical" sound so similar, but they represent two different approaches). In this way of looking at the world, Keynesian theory, which allows for output to vary from its full-employment level, is considered a reasonably good description of how things work in the short and medium run. However, this view holds that, for the reasons set out in the classical model, the economy will tend to return to full employment in the long run.

You may have noticed that in the exposition of the *AS/AD* model, we talked about the short run and the medium run but did not mention the long run. This is because in more decidedly Keynesian thought (to be discussed in what follows), the economy

neoclassical synthesis: A combination of classical and Keynesian perspectives

is really a succession of short and medium runs. Shocks to the economy are so frequent and so pronounced and price and wage adjustments (especially downward ones) so slow that the economy never has a chance to "settle down" at a long-run equilibrium.

In the neoclassical synthesis, however, it is assumed that the economy, if left to its own devices for long enough, would settle back at full employment due to the (eventual) success of classical wage and price adjustments. Models built on this basis would use an analysis much like that presented in the *AS/AD* model used in the body of this chapter but add a vertical *AS* curve such as that shown in Figures 13.17 and 13.18, labeling it "long-run aggregate supply."

To the extent that neoclassical economists and some Keynesians agree on this model, then, debates come down to a question of how long it takes to get to the long run. More classically oriented economists tend to emphasize that excessive unemployment is merely temporary and believe that (at least if government stays out of the way) the long run comes fairly soon. Some Keynesian economists, often called **New Keynesians**, have accepted the challenge from classical economists to present all their analysis in terms of the workings of markets, individual optimizing behavior, and possible "imperfections" in markets. They have built up theories (such as efficiency wage theory, discussed in Chapter 8) to explain why wages do not just fall during a recession to create a full-employment equilibrium. They tend to work within the neoclassical synthesis but claim that due to institutional factors, the long run may be a long, long way away. They believe that government action, then, is often justified.

New Keynesian macroeconomics: a school of thought that bases its analysis on micro-level market behavior but that justifies activist macroeconomic policies by assuming that markets have "imperfections" that can create or prolong recessions

post-Keynesian macroeconomics: a school of thought that stresses the importance of history and uncertainty in determining macroeconomic outcomes

A3. POST-KEYNESIAN MACROECONOMICS

Post-Keynesian economists base their analyses on some of the more radical implications of the original Keynesian theory.* They believe that modern economies are basically unstable and do not accept the idea of a long-run equilibrium at full employment. They stress the view that history matters in determining where the economy is today. They also believe that the future, although it will depend to some extent on the actions we take now, is fundamentally unpredictable due to the often surprising nature of economic evolution and world events.

For example, one post-Keynesian argument is that high unemployment, like high inflation, may also be "toothpaste" that is very difficult to get back into the tube. When people are unemployed for a long time, they tend to lose work skills, lose work habits, and may get demoralized. If this is true, then government action to counter unemployment is even more needed, since high unemployment now may tend to lead to high unemployment in the future, even if the demand situation recovers. (Economists refer to this idea that future levels of unemployment—or any other economic variable—may depend on past levels as "hysteresis" or "path dependence.")

---

* Again, the similarity between the terms "New Keynesian" and "post-Keynesian" can be confusing, but there is a difference in the theoretical perspectives, as noted.

In addition, long periods of high unemployment mean a permanent loss of output and investment—making the economy weaker in the long term. For these reasons, it is essential for the government to act to maintain full or close-to-full employment. Post-Keynesian economists would say that the fiscal expansionary policies put into place in 2009 were a good idea, because they do not believe that an economy left to its own devices will naturally return to full employment, even "in the long run."

Chapter 14

International Linkages and Economic Policy

After several months of heated public debate, on June 24, 2016, the majority of the British electorate voted that the United Kingdom should leave the European Union. When the results became clear the next morning, the value of the British pound against the U.S. dollar dropped sharply, and stock markets all over Europe slumped. Even newspapers catering for the less economically literate described how the British pound had hit a 30-year low. In the days that followed, the fear of an imminent recession grew: Newspapers reported about companies scrapping their investment plans, banks started to be more careful handing out mortgages, and people started to fear for their jobs. In other EU member states, economists revised their growth forecasts downward.

Even though these fears did not materialize and the British economy showed surprising resilience in the second half of 2016, the events around the so-called "Brexit" (for "Britain's exit") referendum demonstrate an important lesson for today's modern economies: The economic fate of different nations is closely interlinked. Events that impact one economy are often also of crucial importance for its trading partners. This is not only true for the countries of Europe, which trade a lot with each other, but increasingly for the global economy as a whole. This could best be observed during and after the global financial crisis of 2008–2009: The crisis started as a mortgage crisis caused by the fall of house prices in the U.S. but quickly pushed the world economy to the brink of a serious depression. During the recovery period, weak economic growth in Europe as a consequence of the euro crisis hindered recovery also in the U.S.

Because of this interconnectedness, economic events abroad and even in places far away sometimes feature heavily in contemporary business media. Elections in Greece, for example, have been watched closely all over Europe in the past years, as a new default of the Greek government on loans had the potential to hurt banks everywhere on the continent and might translate into a new economic crisis in other countries. The Brexit drama was front-page news in most European countries for several days. And economic growth in China is closely monitored, as a slowdown there could implicate a drop in European exports. This chapter is about these economic linkages.

1. MACROECONOMICS IN A GLOBAL CONTEXT

In earlier chapters, our macro model has generally limited its scope to the three main economic sectors: households, businesses, and the government. We have seen how each of these—through consumption, investment, and government spending—contributes to aggregate demand. It is now time to open things up a bit and introduce the foreign sector. Doing so will provide insight into how national economies are linked together and the opportunities and problems that this linkage creates.

1.1 Global Connections

An economy with no international linkages is called a *closed economy*, while one that participates in the global economy is called an *open economy*. The economic linkages among countries can take many forms, including:

- international *trade flows*, when goods and services that have been created in one country are sold in another
- international *income flows*, when capital incomes (profit, rent, and interest), labor incomes, or transfer payments go from one country to another
- international *transactions in assets*, when people trade in financial assets such as foreign bonds or currencies, or make investments in real foreign assets such as businesses or real estate
- international *flows of people*, as people migrate from one country to another, either temporarily or permanently
- international flows of *technological knowledge*, *cultural products*, and other intangibles, which can profoundly influence patterns of production and consumption, as well as tastes and lifestyles
- international sharing of and impact on *common environmental resources*, such as deep-sea fisheries and global climate patterns
- the institutional environment created by international monetary institutions, international trade agreements, international military and aid arrangements, and banks, corporations, and other private entities that operate at an international scale.

Any one of these forms of interaction may be crucially important for understanding the macroeconomic experience of specific countries at specific times. Mexico and Turkey, for example, receive significant flows of income from remittances sent home by citizens working abroad. Biological hazards, such as diseases or insects that threaten human health or agriculture, can travel along with people and goods. Trade in "intellectual property," such as technology patents and music copyrights, is currently an issue of hot dispute.

Thoroughly describing the international economic system is too large a project for one textbook, let alone one or a couple of chapters. As a grounding for the reader's understanding of these matters, this chapter looks at how trade in goods and services affects aggregate demand as well as how it corresponds to a country's international finances. We look at how trade and finance influence the exchange rate of a country's currency. As we will see, these international issues can all affect living standards and macroeconomic stabilization. Later chapters look in more detail at issues of growth and sustainability.

1.2 Major Policy Tools

We say that a country's economy is "open" if it exports and imports large amounts relative to its GDP and "closed" if it exports and imports relatively small amounts. Governments can try to control the degree of openness or "closedness" of their economy through a variety of policy tools. The most drastic way to "close" an economy is to institute a **trade ban**. In theory, a country could prohibit all international trade, but this hardly ever happens. More often, countries make trade in selected goods illegal or ban trade with particular countries (such as the U.S. ban on trade with Cuba). Inspections at the country's borders or at hubs of transportation, such as airports, are used to enforce a ban.

A less drastic measure is a **trade quota**, which does not eliminate trade but sets limits on the quantity of a good that can be imported or exported. A quota on imports, by restricting supply, generally raises the price that can be charged for the good within the country. An import quota thus helps domestic producers by shielding them from lower-price competition. It hurts foreign producers because it limits what they can sell in the domestic market. Some foreign producers may, however, get some benefit in the form of additional revenues from the artificially higher price.

A third sort of policy—which has been used often throughout history and which is still the most widely used tool of trade policy—is a **tariff** (or "duty"). Tariffs are taxes charged on imports or exports.* Tariffs, like quotas, can reduce trade because they make internationally traded goods more costly to buy or sell. Like quotas, import tariffs benefit domestic producers while raising prices to consumers. Unlike quotas, however, import tariffs provide monetary benefit to the government that imposes them. Also unlike quotas, tariffs do not give foreign producers an opportunity to increase prices—in fact, foreign producers may be forced to lower prices in order to remain competitive with domestic producers that do not pay the tariff.

There are also various **nontariff barriers to trade** that can be imposed. These include the use of specific licensing requirements, standards, or regulations on imported goods that permit trade but may limit its extent.

The last important major category of trade-related policies—**trade-related subsidies**—may be used to either expand or contract trade. Export subsidies, paid to domestic producers when they market their products abroad, are motivated by a desire

trade ban: a law preventing the import or export of goods or services

trade quota: a restriction on the quantity of a good that can be imported or exported

tariffs: taxes on imports or exports

nontariff barriers to trade: use of licensing or other requirements to limit the volume of trade

trade-related subsidies: payments given by governments to producers to encourage more production, either for export or as a substitute for imports

---

* Often misunderstood, tariffs are taxes paid to the government of the importing country *by the importing company or entity*, not by the exporting country.

to *increase* the flow of exports. Countries can also use subsidies to promote a policy of **import substitution** by giving domestic producers extra payments to encourage the production of certain goods for domestic markets, with a goal of *reducing* the quantity of imports.

Government policies can also influence international capital transactions (financial flows). Central banks often participate in foreign exchange markets with policy goals in mind, buying or selling foreign currencies, as discussed in detail later in this chapter. Countries sometimes institute **capital controls**, which are restrictions or taxes on transactions in financial assets such as currency, stocks, or bonds, or on foreign owner-ship of domestic assets such as businesses or land. Restrictions on how much currency a person can take out of a country, for example, are one type of capital control. Such controls are usually instituted to try to prevent sudden, destabilizing swings in the movement of financial capital.

Countries may also regulate the form that foreign business investments can take. Some have required that all business ventures within their borders must be at least par-tially owned by domestic investors. Some have required that all traded manufactured goods include at least a given percentage of parts produced by domestic companies. Countries that have adopted such **domestic content requirements** include China, Indonesia, Mexico, and the Philippines. Sometimes such controls are related to a devel-opment strategy, while in other cases, they simply reflect a desire to avoid excessive foreign control of domestic economic affairs.

Some trade policies are enacted to try to attract foreign investment, for example by giving foreign companies tax breaks and other incentives. A popular form of this is the **foreign trade zone**, a designated area of the country within which many tax, tariff, and perhaps regulatory policies that usually apply to manufacturing are suspended. By attracting foreign investment, countries may hope to increase employment or gain access to important technologies. A well-known example is the *maquiladora* policy in Mexico under which manufacturing plants can import components and produce goods for export free of tariffs.

Migration controls are another important aspect of international policy. Countries generally impose restrictions on people who visit or move to their terri-tory, and a few also impose tight regulations on people when leaving the country. Although beliefs about race, national culture, and population size are often the most obvious concerns behind the shaping of these controls, economic interests also play a role. For example, policies may be affected by concerns about the skill composition of the domestic labor force or the desire to receive remittances from out-migrants.

Countries do not necessarily choose sets of policies that consistently lead toward openness or consistently toward "closedness." Often there is a mix—policies are chosen for a wide variety of reasons and can even be at cross purposes. Nor do countries choose their policies in a vacuum. Policy makers need to take into account reactions to their policies by foreign governments. Increasingly, they also need to pay attention to whether their policies are in compliance with international agreements.

import substitution: the policy of subsidizing domestic producers to make products that can be used in place of imported goods

capital controls: the regulation or taxation of international transactions involving assets

domestic content requirement: laws requiring traded goods to contain a certain percentage of goods produced by domestic companies

foreign trade zone: a designated area of a country within which foreign-owned manufacturers can operate free of many taxes, tariffs, and regulations

migration controls: restrictions on the flow of people into and out of a country

457

1.3 The European Union and Trade Policy

It is possible that you have not heard much about any of these trade policy tools discussed so far. Within the European Union, there are no tariffs, no quotas, no trade subsidies, no capital controls, and no migration controls. Regulations have increasingly been harmonized in order to reduce nontariff barriers. Hence, nowadays you can easily order a pair of shoes from a Spanish company and it will be delivered to your house anywhere else in the European Union without you having to pay tariffs or your shoes being delayed by customs controls.

Historically, the formation of the European Union goes back to the years after World War II. After two devastating world wars, the idea in the 1950s was to integrate the countries of Europe economically so that a new war would become materially impossible. A first step was laid out in the Schuman Plan of 1950. Robert Schuman, then foreign minister of France, proposed to place French and German steel production under a common High Authority. Building on this proposal, Germany, France, Italy, the Netherlands, Belgium, and Luxembourg in 1951 signed the Treaty of Paris and formed the European Coal and Steel Community.

In 1957, with the Treaty of Rome, these six countries went one step further and formed the European Economic Community (EEC). Under this arrangement, a 12-year-period was defined over which a number of steps were scheduled to be taken to more strongly integrate the members' economies. A customs union was to be created: Tariffs and quotas between members were set to be abolished, and a common external tariff introduced. The members also designed a common agricultural and transportation policy and agreed on means to ensure fair competition. They also created a pathway to the gradual elimination of obstacles to the free movement of people, capital, goods, and services.

The United Kingdom joined neither the European Coal and Steel Community nor the European Economic Community. In the case of the former, it feared loss of sovereignty, and British politicians criticized lack of democratic control. In the case of the latter, Britain preferred a free trade agreement to a customs union so that the nation could continue to vary national tariffs. The British government was also skeptical of having to contribute to a common agricultural policy. Moreover, the UK wanted to keep European integration decisively intergovernmental, with national governments as the main actors, while the Treaty of Rome gave a more prominent role to pan-European institutions such as the Commission and the European Parliament (originally named Parliamentary Assembly). As an alternative, Britain cofounded the European Free Trade Association (EFTA), a free trade area for industrial goods among (originally) the UK, Norway, Sweden, Denmark, Austria, Switzerland, and Portugal.

A **free trade area** and a **customs union** both remove tariffs between participating countries for goods produced within these countries. However, a customs union goes one step further: It also defines common tariffs toward the rest of the world. This has one important consequence: When goods move across borders within a free trade area, companies still need to go through customs procedures and prove that a certain minimum amount of value has been added within the member states of the free trade area (so-called "rules of origin"), as otherwise importers would chose the country

free trade area: a group of countries that have abolished tariffs and quotas for goods produced in the area and traded between these countries

customs union: a group of countries that have abolished tariffs and quotas among themselves, and have introduced a common external tariff

458

with the lowest external tariff to import into the free trade area, and then "jump" the tariff of the other member states. As you might imagine, it takes a lot of documentation to prove which overall share of value added of (for example) a car has been produced in a given country, as a number of parts might actually have been bought from other suppliers, which again might have bought components yet from other companies. In a customs union, companies do not need to prove that goods have been made within the customs union, and no customs controls between members are necessary.

During the 1960s, intraregional trade in the EEC expanded briskly, and the members experienced higher economic growth than Britain and the U.S. Despite problems in its decision-making mechanism, it was generally perceived as a success. In 1973, Britain, Ireland, and Denmark joined the EEC. In the 1980s, Greece, Spain, and Portugal, all having just ended a prolonged period of dictatorship, were admitted to the EEC.

In parallel, European politicians started to develop the internal market program. The vision was a single market in which goods, services, capital, and labor should be allowed to move freely (the so-called "four freedoms of the single market"). The Single European Act, signed in 1986, reduced nontariff barriers in a number of fields, harmonized regulation, and gave European institutions more powers to further the single market. This act was the first major revision of the Treaty of Rome. In 1993, the Maastricht Treaty went further and created the framework for the introduction of a common currency, the euro (see also Chapter 17). It also formally created the European Union, including integration in new fields such as justice and home affairs. Britain again kept a special role and negotiated opt-outs for important subjects such as the common currency or the Schengen area, a group of countries that have abolished passport controls among them.

The following decade saw a huge wave of new EU members as the fall of communism and the Iron Curtain changed the political scene in Europe. Austria, Finland, and Sweden joined in 1995. The Czech Republic, Estonia, Cyprus, Latvia, Lithuania, Hungary, Malta, Poland, Slovakia, and Slovenia joined in 2004, Bulgaria and Romania in 2007, and Croatia in 2013, bringing up the number of members to 28. In addition, the EU signed a number of free trade agreements and customs unions with other countries in Europe and nearby.

When the British voted to leave the EU in 2016, the Union had become much more than just a free trade agreement. In fact, when describing the EU, scholars often use the Latin term *sui generis*, meaning "of its own kind." It is a construction bearing resemblance both to a supranational organization and to a typical federal nation-state such as the U.S. or Germany. Financial markets are highly integrated and a bank based, for example, in Frankfurt can serve its customers around the whole union. Construction companies from Portugal are allowed to bid for and conduct construction in the Netherlands. Car companies such as Volkswagen or Peugeot have built complex supply chains, sourcing components from a dozen or more European countries.

Yet while the EU has led to a degree of regional economic integration unmatched anywhere else in the world, it is clearly not perfect. Some people criticize the decision-making processes as too complicated and undemocratic, or the regulations created by Brussels as too onerous. Others complain that the EU still lacks some of the economic policy tools usually available to a proper sovereign nation (such as the ability to borrow and run countercyclical fiscal policies) and has hence not been able to deal with the euro crisis adequately (the euro crisis is covered in depth in Chapter 17). Still others are wary of the very openness the EU has created. In the British referendum on whether to leave the EU, the fear of immigration from other EU countries, especially from former communist countries in Central and Eastern Europe, played an important role for voters.

1.4 Patterns of Trade and Finance

World Trade Organization (WTO): An international organization that conducts negotiations aimed at lowering trade barriers and mediates trade disputes between countries

International trade has grown immensely in recent years. Sometimes the sum of a country's imports and exports of goods and services, expressed as a percentage of GDP, is used as a measure of an economy's "openness." Growth in trade according to this measure is shown for 1960–2014 in Figure 14.1. As you can see, openness increased most sharply in the member states of the European Union but has also increased in other parts of the world.

Why has trade grown over time? The first reason is that many governments have, over time, lowered their tariffs and other barriers to trade. This fact is most visible in the European Union, where no tariffs or trade barriers between member states exist anymore. But it is a trend that is present elsewhere, too. Globally, the **World Trade**

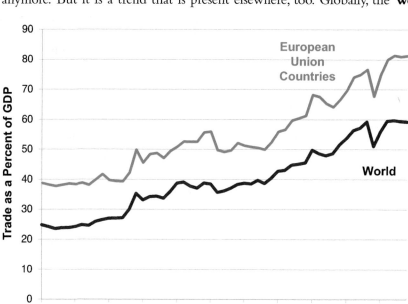

Figure 14.1 *Trade Expressed as a Percentage of Production, World and European Union Countries, 1960–2014*

The worldwide volume of trade, including both imports and exports, expressed as a percentage of global GDP, has been increasing over the past four decades. This trend has been especially strong in the European Union, the members of which are much more open than the world on average.

Source: World Development Indicators, World Bank, 2016.

Note: Since this measure includes both imports and exports, it does not mean that more than 50 percent of all produced goods and services in the world are traded—it counts the same goods both as exports from one country and imports to another.

Organization, with 163 member countries, conducts negotiations aimed at lowering trade barriers and mediates trade disputes between countries. The second reason is improvements in transportation technology. The costs and time lags involved in shipping products by air, for example, are far less now than in 1950. Fruit from South Africa and flowers from Colombia are now flown into the European Union every day—and are still fresh when they arrive. Container ships, first put into service in the late 1950s, have hugely reduced the costs of long-distance transport. Today, transporting a container of apparel from Shanghai to Rotterdam by boat (an almost 22,000-kilometer trip) is not much more expensive than transporting the same container from Rotterdam to Warsaw by truck (a trip of about 1,200 kilometers). The third reason for increased trade is advances in telecommunications. The infrastructure for phone, fax, and electronic communication has improved dramatically. Better telecommunications make it possible for many kinds of services, such as customer support and many technical functions, to be directly imported from, for example, call centers in India.

Figure 14.2 shows the volume of exports that the European Union sells to the top eight buyers of its goods and the volume of its imports that come from the top eight

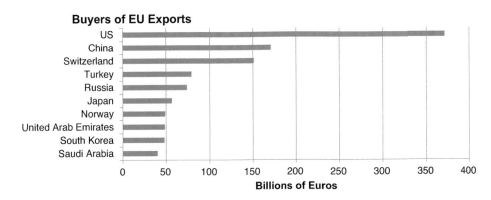

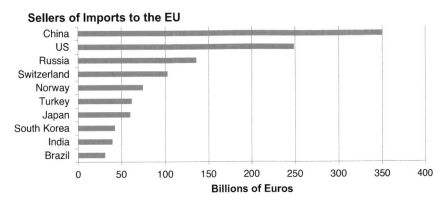

Figure 14.2 *Top Purchasers of Goods From the EU28 and Suppliers of Goods to the EU28, 2014*

The other two large players in world trade, the U.S. and China, are also the main trading partners of the EU.

Source: European Commission, Directorate General for Trade, 2016.

countries that sell to it. You see that the United States is the EU's most important trading partner, followed by China, and—with much smaller trade flows—Switzerland, Turkey, Russia, Japan, Norway, and the United Arab Emirates. On the import side, the most important suppliers for goods sold in the EU have been almost the same countries. The biggest development in recent years has been the emergence of China as a major source of EU imports. Until about 1980, EU trade with China was negligible. Since then, EU importation of Chinese products—especially electronics (including computers and televisions) as well as clothing, toys, and furniture—has boomed.

When we look at individual EU countries, we see that for all of them, trade with other EU countries makes up the most important part of external trade. In 2014, around 63 percent of all trade of EU member states was with other member states. Figure 14.3 portrays the share of trade with other EU countries for a number of

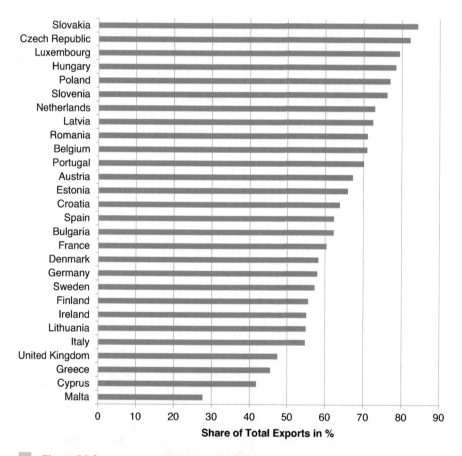

Figure 14.3 *Share of Exports to Other EU Countries as a Share of Total Exports, 2014*

In all EU countries, trade with other countries of the trading bloc is more important than with any other country of the world. In many cases, more than half of the trade is conducted within the EU.

Source: WTO, Country Trade Profiles, 2015.

European Union members. Even for countries at the lower end of the spectrum, the EU market accounts for roughly 50 percent of external trade. Note that Britain actually is at the lower end when it comes to integration with the rest of the continent. However, even for Britain, exports to the other EU member states accounted for roughly 43 percent of exports in 2014, and 55 percent of its imports came from EU partner countries.

The volume of global financial transactions has also exploded in recent years. For example, foreign exchange flows in 2013 averaged about $5.3 trillion (at that time about €4 trillion)—*per day*! This daily figure equates to more than $700 (€525) per person on earth. The volume in mid-2013 was almost four times what it had been in 2001.[1]

Discussion Questions

1. How do international linkages affect your own life? Can you give examples of the sorts of linkages listed in Section 1.1 that have had direct effects on you or your family?
2. Production of apparel has been widely globalized in recent years. Before going to class, check the labels on a number of items of clothing that you own. Which countries are represented?

2. THE TRADE BALANCE: COMPLETING THE PICTURE

How does trade affect the economy? It is certainly an important factor. Consumers who go to any shopping mall cannot help but notice that a large proportion of the goods are imported. Many jobs are in industries that depend on export markets. Tourists from abroad are an important economic factor in many European countries such as Greece, Spain, or Malta. Some people work in other countries than they live in and receive incomes from abroad, which they then spend at home. Again, others have made investments in other countries and receive income and dividends. All this influences the macroeconomy.

The total of imports, exports, and income flows from abroad is summarized in the **current account**. A current account surplus means that a country is receiving more funds by selling goods and services abroad and receiving incomes from abroad than it pays for buying goods and services and paying incomes to foreign workers and investors. A current account deficit means that the funds paid exceed the funds received.

Overall, the euro area currently has a current account surplus. In 2015, this surplus amounted to €329.5 billion, or almost 3 percent of GDP. The large surplus is mostly driven by the surplus in the German current account, which stood at 8.5 percent of German GDP in 2015 (€233.3 billion). On the other hand, there are some countries in the world that have large current account deficits. For example, Britain in 2015 reported a current account deficit of 4.3 percent of GDP (£96.2 billion).

current account: In the current account, all economic transactions other than financial transactions between residents and nonresidents are recorded. This covers sale and purchase of goods and services, income flows and current transfers.

463

2.1 The Circular Flow Revisited

Our current account balance is related to the circular flow discussed in earlier chapters. In this section, we look at the impact of our exports and imports on aggregate demand and GDP. We can introduce trade into our macroeconomic model by adding net exports (*NX*) into the equation for aggregate expenditure:

$$AE = C + I_1 + G + NX$$

As discussed in Chapter 5, net exports (*NX*) equals exports minus imports ($X - IM$). Exports, like intended investment (I_1) and government spending (*G*), represent a positive contribution to aggregate expenditure. More exports means more demand for domestically produced goods and services. Imports, however, are a negative in the equation. That means they represent a *leakage* from domestic aggregate expenditure—a portion of income that is not spent on domestic goods and services.

Negative net exports (when $X < IM$) therefore represent a net subtraction from demand for the output of domestic businesses and a net leakage from the circular flow. A decrease in exports (or an increase in imports) tends to reduce the circular flow of domestic income, spending, and output—unless injections such as intended investment and government spending counteract this contraction. An increase in net exports, on the other hand, encourages a rise in GDP and employment. For example, an increase in purchases of Chinese-made solar panels by euro-area residents and a decrease in purchases of domestic solar panels would lower aggregate demand in the euro area (and raise it in China). But an increase in foreign sales by French car companies would raise euro-area aggregate demand and employment.

Our basic macroeconomic model is completed by the inclusion of exports and imports. We started with a very simple economy, with just consumers and businesses, then added government spending, taxes, and the international sector. We now have a more complex model, with three leakages (saving, taxes, and imports) and three injections (intended investment, government spending, and exports). Imports are considered leakages because, like saving and taxes, they draw funds away from the domestic income-spending flow. Exports, like intended investment and government spending, add funds to the flow. We can modify our original circular flow diagram to show all these flows (Figure 14.4).

Leakages from the circular flow include taxes, saving, and imports. Injections include intended investment, government spending, and exports. The level of macroeconomic equilibrium will depend on the balance of all these flows as well as consumption levels.

Macroeconomic equilibrium involves balancing the three types of leakage with the three types of injection. A change in any one will alter the equilibrium level of output. The model that we have constructed allows us to understand how all these factors are related to levels of income and employment. We will put it to use shortly to explain how saving and investment are linked to the global economy. But first we look at the multiplier effects of exports and imports.

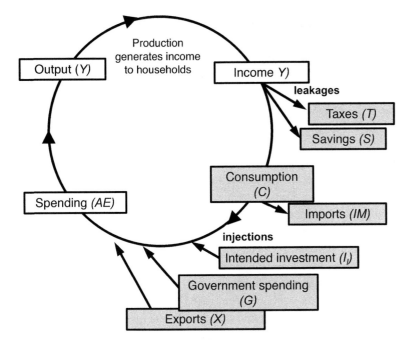

Figure 14.4 *Leakages and Injections in a Complete Macroeconomic Model*

Leakages from the circular flow include taxes, saving, and imports. Injections include intended investment, government spending, and exports. The level of macroeconomic equilibrium will depend on the balance of all these flows as well as consumption levels.

2.2 Effects on the Multiplier

The multiplier effect for an increase in exports is essentially the same as that for an increase in I_I or G. Using the same model as in Chapter 10 (with a multiplier of 5), an increase of exports of 40, for example, leads to an increase of 200 in economic equilibrium.

$$\Delta Y = mult \, \Delta X$$

We can use exactly the same logic for a lump-sum increase in imports—the effect on equilibrium income just goes in the opposite direction. An increase in imports of 40 would lower the equilibrium level of income by 200, and a decrease in imports of 40 would raise the equilibrium by 200.

The multiplier logic becomes a little more complicated, however, when we consider how import levels are determined. In general, when people receive more income in an open economy, they spend some of it on domestically produced goods and some on imports. The proportion spent on imports, as we noted, is a "leakage" that does not

465

add to domestic demand. If we want to account for this fully, we need to modify our multiplier logic. The effect is similar to that of a proportional tax on consumption: It tends to flatten the aggregate demand curve, for the same reason. When people receive additional income, a portion of it "leaks" away into imports. This portion does not stimulate the domestic economy, so multiplier effects are smaller, and the economic response is a bit less dynamic. Multipliers in the neighborhood of 4 or 5 are seldom observed in the real world, because *mpc* is affected not only by our marginal propensity to save but also by the rate of taxation and our marginal propensity to import. For a full treatment of this effect, see Appendix A1.

In an open economy, a portion of any aggregate demand increase goes to stimulate *someone else's economy* via imports. Thus French consumers who buy imported goods from Turkey are creating jobs and income in Turkey, not in France. Does this mean that imports are bad for France? Not necessarily. Two other factors are important to consider.

The first is that French consumers and French industry benefit from cheaper imported goods and services, raw materials, and other industrial inputs. The second is that at least some of the money spent on imports is likely to return to France as demand for exports, which, as we have seen, stimulates an increase in GDP and employment. More generally, the French economy, and overall quality of life in France, improves when other countries have healthier economies and diminishes when other countries are suffering economic setbacks. A prosperous world is a happier world for all. Thus, in the largest sense, if China or Turkey benefit from exporting to the euro zone, to some extent this benefits everyone. Problems can arise, however, when trade deficits (negative net exports) are too large for too long. We explore this issue further later in the chapter.

2.3 Balance Between Savings, Investment, and Net Borrowing

We can use our macro model to demonstrate that saving and investment are related not only to net exports but also to foreign lending and borrowing. Understanding this link is critical to making sense of much that happens in the global economy.

We start with the usual equation breaking down GDP into consumption, investment, and government spending. In addition, we follow the convention—seen earlier in Chapter 5—of breaking government spending down into "government consumption" and "government investment," which results in the following equation:

$$GDP = Personal\ consumption + private\ investment + government\ consumption$$
$$+ government\ investment + net\ exports$$

or

$$GDP = C + I_I + G_C + G_I + NX$$

Rearranging, we obtain

$$GDP - C - G_C = I_I + G_I + NX$$

Because saving is what is left over from income after spending on consumption (the left-hand side of the equation), if we combine private and government savings into a single term S_{total} and private and government investment into a single term $I_{total,}$ we get:

$$S_{total} = I_{total} + NX$$

or:

Total saving = Total investment + net exports

Thinking about these quantities in terms of marketable goods and services, this important identity says, intuitively, that goods and services that are produced in our domestic economy in excess of what we currently use for consumption can become investment goods—additions to our stock of manufactured assets (including replacement of depreciated assets)—or can be sold to foreign countries (in excess of the value of what we import from them).

Another way of understanding this is in terms of macroeconomic equilibrium. If, say, total domestic saving exceeded investment, a net leakage from the circular flow would occur. In order to obtain an equilibrium, this leakage would need to be offset by a trade surplus (an excess of exports over imports, creating a net injection). If total investment exceeded saving, the opposite would result—that is, there would be a trade deficit. In this case, the net leakage from an excess of imports over exports would balance the net injection caused by investment exceeding savings.

Yet another way to look at the relation of saving, investment, and trade is to think of how the various sectors *finance* their purchases of goods and services. In a contemporary economy, goods are rarely traded for goods; rather, money is used as a means of exchange. So, corresponding to any flow of goods and services transacted in exchanges, there is an equivalent flow of monetary funds.

Consider, for a moment, a closed economy. In this case, the last equation would reduce to:

$$S_{total} = I_{total}$$

This says that, in a closed economy, the total amount that is not spent on consumption goods is available for spending on investment goods. How does financial saving get turned into tangible investments?

In the national accounts, it is businesses, the government, and private households (for housing construction) that are counted as investing. They finance their investment expenditures either from their own savings, by borrowing someone else's savings, or by getting a loan of newly created money from their commercial bank. Household and corporate savings, in the form of income not spent on consumption and investment, can be made available for investment by other units—as when the funds in a household's bank deposit are lent to a business or a company buys government bonds. The "saving = investment" identity tells us that at an aggregate national level in a closed

467

economy, in the end, savings and investments will balance, as described in the Keynesian model of Chapter 9.

When we consider an open economy, things get more complicated. Now the country as a whole can also borrow from, or lend to, the foreign sector, and the relevant identity, as noted, is:

$$S_{total} = I_{total} + NX$$

If net exports are positive, we sell more goods abroad than we buy. How would people abroad pay for all our goods if the value of what we sell to them exceeds the value of what they sell to us? They are not earning enough from their sales to pay us! The main way for them to finance their purchases of our goods is by borrowing from us. They would need to borrow the amount by which our exports to them exceed our imports from them. So the identity can be (approximately) rewritten as:

$$S_{total} = I_{total} + net\ foreign\ lending$$

That is, if we had extra savings, above and beyond what is being used for domestic investment, we could lend it to foreigners so that they could buy our goods. This equation is only approximate, because foreigners can also get more goods and services from us than they sell to us by receiving our goods as gifts, paying for them out of transfer income, or selling us their assets, such as land or businesses, in return. We discuss these possibilities in greater detail in the next section.

While the euro area has recently tended to have positive net exports, some countries such as the United Kingdom and the United States have tended to have net exports that are negative—they tended to buy more from foreign countries than they sold. This means that they needed to borrow from foreign countries. The following identity means exactly the same thing as the last one but is easier to use to represent the recent UK or U.S. situation:

$$S_{total} = I_{total} - net\ foreign\ borrowing$$

When a country is in a situation of borrowing from abroad, then the amount the country is really "putting away for the future"—that is, saving—is less than what we would assume if we looked only at what the country is investing. Although the UK or the U.S. may be investing domestically, if they are using "net foreign borrowing" to obtain investment funds, they are also creating future indebtedness to other countries by borrowing from them.

Should we worry if a country has to borrow from foreigners? As in the case of your personal finances, it makes a difference what the purpose of the borrowing is. If the borrowing financed the purchase of productive new private or government investment goods, then it might be a way of actually improving the country's outlook for the future. As mentioned in Chapter 1, for many decades, international authorities encouraged poor countries to borrow heavily for development projects, using exactly this reasoning.

But if the funds borrowed went largely into investments that did not pay off financially, or if the borrowing only financed a high level of consumption, there would be reason to worry. A country that borrows a lot may be in trouble when it comes time to pay back its loans. In recent years, many poor countries have found themselves unable to pay the *interest* on the enormous foreign debts that they have built up over the years—much less repay the principal. In the euro area, some countries such as Spain have also borrowed heavily abroad, and much of the money went into (rather unproductive) real estate. The large foreign debt accumulated by countries such as Spain or Portugal most likely contributed to concerns about the countries' governments ability to continue servicing their debt during the euro crisis (which is covered in detail in Chapter 17).

Discussion Questions

1. What will be the likely effect of increased imports on euro-area GDP? Do imported goods undercut employment in the euro area? What other developments in the economy might counteract this effect?
2. Savings, imports, and taxes are all considered "leakages" from aggregate demand. Are they bad for the economy? Or is there an important function for each? How are their levels related to equilibrium GDP, income, and employment?

3. INTERNATIONAL FINANCE

In addition to trade in goods, countries are also linked through exchange of currencies, flows of income, and purchases and sales of real and financial assets across national borders. As we consider how international finance is related to trade and to domestic macroeconomic policies, the realization that "everything is linked to everything else" can become overwhelming. Most topics that we have discussed earlier in this book—such as supply and demand, interest rates, inflation, aggregate demand, and the Fed—will come back into play. In order to ease into the topic, we focus on relatively simple concepts and models, starting with the difference between purchasing power parity and currency exchange rates.

3.1 Purchasing Power Parity

Purchasing power parity (PPP) refers to the notion that, under certain idealized conditions, the **exchange rate** between the currencies of two countries should be such that the purchasing power of currencies is equalized. Consider, for example, the exchange rate between euros (€) and British pounds (£). As of mid-2016, €1 was worth about £0.83. Equivalently, we could say that one pound was worth €1.20. The two rates are inverses of one another. When we cite "the exchange rate" for the euro in terms of a foreign currency, what we mean is the number of units of the foreign currency that you can get in exchange for a euro.

If currencies could be traded freely against one another, if goods were freely traded across countries, and if transportation costs were not important, then there would be

purchasing power parity (PPP): the theory that exchange rates should reflect differences in purchasing power among countries

exchange rate: the number of units of one currency that can be exchanged for one unit of another currency

a strong logic to the theory of purchasing power parity. Suppose that a winter jacket costs €200 in Paris. If you lived in France and changed €200 into pounds, the theory of PPP says that the number of pounds you would receive in exchange for your euros should be exactly enough for you to buy the identical winter jacket in London. If, indeed, the jacket costs £166 (= €200 × 0.83 euros per pound) in London, PPP holds. If economies really were as smoothly integrated as we are assuming in our idealized world, an item (whether a winter jacket or an hour of labor services) should cost the same, no matter where you are.

If this were *not* true, there should be pressures leading toward change. For example, suppose that the jacket costs €200 in Paris and £166 in London, but the exchange rate is higher, at €1: £1. Why would anyone buy a jacket in Paris if, by changing their money into pounds, they could order it from London and save €34? For jackets to be sold in both locations—in this idealized world—the price in Paris would have to be bid down, the price in London would have to be bid up, or the exchange rate would have to fall.

Of course, in the real world, national economies are not nearly as integrated as this theory assumes. Transportation costs do matter; there are many varieties of goods; markets for goods and services do not work as quickly, smoothly, and rationally as sometimes assumed; and exchange rates are often "managed" (see Section 4.3). Any of these factors can mean that converting monetary amounts from one country to another using the prevailing exchange rates may be misleading. The fact that the price of a jacket is higher in London than in Paris might, for example, reflect a higher general cost of living in London.

purchasing power parity (PPP) adjustments: adjustments to international income statistics to take into account the differences in the cost of living across countries

Sometimes, we see comparisons of international income levels expressed "in PPP terms." Rather than simply using current exchange rates to convert all the various income levels into a common currency, **PPP adjustments** try to take into account the fact that the cost of living varies among countries. For example, converting Polish average per-capita income figures from złoty to euros would probably understate the living standard of the average Pole. Even though the conversion is "correct"—in the sense that there exists a złoty–euro exchange rate that can easily be used for such an adjustment—many of the goods and services in Poland are probably much less expensive than in locations in the euro area such as Paris or Munich. So the euro equivalent of what the average Pole earns each year goes much further in Poland.

The "Big Mac Index" published every year by *The Economist* is a somewhat light-hearted attempt to determine how much exchange rates and the price of goods vary from PPP predictions by comparing the prices (converted into dollars using market exchange rates) of a McDonald's hamburger across various countries. More sophisticated analysis uses a larger "basket" of goods to make such comparisons and estimate appropriate PPP adjustments.

3.2 Currency Exchange Rates

What makes exchange rates go up and down? Currencies are traded against each other all over the world, as people offer to buy and sell. The supply-and-demand model explained in Chapter 4 can be applied to foreign exchange markets once we realize that an exchange rate is really just another kind of price—a price for currency.

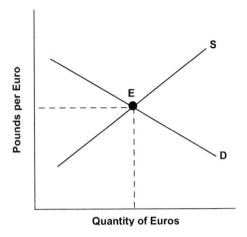

Figure 14.5 *A Foreign Exchange Market for Euros*

When currencies are traded against each other on a market, the "price" is the exchange rate, that is, the number of units of the other currency that are required to buy a unit of the currency in question.

Figure 14.5 shows an idealized foreign exchange market in which euros are traded for pounds. The quantity of euros traded is shown on the horizontal axis, and the "price" of a euro is given on the vertical axis, in terms of the number of pounds it takes to buy a euro.

In a well-behaved foreign exchange market, domestic residents largely determine the supply curve of euros by deciding how many euros they are willing to offer in order to buy foreign-produced goods and services and foreign assets. Because foreign-produced goods, services, and foreign assets must be paid for in the currency of the country from which they will be purchased, euros must be traded in the foreign exchange market. Professional currency traders and banks usually do the actual trading. The more pounds euro-area residents can get for their euros, the cheaper British items are to them, and the more they will want to buy from the UK rather than from euro-area producers. Thus, the higher the exchange rate, the more euros they will offer on the market. The supply curve slopes upward.

It is residents of other countries who largely determine the demand curve for euros. They may want to buy goods and services from the euro area or to invest in German, Spanish, or French bonds or businesses. To make these purchases, they must acquire euros. The more pounds, or other currencies, they have to *pay* to get a euro, the more likely they are to go somewhere other than the euro area for what they want, and the lower will be the quantity of euros that they demand. But if the euro is relatively cheap in terms of pounds, they will want to demand more euros. So the demand curve slopes downward. Market equilibrium is established at point E.

When currencies are traded against each other on a market, the "price" is the exchange rate, that is, the number of units of the other currency that are required to buy a unit of the currency in question.

471

currency depreciation: when a currency becomes less valuable, for example, due to a decrease in demand for a country's exports or an increase in its demand for imports

When the exchange rate falls, we say that the currency has **depreciated**. Suppose, for example, that a UK technology firm comes out with a new device for listening to music that everyone wants to buy. In their desire to obtain pounds to buy the good, people in the euro area will offer more euros on the foreign exchange market, shifting the supply curve to the right. Excess supply will, as in any other market, cause the price to fall, as shown in Figure 14.6. Commentators may say that the euro is now "weaker" against the pound. (Conversely, of course, the pound is now "stronger" against the euro.)

Similarly, an increase in demand for euro-area products or assets would lead to an **appreciation** of the euro. For example, if foreign investors became eager to buy Spanish real estate, the demand curve for euros would shift outward and the euro would appreciate—that is, gain in value. A currency may appreciate or depreciate relative to a specific currency, or it may appreciate or depreciate generally—that is, in relation to all or most other currencies.

currency appreciation: when a currency becomes more valuable, for example, when increased demand for a country's exports causes an increase in demand for its currency

Which factors are most responsible for the depreciation or appreciation of a country's currency? The first potentially important factor is relative prices. If prices in general rose more rapidly in the euro area than in, say, Japan (meaning that inflation is lower in Japan), the Japanese would be less interested in euro-area goods, *ceteris paribus*, and Europeans would be more interested in purchasing theirs. What this means

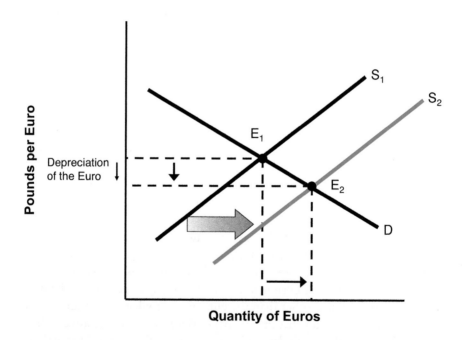

Figure 14.6 *A Supply Shift in a Foreign Exchange Market*

When people become more eager to sell a currency, this causes it to lose value, that is, to depreciate.

472

in terms of the foreign exchange market is that the euro area would supply more euros (in order to obtain yen to make purchases from Japan), and the Japanese would demand fewer euros to purchase our higher-priced goods.

A rightward shift in supply coupled with a leftward shift in demand unambiguously lowers the yen "price" of the euro, meaning that the euro would depreciate relative to the yen (and the yen would appreciate relative to the euro). Note that, in this example, the euro would not depreciate with respect to all other currencies—it would merely depreciate relative to the yen.

When people become more eager to sell a currency, this causes it to lose value, that is, to depreciate.

One might conclude from this discussion that countries that consistently import more than they export should have a persistently weak currency. The United States has, in fact, imported significantly more than it has exported for many years. Yet the value of the dollar not only has not collapsed but remains one of the most stable currencies.

How is this possible? Some economists highlight interest rates as a third key factor in determining exchange rates. If the interest rate on, say, the six-month U.S. Treasury bill were higher than the rate on comparable investments in other countries, the United States might attract flows of money from foreign investors seeking to exploit the interest rate differential. Because Treasury bills are denominated in dollars, the foreign money would be seeking to buy dollars, raising dollar demand. The result would be an appreciation in the value of the dollar. As a general rule, then, higher relative interest rates have a tendency to raise demand for the domestic currency and hence lead to a currency appreciation.

Yet it would be misleading to attribute dollar stability solely, or possibly even at all, to higher interest rates. For example, most countries set interest rates lower in the wake of the 2007–2008 financial crisis, and the United States, as we saw in Chapter 12, has been no exception to this trend. There is a more general foreign appetite for U.S. assets, such as government bonds, that explains the steady and reliable demand for dollars. It is a country's investment attractiveness (or lack thereof) that influences its currency exchange rate; the prevailing interest rate is merely one variable in what makes the country attractive to investors.

This conclusion also explains the sudden weakness of the pound just after the Brexit referendum described at the beginning of this chapter: As the British government had not presented a plan for how exactly Britain's relationship with the EU would look after Brexit, the referendum results created a lot of uncertainty for the British economy. After the Brexit decision, investors felt that UK assets in general were less attractive than they had been before. Hence, the demand for pounds dropped and the pound depreciated.

In addition to currency needs for trade and investment, many traders buy and sell currency for speculative reasons. As discussed in Chapter 4, sometimes people buy something not because they need it (e.g., in this case, for facilitating a trade in real items) but because they are betting that its price will go up or down in the future. Speculative buying and selling of currencies often plays a large role in foreign exchange markets.

473

Unfortunately, because the ability of a country to participate in global trade critically depends on its exchange rate, such "bets" have the potential to produce real economic effects that are not always beneficial. As the role of speculation grows in importance relative to other factors that influence exchange rates, the ability of financial decisions to affect entire economies—especially small, relatively vulnerable economies—only increases. The relationship between speculation and finance, on the one hand, and the "real" economy, on the other, is discussed in Chapters 7 and 11 and is explained further in Chapter 15.

As noted, different countries experience different levels of domestic inflation. To clarify, "inflation" refers to when a currency weakens in terms of domestic purchasing power (higher prices mean that the currency is worth relatively less), while "depreciation" is the weakening of currency in relation to other currencies (a reduction of its exchange rates). As you might expect, the two concepts are related, and what really matters for trade is the **real exchange rate** between currencies. A country with high inflation, for example, will generally experience a steady depreciation of its nominal (money value) exchange rate against the currencies of lower-inflation countries, even without any changes in demand for its items. Foreigners are willing to purchase the country's products at the higher prices resulting from inflation only if they receive more currency units per unit of foreign exchange that they offer, such that the real price remains the same.

Most foreign exchange transactions are made in "strong" currencies or currencies that other countries would generally not hesitate to accept as payment for goods and services or for some investments. The U.S. dollar tops the list, but the euro and the yen also qualify, and probably the British pound as well. Beyond this, the Swiss franc, famed for its remarkable stability, is also considered to be a member of this exclusive club. But the dollar, the euro, and the yen stand out as the top three. These currencies are often referred to as **foreign exchange** due to their general acceptability for foreign transactions.

Weak economies seldom if ever accept one another's currencies, and sometimes not even *their own* currency, as payment for goods, services, or assets. As will become clear, it benefits them to be paid in strong currencies. Thus the overwhelming majority of global currency trades are in dollars, euros, or yen.

3.3 The Balance of Payments

The flows of foreign exchange payments into and out of a country are summed up in its **balance-of-payments (BOP) account**. Table 14.1 shows the BOP account for the euro area in 2015 (tables for individual EU countries as well as other countries such as the UK are available on the companion Web site to this text). The top part of the table tallies the **current account**, which tracks flows arising from trade in goods and services, earnings, and transfers. The **trade account** (not shown separately in Table 14.1) refers exclusively to the portion of the current account related to exports and imports.

Various kinds of transactions lead to payments flowing into the region (and to a demand for euros in the foreign exchange market). When we export goods, we receive payments in return. So the first entry under current account credits is the €2,076.5 billion that the euro area earned from exports of goods. Exports of services

real exchange rate: the exchange rate between two currencies, adjusted for inflation in each country

foreign exchange: the class of currencies that is broadly acceptable by foreigners in commercial or investment transactions. Generally limited to three currencies—the dollar, the euro, and the yen.

balance-of-payments (BOP) account: the national account that tracks inflows and outflows arising from international trade, earnings, transfers, and transactions in assets

current account (in the BOP account): the national account that tracks inflows and outflows arising from international trade, earnings, and transfers

trade account (part of the current account): the portion of the current account that tracks inflows and outflows arising exclusively from international trade in goods and services

Table 14.1 Balance-of-Payment Accounts, Euro Area, 2015, in Billion €

Current and capital account

	Credits	Debits	Net
Goods and services account			
Goods	2076.5	1754.9	321.6
Services	765.1	698.8	66.4
Goods and services	2841.6	2453.7	388.0
Primary income account			
Compensation of employees	36.7	15.4	21.3
Investment income	571.7	538.6	33.1
Other primary income	38.6	18.3	20.4
Primary income	647.1	572.2	74.8
Secondary income account			
Secondary income	103.2	236.4	−133.2
Current account balance	*3591.9*	*3262.3*	*329.5*
Capital account			
Capital account balance			*−14.4*
Balance on the current and capital account			*315.2*

Financial account

	Change in assets	Change in liabilities	Balance
Financial account			
Direct investment	601.5	486.8	114.6
Portfolio investment	394.5	160.5	234.0
Financial derivatives etc.			70.5
Other investment	−263.5	-140.4	−123.2
Reserve assets	10.7		10.7
Total change in assets/liabilities			*306.6*
Net lending/net borrowing			*306.6*
Net errors and omissions			−8.5
Balance of Payments			*0.0*

Source: International Monetary Fund, Balance of Payment Statistics, 2016 (with authors' rearrangements).

(such as travel, financial, or intellectual property) also bring in inflows, as do incomes earned abroad (as profits or interest) by euro-area residents or social security payments made by non–euro-area governments to euro-area residents. Incomes received by an employee or from an investment are recorded under "primary income," while remittances (money sent home to families in the euro area from workers living outside the euro area), taxes, and cross-border social security payments are under "secondary income." All told, credits for the euro area from exports and incomes totaled €3,591.1 billion in 2015.

Other transactions lead to payments going abroad (and to a supply of euros to the foreign exchange market). When we import goods and services, we need to make payments to foreign residents. Foreign residents can take home incomes earned in the euro area. When euro-area governments pay development assistance to poor countries, this is also recorded as a debit in the BOP. All told, outflows of payments from the euro area (debits) in the current account totaled €3,262.3 billion in 2015.

The balance on the current account is measured as credits minus debits. Because credits exceeded debits on the current account in 2015, the euro area had a current account surplus. As you can see from Table 14.1, exports of goods and services exceeded imports, meaning that the euro area had also a positive trade balance, or trade surplus. Even though there was a deficit in the income account (as debits of secondary income were relatively large), this deficit was not enough to turn the overall current account into deficit. Hence, it was the trade surplus that largely accounted for the surplus in the current account of €329.5 billion.

Sometimes, the so-called capital account is lumped together with the current account. In this account, one-time transfers and acquisition and disposals of nonproduced, nonfinancial assets (such as mining rights) are recorded.[2] Examples of one-time transfers might be debt relief for a developing country or investment grants paid to a foreign government after a natural disaster such as a hurricane or an earthquake. As you see in the table, in the case of the euro area, these transactions are not very important. In 2015, the net capital account only amounted to minus €14.4 billion, so that even with these payments, the picture does not change: The euro area received much more in payments for goods, services, and income flows than it paid out.

Yet as you see in Figure 14.7, a sizable current account surplus is a rather new phenomenon for the euro area. In the 2000s, prior to the global economic and financial crisis, the euro area had an almost balanced current account, with minor deficits in some years and surpluses in others. In the global context, a relatively balanced current account is more the exception than the rule. Among the large economies, over the past two decades, we have seen that some countries such as China and Japan have consistently been running current account surpluses, while others such as the U.S. or the UK have run persistent trade deficits.

How can a country steadily import more than it exports? If you, personally, wanted to buy something that costs more than you have the income to pay for, you might take out a loan or perhaps sell something that you own, such as your bicycle or your car. Likewise, countries can finance a trade deficit by borrowing or by selling assets. These are the sorts of transactions listed in the **financial account**.

To the extent the euro area *lends* abroad (e.g., when the government extends loans to other countries, foreigners borrow from euro-area banks, or people in the euro area put money into a foreign bank account), the amount of assets the euro area holds

financial account (in the BOP account): the account that tracks flows arising from international transactions in assets

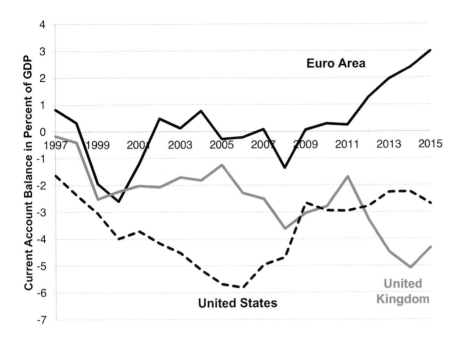

Figure 14.7 *Current Account Balance of the Euro Area, the U.S., and the UK, in Percent of GDP, 1997–2015*

For a long time, the current account of the euro area was roughly in balance. In contrast, the U.S. and the UK have been running persistent deficits.

Source: IMF World Economic Outlook Database, April 2016.

abroad increases. This is recorded as a positive number in the column of change of assets. Similarly, if a euro-area firm engages in **portfolio investment**—investment in the stocks or bonds of a foreign country or company—or **foreign direct investment (FDI)**—the amount of foreign assets held by euro-area residents increases.

In contrast, when a country needs to borrow abroad (e.g., to finance an excess of imports over exports), it increases its liabilities against foreigners. Again, this can happen either by directly borrowing from a foreign bank, by selling domestic bonds to foreigners, or by selling (parts) of domestic firms as portfolio investment or foreign direct investment to foreigners. For all these transactions, you find a positive number in the column on "change in liabilities" in the financial account.

Of course, a country can also pay for imports by selling foreign assets. If, for example, the UK has a current account deficit and needs to finance it, British firms could sell U.S. government bonds purchased in previous years. These transactions turn up as a negative change in assets in the financial account. As you see in Table 14.7, euro-area residents reduced their holdings of "other investments" (a miscellaneous category including bank deposits abroad and loans by euro-area banks to non–euro-area residents and firms) in 2015 by €263.5 billion.

Sometimes, the transactions in the financial account are also discussed as capital outflows and capital inflows. When a country lends abroad, capital *outflows* are generated.

portfolio investment: investment in stocks or bonds of a foreign country or company

foreign direct investment (FDI): investment in a business in a foreign country

477

This terminology may be confusing. Think about capital flows as going *in the direction of* the country that ends up with "the cash" or the power to purchase goods and *away from* the country that "buys something." In the case of a loan, the borrower received "the cash," while the creditor "buys" a bond or other security representing a promise to repay; thus a loan is an outflow from the lender and an *inflow* from the perspective of the borrower. Similarly, if a euro-area firm engaged in portfolio investment—investment in stocks or bonds—from a country outside of the area, or in foreign direct investment—the buying of all or part of a business in another country—it is the people abroad who would end up with "the cash," while the euro-area company would receive the asset. This is also counted as an outflow.

Capital outflows can have widely differing meanings and impacts, depending on where they occur. When a country with a large current account surplus such as Germany invests the proceeds from its exports abroad, this increases the country's claims against the rest of the world but does not necessarily have large negative impacts on the country itself. Weak, unstable economies are much more vulnerable to a specific kind of movement known as **capital flight**, which occurs when investors fear investment losses and rush to move their assets to "safer" countries (mostly the United States, Germany, Switzerland, and Japan). Capital flight may represent Wall Street investors rushing to take their money out of a weak country—as happened with South Korea, Indonesia, and the Philippines during the East Asian financial crisis of 1997—or the local wealthy elite seeking to take money out of their own country. In either case, capital flight has the potential to destabilize economies by making foreign exchange scarce, and governments will often go to great lengths to try to stop it (see Box 14.1).

There is another line in the financial account that we have not covered so far: the change in **reserve assets**. It represents the foreign exchange market operations of the country's central bank (the ECB in the euro area). Why the central bank? Here it is probably more helpful to imagine a somewhat smaller, less-developed country—say, Indonesia. Like any other country these days, it must import some goods and services from other countries. How can it pay for the imports? Its currency, the rupiah, will not do. Most exporters have little faith in the value of the rupiah and will insist on being paid in foreign exchange—that is, dollars, euros, or yen. This presents a problem for Indonesia, because it cannot produce its own dollars. It can, however, obtain them.

For example, when Indonesia exports coffee, it can insist on being paid not in rupiah but in foreign exchange such as dollars. In this way, it has a strong currency available to pay for its imports. It works the same way with the capital account. Indonesia has creditors to whom it owes interest every year (which is reflected in the income section of the current account) that require payment in foreign exchange. Yet Indonesia obtains this foreign exchange not only by exporting coffee and other products but also by attracting foreign capital, which it also insists takes the form of dollars, euros, or yen.

Bank Indonesia, the country's central bank, holds reserves of foreign currency so that it can make up for a balance-of-payments deficit if necessary. Of course, it cannot do so indefinitely. If the central bank runs short of foreign exchange reserves, the country will have to cut back on imports. But in the short term, the central bank can supply foreign exchange to cover a balance-of-payments deficit or acquire foreign

capital flight: rapid movement of capital assets out of a country

reserve assets: a line in the financial account reflecting the foreign exchange market operations of a country's central bank

478

exchange if there is a balance-of-payments surplus. If the central bank supplies foreign exchange, it is recorded as a positive item in the official reserve accounts; if it acquires foreign exchange, it is recorded as a negative item.

BOX 14.1 ARGENTINES TURN CASH INTO CONDOS IN MIAMI

In 2012, brokers selling Miami real estate found that some of their best clients were from Argentina. Argentines were rushing to move their money out of their country and into real estate in Miami and New York. A weakening Argentinian peso and 25 percent inflation led many affluent Argentines to move their money into American real estate by expensive, even sometimes illegal means.

Capital outflow from Argentina nearly doubled from $11.4 billion to $21.5 billion between 2010 and 2011. The Argentine government instituted capital controls to try to stop the outflow, requiring special permits to convert pesos into dollars. Trained dogs were even used to sniff out dollars at ports, airports, and border crossings. Some Argentines were willing to pay a black-market premium of up to 40 percent to convert their money into dollars.

At first, the government controls appeared to have succeeded. Capital flight from Argentina fell to $3.57 billion in the first half of 2012 from $11.7 billion in the second half of 2011. However, the success proved to be only temporary: The Argentinian population grew increasingly discontented with the governments' interventions in the economy, and in 2015 Mauricio Macri was elected president with an explicit platform of economic liberalization. Shortly after taking office, Macri dismantled the capital controls, as promised in the election campaign.

Source: Charles Newbery, "Argentines Turn Cash into Condos in Miami," *New York Times*, September 13, 2012 and other media sources.

Especially in the past two decades or so, changes in foreign reserves often also signal central banks' intervention in the foreign exchange market. For example, for a long time, China's central bank has attempted to keep the renminbi, its national currency, cheap against the U.S. dollar in order to boost exports. To this end, it has printed renminbi and bought hundreds of billions of dollars in U.S. government bonds. As U.S. government bonds held by the Chinese central bank are counted as reserve assets, this would have been recorded as a change in reserve assets in the financial account.

The balance on the financial account is measured as change in assets minus change in liabilities. Thus, the euro area had a €306.6 billion capital account deficit in 2015, meaning that in net terms, euro-area residents have invested more than €300 billion abroad.

One final item is **net errors and omissions**. This represents the inability of statistical authorities to make the accounts balance precisely, given problems in the quality of the data and some small items in the accounts that we do not get into here. Net errors and omissions are included so that the balances of the current account plus the capital account equal exactly the balance of the financial account.

479

4. MACROECONOMICS IN AN OPEN ECONOMY

In earlier chapters, our discussion of how fiscal and monetary policy can be used to influence aggregate demand was limited to a "closed" economy. We are now ready to consider a more complete picture of the effects of such policies. The bottom line of what is laid out in Sections 4.1 and 4.2 is simple to state: The intended effects of monetary policy are strengthened, or amplified, by interactions with the foreign sector, while trade with foreign partners may either strengthen or weaken fiscal policy actions. The reasons why this is so are, however, rather complex. The value of working through them, as we shall do, is that it is a way of showing in action some of the principles of macroeconomic supply and demand that have been laid out thus far.

4.1 Fiscal Policy

Recall from our earlier concept of a macroeconomic equilibrium that, for equilibrium to be present, injections must equal leakages. We know from Chapter 10 that a budget deficit is a net injection because it occurs when government spending (injection) is greater than tax revenue (leakage). If we assume that private savings and investment are in balance, a government budget deficit requires a net leakage from the foreign sector for macroeconomic equilibrium to be achieved—that is, imports must exceed exports (again, disregarding for now the transfers and net income).

In other words, a government's budget balance is correlated with the country's trade balance—a government deficit, not financed from domestic savings, implies a trade deficit. But what is the economic mechanism by which they are related? A country's budget balance can influence its trade balance through at least two separate channels, each related to the exchange rate of its currency.

First, we have seen that deficit spending has the potential, in economies at or near full employment, to lead to higher interest rates—either through the classical argument of crowding out or through the central bank reacting to growing inflationary pressure with rate hikes. In an open economy, the higher interest rates are likely to attract more foreign investment in the form of bond purchases. If foreigners demand more euro-area bonds as a result of their higher interest rates, the demand for euros increases (because euro-area bonds are all denominated in euros). The resulting increase in demand for euros, *ceteris paribus*, leads to an appreciation of the euro compared to other currencies.

We have also seen that a stronger currency makes a country's goods relatively more expensive in the global markets. In other words, if the euro appreciated, we would expect the euro area to be able to export less than before. At the same time, imports would increase, because a stronger euro makes other countries' goods (denominated in their currencies) appear cheaper. Through this sequence, an increase in the budget deficit might increase the size of the trade deficit.

Notice, however, that while both deficits grow, the economic effect of the rising trade deficit is to offset the expansionary effect of the budget deficit. Imports (leakage

480

from the circular flow) increase, while exports (injection) decrease. Because we do not know the magnitude of each of these changes, we are *not* saying that the open economy effect cancels out the original effect of the fiscal stimulus. What we can say is that it probably dampens its effect somewhat.

The other channel is a more direct consequence of the fiscal expansion. Deficit spending boosts aggregate demand, increasing spending and generating greater employment and more income. Yet as the economy grows, *all* spending grows, including spending on imports. The greater demand for imports increases the global supply of euros, as euro-area residents demand more foreign currency to purchase imports. This causes the euro to depreciate, reversing the process, because a weaker euro results in more exports and less imports.

Depreciation of the euro will tend to narrow the trade deficit, resulting in a net injection to the circular flow and *reinforcing* the initial fiscal stimulus. Since the two effects we have described go in opposite directions, we cannot say anything specific about the magnitude of the changes, nor can we say overall whether the "open economy" on balance reinforces or countervails the domestic fiscal policy. But we can say that the effect of deficit spending is complicated by consideration of foreign-sector effects.

4.2 Monetary Policy

In Chapter 12, we discussed monetary policy in a closed economy. In an open economy, monetary policy is more effective in changing aggregate demand because, unlike fiscal policy, its global effects unambiguously reinforce the domestic policy.

Suppose that the ECB believes the euro-area economy needs a boost and lowers interest rates in an attempt to stimulate aggregate demand. As we saw in Chapter 12, the decrease in interest rates should encourage investment spending. But in an open economy, the fall in interest rates should also increase net exports, another component of aggregate demand.

This is because a reduction in euro-area interest rates is likely to drive away some foreign financial capital. If interest rates here fell, people abroad would be less inclined to buy euro-area government bonds or put their money in euro-area bank accounts. As they sent their financial capital elsewhere, the demand for euros would decrease. This would be portrayed as a leftward shift of the demand curve in the foreign exchange market. As discussed earlier (refer to Figure 14.4), a decrease in the demand for euros would cause the euro to depreciate.

A depreciation in the euro means that a euro now buys fewer units of foreign exchange, which, you will recall, discourages spending on imports. Meanwhile, the fact that a euro can be purchased for fewer units of foreign exchange means that euro-area exports become "cheap" for foreign buyers. Exports should increase. Because it is demand for euro-area–produced goods and services minus imports that enters into aggregate demand, the latter rises. Thus, both an increase in exports and a decrease in imports have the effect of raising aggregate demand.

The openness of the economy can be thought of as adding an extra loop to the chain of causation discussed in Chapter 12, as illustrated here:

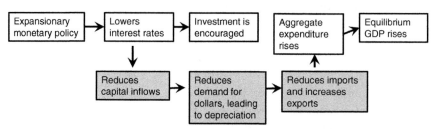

Yet this is not the end of the story. Just as in the earlier case of deficit spending, an increase in aggregate demand tends to produce an increase in imports. As we have seen, this leads to euro depreciation, as euro-area residents trade euros for other currencies so that they can purchase imported products.

Here, also, the effect is to reinforce the initial domestic stimulus, since a weaker euro tends to narrow the trade deficit that, as we have seen, increases aggregate demand, *ceteris paribus*. So in contrast to the fiscal policy case, where "opening up" the economy produces ambiguous effects in relation to a domestic fiscal stimulus, for monetary policy, the international trade consequences clearly reinforce the domestic policy. A monetary stimulus, in other words, is amplified in an open economy. We should note that a monetary contraction would *also* be magnified; the same causal mechanisms would be in effect, only in reverse.

4.3 Managed Versus Flexible Foreign Exchange

So far, we have assumed that exchange rates are determined by market forces, as modeled in Figure 14.5. In a **flexible** or **floating exchange rate system**, countries allow their exchange rates to be determined by the forces of supply and demand. But this is not always the case.

flexible (floating) exchange rate system: a system in which exchange rates are determined by market forces of supply and demand

Flexible exchange rates can create significant uncertainties in an economy. A manufacturer may negotiate the future delivery of an imported component, for example, only to find that exchange rate changes make it much more expensive than expected to complete the deal. Foreign exchange markets can also be susceptible to wild swings from speculation. A mere rumor of political upheaval in a country, for example, can sometimes create a rush of capital outflows as people try to move their financial assets into foreign banks, causing a precipitous drop in the exchange rate. Or an inability to obtain short-term foreign loans may send an economy into crisis—and its exchange rate swinging—even if over a longer period the economy would be considered financially sound. It can be hard to maintain normal economic activities when exchange rates fluctuate wildly.

fixed exchange rate system: a system in which currencies are traded at fixed ratios

Many countries have tried to control the value of their currencies in order to create a more predictable environment for foreign trade. The strictest kind of control is a **fixed exchange rate system**. In this case, a group of countries commits to keeping their currencies trading at fixed ratios over time. Starting in 1944, many countries, including the United States, had fixed exchange rates under what is known as the **Bretton Woods system** (named after the international monetary conference in Bretton Woods, New Hampshire, that created a postwar financial order including the International Monetary Fund and the World Bank).

The exchange rates in such a system, however, do not usually remain perfectly fixed. For one thing, it is impossible to literally fix an exchange rate, because the central bank would need to have perfect (and *continuously* perfect) information about all trades. What the countries that participated in the Bretton Woods conference did—and countries today that fix their currency generally do—is set a "band" or range around a "target rate" and allow the "fixed" rate to fluctuate within this band. In the case of the countries that were part of the Bretton Woods system, the band was very narrow—on the order of plus or minus 1 percent.

Over the long term, the target rate within the band can change, at the government's discretion. When a government lowers the level at which it fixes its exchange rate, what is called a **devaluation** occurs, and when it raises it, a **revaluation** takes place. But the system can be undermined if there are too many changes, and when key currencies such as the dollar come under too much selling pressure, a fixed exchange rate system can break up. This is what happened to the Bretton Woods system in 1972. The U.S. dollar had been the linchpin of the system and had been convertible to gold. When the United States suffered large currency outflows, the U.S. eliminated gold convertibility and allowed the currency to float, which was quickly followed by other major countries floating their currencies also.

After the Bretton Woods system ended, many countries moved to a "floating" system, while others tried to exert some management over their currencies. Such management is performed by trying to maintain certain target exchange rates, by "pegging" the currency to a particular foreign currency, or by letting it "float" but only within certain bounds (something like the Bretton Woods system, only with a much wider band).

How does a country keep its exchange rate fixed, or at least within bounds? A government has at its disposal two main tools. The first is imposing capital controls. For example, a country that wants to limit foreign exchange trading may require that importers apply for licenses to deal in foreign exchange or impose quotas on how much they can obtain. By only allowing highly regulated transactions, it can control the prices at which exchange transactions are made.

The second is **foreign exchange market intervention**. As we saw earlier in our discussion of official reserve accounts, central banks have the power to intervene in foreign exchange markets. They may do this under a floating exchange rate regime, with the object of raising or lowering the rate, or to build up or lower their holdings of foreign exchange. When a country is committed to a fixed exchange rate, it is the responsibility of the central bank to respond to upward or downward pressures on the rate with appropriate intervention in order to keep the rate at the prescribed level.

To see how intervention works, consider Figure 14.8. Suppose that the government would like to keep the exchange rate of its domestic currency at (or above) the level e^*, but market pressures are represented by the curves S_{market} and D_{market}. At the exchange

Bretton Woods system: a system of fixed exchange rates established after World War II, lasting until 1972

devaluation: lowering an exchange rate within a fixed exchange rate system

revaluation: raising an exchange rate within a fixed exchange rate system

foreign exchange market intervention: an action by central banks to buy or sell foreign exchange reserves in order to keep exchange rates at desired levels

483

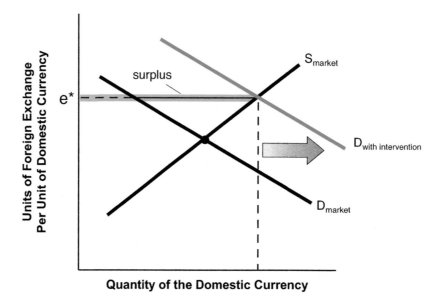

Figure 14.8 *Foreign Exchange Intervention*

In order to keep the exchange rate at the target level e*, the central bank has to buy up the surplus of domestic currency, using in payment its reserves of foreign exchange.

rate e^*, there is an excess supply (surplus) of domestic currency, and so there is pressure on the exchange rate to fall. The central bank must artificially create more demand for the domestic currency, as shown by demand curve $D_{\text{with intervention}}$. It does this by going into the market and exchanging foreign currency for domestic currency—essentially "soaking up" the surplus domestic currency.

The problem is that the central bank can do this only as long as it has sufficient reserves of foreign exchange on hand. If it ran out of foreign exchange, it would be unable to support the currency and be forced to devalue. This is, in fact, fairly common among countries with deficits in their current accounts and an insufficient surplus in the financial account to cover these deficits, and in some cases it leads to a **balance-of-payments crisis**.

balance-of-payments crisis: when a country gets precariously close to running out of foreign exchange and is therefore unable to purchase imports or service its existing debt

Is devaluation a bad thing? The answer to this question is complex. Devaluation is generally thought to be good for exporters, because it makes the country's goods cheaper abroad. But it also means that people in the country will find that imports are now more expensive. And if firms or households have borrowed in foreign currency (as is the case in many developing countries), a depreciation increases the value of this debt in local currency and might push them into default. Because of the potential problems resulting from currency devaluation, many economists have grown cautious about recommending devaluation as a cure for international imbalances.

In contrast, a country can keep its exchange rate *lower* than market forces would dictate by creating domestic currency (either by physically printing currency or by creating central bank reserves by a stroke of a key) and selling it on international financial markets and amassing large amounts of foreign reserves. As mentioned, China has recently used this tactic, keeping the value of its currency, the renminbi, artificially low to stimulate exports. (The value of renminbi is often cited in terms of its most common unit, the yuan). China has, in the process, become a large holder of U.S. dollars as well as other currencies. China has been under pressure from many countries to revalue the renminbi (see Box 14.2).

One complication with fixed exchange rates is that they make it difficult for a country to conduct independent monetary policy. If investors are allowed to move funds freely into and out of the country, the central bank cannot control the domestic interest rate anymore. Hence, if a central bank keeps its exchange rate fixed relative to another currency, the interest rates in the two countries will tend to move together and might not always be appropriate for the country in question.

The adoption of the euro by some member countries of the European Union is a dramatic recent example of fixed exchange rates, as it did not just fix the value of a national currency in another currency but abolished national currencies altogether. We will discuss in greater detail in Chapter 17 on the euro crisis the reasoning behind this step and the problems the euro-area countries have encountered with getting rid of exchange rates between them.

BOX 14.2 UNITED STATES PRESSURES CHINA TO REVALUE ITS CURRENCY

For some time, the United States has put pressure on China to revalue its currency. In May 2012, the U.S. Treasury Department said that China had made progress in allowing its currency to rise against the dollar. This finding averted a formal charge of currency manipulation and a likely trade dispute. But the Treasury still considered China's currency, the renminbi, to be undervalued, meaning that it needed to appreciate further against the dollar.

The renminbi gained 8 percent against the dollar between 2010 and 2012. A currency with a lower value gives China a trade advantage by making its exports cheaper and imports from the United States more expensive. Some American manufacturers have urged the administration to take punitive steps to force China to allow the renminbi to trade freely. The renminbi now trades within a narrow range against the dollar.

The U.S. trade deficit with China was $315 billion in 2012. The continuing trade deficit means that the issue of currency valuation will continue to be a point of dispute between the two countries, with some U.S. legislators urging stronger action to force China to revalue.

Source: Associated Press, "Citing Gains, United States Doesn't Call China Currency Manipulator," May 25, 2012.

5. INTERNATIONAL FINANCIAL INSTITUTIONS

World Bank:
an international agency charged with promoting economic development through loans and other programs

International Monetary Fund (IMF):
an international agency charged with overseeing international finance, including exchange rates, international payments, and balance-of-payments management

The Bretton Woods system of fixed exchange rates was only one aspect of the international financial structure established in the 1940s. Also formed during this period were the International Bank for Reconstruction and Development (IBRD), later expanded into the **World Bank,** with the goal of promoting economic development through loans and programs aimed at poorer countries, and the **International Monetary Fund (IMF),** established to oversee international financial arrangements. Although fixed exchange rates among the major currencies have been abandoned, the World Bank and the IMF continue—with considerable controversy—to play significant roles in international affairs.

When it was created, the IMF was charged with overseeing exchange rates, international payments, and balance-of-payments management and with giving advice to countries about their financial affairs. The IMF has a complicated governance structure based on voting shares allocated to member countries, but in fact its policy making has historically been dominated by the United States and certain countries in Europe. The IMF recently restructured its voting system to give China, South Korea, Turkey, and Mexico slightly larger shares. Both the World Bank and IMF have their headquarters in Washington, DC.

When a country is in financial trouble—for example, when it is unable to pay the interest that it owes on its foreign debts or is experiencing wild swings in its exchange rate—the IMF (in conjunction with the World Bank, if the country is poor) often advises the government on how to remedy the problem. The IMF has tended to encourage low- and middle-income countries with debt problems to remove their barriers to trade and capital flows, arguing that such liberalization promotes economic growth. The countries are also advised to minimize the size of their government and its expenditures as a way to reduce the need for borrowing. They are told to keep their inflation rates down and are often advised about their exchange rate policies as well.

Washington Consensus: specific economic policy prescriptions used by the IMF and World Bank with a goal of helping developing countries to avoid crisis and maintain stability. They include openness to trade and investment (liberalization), privatization, budget austerity, and deregulation.

The policy prescriptions of trade liberalization, privatization, deregulation, and small government became known during the 1980s and 1990s as the **Washington Consensus** (described in more detail in Chapter 17). The policies have also become the source of much controversy, as many economists have come to believe that rigid, "one-size-fits-all" application of such policies often works against rather than for human welfare and international stability (see Box 14.3).

Although the lending power of the IMF gives it considerable say in the affairs of many countries—for better or worse—the powers of any international organization are limited, especially with regard to the countries that are larger and more powerful. For example, many commentators worry about issues such as the undervalued Chinese renminbi/yuan or the volume of foreign debt being taken on by the United States, but there is currently no international institution with the power to force China or the United States to change their policies. The IMF was also unable to prevent the rapid development of the global financial crisis in 2008–2009, although it played a role in putting together bailout packages for some countries after the crisis. While the IMF was involved in lending to Greece and other countries affected by the euro crisis (see Chapter 17), it often was not able to impose its own wishes on the group of creditors.

486

BOX 14.3 THE IMF AND THE ARGENTINE DEFAULT

In December 2001, the Argentine government announced a moratorium on payments on its $155 billion in public foreign debt. This default—at the time the largest by a sovereign nation in history—rocked the international financial world. Was there more that the IMF could have done to prevent this? Or might IMF advice have been part of the reason that the default occurred?

In 1991, Argentina had pegged its currency to the U.S. dollar as a way of bringing hyperinflation to a halt. The IMF, believing that this would lead to more discipline in Argentine policy making, approved the peg. But with the dollar strong against the currencies of Europe and Brazil, Argentina's major trading partners, the peg made Argentina's exports expensive. This discouraged Argentine industry and encouraged the purchase of imports. Trade deficits resulted, financed by borrowing from abroad. Unemployment rose.

The IMF advised the Argentine government to address its financial issues by cutting back on government expenditures and privatizing its social security program. The country's leaders complied, even though the economy was in a downturn. The IMF encouraged Argentina to institute free trade policies, though major markets in the United States and Europe remained closed to its exports. Meanwhile, financial crises in Asia, Mexico, and Brazil made investors more nervous about lending to middle-income countries. The fact that the Argentine economy was visibly struggling caused foreign lenders to demand higher interest rates to compensate them for the risk of default. This, in turn, made the debt even harder to bear, in a vicious circle.

In December 2001, the situation reached a crisis. With official unemployment nearing 20 percent, people demonstrated in the street, which led the government to fall. Unable to make its debt payments, the interim government announced the default. The Argentine economy continued in a downward slide well into 2002.

Some commentators have blamed the default on corruption and mismanagement by the Argentine government and suggested that the crisis might have been avoided if the government had cut its expenditures even *more*. Others, observing that the government budget deficit was actually of a quite reasonable size (less than 3 percent of GDP), believe that inappropriate IMF advice is at least as much to blame. Basic principles of macroeconomics say that a government should raise—not lower—spending during a recession, but the IMF policies went in the opposite direction, pushing the economy into a downward spiral. According to this view, given IMF advice, default was only a matter of time.

Source: Joseph E. Stiglitz, "Argentina, Shortchanged: Why the Nation That Followed the Rules Fell to Pieces," *Washington Post*, May 12, 2002, and other news sources.

Many observers are currently calling for reforms in the international financial system and perhaps for new international institutions. Dissatisfaction over the IMF prescriptions for liberalization has caused some changes within the organization itself. But some argue that these changes are not sufficient and that more radical changes are necessary. Suggestions include greater regulation of international

487

banking, substantial reforms, and increased transparency in multinational corporate governance, restrictions on short-term capital flows, a tax on speculative transactions in foreign exchange (see Chapter 15), and establishment of an international bankruptcy court.

DISCUSSION QUESTIONS

1. To check your understanding of international linkages, consider the following hypothetical scenario. Suppose that people overseas become less interested in buying euro-area government bonds (perhaps because they start to think of them as less secure). What would be the effect on:
   a. The BOP financial account?
   b. The supply or demand for euros?
   c. The value of the euro?
   d. The BOP current account?
2. Have international trade or financial imbalances or actions of the IMF been in the news lately? What are the current controversies?

REVIEW QUESTIONS

1. In what seven ways are economies connected internationally?
2. List four policies related to international trade.
3. List two policies related to international capital transactions.
4. Briefly describe the recent history of the EU and world trade, and list the major European trading partners.
5. What are some international organizations and agreements dealing with trade relations?
6. List six reasons why countries often limit trade.
7. What is the theory of "purchasing power parity"?
8. Who creates the supply of a currency on the foreign exchange market? Who creates the demand?
9. Draw a carefully labeled graph illustrating a depreciation of the euro against the dollar.
10. What are the two main accounts in the balance-of-payment account, and what do they reflect?
11. How and why is an imbalance (surplus or deficit) in the current account related to an imbalance in the capital account?
12. Does having an open economy make monetary policy stronger or weaker? Why?
13. What is the effect of an open economy on fiscal policy?
14. Distinguish between floating and fixed exchange rate systems.
15. How and why might a central bank "intervene" on a foreign exchange market?
16. What is the "Washington Consensus"?
17. What reforms have been suggested for the international financial system?

EXERCISES

1. Singapore is a natural-resource-poor country that has built its economy on the basis of massive imports of commodities and raw materials and similarly massive exports of refined and manufactured goods and services. In Singapore, exports are 178 percent of GDP! But how can a country export *more* than its GDP? (Hint: Remember that imports are subtracted to obtain the measure of *net exports* that is part of GDP.)

2. Classify each of the following as a *trade flow, income flow,* or *asset transaction*:
   a. A U.S. software company sells its products to European consumers
   b. A Saudi investor buys real estate in Europe
   c. A British retailer imports Chinese-made appliances
   d. A worker in the UK sends some of her wages back to her family in India
   e. A Polish manufacturer pays interest on a loan from an Austrian bank

3. Suppose that, due to rising interest rates in the euro area, the Japanese increase their purchases of European securities.
   a. Illustrate in a carefully labeled supply-and-demand diagram how this would affect the foreign exchange market and the exchange rate expressed in terms of yen per euro.
   b. Is this an appreciation or depreciation of the euro?
   c. Would we say that *the yen* is now "stronger"? Or "weaker"?
   d. If the rise in interest rates was due to a deliberate ECB policy, does this international connection make such policy more or less effective? Explain in a few sentences.

4. Determine, for each of the following, whether it would appear in the *current account* or *financial account* section of the euro-area balance-of-payments accounts and whether it would represent an *inflow* or an *outflow.*
   a. Payments are received for airplanes made in the euro area and sold to Thailand
   b. A resident of Nigeria buys a German government bond
   c. A French company invests in a branch in Australia
   d. A Japanese company takes home its profits earned in the Netherlands
   e. The Italian government pays interest to a bondholder in Britain

5. Match each concept in Column A with a definition or example in Column B.

Column A	Column B
a. Tariff	1. Makes international incomes comparable by accounting for differences in the cost of living
b. Current account	2. A rise in the value of a currency in a floating exchange rate system
c. Currency appreciation	3. An organization charged with providing loans for development
d. Purchasing power parity adjustment	4. Investing in a foreign business
e. Balance-of-payments crisis	5. Tracks flows arising from trade, earnings, and transfers
f. Quota	6. A tax put on an internationally traded item

(Continued)

489

Column A	Column B
g. Nontariff barriers to trade	7. When a country runs short of foreign exchange
h. World Bank	8. A rise in the value of a currency under a fixed exchange rate system
i. International Monetary Fund	9. Using measures such as standards and licensing to restrict trade
j. Capital controls	10. When a central bank buys or sells foreign exchange
k. Revaluation	11. A fall in the value of a currency under a floating exchange rate system
l. Foreign direct investment	12. Putting a quantity limit on imports or exports
m. Currency depreciation	13. Government intervention to reduce or eliminate international capital flows
n. Foreign exchange market intervention	14. An organization charged with overseeing international finance

APPENDIX: AN ALGEBRAIC APPROACH TO THE MULTIPLIER IN A MODEL WITH TRADE

Just as we modified the multiplier in the appendix to Chapter 10 to take account of the impact of taxes, we can now go a step further to consider the effect of trade. Suppose that, in addition to consumption's depending on income, imports depend on income according to the equation $IM = mpim\ Y$, where $mpim$ is the marginal propensity to import (the proportion of additional income spent on imports). The $mpim$ is a fraction. Starting with the equation for aggregate expenditure with a proportional tax that we had derived in the appendix to Chapter 10, we can get an equation for aggregate expenditure in an economy including trade, as follows:

$$AE = C + I_I + G + X - IM$$
$$= \bar{C} + mpc(Y - tY + TR) + I_I + G + X - mpim\ Y$$
$$= (\bar{C} + mpc\ TR + I_I + G + X) + [mpc(1-t) - mpim]\ Y$$

The AE curve now has the intercept given by the first term in parentheses. Changes in exports shift the curve upward or downward. The new slope is given by the term in brackets. The slope is flatter due to the subtraction of $mpim$.

Solving for Y (using the same method as in the appendix to Chapter 10—but leaving out some of the intermediate steps) yields:

$$Y - mpc(1-t)Y + mpim\ Y = C + mpc\ TR + I_I + G + X$$
$$Y = \left[\frac{1}{1 - mpc(1-t) + mpim}\right](\bar{C} + mpc\ TR + I_I + G + X)$$

The term in brackets is a new multiplier that includes both proportional taxes and imports that depend on domestic income. This multiplier here is even smaller than the previous two. For example, if $mpc = .8$, $t = .2$, and $mpim = .1$, the new multiplier is $1/(1 - .64 + .1)$ or $1/(0.46)$ or approximately 2.2. This is because any increase in Y now "leaks" not only into saving and taxes but also into increases in imports (which takes away from demand for domestic products).

NOTES

1 Bank for International Settlements, *Triennial Central Bank Survey*, Basle, September 2013.
2 Note, however, that in the literature and even in older documents of international organizations, the term "capital account" is sometimes used differently. In these contributions, "capital account" refers to what today is called "financial account" (see what follows). The confusion stems from a change in the International Monetary Fund's use of the terms over time.

Part IV

Macroeconomic Issues and Applications

Chapter 15

The Financial Crisis and the Great Recession

The financial crisis that commenced in the United States in 2007 and its aftermath have been widely referred to as the "Great Recession"—and with good reason. Never since the end of World War II did economic output contract as quickly or as strongly in the industrialized world as in the winter of 2008–2009, and never were as many jobs lost in such a short period of time. According to UN estimates, between 2007 and 2009, the number of unemployed globally had risen by 27 million, to a total of more than 200 million. In contrast to other economic crises since World War II, high-income countries were especially hard hit. In the rich countries such as the United States and the member states of the EU, more than 14 million jobs were lost. In the U.S., unemployment rose from 4.7 percent to 10 percent (not counting the discouraged and marginally attached workers discussed in Chapter 8). In Europe, unemployment rose most in Spain, Latvia, Estonia, and Lithuania: In Spain, unemployment rose from 8.2 percent in 2007 to 19.9 percent in 2010, in Latvia from 6.1 percent to 19.5 percent, in Estonia from 4.6 percent to 16.7, and in Lithuania from 4.3 to 17.8 percent.

With job losses came economic hardship, as households lost their main source of income. The fate of many households was made worse by their losses of financial assets, and often their homes, when they could not service their mortgage debt anymore and houses went into foreclosure. Globally, it is estimated that $50 trillion (about €35 trillion)—more than the annual GDP of the European Union and the U.S. combined—in financial wealth was wiped out during the crisis. Between 50 million and 100 million people around the world either fell into or were prevented from escaping extreme poverty due to the crisis. Moreover, in Europe, the Great Recession of 2008–2009 became just the prelude to a second crisis, the euro crisis, which led to more contraction in output and more job losses in countries such as Greece, Ireland, Portugal, Italy, and Spain (Chapter 17 will look at the euro crisis in detail).

This chapter will deal with the financial crisis starting in 2007 and the Great Recession of 2008–2009. Why did the crisis happen? Why were its effects so long-lasting? What lessons can be learned for the future? These are complicated questions to which this chapter provides some answers.

1. PRELUDE TO A CRISIS

In retrospect, perhaps it is not difficult to see that something "big" was going to happen. Economic conditions were unusual. Interest rates around the world were at historic lows. This translated into extremely low mortgage rates in the United States and in many countries of the European Union, which motivated an unprecedented rush to buy real estate. Even people who ordinarily would have little hope of obtaining a mortgage got in on the action. As record numbers of people in countries such as the United States, Ireland, and Spain bought homes and investment properties, housing prices surged. Most people—realtors in particular—did not appear to think that house prices could ever go down again.

1.1 The Housing Bubble in the U.S.

The housing bubble in the United States was an archetypal bubble. Like others before it, this bubble began innocently enough, with an increase in demand for real estate. As we learned in Chapter 4, an increase in market demand tends to increase prices, and the housing market proved no exception. Unfortunately, the increase in home prices fed a speculative frenzy, and millions rushed to buy, believing that prices could only go in one direction—up! The buyers included not only would-be homeowners but also speculators who were buying simply with an interest in "flipping" the property (reselling at a higher price). The naive view exhibited by so many was similar to earlier bubbles, during which the lessons of the past were ignored.

To obtain a sense of the magnitude of the housing bubble, consider that average real home prices in the United States—that is, adjusting for inflation—were only 2 percent higher in 1997 than a century earlier (Figure 15.1). But prices skyrocketed starting in the late 1990s, and by the time they peaked in 2006, the average price of a house was nearly *twice* the long-term average price in the previous century. And the subsequent collapse was such that a mere six years later, prices had reverted to their long-term trend.

What fed the speculative flurry that gave rise to such a massive bubble? Economists still do not fully agree on what causes speculative bubbles, but a number of factors are widely believed to have contributed. The main factor was the unprecedented access to credit in the form of mortgages. During the mid-1990s, U.S. households borrowed an annual average of approximately $200 billion in the form of mortgages for home purchases. The figure rose abruptly to $500 billion for the period 1998–2002 and to $1 trillion from 2003 to 2006. While widespread access to credit is arguably critical for a vibrant economy, an exceedingly rapid increase in borrowing has, throughout history, been among the most consistent determinants of financial crises. By inflating bubbles, credit booms have invariably led to financial busts.

Three factors have generally been seen as having been of importance to this development: low interest rates, financial innovations, and capital inflows from the rest of the world into the United States. The key central bank interest rates are decisive in regulating credit availability—in the U.S., particularly the federal funds rate. We saw

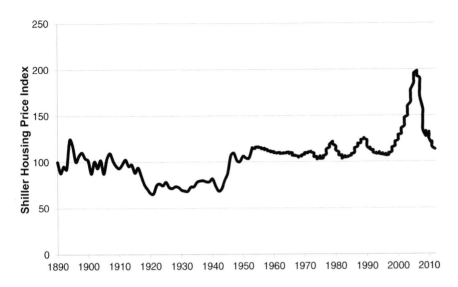

Figure 15.1 *Historical Housing Prices in the U.S.*

This graph shows the real (inflation-adjusted) cost of housing over the long term, with an index of 100 representing the average cost over the twentieth century. The graph shows fluctuation in real housing prices, with dips around 25 percent below average in the 1920s and 1930s, upward spikes of only about 25 percent in later parts of the twentieth century, and then a spike that nearly doubled average house prices in the early years of the twenty-first century.

Source: Shiller dataset. www.econ.yale.edu/~shiller/data.htm.

in Chapter 12 how central banks control interest rates; the critical point to remember in this context is that changes in the central bank's key rates percolate through the economy, because banks that can borrow at lower rates will also lend at lower rates and vice versa. The 2001 recession that followed the collapse of the dot-com bubble prompted the Fed, led by Chairman Alan Greenspan, to lower the target federal funds rate (the Fed's key interest rate) from 6 percent to 1.75 percent. The Fed kept the rate low and in the summer of 2003 lowered it still further—to 1 percent, its lowest level in 50 years. Behind this decision was the observation that the business sector had not increased its investments as much as the central bankers had hoped. After the burst of the dot-com bubble, and given the global uncertainty after the terror attacks and the U.S.–led invasion of Iraq, animal spirits were weak. The low federal funds rate in turn led to rate reductions across the board, including the rates for loans and home mortgages. These reductions fueled the borrowing binge that caused real estate prices to spiral upward (Figure 15.2). Mortgage rates hit a 50-year low of just over 5 percent in 2003, and borrowing to finance home purchases consequently skyrocketed.

There was also a second, less well understood channel through which low rates contributed to the housing bubble. To understand it, you must keep in mind that while low interest rates are attractive to borrowers, they are decidedly unattractive to lenders. Here we are speaking not so much of the commercial banks that are extending

497

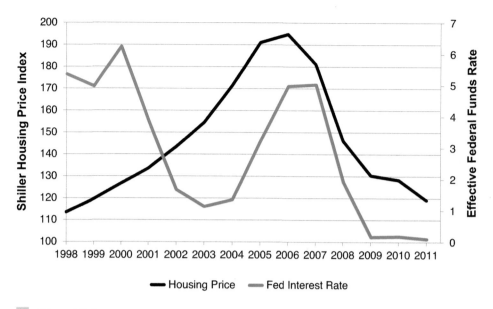

Figure 15.2 *Housing Bubble and Credit Access*

The effective federal funds rate, shown on the right hand vertical axis, plummeted from 2000 until 2004. Although it then began to move back up, the momentum of the housing bubble continued until a softening in housing prices began to be apparent in 2006.

Sources: Federal Reserve (www.newyorkfed.org/markets/statistics/dlyrates/fedrate.html/ and www.federalreserve.gov/releases/h15/data.html); Shiller dataset, www.econ.yale.edu/~shiller/data/ie_data.xls.

mortgages to their customers—because the rate they charge, however low, is always considerably higher than the rate that they must pay to depositors—as of other financial institutions (such as investment banks) or high-net-worth individuals who are seeking higher returns on their money. The Glass–Steagall Act had been put in place after the depression of the 1930s to protect against future bubbles and their bursts. A critical provision of this act, which separated commercial and investment banking, was repealed in 1999, with the result that many more financial players were now able to participate in the mortgage market.

After the 2001 bursting of the dot-com bubble, U.S. Treasury bonds of all types were paying very low rates, and stocks were still not performing well. Financial investors who had grown accustomed to the much higher returns on their money that were available in previous decades were struggling to find more profitable investments. Meanwhile, a rapidly growing number of prospective homebuyers were seeking mortgages at favorable rates. Traditionally, home mortgages involved only the borrower on one side and the bank that provided the funds on the other. But this was to change, as investment banks now saw a unique opportunity to meet both investor and homebuyer interests with a single financial product: a mortgage-backed security (MBS).

A **mortgage-backed security** is a bundle of independently issued home mortgages that an investor may buy in order to obtain a share of the mortgage interest payments; you could think of it as something like a mutual fund, but containing mortgages instead of stocks or government bonds. The investor also takes on the default risk from the individual mortgages that make up the MBS—that is, the risk that the homebuyers might not be able to make their mortgage payments. This risk varies from case to case, and here is where matters become a bit more complex.

mortgage-backed security (MBS): a security composed of a bundle of many home mortgages issued by independent banks

Each MBS is divided into tiers or tranches, with the "senior" tranche the first to be paid in the event of mortgage defaults (hence, the safest). The "lowest tranche" is the riskiest but is correspondingly paid a higher return. Essentially, MBSs are a kind of derivative, constructed by mathematically proficient analysts ("quants") who are paid to calculate the appropriate risk-return balance for each of the individual tranches.*

Following the advent of MBSs in the 1990s, banks increasingly acted as intermediaries that made housing loans and then bundled the mortgages together to be sold for a fee to investors. In the early 2000s, MBSs offered more attractive rates of return to investors than many types of bonds, both because of the Fed's continued low interest rates and the fact that mortgages generally pay higher interest rates than most other types of loans. Private investment banks were selling large quantities of MBSs, and the share of residential mortgages that were bundled into MBSs grew from 50 percent in 1995 to more than 80 percent by 2008.

But financial institutions then went even further. They developed another type of security known as a **collateralized debt obligation** (CDO), which is an even more complex investment product. It packages together a variety of loans, including, especially, MBSs—thus making it a "bundle of bundles" of mortgages. As in the case of MBSs, a hierarchy of tranches is available, each carrying a calculated risk-return balance. The complexity of the bundling that was involved meant that even the analysts entrusted with the construction of CDOs did not always fully understand them, while the investors who bought them and many of the financial executives who approved their use had little idea of the risks involved.

collateralized debt obligation: an investment product that packages together numerous assets including mortgage-backed securities

After packaging mortgages into MBSs and MBSs into CDOs, investment banks also sought to insure the most senior tranches of each of them against default risk. Companies such as American International Group (AIG) sold what are known as **credit default swaps** (CDSs), which are a form of insurance policy against defaults related to MBSs or CDOs. In such an arrangement, the buyer of the CDS (usually an investment bank) pays a fee to the seller (an insurance company or another investment bank), which agrees to cover losses in case of a default.

credit default swap: a security that is effectively an insurance policy against defaults related to MBSs and CDOs

During the early 2000s, it became an increasingly common practice to sell CDSs to insure the top tranches of MBSs and CDOs. As the combination of MBSs or CDOs and CDSs offered seemingly safe, attractive returns, not only American investors piled into these investments, but also banks and other financial institutions from the rest of

---

* As noted in Chapter 7, derivatives are a financial instrument whose value is "derived" from the value of another, underlying asset. In this case, the underlying asset is the original home mortgage.

the industrialized world, and especially Europe, started to buy these papers backed by U.S. mortgages.

In order to satisfy demand for the new products, it was important to maintain a large nationwide pool of home mortgages. And here a problem emerged. Despite the historically low interest rates and unprecedented access to credit, it seemed that new loans could not be issued quickly enough to fulfill investor demand for the new bundled securities. In order to persuade even more people to become homeowners, banks needed not only to continue offering low rates but also to relax some of their lending criteria. This was to be a critical factor in the subprime crisis.

1.2 The Subprime Crisis

Although unbridled optimism about home prices and cheap credit contributed their fair share to the housing bubble, the expansion and deflation of the bubble could not have been so dramatic or damaging in the absence of an extraordinary buildup of risky lending. A new kind of loan, the **subprime mortgage**, became common.

subprime mortgage: a mortgage that does not meet the quality standards of traditional mortgages

Banks typically classify subprime mortgages as those not fulfilling the quality standards of standard mortgages. For example, these may be mortgages to individuals who may lack a regular income, have a poor credit record, or already have a high level of nonhousing debt. Also, subprime mortgages include mortgages to households that have little or no equity to invest in their house. During the subprime boom, banks sometimes lent as much as 120 percent of the house purchased as a mortgage (e.g., $600,000 when the value of the house was only $500,000), with the remainder being spent by the households on furniture, moving costs, or a new car. Historically, banks have turned down applications for most such loans.

During the housing bubble such restrictions were relaxed: The criteria for mortgage eligibility were loosened, and the number of subprime mortgages soared. In 2002, less than 10 percent of U.S. mortgages were subprime; a mere three years later, approximately 25 percent were. While the housing bubble was inflating, many commentators exulted that homeownership was becoming a reality for many for whom it had previously been only a dream. The argument lost credibility several years later, however, when the housing bubble burst. Subprime credit evaporated, and countless borrowers, unable to keep up with their mortgage payments, faced foreclosure.

Evidence supports the claim that the explosion of subprime lending intensified both the rise and the fall of the entire housing bubble. As noted, mortgage borrowing doubled from an annual average of $500 billion from 1998 to 2002 to $1 trillion in the 2003–2006 period. The rapid increase can be attributed largely to the proliferation of subprime lending. When housing prices finally started turning downward in 2006, continuing mortgage payments became especially difficult for subprime borrowers. The resulting wave of subprime foreclosures hastened the downward spiral of prices, because they created a glut in housing supply. Meanwhile, a widespread tightening of credit led to a drop in demand. An increase in supply coupled with a drop in demand is a recipe for lower prices, and that is precisely what was observed after the bubble burst.

1.3 From Housing Crash to Banking Crisis

With borrowers defaulting on their mortgages, the financial sector was also hit. Rapidly falling house prices, combined with limited equity of the homeowners, rendered many mortgages all but worthless. The massive losses in the underlying loan portfolios led to losses in the value of MBSs and CDOs. Issuers of CDSs—designed as insurance policies against defaults of MBSs and CDOs—were not able to cover these unexpected losses and defaulted on their customers' claims. What investors had perceived as safe assets turned out to be highly risky ones, and a number of large banks and funds had to write down the value of their investments. From the spring of 2007 onward, a number of banks and other financial institutions on both sides of the Atlantic got into trouble, and a number had to be closed down because of losses in the U.S. subprime market.

A bad situation turned catastrophic in the late summer of 2008: In July, IndiMac, the largest saving and loan association in the Los Angeles area and seventh largest mortgage originator prior to the crisis, was closed down. On September 7, Fannie Mae and Freddie Mac, two government-sponsored enterprises that had been turning millions of mortgages into MBSs and that were holding billions of dollars in mortgages, were taken over by the U.S. government in order to prevent a default. On September 14, the investment bank Merrill Lynch was on the verge of bankruptcy and was taken over for an almost symbolic price by the Bank of America. Then, on September 15, something unexpected happened: Lehman Brothers, one of the United States' top investment banks, had to file for bankruptcy. This default shocked financial markets globally, as only days before, Lehman Brothers had been perceived as solid, and financial market participants had not expected that a large American investment bank could ever be allowed to fail by the U.S. government.

Suddenly, the solvency of each and every bank in the industrialized world was cast into doubt. Banks stopped lending to each other, and as they noticed that they could not borrow from other banks, they stopped lending to their customers. The problem was that no one knew what kind of assets banks had in their portfolios. Many banks had put at least part of their funds in CDOs. Because it was not only difficult to know what kind of CDOs each bank now held but also which kind of mortgages were actually behind each of these CDOs, the presumption was that every bank was a high-risk borrower. With investment banks and insurance companies (which had sold CDSs as a way to insure losses on CDOs) also on the brink, CDOs turned from safe assets into highly toxic assets.

As businesses suddenly saw themselves unable to obtain loans for investments or just to finance the import and export of goods and services, they cut back on their investment and production plans. The global economy moved to the brink of an abyss, and output contracted sharply.

1.4 Housing Bubbles in Europe

During the time of the development of the U.S. housing bubble, some European countries also experienced housing bubbles. Prime examples here were Ireland, Spain, and Britain. By a number of measures, house prices actually increased more in some

European countries than in the United States. For example, from the mid-1990s to the peak of the bubble, house prices in the U.S. rose by slightly more than 100 percent. During the same time, house prices in Ireland quadrupled and rose by around 200 percent in Britain and Spain.

The underlying factors in Europe were slightly different than in the United States. While speculation certainly played a role in all countries concerned, each country had some idiosyncratic characteristics that can explain the bubble. In Ireland and Spain, an important factor probably was the introduction of the euro. As these countries had a history of inflation and high interest rates, when the euro was introduced, interest rates suddenly were much lower than in the past. This allowed many people who hitherto had been unable to pay mortgage rates to service a loan. Moreover, both countries experienced strong economic growth, which lifted the incomes of the broad population. With higher incomes, households had more funds available to spend on housing. Housing demand soared. Both in Ireland and in Spain, the house price boom went hand in hand with a construction boom as millions of new houses were built.

In Britain, in contrast, it was mainly a combination of strict planning rules, a growing economy, and immigration that pushed house prices up. As the British economy performed relatively well and incomes grew briskly, the country became a magnet for immigration from both the rest of Europe and the rest of the world. At the same time, local councils limited the construction of new houses. As a result, house prices soared—as you would expect when demand increases but the quantity supplied remains constant. What is interesting about Britain is the fact that the housing bubble developed in an environment of moderately high interest rates. The Bank of England's policy rate never fell below 3.5 percent in the early 2000s and was quickly brought above 4 percent again.

If we take the European housing booms together, there was another difference compared to the boom in the United States: In none of the European countries did MBSs and CDOs play a comparably important role in the real estate boom as in the United States. Nevertheless, with the end of the U.S. housing bubble, the real estate bubbles in Europe also burst. With emerging problems in American mortgage portfolios, banks in Europe also started to become more careful in lending to home buyers and real estate developers. With a delay of roughly one year relative to price developments in the U.S., by the spring of 2008, house prices were falling in all European countries that had previously experienced a real estate bubble. Even if the financial systems of these countries had not piled into U.S. subprime mortgages of questionable value, problems still emerged: With falling house prices, households started to default on their mortgages and property developers in turn defaulted on their loans, pulling the banks down with them. As a consequence, and amplified by losses in global financial markets, the European countries experienced their own national banking crises.

Discussion Questions

1. People often refer to the housing "bubble" and even the housing "crisis." Is an increase in the average price of homes not a good thing? What if prices are rising more rapidly than in the past? Explain.

2.   Would you prefer interest rates in the economy to be high or low? On what does it depend? Who benefited from low interest rates during the inflation of the housing bubble in the U.S., Ireland, and Spain? How did the low interest rates create problems?

2.   ECONOMIC IMPACTS OF THE CRISIS

In Chapters 7 and 11, we discussed the relationship between the financial and the "real" economies. The financial crisis clearly demonstrated the importance of this relationship. The disappearance of immense financial wealth in the immediate aftermath of the crisis spilled over into the real economy. As people had less wealth, they were apt to spend less. Even those who preferred to continue spending often found that banks were suddenly much more reluctant to lend them money. Less spending resulted in sharply lower output and a weaker labor market, as our circular flow analysis suggests. (As noted in Chapter 13, Keynesian economists argue that, were it not for an active government policy and the existing social safety net, things could have been much worse.) Both through financial channels and through trade connections, what started as a U.S. financial and banking crisis quickly turned into a global economic crisis.

2.1   Unemployment and the Vicious Recessionary Spiral

As a consequence of the crisis, in the industrialized world, more than 14 million jobs were lost. In many countries, households also saw their wealth diminished. For example, over a particular eight-month period spanning 2008 and 2009, the *average* U.S. household lost nearly $100,000 from its property and retirement portfolio values combined. In Europe, the loss of financial wealth fell especially hard in countries in which the pension system was heavily based on savings, such as the Netherlands, where workers had to accept significant write-offs of their pension entitlements. In the United States alone, around 11 million homebuyers faced foreclosure from 2008 to mid-2012, accounting for about one of every four mortgages in the country. Those who did not lose their jobs were often confronted with pay cuts or involuntarily reduced working hours. In the United States alone, the number of people officially living in poverty rose by almost 10 million in the course of the recession. In the European Union, the number of people at risk of poverty or social exclusion rose by more than 6 million between 2008 and 2012.[1] Clearly, the massive loss of speculative financial wealth on Wall Street (much of it related to depressed MBS and CDO values) translated to a comparable loss of *real* wealth in the wider economy. The financial crisis had turned into a broad-based economic crisis.

Although many families experienced hardship, certain groups were affected disproportionately. Young people, for example, suffered greatly from the unemployment crisis. Each year brought a new wave of recent graduates into the workforce, adding to the masses of young people already facing dismal job prospects. Certain industries, especially construction in countries that had previously experienced a real estate boom, were hit particularly hard.

503

The economic impact of the financial crisis persisted for an unusually long period. In the U.S., the unemployment rate remained above 7 percent through late 2013. In many European countries, a second increase in unemployment during the following euro crisis came on top of the initial increase. Why was this? While the euro crisis will be covered more in detail in the next chapter, to understand the impact of the initial global financial and economic crisis, we need to remember that, as we saw in earlier chapters, the circular-flow economy can, in difficult times, produce a vicious cycle. Unemployed workers generally have less income to spend. Families facing income losses and needing financial assistance can ordinarily borrow money—but after the financial crisis of 2007–2008, banks and financial institutions introduced tougher standards for credit card loans and **home equity loans**, in which an equity stake in a home is posted as collateral. This led to a "credit crunch" in which families and businesses were unable to obtain loans.

Many families were therefore compelled to cut their spending further; in the period from 2008 to 2011, U.S. consumers on average reported spending $175 per month less than they would have in the absence of a recession. Many employers, suddenly facing lower profits, fired workers, contributing to a vicious unemployment cycle. While the values of MBSs and other newfangled securities seemed to plunge overnight, it took longer for the ensuing credit contraction to affect business bottom lines, employment decisions, and consumer spending. Thus the crisis that began in 2007 led to a recession and very slow recovery that in the U.S. lasted more than five years and that turned into an ever-deeper crisis in Europe.

home equity loan: a loan that permits a borrower to offer his or her home (or their equity stake in it) as collateral in case of failure to repay the loan

---

BOX 15.1 THE COSTS OF LONG-TERM UNEMPLOYMENT

The long-term unemployment that followed the Great Recession in the U.S. was unprecedented since the 1930s and has exacted a huge human and economic cost.

Long-term unemployment is experienced disproportionately by the young, the old, the less educated, and African-American and Latino workers. While older workers are less likely to be laid off than younger workers, they are about half as likely to be rehired. [As a result] the number of unemployed people between ages 50 and 65 has more than doubled.

The result is nothing short of a national emergency. Millions of workers have been disconnected from the work force, and possibly even from society. If they are not reconnected, the costs to them and to society will be grim.

(Baker and Hassett, 2012)

Research for the U.S. indicates a 50 to 100 percent increase in death rates for older male workers in the years following a job loss. One reason for this higher mortality is suicide. The longer the period of unemployment, the higher the risk of suicide. Joblessness is also linked to higher rates of serious disease and higher probability of divorce. Effects last into the next generation; children whose fathers lose a job have lower annual earnings as adults than those whose fathers do not experience unemployment.

In the aftermath of the Great Recession, a slow recovery has seen lower job gains for men than for women. By 2013, women's total private-sector employment was slightly higher than before the recession, but jobs for men still lagged 3 percentage points below their previous levels.

Work-sharing programs that encourage companies to cut hours rather than payrolls, as well as retraining and reemployment programs, could help to mitigate the cost of long-term unemployment. Unfortunately, many U.S. state governments have taken the opposite approach, cutting aid to the unemployed. In 2013, North Carolina, with one of the highest jobless rates in the nation, cut both the duration and amount of unemployment benefits. According to economist Paul Krugman, this is "counterproductive as well as cruel—it will lead to lower spending, worsening the economic situation, and destroying more jobs."

Sources: Dean Baker and Kevin Hassett, "The Human Disaster of Unemployment," *New York Times*, May 13, 2012; Floyd Norris, "Gender Gaps Appear as Employment Recovers from the Recession," *New York Times*, July 13, 2013; Paul Krugman, "War on the Unemployed," *New York Times*, June 20, 2013.

Modern economies are, in a certain sense, more vulnerable to events in finance than they were in the past. Due in large part to the proliferation of mutual funds and their increased availability in employee retirement accounts, a higher percentage of the population than ever before have a financial stake in the stock and bond markets.

Today, even if financial instability is mostly speculative in nature and does not have a direct economic cause, it produces very real economic effects, because consumers who feel poorer spend less money, potentially triggering a downturn characterized by reduced economic output and high unemployment. As we saw in Chapter 13, a leftward shift in the *AD* curve during the financial crisis decreased GDP and produced widespread fears of deflation.

2.2 The Great Depression and the Great Recession Compared

Calling the period after the financial crisis the Great Recession invites comparison with the other "great" economic downturn of the past century, the Great Depression. What makes the Great Recession different from previous recessions is the duration of the downturn. During most of the twentieth century, after about 1940, a recession was an almost predictable business cycle downturn followed, after a few quarters, by a solid economic recovery. Although for both the United States and the euro area, business cycle dating committees declared the recession "officially" over by 2009, the general public had the feeling that the "recession" continued much longer. In the U.S., it was the slow pace of recovery in the job market, continued foreclosures, and a continued sense of despondency that contributed to this feeling. In the euro area, the

505

consequences of the global financial and economic crisis of 2008–2009 became just the prelude for the euro crisis that followed shortly afterward and that cast the region into a second recession, lasting from the end of 2011 to early 2013. Even by 2016, many countries in the euro area had not yet reached the GDP level of 2008 again.

Are the current downturn and the Great Depression comparable? Followers of historical trends point out that both downturns were preceded by a period of apparent economic strength. Those who remember the dot-com bubble that preceded the one in housing may not know that Americans experienced a similar asset bubble during the 1920s. In both cases, many banks had been diversifying their services, moving into real estate and other relatively risky investments. As in the more recent period, people were feeling optimistic and were therefore spending, many immoderately, driving prices up. Average annual economic growth during the 1920s in the U.S. is estimated to have been more than 4 percent, so things were looking good. Yet as also occurred before the current downturn, the rapidly inflating asset bubble in the 1920s, most manifest in the main stock indexes like the Dow Jones Industrials (not in housing), inevitably collapsed.

In terms of possible factors that caused each economic downturn, the two episodes may have been more similar than different. But in terms of economic consequences, the differences are noteworthy, and the principal reason relates to government regulation, automatic stabilizers, and discretionary fiscal and monetary policy. For example, thousands of banks failed in the early years of the Great Depression, causing millions of depositors to lose their savings. In contrast, there was not a single such case in the aftermath of the recent crisis. Some banks did fail (though far fewer than in the 1930s), but depositors' accounts were protected by deposit insurances. In response to the crisis, the insurance limit for deposits was raised, helping to prevent depositors' panic: In the United States, the limit for deposit insurance was increased from $100,000 to $250,000. In the euro area, where prior to the crisis only 80 percent of up to €20,000 were insured, the insurance now covers up to €100,000 fully (in Britain, a similar improvement was passed, but the amounts were stipulated in British pounds, not euros).

The existence of a government-financed "social safety net" also made a major difference. Not only was the unemployment rate at the nadir of the financial crisis much lower than during the depths of the Great Depression, but in all major industrialized countries, unemployment benefits were available. In some countries, benefits were actually made more generous during the crisis. For example, under the term "extended benefits," unemployed workers in the United States could receive support for a duration of up to 99 weeks (normally only 26 weeks) during the worst period of the recession. In most countries, there was no unemployment insurance during the Great Depression.

Such benefits enabled many of those involuntarily jobless to function during the worst part of the recent downturn, keeping consumption levels and the broader economy more or less stable despite the slow job recovery. The absence of such basic government support during the 1930s consigned millions to misery and prolonged the depression. In addition to the existence of automatic stabilizers, such as unemployment benefits, in the U.S., aggressive expansionary fiscal and monetary policies were put in place by the federal government and the Fed, starting in late 2008 (discussed in detail in what follows).

Broad statistics support the conclusion that, for all the difficulties caused by the Great Recession, they were significantly less than those during the Great Depression. While the drops in manufacturing output and stock prices initially were rather similar during the two periods, the impact on GDP and employment was very different. During the Great Recession, output stabilized relatively quickly, with the actual period of contracting GDP being relatively short (in many countries, just four quarters). During the Great Depression, the slide in output was more prolonged, from 1929 to 1932. Also, employment contracted by much more during the Great Depression, and unemployment increased much more strongly. The prolonged fall in output during the Great Depression quickly led to a rather strong deflation, with prices falling by more than 10 percent. During the Great Recession, falling prices were halted and a strong deflation prevented.

The principal difference, then, between the two periods is the existence of a social safety net, government regulations to protect ordinary citizens, and activist macroeconomic policy. It is no coincidence that in the United States, programs such as Social Security, food stamps, and unemployment insurance were introduced in the 1930s under the administration of Franklin D. Roosevelt. For all the anxiety over deregulation and the reduction in the social safety net over the past three decades, the financial crisis laid bare the importance of a government presence in the economy. Government programs, first instituted in many countries after the Great Depression, kept the current downturn from becoming far worse.

Table 15.1 *Selected Economic Indicators for 10 Industrialized Economies* in the Great Depression and the Great Recession*

Indicator	Great Depression 1932 vs. 1929	Great Recession 2009 vs. peak 2007–2008
GDP, real, change in percent	−10.0	−4.0
Manufacturing production, change in percent	−23.2	−20.2
Exports, change in percent	−58.5	−20.9
Stock market index, change in percent	−55.4	−53.4
Employment, change in percent	−17.3	−2.5
Unemployment rate (1932 and 2010)	19.6	9.2
Unemployment rate, change in percentage points	13.2	3.1
Inflation, in percent	−12.8	1.0

Source: Karl Aiginger (2010). The Great Recession versus the Great Depression: Stylized Facts on Siblings That Were Given Different Foster Parents. Economics: The Open-Access, Open-Assessment E-Journal, 4 (2010–2018): 1–41.

* Austria, Germany, Belgium, Spain, France, Finland, Sweden, United Kingdom, the United States, and Japan. Numbers are unweighted averages for these 10 countries.

Discussion Questions

1. Do you think changes in the value of "paper assets" like stocks and bonds, or even of homes, should have real economic effects? Why? Why do you think that employment suffered from the disappearance of so much financial wealth following the financial crisis?

2. Do you think that the Great Recession is nearly as bad as the Great Depression was? In what ways is it similar to it? In what ways was it different? Do you know any stories of family members who lived through the Great Depression? Do you know anyone who lost their job during the Great Recession?

3. UNDERLYING CAUSES OF THE FINANCIAL CRISIS

Many factors were behind the Great Recession. We have reviewed the fact that many unqualified borrowers were permitted—often actively encouraged—to buy homes that they could not afford. Other factors include the determination of large banks and the "titans" of finance to maintain high returns for their loans and investments, in the process downplaying the risks that were often, in the end, borne by others. Their ability to do so was greatly increased by a trend toward deregulation of industries, including finance. Economic globalization also provided fuel for the crisis and allowed it to spread more rapidly. These factors combined to produce other effects on the character of the macroeconomy. These other effects range from growing inequality among the population in the U.S. and other industrialized countries to the structure and functioning of large economic institutions to global trends and issues.

3.1 Inequality

In the three decades before the 2007 crisis, the income gap between rich and poor members in many industrialized countries widened. In the U.S., inequality reached levels not seen since the 1920s. During the last two decades of the twentieth century, rising income inequality was mostly due not to real income declines for the poor and middle classes but to relative gains for the wealthy. The low- and middle-income groups were gaining in absolute terms; the problem was simply failure to keep pace with the rich. But starting around 1999, things changed. The median U.S. household income began a real decline, signifying that the low and middle classes were now losing in absolute terms as well. The majority of U.S. families now faced difficulty even maintaining their customary level of consumption.

In a number of European countries, similar trends could be observed. In Germany, the largest economy of the euro area, the inflation-adjusted hourly wages of the poorer half of the population fell in the decade prior to 2007, while the top quarter saw an increase of almost 25 percent.

Policy makers could address the growing disconnect between rising consumption expectations by the low- and middle-income groups and their decreasing real incomes in three ways. The first was the "laissez-faire" option of doing nothing and hoping that market forces would, over time, diminish income inequality. The second option was to alter the tax and spending mix in a way that some income could be either directly or indirectly channeled toward the relatively poor. The third option was to encourage credit expansion and set lower interest rate targets, in the hope that families who did not otherwise possess sufficient income to meet their spending needs might borrow to make up the difference.

In practice, American policy makers rejected the second option of redistributing income in favor of a combination of the first and third options: do nothing about growing inequality but facilitate greater borrowing on the part of middle-class and low-income families. Countless U.S. families—subprime or otherwise—exploited the opportunity to take out home equity loans on generous terms. The trend had broad bipartisan support; indeed, many policy makers greeted it with optimism rather than skepticism. It seemed to be a clever way of addressing the economy's need for sustained consumer spending while avoiding the thornier issue of inequality or unpopular government action.

In the years preceding the crisis, the approach appeared to bear fruit. Consumption in the United States continued to increase despite declining incomes. Expectation of continued appreciation in their home's value encouraged many families to spend more money than they had. But the numbers contained what should have been a warning. In 1980, for example, U.S. households held an average debt level equal to about 60 percent of disposable income; in 2007, this figure exceeded 130 percent. As a result, there was a sharp increase in the number of families who found themselves unable to continue paying their mortgages. For the many thousands whose home values dropped in the subsequent collapse, it often became more economically practical to default and face foreclosure than to continue to pay, because the monthly payments would continue to reflect the original, often much higher, value of the home.

Lower interest rates during these years undoubtedly fueled the credit expansion. But household indebtedness might have ballooned even without such stimulus. A widespread perception of falling living standards, largely a consequence of income inequality, was probably sufficient to provoke a rapid increase in demand for loans.

In some European countries, and especially in Germany, policy makers chose a different approach: They decided to do nothing in the face of growing inequality and also did not encourage borrowing by households. As a result, consumption stagnated over much of the 2000s. At the same time, rich households and corporations were earning more money than they could (or would) spend. As a result, net savings of the German economy increased. As we will discuss further in what follows, these excess savings of economies such as the German one are sometimes seen also as a contributing factor to the growth of the bubble.

3.2 Bank Size and Deregulation

Many believe that the immense size of some of the leading banks in the U.S. and elsewhere was one of the causes of the financial crisis. There is little question that banks have gotten much bigger while banking-sector assets have become more concentrated.

Since around 1980, the steadily increasing frequency of bank mergers has led to a growing number of large banks. In the U.S., from 1984 to 2007, the number of banks with more than $10 billion in assets increased fivefold, from 24 to 119, and the share of banking-sector assets held by large banks increased from 28 to more than 75 percent (Figure 15.3). The consolidation continues to this day. In 2012, in the United States, the five largest banks held almost half of the assets of the sector.

A similar trend could be observed in the euro area: By 2013, the five largest credit institutions also held almost 50 percent of all assets in the currency area. In many of the single member states, the concentration of the five largest banks (not always the same in all member states) was actually even worse: In Estonia, about 90 percent of all bank assets were held by five banks, in the Netherlands more than 80 percent, and in Belgium more than 60. Even in countries in which banking was relatively less concentrated, single banks had gained macroeconomic importance. In Germany, where the top five banks only held about 30 percent of all banking assets, the largest bank, Deutsche Bank, in 2008 had assets with a value of more than 80 percent of German GDP. In France, with the top five banks holding more than 40 percent of all banking assets, BNP Paribas held assets worth the equivalent of about 90 percent of French GDP.

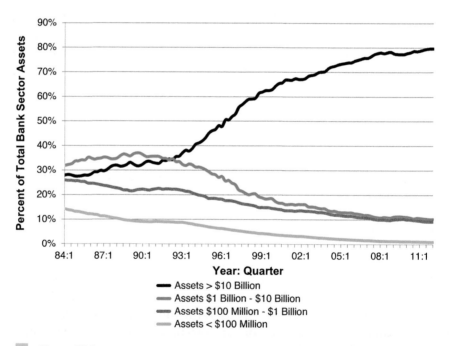

Figure 15.3 *Increasing Bank Size in the U.S.*

This graph shows the proportion of bank assets held by banks of different sizes in the U.S. Over a 16-year period, while medium-sized banks gradually declined in proportion of assets held, smaller banks lost ground even faster. The proportion of banks in the largest size category rose from less than 30 percent to nearly 80 percent.

Source: Federal Deposit Insurance Corporation (www2.fdic.gov/qbp/); www.fdic.gov/bank/statistical/stats/2012dec/industry.html.

510

While the details differ between the development in the U.S. and the euro area, there is a common story behind the growing size of financial institutions and the increasing concentration: On both sides of the Atlantic, the financial sector has been increasingly deregulated since the 1980s (often reversing the safeguards that had been instituted in response to the Great Depression), and the banks were increasingly allowed to conduct business across state lines or across international borders. In the United States, before the 1980s, most states had strict regulations forbidding out-of-state banks from owning subsidiary banks within their borders. The point was to impede excessive bank growth. But beginning in 1980, more states allowed their banks to merge with banks from outside the state. Over the years, Congress passed a number of laws allowing banks to broaden the scope of their activities, culminating in an effective repeal of the Glass-Steagall Act, which had separated commercial and investment banking activities since the Great Depression.

In the euro area, the growth of big banks was partly driven by the wish to create a single European market for capital and financial services. With the introduction of the free movement of capital between EU countries, banks also spread their business. In addition, the introduction of the euro made it easier for banks to borrow from abroad, and the general fashion for financial deregulation led to a relaxation of a number of rules for the financial sector.

At the time, many argued that the financial deregulation trend augured well, claiming that large banks are less prone to risk than small ones and therefore have less of a destabilizing effect on the economy. A large bank would, for instance, lend to borrowers who are more geographically dispersed, thereby making it less vulnerable to locally concentrated defaults. Also, according to this argument, a large bank faces less risk because it possesses a greater diversity of income sources (e.g., stocks and real estate, in addition to loans) as compared to a traditional small bank. Supporters also made so-called **economies-of-scale** arguments, stating that a larger size would allow a bank to operate more efficiently by allowing it to cut costs in many areas. In Europe, many governments thus even tried to protect and nurture at least one "national champion" among its banks—a bank large enough to be of relevance in the global market. On the other side were those who argued that large banks would take on high risk elsewhere by, for example, leveraging highly in order to invest vast sums in potentially risky assets. Empirical studies have generally supported the latter claim.

The principal argument against excessively large banks is related to what is known as "too big to fail." **"Too big to fail"** does not mean that it is impossible for a large bank to fail; as the financial crisis made painfully obvious, it is all too possible. What it means is that it is possible for an enterprise to grow to such a size that its subsequent failure would harm not only the shareholders but also the public at large—and therefore the enterprise may take on excessive risk, relying on the government to bail it out if it encountered problems with macroeconomic consequences.

Large banks count many other large companies among their creditors, so the failure and eventual bankruptcy of any one of them could cause a "domino effect," in which the inability of one bank to pay other creditors could jeopardize the financial standing of others, with potentially catastrophic spillover effects. It was such a fear that

economies of scale: benefits that occur when the long run average cost of production falls as the size of the enterprise increases

"too big to fail": when a company grows so large that its failure would cause widespread economic harm in terms of lost jobs and diminished asset values

511

prompted regulators and governments on both sides of the Atlantic to bail out large financial companies like Citigroup, Bank of America, and AIG in the United States, the Commerzbank in Germany, Anglo Irish Bank and Bank of Ireland in Ireland, or Northern Rock, Lloyds, and the Royal Bank of Scotland in the UK. Although many people did not like the idea of governments granting so much assistance to failed banks—which had failed due mostly to recklessness, not poor fortune—it was generally agreed that the alternative—a potential economic collapse—was much worse.

Despite agreeing with the decision, many banking industry critics point out that we would not have faced the problem in the first place if banks had not been permitted to grow "too big." They argue that after banks (or companies in any sector of our economy) become aware that they are "too big," they have an incentive to take on greater risks, anticipating that they will lose very little regardless of the outcome of their ventures. If the ventures fail to pay off, the large banks would be first in line for government assistance in the form of a bailout. The creation of such perverse incentives is what economists refer to as **moral hazard**.

moral hazard: the creation of perverse incentives that encourage excessive risk taking because of protections against losses from that risk

The moral hazard created by "too big to fail" in effect divorced the public's interests from those of the banks, creating a situation in which the pensions or portfolios owned by many millions of households suffered large losses while major banks were bailed out. In 2008, U.S. Congress passed the Troubled Asset Relief Program (TARP), which authorized the U.S. Treasury to spend as much as $700 billion in loans, stock purchases, and asset buyouts for insolvent banks, in addition to earlier loans provided by the Fed. In Germany, the parliament passed a bank rescue package with a volume of €480 billion, and the British government put together a package with a volume of £500 billion (€625 billion at that time). In many countries, a disproportionate share of these packages supported the "too big" banks; for example, the U.S. Treasury spent $220 billion to purchase stock from the 19 largest financial companies but only $41 billion for all other banks. In Germany, among the banks supported was the Commerzbank, in Britain banks such as Lloyds and RBS. In Switzerland, the giants UBS and Crédit Suisse were bailed out.

In the defense of these bailouts, some of them actually resulted in a profit for the governments: As the U.S. Treasury pointed out in 2012, not only had 94 percent of its TARP investments been repaid, but the value of those investments had increased by $19 billion. Also in other countries such as Switzerland, selling the assets acquired in the bailouts resulted in net profits for the government. Nevertheless, taxpayer money had been used to shoulder trillions worth of risk. And there remain a number of countries such as Ireland and Spain where significant amounts of money from bailing out the banks is irretrievably gone and where ordinary citizens had to bear cuts in public services and increases in taxes to pay for bank bailouts. Although bank bailouts turned out favorably in some countries, the fact that they were even needed vividly illustrates the dangers of a banking sector that is "too big to fail."

3.3 Misguided Corporate Incentive Structure

Although the existence of "megabanks" encouraged financial risk taking, bank managers were facing a changing payment structure that would similarly distort their incentives. Before the 1990s, compensation for bank chief executive officers (CEOs) was mostly unrelated to company fortunes. That is, they were generally paid a salary that would grow at a rate comparable to that of many other employees. If the company performed especially poorly, the CEO might lose his/her job, but otherwise the CEO's salary remained unaffected by company performance.

More recent views, including those taught in business schools, increasingly supported the idea that executive compensation packages should include performance incentives. CEO pay started to come more in the form of stock options, and bonuses were more frequently tied to the company stock value. The rationale for the changes was that they would give CEOs a greater incentive to take steps that would ensure a good return for the company shareholders. Many believed that rapid growth in the stock value would be a reflection of the CEO's ability and understanding of risk.

The new pay structure, however, generated unexpected problems. If CEOs were to be evaluated primarily on the basis of company stock price, they would be motivated to focus on short-term gains in this area, ignoring long-term risks. They would be compensated handsomely—in terms of both the number of stock options and bonus size—if the stock price went up, even if the increase was not sustainable. The CEO might well have left the company before the long-run damage became evident. In the case of the housing bubble, any self-interested CEO could have profited even if he suspected that the rapid increase in home prices could not last. The new pay structure created an incentive for gambling on risky mortgages. It became apparent only later that such an incentive-based pay structure was another example of moral hazard (see Box 15.2).

From 2000 to 2007, the period during which the housing bubble was inflating, Lehman Brothers (which was to be the sole "megabank" to be allowed to fail during the crisis) and Bear Stearns (which also went out of business but was taken over by JP Morgan Chase under pressure from the Fed, thereby technically avoiding bankruptcy) paid their CEOs $61 million and $87 million, respectively, in bonuses, with both citing unprecedented increases in their stock price as justification. These CEOs also earned $461 million and $289 million, respectively, from exercising their stock options during this time. During this period, the companies were engaging in the unsustainable borrowing that would lead to their collapse. By the time the game was up in 2007, and the share prices plummeted, the CEOs had already become immensely wealthy and were under no obligation to return the funds.

BOX 15.2 CEO CAN KEEP BONUS DESPITE GRAVE WRONGDOINGS UNDER HIS LEADERSHIP

In the fall of 2016, the announcement that the U.S. Department of Justice might fine Germany's largest bank, Deutsche Bank, up to $14 billion for misselling mortgage securities in the 2005–2008 period, sent jitters through financial markets. Investors were dumping Deutsche Bank's shares and bonds, and speculation grew whether the German government would be forced to bail out Deutsche Bank. At that time, the allegations of misselling of securities were not the only investigation against the financial institution for illegal conduct: The U.S. Department of Justice was also looking into Deutsche for supporting money laundering through its Moscow branch. Just a few months earlier, Deutsche had been forced to pay a fine of €2.5 billion for participating in manipulation of the Libor, a reference interest rate to which many financial market contracts were tied.

As a result of all these fines but also of past business decisions, Deutsche Bank's shares were selling for roughly two-thirds less than a year earlier. In a drive to restructure, 1 in 10 jobs at Deutsche Bank were set to be cut. Both employees and shareholders were understandably unhappy about the fate of the large German lender.

Under the recently appointed CEO, John Cryan, the bank started to investigate how far it could claw back bonuses paid to managers who had been controlling the bank when the illegal activities were carried out. The result was sobering: While Deutsche Bank cancelled bonuses for its management board for 2015 and froze some bonuses to former managers not yet paid out, funds already transferred remained out of reach. For example, most of the millions of euros in bonuses Josef Ackermann had received for being at the helm of the bank from 2002 to 2012 had already been paid out and could not be easily touched according to German law.

Sources: Birgit Jennen and Nicholas Comfort, "Ackermann Sees No Legal Basis for Returning Paid-Out Bonuses," *Bloomberg*, November 17, 2016; James Shotter and Martin Arnold, "Deutsche Bank eyes bonus clawback for former bosses," *Financial Times*, November 17, 2016; Geoffrey Smith, "Deutsche Bank Wants Bonus Millions Back From Its Former CEOs," *Fortune*, November 17, 2016.

It may not be self-evident *why* shareholders would allow such a skewed incentive structure if it actually threatened their share values. Could it be that the inherent moral hazard in such a pay structure did not occur to anyone? It is highly unlikely. The fact is that shareholders in major companies do not actually possess much influence over CEOs. The boards of directors of companies have historically acted, in theory at least, on behalf of shareholders. And one "action" is determining CEO compensation.

In practice, and especially in recent years, company boards tend to be more aligned with CEO interests than with those of the shareholders whom they are presumed to represent. In some companies, CEOs hold sway over board members' compensation and reelection prospects, generating an incentive for "mutual favors." Moreover, many bank CEOs sit on the boards of other banks, providing ample opportunity for board members to cater to CEO interests, and vice versa. Therefore it should be no surprise that some CEOs were allowed to profit greatly from short-term growth, to the cost of not only shareholders but also the population at large.

3.4 Globalization and Long-Term Economic Trends

As already mentioned, events originating outside the United States also contributed to the bubble in the U.S. housing market and the following financial crisis. First, the progressive globalization of labor markets took its toll on U.S. workers. Beginning around the late 1960s, the United States started to rely more on foreign countries (e.g., China and Mexico) for production of consumer goods, because these countries, which pay a far lower average wage, could produce them at a lower price. As in some European countries, the U.S. manufacturing sector had been in decline from about this time, and real wages in the United States have failed to keep up with gains in productivity since the 1970s. This trend was facilitated by a gradual weakening of labor unions. In the mid-1960s, about one-third of all employees were in a labor union; today only about 12 percent of public-sector workers are, and 7 percent in the private sector. Similar trends were observed in many EU countries, as has been discussed in Chapter 8.

While globalization clearly brought significant advantages to industrialized countries such as the EU member states and the United States (as noted in Chapters 13 and 14), the distribution of the gains and losses tended to reinforce the growing pattern of inequality discussed earlier. As mentioned before, the consequences differed among countries: In the United States, this put pressure on struggling middle-class and low-income families to take on more debt. As we have outlined, easy credit access made going into debt a seemingly attractive option, and as long as house prices were rising, the illusion of increasing wealth encouraged taking on large mortgages. This allowed American families to live beyond their means until the 2008 crisis forced massive retrenchment. In Germany, for a number of reasons, households did not react to the growing inequality with increased borrowing, with the result that total savings increased: When the incomes of the poor came under pressure, they cut back on consumption. The rich, in contrast, did not increase their own consumption in line with their growing incomes, so overall savings in the economy increased. As companies were reluctant to invest in Germany, banks started to use the funds for investments abroad—either lending to banks in countries such as Spain or Ireland, where the funds were used to increase lending to home buyers, or by buying mortgage-backed securities from the U.S. subprime market.

Emerging markets such as China, which benefited from globalization and saw a strong expansion of exports and incomes, experienced another development: Here, incomes rose more quickly, while the population to a certain extent remained in old consumption patterns. While consumption grew briskly, it did so less quickly than incomes. As a result, as in Germany, savings increased.

These savings also contributed to the U.S. housing boom, as they were exported to the United States. This export of savings went through the mechanisms explained in Chapter 14, namely through the persistent U.S. current account deficits. Although the United States did not consistently import more than it exported until the mid-1980s, from then on, the current account grew ever more unbalanced. The deficit increased from about 1 percent of GDP in 1990 to 6 percent in 2006, causing a massive inflow of foreign money that, as we saw in Chapter 14, is necessary to keep international financial flows "in balance." The flood of foreign money was invested in a variety of U.S. assets, intensifying the asset price inflation that was already occurring. Some of it was used to purchase Treasury bonds, but much of it financed borrowing by U.S. homeowners or was directly invested in stocks, MBSs, and CDOs. As noted earlier, the availability of easy credit plays a decisive role in

515

inflating bubbles by fueling consumption and provoking excessive leveraging for purposes of financial speculation. In the case of the foreign inflows resulting from U.S. current account deficits, it is not possible to know whether they would have been sufficient, on their own, to produce a financial bubble in the United States, but we do know that they played an important role.

By the time the housing bubble was close to bursting, the financial sector had been deregulated to an extent not seen since before the Great Depression. Globalization only served to reinforce the inflation of the bubble. Movement of capital by investment banks and hedge funds across borders is only lightly regulated. So the problems discussed earlier, in which there was inadequate oversight of bank investments and loans—and of the management of risk—were magnified because there was no such oversight at all when it came to capital investments from overseas. Because foreign investors were parking their excess funds in the U.S. financial system (recall that they had these funds in no small part as a result of years of trade surpluses with the United States), investment banks and hedge funds possessed more capital with which to take on more risk and more debt (with historically low interest rates serving as another incentive) in order to multiply their returns.

How did finance come to play such an important role in the economy? One possible explanation is that the steady decline in U.S. manufacturing made it increasingly difficult to obtain an attractive return on investments in companies that were manufacturing real products. This downward trend may, at least in part, explain the proliferation of arcane financial products, as discussed earlier. Because expected returns in industry were relatively low, many financial investments seemed relatively more attractive. Thus bubbles are inflated when investors desperate for high returns sink their money into assets with highly questionable foundations, causing their price to rise rapidly, which in turn draws in further investors.

Discussion Questions

1. Have you seen anything in the news in recent weeks or months about the regulation of banking and finance? Do you think, in general, that it is a good idea to allow banks and financial institutions to conduct their business with minimal government interference? Why or why not?
2. Did the financial crisis mostly have to do with banks? Homebuyers? International economics? What do you think is the most important factor that explains it?

4. REMEDIES AND IDEAS FOR AVERTING FUTURE CRISES

The financial crisis called for both short- and long-term responses. Many believe that it was critical, in the short term, to restore at least some semblance of stability to the financial system, lest it collapse and bring the broader economy down with it. This urgent need prompted governments to act by bailing out the institutions deemed most systemically important to the health of the economy and by instituting a "stimulus" program of federal spending. Central banks in many countries followed the U.S. lead, in some cases purchasing not only government bonds but also securities such as MBSs through "quantitative easing" programs (as discussed in Chapter 12).

After the worst had been averted, attention turned to the long-term question—how to prevent future financial crises. This is a more difficult issue. One possible solution is to reverse, at least partially, some of the financial deregulation that helped lead to the crisis. Many have supported calls for more regulation of the financial sector, and some reforms have been implemented, although there has been opposition both from some who think that they go too far and from others who believe that they do not go far enough. In Europe, meanwhile, the financial and economic crisis has morphed into the euro crisis, and the initial reform proposals after the financial crisis have been followed by more comprehensive reforms, substantially changing the setup of banking supervision in the euro area (see Chapter 17).

4.1   Fiscal and Monetary Responses

After the emergency measures taken to forestall a complete economic collapse in late 2008, there remained the task of stimulating the economy, especially with the goal of creating rapid job growth. To this end, governments worldwide passed huge stimulus packages. Relative to the size of its economy, the stimulus in China was strongest, amounting to more than 13 percent of GDP. Among the large industrialized countries, the largest stimulus packages were passed in the U.S., Germany, and Spain, all amounting to at least 3 percent of GDP. The U.S. Congress passed the American Recovery and Reinvestment Act (ARRA), a government-spending bill with a headline figure of $831 billion. In Germany, the "Konjunkturpaket II" was implemented ("stimulus package II," after a small package had been passed slightly earlier), with a headline figure of €50 billion. All of these packages included a combination of tax cuts, increased government spending, and support for households.

Whether the amounts were big enough or too big remains an open question. However, in the immediate aftermath of the crisis, many independent analysts credited the fiscal packages with a halt of the collapse of economic activity and a relatively brisk recovery from late 2009 onward. In fact, many international organizations and private analysts had to revise their GDP forecasts for 2010 *upward* as the packages were implemented and boosted economic growth. In Germany, which experienced an initial drop of GDP of more than 5 percent (by this measure, the deepest recession since World War II), unemployment nevertheless barely increased. (In contrast, countries like Spain seemed at first to have weathered the crisis relatively well but were later hit by the euro crisis.)

Despite some such successes, in the U.S., employment growth remained lackluster through 2013, with the unemployment rate remaining above 7 percent, prompting classical economists to criticize the packages for needlessly fiddling with the economy and Keynesian economists to criticize them for not having been large and decisive enough. Moreover, as we have seen, when the government ramps up spending without a corresponding tax increase, the result is a swelling deficit, increasing the overall national debt. Some critics contend that this policy will lead to even greater problems

517

in the long term, and some economists claim that the debt problems experienced by some euro-area countries since 2010 were exacerbated by deficit spending in 2008–2009 (we review the issue of deficits and debt in Chapter 16). But one indisputable consequence of the crisis, and the bill that followed, is that Keynesian economics once again became an important influence in policy making in the U.S., and—to a lesser extent—in Europe.

During the crisis, a number of innovative policy measures were applied, which significantly helped to stabilize the economy beyond a simple multiplier effect. For example, Germany expanded a subsidy for companies that reduced the hours worked of their employees yet refrained from firing them. This "Kurzarbeitergeld" stabilized workers' incomes while it allowed companies to cut their costs during the crisis. When the economy later recovered, companies could at once ramp up production without having lost human capital. Internationally, this "Kurzarbeitergeld" is now seen as a role model for labor market stabilization in economic crises.

Both the United States and Germany also implemented "cash for clunkers" programs (officially "Car Allowance Rebate System" in the U.S. and "Umweltprämie" in Germany). Under these initiatives, households that replaced an old car with a new one received a subsidy of €2500 in Germany and up to $4500 in the United States. This program had a much higher multiplier effect than usual government transfers, as private households dug into their own savings to buy a new car at a moment when they otherwise would not have done so.

On the other hand, in some cases, central governments ran into the limit of countercyclical policy. In the United States, for example, while the federal government was rapidly boosting spending, many state and local governments were doing the precise opposite. The drop in household income resulting from mass layoffs and stagnant wages meant that state and local governments could collect less tax revenue, resulting in the sharpest drop in state tax revenue in U.S. history. State budget deficits ballooned, peaking at a total of $191 billion in 2010 and remaining high at $55 billion even for fiscal year 2013. States did receive federal assistance, but it covered only about 40 percent of their budget shortfalls from 2009 to 2011. To make up the rest, by 2012, 46 states had cut spending on services, while 30 states had increased taxes. Although appearing fiscally prudent, both policies countervail economic recovery efforts, and some analysts estimate that these "anti-Keynesian" state policies have cost U.S. workers more than 4 million jobs from 2009 to 2012, undercutting the reported job gains from the federal stimulus program.

In the area of monetary policy, all major central banks implemented stimulus plans that were unprecedented in nature. Immediately after the collapse of Lehman Brothers in 2008, the U.S. Fed purchased billions of dollars' worth of shaky assets, including mortgage-backed securities that had lost the largest part of their value. The result was that the assets on its balance sheet jumped from about $950 billion in 2007 to more than $2.5 trillion in 2008.** In Europe, the reaction of the central bank was much

---

**In "quantitative easing," the Fed purchases MBSs from banks and credits them with fresh reserves.

slower. The Bank of England followed the U.S. model and started its own quantitative easing program in the spring of 2009. The ECB, in contrast, in 2008–2009 still perceived the euro area's banking system to be more stable than those in the U.S. and the UK, and it long refrained from quantitative easing, moving to large-scale bond purchases only after the euro crisis had pushed the euro area to the brink of deflation in 2015.

As discussed in Chapter 12, central bank purchases of securities lower the long-term interest rates on bonds. This makes them less attractive for investors. As a consequence, it is hoped that banks will sell their bonds and use the proceeds to lend to firms and households. On the household side, this effect is hoped to induce them to shift their investments toward more risky assets such as equity and corporate bonds, which in turn help companies to increase investment.

At least in the UK and the U.S., these expansionary monetary policies had a major effect in promoting economic recovery, including in the housing market. But employing monetary policy to stimulate the economy has limitations; as noted earlier, one could flood the economy with liquidity and cut interest rates, but if consumers and businesses remain pessimistic, this does not necessarily lead to increases in consumption or investment. In the U.S., despite the Fed's very expansionary policies, banks remain fairly reluctant to lend their excess reserves, except to their most creditworthy borrowers. In the euro area, the euro crisis has overshadowed most if not all of the positive impact of expansionary monetary policies (see Chapter 17).

In addition, some fear that the major central banks, through their efforts, are inadvertently inflating new bubbles. Wall Street, for example, appears ebullient at the efforts of both the fiscal and monetary authorities to reverse the economic decline; in some countries such as the United States and Germany, stock indexes had risen to new record levels by 2017, significantly higher than prior to 2008. In other countries such as the UK, stock prices also exceeded precrisis levels by 2017. At the same time, there was a rush into "junk bonds"—corporate bonds considered at moderate to high risk of default—because of their relatively high interest rates. And we should not forget that sustained low interest rates are always an invitation for speculators to leverage their investment positions inexpensively, as some financial institutions have returned to doing, even in times when commercial banks have cut back their lending to corporations and households.

4.2 Reregulating the Financial Sector

The deregulation that preceded the financial crisis had been developed over many decades. Starting in the 1980s, many government regulations that had been in place for decades were eliminated. The premise for deregulation was the belief that companies would benefit from less government intrusion in their affairs and that the broader economy would gain from an improvement in investment incentives. In many countries, both center-left and center-right parties contributed to the deregulation during the 1990s and 2000s. But in late 2008 the political atmosphere changed rather abruptly. Suddenly, a clamor arose for regulatory reform to protect citizens and public budgets from the recklessness of the financial sector, which only intensified after the financial companies needed billions in government support to keep them afloat.

Regulatory initiatives were pushed on three levels: First, industrialized countries agreed at the G20 level (basically a club of the largest economies) to basic principles of tightening financial regulation. At the same time, in the U.S., a number of issues were addressed in the Dodd-Frank Wall Street Reform and Consumer Protection Act (Dodd-Frank), named after its cosponsors Senator Chris Dodd and Representative Barney Frank (D-MA). In the European Union, the European Commission used its power to regulate the single market for financial services to tighten regulation through a number of regulatory packages.

At the global level, governments agreed to force banks to hold more capital when conducting risky investments. Moreover, they agreed on putting additional requirements on "too-big-to-fail" banks: Large banks would be forced to hold an additional capital buffer. Moreover, they were required to write up "testaments," plans for how to wind banks down without excessive fall-out for the rest of the financial sector. Also on the G20 level, it was agreed that banks should be required to keep part of mortgages in their portfolio when they were bundled and sold off as MBS. To different degrees, these proposals made it into national regulations.

Moreover, in the U.S., Dodd-Frank addressed the deteriorating lending standards that encouraged subprime loans and pumped air into the housing bubble. The legislation required that financial companies that seek to lend money to prospective homeowners use minimum criteria (related to, e.g., credit history and income and debt levels) to determine whether the candidate for a mortgage can reasonably be expected to repay. The law also sought to put a halt to so-called predatory lending, which was increasingly common in the last years of the housing bubble. Predatory lending describes the practice in which financial companies target individuals whom they *know* are unlikely to repay a mortgage. Dodd-Frank created a new Consumer Financial Protection Bureau (www.consumerfinance.gov/) that protects vulnerable borrowers but also monitors loosely regulated lenders known for predatory practices. In July 2013, the Bureau became fully operational with the appointment of a permanent director.

Another key feature of Dodd-Frank is that it directly confronts the moral hazard inherent in the financial system and its pay structure. In order to reduce the extent to which commercial banks transfer risk to investment banks through the use of MBSs and other securities, the legislation requires commercial banks to be exposed to a minimum amount of the mortgage default risk. Dodd-Frank, moreover, puts restrictions on CDSs, requiring companies that seek to insure senior tranches of MBSs or CDOs to post more collateral to back up their value.

In addressing corporate pay structure, Dodd-Frank calls for the Securities and Exchange Commission to ensure that corporate board members who determine CEO compensation do not have private interests in the company that might give them an incentive to favor higher CEO pay over broad shareholder interests.

Dodd-Frank also took on ratings agencies like Moody's and Standard and Poor's, the companies that rate a great variety of debt and debt-related securities, to give investors a clear picture of the riskiness of the asset. The legislation required the agencies to disclose the method used to rate each security, in hopes of increasing transparency for investors. It partially addresses conflict-of-interest concerns stemming from the fact that the agencies are regularly paid by the banks that they rate, possibly creating an incentive to understate the risk of certain securities. Nevertheless, Dodd-Frank does not prohibit ratings agencies from being paid by the firms that they rate.

At the European level, soon after the crisis pan-European institutions were created to coordinate the regulation of the financial sector. To coordinate national banking supervisors, a new European Banking Authority (EBA) was set up. The coordination of national insurance supervisors was delegated to a new European Insurance Authority (EIA). National securities supervisors are now coordinated through the European Securities and Market Authority (ESA). A systemic risk board was created to spot macroeconomic risks through the financial system early on.

Prior to the crisis, differences in regulation had been exploited by financial institutions. For example, the Irish government had followed a hands-off approach in regulating financial institutions incorporated in Ireland but without domestic business in the country. As a result, a number of continental European banks had placed subsidiaries in Ireland that were running risky investments not allowed in their home jurisdiction. When things went wrong during the financial crisis, losses of these subsidiaries had to be covered by their parent banks. For example, the most expensive bank failure in Germany, that of Hypo Real Estate, was caused by losses of its subsidiary Depfa, based in Ireland. The new EU legislation was supposed to make sure that in the future, such "regulatory arbitrage" would not be possible anymore.

Like the Dodd-Frank act, European legislation also put some limits on manager compensation. Moreover, markets for derivatives are more strictly regulated than before, and rating agencies are required to register and follow certain minimum standards of transparency.

Unlike the regulatory regime in the U.S., which has not changed much since the passage of Dodd-Frank, the European Union has continued to reform its financial sector. During the euro crisis, some of the initial reactions were seen as inadequate. Thus, for the euro area, bank supervision was supplemented by moving banking oversight to the European Central Bank when creating the European Banking Union (see next chapter). More changes in the coming years are likely. For example, the European Banking Authority is currently based in London. With Britain leaving the EU, the institution will have to move. If it is moved to Frankfurt, it could become more closely integrated with the ECB.

4.3 Beyond Current Regulations

Like most historic pieces of legislation, financial system reforms have received no shortage of criticism. A familiar argument is one that is commonly heard about regulation in general: that these bills create significant costs for financial firms, slowing down business and job creation. Another point of criticism is that the legislation is too complex, perhaps even contradictory.

A third argument made against currently passed legislation is that it has been "watered down" to a great extent by intense lobbying efforts by the financial industry itself—suggesting, in effect, that the regulators are under the influence of the regulated. In fact, many of the earlier drafts both for the Dodd-Frank Act and for many of the European regulations foresaw much stricter rules than the texts that made it into law. One salient example supporting this claim is the fact that in the United States, in 2012, regulators decided that new CDS regulations would not apply to firms that sell less than $8 billion in CDSs per year. Because of this change, which was a direct result of pressure from the finance lobby, the overwhelming majority of companies are exempt from CDS regulations.

In public opinion, despite thousands of pages of new regulation passed over the past years, there is still a widespread perception that the financial sector has been basically been allowed to continue business as usual after 2008–2009. Behind this perception is the fact that the banks continue to rake in high profits, to pay high bonuses, and to conduct deals with other financial institutions, while credit access for households and corporations remains tight in many countries.

A question not very well addressed in past regulation is how to redirect finance to the goal of increasing overall benefits to society. One way might be to limit speculative activities of banks so that the only way for them to earn profits is to provide loans to firms and households. For example, banks might be prohibited from engaging in speculative activities and loans to other entities which conduct such activities (such as hedge funds). Another possibility would be to ban overly complex products or risky products from being sold by banks to their customers. If banking would be made "boring again" in this way, as the Nobel prize laureate Paul Krugman put it, bank managers might put their energies into devising new ways to help companies in the nonfinancial sector to finance their investments better.

However, such changes, in effect a return to traditional banking, would require addressing the heavy influence that banks have in government today. Pessimists point out that the financial sector still earns large profits and is able to use these profits for lobbying and other ways of influencing legislation.

Another way to redirect finance to serve society would be to require investors to pay a modest tax each time they complete a financial transaction. Keynes proposed such a tax in 1936—at a time when the role of finance vis-à-vis the real economy was minuscule compared to today—as a way of discouraging the short-term speculation that makes the price of company stock highly volatile. Decades later, another prominent economist, the Nobel laureate James Tobin, also argued that financial transactions, particularly currency trades, should be taxed. His idea was that each transaction be taxed at a low rate but that speculators would end up paying much more than long-term investors because they buy and sell securities much more frequently. Today, the term "Tobin tax" is used to refer to any proposed financial transaction tax.

Studies estimate that a financial transactions tax of a fraction of a percentage point would generate billions of dollars in revenue. Within the European Union, 11 member states have agreed to introduce a tax on all stock, bond, and derivative trading under so-called enhanced cooperation (through which a number of member states can integrate more closely than the rest). However, until late 2016, there had been no agreement on the technical details of the tax, and it cannot be predicted when (or if) the tax will actually be implemented.

The financial sector will continue to be the focus of intense debate about regulation, transparency, and the political power of large financial institutions. Economic theory cannot provide definitive answers to these questions, but as this chapter has shown, many of the macroeconomic analyses that we have developed are very relevant to understanding and evaluating the issues.

DISCUSSION QUESTIONS

1. What is "quantitative easing"? Can you think of anything you learned earlier in the book to which it is related? What do you think are the main advantages and disadvantages of such a policy?

2. What would you think about a proposal to tax financial transactions? Would you prefer it to an income or a sales tax? Why or why not?

REVIEW QUESTIONS

1. What was the nature of the housing bubble experienced in the early to mid-2000s? What were its main causes?

2. What is "subprime" lending? How did it contribute to the bubble and the subsequent financial crisis?

3. How can a collapse of the U.S. housing market and weakness in the banking system cause an economic recession and unemployment? How is it possible that the impact spreads around the world?

4. How is the recent economic downturn similar to the Great Depression? How is it different?

5. What are mortgage-backed securities? Collateralized debt obligations? Credit default swaps? Are these "investments" in the traditional sense?

6. Did social inequality play a part in inflating the bubble that led to the 2007 financial crisis? If so, how?

7. What is financial deregulation? How important is it in explaining the financial crisis?

8. Explain "too big to fail" and why it is a potential economic problem in any economic setting. How is "too big to fail" related to moral hazard?

9. Are short-term individual incentives for corporate officers consistent or in conflict with long-run interests of their companies and the economy as a whole?

10. In what ways did globalization contribute to the financial crisis?

11. What have been the principal fiscal and monetary responses to the recession to date? What have been the results thus far?

12. What is the purpose of the financial reregulation such as the Dodd-Frank bill and European initiatives? What were its main measures taken to reregulate the financial sector after the crisis? Have they been favorably received?

13. What is the Tobin tax? What would be its effect on financial transactions?

EXERCISES

1. For this exercise, you need to locate housing price index data for different countries. Go to the Web site of the Bank for International Settlements and locate residential real estate prices (www.bis.org/statistics/pp_detailed.htm). Select three industrialized countries (make sure at least one of them is mentioned as a "housing bubble country" in this chapter) and compare the development of real estate prices over the past 20 years. Now write a short summary of what you've learned. Make sure that you incorporate some specific data into your summary.

2. How does the Great Recession compare to recent economic downturns for the United States of America? To explore this question in further detail, begin at the National Bureau of Economic Research Web site (www.nber.org).

   a. Select "Business Cycle Dates" from the "Data" tab at the NBER site and then record the starting dates (peaks) and ending dates (troughs) for the last four recessions. Assemble these dates in a table.

   b. Now gather some macroeconomic data. You can do this at the Federal Reserve Economic Database (http://research.stlouisfed.org/fred2/). Using the "National Income & Product Accounts" under the "National Accounts" tab within "Categories," locate Real Gross Domestic Product data for each peak and each trough in your table. Record these numbers in a new table. Calculate the percentage change in Real GDP from peak to trough for each of the last four recessions. Report these results in your new table.

   c. Return to the categories page at the FRED Web site. Select the "Current Population Survey (Household Survey)" link under the "Population, Employment, & Labor Markets" category. Select the "unemployment rate" series and record the numbers for each peak and each trough for each of the last four recessions. Organize this data in a table.

   d. Review your tables and calculations. Write a concise summary comparing the Great Recession to the previous three recessions. Make sure that you incorporate specific numbers into your summary.

3. The chapter identifies a series of contributing factors in its exploration of the underlying causes of the financial crisis. Identify the major factors and state which you think were most important.

4. What is the meaning of moral hazard? Give some examples of moral hazard, as discussed in the text, or others that you can think of.

5. Match each concept in Column A with a definition or example in Column B.

Column A	Column B
a. Mortgage-backed security	1. When a company grows so large that its failure would cause widespread economic harm in terms of lost jobs and diminished asset values
b. Collateralized debt obligation	2. A loan that permits a borrower to offer his or her home (or their equity stake in it) as collateral in case of failure to repay the loan
c. Credit default swap	3. A security that is effectively an insurance policy against defaults related to MBSs and CDOs
d. Subprime buyer	4. A would-be home-buyer whose credit-worthiness is suspect because he or she already has a high level of debt and/or a low income and/or a poor credit record
e. Home equity loan	5. Benefits that occur when the long-run average cost of production falls as the size of the enterprise increases
f. "Laissez-faire"	6. The central bank purchases securities from banks and credits them with fresh reserves
g. Economies of scale	7. An investment product that packages together numerous assets, including MBSs
h. Too big to fail	8. Doing nothing
i. Moral hazard	9. A security composed of a bundle of many home mortgages issued by independent banks
j. "Quantitative easing"	10. The lack of any incentive to guard against a risk when you are protected against it

NOTE

1 Note that the figures for the United States and the EU are not directly comparable as official definitions and time period differ.

Chapter 16

Deficits and Debt

You may have seen a debt clock for your country that continually shows how much national debt is increasing each second. The total amount of the debt seems very large—for Germany, the clock shows more than €2.2 trillion—a number with 11 zeros. The numbers for other EU countries are equally mind-boggling: For the UK, the clock shows more than £1.7 billion, for France more than €2.1 trillion, and for the much smaller Netherlands still almost €500 billion. But what does it mean? To whom do we owe all this money? Is it a serious problem? Should we care about government debt when the economy has yet to recover from the financial crisis? Is it possible—or advisable—for our governments to stop borrowing? What are the European rules on government borrowing? This chapter goes into detail in answering these questions.

1. DEFICITS AND THE NATIONAL DEBT

Perhaps because the two terms sound so much alike, many people confuse the government's deficit with the *government debt*. But the two "D words" are very different. For the euro area as a whole, the national governments' deficits added up to €215 billion in 2015, while total debt of national governments stood at around €9.5 *trillion* at the end of 2015. The reason the second number is much larger than the first is that the debt represents deficits accumulated over many years. In economists' terms, we can say that the government deficit is a *flow variable* while its debt is a *stock variable*. (See Chapter 3 for this distinction.)

The government's debt rises when the government runs a deficit and falls when it runs a surplus. Figure 16.1 shows some historical data on government debt, measured as a percentage of GDP, for the U.S., the UK, Italy, Germany, and France. The debt is recorded as **gross general government debt**, that is, an estimate of the total debt outstanding for all levels of government, the most widely used measure for government debt in the EU.* Looking at government debt relative to GDP is more sensible than looking at debt in absolute numbers, as the burden of debt can best be evaluated relative to income. (If you are working on a minimum wage, a debt level of €25,000

gross general government debt: the outstanding debt of all levels of government, including social security systems

---

* For other countries, such as the U.S., it might make sense to use different measures, so you sometimes see them in news articles.

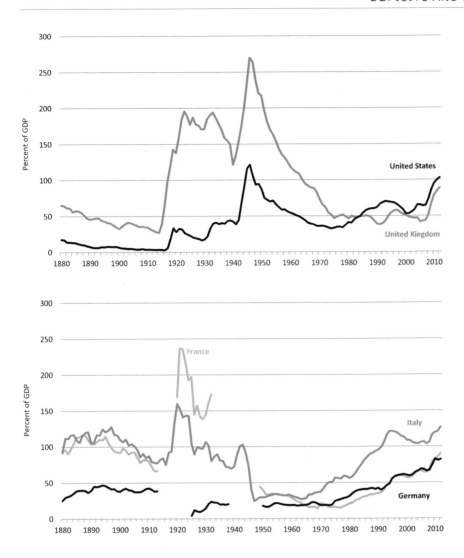

Figure 16.1 *Government Debt of Selected Countries as a Percentage of GDP*

Government debt generally shoots up during wars and comes down afterward. In addition, there has been a general upward trend after the 1970s and a strong increase after the global financial and economic crisis of 2008–2009.

Source: International Monetary Fund.

might be a real problem for you, while if you are the CEO of one of Europe's big corporations with an annual income of a few million euros, owing your bank €25,000 is rather trivial.) Note that for some countries, such as Germany, data is not available for certain crisis and war periods.

In general, we can see that government debt for the European countries shot up during World War I (1914 to 1918) and again during World War II (1939 to 1945).

For the U.S., the increase in World War II was the largest peak. In almost all countries, the debt ratio fell strongly after World War II. (Germany seems to be the exception, but this is because reliable data is not available for Germany during the wars, and, as explained in what follows, because Germany wiped out its government debt immediately after the wars.) All countries have seen an important uptick in public debt after 2008–2009.

What is the impact on the economy of government debt? One commonly expressed view of the government's debt is that it represents a burden on future generations of citizens. There is some truth to this assertion, but it is also somewhat misleading. It implicitly compares the government's debt to the debt of a private citizen. Certainly, if you personally accumulated a huge debt, it could be a danger for your financial future. But government debt is different in some important ways. First, two-thirds of euro-area government debt is, directly or indirectly, owed to euro-area citizens. When people own German bunds, Italian Buoni del Tesoro Poliennali, French Obligations Assimilables du Trésor, or British Gilts, they own government IOUs. From their point of view, the government debt is an asset, a form of wealth. If your grandmother gives you a German government bond, she is giving you a benefit, not a burden. These assets are some of the safest ones that you can own.

Second, government debt does not have to be paid off. Old debt can be "rolled over," that is, replaced by new debt. Provided that the size of the debt does not grow too quickly, the government's credit is good—there will always be people interested in buying and holding government bonds. Most economists use the rule of thumb that as long as the rate of increase in a government's debt is not significantly greater than that of GDP for several years in a row, it does not represent a severe problem for the economy. As Figure 16.1 shows, following the 2007–2009 recession, persistently large deficits have caused the debt to rise much more rapidly than GDP in recent years for all major economies. Nonetheless, at least in countries such as the U.S. and the UK, the debt is still at a lower level relative to GDP than it was immediately after World War II, which was followed by nearly two decades of relative economic prosperity.

Third, most industrialized countries pay their interest in their own currency. The U.S. pays its interest in U.S. dollars, the UK in British pounds. A country such as Argentina that owes money to other countries and must pay interest in a foreign currency (the U.S. dollar) can get into big trouble and go bankrupt. But it is much easier to manage a debt that is denominated in your own currency. Even if some of the debt is owed to foreigners, the United States or the UK do not have to obtain foreign currency to pay it. In cases of temporary lack of sufficient revenue, the governments of these countries could always order the central bank to print some money and lend it to the government to pay interest rates. And so long as foreigners are willing to continue holding U.S. government bonds, it will not be necessary to pay it at all—instead, the debt can be rolled over as new bonds replace old ones.

We have to note, though, that this logic does not fully apply to the euro area. While the euro-area governments' debt is also in the euro area's currency, the euro, individual governments cannot force the ECB to print money and lend it to them. In fact, by the European treaty, the ECB is even prohibited from lending directly to governments.

Hence, in some aspects, the euro-area governments' debt is similar to the Argentinian debt denominated in U.S. dollars. As a consequence, public debt for euro-area countries might be more dangerous than public debt in countries with their own currency, and euro-area countries in fact might be faced with the danger of default. This is a lesson with which policy makers in the euro area were confronted during the euro crisis (which we will cover more in detail in Chapter 17).

Beyond this danger of outright default, there might be some other problems related to rising government debt. First, interest must be paid on the debt. This means that a larger share of future budgets must be devoted to paying interest, leaving less for other needs. It is also true that the largest holders of government bonds tend to be wealthier people, so most of the interest paid by the government goes to better-off individuals. If this payment is not counteracted by changes in the tax system, it encourages growing income inequality. It also creates a problem of generational equity—future taxpayers will have to pay more interest because of government borrowing today. It is a burden on future generations in that debt finance detracts from other important functions that the government could be performing.

An additional problem is that some countries have in recent years increasingly borrowed from banks, individuals, corporations, and governments in foreign countries. The interest payments on this portion of the debt must be made to those outside the country. That means that the country in question must earn enough income from exports and other sources to pay not only for imports but also for interest payments to the rest of the world. Alternatively, the country could borrow more, but it is best to avoid this solution, since it would just make the overall foreign debt problem larger in the long run. Globally, the U.S. has been especially notable for borrowing large amounts from abroad. The euro area as a whole has not borrowed excessively from other parts of the world, but some euro-area countries such as Spain, Portugal, or Greece have borrowed massively from residents of the rest of the euro area.

Large foreign holdings of debt also pose another problem—what if those foreign debt holders decided to sell the bonds that they own? In that case, the government might have trouble finding enough people who are willing to hold government bonds (that is, lend money to the government). This could cause interest rates to rise sharply, which in turn would push the government budget further into deficit—something that has happened during the euro crisis (see Chapter 17).

The question "Is government debt worth it?" can be answered only if we consider what that debt is used to finance. In this respect, an analogy to personal or business debt is appropriate. Most people—including economists—do not reject all consumer and corporate debt. Rather, our judgment about debt depends on the benefits received.

For example, if debt is accumulated for gambling, it is a bad idea. If the bet does not pay off, then it is very difficult to pay the interest on the debt (not to mention the principal). But if the government borrows to pay for intelligently planned investment, it can be very beneficial. If the investment leads to economic growth, the government's ability to collect tax revenue is enhanced. This kind of borrowing can pay for itself, as long as the investment is not for wasteful "pork barrel" spending, poorly planned or unnecessary projects, and so on. Recalling our earlier discussion of the opportunity cost of government borrowing at full employment, the interest-generating capacity of the proposed project is certainly an important—though not the only—consideration.

Even if the debt finances current spending, it can be justifiable if it is seen as necessary to maintain or protect valuable aspects of life. Most people would not be opposed to borrowing to pay for cleanup after a natural disaster or to contain a deadly pandemic. How about for military spending? Opinions differ about whether particular defense expenditures are necessary to maintain or protect valuable aspects of life. But wasteful spending, or spending on unwise defense policies, constitutes a drag on more productive economic activity (as suggested by the production-possibilities curve "guns-versus-butter" analysis introduced in Chapter 2).

The management of debt involves standard principles of wise stewardship of finances. When we apply them to government deficits and debt, we need to weigh the economic benefits of different spending and tax policies.

Discussion Questions

1. What is the difference between the deficit and the national debt? How are they related?
2. "The national debt is a huge burden on our economy." How would you evaluate this statement?

2. PUBLIC DEBT: A HISTORICAL PERSPECTIVE

2.1 Deficits and Debt Since Medieval Times

Deficit financing goes back over centuries: At least since late medieval times, European kings routinely borrowed funds in order to pay for their war efforts. Many of the famous banking families such as the Fuggers and the Medici were deeply involved in war finance toward the end of the Middle Ages (fifteenth and sixteenth centuries), and part of the development of banking in Europe was based on the business between the private wealth owners and the governments. The Bank of England (now Britain's central bank) was founded as a privately owned institution in the 1690s in order to facilitate the English Crown's borrowing for reconstructing its navy.

While exact data is lacking for the extent of indebtedness of governments of that time, war debt in some cases was quite significant, especially if we keep in mind that governments of these times usually lacked a well-developed system of tax collection. The British debt-to-GDP ratio is estimated to have surpassed 100 percent for the first time as early as 1748 (see Figure 16.2). A number of economic historians believe that the efforts of the French court to support the American revolution against France's archenemy Britain, and the related buildup of French public debt during the late eighteenth century, contributed to the outbreak of the French revolution in 1789. Because of the debts accumulated during the independence war, the United States started its history as an independent nation-state in 1790s with a debt-to-GDP ratio of between 30 and 40 percent.

530

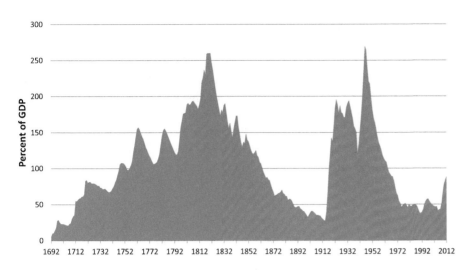

Figure 16.2 *British Government Debt as a Percentage of GDP*

British government debt surpassed 100 percent for the first time in the eighteenth century. It peaked during the Napoleonic wars and after World War II.

Source: International Monetary Fund.

In addition to financing war efforts, government borrowing also became important for the acquisition of territories. When the United States bought the vast Louisiana Territory (which included large parts of what is today known as the Midwest in the United States) in 1803 from France, it issued bonds in international markets to raise a large part of the $15 million purchasing price.

The importance of wars for the historical accumulation of public debt can be well seen for the timeline of British public debt (a country for which we have a relatively reliable estimate for a long historical period): Most of the increases in debt in the nineteenth century can be related to one of the many wars Britain was involved in during this century. The largest peaks over the past centuries can all be attributed to the most important wars: The first massive increase happened during the Napoleonic wars (1803–1815), when Britain fought France's attempts to dominate the continent. The next large increases happened during World War I (1914–1918) and World War II (1939–1945). This trend is mirrored by the development in other European countries and also the United States of America (Figure 16.1): Debt levels tend to increase very strongly during war periods, and the two World Wars led to especially high debt levels.

Another interesting observation is that in many cases, debt-to-GDP ratios tended to fall quickly again after each of the major war-caused increases. The fall of the debt ratios in many countries after World War II was especially rapid: From 1947 to 1957, Britain reduced its debt-to-GDP level by more than 100 percentage points! The U.S. also roughly halved its debt-to-GDP ratio over this time period. This reduction is especially noticeable, as neither the U.S. nor Britain defaulted on their war debt nor went through a hyperinflation.

This reduction of the debt-to-GDP ratio without inflation and default is in stark contrast to what happened in Germany. As you see in the figure, German debt-to-GDP ratio is also reported to have been very low shortly after each of the world wars. For 1923, a debt-to-GDP ratio of only 4.2 percent is recorded, for 1950, a debt-to-GDP ratio of a mere 17.8 percent. The reason for this development is that Germany went through a hyperinflation after World War I, with inflation rates reaching more than 40 percent daily (see also Chapter 12). Government bonds were a promise to repay a certain amount in marks, but the mark lost almost half its value in a single day, so government debt was effectively wiped out. Similarly, after World War II, Germany went through a currency reform in which most of the government's liabilities were again cancelled.

2.2 Public Borrowing in Peace Times: A New Trend Since World War II

It is only in relatively recent times that public debt burdens have increased during peacetime. If you look again at Figure 16.1, you will see that the general decline in the debt-to-GDP ratio in the first couple of decades after World War II was followed by a slow increase in debt levels in many countries. From the late 1970s onward, the debt-to-GDP ratio started to creep upward again for the U.S., Germany, Italy, and France (though not shown in the graph, this was also true of smaller European countries such as Spain, the Netherlands, or Portugal). This trend is briefly interrupted around the mid-1990s before debt levels shoot up again from 2008 onward.

So, what happened from the late 1970s onward? One part of the explanation is that policy makers might have misunderstood the oil shocks of the 1970s and early 1980s. As we discussed in Chapter 13, the oil-price shock can best be understood as a negative supply shock. If policy makers interpreted these shocks as negative demand shocks as well and increased public spending and public deficits as a reaction (as evidently happened in some countries), the result would have been just a higher rate of inflation, but not higher output. As a consequence, the public debt level rose without the expected benefits in terms of higher economic growth, hence pushing upward the debt-to-GDP-ratio.

Some economists also argue that, while it is easy to pass stimulus packages cutting taxes or increasing social benefits, it is politically very difficult to increase taxes again or cut government spending. According to this explanation, the (well-meant) attempt to run countercyclical discretionary policy might end in increasing spending and cutting taxes in bad times but not in reducing the stimulus again once the economy has recovered, as political majorities for these austerity packages might be difficult to forge. In the end, deficits and debts would hence permanently increase.

Another important element for the most recent increase in the public debt-to-GDP ratio in most industrialized countries has been the global economic and financial crisis of 2008–2009. In many countries, governments saw themselves forced to bail out banks. In some cases, these bank bailouts were extremely expensive. For example, estimates indicate that the Irish government increased its outstanding government debt by roughly 40 percent of GDP in order to meet the needs of its bank bailouts. Having been a country with one of the soundest public finances in the EU, it even had to resort to a rescue loan from the International Monetary Fund and the European partners (see Chapter 17). Moreover, the deep recession reduced incomes and hence tax revenue significantly while increasing costs to the governments, for example, through the increase in the number of unemployed who had to rely on public transfers. Finally, the stimulus packages passed in 2008 and 2009 also explain part of the recent increase in government debt.

Yet these explanations probably do not cover the whole story: There have been some important changes in the global macroeconomic environment, first in the late 1970s, then after the Great Recession of 2008–2009, which explain part of the changed trend in public debt. To understand these changes and their consequences, we need to look a little bit deeper into the arithmetic of debt dynamics, which we will do in the next section.

Discussion Questions

1. What have been the main causes of the increase of debt-to-GDP-levels in the past?
2. Some people say that government debt never falls. To what extent is this statement historically correct?

3. ARITHMETICS OF DEBT DYNAMICS

One thing that is striking about the figures presented earlier is the speed with which countries have sometimes reduced their debt burden without resorting to extraordinary measures such as running the printing press or restructuring their debt (a term for changing the terms of debt so that its value is reduced, which can be seen as a partial default). For the discussion of dangers of debt, it is important to understand how debt accumulates and how the debt burden can be reduced again.

At first sight, the dynamics of debt seem simple: If a government spends more than it receives in taxes and other revenues, it runs a deficit. It hence has to borrow the necessary funds, and the debt level increases. If a government receives more in revenues than it spends, it runs a surplus. It can use the funds to pay down debt. Yet in reality, the dynamics are more complicated than this simple example. We can accept the simple logic that deficits lead to an increase in debt and surpluses to a reduction in debt when we consider debt measured in euros; however, it does not necessarily hold when we look at the debt-to-GDP level (which is the most relevant indicator to evaluate the real debt burden). The reason is that in normal times, debt and GDP are both changing. If GDP increases more quickly than the debt level, the debt-to-GDP ratio actually falls, making the debt level less burdensome. Moreover, what is important here is the nominal GDP (measured in current prices). Hence, if inflation is high, everything else being equal, nominal GDP increases more quickly, and the debt-to-GDP ratio falls.

Another important factor is the rate of interest: Especially for countries that already have a large level of public debt outstanding, a change in the interest rate might have a significant impact on the overall deficit. If interest rates increase, overall deficits will increase even if the government has not increased its other expenditures and has not

primary balance:
government net borrowing or net lending, excluding interest payments on government debt

cut taxes. In order to separate the effects of increased government spending from those of increased interest rates, economists have introduced the concept of the **primary balance**, which denotes the government balance without taking into account interest payments. A primary surplus hence means a situation in which the government would run a surplus before accounting for its interest payments and a primary deficit a situation in which it is borrowing already to cover its noninterest expenditure.

We can illustrate the importance of economic growth and inflation for the dynamics of public debt with three examples from a hypothetical economy. In one of our scenarios, the economy in question is experiencing strong growth. In the second scenario, the economy is stagnating. In the last scenario, the economy is growing but faced with deflation (a falling price level). In all three cases, the economy in question starts out with a nominal GDP level of 100 and a debt level of also 100, resulting in an initial debt-to-GDP ratio of 100 percent. In all three cases, the primary deficit of our government is 2 percent of GDP. In all of our cases, the *real* interest rate (nominal interest rate minus inflation, see Chapter 12) is 2 percent.

Let us now first look at the economy that is growing strongly. This economy differs from the other cases because its growth rate is higher. We assume that real GDP grows by 6 percent annually. We also assume that inflation is at 3 percent, and hence the nominal interest rate (real interest rate and inflation) is 5 percent. As we observe in Table 16.1, given these assumptions, both the nominal GDP and the nominal debt are growing, but interestingly, the debt-to-GDP ratio is declining even though the government continues to run a primary deficit! How is this possible? The answer is that nominal GDP increases by 9 percent annually (real GDP growth of 6 percent plus 3 percent inflation), while the debt level only increases by 7 percent (the primary deficit of 2 percent plus 5 percent interest rate on the outstanding debt). The result is a falling debt-to-GDP level.

Table 16.1 Debt Dynamics in an Economy With Strong Economic Growth

Year	Nominal GDP (in national currency)	Debt (in national currency)	Interest payments (in national currency)	Primary deficit (in national currency)	Debt-to-GDP ratio
1	100	100	5.0	2.0	100%
2	109	107	5.4	2.2	98%
3	119	115	5.7	2.4	96%
4	130	123	6.1	2.6	95%
5	141	131	6.6	2.8	93%
6	154	141	7.0	3.1	91%
7	168	151	7.5	3.4	90%
8	183	162	8.1	3.7	88%
9	199	174	8.7	4.0	87%
10	217	186	9.3	4.3	86%

Table 16.2 *Debt Dynamics in an Economy With Stagnating Economic Growth*

Year	Nominal GDP (in national currency)	Debt (in national currency)	Interest payments (in national currency)	Primary deficit (in national currency)	Debt-to-GDP ratio
1	100	100	5.0	2.0	100%
2	103	107	5.4	2.1	104%
3	106	114	5.7	2.1	108%
4	109	122	6.1	2.2	112%
5	113	131	6.5	2.3	116%
6	116	139	7.0	2.3	120%
7	119	149	7.4	2.4	124%
8	123	158	7.9	2.5	129%
9	127	169	8.4	2.5	133%
10	130	180	9.0	2.6	138%

Let us now move on to a situation in which the economic situation is less favorable. In our "stagnation" scenario, we again assume inflation of 3 percent and hence a nominal interest rate of 5 percent. However, now we assume that real GDP is not growing but stagnating (a growth rate of 0 percent). As we see in Table 16.2, the debt-to-GDP ratio develops very differently than in our first scenario: Now nominal GDP only grows by 3 percent (just inflation), but with a deficit as large as in the strong-growth scenario, the debt-to-GDP ratio increases. Within 10 years, it has risen from 100 percent of GDP to about 140 percent of GDP.

Let us now move to the third scenario, that of a deflation. In this scenario, the economy is still growing—much faster than in the stagnation scenario but not as strongly as in the strong-growth scenario. We assume a growth rate for real GDP of 2 percent. However, in this scenario, the general price level *falls* by 2 percent per year. Hence we have a moderate rate of deflation. Given that we assumed a real interest rate of 2 percent, this gives us a nominal interest rate of 0 percent—close to what we have observed for many euro-area countries as an interest rate on their government bonds in 2016. If we now look at the debt dynamics in Table 16.3, we see that the debt-to-GDP ratio also increases in this scenario. Over a 10-year-period, under these assumptions, the debt–to-GDP ratio climbs from 100 to almost 120 percent.

These three examples can help us to understand the debt dynamics of EU countries in some of the historical episodes discussed earlier. After World War II, many countries experienced a situation that was similar to our "strong-growth" scenario but even better. Economic growth was very robust in many countries after World War II (historians often talk about the "economic miracle"). Interest rates were generally rather low, and countries were running only small deficits, if any. The result was a rapid fall

Table 16.3 *Debt Dynamics in an Economy With Deflation*

Year	Nominal GDP (in national currency)	Debt (in national currency)	Interest payments (in national currency)	Primary deficit (in national currency)	Debt-to-GDP ratio
1	100	100	0.0	2.0	100%
2	100	102	0.0	2.0	102%
3	100	104	0.0	2.0	104%
4	100	106	0.0	2.0	106%
5	100	108	0.0	2.0	108%
6	100	110	0.0	2.0	110%
7	100	112	0.0	2.0	112%
8	100	114	0.0	2.0	114%
9	100	116	0.0	2.0	116%
10	100	118	0.0	2.0	118%

in the debt-to-GDP ratio even though the countries did not actually "pay back" a significant part of their debt.

In the late 1970s and into the 1980s, not only did many countries increase their deficits, but many economies also experienced a significant slowdown of economic growth. The decision by many central banks to fight inflation aggressively in the early 1980s additionally led to a strong increase in interest rates. This is a bit like our "stagnation" scenario with an added element of larger deficits and higher interest rates—clearly a recipe for increasing debt-to-GDP ratios.

The recent episode of debt increase since the onset of the Great Recession again can be seen as a combination of the stagnation scenario (the major economies have grown much more slowly than in the decade before), with increased deficits (for bank bailouts, stimulus packages, and because of a fall in tax revenue) and some elements of the deflation scenario (at least in some EU countries, since 2008, we have observed years in which the price level fell). Again, it is clear that such a combination should lead to a sizable increase in debt-to-GDP ratios even without governments actually turning toward an irresponsible fiscal policy. The dynamics of our deflation scenario also give us another reason central banks are so concerned about preventing deflation: Once you are in a deflationary environment, debt becomes more problematic without actual increases in the deficit.

Discussion Questions

1. In historical periods of falling debt-to-GDP-ratios, what has been the predominant mechanism behind the reduction of debt?
2. To what extent is deflation a problem for public debt reduction?

4. POTENTIAL PROBLEMS OF EXCESSIVE DEBTS

In earlier chapters, we saw that when a government borrows money, it issues bonds on which it must pay interest. The interest payments form part of the annual budget. Figure 16.3 shows how these payments as a percentage of the general government budget have varied over time. Note that interest payments accounted for a much greater portion of the economy and the budget during the 1990s than they do now. Considering that public debt as a percentage of GDP has risen quite rapidly over the past decade, how can this be? The answer is that the unusually low interest rates that have prevailed over the same period make this possible.

We have seen in earlier chapters that a weak economy tends to induce lower interest rates, both naturally and as a consequence of policy measures. If interest rates are lower throughout the economy, governments can issue new debt (bonds) at a low interest rate. When it does so, it is effectively reducing the portion of the budget that must be set aside for debt service. The phenomenon is not unlike the low monthly payments a homeowner makes after obtaining a mortgage with a very low interest rate.

As of November 2016, the interest rate on a 10-year German government bond was 0.2 percent (see Figure 16.4). The interest rates on bonds with shorter maturities were even negative. Other European governments had to pay slightly higher interest rates, but by and large, interest rates on government bonds were extremely low in historical comparison. One might think that at this time, borrowing was especially cheap,

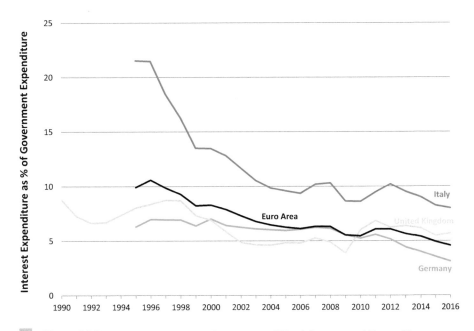

Figure 16.3 *Interest Payments as Percentage of Total Government Expenditure*

Despite increasing debt levels, interest payments on the debt have fallen as a percentage of total government expenditure due to unusually low interest rates.

Source: AMECO.

Figure 16.4 *The Interest Rate on 10-Year German Bonds*

Interest rates on 10-year German bonds have fallen steadily and were briefly even negative in 2016. Yields on other euro-area government bonds have by and large followed this trend.

Source: Macrobond.

making it a good time for the government to run a budget deficit and accumulate debt, at least for countries with relatively low levels of public debt such as Germany or the Netherlands. The argument for adding to public debt seems even stronger if the government spends on programs that produce a high multiplier effect (Chapter 10) or on programs that increase the long-term ability of an economy to grow, such as education (we will come back to factors of long-term growth in Chapter 18). With low interest rates, the gain from the multiplier effect (in terms of the increase in aggregate demand) or long-term growth is potentially larger than the loss (adding to debt burden), making the net gain positive.

However, it may be counterproductive to allow the debt to grow if it is to finance "low-multiplier" activities. An example is tax cuts for the wealthy, which, as we saw in Chapter 10, do not produce as much "bang for the buck" as new spending on constructive activities. A useful way of understanding the problem is to imagine the government as a private business. Would a business borrow money at an interest rate higher than its expected rate of return? Here, the situation is similar, only a bit more complicated; the government needs to assess the projected "social return" of its expenditures.

Another concern with mounting debt is that, if it becomes sufficiently large, lenders may start to doubt the borrowers' ability to repay. If the doubts are severe and widespread, this could affect the bond market and, indirectly, the national economy.

Risk-averse investors would sell their bonds, driving bond prices down. When bond prices go down, bond yields (interest rates) go up (as noted in the Appendix to Chapter 12), because the amount that the government has to pay in interest on the bond becomes higher relative to the value of the bond.

The greater the unease over the borrower's ability to pay, the higher the interest rate that the borrower must offer in order to attract lenders. At some point, the interest rate might become so high that governments are effectively cut off from financial markets. In this case, in order to prevent a default and to continue servicing already outstanding loans (that is paying interest and retiring loans as they come due), governments might be forced to use extraordinary measures such as abruptly cutting public expenditure, borrowing from the International Monetary Fund (IMF), or printing money to service their debt. Such a cutoff from financial markets is exactly what happened to some governments in the euro area during the euro crisis (which will be covered in detail in the next chapter).

This situation can have severe consequences for the economy in question. All options to service debt in such a situation come with severe collateral damage. Austerity measures, such as large cuts in government expenditures and/or increasing taxes, lead to a fall in output, as discussed in Chapter 13. Borrowing from the IMF usually means that the country in question must agree to such measures to reduce the budget deficit, and the national government loses a certain degree of sovereignty over how it can spend its money.

Printing money to service the debt or, more technically, having the central bank purchase government bonds and create the money necessary to do so (called **monetizing the debt**) also is not risk free: As we have discussed in Chapter 12, such a policy risks causing inflation, especially if the increase in the money supply is sufficiently large. If such inflation does occur, the bond markets might then demand higher interest rates on new debt to compensate for the anticipated loss from inflation, which might again force the government to sell more government bonds to the central bank. As many historical instances of hyperinflation were linked to governments trying to monetize debt, economists are generally wary of such a development and see it as a slippery slope toward higher and higher inflation.

monetizing the debt: the purchase of new debt from governments by the central bank

Note that—as briefly mentioned before—monetizing the debt is generally not possible for countries in the euro area. By the rules of the European treaty, single national governments do not have their own central banks that could buy government debt. In fact, the ECB is even prohibited from directly buying newly issued bonds from the governments, and this clause can only be changed by unanimous consent of all EU countries. In contrast, countries outside the euro area such as Britain or the U.S. have their own central banks which have the power to buy government bonds and thus monetize debt.

Finally, not reacting to rising interest rates and potential problems in servicing the debt also is not an option for a government. The problem is that government debt is often strongly interlinked with the financial system. For a number of reasons, banks and other financial institutions in most countries hold a significant share of their assets in government bonds. Government bonds are usually among the most liquid assets in an economy. They are routinely accepted in interbank dealings and dealings between commercial banks and the central bank. They are also among the safest assets in an economy. While in principle one would think that big corporations might be more creditworthy than the government, this notion neglects the fact that faced with a default, government has the power to raise additional money through taxes, unlike individual corporations. As a consequence, rating agencies hardly ever rate a corporation better than the government of the country the firms' headquarters are located in.

Hence, if a government's ability or willingness to service its debt is questioned, financing costs for the firms in the country concerned are also likely to increase, depressing private investment. Moreover, as bond prices are inversely related to interest rates, and interest rates increase when creditors start doubting a government's ability to service the debt, this situation will result in significant losses for banks (which, as we said, own a lot of government bonds). These losses in turn will lead to a deteriorating capital base of banks and will make them more reluctant to lend to private firms and households. This in turn will tend to depress aggregate demand and hence output.

Even if it does not come to the worst, and investors do not question a country's ability to continue servicing the public debt, there are other possible problems related to a very high level of indebtedness. Some economists believe that a high level of government debt reduces private investment: According to this view, firms that consider investing in fixed capital expect that, with a high share of the public budget going to interest payments, the government will not be able to continue to invest in public infrastructure or that the government will have to increase taxes in the future. Deteriorating infrastructure comes with costs for businesses (e.g., when parts cannot be delivered on time because bridges are closed) and lowers private firms' profitability, as would higher corporate taxes. As a consequences, firms will invest less. While many economists accept this argument in principle, there has been a huge dispute about the question of how relevant this mechanism is empirically and at what level of debt it really becomes a problem (see Box 16.1).

BOX 16.1 THE 90-PERCENT-DEBT THRESHOLD AND A SPREADSHEET ERROR

For a long time, most economists agreed that from a certain point onward, public debt would be a drag on economic growth. Yet it remained elusive to show at what point government debt actually would become a problem. In 2010, economists Carmen Reinhart and Kenneth Rogoff published a paper which suggested that from a threshold of about 90 percent debt-to-GDP ratio upward, countries would experience significantly lower economic growth. Policy makers quickly jumped at this conclusion and used the paper to argue for sharp budget cuts in order to bring public debt under control, especially as government debt was close to the 90 percent threshold in many of the important developed countries.

However, the results proved to be less robust than thought: In a class with professor Michael Ash at the University of Massachusetts, Amherst, the graduate student Thomas Herdon was given the task to pick an economics paper and replicate the results. He picked the work of Reinhart and Rogoff but did not manage to replicate the result. Upon closer examination, he found out that Reinhart and Rogoff had made a mistake in their Excel spreadsheet, leaving out five countries in their key calculations.

Including these five countries and also giving more weight to larger countries in the sample fundamentally changed the results of the original paper: While one could still show that economic growth would slow somewhat among countries with higher debt levels, the spectacular result of a dramatic drop in GDP growth once a country's debt-to-GDP-level surpassed 90 percent could not be substantiated.

Subsequently, some economists have also pointed out that the relationship shown between high debt-to-GDP-ratios and low growth does not necessarily imply causality from debt to growth: It is also conceivable that countries experience slow growth for reasons unrelated to the debt level, and this leads to higher deficits and growing debt levels. In that case, low growth would be causing relatively high debt levels rather than vice versa.

Sources: *Economist*, "The 90% question," April 20, 2013; Paul Krugman, "Reinhart-Rogoff, Continued," *New York Times Blog*, April 16, 2013.

Discussion Questions

1. What are possible problems with excessive public debt?
2. What options has a government when it finds itself faced with excessive public debt? Why might one say that there are no good options for dealing with excessive public debt?

5. EUROPEAN RULES ON DEBT AND DEFICITS

Because government debt can be dangerous, and because a high level of government debt can lead to pressure on the central bank to monetize debt, when the member states of the European Union decided in the early 1990s to move forward with the process of introducing a common currency, they tried to limit government debts and deficits. When the Maastricht Treaty was signed in 1992, five **convergence criteria** were defined, which EU countries would have to fulfill before they could join the euro area:

convergence criteria: the requirements that EU countries must satisfy as a condition for introducing the euro, including low levels of inflation, interest rates, government debt, and public deficits

1. Inflation needed to be no higher than in the three EU countries with the lowest rates of inflation plus 1.5 percentage points.
2. Public deficits needed to be below 3 percent of GDP.
3. Government debt-to-GDP-ratio needed to be below 60 percent or at least have "sufficiently diminished and must be approaching the reference value at a satisfactory pace."
4. The country must have kept its exchange rate in a stable corridor with the other currencies of European member states planning to join the euro for two years.
5. Yields on 10-year-government bonds had to be no more than 2 percentage points above the yields in the three EU countries with the lowest rate of inflation.

541

Some of these criteria, of course, had nothing to do with government debt and deficits: The criterion on inflation was supposed to make sure that only countries with (similarly) low rates of inflation would join the euro. The criterion on the exchange rate was supposed to make sure that only countries that could live with a stable exchange rate would be allowed to join.

The other three criteria, however, were designed to ensure that only countries with sound public policies could join the euro: The deficit criterion was supposed to make sure that only countries which have managed to bring down the deficit to a relatively low levels would join the currency union. The yield on government debt was a way to check whether market participants believed that the government would be able to service its debt also in the future: If investors had serious doubts about debt sustainability, they would sell the government bonds in question, sending bond prices down and yields up. Note that the deficit criterion was much more strictly worded than the debt criterion: The wording that the debt level should be below 60 percent of GDP or should have "sufficiently diminished," "approaching the reference value at a satisfactory pace," left a lot of discretion in deciding which country could join.

Shortly after the ratification of the Maastricht Treaty, a debate started over whether the convergence criteria actually were enough to *permanently* guarantee prudent public finances. Originally, especially in Germany, very few experts had believed that given these convergence criteria, a common currency with a large number of European countries would be established anytime soon. There was a consensus that Germany and some economically closely aligned countries such as the Netherlands, Belgium, Luxembourg, and France might form a currency union, but hardly anyone believed that Italy or Spain could meet the criteria. However, with some Southern European countries such as Italy having made huge progress in bringing down inflation and deficits in the 1990s, a larger currency union increasingly became a concrete possibility.

The German finance minister of the time, Theo Waigel, hence proposed an amendment to the rules, forcing members of the currency union to limit borrowing also *after* the introduction of the euro (remember that the convergence criteria were only applied before a country's accession to the euro). In 1997, these ideas were adopted in the **Stability and Growth Pact** (SGP). This pact obliged countries using the euro to run fiscal policies, which confirmed with the original convergence criteria, especially keeping their budget deficit below 3 percent of GDP and making sure that their debt level, if above 60 percent, was falling toward that reference value. They also committed to aim at a national budget "close to balance or in surplus" over the medium term. To make sure that adverse developments were spotted early on, countries agreed to submit annual compliance reports. According to the rules, if countries were running a deficit of more than 3 percent of GDP and had not been victims of severe economic circumstance (such as very deep recessions), they could be fined, yet the actual fining was subject to a complicated voting process, under which the Council of the European Union (representing all EU countries) had to vote to impose a fine. With the introduction of the euro as a virtual currency on January 1, 1999, (coins and notes were introduced three years later) in Germany, France, Italy, Spain, the

Stability and Growth Pact: rules for euro-area countries about government deficit and government debt which can be enforced by imposing fines on member states with excessive deficits

542

Netherlands, Belgium, Austria, Portugal, Ireland, Finland, and Luxembourg, these rules became binding for these 11 countries.

However, the SGP did not work as anticipated. In 2000, a bubble in the tech stock market burst. A year later, terrorists hijacked planes in the United States and steered them into the World Trade Center in New York and the Pentagon in Washington, DC. Both events led to a huge increase in economic uncertainty and, as a consequence, a number of European economies experienced a severe economic slowdown. Portugal went into a recession. Germany was also hard hit, falling into a first recession early in 2002 and experiencing a second one in 2003. Overall, the euro area saw its growth rate collapsing from more than 4 percent in mid-2000 to around 0.5 percent in 2002–2003. With tax revenues falling and costs for unemployment skyrocketing, public deficits shot up. Portugal was the first country to report a deficit above the threshold of 3 percent of GDP. According to data of that time, the deficit for 2001 actually stood at 4.1 percent of GDP. The European Commission invoked the excessive deficit procedure, and Portugal pledged to bring down the deficit again. However, for 2002, and despite cuts in public spending, both Germany and France had to report deficits above the threshold of 3 percent of GDP (it turned out later that Germany had already passed the threshold in 2001).

This situation led to an intense debate about appropriate policy responses. A number of economists pointed out that the Stability and Growth Pact in its original version would induce procyclical fiscal policies: If countries experienced a recession and falling revenues due to the economic slow-down pushed the deficit above the threshold of 3 percent, they would be forced to cut spending. This would result in a procyclical fiscal policy, actually making the recession worse. This group of economists advocated making the SGP more flexible. On the other side of the debate were (mainly German) economists, who warned that fines would be necessary to prevent countries from running irresponsible fiscal policies and who advocated introducing automatic fines for countries reporting a deficit of more than 3 percent of GDP.

In the end, the proponents of more flexibility prevailed. Germany and France used their clout in the Council of Ministers to avoid being fined, and the EU countries changed the rules of the SGP. According to the reformed regulation, the threshold of 3 percent was interpreted in a more flexible way. Deficits above this value were no longer automatically seen as "excessive," but they were accepted if they were deemed to be "exceptional and temporary." Here, long periods of stagnation, the implementation of pension reforms, or high public investments were accepted as exonerating circumstances. On the other side, the commitments to balance the budget over the medium term were made more specific, with a clear commitment to reduce deficits by 0.5 percentage points per year until a budget close to balance was reached. In the short run, however, the reform prevented the sanctioning of countries such as Germany and France for running deficits of more than 3 percent. It was not until 2006 that these countries brought their deficits below the 3 percent threshold again.

However, this was not the last change to the rules. The euro crisis (covered in the next chapter) brought the issue of debt control back on the agenda. As a consequence of what was perceived as a debt crisis, in 2011, the EU member states again overhauled

543

the SGP. On paper, the new rules represented a significant tightening of the SGP. If the debt-to-GDP ratio is above 60 percent, excessive deficit procedures can now be initiated even if the deficit is below 3 percent of GDP. Fines now do not need the approval of the Council of Ministers but can still be vetoed by the Council. Moreover, in a separate treaty, the Treaty on Stability, Coordination and Governance in the Economic and Monetary Union (also known as the **Fiscal Compact**), member states committed to put procedures into national law (preferably their constitutions) to make sure that governments would run budgets that are close to balance. This idea was mainly pushed by Germany which in 2009 had adopted a rule in its constitution ("Schuldenbremse"—debt brake) that prescribed an almost balanced budget for the future.

Fiscal Compact: agreement among euro-area member states to put rules for balanced budget into national law and preferably their constitution

Yet in 2016, the debate about European debt and deficit rules was still not settled. After applying harsh austerity in the first years of the euro crisis, many countries slid deeper into recession. With falling GDP, the debt-to-GDP ratio rose despite cuts in public expenditure and tax increases. As unemployment reached record levels in some countries and populists gained in the polls, countries were given more time to reach the goal of a balanced budget. Into 2016, some countries such as Spain continued to run large budget deficits (for 2015, the Spanish deficit stood at 5.2 percent of GDP), yet it seemed unlikely that they would be fined anytime soon. It seemed that a general consensus was forming that, given the still weak state of the European economy at that time, further budget cuts would not be helpful. However, as has been seen in the past, it is difficult to impose fines once countries have initially been allowed to get away with missing the benchmark. The future of the European rules on debt and deficit is thus still undecided.

DISCUSSION QUESTIONS

1. How did European countries try to make sure that only countries with sound public finances joined the euro area? What were problems with the initial approach?
2. After multiple reforms to the euro area's debt and deficit rules, what are the current rules for government borrowing?

REVIEW QUESTIONS

1. What is the difference between the national debt and a deficit?
2. What years during the twentieth century were debt/GDP levels the highest in Britain, France, Germany, the United States, and Italy? What years were the lowest?
3. What was the role of the national debt in Britain in the sixteenth to nineteenth centuries?
4. How did the national debt picture change with World War II in the countries discussed in this chapter?
5. What factors contributed to the increase in government debt in the 1970s? Which factors to the increase since 2000?

6. Summarize some of the potential problems with government debt.

7. To what extent is government debt a burden for future generations? To what extent is it not?

8. To what extent do potential problems with government debt mean that governments should not borrow at all?

9. What does it mean to monetize the debt?

10. What were the original rules for government debt and deficits in the euro area at the time of the introduction of the euro? What were the problems with these rules?

11. What are arguments for strict rules limiting budget deficits? What are arguments against such rules?

EXERCISES

1. Go to the European Commission's AMECO database (http://ec.europa.eu/economy_finance/ db_indicators/ameco/index_en.htm) and look for recent data on government debt as a percentage of GDP and recent figures on budget deficits for the euro area and your home country. What does this tell you about recent trends? Compare the period 2000–2007 to more recent years. Do the figures indicate that we may be returning to a more "normal" situation regarding debt and deficits?

2. Use the AMECO database and construct a table of Eurozone members and their debt/GDP ratios and the deficit-to-GDP figures. Review the convergence criteria for participation in the euro zone presented in the chapter. What did you discover in this exercise? Explain your answer.

3. The chapter identifies and explains several reasons it is inappropriate to compare the government debt to the debt of a private citizen. Which of these explanations are consistent with the presentation in the chapter?

    a. Governments have the ability to "roll over" their debt more or less endlessly.

    b. Governments cannot default on their debt obligations.

    c. A significant portion of the government debt is owed to citizens of the same country.

    d. Governments with a national currency (such as Britain) pay interest on their debts in currency that they print.

    e. Government debt is always used to finance investment.

4. The chapter identifies and explains several reasons government deficits in the euro area have repeatedly been above the threshold of 3 percent of GDP. Which of these explanations is consistent with the chapter's presentation?

    a. Interest rates for countries having joined the euro were much higher than prior to euro-area membership.

    b. Unexpected recessions have led to lower government revenues and hence have pushed deficits up.

    c. Politicians never cut back deficits.

    d. Interest payments on the debt have risen.

    e. Many governments did not bring down their deficits sufficiently in good times.

5. The chapter is very clear that it's dangerous to assume that "government debt is never a concern." Which of the following are reasons articulated in the chapter for why debt can be a concern?

a. Foreign holders of government debt may decide to sell their bonds.

b. A larger share of future budgets must be devoted to interest payments.

c. It is always unwise for governments to get into debt.

d. Interest payments to high-income individuals could exacerbate income inequality.

e. Deficit spending during a recession will only make the economic downturn worse.

6. Match each concept in Column A with a definition or example in Column B.

Column A	Column B
a. Debt	1. The portion of the gross government debt that is owed to individuals or groups within the country
b. Deficit	2. European rules limiting government deficits
c. Gross public debt	3. The portion of the gross federal debt that is owed to foreign individuals or groups
d. Fiscal Compact	4. A stock variable that represents the accumulation of deficits over many years
e. Internal debt	5. An agreement between European countries to put balanced-budget rules into national law
f. External debt	6. A policy of deficit cutting that reduces public expenditures and/or raises taxes to balance the budget
g. Monetizing the debt	7. A flow variable that measures the excess of spending over revenue collections
h. Stability and Growth Pact	8. The requirements that EU countries must satisfy as a condition for participating in the Eurozone
i. Austerity	9. The purchase of new debt from the governments by central banks
j. Convergence criteria	10. Total amount owed by the government to all claimants, including foreigners, the public, and other government accounts, including the central bank

Chapter 17

The Euro Crisis

In late 2009, policy makers were sighing with relief. The general perception was that their decisive actions had helped to avert the worst during the global financial and economic crisis that started in 2008. Instead of spiraling into a global depression like the one experienced in the late 1920s and early 1930s, the economies of the advanced world had embarked on a brisk recovery. In fact, many forecasters were surprised by how well stimulus packages and monetary easing had worked in improving the global economy in the second half of 2009 and were correcting their forecasts for 2010 upward again.

However, the respite was of short duration: In the spring of 2010, the euro crisis hit Europe. Starting with investor panic about potential debt problems in Greece, the crisis quickly spread over much of the continent. Investors became increasingly afraid of a potential breakup of the common currency. The International Monetary Fund (IMF) was called in to provide rescue loans and help design adjustment programs. Politicians started to pass harsh budget cuts and tax increases to calm investors. Yet the result was not what was hoped for: The euro area fell back into recession, and in many countries, unemployment rate shot up to levels not experienced for decades. EU countries outside the euro area such as the UK were also hit, as demand in their main continental export markets contracted sharply. Investors became ever more spooked. In quick succession, EU and euro-area governments passed new austerity packages, as well as institutional reforms such as new rules for deficit control and common oversight of banks. Only after ECB president Mario Draghi promised to do "whatever it takes" to save the euro, in the summer of 2012, did the panic subside.

As of 2016, the euro-area economy is growing again, but the economic, social, and political damage the crisis has caused in Europe is significant. In Greece, during the crisis, GDP contracted by a quarter. In some countries such as Greece and Spain, youth unemployment reached more than 50 percent, and overall unemployment reached more than 25 percent. Millions of people were pushed into poverty. By early 2016, in many euro-area countries, GDP was still below the 2008 level, and projections show that it might take well into the 2020s before the precrisis levels of output and employment are reached again in the countries most affected.

This chapter will look at the euro crisis in detail. How did the crisis actually evolve? What were the causes? What remedies were attempted, and what worked? Can a replay of the crisis be prevented? As you will see, while the actual timeline of events is clear, the interpretation of what should have been or should be done is still widely disputed.

1. PRELUDE TO THE CRISIS: EUROPEAN MONETARY INTEGRATION

In order to understand the euro crisis, we need to take a step back and have a look at the euro's history. Up until the euro crisis, the euro was seen as one of the crowning achievements of half a century of European integration. While the founding treaty of the European integration project, the Treaty of Rome (signed in 1957), focused mainly on the creation of a common market and a customs union, the discussion about monetary cooperation in Europe began shortly afterward. In the late 1960s, shock waves went through the global Bretton Woods system of fixed exchange rates. Balance-of-payment problems of the United States of America led to wider revaluations of other currencies, and the German mark appreciated, while the French franc depreciated. As these revaluations impacted negatively on the trade of European countries, the members of the European Economic Community (the predecessor of today's European Union) started to think about a solution for more stable exchange rates in Europe. The heads of state or government asked the Council to draw up a plan for monetary integration. In the resulting Werner report, which was published in October 1970, a plan was set up to achieve a monetary union using a common currency within a decade. However, this plan was thwarted by the breakup of the Bretton Woods system in the early 1970s and the first oil shock of 1973. Initially, the European countries tried to limit the fluctuations between their currencies (under an approach called the "snake in the tunnel"). This approach proved unworkable when the oil price shot up. As we have discussed in Chapter 13, countries such as Germany managed to get inflation under control quickly, while countries such as Italy experienced sustained periods of double digit inflation. In such a situation, a common currency or even fixed exchange rates were out of the question, as they would have meant that one country's exports would permanently lose competitiveness while the other country's exports would surge.

A new attempt to stabilize exchange rates in Europe was made in late 1979, when eight European countries (Belgium, Denmark, France, Germany, Ireland, Italy, Luxembourg, and the Netherlands) established the European Exchange Rate Mechanism (ERM). Under this system, exchange rates were allowed to fluctuate only within a given margin, yet there was the possibility of larger corrections if they were deemed necessary. Other European countries joined later. The system brought some stability, but not as much as had been hoped for: Exchange rate realignments were rather frequent and were increasingly seen as an impediment to creating a truly single market for goods and services in Europe, an aim that policy makers were pushing for. As a consequence, a new committee under the chairmanship of European Commission President Jacques Delors was set up in 1988, and the committee delivered the so-called Delors report in 1989, proposing a three-stage path toward monetary union. Based on this proposal, the goal and procedures to move from national currencies to a common

European currency were outlined in the Treaty on European Union in 1991 (also called the **Maastricht Treaty** after the Dutch city it was signed in). According to this plan, a common currency for the European Union was supposed to be introduced during the 1990s but not later than 1999. Countries would join successively as soon as they had met the convergence criteria (see Chapter 16). Denmark and Britain, which feared that they would lose national sovereignty, negotiated opt-out clauses, according to which they could decide whether they would join the euro or not.

The original time line of achieving monetary union was once again delayed. In the early 1990s, Germany was reunited and experienced a strong economic boom. As a consequence, the Bundesbank increased interest rates very strongly. The rest of the EU was faced with a slowing economy, and the other European central banks did not want to follow the Bundesbank's high interest rate policies. As a consequence, speculators were moving large amounts of financial capital from the rest of the EU into Germany, putting currencies such as the Irish punt, the Spanish escudo, the British pound, and the Italian lira under depreciation pressure. In 1992, the ERM system of fixed exchange rates broke down. Inflation and interest rates once more diverged strongly, and the following recession pushed public deficits in most countries beyond the threshold of 3 percent of GDP that had been defined as one of the convergence criteria. The whole project of monetary union was cast into doubt once more.

It was only in the late 1990s that it became clear that many countries did much better than expected with regard to the convergence criteria. While many (especially German) observers had long believed that only some core EU countries such as Germany, France, Austria, Belgium, the Netherlands, and Luxembourg would be able to bring down inflation and public deficits sufficiently to meet the convergence criteria, now also Italy, Spain, Portugal, Ireland, and Finland met the criteria. So monetary union started with these 11 member states in 1999, and Greece joined shortly after.

1.1 The Theory of Optimum Currency Areas

Economists and politicians continued to be deeply divided during the 1980s and 1990s whether it really was a good idea to form a monetary union in Europe. A whole branch of economic research, the **theory of optimum currency areas** (OCA), looked into the question: Under what conditions might it be beneficial for countries to abandon their national currency and form a monetary union? The basic premise was that having a common currency would bring benefits, as it reduced transaction costs and hence promoted cross-border trade, but that a currency union came also with costs. Especially, countries would not be able to set their own interest rate any more or to conduct their own monetary policy. If only one country in a monetary union went into a recession, there would be little that monetary policy could do, since in a monetary union, the common central bank sets the interest rate for all member states. Hence, OCA theory set up criteria under which this drawback would not be very important.

The most famous criterion was defined by Robert Mundell, who later won the Nobel prize in economics for his contributions to this debate: He stated that if workers are sufficiently mobile between countries, these countries could form an OCA. His idea was that an adverse development in one member state of a monetary union could be cured if the unemployed could move easily and quickly to other parts of the monetary union. Other criteria included that of economies being very well diversified (making it less likely that they would be hit by a recession not experienced by their partners) and being very open to trade (meaning that the national economy would be strongly in sync with its partners).

Finally, some economists claimed that one needed some kind of common fiscal policy (sometimes called "fiscal union"), or at least cross-border transfer flows, to make a monetary union viable. According to this view, fiscal policy could substitute for national monetary policies. When a single country was hit by a recession but other countries were not, the downturn could be battled by increased government spending and tax cuts in that country. While single countries might have problems running such a policy for a sustained period of time (as investors might be wary of growing debt levels, as we discussed in Chapter 16), a fiscal union could overcome this obstacle either by paying for the expenditure from a centralized budget or by transferring money from other member states to the country in difficulties.

According to many of these criteria, the European economies did not form an optimum currency area. While workers are allowed to move freely between EU countries, barriers such as different languages, different cultures, and differences in the education system de facto limit labor mobility. Empirically, workers move much more between the single U.S. states than between EU countries. Some of the smaller EU countries clearly are not well diversified. Greece, for example, has strong tourism and strong shipping sectors but not much more. Some of the EU countries also were not very open to trade in 1998, with exports-to-GDP ratios of 16 percent in Greece and around 25 percent in France, Spain, and Portugal. Finally, a fiscal union was not included in the Maastricht plans for a monetary union. Instead, the Maastricht Treaty explicitly ruled out that one member state or the union as a whole might take over obligations from another member state (the so-called **no-bailout clause**). The whole EU budget was limited to a little more than 1 percent of GDP, the largest part of which was allocated well in advance and could not be used to help countries experiencing difficulties.

no-bailout clause: rule laid down in the European treaties that neither the EU nor other member states should assume or be liable for other countries' commitments

Consequently, when the Maastricht Treaty was negotiated, a significant number of economists remained skeptical. However, other researchers asked whether the OCA criteria were really the right way at looking at the issue: They claimed that the introduction of a common currency would by itself change the structure of the participating economies. For example, trade would naturally increase among countries using the same currency, hence making the economies more open. According to this view, OCA criteria would not have to be met *before* the introduction of a common currency, but countries could *become* optimum currency areas once they had introduced a common currency.

Finally, politicians decided: Because of the aim of creating a more closely integrated Europe, especially in a time when Germany was reunited and politicians in some countries were wary of potentially growing nationalist tendencies in Germany, the process of monetary integration in Europe was pushed forward, and the euro was introduced as virtual currency in 1999 and in its physical form in 2002.

In the decade between the introduction of the euro and before the outbreak of the euro crisis, the debate about whether Europe was an optimum currency area had all but disappeared. While some economists were warning that dangerous imbalances were growing in the form of large current account imbalances of some countries, the overall assessment of the monetary integration project was positive. Economies with histories of high inflation such as Italy, Spain, and Greece had experienced a sharp and sustained fall in actual inflation during the transition toward the euro. Interest rates had come down significantly for these countries, and between 1999 and 2007, the governments in these countries could borrow almost as cheaply as the governments of countries such as Germany and the Netherlands. Economic growth was strong, especially in the euro-area periphery (denoting countries such as Greece, Spain, Ireland, and Portugal), and living standards in these countries were increasing robustly. Cross-border trade and financial flows inside the monetary union grew briskly. The EU had managed to overcome the fallout of the U.S. subprime crisis without major tensions between its members and their economies. In other parts of the world such as Africa or the region around the Persian Gulf, countries started to discuss whether they should follow the European model and introduce a common currency.

Discussion Questions

1. Why did European countries decide to move toward a common currency? Do you think the arguments for a common currency in Europe are convincing?
2. What were the initial benefits from the euro received by countries with historically high inflation? Did low-inflation countries also benefit? How?

2. TIMELINE OF THE CRISIS

The euro crisis began in early 2010, when the newly elected Greek government was forced to revise upward data on the public deficit and the public debt level. According to updated figures, the 2009 deficit finally came in at more than 10 percent of GDP. Given the already high level of Greek public debt of more than 120 percent of GDP, market participants started to doubt Greece's debt sustainability, and yields on Greek bonds started to increase (see Figure 17.1). The **bond spread** between Greek bonds and German bonds, a measure of market distrust, increased to almost 10 percentage points, or 1,000 basis points (100 basis points are 1 percentage point). This means that Greece would have had to pay 10 percentage points on a 10-year-bond more than the German government if it tried to borrow in financial markets. Such a high interest rate would be highly problematic, as the interest burden alone would quickly push Greek public debt to a level at which it could not be serviced anymore.

At this point, not only was the Greek deficit large, but government finances in all OECD countries were strained because of the negative effects from the global financial and economic crisis of 2008–2009. In fact, in international comparison, the fiscal

bond spread: the difference in yield between a country's bond and a bond of highest quality (usually a German bond)

551

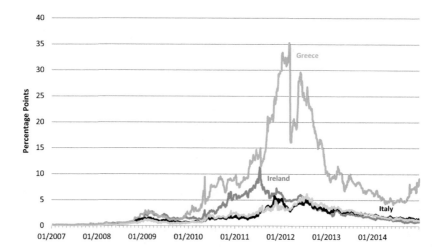

Figure 17.1 *Bond Spreads of Selected Euro-Area Countries*

This graph shows the difference in yields of euro-area bonds relative to German bonds. For most countries, these spreads rose until the summer of 2012 and declined thereafter.

Source: Macrobond Financial Database.

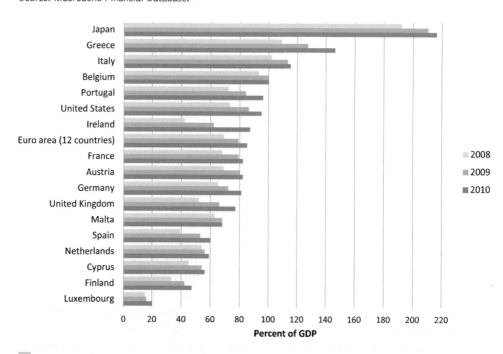

Figure 17.2a *Public Debt for Selected Countries, 2009*

Both debt levels and deficits in the euro area were not especially high by international comparison in 2009. In fact, the public finances in Japan looked much worse. Nevertheless, only the euro area was hit by a confidence crisis.

Source: Ameco Database.

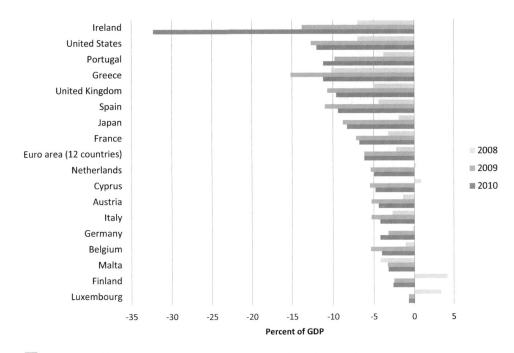

Figure 17.2b *Government Budget Balance for Selected Countries, 2009*

situation of the euro area did not look overly worrying. On average, the euro area in 2009 had a government budget deficit of 6.3 percent of GDP, compared to a deficit of 12.7 percent in the U.S. and almost 11 percent in Britain. With a few exceptions such as Greece and Italy, the public debt-to-GDP level also did not seem overly high in international comparison. Especially the later crisis countries Ireland and Spain, but also Portugal, did not show an excessively high public debt-to-GDP level at the start of the crisis.

2.1   Greece Asks for Assistance

At the beginning, European leaders were opposed to any rescue package for Greece. Their position was that consequences from the Greek financing problems were limited to Greece and that the European treaties actually ruled out support to one member state's public finance by other member states through its no-bailout clause (see earlier). As recommended by the European Commission, Greece started implementing harsh austerity packages in March 2010. The government cut expenditure and increased taxes by a total of about 2 percent of GDP. However, it quickly became clear that Greece would still miss its deficit target by a wide margin. The tough stance of the EU partners started to change when market concerns started to spread to other countries such as Portugal, Spain, Ireland, and Italy. It became obvious that Greece would not be able to borrow the funds necessary to pay for all its expenditure and continue to service its debt. Consequently, in late April 2010, Greece requested assistance from the euro-area member states and the International Monetary Fund, an international organization tasked with supporting countries that have difficulty meeting their external obligations (see Chapter 14). The partner countries and the IMF put together a €110 billion rescue package in early May 2010. These loans relieved Greece from having to borrow directly from the markets at much higher interest rates, but the IMF, the EU Commission, and the ECB (together later referred as "the **troika**") insisted on an economic adjustment program for Greece. As a conditionality for the loans, more budget cuts were demanded and subsequently put into place. The Greek government also agreed on structural reform, liberalizing labor and product markets and privatizing state-owned companies and properties.

troika: term used in the early years of the euro crisis to denote the IMF, the ECB, and the EU Commission, which together decided on conditions for loan packages for countries in crisis

The economic impact of the austerity packages on the Greek economy was in line with what our model from Chapter 13 would predict: The *AD* curve shifted to the left and the Greek economy started to contract sharply from the second half of 2010 onward. Unemployment shot up. Yet the debt-to-GDP ratio did not decline. The deep recession led to a sharp contraction of tax revenue, the continuing large (albeit smaller) deficit added to the outstanding debt, and as nominal GDP (the denominator of the debt-to-GDP ratio) fell, the debt-to-GDP-ratio jumped upward.

2.2 The Crisis Spreads to Portugal and Ireland

Immediately after the first Greek loan package, bond spreads for other euro periphery countries fell but started to increase almost immediately again. Increasingly, market participants did not fear just a default of one or two euro member countries' governments but actually the breaking up of the whole monetary union, as national governments might at some point decide to reintroduce a national currency. According to these scenarios, a default of a government would lead to a banking crisis in the country concerned (as banks hold large quantities of bonds of their national governments), and the government would then be faced with the choice of reintroducing a national currency (which would allow them to use the printing press of their own central bank to finance its deficits) or a meltdown of the national banking system with a deep economic depression to follow.

In order to calm financial markets, the Portuguese government announced severe austerity measures in May 2010. With the impact of these measures (a leftward shift of the *AD* curve), the Portuguese economy slid back into recession, and GDP started contracting from the fourth quarter of 2010 onward. As a consequence, public finances deteriorated further, and Portugal saw itself forced to pass new austerity measures but did not manage to calm financial markets. Spreads on Portuguese bonds continue to increase.

The European partners decided to provide a possibility for countries with difficulties to borrow on a more systematic basis. They set up the European Financial Stability Facility (EFSF) and the European Financial Stabilisation Mechanism (EFSM). These two funds were given guarantees by the member states and could hence borrow cheaply in financial markets to lend this money on to crisis countries. The possible volume of lending of these funds was put at €500 billion.

Meanwhile, concerns about the Irish banking system grew. As discussed in Chapter 15, Ireland had experienced a real estate boom prior to the global financial and economic crisis of 2008–2009. Banks had extended large amounts of loans to households and property developers. During 2009, it became increasingly clear that many of these loans would not be repaid and that some banks would risk default. As the government had guaranteed the banks' debt in 2008, speculation rose about how much money the government would have to inject into the banking system to make good on its promises. Together with a sharp contraction in economic activity, this rattled markets, and spreads on Irish bonds went up, reaching more than 360 basis points by August 2010. After the announcement of bank restructuring costs for the government of up to €50 billion in September 2010, the government saw itself forced to propose a harsh austerity package in October and finally applied for financial assistance from the IMF and European partners in December 2010. With deteriorating economic data and public finances, Portugal followed in April 2011. In both cases, bailout packages came with the conditionality of significant budget cuts and/or tax increases, which in turn led to deep recessions in both countries.

At the same time, it became clear that the first Greek rescue package would not be sufficient. Hence, in 2011, discussions began about a second Greek bailout package. By this point the feeling was that rescue loans alone would not be sufficient for Greece, as government debt was now projected to soon approach 200 percent of GDP. Thus in October 2011, the EU leaders agreed to a debt restructuring for Greece. Private investors who were holding Greek bonds had to accept a "haircut," meaning that the principal of their claim was reduced. This haircut was implemented in 2012, roughly two years after the first provision of liquidity loans from the troika. By this time, however, most of the Greek debt was no longer held by private investors. Many investors had sold their bonds, and since 2010, Greece had basically only borrowed from the IMF and the European rescue funds, the claims of which were not adjusted. Moreover, the debt restructuring rendered large parts of the Greek banking system bankrupt, which had held Greek bonds as part of their assets. The Greek government hence had to bail out the Greek banks and needed to borrow new money from the IMF and its partners to do so. As a consequence, despite the debt restructuring, the Greek debt-to-GDP ratio did not fall much.

2.3 Frantic Attempts by Governments to Calm Markets, and Crisis Solution by the ECB

The decision to restructure Greek debt in 2011 further unsettled markets. Bond spreads of euro periphery countries continued to increase as investors were uncertain if a similar decision could be taken for the outstanding debt of other euro members. In order to ensure markets that euro-area countries would stick to sound fiscal policies, and to increase investors' confidence, the EU tightened budgetary rules for euro members through the so-called six pack, which modified the Stability and Growth Pact. As discussed in Chapter 16, the new rules legislated budgets that structurally had to be broadly balanced along with a path for debt reduction for countries with public debt levels above 60 percent of GDP. The measures came into effect in early December 2011, but financial markets remained unimpressed.

As a reaction, Germany pressed for even tougher measures of budget control. The German government proposed to put the permanently balanced budget requirement into the EU treaty and force national governments to write similar rules into their national constitutions. Even though the rule would not have applied to EU countries not using the euro, Britain's prime minister David Cameron objected to this idea. As a consequence, EU heads of state and government, with the exception of those from Britain and the Czech Republic, decided to put these new rules into a new multilateral treaty, the so-called fiscal compact, which was signed in March 2012.

EU member states also agreed to replace the temporary EFSF with a permanent European Stability Mechanism (ESM) which had a lending capacity of €500bn and was properly integrated into the European Treaties. A limited loan for Spain was initiated in the summer of 2012 to help the country finance the recapitalization of its troubled banks. In addition, EU member states started to draft legislation for a European banking union, a centralization of bank supervision and resolution in the case of crisis. Yet all these steps failed to decisively bring down spreads of European periphery bonds. One of the fears was that the ESM's lending capacity might be too low should Italy or Spain require assistance. In March 2012, the programs for the (small) countries Greece, Ireland, and Portugal already amounted to commitments of €490 billion, while the (re)financing requirements for Spain and Italy over the period of 2012 to 2016 amounted to almost €1800 billion. Consequently, the spreads on periphery bonds continuously climbed upward again during the spring of 2012, reaching again more than 500 basis points for Italy and Spain in the summer.

BOX 17.1 U.S. PRESIDENT BARACK OBAMA TELLS EUROPEAN LEADERS TO GET THEIR ACT TOGETHER

By the early summer of 2012, the U.S. administration was getting increasingly worried about the economic situation in Europe. About two years into the euro crisis, and despite the creation of new funds of hundreds of billions of euros for disbursing emergency loans to euro-area countries with fiscal difficulties, there were few signs of a stabilization of the economic situation.

The team of U.S. president Barack Obama especially feared that the crisis in the euro area could lead to a new global recession, could end the already weak economic growth and job creation in the U.S., and might hence jeopardize the president's chances in the upcoming elections in November.

So when the leaders of the G20 group of the most important industrial countries met for a summit in Los Cabos, Mexico, Obama arranged a separate meeting with the most important leaders of the euro area, including the German chancellor Angela Merkel, the Italian prime minister Mario Monti, and the newly elected French president François Hollande. At this meeting, he told this group that they should finally get their act together. He especially pushed Ms. Merkel to allow the European Central Bank to intervene in government bond markets to stabilize the interest rates for European periphery countries.

> A number of observers see the meeting in Los Cabos as a turning point in the euro crisis. After that meeting, Ms. Merkel backed publicly the ECB president Mario Draghi with his promise to buy bonds of euro-area countries under certain conditions, even though large parts of the German establishment, including important voices at the German Bundesbank, opposed this policy.
>
> Source: Peter Spiegel, "'If the euro falls, Europe falls,'" *Financial Times*, May 15, 2014.

At this point, the European Central Bank's president, Mario Draghi, gave a widely quoted speech in London, saying the ECB would do "whatever it takes" to save the euro. Shortly after, the central bank clarified what it meant: Under the term "outright monetary transactions," it would be willing to buy government bonds of countries that were under an ESM program and in danger of losing access to financial markets. Effectively, Mario Draghi hence promised to make sure that countries that agree to conditionalities under an ESM program would never be faced with a crippling increase in financing costs, as the ECB would buy enough bonds to keep the yield under control. After Draghi's speech, spreads started to fall and have remained under control. This event is now widely regarded as a decisive turning point in the euro crisis.

Yet even though the fears of a euro breakup were widely mitigated by 2016, not all countries have actually escaped the crisis. In Greece, an anti–austerity government led by the left Syriza party was elected in 2015, which caused a standoff with creditors over austerity and reform measures during which again a possible exit of Greece from the euro area (a "Grexit") was discussed and only narrowly averted. In 2016, it was still not clear under what conditions the Greece programs of IMF and the EU partners would continue. Meanwhile, the Greek GDP was stagnating at a level more than 25 percent below its precrisis level, and youth unemployment stood at around 50 percent. More than a third of the Greeks were at risk of poverty or social exclusion. The situation in Spain or Italy might have been better than in Greece, but unemployment in 2016 still was significantly higher and disposable incomes lower than a decade earlier.

Discussion Questions

1. In what respects would you say that European policy makers did a good job in fighting the euro crisis? Would you say they acted in a timely fashion?
2. Would you say the benefits of the euro were worth the costs of the crisis? Is this a relevant question to ask at this point in time?

3. CAUSES OF THE CRISIS

While there are different narratives on what exactly went wrong in the euro area, economists generally agree that the crisis had many dimensions, with different causes in different countries. We will first take a look at possible causes, then turn to specific policy measures used during the crisis to see how they are linked to the underlying causes, and finally discuss remaining disputes.

3.1 Fiscal Profligacy

Especially among the German public, fiscal profligacy in the euro periphery is often seen as the main cause of the crisis. According to this view, the problem was that countries did not follow the EU's budgetary rules and hence had an excessive debt level even before the crisis. When the global economic and financial crisis hit in 2009, the euro-area countries were not in a position to deal with the resulting revenue slumps along with increased costs due to rising unemployment.

Clearly, there is some truth to this description for the case of Greece. After a number of data revisions, it now seems that Greece has neither prior to its accession to the euro area nor after the introduction of the euro actually recorded a public deficit of less than 3 percent of GDP. Had the European institutions been aware of the true state of Greek finances, the country would never have been considered to meet the convergence criteria and would not have joined the euro area. Also, the high debt level of more than 100 percent of GDP even before the global financial and economic crisis of 2008–2009 hints at long-running problems of fiscal discipline. Similarly, the fiscal data of Portugal point at some underlying fiscal problems: According to recent figures, and after a number of revisions, it now appears that Portugal also hardly ever fulfilled the convergence criteria of having a deficit of less than 3 percent of GDP (in fact, according to the EU Commission's database, since 1995, Portugal has run a deficit of 3 percent or less in only one year, 1999).

However, this story is much less convincing for some of the other crisis countries, such as Ireland or Spain. In both of these countries, governments were actually running surpluses for several years prior to the crisis of 2008–2009. Debt-to-GDP ratios had declined and were among the lowest in Europe. In 2007, Spanish public debt stood at 36 percent of GDP, Irish public debt at only 24 percent, not only far away from the Maastricht convergence criteria of 60 percent, but also much lower than Germany's public debt of about 64 percent. Also for the subsequent period, there is little sign of fiscal profligacy: If one looks at detailed data, Spain and Ireland did not see an acceleration of public spending but rather a sharp contraction in tax revenue after 2007, much of which can be explained by the bust in the real estate market and the following recession.

3.2 Insufficient Bank Regulation

For Ireland and Spain, one of the obvious problems has been the difficulties in the national banking systems. The point is most severe in Ireland: During the 2000s, the Irish banking system dramatically increased its lending to households and real estate developers. From 1997 to 2008, outstanding bank loans to households and nonfinancial firms jumped from around 60 percent of GDP to more than 200 percent of GDP. The solvency of many of these borrowers was built on the assumption of ever-increasing real estate prices. When real estate prices started to fall in 2007, and after the default of the U.S. investment bank Lehman Brothers sent shock waves through the global financial system, problems in the Irish banking system started to emerge, and depositors in Ireland started to withdraw their funds. In an attempt to halt this deposit flight and to stabilize the banking system, the Irish government in late September 2008 guaranteed all deposits and most other claims against Irish banks. The hope was that this promise would avert a banking crisis and prevent an ever-deeper recession for the Irish economy. This promise turned out to be extremely costly: Over the following months, it became clear that large parts of the Irish banking sector were de facto insolvent and that the government would have to spend large amounts of money on the guarantee. Ex-post estimates put the total costs of the Irish bank rescue for the Irish government at up to €64 billion or a staggering 40 percent of Irish GDP.

The case of Spain shows some similarities, but the banking crisis there had a much smaller dimension. Spanish banks had also lent freely to house owners and the construction sector, and similarly to Ireland, falling real estate prices at some point led to growing problems in the banking sector. While the Spanish government never issued a blanket guarantee as the Irish government did, it also saw itself pressured into bailing out and recapitalizing a number of banks. The costs were much less than in the Irish case, especially relative to Spanish GDP, but nevertheless quite significant.

Linked to the banks' loan growth is the underlying question of how far the banks have to share at least part of the blame for the real estate bubble of the 2000s and the following crash: A large part of the housing boom was built on credit, and without the lavish credit expansion by Irish and Spanish financial institutions, the bubbles in those countries would never have reached the magnitude they actually did. Less of a bubble, in turn, would have meant a less dramatic downturn after 2007, and hence less costs, for example, in the form of lost government revenue and higher spending on the unemployed. The costs of the banks' imprudent lending in the 2000s is thus more than just the direct costs of bank rescues and might have contributed severely to the fiscal problems experienced in Ireland and Spain. Supervisors and regulators should have been stricter and should have limited part of the excessive boom.

But why did national bank supervisors in both Spain and Ireland not meet this expectation? Part of the reason might have been excessive closeness to the countries' commercial banks, and, potentially, also political pressure. Supervisors have been working closely together with their national banking sector for years. After years of strong house price increases, bankers believed that this trend would continue. These arguments were believed by the regulators. Moreover, if house prices are increasing and the economy is booming, it is extremely unpopular for regulators to ask for tougher requirements for mortgage loans, as part of the population will be prevented from buying a residential property. Stricter loan conditions and fewer loans means also less economic activity, for example in the construction sector—something national politicians are not keen on. It may also be said that belief in the validity of rising real estate prices was in fashion in many parts of the world; it is hard for regulators in a small country to buck the trend set by a large country such as the U.S.

3.3   Doom Loop Between Banks and Governments

Linked to the question of insufficient bank regulation is that of a mechanism often called a doom loop between banks and governments. One problem observed in the euro crisis was the fact that financial problems of the government and problems in the banking system reinforced each other. Governments were concerned about the default of banks in their territory, as bank failures usually lead to households and firms losing access to credit, which in turn leads to a stark drop in aggregate demand and hence a recession. As a consequence, at some point, investors started to anticipate that governments would try to rescue national banks in order to prevent a deep recession. At the same time, banks in all euro-area countries were holding significant parts of their portfolio in government bonds of their own government, an asset generally considered to be highly liquid and extremely safe. As doubts about the solidity of a country's banking system emerged, investors concluded that an expensive bailout might follow and started to doubt the national government's solvency, selling bonds. This bond sale in turn depressed bond prices and reduced the value of the banks' bond holdings, making problems in the banking sector worse.

This problem did not stop with the banks but also had consequences for the real economy: Whenever bond prices fell, banks became more cautious in lending to firms and households, which in turn had to cut back on their investment plans. The resulting drop in aggregate demand meant falling incomes in the economy, resulting in more nonperforming loans and less government revenue, again increasing the problems both in the banking sector and for government finances.

3.4   Divergences in the Euro Area and a Growth Crisis

Another underlying cause for the euro crisis might have been harmful divergences in labor costs and inflation in the euro area. Since the introduction of the euro in 1999, inflation rates and increases in wage costs had been very different between euro-area countries. While prices increased very slowly in Germany, inflation was much higher in Greece, Spain, and Ireland. Figure 17.3 illustrates this problem by showing unit labor cost development in different countries relative to the euro area average from 1999 until before the onset of the euro crisis in 2010. The horizontal line shows the development in the euro area on average. Unit labor costs above this horizontal line signify a loss in cost competitiveness, unit labor costs below this line an improvement in cost competiveness relative to the euro-area partners. What we can see is that some countries such as Greece, Portugal, or Spain significantly lost competitiveness until the onset of the euro crisis, while Germany and Austria have gained competitiveness.

Initially, the stronger inflation and wage growth in the Southern European countries did not cause large problems. Stronger inflation meant that the relevant real interest rate was lower in these countries than in low-inflation Germany (remember that the real interest rate is defined as the nominal interest rate—which was the same everywhere in the euro area—minus inflation). Investment in real capital, especially residential real estate, hence was more attractive in the periphery. As a consequence, while manufacturing firms in these countries were losing ground against their foreign

560

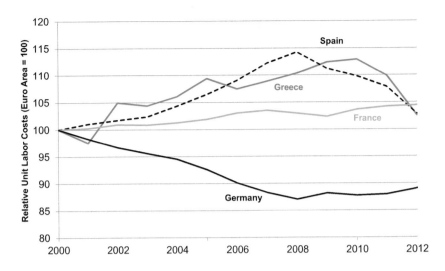

Figure 17.3 *Unit Labor Cost Development in Selected Euro Countries, 2000–2012 (Euro-Area Average = 100)*

In the euro periphery, between 2000 and 2009, unit labor costs increased much more strongly than in the rest of the euro area. These countries hence lost competitiveness. In Germany, in contrast, unit labor costs rose more slowly than in the rest, resulting in an improvement in competitiveness. After the onset of the crisis, labor costs fell strongly in the periphery.

Source: Ameco Database.

competitors (and hence growth was lowered by falling net exports), domestic demand was brisk and for a while more than compensated for the weakness in exports. In fact, in the early 2000s, the economies in these countries often did much better than the German economy.

Linked to these divergences are large current account imbalances that had accumulated before the crisis. Countries that had lost competitiveness were experiencing large current account deficits, while countries that had seen their competitiveness improve were experiencing growing current account surpluses. Table 17.1 shows the current account balances of euro-area countries for 2008. Spain experienced a current account deficit of almost 10 percent of GDP, Portugal and Greece recorded current account deficits of even more than 10 percent of GDP. As we discussed in Chapter 14, a current account deficit means that the country as a whole borrows abroad. Just in order to sustain their imports and domestic expenditure, these countries needed to borrow 10 percent or more of their income abroad. In the euro area, this borrowing was mostly provided through the banking system: German companies and households were accumulating deposits in their German banks. These banks then lent the money to Spanish or Portuguese banks, which in turn extended loans to local firms and households.

With the end of the real estate boom, the onset of the global financial and economic crisis of 2008–2009, and the following euro crisis, banks became reluctant to lend to firms and households. Domestic demand in the deficit countries collapsed. At the same time, these countries had lost so much competitiveness that export demand

Table 17.1 *Current Account Balance, 2008*

Country	% of GDP
Euro area (12 countries)	-0.5
Austria	4.1
Belgium	1.4
Cyprus	-15.6
Finland	2.7
France	-1.4
Germany	5.6
Greece	-15.8
Ireland	-5.8
Italy	-2.9
Luxembourg	7.7
Malta	-1.1
Netherlands	5.2
Portugal	-12.6
Spain	-9.2
United Kingdom	-3.6
United States	-4.7
Japan	3.3

Source: Ameco database (2016).

could not provide a growth engine. This situation led to fiscal problems through two channels: First, the low growth led to falling tax revenues and increasing costs for unemployment. Second, the falling price level led to an increase in the real burden of the existing debt (remember our discussion of the impact of a deflationary environment on debt trends in Chapter 15).

What is less clear (and still disputed) is the question of the origin of the divergences in unit labor costs within the euro area. Some economists believe that different wage-setting institutions and traditions play a decisive role. For example, in Germany, wage negotiations are often conducted at a sector level, and unions do not push aggressively for higher wages, unlike the situation with competing unions in some other countries. Other economists believe that the divergences stemmed mostly from ill-advised lending from banks in the deficit countries, which was financed by imprudent interbank lending.

3.5 Self-Fulfilling Fiscal Crises

Another argument brought forward to understand the euro crisis was the theory of self-fulfilling fiscal crises: According to this theory, from a certain level of public debt onward, shift in investor sentiment by themselves can lead to a default of the government. The logic is as follows: If investors believe a government can service its debt, they will only demand low interest rates. With these low interest rates, servicing the outstanding debt is not a problem. In contrast, if investors believe that the government will have problems servicing its debt, they will demand higher interest rates. These higher interest rate payments then might be enough to actually force the government in question into default. If some investors now see that other investors demand higher interest rates from a government, it is sensible for them also to charge higher interest rates because the risk of default has increased. In the end, the government's ability to service its debt thus depends on investors' expectations.

To understand this logic: Assume you have a monthly income of €4000 and you have a monthly mortgage payment of €1000. If your bank comes and says they have done a reassessment of your risk and have to increase the interest rate they charge you, resulting in a monthly rate of €4000 or even €5000, this would clearly make it impossible for you to continue servicing the loan. Whether or not you are able to pay your mortgage here also depends on whether the bank assumes that you are risky or not—a self-fulfilling prophecy.

Of course, governments usually have debts with longer maturities, so the impact of higher market rates is not as immediate as in our example. However, this model of self-fulfilling fiscal crises seems to explain at least part of what happened to some countries such as Ireland and Spain, which were at different times during the euro crisis suddenly confronted with high interest rates but now do not seem to have problems servicing their debts once the panic subsided and interest rates have fallen.

3.6 Lack of Proper Institutions

Given this argument, one might ask: Why did some euro-area countries experience an increase in bond spreads and the danger of self-fulfilling fiscal crises but not the U.S. or Britain, which at some times had larger deficits than the crisis countries and also significant problems in their banking sectors? The answer might be found in the fact that these countries still have their own central bank. Remember that in the euro area the ECB is prohibited from financing government deficits and buying bonds directly from governments. As these rules are laid down in the European treaties, they can only be changed by unanimous vote of all EU member states. This is a stark difference to the legal basis of the U.S. Federal Reserve or the Bank of England. In principle, the U.S. Congress or the British Parliament can change the law governing their central bank and force the central bank to buy government bonds. It is very likely that a government faced with the threat of a default and a resulting banking crisis will decide to use the central bank to pay for its liabilities or that the central bank itself might even decide that it would be a good idea to extend loans to the government to prevent changes in its statutes. Using the printing press in these instances to patch over liquidity problems of the government might lead to a small uptick of inflation but certainly is much less painful than a government default and a banking crisis. As investors are aware of these considerations and possibilities, they will be reluctant to speculate against the U.S. or the UK government.

This brings us to another argument often brought forward: The euro area is an *incomplete* monetary union. Its institutions are just not (yet) able to secure a smooth working of a monetary union. Different from other currency areas (such as the United States or Britain), it lacks certain features necessary for a survival of a single currency. One of these institutions might be a central bank that acts as a lender of last resort to its government. This option is complicated by the fact that within the euro area there is not just one national government but 19 and that there might be the fear that some countries might abuse the ability to borrow from the central bank.

Other options to make the euro area a more complete monetary union would be the creation of a proper euro-area government with a budget that would be used for stabilizing national economies, either by spending money in regions hit by adverse economic conditions, by transferring money to national governments in financial difficulties, or by taking over the responsibility for resolving ailing national banks to break the doom loop between banks and governments.

Discussion Questions

1. Which of the possible causes of the euro crisis do you think was the most relevant?
2. To what extent do you believe stricter fiscal rules (for example, with automatic sanctions for countries that violate the Stability and Growth Pact) would have prevented the euro crisis?

4. POLICY REACTIONS

If you look at the narrative of the euro crisis presented here, you will notice the frantic reactions of policy makers. In 2011–2012, there really was a feeling of deep crisis and urgency among policy makers, who feared that the euro area might break apart and trigger a new global economic crisis. According to media reports, even U.S. president Barack Obama at that time weighed in and told the key European heads of state and government to get their act together. As a consequence, a number of reforms in the euro area's institutional setup were pushed forward and quickly implemented.

4.1 Austerity and Institutional Changes for Fiscal Policies

As the crisis originated in Greece, which clearly had fiscal problems, policy makers at first focused on limiting government deficits and debt. Countries that asked for emergency loans had to promise to reduce their budget deficit quickly and decisively before they were given loans. While the program countries often missed specific targets, the cuts implemented were significant. For example, under the IMF/EU programs, Greece cut its public expenditure from almost €130 billion in 2009 to around €90 billion in 2016, reducing total public expenditure in this country by almost a third.

At the same time, the EU decided to tighten budgetary rules for the euro-area member states. The Stability and Growth Pact (see Chapter 16) was once again reformed. According to the new rules, national governments now have to present their budget plans to the EU Commission in advance. In the medium term, they have to run a budget close to balance. If their debt-to-GDP ratio is above 60 percent, they have to reduce the gap between the current level of debt and this threshold by 1/20th each year. Even if they are not violating the deficit threshold of 3 percent of GDP, an excessive deficit procedure may now be initiated against them if their debt level is above 60 percent of GDP. For imposing fines, no consent of the Council (the EU body in which member states are presented) is needed any more. In addition, the euro-area member states signed a new multilateral treaty, the "fiscal compact," which required them to put these debt and deficit rules also into relevant national law (in some cases national constitutions, in some cases the laws controlling the budget process).

As the rules were tightened and individual governments were afraid of being cut off from financial markets and having to apply for emergency loans from the IMF and the EU, most European countries cut expenditure and increased taxes. The structural budget deficit for the euro area as a whole was reduced from 5 percent of GDP in 2010 to 1.5 percent of GDP in 2014.

4.2 Structural Reforms

Another element in the conditionality for rescue loans from the IMF and the EU funds was structural reforms. Countries had to pledge to implement certain reforms, mainly liberalizing labor and product markets. For example, Greece had to promise to reform its wage bargaining system, lower minimum wages, and open up a number of formerly regulated markets for services. Countries were also asked to privatize formerly state-owned companies. The logic behind these demands was that the troika hoped that this kind of liberalization would ignite economic growth.

While sometimes media reports claimed that the **program countries** did not really follow through with their promises, research from independent institutions such as the OECD shows that they actually liberalized their markets quite strongly during the crisis years. In fact, this observation is not only true for program countries. For example, Spain (which never was subject to a full troika program) passed a number of labor market reforms in 2012, and France introduced labor market reform legislation in 2016.

program country: country that was forced to implement an economic adjustment program as a conditionality for a loan from the IMF and the European institutions

What remains disputed, however, is how beneficial these structural reforms really were. Skeptics point at the continuing low rate of economic growth continuing into 2017 and the deteriorating social conditions in many parts of the euro area. According to their view, improving supply conditions does not really help if aggregate demand remains depressed. Moreover, they claim that many of the reforms pushed for, especially in labor markets, did not really improve supply conditions but merely worsened the fate of employees.

4.3 The Different Rescue Funds

We have so far mentioned briefly the different rescue funds that were used to provide crisis countries with emergency loans. If you read all the acronyms like EFSF, EFSM, and ESM, they can easily be confusing, and one might ask why so many different funds

565

were needed. To clarify, we will start with the first loans to Greece in the spring of 2010 and work through the way new funds and facilities were created.

Usually, if a country has problems meeting its foreign liabilities, it turns to the International Monetary Fund. The IMF assesses the country's finances and then decides whether to grant a loan. Loans in principle should only be disbursed if there is a probable chance that, with plausible adjustments to the budget and economic policies, the country in question will again be able to service its foreign liabilities on its own. Hence, loans are usually linked to conditionalities under which the government of the country in question promises to cut expenditure, increase taxes, and pass reforms to enhance growth (remember from Chapter 16 that economic growth is a very important variable for debt dynamics). The loans a country can get from the IMF are limited to a certain multiple of that country's capital share in the IMF. When Greece got into trouble in 2010, it needed much more money than the IMF could provide by its rules. At the same time, there was no provision for how to make loans from the EU or euro-area partners. The first rescue package in 2010 was hence constructed of a €30 billion loan from the IMF and €80 billion of bilateral loans from the euro-area partners, which were referred to as the "Greek Loan Facility."

When it became clear that the problems would not be limited to Greece, the EU partners set up two more facilities to be prepared for further requests of support. One facility was the European Financial Stabilisation Mechanism (EFSM), which allowed the EU Commission to borrow €60 billion in capital markets and lend them on to euro-area member states seeking assistance. The second facility was the European Financial Stability Facility (EFSF), which was guaranteed by the euro-area member states and was able to borrow €440 billion to be lent on. Both facilities were designed to be temporary.

Yet these facilities were soon also regarded as insufficient. First, policy makers realized that a temporary solution might not be enough. Second, there were some doubts about the legal foundation of these facilities. The European treaties included a clear no-bailout clause (see earlier), and a number of people claimed that the EFSM and the EFSF were not in line with this clause. Hence policy makers set up the permanent European Stability Mechanism (ESM) and integrated its rules into the European treaties. The ESM was initially designed to be able to lend up to €500 billion.

Economically, these rescue funds all address the problem of self-fulfilling fiscal crises discussed earlier. The idea is that the funds can lend money cheaply to governments that face difficulties in accessing financial markets. As investors know that these funds are available, there is no reason to believe that a country will be pushed into default by simply a market-induced increase in interest rates. The hope is thus that the mere existence of these funds can defuse self-fulfilling crises.

4.4 ECB Interventions

The problem was that these funds were seen to not be sufficiently large. The potential financing needs of countries like Spain and Italy could amount to a multiple of the lending capacity of the ESM. Increasing the volume of the ESM was not seen as a viable solution, as the guarantees for ever-larger loans might actually even have created problems for solvent and economically strong member states such as Germany, pushing their liabilities to uncomfortable levels.

This is where Mario Draghi's promise to do "whatever it takes" to save the euro comes in: Under the ECB's program of **Outright Monetary Transactions**, he promised to buy as many bonds of countries with an ESM program as would be necessary to defuse investor panic. Effectively, this was an equivalent of increasing the lending volume of the ESM. Once a country agreed to an economic adjustment program with the ESM, the ECB would buy government bonds with maturities of up to three years in the secondary markets, putting a cap on interest rates. As investors would know that the ECB was buying these bonds, they would lend money to the government at short maturity (as they could always sell the bonds on to the ECB). And as the ECB can create as much money as it wants with a stroke of a pen (as discussed in Chapter 12), there was no reason that investors should fear that the central bank's purchases might not be sufficient. If we look at Draghi's promise in this context, it is clear why he managed to defuse the crises: His promise effectively increased the combined lending volume of rescue funds to infinity.

4.5 Banking Union

As commercial banks have been singled out as one of the contributing factors for the genesis of the euro crisis, it is not surprising that the EU has also passed a number of reforms for this sector. Specifically, the responsibility for regulating and supervising banks in the euro area has been moved from national authorities to the European level. Since the fall of 2014, the ECB is responsible for specifying the rules for commercial banks and enforcing them. It does so directly for the largest banks and indirectly through the national supervisors for all the other banks. Policy makers hope that the ECB will have a more objective view on national banks' dealings and will be able to look at developments in certain countries in a broader perspective.

A second change concerns the rules on how to deal with banks in trouble. National governments in the euro area now have to follow certain guidelines when it comes to bailing out banks. Specifically, they are now prohibited from using public funds to bail out banks before the banks' creditors have contributed their share to a bank rescue. A common fund for bank rescues in the euro area will be built up, relieving national governments of the cost of potential bailouts. Decisions on how to deal with banks in trouble are now taken at the EU level, not at the national level. The hope here is that, first, the doom loop between banks and national governments is severed and, second, bank creditors will force the banks to behave more prudently if they face the certainty of losing money when a financial institution needs to be bailed out.

Discussion Questions

1. Which policies did European policy makers introduce in order to deal with the crisis? Which were successful? Which were not? Do you think the more

successful policies would have worked in isolation (that is, without the other policies implemented)?

2. Do you think it was right that Mario Draghi promised to do "whatever it takes" to save the euro? Why or why not?

5. DISPUTED ISSUES

Not only are the exact underlying causes of the euro crisis disputed, but also the remedies applied during the crisis as well as the steps necessary to make the euro area crisis-proof in the future.

5.1 Austerity Policies

The most strongly disputed part of the euro area's approach to deal with the crisis has been austerity imposed through the EU budget rules for all euro member states and—more strictly—through conditionalities of the economic adjustment programs for program countries. While some German economists (and government officials) claim that there has been no alternative to budget cuts in crisis countries, opponents point out that austerity policies in Europe did not really deliver what was hoped for, while creating huge social costs.

The first challenge of austerity policies is economic: Opponents claim that austerity failed in that the debt-to-GDP ratios continued to climb strongly during the years of strong austerity, 2010 to 2013. GDP fell by much more in the crisis countries than originally predicted by the IMF and the EU Commission. Falling GDP then contributed to missing deficit targets as tax revenue fell and costs for unemployment surged. Moreover, with falling GDP, the debt-to-GDP ratio increased. According to the advocates of this view, a less harsh approach of budget consolidation (e.g., with smaller budget cuts implemented later when the economy was on a more solid footing) would in the end have led to a lower debt-to-GDP ratio. They see support for their position in modern research, pointing out that the fiscal multiplier is larger in a recession than in normal times (see Chapter 10). In contrast, defenders of the austerity policies during the euro crisis argue that politicians would not have actually cut budget deficits decisively after the crisis without market pressure and that the demonstration of commitment was necessary to regain the trust of financial markets.

The second challenge to austerity policies is the social outcome: Unemployment and poverty increased significantly in some of the euro-member states during the crisis. From 2009 to 2014, the share of the population at risk of poverty or social exclusion jumped from 27.6 percent to 36 percent in Greece and from 26.1 to 29.2 percent in Spain. In the euro area as a whole, the number of people living at risk of poverty increased by almost 7 million. Opponents of austerity policy put the blame for this development on cuts in public expenditure, while proponents defend austerity as having been without alternative.

568

BOX 17.2 THE SHORT-LIVED GREEK UPRISING AGAINST AUSTERITY

The deep economic crisis Greece experienced since the beginning of the euro crisis in 2010 quickly turned the whole political system of the country upside down. While the large traditional parties, the left-of-center Pasok and the liberal-conservative New Democracy, saw their share of votes crumble, the coalition of the radical left under the name Syriza became rapidly the focal point and main benefactor of discontent. Founded as an electoral coalition in 2004, Syriza quickly gained in the polls during the crisis. After getting less than 5 percent of the popular vote in the 2009 election, it managed to more than triple its share in 2012, receiving 16 percent of the votes cast.

For the snap election of January 2015, it ran under its charismatic leader Alexis Tsipras with the promise to end austerity imposed by the European partners, the European Commission, and the International Monetary Fund. These promises were highly successful: Syriza became the largest party, with a share of 36.3 percent of the popular vote. Because of specific rules of the Greek electoral system, this result gave Syriza 149 out of 300 seats in the parliament. To the surprise of many observers, within days, Tsipras formed a coalition government with the Independent Greeks, a national conservative party.

Over the coming months, the Greek government tried to renegotiate the bailout terms for the loans from European and international institutions. However, the lenders did not budge in their demand for austerity to continue. On June 27, 2015, Alex Tsipras announced that he would hold a referendum on the terms of the bailout loans demanded by the European Commission, the IMF, and the ECB, indicating that he would recommend a "no" vote.

In the referendum on July 5, 61 percent of the voters followed this recommendation. Immediately after the vote, the European Central Bank said it would not extend further emergency loans to Greek banks. The Syriza government was forced to impose a bank holiday, and all banks in the country remained closed. Withdrawals from ATMs were limited to €60. The Greek economy, already heavily damaged by years of austerity and recession, was further hit with people trying to keep their cash together.

A week of frantic negotiations between Greece, the European institutions, and European partner countries began. The partners, enraged by Tsipras's unilateral call of a referendum, remained uncompromising. Arguing that now the economic situation in Greece had deteriorated and thus the expected budget shortfall had grown, they demanded even tougher austerity measures than before. Confronted with the growing economic chaos at home, Tsipras agreed to the new bailout terms, and on July 13, his government accepted a bailout package that contained larger pension cuts and tax increases than the one rejected by Greek voters in the referendum.

Over Tsipras's dealing with the European partners, a number of senior figures left Syriza. Tsipras decided to call for another national election to get legitimization for his policies. In the election on September 20, Syriza again became the strongest party, this time with 35.5 percent of the vote, and Tsipras managed to form a new government, which was set to implement new austerity measures over the following years.

Sources: Mark Thompson, "Greece shuts banks in bid to prevent collapse," *CNN Money Online*, June 29, 2015; Mark Lowen, "Greek debt crisis: What was the point of the referendum?," *BBC News*, July 11, 2015; Kerin Hope and Henry Foy, "Syriza secures clear victory in Greek general election," *Financial Times*, September 20, 2015.

5.2 A Fiscal Capacity

fiscal capacity:
public revenues that
can be spent within a
given jurisdiction

In order to prevent countries in the future from having to impose as much austerity as in the past crisis, a number of proposals have been made for a **fiscal capacity** for the euro area. In 2016, a number of options were discussed. One possibility would be to create a euro-area budget which would implement investment programs in countries with weak economic growth. Another possibility would be to create euro area–wide transfer systems that would channel funds from member states in which the economy is growing briskly to those which experience a shortfall of aggregate demand. One widely discussed option here would be to introduce a European unemployment insurance (see Box 17.3). Under this scheme, funds would flow from countries with low unemployment to those with high unemployment, effectively creating a new automatic stabilizer for the euro-area member states.

The basic notion behind all of these proposals is to make fiscal policy more anticyclical than in the past years: Countries that are hit by a crisis and have to cut national public expenditure would see their aggregate demand stabilized by payments from the European Union. The hope is that, first, this would make future recessions and crises less painful. Second, such a mechanism would potentially help to limit harmful divergences (discussed earlier) from the very beginning: As fast-growing economies would have to make transfers to the rest of the euro area, growth would be dampened in a boom, and excessive inflation in a single country becomes less likely. As a consequence, inflation and wage developments should not deviate as much from the euro-area average as they did in the time between 1999 and 2008.

While such transfer systems are supported by a significant number of economists, politicians especially in member states such as Germany, the Netherlands, or Finland fear that their countries would become permanent net payers into such systems. This explains why until 2016, no real progress on a fiscal capacity has been made.

BOX 17.3 TOWARD A EUROPEAN UNEMPLOYMENT INSURANCE?

Since the onset of the euro crisis in 2010 and its spread to large parts of the euro periphery, a debate has flared up on how far the architecture of the monetary union needed to be revised. One argument commonly made was that the euro area would need a so-called "fiscal capacity" through which aggregate demand in crisis countries should be bolstered, while countries doing better should contribute to this stabilization.

One proposal widely discussed was a so-called basic European unemployment insurance. Under this proposal, all employees in the euro area would be insured in a European system. They (and their employers) would pay part of their monthly wages into the European system, and, if they became unemployed, they would receive for a limited number of months unemployment benefits from the European system.

The European Unemployment Insurance would replace part of the existing national systems and provide a basic safety net for the unemployed. Beyond this, national governments would still be allowed to provide better protection for unemployed workers in their countries by topping up the European payment with national funds or paying benefits for a longer period of time.

Compared to the existing independent national systems, the advantage would be that, by pooling funds, countries experiencing a deep recession would not (as in the past) have to increase contributions to their national unemployment insurance or cut benefits to balance their budgets. Instead, in bad times, they would get the funds from the European system and pay in more in good times. With less procyclical benefit cuts or contribution increases, recessions would become less deep.

According to some estimations, almost a third of the fall of GDP in the Spanish recession in 2007–2009 could have been prevented had such a system been in place.

While the EU commissioner for employment at that time, László Andor, supported the idea of a European unemployment insurance, some of the EU member states were very skeptical. In Germany and the Netherlands, many politicians feared that they would become permanent net payers, subsidizing Southern European unemployed people forever. As a consequence, when the five presidents' report on the future of the euro area was published in 2015 the focus was more on integrating financial markets than on pushing for a fiscal capacity.

Sources: László Andor, Sebastian Dullien, H. Xavier Jara, Holly Sutherland, and Daniel Gros, "Forum: Designing a European Unemployment Insurance Scheme," *Intereconomics* 2014/4, pp. 184–203.

5.3 Debt Mutualization

A final possibility that has been widely debated is the idea of debt mutualization. Behind this idea is the observation that the debt level for the euro area as a whole is less than that of the U.S. or Japan, yet the euro area was the only entity that experienced investors' fear of default. According to this view, a shared liability for all debt would have prevented and solved the crisis, because there would not have been any speculation about individual countries defaulting on their debt. Such debt mutualization has usually been discussed under the term "euro bonds," bonds for which all euro members would be liable. Some of these proposals called for a complete mutualization of debt; some other proposals included the mutualization of only part of the debt or up to a certain limit per country.

Debt mutualization, however, is highly unpopular, especially in countries with comparably low debt-to-GDP levels such as Germany, the Netherlands, Estonia, or Finland. The fear in these countries is, first, that they would have to pay for the profligacy in other member states such as Greece, Italy, or Portugal with high debt levels and, second, that governments would increase their own borrowing if they knew that others might in the end be held liable for the newly accumulated debt. As of 2016, the debate on debt mutualization has hence made no progress and seems unlikely to do so soon.

DISCUSSION QUESTIONS

1. To what extent would you agree that austerity was inevitable during the euro crisis?
2. Do you think it is a good idea to have a proper euro-area government with its own budget? What about having common debt for the euro area?

REVIEW QUESTIONS

1. What was the main concern during the euro crisis? What were the main causes of the euro crisis?
2. What have European policy makers done to solve the euro crisis? Which reforms of the euro-area structures have they initiated and implemented?

EXERCISES

1. For this exercise, you need to locate GDP and debt data for euro-area countries. Use the EU Commission's Annual Macroeconomic (Ameco) Online database (http://ec.europa.eu/economy_finance/db_indicators/ameco/index_en.htm).
   a. Extract data on real GDP ("constant prices") for the euro-area countries. Which five countries saw their GDP decline most during the euro crisis? By how many percent did GDP decline before it started to grow again? (Hint: start with the last year after 2009 in which GDP did not fall relative to the year before and end with the last year before GDP grew again.)
   b. According to the EU Commission's data and forecast in the Ameco database, when has/will the GDP level of those five countries have reached again at least the precrisis level?
   c. Now locate the debt-to-GDP ratio in the Ameco database. Compute by how much this ratio has changed for each euro-area country between 2009 and 2014. Can you see any correlation between this change in the debt level and the depth of the crisis which you have computed in question a?
2. How did the euro area perform economically relative to other countries during the Great Recession and the euro crisis? Again use the Ameco database and check by how much the following variables have changed between 2007 and 2015 for the euro area as a whole, the UK, the U.S., Sweden, and Japan:
   a. Real GDP (in national currency; please compute percentage change)
   b. Debt-to-GDP ratio (please compare change in percentage points)
   c. Unemployment (please compare change in percentage points)
3. The chapter identifies a series of contributing factors in its exploration of the underlying causes of the euro crisis. It also explains some policy measures taken during the crisis. Identify the major factors and state which of the policy measures address which factor.
4. Use the *AS/AD* model we have used in former chapters. Assume now a combination of strong austerity and structural reforms in goods and labor markets (as they were combined in the

economic adjustment programs). What would you expect to happen? To what extent is it sensible to assume that structural reforms can compensate for the negative effects of austerity? Which factors might influence whether such a compensation is possible or not?

5. Match each concept in Column A with a definition or example in Column B.

Column A	Column B
a. International Monetary Fund	1. ECB program to buy government bonds
b. European stability mechanism	2. Difference between yield on a specific bond and yield on a high-quality bond
c. Bond spread	3. Prohibition in EU treaties to assume other countries' liabilities
d. Outright monetary transaction	4. European fund giving emergency loans to euro-countries
e. Austerity	5. International organization providing emergency loans to countries
f. No-bailout clause	6. Cuts in expenditure and increases in taxation
g. Denmark	7. Research asking under which circumstances forming a monetary union is beneficial
h. Optimum currency area theory	8. Bonds jointly guaranteed by euro-area members
i. Euro bonds	9. Changing the debt burden by reducing the principal, reducing interest rate payments, or increasing maturity
j. Debt restructuring	10. An EU country not having joined the euro

Chapter 18

How Economies Grow and Develop

What do people mean by economic development? How can the economic status of countries and the well-being of their people change over time? Most of the macroeconomic theory that we have presented so far relates to advanced economies such as the member states of the European Union or the United States. But if we think back a hundred years, all of these countries were very different places than they are today. Most transportation was still horse drawn, with only a few cars operating on a poor-quality road system. Most rural areas did not have electricity or telephone service. In 1900, measured in today's prices, real *annual* per-capita income in Germany and France was the equivalent of less than €4,000, in Spain only around €2,000, and even in the then more prosperous United States only $6,700 and in England around £5,000. During the twentieth century, real per-capita income in all these countries rose at least fivefold and even eightfold in Spain and now stands in all of these countries at more than €30,000.

The median income in the world today is about equal to that of the United States in the early 1900s—and significantly above the median income in France, Germany, or Spain at that time. Although billions of people still live in severe poverty, some formerly poor countries—such as South Korea, China, and India—are rapidly developing. Many others have experienced little economic progress. It is both interesting and important to evaluate how economies grow, how the growth process differs in different cases, and why some countries are very successful at promoting rapid growth, while others seem to be "stuck" at a low level of income.

As we will see in what follows, *economic growth* and *economic development* are not always the same thing, and the differences become more pronounced at higher levels of income. One important theme in this chapter is that, contrary to some earlier theories, there is nothing "automatic" about poor countries becoming developed. Another is that even rapid and sustained GDP growth may not be sufficient to ensure broad-based well-being improvement.

1. DEVELOPMENT AND ECONOMIC GROWTH

Economic development is an idea that became formalized in the mid-twentieth century, as the colonial empires began to break down and the more industrialized countries gradually took on a changed set of attitudes toward the parts of the world that had not experienced industrialization.* The economic relations between colonies and their rulers had been dominated by the desire of the ruling countries to enrich themselves, first, through extraction of raw materials, and, second, through the creation of markets for goods that they wished to export. By the mid-twentieth century, resistance to imperial domination and strong movements for independence had made it impossible for the ruling countries to maintain their control. The emergence of many newly independent countries required a change in attitude.

On the economic side, it was recognized that countries make better trading partners if they can escape from poverty. On the moral side was the recognition that, considering the improvement in living conditions that had accompanied industrialization for the richer countries, it was only right that the "underdeveloped" countries should have a chance to develop their economies and to gain greater wealth and well-being. Some theorists of "neocolonialism" have argued that the former colonial powers continued to use political and economic power to maintain their dominant position. Nonetheless, newly independent countries were determined to promote economic progress, and the economic theory of development emerged with the purpose of helping to achieve this goal.

The idea of development initially focused on the question: How can poor countries most rapidly follow in the steps of the rich ones? The answers to this question are the subject of a large part of this chapter. We focus especially on the countries in which there is a clear need for increased economic development to satisfy people's basic needs for food, shelter, health care, and education. But it is also worth noting that the term "development" can be used for *all* kinds of positive economic change and, thus, could also be applied to the countries that have successfully achieved greater wealth and industrialization. That is an issue to which we return in Chapter 19, where we will take a look at the changes that will be required both in wealthier countries and in rapidly developing countries such as China if the global economy is to achieve a sustainable balance with its ecological context.

1.1 Standard Economic Growth Theory

As we noted in Chapter 6, there are many criticisms of the use of GDP as a measure of economic progress. Standard models of economic growth, however, are all based on this measure, and we begin by reviewing some of these models.

The simplest definition of economic growth is an increase in real GDP (i.e., GDP adjusted for inflation). The growth rate of real GDP is the percentage change in real GDP from one year to the next. Using what we learned in Chapter 5, we can express the rate of growth in, for example, the period 2014–2015, as follows:

$$\textit{growth rate of } GDP = \frac{GDP_{2015} - GDP_{2014}}{GDP_{2014}} \times 100$$

---

* In the first half of the twentieth century, a number of Western countries, including Britain, Germany, France, the Netherlands, Portugal, and Spain, were colonial powers, exerting control over many colonies in Africa, Asia, and South America. Japan was also a colonial power, ruling South Korea and, at various times, parts of China. Most of the colonies had become independent countries by the 1960s.

For example, euro-area real GDP in 2015 (in chained 2005 dollars) was €9.827 trillion, and in 2014 it was €9.668 trillion.[1] Thus the growth rate of euro-area real GDP from 2014 to 2015 was

$$= \frac{9.827 - 9.668}{9.668} \times 100 = \frac{159}{9.668} \times 100 = 1.6 \, \text{percent}$$

For purposes of evaluating how economic growth is related to economic development, it is often helpful to focus on the growth rate of GDP *per capita*—that is, output *per person*—rather than simply on overall output. Mathematically, GDP per capita is expressed as:

GDP per capita = GDP/population

The growth rates of GDP, population, and GDP per capita are related in the following way (where the sign ≈ means "approximately equals"):

Growth rate of GDP ≈ Growth rate of population + growth rate of GDP per capita

or:

Growth rate of GDP per capita ≈ Growth rate of GDP − growth rate of population

Economic growth increases the maximum productive capacity of the economy. It involves both supply-side and demand-side expansions and does not necessarily involve a change in the rate of inflation.

Thus, for example, an economy that has a GDP growth rate of 4 percent and a population growth rate of 2 percent would have a per-capita GDP growth rate of approximately 2 percent. The per-capita GDP growth rate is especially important because it indicates the actual increase in average income being experienced by the people of the country. If a country had a 2 percent GDP growth rate but a 3 percent population growth rate, its per-capita GDP growth rate would actually be negative, at −1 percent. The people would on average be getting poorer each year, even though the overall economy is growing. Thus for people's incomes on average to increase over time, the GDP growth rate must exceed the rate of population growth.

In terms of the aggregate supply-and-demand graphs that we used in Chapter 13, economic growth can be shown as a rightward shift of the aggregate supply (*AS*), increasing the economy's maximum capacity (Figure 18.1). If this kind of increase in aggregate supply took place without any shift in aggregate demand (*AD*), its effects would include growth in output and a declining rate of inflation. In practice, however, economic growth is almost always accompanied by, and is often caused at least in part by, an increase in aggregate demand. Thus a more typical pattern for economic growth would be for *both* the *AD* and *AS* curves to shift to the right, as shown in Figure 18.1. In this case, output clearly rises, but the effect on inflation is ambiguous.

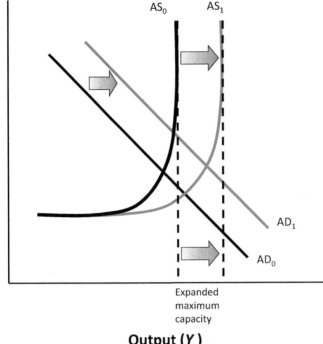

Figure 18.1 *Economic Growth in the* AS/AD *Model*

Economic growth increases the maximum productive capacity of the economy. It involves both supply-side and demand-side expansions and does not necessarily involve a change in the rate of inflation.

What causes economic output to increase? One way that output could increase is if there is an expansion in the inputs used to produce it. Recall that in Chapter 3, we outlined five kinds of capital. Land and natural resources are *natural capital*. The stock of productive resources that have been produced by people is called *manufactured capital*. All the skills and knowledge possessed by humans are *human capital*, while *social* and *financial capital* both refer to cultural and institutional arrangements that make production possible.

Capital expansion is related to the production-possibilities frontier (PPF) that we first saw in Chapter 2. Recall that any point "outside" the PPF is unattainable—impossible to achieve with the *present* endowment of inputs and available technology. So another way of seeing GDP growth is in relation to the capital expansion required to "shift" the PPF outward, to where previously unattainable combinations of, say, guns and butter become possible. Such an outward shift could require an increase in any one of the capital types: for example, if all the material and technological resources are in place but are being used inefficiently, an outward shift could be achieved through an increase in social capital that allows better coordination and cooperation among workers and managers.

Economists sometimes think about output as being generated according to a "production function," which is a mathematical relation between various inputs and the level of output. In the most general sense, we might say that the output of an economy should be expressed as a function of flows from *all* the different types of capital that make production possible. The inputs to the production function are commonly referred to as **factors of production**. In the production functions most commonly used by economists, the factors that are emphasized are manufactured capital and labor. Sometimes, but not always, natural resources are also included.

factors of production: the essential inputs for economic activity, including labor, capital, and natural resources

Technology is the other important variable that influences economic output. We say that a point outside the PPF is unattainable "given available factors of production (i.e., inputs) and the present state of technology." In other words, it matters not only how much of the different factors we possess but also how productive on average each is—and productivity depends crucially on the level of technology.

total factor productivity: a measure of the productivity of all factors of production. It represents contributions to output from all sources, not just quantities of manufactured capital and labor.

In their production functions, economists often include a term that captures **total factor productivity**, which includes all contributions to total production not already reflected in the input levels. "Total factor productivity" has often been interpreted as reflecting the way in which technological innovation allows inputs such as capital and labor to be used in more effective and valuable ways. For example, the development of word-processing software greatly increased efficiency compared to the use of typewriters. Typewriters, which seem antique to us today, were themselves a huge productive advance over clerical work using pen and paper. This process of improved technological methods has resulted in an increase in labor productivity—more output can now be produced with fewer inputs. The input most often measured in productivity statistics is labor-hours; however, total factor productivity also takes into account natural capital, machinery, and any other relevant inputs.

1.2 Historical Overview and Twentieth-Century Theory

Industrial Revolution: a process of social, technological, and economic change, beginning in Western Europe in the eighteenth century that developed and applied new methods of production and work organization, resulting in a great increase in output per worker

The **Industrial Revolution**, a process of rapid social, technological, and economic change, which began in Britain and Western Europe, dramatically changed the nature of economic production. Although, as we discuss later, the applicability of this model to current development issues has been subject to criticism, its strong influence on standard views of economic growth makes it an important starting point for understanding development.

Several elements were critical in creating the Industrial Revolution. First, new agricultural techniques, along with new kinds of tools and machines, made agriculture more productive. Because farmers became more productive, fewer were needed to produce the necessary food, and many migrated to the growing urban areas. Second, the invention and application of technologies using fossil-fuel energy (especially coal) contributed not only to the productivity gains in agriculture but also to growth in the number of factory jobs and the development of transportation networks. Third, Britain's increasing reliance on other countries, including its extensive network of colonies, for supplies of raw materials and as markets for its goods, was critical in the development of its industrial sector. Britain imported cotton fiber from India, for example. It discouraged the further development of cotton manufacturing within

India by putting high import tariffs on Indian-made cloth while requiring that India let in British-made cloth tariff free.

While the Industrial Revolution began in Britain, by the nineteenth and early twentieth centuries, it was well along in much of Western Europe and other "early industrializing" countries, such as the United States, Canada, and Australia. It is important not just as a historical episode but because the pattern of economic development that it established has become, in many people's minds, the model for how development should proceed worldwide. The vocabulary of referring to rich countries as "developed" and poorer countries as "developing," for example, involves an implicit assumption that poorer countries are on a path of industrialization, on the road to perhaps eventually "catching up" to rich countries' lifestyles and levels of wealth.

Starting in the early 1950s, a number of economists began to develop theories on how economies develop. The economic historian W. W. Rostow, for example, advanced the thesis that progress from "underdevelopment" to development invariably went through five stages. The first he referred to as "traditional, agrarian society," meaning not only an economy based on farming but also one that was stagnant—that is, not in an active process of development. The second stage, "preconditions for takeoff," is similar to the first, with the important exception that the country now possesses a critical mass of entrepreneurs and educated people, signifying the country's *potential* for development. Although he did not use these terms, for Rostow, "human capital" was indispensable for development, and "natural capital" (which even the least developed countries possess), while important, was insufficient.

The third stage was "takeoff" (into self-sustaining growth). At this point, the country realizes its development "potential" by achieving a sufficiently high level of *savings* to finance the *investment*—specifically, the accumulation of manufactured capital—necessary for growth. From there, growth and development was expected to sustain itself. The fourth stage is the "drive to maturity," and the final stage, in which the rich countries currently find themselves, is the "age of high mass consumption."

The main conclusion from Rostow's theory is that after the necessary "preconditions" (education and entrepreneurship) are present, investment in manufactured capital and technology is sufficient to propel a country to a high living standard. A very similar conclusion was reached by the more mathematical Harrod-Domar model, named after the economists Roy Harrod and Evsey Domar.

An important corollary to Rostow's theory is that if domestic savings were insufficient to enable a country to reach the "takeoff" stage, "foreign saving" should help compensate for the shortfall. This could come from private investment, assuming that countries had stable enough conditions to attract foreign investors. The theory also supported the then-widespread view that countries like the United States should provide foreign aid to developing countries to help them raise their living standard (and also, given the reality of the Cold War, to lure them into the U.S. "sphere of influence"). Yet as we will see, success in this effort was far from universal. The failure of aid to stimulate sustained growth in many countries caused a great deal of frustration among policy makers.

By the 1980s, a new idea gained ground: that countries should engage in "structural reforms" as a precondition for being granted aid. Multilateral institutions such as the

International Monetary Fund (IMF) and the World Bank, which provided loans for development or to assist countries in financial difficulties, began to insist that *all* recipient governments undertake a broad swath of policy changes to qualify for further loans. The set of favored policies came to be known as the Washington Consensus. The main principles of the Washington Consensus were:

- *Fiscal discipline.* Developing countries were urged to end fiscal deficits and balance government budgets by developing reliable sources of tax revenue and limiting spending.
- *Market liberalization and privatization.* Abolition of government-controlled industries, price controls, and other forms of intervention in domestic markets were seen as essential to promoting growth.
- *Trade liberalization and openness to foreign investment.* Countries were pressured to remove tariffs and other barriers to trade, as well as capital controls and other restrictions on foreign investment flows.

Loans from the World Bank, the IMF, and other institutions were made conditional on moving toward making such "structural reforms" or "structural adjustments" in a country's economy. The slogan "stabilize, privatize, and liberalize" governed the thinking of development policy makers. The implicit promise was that if these policies were followed, the conditions for rapid growth would be created. As in Rostow's theory, the emphasis was on making developing economies appealing and "safe" for foreign investment; also, the presumption was that the same guidelines applied to every developing country. A new element that arrived with the Washington Consensus was a set of limitations on the autonomy of developing-country governments.

Recent growth performances seriously call into question the validity of these policy prescriptions. The region of the world most influenced by the Washington Consensus has been Latin America, and, as can be seen in Table 18.1, its growth rates over the

Table 18.1 *Per-Capita Annual Real GDP Growth in Select Latin American Countries, 1980–2015 (%)*

Bolivia	0.9
Brazil	1.2
Chile	3.3
Colombia	2.0
Ecuador	1.1
Mexico	0.8
Peru	1.4
Venezuela	−0.3
All Middle-Income Countries Average	2.7

Source: World Bank, World Development Indicators Database, 2016.

past three decades compare rather unfavorably to the average growth rate for middle-income countries as a whole (with few exceptions, Latin American countries are in the "middle-income" category). Only Chile, which had 3.3 percent growth from 1980 to 2015, has a growth rate similar to the global average for middle-income countries. All the other listed countries (with the possible exception of Colombia) grew anemically. The entire Latin America and Caribbean region had an annual average growth rate of only about 1 percent.

The poor performance of this region of the world is, to date, the strongest indictment of the Washington Consensus. As we will see, however, even where growth in other regions has been stronger, it was quite imbalanced, often widening the gaps between rich and poor. One of the challenges in development economics is to address the growing inequality that results—both within and among countries.

Discussion Questions

1. How, according to twentieth-century theory, can a country achieve GDP growth? How is growth related to the capital endowments—and which kinds of capital are most important?
2. What, according to Rostow, are the five "stages of growth" through which all countries must pass in order to become developed? Do you think this theory fits with the actual experience of development? Can you name a country at each stage?

2. COUNTRY GROWTH EXPERIENCES

The Rostow and Harrod-Domar models were largely based on the phenomenal economic growth record of the industrialized countries. This section briefly reviews that record and then compares more recent growth rates of different countries.

2.1 Growth Comparisons Across Countries

During the twentieth century, real income in Western Europe rose about sixfold (despite two devastating wars), that in the United States about sevenfold, and world per-capita economic output grew about fivefold. Most of this growth came in the second half of the twentieth century. Figure 18.2 shows the record of global growth since 1971. Gross world product went up by a factor of 4 during this period (in inflation-adjusted terms). This was accompanied by a more than doubling in the use of energy, primarily fossil fuels. Even though world population nearly doubled over the period 1971–2011, food production and living standards grew more rapidly than population, leading to a steady increase in per-capita income.

This economic growth has been very unevenly distributed among countries, as well as among people within countries. Table 18.2 shows the per-capita national incomes and rates of economic growth for selected countries and income category groups during the period 1990–2015. The table gives national income in purchasing power parity (PPP) terms, comparing countries based on the relative buying power of incomes (see Chapter 14, Section 3.1, for an explanation of PPP).

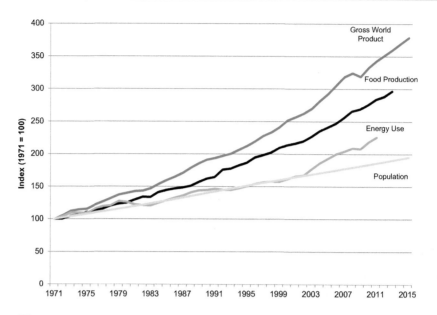

Figure 18.2 *World Economic Growth, 1971–2015*

All series are shown using an index of 100 for 1971 levels. During the period 1971–2015, population nearly doubled, energy use more than doubled, food production tripled, and gross world product increased by 280 percent.

Source: World Bank, World Development Indicators Database, 2016.

As Table 18.2 shows, the record is highly variable, with some countries achieving less than 1 percent annual per-capita economic growth, and others achieving more than 4 percent, with China in the lead at a sizzling 8.8 percent. Some already-poor countries, such as Haiti and the Democratic Republic of Congo, are becoming even poorer. While the table indicates that the middle-income countries are the fastest-growing group, this is largely a result of high growth rates in China and India, which together account for more than half the population of all middle-income countries.

What accounts for the striking differences in economic fortunes across countries? And can we expect such differences to increase or decrease?

Economies such as those of the United States, Europe, and Japan have benefited from many decades of economic growth. Such growth has not been uniform; periods of expansion have alternated with periods of slowdown or recession. (The Japanese economy and the euro-area economy, for example, have grown very slowly in recent years.) But overall, GDP in these countries has increased due to a combination of factors including growth in aggregate demand and—as discussed earlier—labor productivity, technological innovation, and investment in manufactured capital.

In addition, successful economic growth has often resulted from taking advantage of trade opportunities. Although industrialized countries have generally benefited from openness to trade, they have also typically used protectionism—tariffs and quotas

Table 18.2 *Income, Growth, and Population Comparisons, Selected Countries and Country Groups*

Country or Category	GDP per capita, 2015 (PPP, constant 2011 international $)	Percent growth in GDP per capita (PPP, annual average, 1991–2015)	Percent of world population (2011)
High Income	42,261	1.4%	16.2%
Hong Kong	53,380	2.6%	0.1%
United States	52,549	1.5%	4.4%
Japan	35,804	0.7%	1.7%
France	37,306	0.9%	0.9%
South Korea	34,387	3.9%	0.7%
Middle Income	10,104	3.3%	74.6%
Russia	23,895	0.8%	2.0%
Turkey	18,959	2.4%	1.1%
Brazil	14,455	1.4%	2.8%
China	13,400	8.8%	18.7%
India	5,730	4.8%	17.8%
Low Income	1,548	1.1%	8.7%
Bangladesh	3,137	3.6%	2.2%
Nepal	2,313	2.5%	0.4%
Haiti*	1,658	−0.3%	0.1%
Ethiopia	1,530	3.9%	1.4%
Congo, DR	737	−1.7%	1.1%

Source: World Bank, World Development Indicators Database, 2016.

*Data for Haiti growth rate is for 1999–2015.

to limit trade—to foster the development of important domestic industries. Critics such as economist Ha-Joon Chang claim that such countries have "kicked away" the (protectionist) ladder that they have used to ascend to higher living standards and now insist that poor countries seeking to develop their economies follow "free trade" rules and not use tariffs or quotas to protect their industries.

Japan and other "Asian Tigers" (South Korea, Hong Kong, Taiwan, and Singapore), starting in the mid-twentieth century, demonstrated a pattern of **virtuous cycles** in which high savings and investment lead to greater productivity, a competitive export industry, and growth of domestic industries. The resulting financial capital is then invested in machines, tools, factories, and other equipment that can further enhance productivity—and the cycle begins again. In addition, as the economy grows, more resources are available to invest in the development of health-care and educational systems. It sounds simple and obvious—yet many countries have had great trouble in achieving such virtuous cycles.

virtuous cycles (in development): self-reinforcing patterns of high savings, investment, productivity growth, and economic expansion

583

One factor that appears to be essential in almost every case for promoting growth and development is human capital. For example, while the U.S. savings rate is low, American investment in human capital is relatively high. Only Sweden, Korea, and Finland have college enrollments beyond high school that are higher than those in the United States. The Asian Tigers have also benefited from generally excellent educational systems, along with industrial structure that (especially in Japan) motivated workers through good employment benefits linked to company profitability.

Early theories of development such as Rostow's assumed that the lessons from industrialized economies simply needed to be applied to countries at lower levels of income so that they could follow a similar path of economic growth. But the global record of uneven development and inequality makes the picture significantly more complex. For example, the global distribution of per-capita GDP across countries is shown in Figure 18.3, where each country's per-capita GDP in 2015 has been translated into U.S. dollars and adjusted for PPP for the sake of comparability. The United States, along with Canada, most of Europe, Australia, Japan, and a few other countries, enjoys a per-capita GDP of more than $30,000. The poorest countries on earth tend to be in Africa and Asia, where annual income per capita can be below—sometimes much below—$1,000.

Traditionally, many economists have taken an optimistic view concerning the future of global income inequality. They have argued that a given increase in the manufactured capital stock should lead to a greater increase in output in a country that is capital poor than in a country that is already capital rich. Therefore, as developing countries build up their capital stocks, it is just a matter of time until "less developed" countries catch up with the countries that have already "developed." The idea that poorer

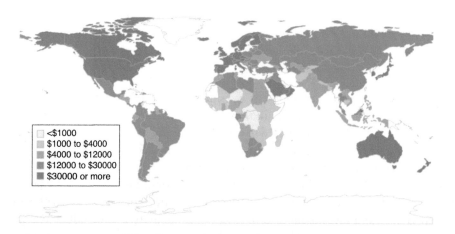

Figure 18.3 *GDP per Capita in 2015 (in Current PPP $ per Person)*

Income per person is highest in the industrialized countries of North America and Europe, along with Japan, Australia, and New Zealand. Income per person is lowest in many African and Asian countries.

Source: World Bank, World Development Indicators Database, 2016.

countries or regions are on a path to "catch up" is often referred to as **convergence**. Describing low-income countries as "developing" assumes that they are on a one-way path toward greater industrialization, labor productivity, and integration into the global economy.

Is it true that "developing" countries are, in general, catching up with the "developed" countries? Some studies of GDP per-capita growth rates, using data such as that in Table 18.2, emphasize that even the low-income countries have grown more rapidly, on average, than the high-income ones. However, this has largely been due to the strong growth rates experienced by more populous countries (as noted, the rapid growth of China and India significantly raises the average for the middle-income group of countries). If we look at every country individually, the conclusion on convergence appears more ambiguous.

The evidence suggests that, while some developing countries are on a path to catch up with the richer ones in GDP terms, others are not. In fact, if we count each country equally, the average annual growth rate of real GDP per capita (PPP) in 1990–2015 was 0.7 percent in the low-income countries, 2.3 percent in the middle-income countries, and 1.7 percent in the high-income countries—suggesting further divergence rather than convergence, at least for the low-income countries. It is also true that if a rich country and a poor one are experiencing the same *percentage* growth rate, this adds a great deal more income in the rich country than in the poor one. Thus in absolute terms, the gap between them grows wider unless the poor country has a very much higher growth rate.

In spite of all this, when GDP per capita of certain developing countries is expressed as a proportion of average GDP per capita in the United States (the largest high-income country), some countries do appear to be "catching up" (Figure 18.4a). South Korea, for example, is well on its way to joining the ranks of the rich countries, as its per-capita GDP rose from as little as 10 percent of U.S. GDP in 1970 to almost 70 percent today. Botswana's per-capita income also rose considerably over this period, from less than 5 percent of U.S. GDP to more than 30 percent. At a lower level, the rise in China's per-capita GDP has been the most rapid, from little more than 5 percent of U.S. GDP as late as 1990 to about 25 percent today. India is also "catching up," albeit somewhat more slowly and from a lower starting point.

Other developing countries exhibit trends such as those seen in Figure 18.4b. Brazil, often touted as one of the most important "newly industrializing countries" (NICs), experienced a growth spurt in the early 2000s, but has fallen back since 2010. Bolivia's relative income position deteriorated slightly from the 1960s onward but has rebounded during the times of high commodity prices of the first years of the 2000s. Nigeria and the Democratic Republic of Congo, among many other countries, have suffered significant losses, with the relative standard of living today much worse than in the 1960s. A consistent pattern among the countries "falling behind" is a particularly sharp drop in the 1980s, followed by more or less of a leveling off after 2000.

Rapid growth in China and India, along with some gains in other countries, suggests growing progress toward convergence. A recent study optimistically reports: "the last decade witnessed a sharp reversal from a pattern of divergence to

convergence (in reference to economic growth): the idea that underlying economic forces will cause poorer countries and regions to "catch up" with richer ones

585

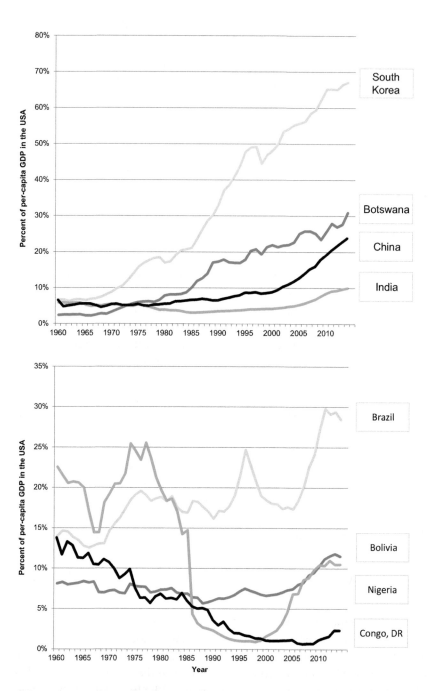

Figures 18.4a and 18.4b *Per-Capita GDP Expressed as a Percentage of per-Capita GDP in the USA*

If poor countries are "converging" or "catching up" to rich countries, their incomes should be rising when expressed as a percentage of rich country incomes. This has happened for South Korea, China, and Botswana, and also, though much more slowly, for India. Brazil, Bolivia, Nigeria, and the Democratic Republic of the Congo, in contrast, show a much more volatile development, with especially the African countries having fallen further behind in the 1980s and 1990s.

Source: Feenstra, Robert C., Robert Inklaar and Marcel P. Timmer (2015), "The Next Generation of the Penn World Table" American Economic Review, 105(10), 3150–3182, available for download at www.ggdc.net/pwt.

convergence—particularly for a set of large middle-income countries."[2] But even if convergence is sustained, global inequalities will continue for a long time. The United Nations notes that were "high income countries to stop growing today and Latin America and sub-Saharan Africa to continue on their current growth trajectories, it would take Latin America until 2177 and Africa until 2236 to catch up."[3]

How rapidly are countries growing now? Figure 18.5 summarizes a wealth of information about economic growth across countries since 1980. The horizontal axis measures GDP per capita in 2015, in constant chained 2010, PPP–adjusted dollars. The size of the spheres is proportional to the population of the country represented, so that the United States is a medium-size sphere, while China and India—together, home to nearly 40 percent of the world's population—are represented by very large spheres. Spheres on the right represent the United States and other industrialized countries, and spheres on the left represent poorer countries.

The vertical axis measures average annual real GDP per capita growth rates from 1980 to 2015. Thus more rapidly growing countries, including China, India, and South Korea, are high on the graph, while slower-growing countries are represented by spheres closer to the horizontal axis. Some countries have experienced negative growth—that is, their levels of income per person have actually fallen in recent years after adjusting for inflation. High-income countries have generally experienced

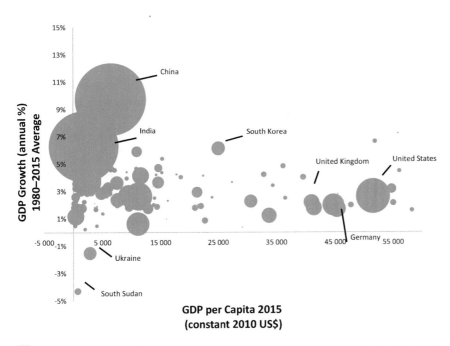

Figure 18.5 *Growth and Income Relationship With Area Proportional to Population*

Each circle represents a country. The size of the circle corresponds to the size of the country's population. The location of the circle shows GDP and GDP growth rate.

Source: World Bank, World Development Indicators Database, 2016.

587

moderate, positive average growth rates (on the order of 1 percent to 2 percent), while growth rates diverge much more as one moves down the income scale. For developing countries, average growth rates diverge dramatically (ranging from 10 percent for China down to minus 3 percent for DR Congo).

2.2   The Variety of Sources of Economic Growth

What accounts for the striking differences in economic fortunes across countries? If there were just one simple story about how economic growth occurs, economic analysis would be much easier. In fact, however, one can point to a great variety of factors, all of which may play a role in development. But their significance—and even the direction of their effect, positive or negative—may vary greatly from country to country. For this reason, it is impossible to make all-encompassing statements about why many developing countries have failed to achieve sustained growth. The following observations summarize a range of reasons for growth; their relevance varies from one situation to another.

Natural Resources

Often, one of the first things that students of development think of is the role of natural resources. Indeed, large expanses of arable land, rich mineral and energy resources, good natural port facilities, and a healthy climate may make it easier for a country to prosper, while a poor natural endowment, such as a climate that makes a country prone to malaria or drought, can be a serious drag on development. But the historical record includes some surprises. Hong Kong and Singapore have prosperous trade-based economies even though they have scant domestic resources, with little land or energy of their own.

In fact, the overexploitation of natural resources can lead both to environmental degradation and to economic distortion. Countries such as Nigeria have found that oil reserves, seemingly a source of wealth, can easily be misappropriated, with very damaging effects on development. Misdirected oil revenues can lead to massive corruption and waste. Other sectors of the economy are starved of investment and resources, as available resources go primarily toward oil production. And because oil is an exhaustible resource, the country can eventually run out of oil and find itself worse off than before. Nigeria's experience is symbolic of what many have referred to as the "resource curse" (the idea that countries endowed with abundant natural resources often do worse than countries with fewer resources).

Savings and Investment

Investment in manufactured capital requires financial capital that, as we have seen, comes from savings. Yet investment in industrial manufactured capital is not the only important kind of investment. Investments in agriculture, through improvement of seeds, irrigation, and the like, are also essential to growth. Countries can also invest in human capital by improving their systems of education and health care. Workers who are skilled and healthy are more able to be productive. Many economists stress that education in science and technology, in particular, is likely to have significant effects on growth.

Additions to capital, however, do not automatically lead to growth. Technologies that are highly automated or "**capital intensive**" may sometimes be inappropriate in countries with much unemployment. In such countries, more appropriate investments might be made in technologies that make greater use of its abundant potential workers—in other words, technologies that are more "**labor intensive**."

capital intensive: a process or procedure that makes use of more capital relative to other inputs such as labor

This claim is not without some controversy, because goods produced under labor-intensive processes tend to be less sophisticated, with less high technology, and therefore promise less export revenue than other products made with modern equipment. Indeed, one of the conflicts regularly confronted by developing countries is the need to balance economic diversification (especially into "higher-end" products) with the need to provide employment opportunities. There is also a significant tension between the motivations to provide more sophisticated products for export versus products that will be of more use to people in the country. In extreme cases, countries export food that their people cannot afford to buy for themselves.

labor intensive: a process or procedure that makes use of more labor relative to other inputs such as capital

Allocation of Investment

According to market theory, investors should be attracted to the most profitable opportunities. But market allocation of investment may ignore social priorities and will not necessarily contribute much to the development of infrastructure (things like roads, ports, railroads, and electronic networks). These and other important public goods such as environmental quality and water supplies require a public role in directing investment.*

In addition to investing in public goods, governments have often played a role in planning other industrial investments. Known as **industrial policy**, this approach can involve promoting particular industries, using tariffs, subsidies, and other economic tools as needed, even when this implies active government modification of market outcomes. These tools may be applied to protect or subsidize industries that are not yet competitive in the hope that they may become so over time; this is sometimes referred to as an **infant industry** policy.

industrial policy: a set of government policies designed to enhance a country's ability to compete globally

Virtually all currently high-income countries used such policies in earlier stages of growth. Britain and the United States consciously formulated tariff policies to encourage domestic industries. Similar industrial policies employed by Japan and the Asian Tigers (Hong Kong, Singapore, South Korea, and Taiwan) were essential to their rapid development between the 1960s and 1990s. Ironically, Western countries that aggressively used industrial policies in earlier stages of development now often preach free trade and fiscal reform to others.

infant industry: an industry that is not yet globally competitive but receives government support with the expectation that it may become so

---

* See the definitions of infrastructure and public goods in Chapter 2.

Foreign Sources of Financial Capital

If a country is not able to finance the investments it needs for development out of its own domestic savings, it generally seeks grants, loans, or investments from abroad. The sources of foreign capital for development can be either public or private. Public aid for development can take the form of either bilateral assistance or multilateral assistance. **Bilateral development assistance** consists of grants or loans made by a rich country's government to a poorer country. Many developing countries also receive **multilateral development assistance** from institutions such as the World Bank, regional development banks such as the Inter-American Development Bank, and UN agencies such as the United Nations Development Programme (UNDP). Countries may also borrow from the IMF, particularly during times of crisis.

Private foreign investment is carried out by private companies or individuals. Foreign direct investment (FDI) occurs when a company or individual acquires or creates assets for its own business operations (e.g., a German company building a factory to produce televisions in Mexico). FDI may or may not actually increase the capital stock in the recipient country, because it can include acquisitions of existing capital. Private flows also include loans from private banks. From 2000 to 2010, private flows of investment to developing countries increased dramatically, from $200 billion to more than $1 trillion, but have since leveled off at about $700–800 billion.[4]

The empirical evidence concerning the contribution of public and private foreign capital to economic growth is mixed. Some of the countries that are still among the poorest have also been the heaviest recipients of concessional aid (meaning aid without any requirements for repayment). In some cases, aid went to corrupt leaders who spent it on their own luxurious lifestyles rather than on benefits for their people. Many poor countries are now highly indebted and spend more on debt service (payment of principal and interest) than on health care for their populations.

Foreign investment can sometimes play an essential role in spurring development, but welcoming foreign businesses also can have a downside. When a large, powerful transnational corporation moves into a developing country, it may "crowd out" local initiatives by competing with them for finance, inputs, or markets, sometimes in effect replacing a viable, though small-scale, local business sector with an international corporation producing for international sales. It may also be disruptive politically or culturally. Some of the most oppressive actions in development history (such as peasants being forced off their land or union organizers repressed with violence) have come about through alliances between large transnational corporations and corrupt governments.

Domestic Demand Versus Export Orientation

Because there would be little point in increasing production if what is made cannot find a market, the level of aggregate demand in an economy is also of great importance for growth. One reason that developing countries sometimes fail to achieve sustained growth is that, while production for export is emphasized, not enough is done to

bilateral development assistance: aid (or loans) given by one country to another to promote development

multilateral development assistance: aid or loans provided with the announced intention of promoting development by the World Bank, regional development banks, or UN agencies such as the United Nations Development Programme (UNDP)

develop domestic markets. There are counterexamples to this statement: countries such as Japan and South Korea broke into the ranks of more advanced economies by developing powerful export industries, and China is now following this same path. But export dependence can become a trap that stifles economic development when countries depend on exporting products for which world demand is limited. Producers of agricultural exports, in particular, often suffer when world **terms of trade** turn against them, so that the value of what they can sell on the world market drops relative to the value of what they want to import.

terms of trade: the price of exports relative to imports

Financial, Legal, and Regulatory Institutions

Recently, policy makers have gained a greater appreciation of the role played by financial, legal, and regulatory institutions (which fit into the category of social capital) in encouraging—or discouraging—growth. Very poor countries sometimes have banking and legal systems that do not reach very far into rural areas and provide credit only for the well connected or well-to-do, making it difficult for small businesses and entrepreneurs to finance new or growing enterprises. The experience of Russia, where GDP fell more than 40 percent during its emergence from communism in the 1990s, highlighted the need for markets to be based in a good institutional framework.

Countries that have been successful in maintaining growth generally have effective systems of property rights and contract enforcement, which allow entrepreneurs to benefit from their investments, as well as effective corporate and bank regulation. Even in the case of property rights, however, the conventional wisdom does not always hold. China and Vietnam, for example, have been able to attract significant amounts of investment, even though, being at least nominally still communist countries, they do not have systems of private property rights. Nevertheless, they are able to assure firms that they will benefit from their investments by other means.

Some developing countries suffer from severe corruption, internal conflict, and other factors that make it difficult for effective institutions to take root. Political instability leads to economic inefficiency, difficulty in attracting foreign investment, and slow or no growth. This, in turn, means that less saving is available for future investment, reinforcing the problems. Breaking this vicious cycle is essential for development but can be very difficult to do.

2.3 Different Kinds of Economies

The previous section focused on the importance of investment—whether in agriculture or industrialization, in human and social capital, or in technology, infrastructure, or other physical capital. This raises the question: Who decides what are the most important investments to make? Should investment decisions be left to private markets or controlled by the government or some combination of the two? Historical experience offers a number of models.

The most extreme form of government control, represented by the experience of the Soviet Union from 1917 to 1989 and often referred to as a "command economy," has generally been discredited as an economic model. Its achievements in areas such as military production and some public goods (such as the Moscow subway system and elements of public education) came at a terrible human cost. Comparisons of Communist North Korea and East Germany with market-oriented South Korea and West Germany showed starkly that markets had a far better chance of achieving a more humane kind of development.

However, these alternatives are not, in fact, the only possibilities. Indeed, there are not only differences between market and command economies, but within each of these categories, there is more than one alternative—and relative development successes or failures do not all fall neatly into one place. We can categorize economic organizations according to *forms of ownership*, making a basic distinction between capitalist versus socialist economies. Then we may further subdivide each of these.

laissez-faire capitalism: a national system characterized by private corporate ownership and a great reliance on exchange as a mode of coordination (with relatively little coordination by public administration)

Capitalism is a system characterized by predominantly *private ownership* of productive assets; owners may be either private individuals or businesses. Under **laissez-faire capitalism**, the role of the state is supposed to be relatively small; at least in theory, it is confined to maintaining a legal-institutional environment conducive to corporate ownership and market exchange. The United States and the United Kingdom are the two advanced countries that lie closest to this end of the spectrum. In contrast, **administrative capitalism** involves a more substantial amount of state activity alongside market-coordinated activity. Germany, Italy, France, the Scandinavian countries, and also Japan fit this description. Canada, Australia, and New Zealand have tended to be somewhere in the middle, between these two varieties of capitalism.

administrative capitalism: a national system characterized by private corporate ownership and a substantial reliance on public administration as a mode of coordination

Socialism is a system that relies much more on *public ownership*, where the owners may be either government or various kinds of cooperatives. The former Soviet Union and North Korea exemplify **administrative socialism**, which centralizes a very large proportion of economic power in the government. In contrast, China and Vietnam have been experimenting with a hybrid—**market socialism**—that keeps *political* power centralized, with state ownership predominating, but releases a growing amount of *economic* decision-making power to market forces.

administrative socialism: a national system in which state ownership predominates and activity is coordinated primarily by public administration ("command")

Which of these systems is most conducive to development? And what kind of development? To compare the success of various types of economies, review some of the data presented in Chapter 0. How do the laissez-faire economies of the United States and United Kingdom perform compared to the administrative capitalist economics of Japan, France, and the Scandinavian countries? Or to the market socialism of China or Vietnam?

market socialism: a national system in which state ownership predominates but much economic activity is coordinated through markets

Consider the clearly economic categories (2 through 7 in Chapter 0): recent growth rate of GDP per capita, net national savings, government debt, labor productivity, average annual hours worked, and unemployment rate. Or what about the more well-being–related categories of income inequality: Internet users, educational performance, life expectancy, and subjective well-being—how do the different types of economies compare in these respects? Finally, consider the last two categories (CO_2 emissions per capita and local air quality), which say something about the hidden environmental and health costs of high levels of production and consumption.

592

Clearly, there is not a single winner. The United States does relatively well in some areas: It is among the world's richest countries and has very high labor productivity and currently low inflation. It performs poorly on some other measures. The U.S. savings rate is near the bottom. Especially when compared to other developed countries, U.S. educational performance is mediocre, life expectancy is somewhat shorter, and inequality is relatively high.

If you look at the ranking of the countries whose economies are described as administrative capitalism (for example, Japan and the Scandinavian countries), you will find a different pattern—one that, to some people, looks appealing in terms of greater equality as well as health and educational measures.* And China, the nearly unique exemplar of market socialism, is virtually in a class by itself. Its extraordinarily high savings and GDP growth rates make it the winner among major countries in those categories. Its debt is low and its trade balance positive. But its income inequality, which used to be very low, has climbed to equal that of the United States. While China has a developing middle class, it still has many extremely poor people. On the environmental front, as is well known, it has become a major emitter not only of greenhouse gases but also of other harmful pollutants.

The debate on development continues. As the experience of the twentieth century reveals, there is nothing "automatic" about achieving sustained growth and a high standard of living. Undoubtedly, a combination of market- and government-led policies will be used as countries continue to strive to develop. The unsettled questions are how to determine the combination that will work best for a particular country and how best to promote a combination of goals that include economic development and social well-being. The fact that each country is unique and therefore requires a unique "playbook" of strategies makes the task of development economists all the more challenging.

Discussion Questions

1. Do you think that the economic challenges faced by developing countries today are the same as those faced by industrialized countries when they were starting out? If not, how are they different?
2. Think of a poor country that you know a little about—even if what you know is just where it is on a world map and who its neighbors are. Considering the varieties of sources of economic growth, where would you propose starting to design a development plan for that country?

3. UNDERSTANDING POVERTY

From the early days of development economics, the eradication of poverty has always been a goal—sometimes the primary goal, at other times taking second or third place to other goals, but always an important consideration. However, the understanding of

---

* If you want to look into this further, you can go to the Web site www.gdae.org/macro/, which provides figures for all countries for which there are reliable statistics, not just those that are presented in Chapter 0.

poverty is not as obvious as it might at first appear. This section uses the lens of measurement to show how different groups have tried to understand the issue.

3.1 GDP Growth and Poverty Reduction

There is a close relationship between the goals that we set ourselves and the metrics that we use to assess where we are and how well we are progressing toward our goals. Joining a growing (new) consensus, the IMF and World Bank have replaced their focus on "structural adjustment" with an emphasis on "poverty-reduction" policies that are intended to give countries more voice in creating their own development solutions.* To reach such a goal, the first requirement is to define and measure the thing that we want to change.

As noted earlier, the simplest way of defining poverty is according to average income, or GDP per capita. Yet averages hide a great deal. An average GDP per capita of €10,000 could exist in a country where most people are able to cover their basic needs for nutrition, basic health care, and shelter, along with some access to education and communications. Alternatively, most of the people in such a country could be living in dire poverty, with a small percentage being quite rich, leading to the same *average* GDP per capita of €10,000. We must therefore consider some other poverty measures as additional ways of understanding where economic growth is most needed and what role it plays in the larger topic of development.

One common approach is to define poverty as the percentage of the population below what is known as the **poverty line**. One international poverty line that is often used as a minimum standard to escape extreme poverty is $1.90 per day (updated in 2015 from a formerly used figure of $1.25 per day). According to this measure, many developing countries experiencing at least modest growth rates have succeeded in reducing the incidence of poverty in their countries. For example, from 1984 to 2012, Mexico had an average annual growth rate in per-capita GDP of only 0.8 percent yet was able to work within this growth rate to reduce its poverty rate from 9.7 to less than 1 percent (Table 18.3). Similarly, Brazil managed to bring down its poverty rate from 1981 to 2013 from 9.8 percent to 2.8 percent despite a growth rate of only 1.1 percent. Of the countries shown, Nigeria is the only one experiencing growth and an *increase* in poverty.

In comparing countries, it is necessary to use a universal standard, such as the $1.90-per-day threshold on which the poverty rates shown in the table are based. Many countries also have their own (national) poverty line. The threshold for the United States, for example, was about $20,000 per year for a family of four in 2016—or $2,000 per month. In the European Union, instead of an explicit poverty rate, a rate is computed of those "at risk of poverty and social exclusion" to underline the difference of absolute poverty rates and conditions of poor people in developed countries.

poverty line: the income threshold below which members of a population are classified as poor

---

* See International Monetary Fund, "Poverty Reduction Strategy in IMF-supported Programs," 2017, retrieved from www.imf.org/external/np/exr/facts/prsp.htm; or World Bank, "Poverty, 2017," retrieved from www.worldbank.org/en/topic/poverty.

Table 18.3 *Growth Rates and Changes in Poverty Rates, Select Countries*

	Period	Annual growth rate in per-capita GDP, %	Poverty rate at beginning of period, %	Poverty rate at end of period, %
Bangladesh	1983–2010	2.6	22.4	11.2
Brazil	1981–2013	1.1	9.8	2.8
China	1981–2010	8.9	43.2	2.7
Ethiopia	1982–2010	1.1	24.3*	9.0
India	1983–2011	4.3	16.1	4.3
Indonesia	1984–2010	3.5	27.9	2.9
Mexico	1984–2012	0.8	9.7	0.7
Nigeria	1985–2009	1.7	17.4	21.8
Philippines	1985–2012	1.3	9.3	2.7
South Africa	1992–2011	1.0	11.0	4.9
Thailand	1981–2012	4.3	5.0	0.0

Source: World Bank, World Development Indicators Database, 2013.

Note: The poverty rate is based on a poverty line of $1.90 per day.

The threshold for being considered at risk of poverty is calculated relative to national incomes. For example, in 2014, a family of two adults and two children under the age of 14 was considered being at risk of poverty in Germany if the household's net disposable income was below €2,072 per month. The threshold for the United Kingdom was £1,742, for Spain €1,393, and for Estonia €752.

While not useful for comparing across countries, the advantage of a national poverty line is that it allows a country to define poverty according to its own standard of living. An income that classified someone as poor in the United States would almost certainly not be considered living at the poverty level in India. The international standard of $1.90 per day may help in classifying poor countries but would be useless for rich countries, where the poverty rate using this standard would be nearly zero.

Both approaches are typically referred to as "headcount" measures, since they simply require the "counting" of people who fall below the poverty line. But many find that measuring poverty based exclusively on income reflects only a small part of the poverty picture. In what follows, we consider a more broad-based measure of poverty.

3.2 The Multidimensional Poverty Index

Amartya Sen, a Nobel Prize–winning economist, has argued that basing poverty on income deficiencies is exceedingly narrow and often does not provide an accurate picture of how poor a population may be. He has proposed that one's **capabilities**—that is, the opportunities that people have to be well nourished, decently housed, have

capabilities: the opportunities that people have to pursue important aspects of well-being, such as being healthy and having access to education

595

access to education, and in many other ways live lives that they find worthwhile—are more important than a simple income measure. Sen emphasizes the goal of enlarging people's choices, which depends fundamentally on building their capabilities.

The Multidimensional Poverty Index (MPI), based on Sen's work, was developed in 2010 by the Oxford Poverty and Human Development Initiative for the United Nations Development Programme's *Human Development Report*. The MPI considers several elements that are critical for a decent life in the areas of physical living standards, education, and health, as outlined in a study by Oxford University (see Box 18.1). Although the 10 items on the list are not the only essentials, they are good proxies; people who do not have these can reasonably be considered deprived, or poor.

The study found that a total of 1.6 billion people are living in multidimensional poverty. This is more than 30 percent of the people living in the 104 countries surveyed. Among these, South Asia leads the world in poverty, with between 52 percent and 62 percent of those defined in the MPI as being in the world's bottom billion.* About 40 percent of the total are in India. Most of the rest live in sub-Saharan Africa, which is home to between 33 percent and 39 percent of the poorest billion. Of the 104 countries in the survey, only four—Belarus, Hungary, Slovenia, and Slovakia—were not home to any of the poorest billion people. Surprisingly, 41,000 of the poorest billion people live in countries defined, in this study, as high income: Croatia, Estonia, United Arab Emirates, Trinidad and Tobago, and the Czech Republic.

BOX 18.1 HOW THE MPI DEFINITION OF POVERTY IS CONSTRUCTED

A person is identified as multidimensionally poor if he or she is deprived in one-third or more of the following weighted indicators:

Education (each indicator is weighted equally at 1/6)

- *Years of Schooling:* deprived if no household member has completed five years of schooling
- *School Attendance:* deprived if any school-age child is not attending school in years 1 to 8

Health (each indicator is weighted equally at 1/6)

- *Child Mortality:* deprived if any child in the family has died
- *Nutrition:* deprived if any adult or child for whom there is nutritional information is malnourished

Living standards (each indicator is weighted equally at 1/18)

- *Electricity:* deprived if the household has no electricity
- *Drinking Water:* deprived if the household lacks access to clean drinking water or clean water is more than a 30-minute walk from home, round trip

---

* The imprecision is due to three alternative regional divisions used: national, subnational, and individual.

- *Sanitation:* deprived if the household does not have adequate sanitation or their toilet is shared
- *Flooring:* deprived if the household has a dirt, sand, or dung floor
- *Cooking Fuel:* deprived if the household cooks with wood, charcoal, or dung
- *Assets:* deprived if the household does not own more than one of: radio, TV, telephone, bike, motorbike, or refrigerator and does not own a car or tractor

Technical note: The MPI is the product of two components: (1) Incidence, the percentage of people who are disadvantaged (or the headcount ratio, H); and (2) Intensity of people's deprivation, the average share of dimensions in which disadvantaged people are deprived (A). Thus $MPI = H \times A$.

Source: Sabina Alkire, José Manuel Roche and Suman Seth, Oxford Poverty & Human Development Initiative, Multidimensional Poverty Index 2013, www.ophi.org.uk, March 2013.

It is interesting to compare the results of the MPI study with the "less than $1.90 a day" (income-poor) approach. In some countries, there are large discrepancies between the percentage of the population that is "MPI poor" and the percentage that is income poor. At one end of the scale are the countries that are the least poor in MPI terms. Some of these—for example Georgia—are nevertheless identified as having between 10 percent and 20 percent of their population earning less than $1.90 a day.

The two largest discrepancies in the middle group are Morocco, with income poverty rates in single digits but more than 15 percent MPI poor; and Swaziland, with over 40 percent income poor but about 20 percent MPI poor.

Such discrepancies reveal the potential limitations in relying exclusively on income-based poverty measures. Clearly, based on the Oxford study, being above the income poverty line is neither necessary nor sufficient for escaping multidimensional deprivation. If income is a means to an end, and the "ends" include the health, education, and physical living standards criteria outlined in the MPI report, then multidimensional poverty may be more relevant than income poverty in the assessment of deprivation within countries. As we see in the following section, this "multidimensionality" is also present in any evaluation of a country's progress in achieving development.

3.3 Human Development and the Millennium Development Goals

There are alternatives to measuring development primarily in terms of GDP. Bearing in mind the "capabilities" approach and multidimensional approaches to defining poverty, some have argued that development should be geared primarily to meeting basic needs for food, shelter, and health care. The **human development** approach includes attention to such basic needs but goes further to encompass other dimensions of a worthwhile life.

Recent UNDP reports have, for example, examined how widespread, socially accepted domestic violence limits the human development of women in many regions

human development: an approach to development that stresses the provision of basic needs such as food, shelter, and health care

597

and how human development may be limited by political oppression along ethnic or other lines. Such issues affect countries with high material standards of living, as well as those still unable to supply basic goods.

In September 2000, the member states of the United Nations unanimously declared their intention to try to reach a set of development objectives called the **Millennium Development Goals (MDGs)**. These goals focused on improvements in the life of the very poorest people in the world, emphasizing food security, education, gender equity, and health care (see Box 18.2). The MDGs included mention of environmental sustainability (discussed in Chapter 19). Most of the goals set a deadline of 2015 for achievement.

Each of the eight main *goals*, such as "reduce child mortality," was accompanied by one or more specific *targets*, such as "reduce the under-five mortality rate by two-thirds between 1990 and 2015." These targets, in turn, may relate to a number of policy actions, such as increasing education for mothers, vaccinating against measles, and distributing malaria-fighting mosquito nets. The eighth goal, "develop a global partnership for development," pointed to some policies that the richer countries should enact. They included eliminating tariff barriers to poor countries' products, canceling or restructuring debts, increasing foreign aid, easing the flow of essential drugs, and sharing technology.

As a high-profile, specific commitment of UN members, the MDG declaration has served to increase the global attention paid to the promotion of human development. Some have nevertheless criticized the MDGs, believing that the goals do not go far enough in addressing inequalities and injustices between rich and poor countries. While the follow-through of the MDG since their declaration in 2000 has had mixed results, most experts were surprised how well they actually worked, as during the period of 2000 to 2015, globally, many dimensions of human development improved much more quickly than in the previous 15 years.

For example, according to the UN, the first MDG of halving the proportion of people living on less than $1.25 a day (the threshold in 2000) was met three years *before* the target date. By 2015, the global poverty rate had decreased from 47 percent to 14 percent. This progress has been very uneven, with regions such as South and East Asia having seen considerable gains (China and India contributing most to the improvement in the global picture), while conditions in parts of sub-Saharan Africa have deteriorated (see Figure 18.5 and Table 18.3), in 2015, globally, about 1 billion fewer people were living in poverty than in 1990. While the goal of reducing child mortality by two-thirds was not quite reached, most regions, including Sub-Saharan Africa, saw a decrease of child mortality by more than half.

Millennium Development Goals (MDGs): a set of goals declared by the United Nations in 2000, emphasizing eradication of extreme poverty; promotion of education, gender equity, and health; environmental sustainability; and partnership between rich and poor countries

---

BOX 18.2 THE MILLENNIUM DEVELOPMENT GOALS

1. Eradicate extreme poverty and hunger—Halve, between 1990 and 2015, the proportion of people whose income is less than $1 a day or who suffer from hunger
2. Achieve universal primary education—Ensure that, by 2015, children everywhere, boys and girls alike, will be able to complete a full course of primary schooling

3. Promote gender equality and empower women—Eliminate gender disparity in all levels of education no later than 2015

4. Reduce child mortality—Reduce by two-thirds, between 1990 and 2015, the under-five mortality rate

5. Improve maternal health—Reduce by three-quarters, between 1990 and 2015, the maternal mortality ratio

6. Combat HIV/AIDS, malaria, and other diseases—By 2015 have halted and begun to reverse the spread of HIV/AIDS, malaria, and other major diseases

7. Ensure environmental sustainability—Integrate the principles of sustainable development into country policies and programs and reverse the loss of environmental resources. Halve, by 2015, the proportion of people without sustainable access to safe drinking water and basic sanitation. Have achieved, by 2020, a significant improvement in the lives of at least 100 million slum dwellers

8. Develop a global partnership for development—including fair trade, debt relief, and access to health and information technology

Source: United Nations Development Programme, www.undp.org/content/undp/en/home/mdgoverview/.

Yet as the Millennium Development Goals in many dimensions described a reduction of deprivation, much misery and poverty remained. For example, in 2013, a UN report noted that 57 million children still do not have access to primary education, and 2.5 billion people still lack adequate sanitation facilities.

Also, by and large, developed countries had not followed through with their commitments. In 2015, only six countries (Denmark, Luxembourg, the Netherlands, Norway, Sweden, the United Kingdom, and the United Arab Emirates) have met the UN target for offering international aid of at least 0.7 percent of GDP. Many countries such as Spain cut their ODA spending during the euro crisis. The Doha round of World Trade Organization negotiations, intended to achieve reforms that would help developing countries, remains stalled after more than 10 years.

Little progress has been made in opening up rich countries' markets to the products of poorer countries. The spread of some kinds of technology (particularly cell phones) has been rapid in some areas, but a technological gulf between rich and poor countries persists. In short, while there has been progress in certain areas, it is not clear that poor countries as a whole are "converging" to the levels of human development enjoyed in the industrialized world. For many countries, it seems that the opposite is true.

In addition to inadequate funding, another reason for limited success in achieving the MDGs may be a degree of incompatibility between their goals and the macroeconomic strategies employed by donor countries and multinational agencies, such as the IMF and the World Bank. The MDGs were derived from the UN work in defining and assessing human development. While, as noted, the World Bank and IMF have recently shifted their focus to incorporate poverty reduction, for much of the last several decades, development efforts were still dominated by the "neoliberal" Washington Consensus (discussed earlier).*

The neoliberal strategy was poorly suited to achieving the MDGs because, in effect, it has different goals (see Box 18.3). It does not concern itself with issues that are central to the UN concept of human development, such as care for children and the aged, inequality in general, or gender equity, including intrahousehold distribution of income and assets.**

BOX 18.3 COMPARISON OF NEOLIBERAL AND UNITED NATIONS APPROACHES TO DEVELOPMENT

Multilateral agencies in charge of development have often acted at cross purposes, with public statements of goals coming from the United Nations but implementation carried out by agencies with a "neoliberal" orientation toward development. Some of the differences were summarized in a UN Briefing Note written by advocates of the human development approach:

The human development approach emphasizes three areas of concern. First, it underlines the need for the inclusion of a broader group of governmental and nongovernmental actors in decision-making processes. In government, policy making cannot be left to economic and financial decision makers alone. Other ministries or departments, particularly those concerned with nutrition, health, and education, need to be a part of the process. Outside government, local communities need to be included to ensure a human focus and a clear understanding of available options.

Second, the human development approach broadens the scope of indicators used to monitor development. In place of neoliberalism's sharp focus on economic and financial indicators as a means to human ends, human development relies on a wider range of human and social indicators that are given primary place as ends in themselves. Thus special importance is given to indicators that track the human situation: life expectancy, nutritional status, and ultimately of well-being and happiness. In this regard, human development is similar to the basic needs approach of the 1970s.

Third, there are differences in the two approaches that reflect different attitudes toward international policy. The urgency of human development needs requires stronger international action and more rapid and flexible support, financially in access to markets and in other forms such as peace operations. Moreover, the values and principles at

---

* "Neoliberal" here refers to market-oriented development theory. It is derived from an older sense of the word "liberal," meaning freeing markets from government controls. This can be confusing since "liberal" in politics today often means using government action to help the poor.

**"Intrahousehold distribution" refers to the role of women in managing household income and assets. Often control over income and assets remains in the hands of men, while women are required to do most of the household labor.

the heart of the human development approach extend far beyond neoliberalism's preoccupation with economic efficiency and include human rights, justice, and human solidarity.

Source: Richard Jolly, Louis Emmerij, and Thomas G. Weiss, *UN Intellectual History Project Briefing Note Number 8*, July 2009, http://hdr.undp.org/en/media/Jolly%20HDR%20note%20%20UN%20Intellectual%20History%20Project%20 8HumDev.pdf, accessed April 2, 2013.

Based on these experiences, in 2015, the United Nations initiated a follow-up to the Millennium Development Goals, the so-called Sustainable Development Goals (SDGs). These have replaced the eight MDGs with 17 "focus areas" (see Box 18.4). These focus areas are much broader than the original MDGs. For example, the SDGs do not only address the conditions in developing countries, but also living conditions in rich countries, including goals such as "reducing inequality" or promoting "just, peaceful and inclusive societies." The SDGs are further specified in targets, such as "by 2030, eradicate extreme poverty for all people everywhere" or "promote development-oriented policies that support productive activities, decent job creation, entrepreneurship, creativity and innovation."

However, while this widening in focus and ambition clearly addresses dimensions neglected in the MDGs, it also has its critics. Some commentators have pointed out that one of the MDGs' merits was the limited scope of clearly defined goals that could be effectively targeted by specific policy measures. In contrast, some of the SDGs' targets are formulated such that monitoring progress becomes difficult. Moreover, what remains is a potential conflict between the new Sustainable Development Goals and the global financial and economic order. For example, the austerity imposed during the euro crisis (a result of the institutional setup in Europe but also of the International Monetary Fund) has led to a strong increase in unemployment in some countries—which is a clear violation of the proclaimed SDG target of "decent work for all."

Sustainable Development Goals (SDGs): a set of goals set forth by the United Nations in 2015, building on and expanding the Millennium Development Goals, including goals such as battling inequality worldwide, promoting inclusive growth, and limiting climate change

---

BOX 18.4 THE SUSTAINABLE DEVELOPMENT GOALS

1. End poverty in all its forms everywhere
2. End hunger, achieve food security and improved nutrition and promote sustainable agriculture
3. Ensure healthy lives and promote well-being for all at all ages
4. Ensure inclusive and equitable quality education and promote lifelong learning opportunities for all
5. Achieve gender equality and empower all women and girls
6. Ensure availability and sustainable management of water and sanitation for all
7. Ensure access to affordable, reliable, sustainable and modern energy for all

8. Promote sustained, inclusive and sustainable economic growth, full and productive employment and decent work for all

9. Build resilient infrastructure, promote inclusive and sustainable industrialization and foster innovation

10. Reduce inequality within and among countries

11. Make cities and human settlements inclusive, safe, resilient and sustainable

12. Ensure sustainable consumption and production patterns

13. Take urgent action to combat climate change and its impacts

14. Conserve and sustainably use the oceans, seas and marine resources for sustainable development

15. Protect, restore and promote sustainable use of terrestrial ecosystems, sustainably manage forests, combat desertification, and halt and reverse land degradation and halt biodiversity loss

16. Promote peaceful and inclusive societies for sustainable development, provide access to justice for all and build effective, accountable and inclusive institutions at all levels

17. Strengthen the means of implementation and revitalize the global partnership for sustainable development

Source: United Nations, www.un.org/sustainabledevelopment/sustainable-development-goals/.

Discussion Questions

1. Do you think the categories in the Multidimensional Index of Poverty do a good job of reflecting who is truly poor? If you were asked to add one item to this list, what would it be?
2. Do you think the Sustainable Development Goals are realistic or achievable?
3. What does the mixed success in achieving the Millennium Development Goals say about current development policies?

4. INEQUALITY

We have discussed the issue of inequality *between* countries. Also important is the level of inequality *within* countries. As we have seen, many countries have very high levels of inequality (as measured by the Gini coefficient, shown for selected countries in Chapter 0), meaning that the poorest 40 percent of the population receive a meager share of national income, while in other countries the "pie" is more equally shared. Apart from any potential ethical issues, inequality within countries should concern us if it significantly influences a given country's prospects of achieving sustained growth and development.

4.1 Growth, Inequality, and the Kuznets Curve

Although economic growth and poverty reduction have most often been the primary goals of development, there have also been many thinkers—in philosophy as well as in economics and other social sciences and humanities—who have placed equality, equity, or fairness high on their list of end goals: objects worth achieving for their own sake. Yet not everyone considers such matters paramount, especially economists. For some, equality is regarded as an intermediate goal—something worth achieving if it leads to other desirable outcomes. And some have argued that *in*equality may have a role to play at least at some stages in efforts toward economic development.

Although we have seen (e.g., in Chapter 0) that the extent of income inequality within countries is highly variable, it turns out that world income inequality is more extreme than in any individual country. In Figure 18.6, the world's population is organized into successive income quintiles, each representing 20 percent of the world's population. Thus the bottom quintile represents the poorest 20 percent of humanity, the next quintile represents the second-poorest 20 percent, and so on. The area associated with each quintile is in proportion to how much of the world's income it receives. Remarkably, 82.8 percent of the world's income goes to the richest 20 percent. Meanwhile, the poorest 40 percent receive only 3.1 percent of the world's income. This outcome is a product of *both* growing income inequality within many countries and growing inequality between countries (e.g., poor countries "falling behind").

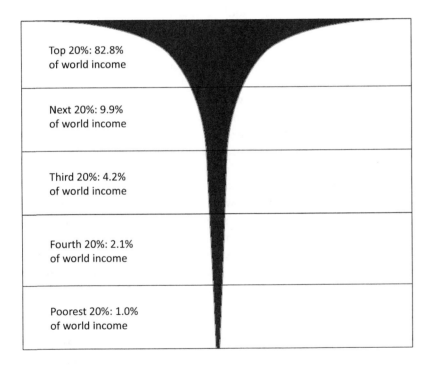

Figure 18.6 *The Unequal Distribution of the World's Income, 2007*

The "champagne glass" shape of the world's income distribution is based on more than 80 percent of the world's income going to the top 20 percent of the world's population, while the poorest 20 percent get only 1 percent of total income.

Source: I. Ortiz and M. Cummings, "Global Inequality: Beyond the Bottom Billion," UNICEF Social and Economic Policy Working Paper, April 2011.

Early in the history of development theory, Simon Kuznets (the same economist who initiated work on National Income and Product Accounts, as discussed in Chapter 5) discussed the issue of inequality in a famous paper.[5,6] He proposed that during the initial stages of economic growth, inequality would increase as investment opportunities created a wealthy class, while an influx of rural laborers into cities would keep wages low. Eventually, according to Kuznets, further industrialization would lead to democratization, widespread increases in education, and safety-net policies that would lead to lower inequality. This **Kuznets curve hypothesis** suggests an inverted-U relationship between economic growth and inequality—inequality would first rise then fall with economic growth.

Kuznets curve hypothesis: the theory that economic inequality first increases during the initial stages of economic development but then eventually decreases with further economic growth

Some countries' development paths roughly correspond to the Kuznets curve hypothesis, especially the early industrializers, such as England, France, Sweden, and Germany—however, the evidence is more mixed when we consider a broader range of countries. Some countries, such as Norway, Japan, and South Korea, have experienced economic growth with a continual decrease in economic inequality. And as we have seen in earlier chapters, economic growth in the United States since the 1970s has been associated with an increase in inequality, which also contradicts the basic Kuznets curve hypothesis.

Although the Kuznets curve hypothesis looks primarily at the influence of economic growth on inequality, we can also look at the relationship in the opposite direction—how the level of inequality influences economic growth. Here the evidence is also mixed: Some studies find that countries that are highly unequal at the start of development have a difficult time achieving rapid growth, and others support the view that inequality correlates positively with growth. The latter conclusion conforms to a view sometimes associated with traditional economics: that the existence of economic inequality creates an incentive for hard work, thereby helping the economy grow. In other words, if the economic outcomes in a society were too equal, there would be little reason to seek to improve one's economic situation.

More recently, however, economists have debated whether the high level of inequality in rich countries is slowing economic growth. Nobel Prize–winning economist Joseph Stiglitz, for example, argues that in the recent case of the United States, high inequality has impeded the economic recovery after the financial crisis of 2007–2009. He claims that the U.S. middle class is now weaker than in the past and is therefore unable to fuel a recovery adequately with consumer spending. A weakened middle class is also less likely to invest sufficiently in education or start enough new businesses.

According to research by the IMF, inequality is associated with greater economic instability.[7] It may be no coincidence that the most significant economic downturns in the industrialized world over the past 100 years, the Great Depression and the Great Recession, both occurred during peaks of inequality in the United States and elsewhere.

Others, such as Paul Krugman (another Nobel Prize–winning economist), believe that it is not income inequality per se that impedes economic recovery. The problem is that extreme income inequality gives rise to *political* inequality, and this is what can impede recoveries. Krugman suggests that the recent slow economic recovery is due mostly to political problems. According to this view, wealthy individuals and powerful corporations, interested in their own economic welfare and wielding significant political power, can effectively prevent the policies that would promote a broad-based economic recovery.

According to a recent OECD report,[8] such policies for broad-based recovery should include:

1. *Promoting education:* policies that increase high school and college graduation rates as well as policies that promote equal access to education, reduce inequality, and increase long-term economic growth.
2. *Well-designed labor market policies and institutions:* For example, as long as the minimum wage is not too high to reduce overall employment significantly, it can reduce wage inequality. Strong unions can also reduce wage inequality.
3. *Immigration and discrimination policies:* Policies that promote the integration of immigrants and that prohibit all forms of discrimination reduce inequality and can increase growth.
4. *Tax policies:* Eliminating tax loopholes that benefit primarily high-income households, such as the mortgage interest deduction, would increase the overall progressivity of the tax system and allow for a reduction in marginal tax rates, which increase the incentive for working.

The OECD report notes that some policies to promote economic growth are likely to increase inequality, such as shifting from taxation of income to taxation of consumption, using a sales tax or value-added tax (VAT).* Thus the challenge becomes one of identifying policies that offer "win-win" outcomes—that is, those that promote both GDP growth and a reduction in the degree of income inequality.

Up to what point should inequality be reduced? Just as no one would be likely to advocate the extreme position of "the more inequality the better," few would support the idea of attempting to achieve perfectly equal income distribution throughout a society. Yet there is widespread concern that inequality has become excessive in many countries. High inequality exists in many developing countries but has also become increasingly evident in many countries of the European Union as well as the United States. As noted, the evidence remains inconclusive regarding its effect on growth. But when we broaden our scope to consider the well-being aspects of development instead of just economic growth, the negative effects of inequality become more apparent.

4.2   Recent Studies of Inequality

Even if the relationship between income inequality and GDP growth remains somewhat ambiguous, the same is not true for the relationship between inequality and broad-based well-being. Countries that are more unequal in terms of income generally perform more poorly on many well-being indicators.

---

* A value-added tax, or VAT, is imposed on the net value added in an industry (revenues minus costs of intermediate inputs). The concept of value added was discussed in Chapter 5.

One way in which inequality affects people is in its impact on population health. Figure 18.8 plots one proxy for health—average life expectancies—against GDP per capita, with spheres, as before, proportional to the population of the country represented. A curve is drawn to fit the general pattern made by the data points. Looking at the far left-hand side of the figure, it is clear that living in a very poor country, such as Nigeria, dramatically increases the chance that one will die prematurely, compared with living in a country with somewhat higher GDP per capita, such as India or China. On the left-hand portion of the graph, we can see that substantial inequality *between* countries plays an important role in determining longevity.

In the middle section of the graph, moving from left to right, we see countries such as Mexico, which has achieved a life expectancy fairly close to those of the richest countries, even though its average income per capita is not even half as high. But South Africa lies far below the line, reflecting a case in which inequality makes it difficult to translate a moderate *average* level of income into well-being and longevity.

Looking at the spheres representing Western Europe, Japan, and the United States at the right-hand side of the figure, we see that the positive relationship between income

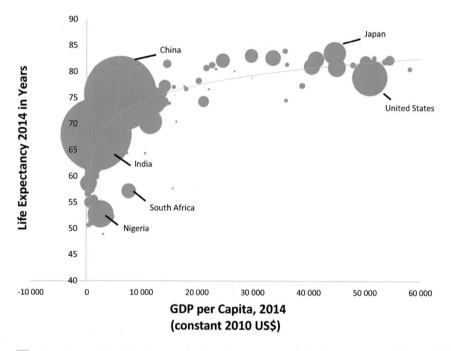

Figure 18.7 *The Relation Between Life Expectancy and Income, With Area Proportional to Population*

At very low levels of income per head, increases in per-capita income are associated with steep increases in life expectancy. After a middle-income level of per-capita GDP is reached, however, increases in income are associated with much more modest increases in life expectancy, and at high incomes the relationship flattens out.

Source: World Bank, World Development Indicators Database, 2013.

606

and life expectancy essentially disappears. At high incomes, in fact, inequality within countries—not income per capita—may be an important factor in determining health and life expectancy. For example, according to a recent study, despite the fact that the average U.S. citizen can expect to live about 77 years—which is considerably better than the global average of about 70 years—U.S. life expectancy is lower than most other (generally more equal) industrialized countries, which are in the 78- to 82-year range. Infant mortality also appears to be higher in countries with greater inequality.[9] The authors of this study argue that inequality is positively associated with a range of negative social outcomes, including mental health and incidence of violence.

Another recent study emphasizes the enormous inequality *between* countries in outcomes other than income:

> The differences in life expectancy between countries dwarf those between different groups within countries. (This is true for income inequality, too.) There is an eight-year difference in life expectancy between Japanese women (86.1 years) and Japanese men (78.0 years), but both Japanese men and women can expect to live almost twice as long as a newborn in the countries with the lowest life expectancy in sub-Saharan Africa (Zambia, Angola, and Swaziland).
>
> Infant mortality rates—which are the main drivers of differences in life expectancy between rich and poor countries—vary from 3 per 1,000 in Iceland and Singapore to more than 150 per 1,000 in Sierra Leone, Afghanistan, and Angola. In 1990, more than a quarter of children in Mali did not live to see their fifth birthdays, a marked improvement over 1960, when around half died in childhood—or put even more starkly, when median life expectancy at birth was only five years.[10]

Thus it seems clear that a special focus of development should be on increasing incomes for the poorest and eliminating the kinds of inequality that lead to major human suffering. These goals need to be balanced with the more general objectives of development discussed in Sections 1 and 2.

4.3 Economic Development and Human Development

Over the past century, the world has seen dramatic economic growth, but the benefits of this growth have been unevenly distributed. Some developing countries, such as India and China, have experienced rapid growth rates. * Others, such as most countries in sub-Saharan Africa and some countries in Latin America and Central Asia, are still struggling with low or even negative growth rates. In terms of living standards and well-being, much of the world's population has been left out of the significant progress that appears in aggregate statistics. In the future, further development is clearly

---

* Both China and India experienced extremely high growth rates of up to 10 percent per year or more during the decade 2000–2010, although growth rates in both countries have recently slowed somewhat. See http://data.worldbank.org/indicator/NY.GDP.MKTP.KD.ZG.

essential, but simple models of economic growth may fail to capture important elements of the development challenge (see Box 18.5).

A growing number of development economists recognize the need to rethink development more in the direction of broad-based human development, with increased emphasis on inequality at all levels of development. For those suffering material deprivation, GDP growth is often but not always or only the first solution, and policies to achieve GDP growth should be balanced with promotion of human development goals.

There is another important reason for a shift in paradigms regarding economic development. We cannot assume that indefinite GDP growth will in the long term be *ecologically sustainable*. This is the focus of Chapter 19, in which we consider some of the issues relating to the environmental and resource limits that we face in the twenty-first century.

BOX 18.5 COMPARING INDIA AND CHINA IN HUMAN DEVELOPMENT

Both India and China have experienced rapid economic growth since 2000, but there are significant differences in their human development levels. Nobel Prize winner Amartya Sen, who originated the "capabilities" approach to development, comments that the most significant gap between China and India is not in growth rates but in the provision of essential public services:

> Inequality is high in both countries, but China has done far more than India to raise life expectancy, expand general education, and secure health care for its people. India has elite schools of varying degrees of excellence for the privileged, but among all Indians 7 or older, nearly one in five males and one in every three females are illiterate. And most schools are of low quality; less than half the children can divide 20 by 5, even after four years of schooling. . . . The poor have to rely on low-quality—and sometimes exploitative—private medical care, because there isn't enough decent public care. . . .
>
> India's underperformance can be traced to a failure to learn from the examples of so-called Asian economic development, in which rapid expansion of human capability is both a goal in itself and an integral element in achieving rapid growth.

Despite a lack of democratic process in China, its leaders have placed a priority on eliminating hunger, illiteracy, and medical neglect. According to Sen, if India is to match China's economic record, it needs a "better-educated and healthier labor force at all levels of society," as well as "more knowledge and public discussion about the nature and huge extent of inequality and its damaging consequences for economic growth."

Source: Amartya Sen, "Why India Trails China," *New York Times*, Op-Ed, June 19, 2013.

DISCUSSION QUESTIONS

1. How important to you are your income goals relative to your other goals? A recent survey, for example, asked respondents to say whether each of the following was absolutely necessary, very important, somewhat important, not very important, or not at all important "for you to consider your life as a success." How would you answer?

Earning a lot of money	Having an interesting job
Seeing a lot of the world	Helping other people who are in need
Becoming well-educated	Living a long time
Having a good marriage	Having good friends
Having a good relationship with your children	Having strong religious faith

2. How would you balance the issue of human development with the issue of economic growth? Is growth essential for human development? Could the answer differ for different countries? What kinds of policies do you think are best for promoting human development?

REVIEW QUESTIONS

1. Which two variables can be added together to obtain the growth rate of GDP in a country?
2. How can economic growth be represented using the *AS/AD* graphs discussed in Chapter 13?
3. What was the Industrial Revolution? What factors were essential in creating the Industrial Revolution?
4. How evenly has economic growth been distributed among different countries in recent decades?
5. What factors are generally considered responsible for GDP growth in developed countries? Have the factors responsible for growth been the same in all developed countries?
6. About how much of the world's income goes to the richest 20 percent? How much goes to the world's poorest 40 percent?
7. What is the concept of convergence in economic growth?
8. What is the evidence for and against economic convergence?
9. How can investment be used to promote economic development?
10. Is an abundance of natural capital a prerequisite for economic development?
11. How can export development both promote and threaten economic growth?
12. By what different methods can foreign capital be provided to promote economic development?
13. What has been the most significant source of foreign capital for economic development in recent years?
14. What are the main principles of the Washington Consensus?
15. What is the evidence regarding the performance of the Washington Consensus recommendations?

EXERCISES

1. Suppose the real GDP of Macroland is €1.367 trillion in Year 1 and €1.428 trillion in Year 2. Also, assume that population in Macroland grew from 128 million in Year 1 to 131 million in Year 2.
   a. What is the growth rate of real GDP in Macroland during this period?
   b. What is the growth rate of real GDP per capita in Macroland?
   c. What is real GDP per capita in Macroland in Year 2?

2. Suppose we know that the growth rate of output per worker in Macroland is 1.7 percent per year and the growth rate of total factor productivity is 0.8 percent per year. Using the growth accounting equation, calculate the growth rate of manufactured capital per worker in Macroland.

3. Using the data for each country in Table 18.2, create a graph similar to Figure 18.5 showing real GDP per capita in 2015 on the horizontal axis and the rate of real GDP per capita growth for 1991–2015 on the vertical axis. (You don't need to include the three country income groups.) Draw each data point as a sphere approximately equal to the population of the country. Does your graph support economic convergence? Explain.

4. Match each concept in Column A with a definition or example in Column B:

Column A	Column B
a. Factors of production	1. Nigeria
b. A country that has shown significant economic convergence in recent decades	2. Development assistance from one country to another
c. Foreign direct investment	3. 3.1 percent
d. The percentage of global income going to the top 20 percent of the world's population	4. Singapore
e. Fiscal discipline	5. A characteristic of the Industrial Revolution
f. An example of a country that has grown despite a low savings rate	6. Income inequality first increases, then decreases, with development
g. Total factor productivity	7. The effect of technology on the productivity of capital and labor
h. The percentage of global income going to the bottom 40 percent of the world's population	8. A structural reform under the Washington Consensus
i. Bilateral development assistance	9. 2 percent
j. A country that has grown despite a lack of natural resources	10. China
k. High savings and investment rates	11. 82.8 percent
l. Growth in GDP per capita if population grows by 2 percent and GDP grows by 4 percent	12. A common factor in the economic development of the "Asian Tigers"

(Continued)

Column A	Column B
m. A country that has not shown economic convergence in recent decades	13. United States
n. The use of technologies employing fossil fuel energy, especially coal	14. Labor, capital, and natural resources
o. Kuznets curve hypothesis	15. A European company purchases a factory in an African country

NOTES

1 Note that these numbers differ from those in Chapter 5 as we are looking at real (inflation-adjusted) numbers here, but looked at nominal figures in Chapter 5.

2 Justin Yifu Lin and David Rosenblatt, "Shifting Patterns of Economic Growth and Rethinking Development," *Journal of Economic Policy Reform* 15(3) (2012): 171–194.

3 United Nations Development Programme (UNDP), *Human Development Report 2005: International Cooperation at a Crossroads*, New York, UNDP, 2005, p. 37.

4 "Capital Flows to Developing Countries," *The Economist* (June 16, 2012), retrieved from http://www.economist.com/node/21556965.

5 United Nations, *The Millennium Development Goals Report 2013* (New York: United Nations, 2013). Retrieved from www.un.org/millenniumgoals/pdf/report-2013/mdg-report-2013-english.pdf.

6 Simon Kuznets, "Economic Growth and Income Inequality," *American Economic Review* 45 (1955): 1–28.

7 See International Monetary Fund, "IMF Survey: Broad-Based Growth Can Counter Inequality, Instability — Stiglitz," October 11, 2011, retrieved from: www.imf.org/external/pubs/ft/survey/so/2011/INT101111A.htm.

8 OECD, "Job-rich growth essential for G20 recovery, say OECD and ILO," May 17, 2012, retrieved from www.oecd.org/employment/job-richgrowthessentialforg20recoverysayoecdandilo.htm.

9 Richard Wilkinson and Kate Pickett, *The Spirit Level* (New York: Bloomsbury Press, 2010).

10 Angus Deaton, "What Does the Empirical Evidence Tell Us About the Injustice of Health Inequalities?" In Nir Eyal, Samia Hurst, Ole Frithof Norheim, and Daniel Wikler (eds.), *Inequalities in Health: Concepts, Measures and Ethics* (Oxford, UK: Oxford University Press, 2013), pp. 263–281.

Chapter 19

Growth and Sustainability in the Twenty-First Century

What will the world be like in 2050 or 2100? Will the world situation be characterized as one of widespread material affluence and social peace? Or will the gap between the "haves" and the "have-nots" be even bigger and the planet afflicted by widespread social conflict and environmental damage? Of course, no one can foresee the future. But we can at least consider how some especially pressing social and environmental challenges will affect the macroeconomics of the future.

1. MACROECONOMIC GOALS: LOOKING FORWARD

As we have seen throughout this text, macroeconomics is, at its base, concerned with human well-being. The goals of macroeconomic institutions and policies are (as described in Chapter 1) the achievement of good living standards, stability and security, and financial, social, and ecological sustainability.

Much of traditional macroeconomics, as we have seen, tends to focus on the stability and growth rate of real GDP. To the extent that growth in GDP leads to growth in well-being, this is a sensible strategy. But as we saw in Chapter 6 on alternative national accounts, GDP does not measure or report on many important issues of well-being such as environmental deterioration, unpaid home production, and inequality in the distribution of wealth and income. GDP rises when there is increased production of goods that are damaging to society or the environment or that simply make up for damage already done. A narrow focus on stability and growth in GDP also ignores changes in the conditions of work, stresses imposed on families, and developments in the social and financial infrastructure of an economy.

Some people believe that continued GDP growth and technological innovation will solve the social and environmental problems of the present and future. Others, however, believe that many of the social problems of today—including environmental degradation, growing inequality, and inadequacies in health care, child care, and education—can be traced to the fact that existing forms of economic growth and development have in some ways worked against "true" or sustainable well-being.

In Chapter 18, we examined concepts of human development based on a broader perspective suggesting that economic growth alone is not sufficient—though it is

612

often necessary—for fostering and maintaining human well-being. In this chapter, we look at a second challenge to standard economic growth, relating to the impacts of economic growth on the environment and the extent to which finite planetary limits might make unlimited GDP growth infeasible.

2. MACROECONOMICS AND ECOLOGICAL SUSTAINABILITY

In Chapter 18, we noted that world economic production has more than tripled since the early 1970s. Further economic growth is clearly desirable in developing countries to improve the well-being of the roughly one billion people who are now living in desperate poverty. Continued economic growth has been a principal policy objective in industrialized countries.

But as the twenty-first century proceeds, we must consider whether it is possible, or even desirable, to continue along the economic growth trajectory of the twentieth century. Economic growth has been accompanied by an increasing demand for natural resources, as well as increases in waste, pollution, and ecosystem damages. Many ecologists warn us that the current scale of human impact on the natural world is already unsustainable. Yet the ecological implications of a further doubling, quadrupling, or more of human economic activity is an issue that, to date, has received little attention from macroeconomists.*

In this section, we consider the implications of current environmental issues for economic growth and development. First, we present an overview of some of the most pressing global environmental problems. Then we explore the relationship between economic growth and environmental quality and discuss policies to promote ecologically sustainable development.

2.1 Major Environmental Issues

A number of environmental issues are closely related to economic growth, including:

Global Population

Economic and technological growth since the Industrial Revolution has fostered a dramatic increase in world population. Global population was approximately 1 billion in 1800 and increased to 2 billion around 1930 and 3 billion in 1960. In 2000, it increased to 6 billion, and in 2011 it passed 7 billion. Human population growth contributes to increases in many environmental pressures, including those related to food production. Although so far intensification of food production has kept pace with population growth, it has led to significant costs in terms of land degradation, pollution from fertilizers and pesticides, and overtaxing of water supplies.

---

* At a GDP growth rate of 3 percent, a doubling of GDP takes about 24 years. A quadrupling would take 48 years.

613

Global population growth rates are currently declining, and many projections indicate that the human population will peak sometime in the twenty-first century (see Appendix). A stable or declining global population would eventually ease environmental pressures, but a substantial population increase is still predicted in the coming decades. Medium-range projections by the United Nations show a global population of 9.7 billion people in 2050, with almost all future population growth occurring in developing countries.

Resource Depletion

As noted in Chapters 7 and 18, depletion of important renewable and nonrenewable resources has accompanied economic growth. Many of the world's fisheries are in decline due to overfishing. Tropical forests are being lost at a rapid rate. Nearly a billion people live in countries where usable water is in scarce supply and water sources continue to be overdrawn and polluted. Stocks of key mineral resources, such as aluminum and copper, are for the most part not close to exhaustion, but high-quality reserves are being depleted, and recovery of lower-quality reserves tends to involve higher energy and environmental costs.

Probably no other natural resource has been more critical for modern economic growth than fossil fuels. These fuels (oil, coal, and natural gas) currently provide more than 80 percent of global energy supplies. The U.S. Department of Energy projects that global demand for fossil-fuel energy will increase approximately 60 percent between 2006 and 2030. However, many estimates suggest that global production of conventional oil, the most-used energy source, will peak within the next few decades. While "unconventional" sources of oil and gas, such as shale oil and natural gas obtained through hydraulic fracturing or "fracking," may expand supplies, these sources are likely to be more expensive and come at higher environmental cost. All of these fuels contribute to CO_2 emissions that cause global climate change (discussed in detail in what follows). Given the current dependence on fossil fuels, limitations on their use, for economic or environmental reasons, could challenge both the potential for industrialized countries to maintain their living standards and for developing countries to reduce poverty.

Pollution and Wastes

As discussed in Chapter 6, damage from pollution is not reflected in traditional national accounting measures, even though it clearly reduces welfare. Industrial countries generate the vast majority of the world's pollution and waste. Although rich countries are home to only about one-sixth of the world's population, they generate about two-thirds of global industrial wastes by volume. But pollution also jeopardizes economic development in poorer countries. A 2016 World Bank study estimated the global welfare cost of air pollution alone for 2013 as a staggering $5.1 trillion. According to the study, the heaviest burden was borne by countries in Asia, with air pollution cost reaching an equivalent of 7.5 percent of GDP in East Asia and 7.4 percent of GDP in South Asia.[1]

In some cases, toxic wastes are exported from industrialized countries to low-income countries that need the income they earn as compensation for accepting wastes but that are ill equipped to receive and process them. Rapid future development will mean that pollution and waste management problems, both domestic and trade related, are likely to grow, despite efforts to control them with environmental regulations.

2.2 The Race Between Technology and Resource Depletion

In the history of economic development, when one resource became scarce, another has been found to replace it. Thus, as wood and whale oil became scarce as energy sources, fossil fuels were discovered and developed to take their place. Another example is the development of a variety of plastics that have replaced metal or wood inputs in countless products. Even when resources are abundant, there may be substitutes (or potential substitutes) that can be used more inexpensively. Much of the story of economic growth is associated with productivity gains from being able to produce goods and services with progressively cheaper resources.

Yet there is some debate about possible limits to such a process. Some "technological optimists" believe that human ingenuity is virtually limitless and that humans will always be capable of finding economic substitutes for existing resources as they grow scarcer. But do substitutes exist for *all* resources? And are some resources more essential than others?

There is no substitute for potable fresh water, which is absolutely essential for humans and many other species. Even where a resource is not essential and substitutes are conceivable, it may be necessary to contend with the difficulty of obtaining the substitutes and the associated costs in terms of money or energy.

The minerals sector is an example of a significant area in which costs have recently been rising. Mineral prices increased significantly from 2000 to 2016 (even though the 2016 level in general has been much lower than the peaks shortly after 2010), and growing demand from developing economies suggests that they may continue to remain high or even rise over the medium to long term.

Copper is one important mineral for which technology had seemed for a long time to be winning the race against resource depletion. Plastic has replaced copper in many uses, such as plumbing, and plastic fiber-optic cables (as well as wireless technologies) have displaced copper wires for long-distance information transmission. Yet global demand for copper continues to grow, and copper prices tripled between 2000 and 2012. Copper in the ground remains in reasonably plentiful supply, but what is left to mine is of lower quality than what has already been taken. This is economically and ecologically important because when ore quality drops, more energy is typically required to extract and refine it. And generally the more energy-intensive the extraction of the mineral is, the more adverse the environmental impacts (e.g., pollution) that are produced.

Another important example is phosphorus, which is a critical input in the fertilizer used in the mass production of food. It has no known substitutes and there are no synthetic ways of creating it. Researchers are therefore focusing on methods of reducing dependence on the element or looking for ways of reusing it, conserving it at the point of use, or recycling it from plant and animal wastes.

2.3 A Biological Example: Fish Stocks

Unlike minerals, fish are a renewable or reproducible resource. Yet renewable does not mean inexhaustible: It is quite possible for us to run out of fish in the wild if we harvest them more rapidly than they are able to reproduce.

Many deep-sea fish (e.g., Atlantic halibut, bluefin tuna, and cod) are seriously depleted. If the danger is recognized early enough and steps are taken to reduce fishing activity sufficiently in areas where they spawn, fish populations can often recover. Since the inception of the common fisheries policies in the European Union in the 1970s, attempts have been made to limit overfishing, first by limiting the nations' fleet size, then by regulating the number of fish caught. Today, the European Union sets total allowable catches (TACs) and distributes these quotas to member states. The stated goal is that by 2020 at the latest, all fish stock should only be exploited at a level that will let them reproduce the "maximum sustainable yield for the long term." As a consequence, a number of fish stocks are recovering, but many species, including the Atlantic salmon, the Atlantic bluefin tuna, and the Atlantic halibut, are still in danger. Many other species around the world suffer from overfishing as well as habitat destruction. According to the United Nations Food and Agriculture Organization, 80 percent of the world's marine fish stocks are fully exploited or overexploited.[2]

Ironically, technological change has contributed to the decline. The introduction of bigger boats, sonar technology for finding fish, and large-scale "drift nets" have all increased depletion rates. Increasing scarcity has raised the market price for most wild-caught fish, generating incentives to expand aquaculture (fish farming). But there are also adverse ecological impacts from aquaculture, especially with the farming of saltwater species, such as shrimp and salmon. At least under traditional farming methods, five kilograms of wild-caught fish are used as feedstock in the production of each kilograms of farmed salmon, while shrimp farming has led to widespread destruction of coastal mangrove forests. The hope is that in the future, closed-system aquaculture, in which the fish is nourished with farmed insects and worms, can solve some of these sustainability issues.

Discussion Questions

1. Are you concerned about the future impacts of population growth and resource and environmental impacts? Do you think there should be some limits to population and/or economic growth?

2. Do you consider yourself a "technological optimist"? Do you believe that natural resource constraints represent a serious threat to economic production in the future? If so, which resources do you think we should be most concerned about?

3. CLIMATE CHANGE

The resource and environmental issues discussed earlier all pose serious problems. But perhaps the primary environmental challenge of the twenty-first century is global climate change. Global climate change combines issues of resource use and environmental impact and is strongly related to economic growth.

3.1 Greenhouse Emissions and Global Temperature Change

Recent research, summarized 2007 and 2014 reports by the Intergovernmental Panel on Climate Change (IPCC), has virtually eliminated any doubts that human activities are affecting the earth's climate, and these results have been further confirmed by follow-up reports.[3] Emissions of various greenhouse gases, particularly CO_2, trap heat near the earth's surface, leading not only to a general warming trend but to sea-level rise, ecological disruption, and an increase in severe weather events, such as hurricanes, floods, and droughts.

Greenhouse gases persist for decades or more in the earth's atmosphere. In addition, there is a lag between the time a gas is emitted and the time when its effects are fully realized. Thus, even if annual emissions of greenhouse gases were immediately stabilized at current levels, the concentration of these gases in the atmosphere would continue to rise, with effects such as sea-level rise continuing for centuries. Global emissions of greenhouse gases will eventually need to be reduced significantly—as much as 80 or 90 percent lower than current levels by 2050—if we are to avoid the most dangerous effects of climate change. But rather than declining, emissions of the major greenhouse gases are rising rapidly, primarily driven by fossil fuel–based economic growth.

According to BP's Energy Outlook, global emissions of CO_2 rose by 40 percent between 2000 and 2015. This growth came entirely from developing countries and emerging markets: Estimated EU emissions actually *declined* by 15 percent over the same period (and those in the U.S. by 8 percent), partly as a result of the global financial and economic crisis of 2007–2008 and the following euro crisis and partly due to a shift to renewable energy sources in some European countries.

Predicting the precise effects of climate change is subject to substantial uncertainty. The IPCC report summarizes the predictions of various climate change models. They reported a range in which the average global temperature was expected to be between 1.1 and 6.4°C warmer in 2100 compared to preindustrial levels, with the most likely range being between 1.8°C and 4°C. This range of possible temperature increases is shown in Figure 19.1.

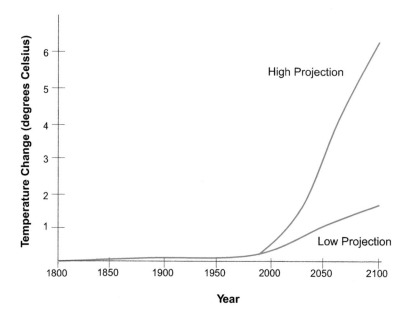

Figure 19.1 *Global Temperature Trends, 1900–2100*

Global average temperature is predicted to be between 3 and 7 degrees Fahrenheit warmer in 2100 compared to preindustrial levels.

Source: U.S. Global Change Research Program. www.globalchange.gov.

The likely effects of a 2°C increase in global average temperature (toward the lower end of the projected range) include:

- A 20–30 percent decrease in water supplies in already vulnerable regions such as southern Africa and the Mediterranean;
- Significant declines in crop yields in tropical regions;
- 40–60 million more people exposed to malaria in Africa;
- As many as 10 million more people affected by coastal flooding each year, with major low-lying areas swamped and coastal cities endangered;
- 15–40 percent of species in danger of extinction.

A report sponsored by the British government in 2006 found that, under a "business-as-usual" (BAU) scenario, there is at least a 50 percent chance of an average temperature increase of more than 5°C (9°F) by the early twenty-second century. Climate change of this magnitude could lead to catastrophic effects such as the irreversible melting of the Greenland ice sheet, the collapse of the Amazon forest, and flooding of major cities including London and New York (see Box 19.1). This report specifically examined the economics of climate change. It estimates the costs of climate change in the twenty-first century as between 5 percent and 20 percent of global GDP, while the most severe effects of climate change could be avoided at a cost of approximately

1 percent of GDP. Thus, the report concludes that it appears that the benefits of immediate action to minimize climate change significantly exceed the costs.

Although the most dangerous impacts of climate change are not likely to occur for several decades or more, the actions taken in the next few decades will almost surely have a profound effect on those ultimate impacts. Delaying action for even a decade would lead to a greater risk of catastrophic effects. This has significant implications for global equity. The impacts of climate change—including coastal flooding, agricultural yield reductions, spreading of tropical diseases, and water shortages—are poised to fall disproportionately on the developing countries. While the rich countries would, to some extent, be able to adapt to many of the effects of climate change, most developing countries lack the financial and technical resources to do so. The 2007 IPCC report notes that climate change is likely to exacerbate global inequalities and impede economic development in poorer countries.

BOX 19.1 THE STERN REVIEW—THE ECONOMICS OF CLIMATE CHANGE

Published in October 2006, the British government report written by former World Bank chief economist Nicholas Stern presents an urgent case for strong and immediate action to respond to the threat of global climate change. According to this report:

> The scientific evidence is now overwhelming: climate change presents very serious global risks, and it demands an urgent global response. . . . Under a BAU [business as usual] scenario, the stock of greenhouse gases could more than treble by the end of the century, giving at least a 50 percent risk of exceeding $5°C$ global average temperature change during the following decades. This would take humans into unknown territory. An illustration of the scale of such an increase is that we are now only around $5°C$ warmer than in the last ice age. Such changes would transform the physical geography of the world. A radical change in the physical geography of the world must have powerful implications for the human geography—where people live, and how they live their lives.
>
> The evidence gathered by the Review leads to a simple conclusion: *the benefits of strong, early action considerably outweigh the costs*. The evidence shows that ignoring climate change will eventually damage economic growth. Our actions over the coming few decades could create risks of major disruption to economic and social activity, later in this century and in the next, on a scale similar to those associated with the great wars and the economic depression of the first half of the twentieth century. And it will be difficult or impossible to reverse these changes. Tackling climate change is the pro-growth strategy for the longer term, and it can be done in a way that does not cap the aspirations for growth of rich or poor countries. The earlier effective action is taken, the less costly it will be.
>
> In summary, analyses that take into account the full ranges of both impacts and possible outcomes—that is, that employ the basic economics of risk—suggest that BAU

619

climate change will reduce welfare by an amount equivalent to a reduction in consumption per head of between 5 and 20 percent. Taking account of the increasing scientific evidence of greater risks, of aversion to the possibilities of catastrophe, and of a broader approach to the consequences than implied by narrow output measures, the appropriate estimate is likely to be in the upper part of this range. . . . It is still possible to avoid the worst impacts of climate change; but it requires strong and urgent collective action. Delay would be costly and dangerous.

Source: Excerpted from the Stern Review, available at http://webarchive.nationalarchives.gov.uk/20130129110402/ www.hm-treasury.gov.uk/sternreview_summary.htm (emphasis added).

3.2 National and Global Responses to the Climate Challenge

Because many modern environmental problems are global in scope, they require a coordinated international response. The challenge of global climate change presents an illustration of how difficult this can be in practice. The Kyoto Protocol, drafted in 1997, committed industrialized countries to reduce their greenhouse gas emissions by an average of 5 percent below their 1990 emissions by the period 2008–2012. But it was not until 2005 that enough countries ratified the treaty to enable it to enter into force. The United States, the world's largest emitter of greenhouse gases, refused to ratify the treaty on the grounds that it would hurt the U.S. economy and because it does not bind developing countries to any emissions targets. Many of the countries that had ratified the treaty, moreover, did not meet their emissions targets.

International negotiations tried to draft a "roadmap" for a new treaty to succeed the Kyoto Protocol since it expired in 2012. For a while, it looked as if international efforts did not lead anywhere, especially as it seemed dubious whether China and the U.S. could be brought on board. Things began to change when, in November 2014, U.S. President Barack Obama and China's Communist Party's General Secretary Xi Jinping agreed to limit greenhouse gas emissions. This public statement cleared the path to an agreement at the United Nations Climate Change Conference in Paris in December 2015 (the "Paris Agreement") to limit climate change by reducing global carbon dioxide emissions. Under this treaty, 195 countries agreed to limit the increase of the global temperature to "well below 2°C" and to aim at reaching "global peaking of greenhouse gas emissions as soon as possible."

While environmental activists lauded the fact that a global treaty had been signed, they warned against potential weaknesses in the agreement. For example, under the Paris Agreement, each country is supposed to set its own goal for the reduction in greenhouse gas emission. Moreover, the treaty does not include any mechanism to actually enforce the commitments. If a country fails to live up to the agreement, there is little other countries can do to force it into complying. It hence remains to be seen how much reduction of greenhouse gases the treaty will actually deliver in the end.

The best hope for avoiding the worst impacts of climate change is to replace fossil-fuel energy sources with plentiful, less ecologically destructive resources, such as wind and solar power. There is also great potential to reduce energy demand through greater efficiency. Currently, technological progress reduces energy use per unit of GDP by about 2 percent per year in the United States and other advanced countries. But combined with an economic growth rate of about 2 percent per year, this still only results in stabilizing energy use. Doubling the rate of energy efficiency gain would mean a 2 percent *decrease* in energy use per year—making it much easier to achieve carbon emissions reduction targets.

Opportunities for reducing emissions have been described in a number of studies. For example, the consulting firm McKinsey and Company has designed a scenario under which the European Union could reduce its greenhouse gas emission by 80 percent relative to the 1990 level by 2050, increase the use of renewables in power generation to 80 percent, and reduce carbon dioxide emission in the power production sector by 95 percent. According to the report, such an achievement is technically feasible, and the costs are economically bearable, if the transition is managed efficiently. Among the issues that would need to be tackled would be the construction of powerful cross-border power grids (which help funnel electrical power from areas where renewable energy can be produced easily due to good wind or sun conditions to areas where it is needed), as well as solar parks in Northern Africa and the Middle East.

For Germany, a highly industrialized country, the German Federal Environmental Agency ("Umweltbundesamt") has provided an even more ambitious scenario. According to a study published in 2013, it is technically feasible to reduce German CO_2 emissions to 1 ton per capita by 2050 (which would be the equivalent of a 95 percent reduction relative to the 1990 level). To reach this goal, however, massive changes in the insulation of houses would be needed as well as in the organization of traffic and transport, shifting a portion of the goods transported from roads to trains and boats.

3.3 The Cost of Responding Versus the Cost of Inaction

A report from the World Economic Forum in Davos, Switzerland, has estimated that $700 billion in public and private investments will be needed each year to shift the global economy away from its dependence on fossil fuels. The study by McKinsey discussed earlier puts the cumulative costs of the 80 percent reduction in greenhouse gas emission and 80 percent share of renewables in power production at €900 billion for the EU alone.

Although a large-scale energy transition away from fossil fuels would have significant costs, they may be quite modest on a macroeconomic scale and should be balanced against the growing costs likely to be caused by climate change, including damage from extreme weather events, agricultural output losses, and possible effects of famine, armed conflict, and mass migration if large areas are affected by sea-level rise or desertification. As quoted by McKinsey, €900 billion is the equivalent of less than 2 percent of the EU's GDP for the time period under consideration. Extreme weather events alone might cause a comparable degree of damage by 2050. For example,

621

Hurricane Sandy, which hit the East Coast of the United States in 2012 (and which has been linked by some experts to climate change) was alone responsible for more than \$70 billion (€50 billion) in damage. At the same time, looked at from the point of view of Keynesian macroeconomic analysis, the policies and actions suggested for preventing further climate change could bring potentially large economic benefits in terms of employment creation.

Discussion Questions

1. How do you think we should evaluate the economic impacts of climate change? Check the short executive summary of the Stern Review on the Economics of Climate Change (see Box 19.1). Do you agree with the conclusions of the report?
2. What do you think should be done by the European Union and your country in response to global climate change? Can you think of specific policies that would reduce carbon emissions without resulting in significant economic disruption?

4. ECONOMIC GROWTH AND THE ENVIRONMENT

4.1 The Environmental Kuznets Curve Hypothesis

Some researchers have suggested that, in the long run, economic development reduces per-capita environmental damages. The logic behind this assertion is that sufficient wealth and technology allow countries to adopt clean production methods and move to a service-based economy. Further, environmental quality is generally considered a "normal good," meaning that people will demand more of it as they become wealthier.

The environmental Kuznets curve (EKC) hypothesis posits an inverted U-shaped relationship between economic development and environmental damages.* It states that environmental damage per capita increases in the early stages of economic development, reaches a maximum, and then diminishes as a country attains higher levels of income. If the evidence supported this hypothesis, it would imply that economic growth would eventually promote a cleaner environment.

Does this principle really work? The EKC relationship does seem to hold for some pollutants. Figure 19.2 shows the findings of a study that estimated the relationship between per-capita sulfur dioxide emissions (the primary cause of "acid rain") and a country's per-capita income. Sulfur dioxide emissions per capita appear to peak at an income level of around \$5,000 and decline as incomes rise further. Studies of some other pollutants, mostly air pollutants, have also given limited support to the EKC hypothesis.

However, the EKC relationship does not appear to hold for many other environmental problems. Studies of municipal waste and energy use find that environmental impacts generally continue to rise as incomes rise. Perhaps most importantly, CO_2

---

* This hypothesis was not devised by Simon Kuznets but is similar to his hypothesis, discussed in Chapter 18, that inequality first increases, then decreases with growing national wealth.

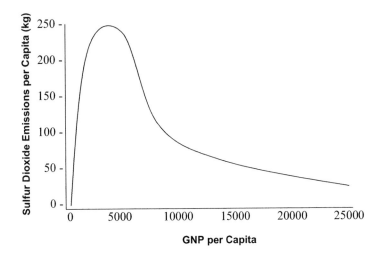

Figure 19.2 *Environmental Kuznets Curve for Sulfur Dioxide Emissions*

The empirical relationship between sulfur dioxide emissions and the level of economic development in a country supports the EKC hypothesis.

Source: T. Panayotou, "Empirical Tests and Policy Analysis of Environmental Degradation at Different Levels of Development," International Labour Office Working Paper, 1993.

emissions show a positive relationship with average income, as shown by the upward-sloping trend line in Figure 19.3, with no apparent turning point. This means that carbon emissions can be generally expected to increase as economies grow unless current dependence on fossil-fuel energy is dramatically altered. The graph, however, also gives reason for hope that this is possible. Carbon dioxide emissions vary by countries of similar levels of development. The emissions per capita in the U.S. are more than three times those in France, even though U.S. GDP per capita is only about 30 percent higher. China by now has a carbon dioxide emission per capita that *exceeds* that of France by 30 percent, even though per-capita incomes in China are not even one third of those in France.

Thus, contrary to the EKC hypothesis, economic growth appears unlikely to provide a guaranteed path to environmental sustainability. The relationship between growth and the environment is, in reality, more complex. Average income is not the only relevant factor in determining environmental impacts; the structure of the economy and lifestyles are important. Also, the distribution of wealth and income plays a key role. Sustainable development needs to include reducing economic inequalities along with preserving the environment.

Some environmental damage, such as soil erosion and deforestation, may occur because poor people engage in unsustainable practices simply to survive. Programs to eliminate poverty in developing countries can provide people with choices that are less environmentally destructive. Meanwhile, environmental degradation typically hits the poorest people the hardest, because many rely heavily on the natural environment for their subsistence.

623

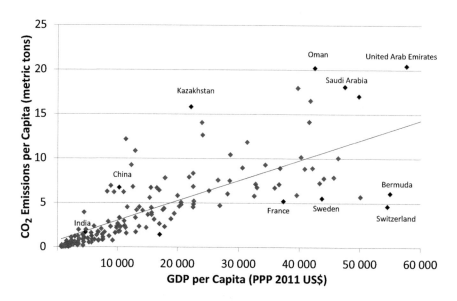

Figure 19.3 *Carbon Dioxide Emissions Versus GDP per Capita, 2009*

Carbon dioxide emissions per capita tend to increase with higher levels of economic development in a country.

Source: World Bank, World Development Indicators Database, 2013.

Policies that improve the environment can thus also serve to reduce poverty and economic inequality. The objectives of human development and environmental protection are actually interlinked. The promotion of human development in poor countries can improve environmental quality, while policies to improve the environment can also reduce economic disparities. This suggests the need for a coordinated policy response that considers the linkages between human development and the environment.

4.2 Policies for Sustainable Development

Much of macroeconomic theory and policy is currently oriented toward promoting continuous economic growth. What kind of policies would be required to promote ecological sustainability? How can these policies be designed so that they also maintain well-being and promote human development, especially in developing countries?

Some ecologically oriented economists view "sustainable growth" as a contradiction in terms. They point out that no system can grow without limit. Yet it seems that some kinds of economic growth are essential. For the large number of people in the world who cannot satisfy their basic needs, for example, an increase in consumption of food, housing, and other goods is clearly required. For those who have already achieved a high level of material consumption, there are possibilities for continued improvements in well-being through expanded educational and cultural services that do not necessarily have a large negative environmental impact. But there is nothing in standard macroeconomics to guarantee that economic growth will be either equitable or environmentally benign. Specific policies for sustainable development are therefore needed.

What might such policies involve? There are numerous possibilities, including what follows.

Green Taxes

"Green" taxes make it more expensive to undertake activities that deplete important natural resources or contribute to environmental degradation. They discourage energy- and material-intensive economic activities while favoring the provision of services and labor-intensive industries. One example of a green tax is a tax on the carbon content of energy supplies, favoring renewables and efficiency over carbon-based fuels. All countries have implemented environmentally based taxes to some extent. As shown in Figure 19.4, environmental taxes in industrial countries can range from as little as 3 percent to 9 percent of total tax revenues.

Green taxes are strongly supported by economic theory as a means of internalizing negative externalities such as pollution. When a negative externality such as pollution exists, an unregulated market will result in an inefficient allocation (as discussed in Chapter 2). Because all taxes, in addition to raising revenue, discourage the "taxed" activity, it is economically desirable to discourage "bads" such as environmental

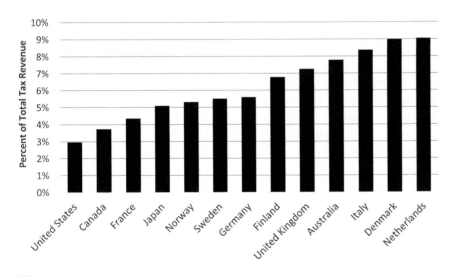

Figure 19.4 *Environmentally Based Taxes as a Share of Total Tax Revenue, Select Industrialized Countries, 2013*

Environmentally based taxes account for 9 percent of total tax revenue in Denmark and the Netherlands but only about 3 percent of total revenue in the United States.

Source: OECD, 2016.

pollution and natural resource depletion by placing taxes on them rather than on positive economic activities like investment and the earning of income.

Two common objections to green taxes frequently arise. First, it is likely that green taxes would fall disproportionately on lower-income households. Low-income households usually own older appliances and live in poorly insulated dwellings, increasing their heating bills. However, a rebate or credit to these households could be implemented to avoid making a green tax regressive. The other criticism is that green taxes are politically unpopular—no one wants higher taxes. Increases in green taxes can be offset, also, by reductions in other taxes (such as income taxes or social security contributions) so that the tax burden on a typical household remains unchanged. Households and businesses can also be given the option to lower the amount of green taxes they pay if their government assists with the cost of undertaking energy conservation measures and other environmentally friendly practices.

Eliminating Subsidies

Agricultural and energy subsidies that encourage the overuse of energy, fertilizer, pesticides, and irrigation water could be reduced or eliminated. This would reduce government expenditures, and the money saved could be used to lower taxes or to promote more sustainable agricultural systems that rely on the recycling of nutrients, crop diversification, the use of natural pest controls, and minimizing the use of artificial chemicals and fertilizer. Such systems also tend to be more labor intensive, so they also have the potential to boost employment. They can also increase the ability of the soil to take up and store CO_2, one of the major gasses causing climate change.

Recycling and Renewable Energy

Policies such as deposit/refund systems or targeted subsidies can be used to promote greater recycling of materials and the use of renewable energy. Through research and development grants, subsidies, and tax breaks, governments can support the expansion of energy from solar power, wind, and geothermal heat. Strategic public investment in new technologies such as fuel cells and high-efficiency industrial systems can eventually make these technologies cost competitive.

Tradable Permits

Tradable permit systems (often called "cap-and-trade") can set an overall limit on pollution by offering a limited number of permits allowing the emission of specific quantities and types of pollution. These plans are based on the principle that a process of pollution reduction may be most efficiently achieved by allowing businesses to choose between finding low-cost ways to reduce their emissions and paying to buy permits. After the permits are distributed to firms, they can then buy them from or sell them to other firms. Pollution reduction will occur first where it can be done most economically.

This efficiency characteristic makes tradable permit systems popular among economists. Although environmentalists have sometimes objected, on principle, to the idea of government issuing "permits to pollute," it is recognized that tradable permits have been used successfully in several instances, most notably in reducing sulfur dioxide emissions in the United States. Such permits can also be purchased by environmental groups or private citizens in order to retire them and thus reduce the overall level of pollution. Carbon trading systems apply the same principle to carbon reduction.

Among other regions, the EU introduced such a system in 2005. However, after operating for more than a decade, the EU Emissions Trading System (EU ETS) is subject to a number of criticisms. The main problem seems to be that the price for emission permits has fluctuated sharply, falling from a peak of more than €30 to little more than €5 per ton. According to critics, the volatility and the sharp drop in emission prices have discouraged companies from investing in emission-reducing technologies. Two underlying reasons are usually given for the problems of the system: First, too many permits have been issued, partly due to the fact that policy makers failed to predict the global financial and economic crisis that depressed economic activity and hence the demand for emission permits. Second, the very nature of a system of tradable permits can lead to high uncertainty about the future benefits of emission-reducing investments.

Nudging Toward Sustainable Transportation

Efficient transportation systems can replace energy-intensive automotive transport with high-speed trains, public transit, greater use of bicycles, and redesign of cities and suburbs to minimize transportation needs. In countries such as the United States, where automobile-centered systems are already extensively developed, the use of highly fuel-efficient cars, or electric cars charged with electricity from renewable sources, can reduce fuel needs; in some developing countries, automobile dependence might be avoided altogether.

In many cases, the construction of the infrastructure needed for such a shift in transport requires huge investments that cannot be expected to be done by the private sector, such as for bicycle lanes or railroad networks or possibly a country-wide network of high-power charging stations for e-cars. In these cases, the government needs to finance and conduct these investments. Subsidies for first adopters of certain technologies could get them moving more quickly.

Feed-In Tariffs

Feed-in tariffs are often used to promote the construction of renewable energy supplies. Under such a scheme, suppliers of power from renewable energies get the right to feed their electricity into the grid at a predetermined rate which is usually above the market rate for electricity. This markup over the market rate allows renewable electricity production (much of which still has higher production costs than traditional electricity production) to be competitive while creating an incentive for the installation of

627

renewable energy capacities. The difference between the feed-in tariff and the market rate for electricity is usually covered by a surcharge on all electricity consumption.

Feed-in tariffs have been used in a number of countries such as Spain, the United Kingdom, and Germany. They have been widely credited as being crucial for Germany's quick expansion of the share of renewables in energy production, but have also been criticized as leading to excessive and sometimes inefficient investments (such as solar panels on house roofs in Northern Germany, where there is little sun in the winter) and to a burden on low-income households due to higher electricity prices.

Debt-for-Nature Swaps

Debt-for-nature swaps work by forgiving the debt of developing countries in exchange for agreements to protect nature reserves or pursue environmentally friendly policies. For example, in 2002, the United States canceled $5.5 million in debt owed to it by Peru in return for Peru's agreement to conserve 10 rainforest areas covering more than 27.5 million acres. This innovative form of international fiscal policy was authorized by the Tropical Forest Conservation Act of 1998.

4.3 Sustainability and Consumption

As discussed earlier, global inequalities currently mean that many people in the world have too little to live on, while others consume at high levels. Some theorists have suggested replacing the goal of ever-increasing consumption with the goal of *sufficiency*. This idea can be developed at two levels. At the individual level is the question of the amount of consumption that is sufficient to support human well-being. At the macro or global level is the question of what kinds and amounts of consumption can be sustained, by humanity as a whole, without destructive environmental consequences. Note that the second question includes two different issues: the *kinds* of consumption and the aggregate *quantities* consumed.

Alan Durning, the author of *How Much Is Enough: The Consumer Society and the Future of the Earth*, has proposed dividing the global population into three groups classified according to their consumption levels and environmental impacts.[4] Table 19.1 presents a similar classification using updated data. We see that energy use, carbon emissions, and vehicle use are all much lower for those in the global lower-income class than in the rest of the world. Although these households are often forced to undertake ecologically unsustainable actions simply to survive, their overall impact on global environmental problems is relatively minor.

The global "middle class" uses more resources than the poor, but its lifestyle is still relatively environmentally sustainable. Those in this class rely primarily on bicycles and public transportation, eat a grain-based diet, and use a moderate amount of energy. Durning suggests that the entire world population could live at this level of affluence without exceeding the ecological capacity of the planet.

628

Table 19.1 *Global Population Classification by Income and Environmental Impacts, 2013*

	Global lower income	Global middle income	Global high income
Population (millions)	817	5,022	1,135
Average income per capita (U.S. dollars)	571	4,148	39,860
Energy use per capita (kg oil equivalent)	363	1,310	5,000
Electricity power consumption per capita (kWh)	242	1,823	9,415
Carbon dioxide emissions per capita (metric tons)	0.3	3.5	11.4
Passenger cars per 1,000 population	10	60	620

Each of the three groups defined here needs to approach environmental sustainability with different objectives.

- For the lower-income group, the focus must be on improving material living standards and expanding options while taking advantage of environmentally friendly technologies.
- The challenge for the middle-income group is to keep overall environmental impacts per capita relatively stable by pursuing a development path that avoids a reliance on fossil fuels, disposable products, and ever-increasing levels of material consumption.
- Finally, the high-income group must find a way to reduce environmental impacts per capita through technological improvements, intelligently designed policies, and changes in lifestyle aspirations.

Source: World Bank, *Little Green Data Book 2013; World Development Indicators 2013.*

The global upper-income class relies on private vehicles and air transportation, eats a diet including daily consumption of meat, and uses a significantly higher amount of energy than the other classes. The rest of the world can not possibly emulate the lifestyle of this class without exceeding the capacity of the global environment.

The problem may not be as intractable as it appears. In addition to the question of what is possible—that is, ecologically sustainable—we need to ask what is *desirable*. In rich countries, it has become increasingly important to recognize that "too much" can be just as much of a problem as "too little." Increasing consumption may bring little benefit and can actually be worse for individuals, who may suffer ill health from overeating, sedentary lifestyle, and reliance on automobiles and, according to some social scientists, spiritual malaise from exclusive or excessive attention to material things. At high income levels, other dimensions of human development, such as freedom from violence, closer and more peaceful families and communities, a satisfying work life and leisure-time (including volunteer) opportunities, cultural activities, and investments in the productive and creative capacities of the next generation may be more important than having more marketed goods and services. To the extent that we trade material consumption for these other objectives, sustainability becomes less of a challenge.

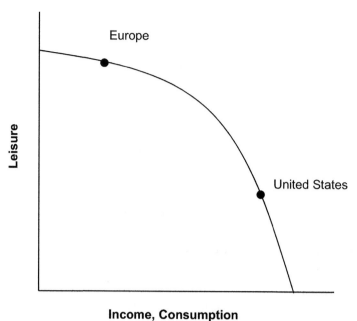

Figure 19.5 *A Consumption Possibilities Frontier*

The diagram illustrates the trade-off between consumption and leisure time. Europeans on average live at a lower material standard than people in the United States, because they do not work as many hours and hence earn less income. On the plus side, they enjoy more leisure time, which Americans sacrifice in order to be able to consume more.

Moreover, a large portion of every country's social and individual well-being depends on the maintenance of homes and families, including care of sick and elderly people, along with other productive activities that take place in homes and communities but are not bought and sold in formal markets (as discussed in Chapters 3 and 6). Many adults today feel squeezed between the demands of conventional 40 hours (or more) per week of paid employment and the time requirements of their families. Full-time employment in Europe requires the equivalent of five fewer weeks of work per year, on average, than full-time employment in the United States. Europeans have in effect chosen to translate part of their increased labor productivity into increased leisure instead of using it all to increase earnings and consumption. As shown in Figure 19.5, there is a trade-off between leisure time and money earned, each one being, in effect, the opportunity cost for the other. Where a country situates itself on the "consumption-possibilities frontier" depends on the culture and the prevailing attitudes toward work.

Economic practices that make people "rich" as consumers but "poor" as family and community members are not consistent with the human development goal of having the freedom to live a valuable life. They are also not ecologically sustainable in the long run, at least if every human on earth aspires to the highest levels of consumption.

Fortunately, it is growing increasingly apparent that scaling back in the area of material consumption not only is good for the natural environment but also—at least beyond a certain level of income—can enhance our overall well-being.

4.4 Sustainability and Investment

If an ecological perspective implies limits on consumption, what happens to investment? As we have seen earlier in this book, investment spending has often been crucially important for aggregate demand and employment. Yet additional investments in traditional kinds of plants and equipment, which rely heavily on fossil fuels, may work against environmental sustainability. This dilemma can be resolved only by forms of investment that improve well-being but do not increase what has been called **throughput**—the use of raw materials and energy as inputs, resulting in the creation of wastes as system outputs. The social and environmental challenges that have been outlined in this chapter suggest the need for large investment expenditures, many of which are not directly related to increasing material consumption. Rather than being a burden or threat, such investment expenditures may be the solution to maintaining employment with limited consumption.

throughput: the flow of raw materials and energy through the economy, leading to outputs of waste

As we saw in Chapter 18, many countries in the past used industrial policies successfully to push an economy from one phase to another. Britain sheltered its textile industry against Indian competition in the early stages of the Industrial Revolution. The United States could not have gone from a mostly agrarian economy to an industrial one without government assistance in developing transportation and communication systems. Japan's government carefully selected a sequence of industries to support, going from low tech and labor intensive to high tech and information intensive. All of the successful European, Asian, and North American economies have depended on essential support from national investments in education and public health. Many such investments are "public goods" (as discussed in Chapter 2) because, although they provide widespread benefits, it is hard to collect payment from the people who benefit from them; hence, if they are to occur, they must be supported through national action.

A similar set of strategic investments, focused on areas such as alternative energy, public transportation, sustainable agriculture, education, and health services could move countries toward a more environmentally sustainable economy. Such investments contribute to economically and environmentally positive development but may not pay the kind of return that would encourage private companies to undertake them. Yet with such strategic investments in place, the private sector can be relied on for much of the follow-through—much as, in the past, governments provided highways while the private sector supplied cars and trucks.

It is also important to remember that, as discussed in Chapter 6, "investments" should really refer to much more than just factories and equipment. Environmental policy is concerned with protecting, or avoiding *dis*investment in, the global commons—the oceans, the atmosphere, the world's store of living species, and other aspects of natural and social capital that greatly affect the possibilities and the quality of life for present and future human generations.

631

BOX 19.2 DISCOUNTING THE FUTURE

In economic theory, future costs and benefits are often evaluated with a technique called discounting. The theory behind discounting is that a dollar today is worth more than a dollar tomorrow—even after correcting for inflation. The discount rate, sometimes referred to as the "time discount rate," is the annual rate at which dollar values are considered to change over time (this is a different, broader use of the term than the Federal Reserve's discount rate offered to member banks, discussed in Chapter 11). Use of a discount rate often depends on the assumption that people of the future will be better off than people today—therefore, a dollar is worth more to us now than it will be to our great-grandchildren, even after accounting for possible inflation. For most commercial and financial calculations, the use of a discount rate makes sense. However, its application to social and environmental costs and benefits is more complicated.

To illustrate the impact of discount rate calculations, at an 8 percent discount rate, €1.00 today becomes worth €1.08 next year and $(€1.00)(1.08^{10}) = €2.16$ 10 years from now. Similarly, €1.00 to be received 10 years from now is worth only $(€1.00)/(1.08^{10}) = €0.46$ today.

For longer periods, the impact of discounting becomes much more dramatic. The present value of €1,000 50 years from now is only €87.20 at a 5 percent discount rate, and the value of €1,000 100 years from now is only €7.60. At a 10 percent discount rate, the value of €1,000 100 years from now is only 7 cents! This would mean that, applying a discount rate of 10 percent, it is not worth spending more than 7 cents today to avoid €1,000 worth of damages 100 years from now. This has led to a serious criticism of the discounting approach. How can we justify a technique that might implicitly consider serious damages to future generations less important than moderate costs today?

Discounting is essential if we are considering the economics of, for example, taking out a mortgage to buy a house or a loan to finance a business investment. The benefits of being able to own and live in the house starting today may well outweigh the future costs of paying interest on the mortgage over the next twenty years. Similarly, the income generated by the business investment can be compared to the annual payments on the loan—if the rate of return on the investment exceeds the discount rate, it brings net benefits.

In such cases, it makes sense to use the commercial discount rate, determined in current markets, to compare present and future costs and benefits. But can we say that a GDP gain today, or in the near future, outweighs major damage in the next generation? How should we evaluate broader environmental impacts that will continue over long periods?

social discount rate: a discount rate that reflects social rather than market valuation of future costs and benefits; usually lower than the market discount rate

We can try to resolve the problem by defining a **social discount rate**—a rate that attempts to reflect the appropriate social valuation of future costs and benefits. Estimates of social discount rates vary but are usually significantly lower than commercial discount rates and include a rate of zero. But, of course, private-market actors such as corporations will base their decisions on the current market rate of interest, not a social discount rate. Public investments, by contrast, can be based on a judgment that the appropriate social discount rate is lower—which means that the future should be weighted more heavily. This might justify, for example, more investments in energy efficiency and carbon-free energy sources today, to avoid damages from climate change that are likely to occur in future decades.

This kind of long-term investment requires a more future-oriented perspective than is used for most business investments. The use of market discount rates (see Box 19.2) tends to limit the planning horizons of most businesses and individuals to about 20 to 30 years. But long-term sustainability demands a generational perspective, because many of the most severe impacts of problems such as global climate change will take decades or even centuries to unfold.

Discussion Questions

1. How do you think your environmental impacts compare with those of the average person in the world?
2. Does reducing environmental impacts require sacrifice, or can it be done in ways that increase overall well-being?

5. ARE STABILIZATION AND SUSTAINABILITY IN CONFLICT?

Earlier chapters have emphasized that a high level of aggregate demand is necessary to support a high output level, keeping income levels up and unemployment down. Is this goal in conflict with the goal of environmental sustainability? In some ways, it appears that it is, given the evidence that we have reviewed on how environmental problems increase with higher consumption. But there may be ways to reconcile the goals of higher living standards, full employment, and environmental sustainability. To do so, we have to reexamine some of our assumptions about economic growth.

5.1 What Do We Really Want From Employment?

The macroeconomic models that we have developed starting in Chapter 9 have implicitly assumed that more employment is better. There is no doubt that needing a job and not being able to find one can be very tough on the unemployed. In addition to the lack of income—which can cause severe hardship and poverty for a worker and his or her family—unemployment can also have serious psychological repercussions. People often feel demoralized and depressed when they find that they are not wanted. Studies of the effects on health and mortality of business cycle swings show that suicide rates rise during economic downturns (see Chapter 15, Box 15.1). Clearly, a humane society should want to keep such suffering at a minimum to the extent possible.

Rather than just thinking about "employment" and "unemployment," perhaps macroeconomists should be thinking more about the *quality*, *types*, and *intensity* of employment that an economy offers and what these mean for people's well-being. Being pushed out of the wage-earning system is clearly injurious to the involuntarily unemployed, and being deprived of sufficient income is very tough on the working poor. But the solution need not mean that everyone should always work 40 or more hours a week.

As discussed in Chapter 8, people also benefit from hours that they spend away from paid employment; this time provides opportunities to do unpaid work, including family care, and also to pursue leisure activities. It may be possible to keep employment *levels* high while reducing material and energy throughput if we, as a society, think creatively enough about what sorts of as well as *how much* employment we really want.

The Dutch government, for example, responded to an economic downturn in the 1980s by stabilizing wages and allowing work hours to decline in order to reduce the unemployment rate. The idea, in other words, was to "share" available work hours among more people. New government employees were hired for four instead of five days per week. Other sectors soon followed, and eventually even Dutch banks adopted 80 percent schedules and a four-day workweek. In July 2000, the country passed the Working Hours Adjustment Act, landmark legislation that granted employees the right to reduce their weekly hours (even below 80 percent in many cases) without losing their job or suffering a reduction in hourly pay or employment benefits.[5]

In the same year, the French government reduced the standard workweek from 39 hours to 35 hours. Both the Dutch and French policies were motivated primarily by the desire to reduce the unemployment rate, but they also served to enhance workers' quality of life by affording them more leisure time. Because more leisure time and lower earnings on average leads to less consumption (and less throughput), both policy initiatives are examples of innovative macroeconomic policy that takes into account both stabilization and sustainability concerns.[6]

5.2 What Do We Really Want From Production?

The model that we developed in earlier chapters works only with the *level* of output, Y, and says nothing about the *composition* of output. From a sustainability perspective, however, the composition of output makes a very big difference. Some things that we benefit from and enjoy require relatively little use of material and energy inputs. Eating locally grown produce, taking a bike ride with friends, or engaging in educational and cultural activities, for example, puts little stress on the natural environment. Other activities, such as heating and furnishing a very large house, driving an SUV, or maintaining a perfect lawn using chemical fertilizer, have more negative impacts. Shifting away from producing goods and services that are most damaging to ecological systems and toward producing goods and services that are less destructive—or even environmentally beneficial—could allow an economy to maintain consumption, investment, and employment in a less environmentally damaging way.

Another important macroeconomic issue relates to population stabilization. As discussed further in the Appendix to this chapter, the countries of the European Union (like many other countries in the world) are already experiencing a growing ratio of retirees to active workers. Many elderly people need extra medical care and personal care. This suggests that while an economy may need to release some workers from high-throughput jobs for sustainability reasons, there will also be an increased demand for workers in medical and social services.

Similarly, while some opportunities for investment would no longer be available in a more sustainable economy, many more would open up. Investments in energy-saving infrastructure for transportation, in wetland restoration, and in conversion of residential and commercial buildings to more environmentally friendly patterns of energy

634

and chemical use, for example, would create additional employment opportunities. While employment might decline in fossil-fuel and high-polluting industries, these possibilities for expanded job creation suggest that pursuing sustainability goals need not conflict with the goal of full employment.

The problems of transitioning to a more sustainable macroeconomy should not be minimized. People who build SUVs today, for example, cannot simply start building solar panels tomorrow—changes in human and manufactured capital must take place first. But neither should these problems be exaggerated. Scientific evidence suggests that a conversion to a less resource-intensive economy is not a matter of *if* but, rather, a matter of *when* and *how*. And the longer the conversion is put off, the more difficult it is likely to be.

5.3 Sustainability at the Local Level

Sustainable development does not depend only on national policies; it can also be developed from the bottom up, starting at the local level. In fact, many changes in the organization of modern human life that are central for a shift toward more sustainability can only be brought about at the initiative (or at least with the cooperation) of the local level. For example, if the goal is to enable people to go to work, take their children to school, and do their shopping without the excessive use of cars, local planning is key. Residential and commercial areas need to be planned to be reached easily, and noncar transportation links such as bicycle lanes or trams need to be provided.

By now, there are a number of initiatives that try to support cities in becoming more sustainable. One of the best known has been the Aalborg Charter, drafted in 1994 and by now signed by more than 3,000 local authorities from more than 40 countries. The initiative was inspired by the Rio Earth Summit's Local Agenda 21 plan from 1992. The signatories committed to "integrate principles of sustainability" into all their policies and design strategies to make their towns and cities more sustainable and have followed up with further conferences and platforms to share individual experiences.

There are some cities that have actively tried to use the transformation toward more sustainability to market themselves nationwide and internationally. Perhaps the most widely cited example of such a "sustainable" city has been Freiburg in Southern Germany (population in 2015: 226,000). The city has not only pledged to reduce CO_2 emission by 50 percent by 2030 but has also set itself the long-term goal to become climate neutral by 2050. In order to reach this goal, the city has invested heavily in renewable energy. Traffic planning for years has given priority to pedestrians, bicycles, and public transport. A "Freiburg standard" of higher energy efficiency for new buildings has been introduced, and the city houses a number of pilot projects of so-called passive buildings, buildings that do not use any heat energy, including Germany's first passive high-rise building. For constructing new houses, Freiburg has strongly supported efforts of small-scale cooperative groups to provide affordable but still ecologically sustainable housing.

Such initiatives can serve as role models for other cities and towns and actually help to convey a feeling of ownership for sustainability measures. This is extremely crucial since the shift toward a more sustainable economy will produce losers (such as workers currently producing SUVs) as well as winners. Only if the population at the local level feels that the transformation process is something that benefits them and that they want can the process be continued over the long time span necessary to get significant results.

5.4 Macroeconomic Policies for Stabilization and Sustainability

In Chapter 10, we saw how government spending and taxing policies can contribute to stabilization, and in Chapters 11 and 12, we looked at issues of money and credit. A society committed to both stabilization and sustainability could find ways to use these standard macroeconomic tools to work toward both goals.

Some economic policies aimed at promoting sustainability might actually represent a return to well-known Keynesian-style policies but with a new ecological twist—a strong emphasis on government and private investment in green technologies and a tax structure that shifts the tax burden from income, labor, and capital to the use of fossil fuels and resources.

As discussed in Chapter 13, the stimulus plans passed by many of the EU countries as well as the United States in 2009 were classic Keynesian expansionary policy. Yet in some of the large countries, up to 20 percent of the stimulus specifically targeted environmental objectives (see Box 19.3). Such "green Keynesian" policies could be widely adopted and expanded to promote the transition to a more sustainable economic system.

Some ecologically oriented economists have suggested that, rather than growing indefinitely on an exponential path—say of 4 percent GDP growth per year—national and global economic systems must follow what is called a logistic pattern, in which growth is eventually limited, at least in terms of resource consumption. This would lead to what is called a **steady-state economy**, in which population and economic output are stabilized (see Figure 19.6).

steady-state economy: an economy with no increase in population or in the rate of use of raw materials and energy

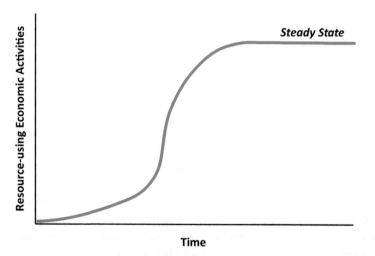

Figure 19.6 *Growth Reaching a Steady State*

After starting with an exponential growth pattern, an economy adapting to a steady state reduces its rate of growth in what is called a logistical pattern, approaching a maximum level at which economic activity stabilizes.

BOX 19.3 "GREEN" KEYNESIAN POLICIES IN THE GREAT RECESSION

During the global financial and economic crisis of 2008–2009, the economically most important countries (known as the G20) passed stimulus packages with a total volume of more than $2 trillion. Many of these packages included large elements of "green" investments or "green" tax incentives. Some examples:

- *Germany:* From a stimulus package of €80 billion, about 13 percent can be considered "green." Germany supported the upgrading of heating and insulation through subsidized loans to households. Also, schools and universities were refurbished for energy efficiency. The development of clean technologies in the automotive sector was supported. Moreover, a car scrappage scheme was introduced, subsidizing new cars with €2,500 when the buyer got rid of a car that was more than nine years old.
- *France:* Out of a stimulus package of €26 billion, 8 to 20 percent are considered "green elements." France subsidized new cars with high fuel efficiency with €1000 each, supported insulation of private houses and public buildings, and invested in mass transit and rail infrastructure. Some money went into subsidizing sustainable farming.
- *United Kingdom:* Out of a stimulus package of around £26 billion, about 5 percent was considered "green." The government subsidized insulation and heating improvements for private houses and public buildings, invested in rail infrastructure, and subsidized (to a small extent) offshore wind power.
- *United States:* Out of a stimulus package of $977 billion, about 12 percent can be considered "green." Among other things, the government spent funds on energy efficiency in federal buildings and Department of Defense facilities, smart-grid infrastructure investment, energy efficiency, and renewable energy research and loan guarantees for wind and solar projects. It also gave tax breaks for plug-in electric vehicles and for nonpetrol refueling infrastructure.

The double benefit of such policies is that they promote employment and also advance a transition to a more environmentally sustainable economy. It is easily possible to envision much larger programs of this nature. For example, the British stimulus program included £150 million in the Warm Front Programme, which subsidized insulation and heating improvements in private housing. A major nationwide program for energy efficiency retrofit in houses and commercial buildings could easily be 10 times as large. In the U.S., the stimulus program temporarily quadrupled U.S. spending on energy and environmental research and development; a permanent increase of this magnitude would have enormous long-term benefits in promoting a transition to efficiency and renewables.

Sources: Cambridge Economics, "Assessing the Implementation and Impact of Green Elements of Member States' National Recovery Plans," Final Report for the European Commission, 2011, Cambridge; Jonathan M. Harris, "Green Keynesianism: Beyond Standard Growth Paradigms," in Robert B. Richardson ed., *Building a Green Economy: Perspectives from Ecological Economics* (East Lansing, MI: Michigan State University Press, 2013).

These environmental limits on growth would apply to resource and energy consumption; at the same time, activities that do not involve resource consumption, which are environmentally neutral or environmentally friendly, could continue to grow. Such activities could include services, arts, communication, and education. After basic needs are met and reasonable levels of consumption achieved, the concept of sustainable development implies that economic development should be increasingly oriented toward this kind of inherently "sustainable" activities.

One model of a transition to a steady-state economy has been presented by the Canadian economist Peter Victor. An economic model called LOWGROW, when applied to the Canadian economy, models "socio-eco-environmental" paths that offer attractive social and environmental outcomes without requiring economic growth.[7] In the scenario presented in Figure 19.7, the Canadian government is assumed to introduce a tax on greenhouse gas (GHG) emissions, creating incentives to switch from high-GHG sources of energy to lower ones, making energy in general more expensive and encouraging conservation and efficiency. The revenues from the GHG tax are used to reduce other taxes so that the net effect on revenues is zero.

In this scenario, GDP per capita stabilizes after 2025, and GHG emissions decrease by 22 percent by 2035. Poverty levels as well as unemployment decrease significantly, and fiscal balance is reached, with a steady decrease in the debt-to-GDP ratio. A shorter workweek allows for full employment, with less growth in material consumption but more spending on health care and education. Such models suggest that slower growth

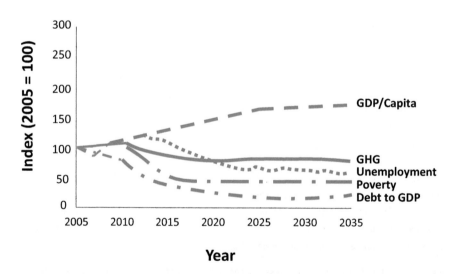

Figure 19.7 *A No-Growth Scenario for the Canadian Economy*

Even though projected GDP per capita stops growing in this macroeconomic model, well-being continues to increase, with declining unemployment, poverty, and debt, and improved environmental conditions.

Source: Adapted from Peter Victor, *Managing Without Growth: Slower by Design, not Disaster.* Northampton, MA: Edward Elgar, 2008, p. 182.

638

leading to no growth can be consistent with full employment, virtual elimination of poverty, more leisure, considerable reduction in GHG emissions, and fiscal balance.

However, Victor's proposal also comes with a number of potentially highly unpopular measures. In order to reduce private spending on status goods such as large cars, he proposes large tax increases (by almost half in the case of personal taxes), the revenue of which will be used by the government to provide more public services. Moreover, critics have pointed out that the model does not take into account how far such a no-growth economic path would be compatible with modern financial and capital markets and an open economy, raising the question of its compatibility with a modern capitalist society.

Discussion Questions

1. Cutting the length of the standard full-time workweek could be one way to keep people employed while cutting down on the "throughput" of materials and energy. Can you think of other policies that might also have this effect?
2. Do you think that an economic system can prosper without growth? Can we distinguish among growth in GDP, growth in employment, and growth in well-being? To what extent do these necessarily go together, and to what extent can improvements in employment and well-being be separated from GDP growth?

6. CONCLUDING THOUGHTS

Throughout the twentieth century, the main objective of macroeconomics was steady, strong economic growth. Considering the challenges that we face in the twenty-first century, macroeconomics itself will need to adapt to new realities. Employment, price stability, and GDP growth will continue to be issues of great importance—not as ends in themselves, however, but as the means to the broader goals of human development and sustainability. Keeping the ultimate well-being goals in mind, macroeconomics must look beyond the experience of the past and ask new questions.

A fundamental question confronting macroeconomics in the twenty-first century is how the majority of people in the world, currently at relatively low standards of living, can improve their well-being. The issues of "human development" discussed in Chapter 18 involve a combination of traditional economic growth and new approaches more oriented toward dealing with problems of poverty, inequality, and ecological sustainability.

Economic analysis must take into account the need for technologies that can provide energy and materials for human consumption in ways that are ecologically sound and that help to remedy past damages (Box 19.4). The transition to a more sustainable economy will have economic costs but also significant benefits, such as increased employment and improved quality of life. Another set of essential questions relates to how macroeconomics can be reformed to take into account the distant future. A first step in this direction must be recognition that in important areas, it is inappropriate to discount the future (see Box 19.2). When our great-great-grandchildren are alive, their lives and well-being will be as important to them as ours are to us. (This perspective, though often neglected in economics, is not new and was emphasized by John Maynard Keynes in the 1930s—see Box 19.5.)

BOX 19.4 TECHNOLOGIES FOR A SUSTAINABLE ECONOMY

Technological progress can reduce the need for resource inputs and mitigate or eliminate environmental impacts. For a new technology to be adopted in the marketplace, it must be cost effective. Recent developments have encouraged hope that some environmentally sound technologies are or may soon become competitive with more energy and resource-intensive and fossil fuel–based technologies.

- Renewable power sources have steadily declined in cost. Land-based wind power is now fully competitive with coal and nuclear power (Ailworth, 2013). While solar and offshore wind power remain more expensive than conventional power, their costs have declined also. Technologies such as solar roof tiles make it possible for buildings to generate much or all of their own power, thus adding to the asset value of the building.

- In many EU countries, modern houses are built with very high energy standards, using triple-glazed windows and elaborate heat pumps. They now often use less than 15 KWh of energy per square meter per year, a huge improvement from buildings from the 1980s, which needed 300 KWh in energy per square meter/year. As in Northern Europe, heating energy is a significant part of total energy consumption (in Germany, 80 percent of household energy use is for heating and hot water), so this technological improvement helps to sharply reduce energy use.

- Engineers at Lockheed Martin are creating a better way to desalinate water to meet the growing global demand for potable water by using filters embedded with sheets of graphene, which are 500 times thinner than others, taking much less energy to push water through them to remove salt.

- Rentricity is a New York–based company that uses water pressure in municipal pipes to create electricity. Using this otherwise untapped resource for energy also reduces costs for water utility companies.

- The spread of modern car-sharing offers (often app based) has in a number of cities led to fewer people owning their own cars. With the development of driverless cars, some people imagine a future in which most households do not own a car at all anymore, with huge savings in material and energy used in car production.

Sources: Erin Ailworth, "Massachusetts Utilities Go for Wind Power," *Boston Globe*, September 23, 2013; John A. Laitner, "Linking Energy Efficiency to Economic Productivity," American Council for an Energy-Efficient Economy www.aceee.org/research-report/e13f; Rachel Feltman, "Lockheed's Better, Faster Way to Desalinate Water," *Popular Mechanics* March 14, 2013; Rentricity and Disappearing Package, and other examples from www.dmass.net.

The macroeconomics of the twenty-first century must be truly global. The social problems of poverty reduction, as well as major environmental problems such as global climate change, can be partly addressed at the national level, but the roles of international trade and global institutions are critical. Our earlier analyses of national income, fiscal and monetary policy, unemployment and inflation, and other macroeconomic issues remain relevant, but must be placed in the context of global developmental and environmental challenges.

BOX 19.5 ECONOMIC POSSIBILITIES FOR OUR GRANDCHILDREN

What can we reasonably expect the level of our economic life to be a hundred years hence? What are the economic possibilities for our grandchildren? John Maynard Keynes thought that:

> a point may soon be reached, much sooner perhaps than we are all of us aware of, when these needs are satisfied in the sense that we prefer to devote our further energies to non-economic purposes. . . . I draw the conclusion that, assuming no important wars and no important increase in population, the economic problem may be solved, or be at least within sight of solution, within a hundred years. This means that the economic problem is not—if we look into the future—the permanent problem of the human race.
>
> Thus for the first time since his creation man will be faced with his real, his permanent problem—how to use his freedom from pressing economic cares, how to occupy the leisure, which science and compound interest will have won for him, to live wisely and agreeably and well.
>
> When the accumulation of wealth is no longer of high social importance, there will be great changes in the code of morals. . . . The love of money as a possession—as distinguished from the love of money as a means to the enjoyments and realities of life—will be recognized for what it is, a somewhat disgusting morbidity, one of those semi-criminal, semi-pathological propensities which one hands over with a shudder to the specialists in mental disease. All kinds of social customs and economic practices, affecting the distribution of wealth and of economic rewards and penalties, which we now maintain at all costs, however distasteful and unjust they may be in themselves, because they are tremendously useful in promoting the accumulation of capital, we shall then be free, at last, to discard.
>
> Of course there will still be many people with intense, unsatisfied purposiveness who will blindly pursue wealth—unless they can find some plausible substitute. But the rest of us will no longer be under any obligation to applaud and encourage them.

Source: John Maynard Keynes, "Economic Possibilities for Our Grandchildren," *Essays in Persuasion*. New York: Classic House Books, 2009 [original publication 1930].

641

DISCUSSION QUESTIONS

1. Are you optimistic or pessimistic about the future when it comes to reducing global inequalities? Do you believe that the world will be less or more unequal in 50 years? What about environmental problems—do you think they will grow better or worse in your lifetime?

2. Do you agree with Keynes's belief that industrialized countries will soon reach a point at which needs will be "satisfied in the sense that we prefer to devote our further energies to non-economic purposes"? Do you think that we are any closer to this point than in 1930, when Keynes wrote his essay? Do you see any evidence that this is starting to occur?

REVIEW QUESTIONS

1. What are some of the environmental issues related to economic growth?
2. What are some of the projected effects of future climate change?
3. What is the environmental Kuznets curve (EKC) hypothesis? What is the evidence regarding this hypothesis?
4. What are "green" taxes?
5. What are tradable permit systems?
6. What is a debt-for-nature swap?
7. What is the idea of sufficiency?
8. How do environmental impacts differ across the three global income classes?
9. What are some examples of local sustainability?
10. What are "green Keynesian" policies? Give some examples.
11. What is a steady-state economy?

EXERCISES

1. Issues of environmental sustainability can sometimes be a bit abstract. This exercise is designed then to an individual level. Start at www.footprintnetwork.org/ and familiarize yourself with the notion of "ecological footprints," then take the quiz at www.ecologyfund.com/ecology/res_best-foot.html to discover what your personal footprint looks like. What did you learn that was new information to you? What specifically can you do about this new information?

2. Begin at the Web site of the Global Footprint Network (www.footprintnetwork.org) and locate the "Footprint for Nations" under Footprint Basics. Access (or download) the latest Data Tables (in Excel format) and familiarize yourself with this data to complete the following:
   a. What was the per-capita ecological footprint of consumption for your country?
   b. What was the per-capita biocapacity in your country?
   c. Explain the meaning of the two numbers you just located. What are the implications?

d. Search through the database to locate the nations that had a larger footprint than your country in the last year available. Identify these nations and their footprints.

e. Study the income and continent category summaries in the database. What conclusions can you draw from these summaries? Explain your answer.

3. Match each concept in Column A with a definition or example in Column B:

Column A	Column B
a. "Green" taxes	1. Opportunity for developing countries to protect nature reserves or pursue environmentally friendly policies
b. Tradable permit systems	2. An inverted U-shaped relationship between economic development and environmental damages
c. Debt-for-nature swaps	3. A situation in which population and the use of raw materials and energy have stabilized
d. Throughput	4. Based on the principle that a process of pollution reduction may be most efficiently achieved if businesses have choices
e. Social discount rate	5. Designed to discourage pollution and natural resource depletion by making them more expensive
f. Environmental Kuznets curve	6. Reflects social rather than market valuation of future costs and benefits
g. Steady-state economy	7. The flow of raw materials and energy into the economic system and the flow of wastes from the system

APPENDIX: DEMOGRAPHIC CHALLENGES

One of the important issues in the area of human development and environmental sustainability is the question of *how many* people we need to be concerned about. In 1700, the human population was about 600 million. In 1927, it was 2 billion. Currently, more than 7 billion people live on this planet. Will national and global populations continue to grow, level off, or even shrink? What are the macroeconomic challenges presented by likely demographic changes in the coming century?

The relationship between demographic and economic issues is multifaceted. On the one hand, growth in the size of economies is often associated with population growth, because a growing population means more workers and hence greater ability to produce. On the other hand, human well-being can be endangered when population growth outpaces available resources, including environmental resources. If the production of needed goods and services cannot keep pace with population, lower standards of living can result. In addition to the question of population size, issues about the composition of a population, when considered according to characteristics such as age, can also be important in explaining economic change. After introducing some basic concepts in demography (the study of populations), this appendix examines the macroeconomic challenges posed by continued growth in global populations and the dramatic aging of populations in many countries.

A1. BASIC DEMOGRAPHIC TERMS AND HISTORY

birth rate: the annual number of births per 1,000 population

fertility rate: the average number of births per woman of reproductive age

death rate: the annual number of deaths per 1,000 population

mortality rate: the average number of deaths among a specific group

replacement fertility rate: the fertility rate required for each generation to be replaced by a subsequent generation of the same size

population momentum: the trend in population size that results from its age profile, in particular the number of women who are of childbearing age or younger

demographic transition: the change over time from a combination of high birth and death rates to a combination of low birth and death rates

net migration rate: the net gain in population from migration, per 1,000 population

Although the terms "birth rate" and "fertility rate" may seem as if they should mean the same thing, in the field of demography they have different meanings. The **birth rate** is the annual number of births per 1,000 *people* in a population. The **fertility rate** refers to the average number of births *per woman of reproductive age* in a population. The birth rate in any country will depend on two things: first, the proportion of people in the country who are women of reproductive age, and, second, the rate of fertility among these women. Similarly, the **death rate** is the annual number of deaths per 1,000 people, while a **mortality rate** refers to deaths within a specific group.

If the fertility rate is equal to what is called the **replacement fertility rate**, then the next generation will be the same size as the current one—women will, on average, produce just enough children to replace themselves and one other adult. Currently, the replacement fertility rate for industrialized countries is about 2.1 children per woman. (It is slightly higher than 2 because slightly more males than females are born, and some female children will die before reaching reproductive age.) In countries with higher mortality rates or larger ratios of men to women, the replacement fertility rate is somewhat higher.

It might seem that a country with fertility rates that are exactly equal to the replacement rate should have a stable population. However, this is not necessarily so, due to a phenomenon called **population momentum**. Recall that the birth rate depends not only on the fertility rate but also on the size of the childbearing population. Suppose that a country has relatively few older people and large numbers of people of childbearing age. Its population will continue to grow even with a replacement fertility rate because the birth rate will be high (reflecting the size of the childbearing group), while the death rate will be low (because only a small proportion of the population will be reaching the end of life). Only when birth rates and death rates are equal does a population stabilize.

In the past 200 to 300 years, the industrialized countries have experienced a **demographic transition** from a combination of high birth rates and death rates to a combination of low birth rates and death rates. But this transition has not been smooth. Table 19.2 outlines the four—or perhaps five—stages of demographic transition.

In the first stage of the demographic transition, which characterized much of human history, women spend a great deal of time and effort in bearing and raising children, at much risk to their own health, only to see many of their children die young. Thus moving away from the first stage is an important goal of human development. Populations in the third and fourth stages have moved past the highest birth and death rates, making a higher quality of life possible.

Although birth and death rates are crucially important for explaining population trends in any country, for some countries, the net migration rate is also important. The **net migration rate** is the number of people gained by migration over a year

Table 19.2 *Stages of Demographic Transition*

First Stage	Both birth and death rates are high. On average, the number of children that survive in each family is just enough to keep the population stable or growing very slowly.
Second Stage	Death rates are reduced, while birth rates stay high, so parents are typically survived by significantly more than the two children required to replace them. From the eighteenth to the twentieth centuries, this second stage occurred in industrializing countries due to the nutritional advances that followed increased agricultural productivity and (especially after about 1850) better medical care and sanitation.
Third Stage	Birth rates start declining but are still higher than death rates. The increased availability of contraception and improvements in female education contribute to this stage. In the third stage, fertility rates are initially above replacement level but will eventually drop to or possibly below replacement level. Population growth slows down, though it continues to grow because of the number of women of childbearing age.
Fourth Stage	Birth rates and death rates equalize at a low rate. Population growth is zero—but the population is considerably larger than it was when the process began.
Fifth Stage	Birth rates are lower than death rates. When the demographic transition was first conceptualized, the process was expected to stop at the fourth stage. In fact, however, some countries may move fairly rapidly from above- to below-replacement birth rates, passing through the fourth stage of equal birth and death rates. Population actually declines.

(calculated as the number of people who move into an area minus the number of people who moved out of the area), usually expressed per 1,000 people.

A2. GLOBAL POPULATION PATTERNS AND POLICIES

The industrialized countries are generally in the third or fourth stage of the demographic transition. The fertility rate in all important industrialized countries has by now dropped below 2, and in some countries it has fallen far below this number. Italy was one of the first countries to be recognized as having a below-replacement birth rate, entering the third stage in about 1960. Its population, nevertheless, continued to increase, from 50 million to about 57 million now (due to population momentum). Given current trends, Italy's fifth stage is about to begin; unless fertility rates rebound, the population is predicted to sink to 54 million in 2025 and 38 million in 2050—a 33 percent decline from the peak. Germany and Japan are other countries where population decline has just begun. Government policies in such countries now often seek to increase births (see Box 19.6).

Throughout most of the world, populations are still growing. Many governments and international agencies working in poorer countries have tried to bring down fertility rates in order to ease the stress that a rapidly growing population puts on resources and productive capacities. These programs have often been successful, at least to a degree, and some population policies simultaneously serve other human development ends.

645

BOX 19.6 SHRINKING ITALY

Although many environmentalists fret about overpopulation, Italians are fretting over the opposite. Despite the stereotype of its massive Catholic clans, Italy actually has one of the lowest birth rates in the world, a population set to shrink by a third by 2050, and the world's highest percentage of population aged 65 or older (21 percent in 2013). The country wants babies. Badly. [In 2004] the Italian government offered a €1,000 one-time payment to couples who had a second child. The rural village of Laviano, fearful of disappearing altogether, is offering €10,000 for every baby produced. Studies show, however, that while cash payments may accelerate breeding schedules, they don't persuade tot-averse citizens to procreate. Some activists say what's really needed is more public-policy support for working mothers. If serious steps aren't taken, says Franca Biglio, mayor of Marsaglia (population 400), "Our bella Italia will become a deserted wilderness."

Source: Tracy Wilkinson, "Mayor of Shrinking Italian Town Pays Women to Give Birth," *Los Angeles Times*, February 13, 2005; Population Resource Bureau, *World Population Data Sheet 2013*. www.prb.org.

Increasing women's access to health services and education has often played a crucial role, not only delivering knowledge about family planning but also giving women the power to play a greater role in household decisions. Other policies, such as China's long-time policy of penalizing families with more than one child, are more coercive. Forced sterilizations, forced abortions, and infanticide (especially of girls in cultures that prize boys) are the darker side of a compulsory approach to population control.

Population trends in China and India are followed closely, because together they are home to nearly 40 percent of the world's population. Even though China has put downward pressure on population with its one-child policy and had a fertility rate estimated at 1.56 in 2010, its population is still growing due to population momentum. The UN projections suggest that its population will continue to grow until 2030, peaking at 1.45 billion. India currently has a smaller population than China, and its fertility rate has fallen by half since the 1960s. But with a current fertility rate of 2.43, India is expected to displace China as the world's most populous country within the next 50 years. Populations are also still growing in most middle-income countries, though their fertility rates vary, some above and others below replacement.

Sub-Saharan Africa has had some of the world's highest fertility rates in modern times—as many as seven children per woman in some countries. Tragically, however, the HIV/AIDS pandemic has drastically increased mortality rates in many of these countries. The population story in the Russian Federation is also rather grim. Suffering from the special conditions of a poorly managed transition from socialism to a market economy, it has experienced both high death rates and low birth rates. Its population, which reached a high of 148 million in 1990, had fallen to 143 million by 2013 (although birth rates have recently started to rise).

On the global scale, projections about population made by the United Nations Population Division forecast world population rising from its current level of 7 billion to almost 10 billion by 2050. Most of the additional people will live in the less industrialized parts of the world. The projections assume that life expectancy will increase except where a population is affected by HIV/AIDS.

The UN projections, however, do not take into account the consequences of environmental degradation. Whether the resources of the world will be able to continue to support such a growing population remains to be seen. If population ceases to grow in this century, will it be because of individual choices and human development–oriented policies, such as increasing people's power to control their family size? Or because of coercive policies or high death rates due to flood, famine, conflict, and disease? Macroeconomic policies concerning resource use, development, and international economic relations hold part of the key to these important questions.

A3. THE ISSUE OF AGING POPULATIONS

To those who have been concerned about the ecological, economic, and social impacts of rapid population growth or excessively high population density, stabilizing populations are good news. But there are also significant threats and challenges inherent in the fourth and fifth stages of the demographic transition. The most obvious problems arise from the fact that rapidly falling birth rates lead to changes in the age structure of a population.

A convenient way to visualize the age structure of a population is to chart the numbers of men and women in different age categories, as shown in Figure 19.8 for the case of the European Union. Such figures are sometimes called "population pyramids," because in populations with sizable, steady birth rates and regular, steady death rates among the elderly, they take on the triangular shape shown in the first part of Figure 19.8, representing the European population in 1960 (there are some "dents" in the pyramid as a consequence of the two world wars Europe experienced).

Although fertility rates fell in the European Union after World War II, this fall was not steady. Fertility in many countries first increased after the war and then collapsed after the late 1960s (a development that is often dubbed "pill kink," as it appeared after the introduction of the birth control pill). As a result, the "pyramid" by 2000 did not look so triangular anymore. At the turn of the twenty-first century, a high proportion of people were in their prime working years, with relatively small numbers of the elderly and children, as shown in the second part of Figure 19.8.

As the bulge created by middle-aged people born in the 1960s moves farther up the pyramid over the coming decades, the proportion of the population in retirement years will rise. (The first baby boomers turned 65 in 2011.) Projections suggest that the age structure of the EU population will look like the third part of Figure 19.8 in 2040—much more like a tower with a bulging head than a triangle.

Other countries that have experienced a "baby bust" will face a similarly top-heavy age structure. This means that there will be fewer people of working age to support people who have retired. The **old-age dependency ratio** is often defined as the

old-age dependency ratio: the number of retirees relative to the number of active workers

647

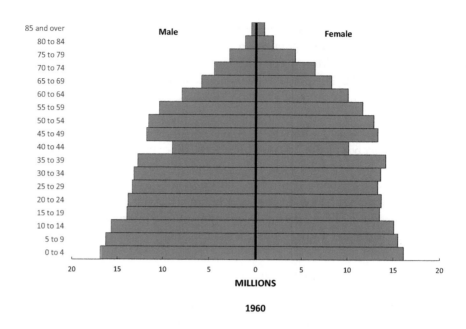

1960

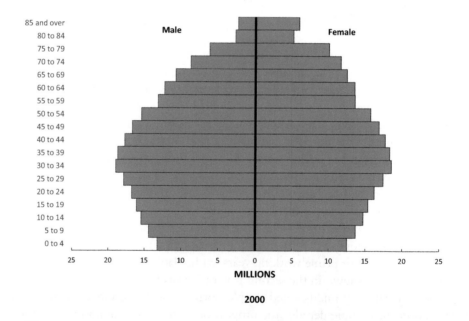

2000

▨ **Figure 19.8** *Population by Age and Sex, European Union, 1960, 2000, and 2040 (Projected)*

In 1900, the "population pyramid" shows a small elderly population, a larger middle-aged population, and an even larger population of children. By 2000, falling birth rates made the middle tiers of the "pyramid" bulge outward. The proportion of older people in the population is forecast to be much higher in future decades.

Source: Eurostat.

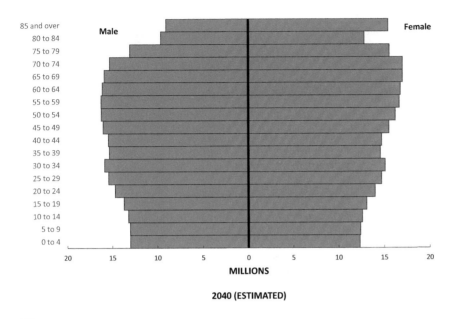

Figure 19.8 (Continued)

number of people age 65 and over for each hundred people age 15 to 64. Figure 19.9 shows the projected rises in the old-age dependency ratio for the currently economically most important regions and countries in the world: Europe, China, and the United States: As the U.S. still has the highest birth rate among these, it is least hit by the aging, but even there, the number of old people relative to the young will increase from around 20/100 in 2010 to almost 40/100 by 2050.

Such a changing age structure has a number of implications for national macroeconomics:

■ First, each future worker will have considerably more retired people dependent on his or her services. The needs of the elderly for health and social services may lead to a further sectoral shift toward service-sector employment. In some countries, the need for workers may be filled, in part, by increased immigration.

■ Second, there are implications for savings rates. With more people drawing down their retirement savings and fewer people in the process of building up their savings in preparation for retirement, one can expect national savings to be depressed. This may boost consumption and aggregate demand but may also cause a lack of loanable funds needed for investment purposes.

■ Third, there are implications for government budgets. An aging population means fewer people paying taxes at the same time that more people become reliant on public retirement programs and publicly provided social services and medical care. Such strains on public finances may lead to higher taxes or lower benefits or cuts in other areas.

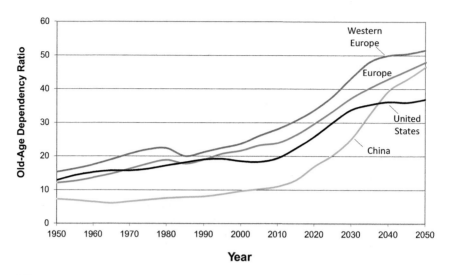

Figure 19.9 *Old-Age Dependency Ratios, 1950–2050*

Countries with sharp declines in birth rates can expect to have a rising ratio of older people to working-age people over the next several decades.

Source: United Nations, *World Population Prospects: The 2015 Revision*, Population Database. Figure based on medium-variant projections.

In countries such as most of the European Union members, where there has been a long history of retirement support, the effect may be felt primarily through strains in public budgets—as current controversies over the pension reforms in many countries already demonstrate. The aging of the population may be felt even more acutely in China, where pensions, medical care, and other support for the elderly are looming as possibly the leading social crises.

A4. DEMOGRAPHIC CHALLENGES AHEAD

The population pyramids shown in Figure 19.8 can be used, with a little assistance from your imagination, to illustrate another, very important point. The first part of Figure 19.8 showed the European Union in 1960; it can also serve as a generalized picture of any country that has a growing population impelled by fertility rates above replacement. More than half the world's population—about 3.5 billion people—fit this picture. At the same time, the third part of Figure 19.8 is a reasonably good picture of the squared-off "pyramids" that will, in the foreseeable future, characterize nearly all the rich countries of the world: Western Europe, Japan, and a few other highly industrialized countries.

As the developing countries gradually stabilize, their population "pyramids" will fill out just as those for the United States did over the past century, representing the additional 2 billion people in the UN's population projections for 2050. These population images and the underlying realities, including growing inequalities of living standards, will be of great global significance for at least the next 50 years.

Although there is no certainty that inequalities between rich and poor will diminish in the foreseeable future, by midcentury, there will be some important factors to add to the situation just described. China's population (as noted earlier) will have begun to decline by 2050. It also seems likely that India's declining fertility rate will not stop when it reaches 2.1 but will continue to fall, so that sometime in the second half of the twenty-first century, India will join China in a new category of countries that, even if not yet rich, have nevertheless reversed the long growth trend of the second stage of the demographic transition.

With China and India, and a number of other countries as well, eventually joining the list of countries with below-replacement fertility, it seems likely that within this century, we will see a stabilization of the global human population. It is also possible that, beyond stabilization, the shrinking of populations will continue in the richer countries and spread to others as well. In terms of resource demands, pollution generation, and pressure on the earth's ecological capacity, stabilization of population is desirable. However, significant changes will be required in how people conceptualize and pursue their goals if a shift toward smaller populations is to be felt as positive rather than severely negative.

Macroeconomic theory has a significant role to play in helping to understand and plan for these changes, including the need to revise expectations, behaviors, policies, and theories to assist populations in adapting to a changing age profile. This has potentially large implications for medical care and other services, GDP, policy, and culture. One important challenge is discovering how the elderly can be more of a resource than a drain; this is desirable from an economic point of view as well as in terms of the psychological well-being (sense of meaning and purpose in life) of the elderly.

An overriding concern in the first half of the twenty-first century must be the need to provide food, energy, education, and productive work for a likely sizable increase in the number of people on earth—with virtually all of that increase occurring in areas where economic as well as social, cultural, and political systems are already hard pressed to adapt to past and present population growth.

The record of the past 300 years is one of astonishing achievement, in which the total human population has multiplied more than tenfold, with more than half of those now alive enjoying a level of material consumption that would have been considered great riches in any previous era. But the number now living in extreme poverty is greater than the entire human population at the beginning of the demographic transition. And the natural capital on which humanity can draw is now significantly degraded. The moral of the demographic story is sobering: It is the need to find ways to provide better lives for more people, with limited natural resources.

NOTES

1 The World Bank and Institute for Health Metrics and Evaluation, *The Cost of Air Pollution: Strengthening the Economic Case for Action* (Washington, DC: World Bank, 2016).
2 Food and Agriculture Organization of the United Nations (FAO), *Review of the State of World Marine Fishery Resources* (Rome, Italy: FAO, 2012).

3   Intergovernmental Panel on Climate Change, *Climate Change 2007: The Physical Science Basis* (Cambridge, UK, and New York: Cambridge University Press, 2007); Intergovernmental Panel on Climate Change, Climate Change, *Synthesis Report. Contribution of Working Groups I, II and III to the Fifth Assessment Report of the Intergovernmental Panel on Climate Change* (Geneva: IPCC, 2014).

4   Alan Durning, *How Much Is Enough: The Consumer Society and the Future of the Earth* (New York: Norton, 1992).

5   Juliet Schor, "Tackling U.S. Unemployment: The 80% Solution," 2011, retrieved from http://blogs.worldwatch.org/sustainableprosperity/the-80-percent-solution/.

6   It should be noted, however, that the 35-hour workweek in France has also been criticized. As minimum monthly incomes were regulated not to decrease with the shortening of the workweek, labor costs for low-income earners increased. Moreover, companies complained about growing inflexibility. As a consequence, employers in France have been criticizing the 35-hours week up until today.

7   Peter Victor, *Managing without Growth: Slower by Design, not Disaster* (Northampton, MA: Edward Elgar, 2008).

Glossary

abundance: resources are abundant to the extent that they exist in plentiful supply for meeting various goals (2)

accelerator principle: the idea that high GDP growth leads to increasing investment, and low or negative GDP growth leads to declining investment (12)

accommodating monetary policy: loose or expansionary monetary policy intended to counteract recessionary tendencies in the economy (12)

activity rate or labor force participation rate: the percentage of potential workers either with a job or actively seeking a job or the labor force as a percentage of the civilian noninstitutional population (8)

administrative capitalism: a national system characterized by private corporate ownership and a substantial reliance on public administration (as well as exchange) as a mode of coordination (18)

administrative socialism: a national system in which state ownership predominates and activity is coordinated primarily by public administration (command) (18)

aggregate demand: the total demand for all goods and services in a national economy (1, 8)

aggregate expenditure (*AE*): the total demand for all goods and services in a national economy; (in a simple model without government or foreign trade): what households and firms *intend* to spend on consumption and investment: $AE = C + I_I$ (1, 9)

assets: property owned by an individual or company (1)

automatic stabilizers: tax and spending institutions that tend to increase government revenues and lower government spending during economic expansions but lower revenues and raise government spending during economic recessions (10)

balance–of–payments (BOP) account: the national account that tracks inflows and outflows arising from international trade, earnings, transfers, and transactions in assets (14)

balance–of–payments crisis: when a country gets precariously close to running out of foreign exchange and is therefore unable to purchase imports or service its existing debt (14)

balanced budget multiplier: the impact on equilibrium output of simultaneous increases of equal size in government spending and taxes (10)

bank reserves: funds not lent out or invested by a private bank but kept as vault cash or on deposit at the European Central Bank (11)

barter: exchange of goods, services, or assets directly for other goods, services, or assets, without the use of money (11)

base year (in the constant-price method of estimating GDP): the year whose prices are chosen for evaluating production in all years. Normally real and nominal GDP are equal only in the base year (5)

basic neoclassical (traditional microeconomic) model: a model that portrays the economy as a collection of profit-maximizing firms and utility-maximizing households interacting in perfectly competitive markets (2)

behavioral equation: in contrast to an accounting identity, a behavioral equation reflects a theory about the behavior of one or more economic agents or sectors. The variables in the equation may or may not be observable. (9)

bilateral development assistance: aid (or loans) given by one country to another to promote development (18)

birth rate: the annual number of births per 1,000 population (19, Appendix)

bond: a financial instrument that pays a fixed amount every year (the coupon amount), as well as repaying the amount of principal (the face value) on a particular date (the maturity date) (12)

bond spread: the difference in yield between a country's bond and a bond of highest quality (usually a German bond) (17)

Bretton Woods system: a system of fixed exchange rates established after World War II, lasting until 1972 (14)

budget deficit: an excess of total government outlays over total government revenues (10)

budget surplus: an excess of total government revenues over total government outlays (10)

building society: a financial institution which collects savings from its customers and offers them at preferential rates to other customers so that they can buy or build a residence (11)

business sphere: firms that produce goods and services for profitable sale (3)

business (trade) cycle: recurrent fluctuations in the level of national production, with alternating periods of recession and boom (1)

capabilities: the opportunities that people have to pursue important aspects of well-being, such as being healthy and having access to education (18)

capital controls: the regulation or taxation of international transactions involving assets (14)

capital flight: rapid movement of capital assets out of a country (14)

capital gain: an increase in the value of an asset over time (3)

capital income: rents, profits, and interest (3)

capital intensive: a process or procedure that makes use of more capital relative to other inputs such as labor (18)

capital stock: a quantity of any resource that is valued for its potential economic contributions (3) *ceteris paribus:* a Latin phrase meaning "other things equal" or "all else constant" (2)

chain-type quantity index: an index comparing real production in the current year to the reference year, calculated using a series of year-to-year Fisher quantity indexes (5, Appendix)

change in demand: a shift of the demand curve in response to some determinant other than the item's price (4)

change in quantity demanded: movement along a demand curve in response to a price change (4)

change in quantity supplied: movement along a supply curve in response to a price change (4)

change in supply: a shift of the supply curve in response to some determinant other than the item's price (4)

classical economics: the school of economics, originating in the eighteenth century, that stressed issues of growth and distribution, based on an image of smoothly functioning markets (1)

closed economy: an economy with no foreign sector; i.e., it neither purchases goods or services from outside its borders, nor does it sell goods or services abroad (5)

collateralized debt obligation (CDO): an investment product that packages together numerous assets including mortgage-backed securities (15)

collective investment vehicle or pooled fund: an investment vehicle that pools investments from many different sources, making investment decisions for them all as a group (11)

commodity money: a good used as money that is also valuable in itself (11)

complementary good: a good that is used along with another good (4)

consumer durable goods: consumer purchases that are expected to last longer than one year. These are generally items of equipment, such as vehicles and appliances, used by households to produce goods and services for their own use (5)

consumer price index (CPI): an index measuring changes in the prices of goods and services bought by households (5)

consumption: the final use of a good or service to satisfy current wants (3)

contractionary fiscal policy: reductions in government spending or transfer payments or increases in taxes, leading to a lower level of economic activity (10)

contractionary monetary policy: the use of monetary policy tools to limit the credit and money supply, raise interest rates, and encourage a leveling off or reduction in economic activity (12)

convergence criteria: the requirements that EU countries must satisfy as a condition for introducing the euro, including low levels of inflation, interest rates, government debt, and public deficits (16)

convergence (in reference to economic growth): the idea that underlying economic forces will cause poorer countries and regions to "catch up" with richer ones (18)

core sphere: households, families, and communities (3)

countercyclical policy: fiscal policy in which taxes are lowered and expenditure is raised when the economy is weak, and the opposite occurs when the economy is strong (10)

credit default swap: a security that is effectively an insurance policy against defaults related to MBSs and CDOs (15)

credit money: money that is backed by a promise to pay by someone other than the central bank (11)

credit rationing: when banks deny loans to some potential borrowers in the interest of maintaining their own profitability (12)

crowding in: the process in which government spending leads to more favorable expectations for the economy, thereby inducing private investment (10)

crowding out: a reduction in the availability of private capital resulting from government borrowing to finance budget deficits (10)

currency appreciation: when a currency becomes more valuable, for example, when increased demand for a country's exports causes an increase in demand for its currency (14)

currency depreciation: when a currency becomes less valuable, for example, due to a decrease in demand for a country's exports or an increase in its demand for imports (14)

current account: In the current account, all economic transactions other than financial transactions between residents and nonresidents are recorded. This covers sale and purchase of goods and services, income flows and current transfers (14)

customs union: a group of countries that have abolished tariffs and quotas among themselves, and have introduced a common external tariff (14)

cyclical deficit (surplus): the portion of the deficit (or surplus) that is caused by fluctuations in the business cycle (10)

cyclical unemployment: unemployment caused by a drop in aggregate demand (8)

damage-cost approach: assigning a monetary value to an environmental service that is equal to the actual damage done when the service is withdrawn (6)

death rate: the annual number of deaths per 1,000 population (19, Appendix)

defensive expenditures: money spent to counteract economic activities that have caused harm to human or environmental health (6)

deficit spending: government spending in excess of revenues collected (10)

deflation: when the aggregate price level falls (11)

demand curve: a curve indicating the quantities that buyers are ready to purchase at various prices (4)

demographic transition: the change over time from a combination of high birth and death rates to a combination of low birth and death rates (19, Appendix)

dependency needs: the need to receive care, shelter, or food from others when one is unable to provide these for oneself (3)

deposit facility: a facility in which commercial banks can deposit excess reserves and on which interest is paid (12)

depreciation: a decrease in the quantity or quality of a stock of capital (3, 5)

devaluation: lowering an exchange rate within a fixed exchange rate system (14)

direct public provision: the supply of goods or services from government or non-profit institutions (3)

discouraged workers: people who want employment but have given up looking for a job (8)

discretionary fiscal policy: changes in government spending and taxation resulting from deliberate policy decisions (10)

disposable income: income remaining for consumption or saving after subtracting taxes and adding transfer payments (10)

distribution: the allocation of products and resources among people (3)

division of labor: an approach to production in which a process is broken down into smaller tasks, with each worker assigned only one or a few tasks (1)

domestic content requirement: laws requiring traded goods to contain a certain percentage of goods produced by domestic companies (14)

double dip recession: two recessions in very short succession

dynamic analysis: analysis that takes into account the passage of time (2)

economic actor (economic agent): an individual, group, or organization that is involved in economic activities (1)

economic development: the process of moving from a situation of poverty and deprivation to a situation of increased production and plenty through investments and changes in the organization of work (1)

economic growth: increases in the level of marketed production in a country or region (1)

economic liability: anything that one economic actor owes to another (11)

economics: the study of how people manage their resources to meet their needs and enhance their well-being. The four essential economic activities are resource maintenance and the production, distribution, and consumption of goods and services (1)

economies of scale: benefits that occur when the long run average cost of production falls as the size of the enterprise increases (15)

efficiency: the use of resources in a way that does not waste any inputs. Inputs are used in such a way that they yield the highest possible value of output, or a given output is produced using the lowest possible value of inputs (2)

efficiency wage theory: the theory that an employer can motivate workers to put forth more effort by paying them somewhat more than they could get elsewhere (8)

empirical investigation: observation and recording of the specific phenomena of concern (2)

employed person (Eurostat definition): a person who did any work for pay or profit during the week before he or she is surveyed or who worked in a family business (8)

environmentally adjusted net domestic product (EDP): GDP less depreciation of both manufactured and natural capital (6)

equilibrium: a situation of rest, in which there are no forces that create change (4)

Euro area: The countries of the European Union which use the euro as their currency (5)

European Exchange Rate Mechanism: a system of quasi-fixed exchange rates between the currencies of European countries (17)

European Statistical System (ESS): partnership between the Community statistical authority, which is the Commission (**Eurostat**), and the national statistical institutes and other national authorities responsible in each European Union member state for the development, production and dissemination of European statistics (5)

European System of National and Regional Accounts (ESA): a set of statistics compiled by the national European statistical agencies concerning production, income, spending, prices, and employment (5)

Eurostat: European Union statistical authority (5)

exchange: trading one thing for another (3)

exchange rate: the number of units of one currency that can be exchanged for one unit of another currency (14)

exchange value: value that corresponds to the value of goods or services for which the item can be exchanged (11)

expansionary fiscal policy: the use of government spending, transfer payments, or tax cuts to stimulate a higher level of economic activity (10)

expansionary monetary policy: the use of monetary policy tools to increase the money supply, lower interest rates, and stimulate a higher level of economic activity (12)

expected real interest rate: the nominal interest rate minus expected inflation, $r_e = i - \pi_e$ (12, Appendix)

explicit contract: a formal, often written agreement that states the terms of exchange and may be enforceable through a legal system (2)

externalities: side effects or unintended consequences, either positive or negative, that affect persons or entities such as the environment that are not among the economic actors directly involved in the economic activity that caused the effect (2)

factors of production: the essential inputs for economic activity, including labor, capital, and natural resources (18)

fertility rate: the average number of births per woman of reproductive age (19, Appendix)

fiat money: a medium of exchange that is used as money because a government says it has value and that is accepted by the people using it (11)

final good: a good that is ready for use, needing no further processing (5)

financial account (in the BOP account): the account that tracks flows arising from international transactions in assets (14)

financial assets: a variety of holdings in which wealth can be invested with an expectation of future return (7)

financial capital: funds of purchasing power available to facilitate economic activity (3)

financial institution: Any institution that collects money and holds it as financial assets (7)

financial intermediary: an institution such as a bank, savings and loan association, or life insurance company that accepts funds from savers and makes loans to borrowers (11)

financialization: a process in which the financial sector of the economy is increasingly able to generate and circulate profits that are not closely related to the real economy (7)

fiscal capacity: public revenues that can be spent within a given jurisdiction (17)

fiscal compact: agreement among euro-area member states to put rules for a balanced budget into national law and preferably their constitution (16)

fiscal policy: government spending and tax policy, involving the manipulation of levels of government spending and taxation to raise or lower the level of aggregate demand (1, 10)

Fisher quantity index: an index that measures production in one year relative to an adjacent year by using an average of the ratios that would be found by using first one year, and then the other, as the source of prices at which production is valued (5, Appendix)

fixed assets: equipment owned by businesses and governments, structures, dwellings, software, weapons systems, cultivated biological resources, and intellectual property products (5)

fixed exchange rate system: a system in which currencies are traded at fixed ratios (14)

flexible (floating) exchange rate system: a system in which exchange rates are determined by market forces of supply and demand (14)

flow: something whose quantity can be measured over a period of time (3)

foreign direct investment (FDI): investment in a business in a foreign country (14)

foreign exchange: the class of currencies that is broadly acceptable by foreigners in commercial or investment transactions. Generally limited to three currencies—the dollar, the euro, and the yen (14)

foreign exchange market intervention: an action by central banks to buy or sell foreign exchange reserves in order to keep exchange rates at desired levels (14)

foreign trade zone: a designated area of a country within which foreign-owned manufacturers can operate free of many taxes, tariffs, and regulations (14)

free riders: people who seek to enjoy the benefit of a good without paying for it (2)

free trade area: a group of countries that have abolished tariffs and quotas for goods produced in the area and traded between these countries (14)

frictional unemployment: unemployment that arises as people are in transition between jobs (8)

"full-employment output" ($Y\star$): For modeling purposes, a level of output that is assumed to correspond to a case of no excessive or burdensome unemployment but the likely existence of at least some transitory unemployment (9)

GDP deflator (implicit price deflator): a price index created by dividing nominal GDP by real GDP (5, Appendix)

Gini ratio (or Gini coefficient): a measure of inequality, based on the Lorenz curve, that goes from 0 (perfect equality) to 1 (complete inequality). Greater inequality shows up as a larger area between the curved line and the diagonal (3)

659

global economy: the system of economic rules, norms, and interactions by which economic actors and actions in different parts of the world are connected to one another (1)

goods: tangible objects that are produced for human use (3)

government bond: an interest-bearing security constituting a promise to pay at a specified future time (10)

government outlays: total government expenditures, including spending on goods and services and transfer payments (10)

government spending (G): the component of GDP that represents spending on goods and services by federal, state, and local governments (10)

gross domestic product (GDP): a measure of the total market value of final goods and services newly produced within a country's borders over a period of time (usually one year) (5)

gross general government debt: the outstanding debt of all levels of government, including social security systems (16)

gross investment: all flows into the capital stock over a period of time (3, 5)

hedge fund: a type of pooled fund that often engages in highly speculative investments and to which access is generally restricted to wealthy clients (11)

historical investigation: study of past events (2)

home equity loan: a loan that permits a borrower to offer his or her home (or their equity stake in it) as collateral in case of failure to repay the loan (15)

human development: an approach to development that stresses the provision of basic needs such as food, shelter, and health care (18)

Human Development Index (HDI): In indicator for a country's development, calculated based on only three components of well-being: life expectancy at birth, years of formal education, and real per-capita GDP (18).

human capital: people's capacity for work and their individual knowledge and skills (3)

identity (accounting identity): an equation in which the two sides are equal by definition (5)

implicit contract: an informal agreement about the terms of exchange, based on verbal discussions and on common norms, traditions, and expectations (2)

import substitution: the policy of subsidizing domestic producers to make products that can be used in place of imported goods (14)

imputation: a procedure in which values are assigned for a category of products, usually using values of related products or inputs (5)

inactive person (Eurostat definition): someone who is neither "employed" nor "unemployed" (8)

index fund: a type of pooled fund that tries to replicate a common stock or bond market index. As this fund does not require active management by a manager, fees are usually lower than in other types of pooled funds (11)

index number: a figure that measures the change in magnitude of a variable, such as a quantity or price, compared to another period (5)

industrial policy: a set of government policies designed to enhance a country's ability to compete globally (18)

Industrial Revolution: a process of social, technological, and economic change, beginning in Western Europe in the eighteenth century, that developed and applied new methods of production and work organization, resulting in a great increase in output per worker (18)

infant industry: an industry that is not yet globally competitive but receives government support with the expectation that it may become so (18)

inflation: a rise in the general level of prices (1)

informal sphere: made up of businesses operating outside government oversight and regulation. In less industrialized countries, it may constitute the majority of economic activity (3)

in-kind transfers: transfers of goods or services (3)

inputs: resources that go into production (3)

institutions: ways of structuring interactions between individuals and groups, including both formally constituted establishments and patterns of organization embodied in customs, habits, and laws (2)

insurance company: a company that pays to cover all or part of the cost of specific risks against which individuals and companies chose to insure themselves (11)

intermediate good: a good that will undergo further processing (5)

International Monetary Fund (IMF): an international agency charged with overseeing international finance, including exchange rates, international payments, and balance-of-payments management (14)

intrinsic value: value related to the tangible or physical properties of the object (11)

inventories: stocks of raw materials or manufactured goods held until they can be used or sold (5)

investment: actions taken to increase the quantity or quality of a resource now in order to make benefits possible in the future (3)

Keynesian economics: the school of thought, named after John Maynard Keynes, that argued for the active use of fiscal policy to keep aggregate demand high and employment rates up (1)

Kuznets curve hypothesis: the theory that economic inequality first increases during the initial stages of economic development but then eventually decreases with further economic growth (18)

labor force (Eurostat definition): all those who are either employed or unemployed (8)

labor income: payment to workers, including wages, salaries, and fringe benefits (3)

labor intensive: a process or procedure that makes use of more labor relative to other inputs such as capital (18)

labor productivity: the level of output that can be produced per worker per hour. The market value of the output that results from a given amount of labor (1, 8)

laissez-faire capitalism: a national system characterized by private corporate ownership and a great reliance on exchange as a mode of coordination (with relatively little coordination by public administration) (18)

laissez-faire economy: an economy with little government regulation (1)

leverage: the use of borrowed money to increase the investment power of one's own money (7, 11)

liquidity: the ease of use of an asset as a medium of exchange (11)

liquidity trap: a situation in which interest rates are so low that the central bank finds it impossible to reduce them further (12)

living standards growth: improvements in people's diet, housing, medical care, education, working conditions, and access to transportation, communication, entertainment, and other amenities (1)

Lorenz curve: a line used to portray an income distribution, constructed on a graph by having percentiles of households on the horizontal axis and the cumulative percentage of income on the vertical axis (3)

M1: a measure of the money supply that includes currency and overnight deposits (11)

M2: a measure of the money supply that includes all of M1 plus deposits with an agreed maturity of up to two years and deposits redeemable at a notice of up to three months (11)

Maastricht Treaty: treaty from 1991 between European countries transforming the European Community into the European Union and outlining the path toward the introduction of the euro (17)

macroeconomics: the study of how economic activities at all levels create a national (and global) economic environment (1)

macroeconomy: an economic system whose boundaries are normally understood to be the boundaries of a nation or an area, such as the euro area, when it is operating, in economic terms, like a nation (1)

maintenance–cost approach: assigning a monetary value to an environmental service that is equal to what it would cost to maintain the same standard of services using an alternative method (6)

manufactured assets: goods that are produced for investment purposes to assist in the production of other goods and services (3)

manufactured capital: physical assets generated by applying human productive activities to natural capital (3)

manufacturing productivity: an index of the value of the goods produced per hour of labor in the manufacturing sector (7)

marginal lending facility: a facility under which commercial banks can always borrow reserves at short notice from the ECB (12)

marginal propensity to consume: the number of additional dollars of consumption for every additional dollar of income (typically a fraction between 0 and 1) (9)

marginal propensity to save: the number of additional dollars saved for each additional dollar of income (typically a fraction between 0 and 1) (9)

market (first meaning): a physical place or Web location where there is an expectation of finding both buyers and sellers for the same product or service (2)

market (second meaning): an institution that brings buyers and sellers into communication with each other, structuring and coordinating their actions (2)

"the market" (third meaning): a phrase that people often use to mean an abstract situation of pure exchange or a global system of exchange relationships (2)

market disequilibrium: a situation of either shortage or surplus (4)

market failure: a situation in which markets yield inefficient or inappropriate outcomes (2)

market socialism: a national system in which state ownership predominates but much economic activity is coordinated through markets (18)

market power: the ability to control or significantly affect the terms and conditions of the exchanges in which one participates (2)

market-clearing equilibrium: a situation in which quantity supplied equals quantity demanded (4)

maximum capacity output: the level of output an economy would produce if every resource in the economy were fully utilized (13)

means-tested programs: programs designed to transfer income to recipients based on need (3)

menu costs: the costs to a supplier of changing prices listed on order forms, brochures, menus, and the like (4)

microeconomics: the study of the economic activities and interactions of individuals, households, businesses, and other groups at the subnational level (1)

migration controls: restrictions on the flow of people into and out of a country (14)

Millennium Development Goals (MDGs): a set of goals declared by the United Nations in 2000, emphasizing eradication of extreme poverty; promotion of education, gender equity, and health; environmental sustainability; and partnership between rich and poor countries (18)

model: an analytical tool that highlights some aspects of reality while ignoring others (2)

monetarism: a theory associated with Milton Friedman, which claims that macroeconomic objectives are best met by having the money supply grow at a steady rate (see also monetarist economics) (12)

monetarist economics: the school of economic thought that focused on the effects of monetary policy and argued that governments should aim for steadiness in the money supply rather than playing an active role (1)

monetary base: the sum of total currency plus bank reserves (12)

monetary neutrality: the idea that changes in the money supply may affect only prices while leaving output unchanged (12)

monetary policy: the use of tools controlled by the central bank, such as interest rates on funds commercial banks borrow from the central bank, or the purchase of government bonds by the central bank to affect the levels of interest rates, credit, and money supply (1, 11)

monetizing the debt/monetizing the deficit the purchase of new debt from governments by the central bank (12, 16)

money multiplier: as the ratio of the money supply to the monetary base, it tells how much bigger the money supply is relative to the monetary base (12)

money supply rule: committing to letting the money supply grow at a fixed rate per year (12)

moral hazard: the creation of perverse incentives that encourage excessive risk taking because of protections against losses from that risk (15)

mortality rate: the average number of deaths among a specific group (19, Appendix)

mortgage-backed security (MBS): a security composed of a bundle of many home mortgages issued by independent banks (15)

multilateral development assistance: aid or loans provided with the announced intention of promoting development by the World Bank, regional development banks, or UN agencies such as the United Nations Development Programme (UNDP) (18)

national accounting conventions: habits or agreements adopted by government agencies in order to make national accounts as standardized and comparable across different countries and periods as possible (5)

national income (NI): a measure of all domestic incomes earned in production (5)

natural capital: physical assets provided by nature (3)

negative (or inverse) relationship: the relationship between two variables if an increase in one variable is associated with an decrease in the other variable (or vice versa) (2)

neoclassical synthesis: A combination of classical and Keynesian perspectives (13, Appendix)

net exports: the value of exports less the value of imports (5)

net investment: gross investment minus an adjustment for depreciation of the capital stock (3, 5)

net migration rate: the net gain in population from migration, per 1,000 population (19, Appendix)

net domestic product (NDP): a measure of national production in excess of that needed to replace worn-out manufactured capital, calculated by subtracting depreciation from GDP (5)

net taxes: taxes minus transfer payments (10)

New Keynesian macroeconomics: a school of thought that bases its analysis on micro-level market behavior but that justifies activist macroeconomic policies by assuming that markets have "imperfections" that can create or prolong recessions (13, Appendix)

nominal (current euro) GDP: gross domestic product expressed in terms of current prices (5)

no-bailout clause: rule laid down in the European treaties that neither the EU nor other member states should assume or be liable for other countries' commitments (17)

nonbank financial institution: a financial institution that performs a number of services similar to those offered by banks but that is not a licensed bank and is not subject to banking regulations (11)

nonrenewable resource: a resource that cannot be reproduced on a human time scale, so that its stock diminishes with use over time (3)

nontariff barriers to trade: use of licensing or other requirements to limit the volume of trade (14)

normative questions: questions about how things should be (1)

Okun's "law": an empirical inverse relationship between the unemployment rate and real GDP growth (9)

old-age dependency ratio: the number of retirees relative to the number of active workers (19, Appendix)

open economy: an economy with a foreign sector (5)

opportunity cost: the value of the best alternative that is forgone when a choice is made (2)

opportunity-cost method (for estimating the value of household production): valuing hours at the amount that the unpaid worker could have earned at a paid job (6)

output sectors: divisions of a macroeconomy based on what is being produced (7)

outputs: the results of production (3)

pension fund: a fund with the exclusive purpose of paying retirement benefits to employees (11)

perfectly competitive market: a market in which there are many buyers and sellers, all units of the good are identical, and there is free entry and exit and perfect information (4)

physical infrastructure: the equipment, buildings, physical communication lines, roads, and other tangible structures that provide the foundation for economic activity (2)

population momentum: the trend in population size that results from its age profile, in particular the number of women who are of childbearing age or younger (19, Appendix)

portfolio investment: the purchase of financial assets such as stocks and bonds; in international finance, investment in stocks or bonds of a foreign country (11, 14)

positive (or direct) relationship: the relationship between two variables if an increase in one variable is associated with an increase in the other variable (2)

positive questions: questions about how things are (1)

post-Keynesian macroeconomics: a school of thought that stresses the importance of history and uncertainty in determining macroeconomic outcomes (13, Appendix)

poverty line: the income threshold below which members of a population are classified as poor (18)

precautionary principle: the principle that we should err on the side of caution when facing a significant possibility of severe damage to human health or the natural environment (1)

price elasticity: a measure of the sensitivity or responsiveness of quantity supplied or demanded to changes in price (4)

price elasticity of demand: a measure of the responsiveness of quantity demanded to changes in price (4)

price elasticity of supply: a measure of the responsiveness of quantity supplied to changes in price (4)

primary balance: government net borrowing or net lending, excluding interest payments on government debt (16)

primary sector: the sector of the economy that involves the harvesting and extraction of natural resources and simple processing of these raw materials into products that are generally sold to manufacturers as inputs (7)

private property: ownership of assets by nongovernment economic actors (2)

procyclical policy: fiscal policy in which taxes are lowered and expenditure is raised when the economy is strong, and the opposite is done when the economy is weak (10)

production: the conversion of resources to goods and services (3)

production-possibilities frontier (PPF): a curve showing the maximum amounts of two outputs that society could produce from given resources over a given time period (2)

program country: country that was forced to implement an economic adjustment program as a conditionality for a loan from the IMF and the European institutions (17)

progressive income tax: a tax in which a larger share of income is collected from those with higher incomes (3)

proportional income tax: a tax in which the same share of income is collected from households, irrespective of income level (3)

public goods: goods for which (1) use by one person does not diminish usefulness to others and (2) it would be difficult to exclude anyone from benefiting (2)

public-purpose sphere: governments and other local, national, and international organizations established for a public purpose beyond individual or family self-interest and not operating with the goal of making a profit (3)

purchasing power parity (PPP) adjustments: adjustments to international income statistics to take into account the differences in the cost of living across countries (14)

purchasing power parity (PPP): the theory that exchange rates should reflect differences in purchasing power among countries (14)

quantitative easing (QE): the purchase of financial assets including long-term bonds by the ECB, creating more monetary reserves and lowering long-term interest rates (12)

quantity adjustments: a response by suppliers in which they react to unexpectedly low sales of their good primarily by reducing production levels rather than by reducing the price and to unexpectedly high sales by increasing production rather than raising the price (4)

quantity equation: $M \times V = P \times Y$, where M is the money supply, V is the velocity of money, P is the price level, and Y is real output (12)

quantity theory of money: the theory that money supply is directly related to nominal GDP, according to the equation $M \times \bar{V} = P \times Y$ (12)

quantity index: an index measuring changes in levels of quantities produced (5)

rational expectations theory: the theory that people's expectations about ECB policy cause predictable monetary policies to be ineffective in changing output levels (13, Appendix)

real business cycle theory: the theory that changes in employment levels are caused by change in technological capacities or people's preferences concerning work (13, Appendix)

real depreciation: domestic products gaining price competitiveness because of lower inflation than in partner countries or because of a depreciation of the nominal (money value) exchange rate (13)

real economy: the part of the economy that is concerned with actually producing goods and services (7)

real exchange rate: the exchange rate between two currencies, adjusted for inflation in each country (14)

real GDP: a measure of gross domestic product that seeks to reflect the actual value of goods and services produced by removing the effect of changes in prices (5)

real interest rate: nominal interest rate minus inflation, $r = i - \pi$ (12, Appendix)

recession: a downturn in economic activity, usually defined as lasting for two consecutive calendar quarters or more (1, 8)

regressive income tax: a tax in which a larger share of income is collected from poorer households (3)

regulation: setting standards or laws to govern behavior (3)

reinsurer: a company that sells insurance to insurance companies to share the risk in case of large damages caused, for example, through natural disasters (11)

renewable resource: a resource that regenerates itself through short-term processes (3)

rent: payments for the use of any capital asset (3)

reserve requirements: the fraction of bank deposits that banks *must* keep as reserve (11)

replacement-cost method (for estimating the value of household production): valuing hours at the amount it would be necessary to pay someone to do the work (6)

replacement fertility rate: the fertility rate required for each generation to be replaced by a subsequent generation of the same size. (19, Appendix)

reserve assets: a line in the financial account reflecting the foreign exchange market operations of a country's central bank (14)

resource maintenance: the management of capital stocks so that their productivity is sustained or improved (3)

restorative development: economic progress that restores economic, financial, social, or ecological systems that have been degraded and are no longer adequately supportive of human well-being in the present and the future (1)

restorative socioeconomic system: a system in which successful efforts are made to restore social, environmental, manufactured, or human capital that has deteriorated (3)

revaluation: raising an exchange rate within a fixed exchange rate system (14)

rule of 72: a shorthand calculation that states that dividing 72 by an annual growth rate yields approximately the number of years it will take for an amount to double (5)

satellite accounts: additional or parallel accounting systems that provide measures of social and environmental factors, often in physical terms, without necessarily including monetary valuation (6)

saving: refraining from consumption in the current period (3)

Say's Law: the classical belief that "supply creates its own demand" (1)

scarcity: resources are scarce to the extent that they are not sufficient to allow all goals to be accomplished at once (2)

secondary sector: the sector of the economy that involves converting the outputs of the primary sector into products suitable for use or consumption. It includes manufacturing, construction, and utilities. (7)

securities broker: an agent responsible for finding a buyer for sellers of different securities, thereby offering enhanced liquidity to the seller (11)

self-correcting market: a market that automatically adjusts to any imbalances between sellers (supply) and buyers (demand) (4)

services: intangibles that are produced by one individual or organization and offered to others (3)

shadow bank: credit intermediation that involves entities and activities outside the regular banking system (11)

shortage: a situation in which the quantity that buyers wish to buy at the stated price is greater than the quantity that sellers are willing to sell at that price (4)

skill-biased technical change: the theory that relative wage gains will be the greatest for those workers possess the education and skills to use modern technologies (8)

social capital: the institutions and the stock of trust, mutual understanding, shared values, and socially held knowledge that facilitate the social coordination of economic activity (3)

social discount rate: a discount rate that reflects social rather than market valuation of future costs and benefits; usually lower than the market discount rate (19)

social insurance programs: programs designed to transfer income to recipients if and when certain events (like retirement or disability) occur (3)

specialization: in production, a system of organization in which each worker performs only one type of task (1)

speculation: buying and selling assets with the expectation of profiting from appreciation or depreciation in their value (4)

speculative bubble: the situation that occurs when mutually reinforcing investor optimism raises the value of an asset far above what can be justified by fundamental value (4)

Stability and Growth Pact: rules for euro-area countries about government deficit and government debt which can be enforced by imposing fines on member states with excessive deficits (16)

stagflation: a combination of rising inflation and economic stagnation (13)

static analysis: analysis that does not take into account the passage of time (2)

steady-state economy: an economy with no increase in population or in the rate of use of raw materials and energy (19)

"sticky wage" theories: theories about why wages stay at above-equilibrium levels despite the existence of a labor surplus (8)

stock: something whose quantity can be measured at a point in time (3)

stock-flow diagram: an illustration of how stocks can be changed, over time, by flows (3)

structural deficit (surplus): the portion of the deficit (or surplus) that results from tax and spending policy dictated by the government at its discretion (10)

structural unemployment: unemployment that arises because people's skills, experience, education, or location do not match what employers need (8)

subjective well-being: a measure of welfare based on survey questions asking people about their own degree of life satisfaction (6)

subprime mortgage: a mortgage not meeting the quality standards of traditional mortgages (4, 15)

substitutability: the possibility of using one resource instead of another (3)

substitute good: a good that can be used in place of another (4)

supply curve: a curve indicating the quantities that sellers are willing to supply at various prices (4)

supply shock: a change in the productive capacity of an economy (13)

supply-side economics: an economic theory that emphasizes policies to stimulate production, such as lower taxes. The theory predicts that such incentives stimulate greater economic effort, saving, and investment, thereby increasing overall economic output and tax revenues. (10)

surplus: a situation in which the quantity that sellers wish to sell at the stated price is greater than the quantity that buyers will buy at that price (4)

Sustainable Development Goals (SDGs): a set of goals declared by the United Nations in 2015, building on and expanding the Millennium Development Goals, including goals such as battling inequality worldwide, promoting inclusive growth, and limiting climate change (18)

sustainable socioeconomic system: a system in which the overall quality and quantity of the resource base required for sustaining life and well-being do not erode (3)

tariffs: taxes on imports or exports (14)

tax multiplier: the impact of a change in a lump-sum tax on economic equilibrium, expressed mathematically as $\Delta Y/\Delta \overline{T} = (mult)(mpc)$ (10)

technological progress: the development of new products and new, more efficient methods of production (2)

technological unemployment: unemployment caused by reduced demand for workers because technology has increased the productivity of those who have jobs, effectively reducing the demand for workers (8)

terms of trade: the price of exports relative to imports (18)

tertiary sector: the sector of the economy that involves the provision of services rather than of tangible goods (7)

theoretical investigation: analysis based in abstract thought (2)

theory of market adjustment: the theory that market forces will tend to make shortages and surpluses disappear (4)

theory of optimum currency area: research about under which conditions a monetary union between different countries is beneficial (17)

three major macroeconomic goals: the achievement of good living standards, stability and security, and environmental sustainability (1)

throughput: the flow of raw materials and energy through the economy, leading to outputs of waste (19)

time lags: the time that elapses between the formulation of an economic policy and its actual effects on the economy (10)

time-series data: observations of how a numerical variable changes over time (2)

"too big to fail": when a company grows so large that its failure would cause widespread economic harm in terms of lost jobs and diminished asset values (15)

total factor productivity: a measure of the productivity of all factors of production. It represents contributions to output from all sources, not just quantities of manufactured capital and labor. (18)

trade account (part of the current account): the portion of the current account that tracks inflows and outflows arising exclusively from international trade in goods and services (14)

trade ban: a law preventing the import or export of goods or services (14)

trade quota: a restriction on the quantity of a good that can be imported or exported (14)

trade-related subsidies: payments given by governments to producers to encourage more production, either for export or as a substitute for imports (14)

transaction costs: the costs of arranging economic activities (2)

transfer: the giving of something with nothing specific expected in return (3)

transfer payments: payments by government to individuals or firms, including pension payments, unemployment compensation, interest payments, and subsidies (10)

troika: term used in the early years of the euro crisis to denote the IMF, the ECB, and the EU Commission, which together decided on conditions for loan packages for countries in crisis (17)

underemployed part-time workers: part-time workers who would like to work additional hours and are available to do so (8)

unemployed person (Eurostat definition): a person who is not employed but who is actively seeking a job and is immediately available for work (8)

unemployment rate: the percentage of the labor force made up of people who do not have paid jobs but are immediately available and actively looking for paid jobs (8)

unemployment: a situation in which people seek a paying job but cannot obtain one (1)

utility: the level of usefulness or satisfaction gained from a particular activity such as consumption of a good or service (2)

value added: the value of what a producer sells less the value of the intermediate inputs it uses, except labor. This is equal to the wages paid out by the producer plus its profits (5).

670

velocity of money: the number of times that a euro would have to change hands during a year to support nominal GDP, calculated as $V = (P \times Y)/M$ (12)

virtuous cycles (in development): self-reinforcing patterns of high savings, investment, productivity growth, and economic expansion (18)

wage and price controls: government regulations setting limits on wages and prices or on the rates at which they are permitted to increase (13)

wage-price spiral: when pressure on wages creates upward pressure on prices and, as a result, further upward pressure on wages (13)

wage–productivity gap: the gap between the growth of labor productivity and the growth of wages (8)

Washington Consensus: specific economic policy prescriptions used by the IMF and World Bank with a goal of helping developing countries to avoid crisis and maintain stability. They include openness to trade and investment (liberalization), privatization, budget austerity, and deregulation. (14)

waste products: outputs that are not used either for consumption or in a further production process (3)

well-being: a term used to describe the overall quality of life (1)

World Bank: an international agency charged with promoting economic development through loans and other programs (14)

World Trade Organization (WTO): An international organization that conducts negotiations aimed at lowering trade barriers and mediates trade disputes between countries (14)

Index